❧ At last those of us who regularly teach courses in American religious history have readily available a set of readings that puts students in touch with the field as it is being constituted now. Here is all the best new scholarship in lively and accessible form. Hackett gives us multicultural religious America in a format that communicates. I'm delighted and will surely use the reader in my own courses.

—Catherine L. Albanese, University of California at Santa Barbara

❧ Hackett has chosen splendid, sparkling examples of the kind of historical writing that draws our attention to previously marginalized groups. He has, wisely, not attempted to deal in one collection with both the "outsiders" and the putative mainstream. Instead we have, collected in one place, supplementary readings that will extend and enrich the accounts offered in the best textbooks on American religious history.

—William R. Hutchison, The Divinity School at Harvard University

❧ This book should be read by all who teach and study in America because it models academic justice in its trreatment of the broad range of cultural per-spectives and religious traditions.

—Peter Paris, Princeton Theological Seminary

❧ The volume communicates a strong sense of the religious diversity of the American past.

—Nancy F. Cott, Yale University

❧ This reader provides an outstanding collection of articles that reflect the diversity of new approaches to non-mainstream Protestant religious groups in the American context. The reader nicely complements standard textbooks in American religious history, provides relevant supplementary reading for a number of widely assigned primary sources, and allows students to engage with cutting-edge scholarship in the field.

—Ann Taves, School of Theology at Claremont

❧ This reader is a rich feast of little-known American religious delicacies often squeezed off the table by an older understanding of the proper menu. It brings together some of the best in recent scholarship and introduces its readers to just how wonderfully varied and complicated our story is.

—Nancy Ammerman, Hartford Seminary

RELIGION
AND
AMERICAN
CULTURE

RELIGION AND AMERICAN CULTURE

A Reader

David G. Hackett

Editor

Routledge
New York & London

Published in 1995 by

Routledge
29 West 35th Street
New York, NY 10001

Published in Great Britain by
Routledge
11 New Fetter Lane
London EC4P 4EE

Copyright © 1995 by Routledge

Printed in the United States of America on acid-free paper.

All rights reserved. No part of this book may be reprinted or reproduced or utilized in any form
or by any electronic, mechanical or other means, now known or hereafter invented, including
photocopying and recording, or in any information storage or retrieval system, without
permission in writing from the publisher.

Library of Congress Cataloging-in-Publication Data

Correct Information to come from Routledge
Altared ground: Levinas, history, and violence / Brian S. Schroeder.
        p. cm.
Includes bibliographical references.

ISBN 0-415-91452-3 (cl) — ISBN 0-415-91453-1 (pbk)
    1. Philosophy. 2. Religion. 3. History—Philosophy. 4. Violence. 5. Subjectivity.
6. Self (Philosophy). 7. Levinas, Emmanuel. I. Title.

B945.S33A48 1995   95-36343
179'.7 —dc20   CIP

CONTENTS ❦

ACKNOWLEDGMENTS ❦

A NUMBER OF FRIENDS AND COLLEAGUES have taken the time to offer their thoughts on the organization and content of this book. For their helpful advice and encouragement, I particularly want to thank: Mary Bednarowksi, Jim Bratt, Ann Braude, John Corrigan, Fred Denny, Jay Dolan, Diana Eck, Cynthia Eller, Tracy Fessenden, Will Gravely, Ramón Gutiérrez, Yvonne Haddad, David Hall, Nathan Hatch, Sam Hill, Brooks Holifield, Charles Joyner, Laurie Maffly-Kipp, Joel Martin, Colleen McDannell, Deborah Dash Moore, Azim Nanji, Stephen Nissenbaum, Bob Orsi, Amanda Porterfield, Steve Prothero, Al Raboteau, Elizabeth Reis, Dan Richter, Jonathan Sarna, Leigh Schmidt, Jan Shipps, Steve Tipton, Roberto Trevino, Tim Tseng, Tom Tweed, Chris Vecsey, Grant Wacker, Margaret Washington, David Watt, Jack Wertheimer, David Wills, John F. Wilson, Bob Wuthnow, Wendy Young and the 1994–95 members of Princeton's Center for the Study of American Religion Friday workshop. None are responsible for the final selection and organization of the readings. I also want to thank my editor Marlie Wasserman, her assistant Mary Carol De Zutter, and Adam Bohannon and Carter Craft who have been a wonderfully helpful and supportive team. Finally, I married Wendy Young in the midst of this project and I thank her for making everything so much more delightful.

INTRODUCTION ❦

TODAY THE STUDY OF AMERICAN RELIGION continues to move away from an older, European American, male, middle-class, northeastern, Protestant narrative concerned primarily with churches and theology and toward a multicultural tale of Native Americans, African Americans, Catholics, Jews and other groups. Many of these new studies cut across boundaries of gender, class, and region, and pay particular attention to popular religion. Most current textbooks remain wed to the older Protestant narrative. The purpose of this reader is to expose students to a broad overview of the new work emerging from this rapidly changing field.

At the outset we need to recognize that the field of American religious history is in the midst of substantial revision. As recently as the 1970s what we knew about the American religious past came primarily from the study of formal theology and the histories of the established churches. The crowning achievement in this tradition was the publication of Sydney Ahlstrom's magisterial *A Religious History of the American People* in 1972.[1] The great and continuing strength of church history is its attention to the influence of religious ideas and to the relationship between religion and political affairs. All of the major textbooks are written by historians schooled in this genre and their narratives largely reflect the dominant Protestant point of view. It is, of course, foolish to simply ignore the importance of Protestant churches in American religion. Nevertheless, as a recent president of the American Society of Church History concluded in a review of the available textbooks: "There is a widespread feeling among professionals in the field that the text resources available in the past are unsuitable for the present."[2]

Religious history started breaking away from church history in the 1960s, when social historians began to see religion as playing a more active role in social change. Influential historians, such as E. P. Thompson and Eugene Genovese, emphasized the power of popular religion in helping ordinary people to oppose the institutional religion of the ruling classes. By the 1970s, this conflict model was largely superseded by the insights of anthropologists who directed historians' interest to the meaning and order conveyed to believers by religious symbols. In particular, Clifford Geertz's understanding of "religion as a cultural system" was widely read and appropriated throughout the discipline. By the late 1970s, this mixture of social history and cultural anthropology led to the emergence of the new area of "popular religion." Works by Jon Butler on magic and the occult, Rhys Isaac on the religious culture of eighteenth-century Virginia, as well as new research on revivalism and slave religion, all suggested the arrival of a new "popular" approach to the American religious past.[3]

During the 1980s, and up to the present, the thrust of this work has dramatically expanded the area of research. Regional religious stories of the West and the South are coming into view. Native American religious history, non-existent as a field until the 1980s, is an exciting and rapidly emerging new discipline. Dramatic revisions are being made in our understanding of the African American religious past. Mormons, Masons, Pentecostals, ethnic Catholics, sunbelt Jews, followers of Islam, Asian religions, and Haitian Vodou are now on the scene. Attention is being given to the relationship between religion and commercial culture. The complex view of women in today's women's studies is echoed in new works on women across class and racial lines. In many of these studies we can see a new interest in ritual and ceremony.

The result of this scholarship is not to offer a new interpretation of the American religious past. It is still not at all clear what should be the proper subject matter of religious history nor which methods and theories ought to be applied. Still, the sheer number of new works that demonstrate the existence and vitality of religious peoples and practices outside the domain of the Protestant middle class is sufficient to throw into doubt the explanatory power of the older view. Because a new paradigm is not yet clear, it is not the time for a new textbook. The older texts are valuable for providing the Protestant narrative. But exactly because the field is currently so rich and diverse, now is the time for an anthology that gives clear voice to these new studies.

The organization of the following readings is loosely chronological: four broad periods, with a particular focus on recurrent themes. Two different organizational schemes, one chronological and the other thematic, are currently followed in American religion courses. Both of these schemes have advantages and limitations; many who teach these courses use a combination of the two.

The chronological approach has the great advantage of providing a coherent overview of the development of American religion. This approach also has the disadvantage of favoring a Protestant periodization of the American past, though recent scholars have incorporated the chronological stories of Native Americans, European Americans, and African Americans into a larger scheme.[4]

Advocates of the thematic approach, in contrast, hold that a focus on themes rather than chronology allows for a decisive break from the older Protestant narrative, leaving more room for other stories to emerge. The drawback to this approach is that it risks a presentism and impressionism, intriguing students with all sorts of interesting issues, but perhaps failing to explain these issues very well (where do they come from and why are they this way and how do they relate to the other elements of the course?).

The solution suggested by this reader is to combine these two approaches by employing a loose chronological framework while paying attention to recurrent themes. The Native American story, for example, is introduced at the beginning but, unlike most traditional histories, does not disappear. It returns as that story changes through each successive historical period. Similar attention is given to the African American story through each stage of the chronology. Themes like "women and religion" are given particular attention not only during the period in which they become prominent, but also when they recur at later times. Issues of region and class are similarly prominent in many of the readings.

The intention of the following readings is neither to provide a new narrative nor simply assemble a random assortment of readings. Rather, through a loose chronology, attention to recurrent themes, and brief introductions to each selection, this reader offers a selection of the new work emerging in this dynamic and changing field.

NOTES

1. Sydney E. Ahlstrom, *A Religious History of the American People* (New Haven: Yale University Press, 1972).

2. Stephen J. Stein, "'Something Old, Something New, Something Borrowed, Something Left to Do': Choosing a Textbook for Religion in America." *Religion and American Culture* 3:2 (Summer 1993), 224.

3. For a sustained treatment of these developments, see Thomas Kselman ed., *Belief in History: Innovative Approaches to European and American Religion.* (Notre Dame: University of Notre Dame Press, 1991), 1–15.

4. See especially the inclusive chronological approaches used by Catherine L. Albanese, *America: Religions and Religion* (Belmont, Calif.: Wadsworth Publishing Company, 2nd edition, 1992) and Peter W. Williams, *America's Religions: Traditions and Cultures* (New York: Macmillan Publishing Company, 1990).

PART ONE

EARLY AMERICA
1500–1750

THE PUEBLO INDIAN WORLD IN THE SIXTEENTH CENTURY

Ramón A. Gutiérrez

The triumph of America's first European settlers over the Indians is a tale often told. According to most textbooks, American history "begins" with the defeat of the Native Americans. This story is usually told from the colonists' point of view. Rarely are we given the Indians' perspective. Since the 1980s a new generation of scholars has shown that the European encounter with America's Indians was not as one-sided as historical accounts have led us to believe. There was actually a dialogue between cultures, each of which had many voices. One insight of these new studies is that the Indians had their own point of view, a distinct historical voice that previous historians had unconsciously denied them.

In the following historical reconstruction of sixteenth-century Pueblo culture and society, Ramón Gutiérrez presents the world view of one of the more than five-hundred Indian tribal worlds. He does this by weaving together a variety of sources into a rich tapestry that depicts the ideological, economic, cosmic, spatial, ritual, and sexual relations within the Pueblo community. This story comes from the Acoma Pueblo, the oldest continuously settled community in the United States. Nestled atop a steep rock formation in western New Mexico, the town of Acoma has a history that reaches back to 1300. Since that time the town has resisted neighboring aggressors; defeat by the Spanish, annexation by the United States, and recently, the invasion of modern technology. The myth that begins this essay reveals the origins and structure of their Pueblo Indian world.

Adapted by permission from Ramón A. Gutiérrez, "The Pueblo Indian World in the Sixteenth Century," in his *When Jesus Came, the Corn Mothers Went Away: Marriage, Sexuality, and Power in New Mexico, 1500-1846* (Stanford University Press, 1991), 3–36.

I am glad I have seen your nakedness; it is beautiful; it will rain from now on.
—Talashimitiwa, Hopi Indian from Oraibi, 1920

1

THE PUEBLO INDIAN WORLD
IN THE SIXTEENTH CENTURY

Ramón A. Gutiérrez

IN THE BEGINNING two females were born underneath the earth at a place called Shipapu. In total darkness Tsichtinako (Thought Woman) nursed the sisters, taught them language and gave them each a basket that their father Uchtsiti had sent them containing the seeds and fetishes of all the plants and animals that were to exist in the world. Tsichtinako told the sisters to plant the four pine tree seeds they had in their basket and then to use the trees to ascend to the light. One grew so tall that it pushed a hole through the earth. Before the sisters climbed up the tree from the underworld, Thought Woman taught them how to praise the Sun with prayer and song. Every morning as the Sun rose, they would thank him for bringing them to the light by offering with outstretched hands sacred cornmeal and pollen. To the tones of the creation song, they would blow the offering to the sky, asking for long life, happiness, and success in all their endeavors.[1]

When the sisters reached the earth's surface it was soft, spongy, and not yet ripe. So they waited for the Sun to appear. When it rose, the six directions of the cosmos were revealed to them: the four cardinal points, the earth below, and the four skies above. The sisters prayed to the Sun, and as they did, Thought Woman named one of the girls Iatiku and made her Mother of the Corn clan; the other she named Nautsiti, Mother of the Sun clan.

"Why were we created?" they asked. Thought Woman answered, "Your father Uchtsiti made the world by throwing a clot of his blood into space, which by his power grew into the earth. He planted you within it so that you would bring to life all the things in your baskets in order that the world be complete for you to rule over it."

When the first day ended, the girls slept. They awoke before dawn to greet the Sun with a prayer on their lips and an offering of cornmeal and pollen. When Sun rose and gave them warmth, the sisters were very happy. Tsichtinako then took several seeds from their baskets and showed the sisters how to plant corn. With a dig stick she poked holes into Mother Earth and deposited seeds in her womb. The corn germinated and grew. When its ears were ripe and plump, Thought Woman showed them how to pick it, how to collect its pollen, and how to mill its kernels into the meal they would offer their father daily.

That night a flash of brilliant red light fell from the sky and when it touched the earth, it exploded into fire. "Your father Sun gives you fire to cook your food and to keep you warm," explained Thought Woman. "The fire's tongues will stay alive if fed branches from the pine tree that gave you passage from the underworld." From that day forward, Iatiku and Nautsiti had fire with which to cook corn. They flavored the corn with the salt they found in their baskets and ate to their hearts' content.

Next, Thought Woman taught the sisters how to give life to the animal fetishes in their baskets so that the animals would give them life in return. Mice, rats, moles, and prairie dogs were created and were given grasses on which to forage and multiply. The sisters cast pebbles in various directions and from these emerged mountains, plains, mesas, and canyons. From the seeds they next strewed about, pine, cedar, oak, and walnut trees grew and underneath them beans and squash sprouted and yielded their fruit. Rabbits, antelope, bison, and deer were dispatched to the open plains. To the mountains went the elk with their predators the lions, wolves, wildcats, and bears. Eagle, hawk, and turkey were cast into the sky, but turkey fell back to earth and never learned to fly. In the earth's waters fish, water snakes, and turtles were placed, and there they flourished and multiplied. Now Thought Woman told the sisters to kill an animal. "Roast meat and corn together and flavor it with salt," she instructed. "Before you eat, always pray and offer morsels of these to your father Uchtsiti who created the world and lives in the fourth sky above."

Tsichtinako cautioned Iatiku and Nautsiti to handle their baskets carefully. At first they did. But as they were giving life to the snakes one fetish fell out of a basket unnoticed and came to life of its own power as the serpent Pishuni. Pishuni bred selfishness and competitiveness between the sisters. Soon Nautsiti became sullen and refused to associate with Iatiku. When this occurred, Pishuni asked Nautsiti: "Why are you lonely and unhappy? If you want what will make you happy, I can tell you what to do. If you bore someone like yourself, you would no longer be lonely. Tsichtinako wants to hold back this happiness from you," he said. Nautsiti believed Pishuni and agreed to meet him near a rainbow. On a rock near the specified rainbow, Nautsiti lay on her back, and as she did drops of rain entered her body. From this rain she conceived and bore twin sons. Father Sun had strictly forbidden the sisters to bear children, and when he learned that Nautsiti had, he took Thought Woman away.

When Nautsiti's sons grew up, the sisters separated. Nautsiti departed East with her favorite child; Iatiku remained with Tiamuni, the son Nautsiti disliked. Iatiku and Tiamuni eventually married and had many daughters to whom they gave clan names representing all the things that their father had given them at emergence: Sky, Water, Fire, and Corn.

After Thought Woman departed, Iatiku took earth from her basket and made the season spirits: Shakako, the ferocious spirit of winter, Morityema, the surly spirit of spring, Maiyochina, the warm spirit of summer, and Shruisthia, the grumpy spirit of fall. Iatiku told the people that if they prayed properly to these spirits they would bring moisture, warmth, ripening, and frost, respectively.

Next Iatiku, their Corn Mother, took dirt from her basket and created the katsina, the Cloud-Spirits or ancestor dead who were to live beneath a lake in the West at Wenimats. Tsitsanits (Big Teeth) was brought to life first as ruler of the katsina, then many other katsina were brought to life. Some looked like birds with long beaks and bulging eyes, others had large animal snouts, and still others were moon creatures with horns sticking out of their heads like lunar crescents. "Your people and my people will be combined," Iatiku told the katsina. "You will give us food from your world and we will give you food from our world. Your people are to represent clouds; you are to bring rain." Iatiku then took cornmeal and opened a road four lengths long so that the katsina could travel to Wenimats and along which they would return when called.[2]

"Now we are going to make houses," said Corn Mother. Suddenly a house made of dirt and trees grew out of the earth resembling in shape the mesa and mountain homes of the season deities. Each of Iatiku's daughters constructed a house for their children and when they were all ready, Iatiku laid them out into a town. "All is well but…we have no sacred place, we have no *kaach* [kiva]," Iatiku said. She taught the oldest man of the Oak clan how to build religious houses underneath the earth's surface to resemble Shipapu, the place of emergence.

The people did not have a father of the game animals, so Iatiku appointed a Shaiyaik (Hunt Chief), taught him the songs and prayers of the hunt, gave him an altar, and showed him how to make stone fetishes and prayer sticks to secure the power of the prey animals. Hunt Chief eventually became overburdened with work and so Corn Mother made Tsatia hochani (War Chief or Outside Chief) to rule over everything outside the pueblo. Iatiku gave him a broken prayer stick with four tails marked on four sides to extend from the earth to the sky. "When you hold [the prayer stick] clasped in your hands," Iatiku told Tsatia hochani, "you are drawing all the people together so they will not be scattered. With this you will have great power over all the rest of the people." Iatiku gave the War Chief twin sons, Masewi (Wren Youth) and Oyoyewi (Mocking Bird Youth), to assist him. The boys were the Twin War Gods, sons of Father Sun.

The people had never known sickness until the serpent Pishuni returned as a plague. The people tried to cure themselves, but could not. To break Pishuni's spell Iatiku created the *chaianyi*, the Medicine Man. The oldest man of the Oak clan was made Fire Medicine Man because fire was the strongest thing that Sun had given them and oak burned hottest. Corn Mother told Oak Man to go to North Mountain and there in a pine tree that had been struck by lightning he would find an obsidian arrowhead that would be his heart and his protection. She taught him how to make black prayer sticks as symbols of the night in which he would work, and then made him an altar. Iatiku taught the Medicine Man how to mix medicines and how to secure the power of bears to destroy disease-causing witches. "Now I will make you *honani* [corn fetish] so that you will remember me," Iatiku said to the chaianyi, "it will have my power." Into a corn cob she blew her breath along with a few drops of honey to symbolize all plant food. The cob was wrapped in four husks and dressed with the tail feather of a roadrunner and of a magpie to make it useful in prayers. Iatiku also placed turquoise on the corn fetish so that it would always have the power to make one attractive and loved.

Everything was ready for a cure so Iatiku said to Fire Medicine Man, "Let us try it out." For four days the medicine man did not touch women, salt, or meat, and only sang and prayed. On the fourth night he performed a cure. The people quickly recovered. When Iatiku saw this, she also created the Flint, Spider, and Giant Medicine Societies.

Eventually it came to pass that the young people no longer respected Iatiku. So she returned to Shipapu. After she departed, Outside Chief led the people in search of their home at Haako (Acoma), "the place where the echo returned clearest." They settled at White House for a while but the katsina refused to visit because the young had insulted Iatiku. Rain clouds would not form and famine came. Flint Medicine Man and an ordinary man worked very hard, prayed, and fasted, and finally got the katsina to visit, bearing rain and gifts.

Iatiku's people were happy for a long time until sickness again befell them. The War

Twins believed that this was a sign from Iatiku that they should move to Haako, and so they did, gathering everything in four days and traveling until they reached Washpashuka. They settled there until the people began to quarrel. When this occurred, Outside Chief told the people that it was time to move again. They walked south for many moons until they reached Tule Lake. The people settled at Tule Lake for a while too. But after they suffered a severe famine there, they decided to continue their search for Haako.

They traveled south until they reached Dyaptsiam, a place of many turkeys and antelope. There they built a town. The people lived very happily until Outside Chief reminded the Medicine Men and the War Twins that they still had not reached Haako. The chiefs searched in the south and came upon a large rock. Outside Chief yelled out, "Haako!" and listened. Four more times he yelled and each time the echo came back clearly. After four days of preparation the people moved to Haako and were happy knowing that their journey had ended.

PUEBLO IDEOLOGY

The origin myth of the Acoma Indians just presented likened human life to plant life. Seeds held the potential to generate life. When planted deep within Mother Earth and fertilized by the sky's vivifying rain, seeds germinated, grew into plants, and eventually bore seeds that repeated the cycle of life. Like a sprouting maize shoot rooted in the earth or a child coming forth from its mother's womb, so the Pueblo Indians described their emergence from the underworld.[3]

All of the Pueblos have origin myths that dramatically depict the ideological structure of their world. Myths express the values and ideals that organize and make people's lives meaningful. They explain how the universe was created, its various components, and the tensions and balances that kept it intact. Whether through the deeds of gods, the feats of heroes, or the abominations of monsters, the Pueblo origin myths expressed life's generic prospects: birth, marriage, sex, quarreling, illness, migrations, and death. The Pueblo Indians conceived their history as instances of these generic forms. When pestilence struck, when famine engulfed the land, or when invading warriors demanded submission, it was through comparison with patterns in remote mythological events that the particular was understood.

The Western mind's linear concept of time imposes chronology on all events and struggles to comprehend the causes and consequences of moments that have irrevocably altered history. Such a concept of time was alien to the Pueblo Indians until quite recently. Time to them was not linear but cyclic: in the words of Mircea Eliade, it eternally returned. No event was deemed unique or serendipitous; the particular was simply comprehended through those experiences of mythic progenitors. Like the life contained within a seed that sprouts, bears fruit, and dies, only to be reborn again from a seed, so the Pueblo Indians conceived of time and of their historical past.[4]

PUEBLO RITES

From birth until death every phase of a Pueblo Indian's life was marked by rites of transition and incorporation. Before children of either sex could be considered adults they needed a host of essentials. Girls needed religious fetishes, esoteric knowledge in curing, pottery production, household construction, basket making, and a husband. Boys likewise needed sacred fetishes, knowledge in hunting, warfare, curing, rain-conjuring, and a wife. Boys and girls, however, were incapable of obtaining these goods for themselves. Seniors had to secure them for their children and did so by offering gifts to those seniors who could provide the required goods. For example, four days after a child was born at Acoma, a medicine man had to present the infant to the rising sun, to give it a name, and to endow it with a perfect ear of corn, and if a boy, also with a flint arrowhead. Early on the fourth day, with four arm-gathering motions, the medicine man presented the child to the sun and gave it the sun's strength saying: "Now you have become a member of the ___ clan." When the medicine man returned the child to its mother he would announce: "Here comes [child's name]…she is bringing food, beads, game, and a long life into her house." The mother welcomed the abundance and prosperity her daughter brought with four arm-gathering motions. Then the medicine man sprinkled the baby's cradle board with medicines, attaching a perfect ear of corn, and if it was a boy, a flint arrowhead too. For the blessing and gifts the medicine man gave the child, the parents reciprocated with gifts of cornmeal and food.[5]

Thus when girls and boys began life they were already indebted to their parents for the payment of gifts to the medicine man on their behalf. As a result of this debt and the many others they would incur to reach adulthood, juniors had to reciprocate with obedience and respect toward their parents. Concretely, respect meant that girls had to work for their mothers grinding corn, cooking, and tanning hides; boys had to tend to the corn crops, hunt, and weave cloth. Seniors, by appropriating the products of their children's labor, obtained gift stuff to offer seniors of other households so that their children could receive those blessings, knowledge, and gifts they needed to become adults.[6]

Gift exchange in Pueblo society created dyadic status relationships between givers and receivers. A gift properly reciprocated with a countergift established the exchanging parties as equals, there being no further claim one could make of the other. If a gift giver initiated an exchange with a highly respected or knowledgeable person to obtain blessings, religious endowments, or ritual knowledge, such as when a parent offered a medicine man gifts so that he would present their child to the rising sun, the obligation created was fulfilled through a proper countergift. But if only one side gave and the other side could not reciprocate, the receiver out of gratitude had to give the presenter unending obedience and respect.[7]

The rules of reciprocity that governed gift exchange among the Pueblos are revealed in a variety of historical sources. The Acoma origin myth explains that when Tsichtinako gave life to Iatiku and Nautsiti, she presented each with a basket their father Uchtsiti had given them containing the seeds and fetishes of all the plants and animals in the world. As a result of this paternal gift the girls had to welcome him daily with songs and prayers, offering him the products of their labor—maize ground into cornmeal and sacred pollen. From the moment of their creation the Corn Mothers were indebted to their father for the baskets he had given them. Since they had nothing to give him in return, they did as Tsichtinako instructed, daily singing his praises and offering him food.

The Acoma origin myth also describes what could happen if the rules of reciprocity that governed gifting and structured generational obligation faltered. These themes surface in reference to the katsina, the beneficent rain spirits that represented the ancestral dead. In Pueblo thought, with increasing age one approached the godliness of katsina. The myth explains that the katsina first fought with the people, abandoned them, refused to shower them with rain and happiness, and ultimately severed the ties that bound them with the people because the young no longer respected the katsina and instead mimicked their gestures, burlesqued their dances, and refused to call them properly with gifts. Seniors scolded juniors for their disrespect, but the juniors continued to misbehave. When the katsina discovered this, they became very angry and refused to accept the peoples' prayer sticks. When the katsina finally visited they killed many people. The Twin War Boys retaliated by killing many katsina, explaining that they did so because "the katsina on their part should care for the people." The town chief told the Twins that the people were at fault because they had not respected the katsina. He urged the War Twins to use their magical powers to bring the katsina back to life. The Twins agreed because it was "by them [i.e., the katsina] that we have lived and been happy." The magic worked. The katsina came back to life. To teach the young the respect they had to show the katsina, that is, the reciprocity which regulated generational relations and labor exchange between juniors and seniors, every adolescent had to be initiated into the katsina cult and learn what death and destruction awaited those juniors who did not observe these rules.[8]

Marriage, the mark of transition from junior to senior status, was similarly enmeshed in gift exchanges. Girls married when they were about seventeen years old, said Hernan Gallegos in 1582, boys when they were about nineteen. This occurred in the standard boy-meets-girl way. The young man would then inform his parents that he wanted to marry. If the parents and kin agreed to the match, the senior members of his household gathered the necessary marriage-validating gifts on the boy's behalf. The willingness of elders to gather these gifts testified that the boy had been respectful of his elders, had toiled for them tirelessly, and had been obedient. Had he not, they could withhold the gifts he needed to present to his prospective in-laws, reminding him of his past failures and of their anger at him, much like when the katsina became angry at disrespectful juniors and refused to bless them.[9]

When the boy's elders had gathered their marriage-validating gifts, they took them to the girl's household. If the girl's kin agreed to the marriage and accepted the gifts, each person that accepted a gift had to give one in return. The gifts the bride's kin collected for her in-laws were usually taken to them on the fourth day after the initial gifts were received. Jane Collier characterizes this marital system as one of "equal bride-wealth" because "equal" amounts of wealth are exchanged between the boy's and girl's households to validate the marriage. When these exchanges were complete a marital rite followed.[10]

Marriage and procreation marked one as an adult. Children triggered a new cycle of indebtedness. But if because of few or sickly children a couple was unable to produce those socially desired goods exchanged as gifts, then these unsuccessful seniors would have to indebt themselves to successful seniors in order to provide their own children with the prerequisites for adulthood. Unsuccessful seniors who obtained gifts they could not reciprocate for their child from successful seniors were indebted to them and could be expected to render labor, respect, and obedience. Heads of successful households, by having numerous juniors as well as unsuccessful seniors whose labor they could appropriate to accumulate gift-stuff, were thus in a position to support large extended households consisting of secondary wives, widows, orphans, and strays.

Relationships of superordination and subordination among the Puebloans were based on age and personal characteristics. Such societies are often called egalitarian because theoretically all men and women had equal access to those things a person of either sex needed in life, be it ritual blessings, esoteric knowledge, tools, land, or seeds. "I have not seen any principal houses by which any superiority over others could be shown," said Francisco

Vásquez de Coronado in 1540, as he tried to assess the differences between the Aztecs and the Pueblos. Diego Pérez de Luxán visited the Hopi and Zuñi Pueblos in 1582 and concluded that no discernible differences in material trappings existed between the caciques, or chiefs, and others: "They are all equal." Age grading was one source of inequality in the Pueblos, but as one advanced through life and married, became a parent, a household head, and finally an elder, one's power and prestige also grew. Senior men, successful or unsuccessful, controlled social well-being. Senior women likewise commanded great respect and authority through ownership of the household, of its sacred fetishes, and of its seeds, whatever the household's size or productivity. "The old men are the ones who have the most authority," reported Hernando de Alvarado and Fray Juan de Padilla in 1540. Pedro de Castañeda observed that same year that the Hopi were governed "by an assembly of the oldest men."[11]

According to Jane Collier, "leadership is a creation of followership" among tribesmen. When a chief died or became so senile that he was no longer able to accumulate the gift-stuff to stage ceremonials and to indebt others, his following dissolved. The chief's children might be advantaged in obtaining ritual knowledge, blessings, and gifts, but every person who aspired to leadership had to obtain his own ritual knowledge, his own bride, and his own following. Leadership was not hereditarily based in one household or matrilineage until the eighteenth century, thus minimizing inherited inequalities. Additionally, the Pueblos prized generosity and equated conspicuous wealth with witchcraft. Chiefs were above all successful seniors who generously gifted those who sought their help and selflessly provided all the goods necessary to stage religious ceremonials through which the gods' blessings were obtained.[12]

The Pueblo Indians viewed the relations between the sexes as relatively balanced. Women and men each had their own forms of wealth and power, which created independent but mutually interdependent spheres of action. The corn fetish every child was given at birth and the flint arrowhead with which boys were endowed symbolized these relations and expressed the basic preoccupations of a people living in a semi-arid environment. Corn and flint were food and water, but they were also the cosmic principles of femininity and masculinity. Female and male combined as corn seeds and rain combined to perpetuate life. Corn plants without rain would shrivel and die; water without corn was no life at all. The ear of corn infants received represented the Corn Mothers that had given life to all humans, plants, and animals. At Acoma Pueblo this corn fetish is still called Iatiku, because it contains her heart and breath. For this reason too the Hopi called this corn fetish "mother." "Corn is my heart, it will be to [you]…as milk from my breasts," Zia's Corn Mother told her people. Individuals kept this corn fetish throughout their entire lives, for if crops failed its perfect seeds held the promise of a new crop cycle.[13]

If the corn ear represented the feminine generative powers latent in seeds, the earth, and women, the flint arrowhead represented the masculine germinative forces of the sky. Father Sun gave men flint arrowheads to bring forth rain, to harness heat, and to use as a weapon in the hunt. The noise emitted by striking together two pieces of flint resembled the thunder and lightning that accompanied rain. Rain fertilized seeds as men fertilized their women. Without rain or semen life could not continue. The flint arrowhead was the sign of the hunter and warrior. Sun gave his sons, the Twin War Gods, arrowheads with which to give and take away life. From flint too came fire. When men struck flint and created that gift Sun gave them at the beginning of time, they transformed that which was raw into that which was cooked. To the Pueblo Indians flint, rain, semen, and hunting were to male as corn, earth, and childbearing were to female. This idea is conveyed in the Hopi word *posumi*, which means both corn seed and nubile woman. We see this too in the ceremony Zuñi women perform to celebrate the sex of their babies. Over a girl's vulva the women place a large seed-filled gourd and pray that her sexual parts grow large and her fruit abundant. The boy's penis is sprinkled with water, and the women pray that it remains small. Men became very angry when they saw this ritual, for through it women asserted that their life-bearing capacity was immense in comparison to that of men. Men vigorously contested this claim in their rituals to vivify the earth, sporting large artificial penises to show women that their fructifying powers were really more immense, "singing about the penis being the thing that made the women happy."[14]

The natal home was the primary unit of affiliation in Pueblo society. Everyone belonged to a home. Humans, animals, deities, and even the natural forces were believed to each have a home within which they lived. In the sixteenth century the Pueblos were matrilineal, anchoring maternity to matrilocal households. "The houses belong to the women, they being the ones who build them," observed Espinosa in 1601.[15]

The typical household unit consisted of a grandmother and her husband, her sisters and their husbands, her daughters and their husbands, various young children, and perhaps an orphan, slave, or stray. Women were attached to their natal dwelling throughout their lives, said Hernán Gallegos in 1582, and did "not leave except when permitted by their mothers." Men moved from house to house according to their stage of life. During childhood boys lived with their mothers, and at adolescence they moved into a kiva to learn male magical lore. When they had mastered these skills, and were deemed worthy of marriage by their kin, they took up residence in their wife's home. A man nonetheless remained tied to his maternal home throughout his life. For important ceremonial events, men returned to their maternal households. When this occurred the household became a matrilineage. Matrilineages that acknowledged descent from a common ancestor, usually through ownership of a similar animal or spirit fetish, formed larger, primarily religious aggregations known as clans.[16]

Large portions of a woman's day were spent preparing meals for her household. Corn, beans, and squash were the main staples of the diet. Corn was the most important and symbolic of these. It was boiled whole, toasted on the cob, or dried and ground into a fine powder easily cooked as bread or gruel. Every day a woman and her daughters knelt before metates, grinding corn to feed their gods, their fetishes, and their kin. The women worked joyfully at this task, observed Castañeda in 1540. "One crushes the maize, the next grinds it, and the third grinds it finer. While they are grinding, a man sits at the door playing a flageolet, and the women move their stones, keeping time with the music, and all three sing together."[17]

> *Oh, for a heart as pure as pollen on corn blossoms, And for a life as sweet as honey gathered from the flowers, May I do good, as Corn has done good for my people Through all the days that were. Until my task is done and evening falls, Oh, Mighty Spirit, hear my grinding song.*

WITHIN THE HOUSEHOLD an age hierarchy existed, for as Hernán Gallegos observed in 1582, "women, if they have daughters, make them do the grinding." The production of pottery (e.g., storage jars, cooking utensils, ritual medicine bowls), moccasins, ceremonial apparel, and turkey-down blankets was also women's household work. Men appropriated and circulated some of these goods throughout the Southwest. Pottery was widely coveted and brought a handsome barter in hides, feathers, and meat.[18]

After feeding, the activity of greatest cultural import to Pueblo women was sexual intercourse. Women were empowered through their sexuality. Through sex women bore the children who would offer them labor and respect in old age. Through sex women incorporated husbands into their maternal households and expected labor and respect from them. Through sex women domesticated the wild malevolent spirits of nature and transformed them into beneficent household gods. Accordingly, then, sexuality was deemed essential for the peaceful continuation of life.

Female sexuality was theirs to give and withhold. In marriage a woman gave her husband her love and her body because of the labor he gave her mother, and because of all the marriage-validating gifts that had been given on her behalf to her in-laws. When women gave the gift of their body to men with whom no obligational ties existed, they expected something in return, such as blankets, meat, salt, and hides. For a man to enjoy a woman's body without giving her a gift in return was for him to become indebted to her in a bond of obligation.[19]

Erotic behavior in its myriad forms (heterosexuality, homosexuality, bisexuality) knew no boundaries of sex or age. Many of the great gods—the Zuñi Awonawilona, the Navajo First Man/First Woman, the Hopi Kawasaitaka katsina—were bisexual, combining the potentialities of male and female into one—a combination equally revered among humans. If the Indians sang of sex, copulated openly, staged orgiastic rituals, and named landmarks "Clitoris Spring," "Girl's Breast Point," "Buttocks-Vagina," and "Shove Penis," it was because the natural world around them was full of sexuality.[20]

Sexuality was equated with fertility, regeneration, and the holy by the Pueblo Indians, a pattern Mircea Eliade has found to be common to many societies. Humanity was dependent on sexuality for its continuation. The Acoma Indians say they were conceived when Pishuni, the serpentine deity of water, entered Nautsiti's body as rain. At the beginning of time, too, Thought Woman taught the Corn Mothers that maize would give them life if planted deep within Mother Earth's womb. When the clouds (men) poured down their rain (semen) the seeds (women) would germinate and come to life. The reader will recall that this is why a boy's penis was sprinkled with water at birth and a girl's vulva was covered with a seed-filled gourd.[21]

With the onset of menses Hopi girls were initiated into the clan-based Marau, Lakon, or Oaquol societies. Since the Hopi say that the Lakon and Oaqol ceremonies are derived from the Marau ceremony, let us focus on it. According to myth, the Marau Society was created by the Sun. He met a woman in the underworld and abducted her, and from their union came many children. Sun taught one of his sons the mysteries of the Wuwutcim (men's society) and one of his daughters those of the Marau.[22]

Twice a year, in January and in September, the Marau Society conducted a ceremony at which women officiated; at no other time did this occur. The January ceremony, which celebrated female fecundity, sexuality, and reproduction, began with four days of prayer-stick making, songs, prayers, and smokes. On the fifth day the society's initiates were inducted with a hair-washing. Throughout the next two days the women danced to awaken the sky's (men's) desires so that it would pour forth its rain (semen). Dancing naked in a circle with their backs to the community, the women would fondle clay phalluses and taunt the men with lewd songs to the clouds (rain, semen) and lightning (penis), repeatedly bending over to expose their genitals to the men. "Iss iss, iss iss," the men would cry excitedly. "I wish I wish, I wish I wish!"—wishes the women satisfied at the dance's end, cooling the passion of the men through intercourse, the symbol of cosmic harmony.[23]

The September Marau celebration was identical except for a ritual confrontation between the society's women and two men who impersonated the Twin War Gods. While the women danced holding corn-stalks with young ears of corn on them, the War Twins approached the circle and shot arrows at a bundle of produce that represented the feminine reproductive earth. The arrows symbolized lightning (penis), and their strikes germination (intercourse). The dancers then encircled the Twins and fed them cornmeal, the substance of female labor, which when exchanged as a gift symbolized peace, established affinity, and incorporated individuals into a household. When the dance ended, the women deposited the arrows at the shrine of the war gods.[24]

Warfare was a male activity among the Pueblos that was outside and beyond the moral order of society. In the continuum of reciprocities that regulated a pueblo, the taking of human life through violence was at the negative end; gifting was at the positive end, signifying the avoidance of war. Through the gifting of food and the offering of hospitality in the form of intercourse women assured communal peace. Violence was domesticated and tamed through such female ritual. And through the issue of women's bodies—children— foreigners and natives became one and were incorporated into households.[25]

These ideas were expressed poignantly during the scalp dance performed by Pueblo women when their men returned from war. Women would jubilantly greet returning war parties outside the pueblo, reported Fray Atanasio Domínguez in 1776, and together with their men would carry the scalps of the enemy dead, "singing on the way about the events of the battle... [with] howls, leaps, shouts, skirmishes, courses back and forth, salvos, and other demonstrations of rejoicing." When the scalps entered the pueblo, said Domínguez, "the women scornfully touch their private parts with the scalp." Another observer said that the women "bared their buttocks to it [the scalp]. They said it was their second and third husband and lay down on it as if having sexual intercourse. All of this was to take power away from the enemy." After the scalps had been robbed of their power in this way, they were attached to a large wooden pole and a dance was performed for them, which included much singing about the feats of battle and the prowess of Pueblo warriors.[26]

The Pueblos believed that an enemy's head and scalp were invested with the person's spirit; if not properly adopted, they would wreak havoc. To forestall this possibility, after the scalps were robbed of their power through intercourse, they were entrusted to women who fed them cornmeal and thereby incorporated into a household. Beneficent fetishes now, the scalps were considered potent rain makers. "We are going to have a little rain," the Keres say, "the scalps are crying."[27]

Finally, we see the cultural importance that feeding and sexual intercourse played in domesticating all those alien and dangerous forces outside the pueblo in the deer butchering practices of the Acoma Indians. After the men killed a deer, usually through suffocation, they began the butchering by splitting open the deer's cavity. Then they removed the deer's penis, if it was male, or the vulva, if female, and placed the genitals in the stomach. This joining of genitals and stomach in a wild animal that is about to enter the village underscores the close symbolic association between sexuality and feeding. Women performed a similar rite for the deer when it entered the pueblo. First the women sexually taunted the dead deer with lewd speech, they "had" intercourse with it, fed it, and finally welcomed it into their home.[28]

The power women enjoyed by virtue of their control over the household, feeding, and sexuality was rivaled by the power men enjoyed as a result of their control over the community's relationships with its gods, which made hunting, warfare, rain making, and trade possible.

The space outside and beyond the pueblo was authentically the province of men and gained meaning in opposition to the space men controlled at the symbolic center of the town. The male conceptualization of space outlined here comes from Pueblo origin myths. Bear in mind that such myths are products of the male imagination. They are sacred knowledge that men transmitted to other men and as such were profoundly political narratives. By outlining the organization of society in mythic times, detailing who helped whom emerge when and where, men asserted their spatial claims, their rights, and their precedence in their relationships both with women and with the members of other households and clans.[29]

The men of every pueblo considered their town to be the center of the universe and placed their main kiva at the vortex of a spatial scheme that extended outward to the four cardinal points, upward to the four skies above, and downward to the underworld. Kivas were usually round (sometimes square) subterranean structures that conjoined space and time to reproduce the sacred time of emergence. Located at the center of the kiva's floor was the shipapu, the earth's navel, through which the people emerged from the underworld and through which they would return.[30]

The kiva was circular to resemble the sky. A hole in the center of the roof, the only entrance and source of light, symbolized the opening through which the Corn Mothers climbed onto the earth's surface. The profane space outside and the sacred space within the kiva were connected by a ladder called "rainbow" made of the same pine tree the sisters had used to emerge. The kiva floor had a fire altar that commemorated the gift of fire, and a hollow, dug-out place that represented the door to the house of the Sun, the Moon, and the mountains of the four cardinal points. The walls had altars on which were placed stone fetishes representing all the animals and deities of the world. Around the entire base of the kiva was an elevated ledge covered with bear and lion skins known as "fog seats." When the spirits that lived outside the pueblo were invoked and came to participate in ceremonials, they sat on these. Men's claims to precedence over women lay precisely in this capacity to bring what was outside the village into its core during religious rituals, to communicate with the gods, and thereby to order and control an otherwise chaotic and hostile natural world.[31]

Radiating outward horizontally from the kiva toward the four cardinal points were a series of tetrads that demarcated the sacral topography. The outermost tetrad was formed by the horizontal mountain peaks in which the seasonal spirits lived. In between the horizon and the pueblo were the shrines of the outlying hills and mesas. Shrines were "heaps of small stones which nature [had] formed," reported Hernán Gallegos in 1582, or holes in the earth's surface that resembled navels. People "worshiped and offered sacrifices" at these places, said Diego Pérez de Luxán, when they were "weary from their journey or troubled with any other burdens." Within the town the tetrad was repeated as directional points that all ceremonial dance circuits touched. At the center of the pueblo, the kiva united the cosmic six directions.

Men owned the kivas and the sacred fetishes, altars, masks, and ritual paraphernalia contained therein.[32]

The kiva, as the navel that tied the people with their gods, was the physical symbol of political society. Each pueblo was a theocracy. At the center of political life stood the cacique, the town chief or Inside Chief, who exercised broad authority over all matters. Around him stood men of superlative knowledge in hunting, warfare, medicine magic, and rain-conjuring who by virtue of their abilities had accumulated large followings as well as large amounts of gift-stuff with which they could stage communal rites and offer gifts to others on behalf of unsuccessful villagers. Next were the unsuccessful seniors, their veneration increasing with age. Young male aspirants to the religious knowledge that would translate into political power came next. And finally, at the margins, as men saw it, were women, children, slaves, and strays.[33]

The forces of dispersion that could destroy Pueblo society were centrifugal. The political discourse that religious ritual made possible was centripetal. Men mechanistically created cosmic harmony, a requisite for social peace, only by coming together in unison at the center. Junior men moved from the margins to the center to obtain the blessings and ritual knowledge that would bring them adult status, a wife, and social power. But unlike the path of the young toward the old, of the human toward the godly, which was symbolized by movement from the margins to the center, our journey through the male world of ritual goes in the opposite direction, from the center outward. This expository strategy helps us to localize social groups in space.

Presiding over the town's main kiva, the quasi-divine Inside Chief was simultaneously a lawgiver and a peacemaker, a war lord and a high priest. He symbolized cosmic harmony and the embodiment of those forces of attraction that constituted society. He conjoined the human and the divine, the cosmological and the political, the mythic and the historic, and organized those three functions on which Pueblo religio-political life depended: administration of the sacred, exercise of physical force, and control over well-being and fecundity.[34]

The Inside Chief controlled the sacred in Pueblo society. He was the town's chief priest, a direct descendant of the Sun, "the holder of all roads of men," and the person who brought order to an otherwise chaotic cosmos. The people "esteemed and venerated the sun above all things," said Hernando de Alarcón in 1540, "because it warmed them and made the seeds germinate." Associated with the sky's greatest deity, the cacique regulated life's rhythms and assured happiness, prosperity, and long life. Appropriately, the Zuñn town chief was called Sun Speaker (*Pekwin*), and the Hopi chief, Sun Watcher (*Tawawunitaka*).[35]

The religious system the Inside Chief administered was fundamentally monistic. Humans, animals, natural forces, and supernatural spirits were all intricately related in balanced ties of reciprocity. The cosmic harmony every person desired was subject to human mechanistic control. So long as people performed religious rites joyfully and precisely, careful that every prayer was word-perfect and full of verve, and that the ritual paraphernalia was exact to the last detail, the forces of nature would reciprocate with their own uninterrupted flow. The sun would rise and set properly, the seasons of the year would come and go, bringing rainfall and verdant crops in summer, and in the winter, game and snow.[36]

The cacique's central imperative was to keep the cosmos properly balanced so that humanity did not swerve from life's road. So long as the forces of evil that threatened to disrupt society were rendered impotent through ritual, peace and prosperity reigned. The Inside Chief accomplished this by calling together the men in the town's households and clans for ritual purposes and by acting as arbiter of law and order. As high priest, the cacique was the keeper of sacred time. From the heights of the town's dwellings he watched the courses of the sun and moon and with amazing accuracy announced the summer and winter solstices, the vernal and autumnal equinoxes, and all the dates for planting, harvest, initiations, and rain and curing rites. At appropriate points in the lunar year, the cacique entered the town's main kiva, and by ritually recreating the primordial time of emergence when humans and gods were one, and when all a town's clans, kivas, and esoteric societies were in harmony, he temporarily obliterated local enmities and tensions.[37]

If the Inside Chief's administration of the sacred was a harmonizing power, the antithesis—violence, human domination, and the negation of the community's moral order, what we will call physical force—was in the hands of the Outside Chiefs, war chiefs who protected the village from external, natural, and supernatural enemies.[38]

The Outside Chiefs were the divine sons of Father Sun, Masewi (Wren Youth) and Oyoyewi (Mockingbird Youth), also known as the Twin War Gods, say the Acoma Indians. The Twins were conceived miraculously when an ordinary woman ate two pine nuts the Sun gave her. As youngsters the Twins were fearless warriors, roving the countryside, causing mischief, terrorizing others, and killing with those instruments of war their father had given them: bows, arrows, and flint arrowheads.[39]

The mythic tales of the Twin War Gods explained the use of force in Pueblo life. Physical force was born of the godhead through an act of copulation with a woman who represented the land's people. The sons were of their father's essence but were also his antithesis. At the center of society such brutish and terrorizing boys would have wreaked havoc. And so they were pushed to the peripheries as the Outside Chiefs to rule over all that was outside of the village. There, their violence befitted external threats to tranquillity. Localizing functions and social groups in space, we find that warfare was conceived of as marginal, young, and outside the pueblo, while the sacred was at the center, old, and inside the town.

Warfare was the most generalized masculine task in Pueblo society. Before boys could become men, they had to establish themselves as competent warriors. To do this, young men sought out a "warrior father" (usually the war chief or Outside Chief) of great bravery and skill to teach them the prayers, songs, dances, and esoteric lore that would give them power over enemies. Through offering the warrior father numerous gifts, aspiring warriors were gradually taught how to harness the power of the prey animals for success in battle. I want to emphasize the word gradually here, because knowledge was power, and as such it was in the interest of the warrior father to dispense his knowledge slowly. By so doing he maintained a large following and acquired numerous gifts with which he could indebt others and gather the means to stage large raids.[40]

Besides the town's main kiva, male ritual associations devoted to war, curing, hunting, and rain-making each had its own kiva that doubled as a lodge house. Warrior novices lived in the warrior society kiva and there their warrior father taught them bravery, endurance, and agility. Before the arrival of European horses in the Southwest, all warfare was conducted on foot, so running fast was also a cultivated skill.[41]

When men practiced war magic they had to have pure minds and hearts. For the four days before and after war, they refrained from sexual intercourse and purified themselves with sweat baths and emetic drinks. Offering smokes to the war gods and singing war songs, they prayed for success. To obtain the ferocity and strength of bears, the cunning of lions, and the sharp vision of eagles, the warriors took their war fetishes shaped in the likeness of animals, bathed them in human blood and fed them pieces of human hearts that had been torn from the breasts of enemies in previous victories. When all the ritual preparations for warfare were complete, the warriors marched into battle.[42]

Once a young man had proven himself by killing an enemy he was inducted into the warrior society through an ordeal. The Zuñn Bow War Society required its initiates to sit naked atop a large ant hill for a day and submit stolidly to the insects' bites. Members of the Hopi, Zuñi, and Tewa Cactus War societies whipped themselves with cacti. Such a benumbing ordeal also marked the installation of a war chief.[43]

The opposing forces harmonized by the town chieftaincy—Inside Chief versus Outside Chiefs, center versus margin, old versus young, native versus foreign, law versus force—were dependent on the existence of fecundity and well-being. This third essential component of religious life was controlled competitively by three chieftaincies: the rain chiefs, the hunt chiefs, and the medicine men.

The chiefs who directed the hunt, rain, and medicine societies knew well the godly transmitted mysteries of life and death. Women might know the life-giving secrets of Mother Earth, seeds, and child-bearing, but through ritual men controlled the key to the positive and negative reciprocities in their world, which at any moment could be turned to life or death. The heart (which contained the breath and spirit of humans, animals, and deities) and blood were the symbols of the rituals staged by men to assure communal peace and fertility. Just as feeding was a central part of female ritual, so too men regularly gave life to their fetishes, bathing them in nourishing blood and symbolically feeding them bits of heart. Men also fed the earth with their own blood, whipping themselves crimson when they sought those blessings that assured fertility.

Rain was the Pueblo Indians' central preoccupation and the essential ingredient for fecundity. Men recognized that Mother Earth and women had immense capacities to bring forth life, but to realize this potential the sky had to fructify the earth with rain and men their wives with semen. Thus what the people worshipped most, said Hernando de Alarcón in 1540, was "the sun and water." Why did they worship water? According to Coronado it was "because it makes the maize grow and sustains their life, and that the only other reason they know is that their ancestors did so.[44]

The rain chief was one of the most powerful men in every village because he knew how to conjure rain both by calling Horned Water Snake and the katsina. The Pueblos equated serpentine deities with rain. The Horned Water Serpent of the Pueblos united the vertical levels of the cosmos. He lived both upon the earth and below it and so combined the masculine germinative forces of the sky (rain) with the feminine generation power of the earth (seeds). The phallic representations of Horned Water Snake were cloaked in feathers as a god of lightning and rain. The earliest Pueblo rock drawings depict him as a zigzag line with a horned triangular head and as a lightning snake attached to a cloud burst.[45]

The Pueblo Dead—the katsina—were also potent rain spirits tied to the living in bonds of reciprocity. It was the rain chief who knew how to call the katsina and did so by offering them prayer sticks and gifts, asking them to visit with rain, food, and fertility. Katsina lived at the place of emergence underneath lakes and on mountain tops. Missives to the katsina were dispatched as puffs of smoke, which as mimetic magic beckoned the cloud spirits to visit. At death Puebloans became clouds. That is why to this day the Hopi harangue their dead saying: "You are no longer a Hopi, you are a Cloud. When you get yonder you will tell the chief to hasten the rain clouds hither."[46]

After warfare, hunting was the broadest male task in Pueblo society. Men contributed meat to the maize diet at every pueblo, but it was at those villages dependent exclusively on rainfall for crop irrigation that hunting magic was most important. Boys learned hunting techniques by observing renowned hunters and by listening to their animal stories. When a boy killed his first rabbit, he was initiated into a hunt society and apprenticed to a hunt father who gradually taught him the prayers, songs, and magical ways of the hunt in return for gifts of corn and meat. The novice became a full member of the society when he captured a large game animal (deer, antelope, or mountain sheep). If by chance he killed a prey animal (bear, lion, or eagle), he automatically became a member of the warrior society, because hunting and warfare were considered very similar activities.[47]

Hunting practices for rabbit, antelope, deer, and buffalo were all very similar. We focus here on deer hunting because deer meat was the most abundant and highly prized, and because men thought of women as two-legged deer. A deer hunt was organized whenever food reserves were low, when a ceremonial was to be staged, or when the katsina were going to visit.

For four days the hunt chief led the hunt society's members in song, prayer, prayer-stick making, and smokes. During this time the eldest male of each household brought his lineage "offspring" animal fetish to the kiva and placed it next to the hunt chief's "mother" fetish on the society's altar. There the hunt chief empowered the fetishes with animal spirits for a successful hunt by bathing them in nourishing blood and feeding them small bits of the animal they were going to hunt. These fetishes contained the living heart and breath of the animals they depicted. When the hunt chief empowered them, he unleashed the fetish's heart and breath. The fetish's breath immediately pierced the heart of the hunted animal, sapped its soul's energy and immobilized it. In this state the hunted animal was easily overcome.[48]

During these four days, and for four days after the hunt, men were sexually continent. Hunters believed that animals disliked the smell of women and would not allow themselves to be captured by a man so contaminated. To rid himself of such odor, a hunter purified his body with emetic drinks and smokes. If a man was to accomplish his goal, neither his mind nor his heart could be dissipated by the thought of women.[49]

The hunt began on the fourth day. Transformed into the animals they hunted, the hunters donned deerskins with the head and antlers still attached. The hunt chief selected the hunting ground and dispersed the men around its edges, forming a large circle. Slowly the circumference of the circle tightened and the deer became exhausted. Finally the deer were wrestled to the ground and choked. A deer was suffocated so that its breath and spirit would be reborn as more game, and because only the skins of suffocated animals could be used as hunt costumes.[50]

The deer was immediately skinned and disemboweled. First its heart was cut out and its blood was fed to the animal fetishes the hunters carried in their pouches. Next the stomach was removed and opened. If a doe, its vulva was placed in the stomach and sprinkled with corn pollen; if a buck, the penis and testicles were similarly treated. The carcass was then carried back to the pueblo, where it was adopted into the hunter's maternal household through ritual intercourse and ritual feeding. "We are glad you have come to our home and have not been ashamed of our people," Acoma's women would tell the deer as they offered it cornmeal. The hunter's relatives rubbed their hands over the deer's body and then across their own faces to obtain its beauty and strength. Finally, the hunter purified himself with juniper smoke so that the deer spirit would not haunt him. The meat was divided between the hunt chief who had taught the boy how to hunt and the hunter's household of affiliation.[51]

A pueblo's prosperity was fundamentally dependent on the physical and psychological well-being of its members. Thus every village had several *chaianyi*, medicine men who cured illnesses and exorcised disease-causing witches who robbed human hearts of their breath and spirit. As knowledgeable herbalists, the *chaianyi* cured minor ailments; but if a disease seemed unique, longlasting, or particularly debilitating, witchcraft was its cause. Witches wrought calamities and illnesses by shooting objects into the body of their victim or by stealing their heart. Using tactics similar to those of hunters, witches sapped people of their strength by attacking their heart. Since witches plied their craft disguised as animals, medicine men had to fight them as animals. That is why *chaianyi* were known as bears (the fiercest animal humans knew) and their magic as "bear medicine." In such form medicine men could help people regain their health, winning back their heart and sucking out the objects shot into them by the witch.[52]

When an individual or a community was afflicted by disease, a cure by the medicine man known to have power over that illness was requested through gifts. For four days the medicine man prepared himself, smoking, making prayer-sticks, reciting the necessary prayers and songs, and abstaining from meat, salt, and sex. He made offerings at appropriate shrines, obtained water for medicines from sacred springs, erected an altar, and arranged on it fetishes, medicine bowls, and curing paraphernalia. When all was ready, the sick individual was placed on the floor before the altar. Near the patient, the medicine man made a circular sand painting representing all the powerful forces in the cosmos. Then, to obtain the power to cure from the "real" medicine men, the animals, he prayed to the bear fetish for the power of all the animals on earth, to the eagle fetish for the power of the animals in the air, and to the weasel fetish for the power of the animals in the ground. Each of these fetishes was fed and bathed in blood from the heart of the animal they represented. Wearing a bear claw necklace with four claws, and holding eagle plumes in each hand, the medicine man "whipped away" the disease with cutting motions. If a quartz crystal with which the person's body was examined revealed foreign objects, the medicine man sucked them out. If the patient's heart had been stolen, the *chaianyi* fought with the witches to retrieve it. When the ceremony ended, the patient drank medicines and returned home cured. If for some reason the patient died, the presumption was that the ceremony had not been properly conducted or that the *chaianyi's* heart was impure.[53]

In sum, entering male ceremonialism from the edges and moving toward the center, we first find the chiefs who controlled well-being and fertility (rain, hunt, and medicine chiefs), then the Outside Chiefs who organized physical force, and finally at the core the Inside Chief who represented the sacred powers of attraction that constituted political society. Through apprenticeship in a town's various societies, junior men gradually learned the religious knowledge they needed to assure prosperity and guarantee their personal advance to senior status. Religious knowledge allowed men to harness and control those natural forces outside the pueblo, which the gods ruled, and to bring them peacefully into the core; it gave them the power to kill, and by so doing assured life. By carefully executing prescribed ritual formulas, they preserved the relationship of reciprocity that existed between men and the spirit world and kept the fragile structure of the cosmos intact.

Men envisioned a cosmos in which masculinity and femininity were relatively balanced. But the social world really was not so. In a largely horticultural society women asserted and could prove that they had enormous control and power over seed production, child-rearing, household construction, and the earth's fertility. Men admitted this. But they made a counterclaim that men's ability to communicate with the gods and to control life and death protected the precarious balance in the universe by forestalling village factionalism and dissent. The tendency of women to overproduce had to be properly controlled through the religious activities of men. Women's voraciousness for semen and the earth's infinite capacity to soak up rain sapped masculinity of its potence. This was indeed the case, explains Jane Collier, regarding gender concepts in "equal bridewealth" societies. On a daily basis women appropriated men's vital energies: the crops they planted, the children they engendered, and the meat from their hunts. Men thus frequently renewed their energies by segregating themselves from women and staging ceremonials to assure successful hunts, war, curing, and rain-making. Because potent feminity polluted and rendered male magic impotent, men abstained from sex with women for a prescribed period before and after their rituals. It is easy to understand the roots of these gender concepts in the social division of labor. The ecological constraints of the habitat in which men pursued their productive activities made their world precarious. Who could predict defeat in battle, disease, factionalism, drought, or poor hunting?[54]

It is as part of this contestation between the sexes over the cosmic power of men and women, and the masculine assertion that ritual give them a dominant hand, that we can best understand the place and function of the "third sex" in Pueblo life, the half-men/half-women, as the natives still know them, or the berdache (from the Arabic *bradaj*, meaning male prostitute), as the sixteenth-century Europeans called them.[55]

The berdache were biological males who had assumed the dress, occupations, mannerisms, and sexual comportment of females as a result of a sacred vision or community selection. Hernando de Alarcón in 1540 observed that in those villages where he found berdaches, they numbered four. Four was a sacred number to the Pueblo Indians; there were four horizontal directions, four seasons, four lengths to Wenimats, four days of preparation before ritual, etc. Alarcón was told that if one of the four berdaches died, "a search was made for all the pregnant women in the land, and the first born was chosen to exercise the function of women. The women dressed them in their clothes, saying that if they were to act as such they should wear their clothes."[56] Alvar Núñez Cabeza de Vaca observed berdaches during his 1523-33 trek across Texas and New Mexico: "I saw one man married to another and these are impotent, effeminate men and they go about dressed as women, and do women's tasks, and shoot with a bow, and carry great burdens…and they are huskier than the other men and taller."[57]

That the berdache were consistently described as men abnormally tall and heavy led Fray Juan Agustín de Morfi in the 1770s and Dr. William A. Hammond, the U.S. Surgeon-General, in the 1850s to wonder if they were intersexuals. Morfi pondered the matter and admitted uncertainty; Hammond uncovered the "facts," examining the genitals of an Acoma and a Laguna berdache. To Hammond's amazement, neither was a hermaphrodite. Both had large mammary glands, scant pubic hair, small penises ("no larger than a thimble," "not…over an inch in length"), and small testicles ("the size of a small filbert," "about the size of a kidney bean"). More significant were the comments Hammond elicited from the Acoma berdache: "He told me that he had nursed several infants whose mothers had died, and that he had given them plenty of milk from his breasts. I expressed my doubts of the truth of this assertion, but he persisted with vehemence that it was true…he informed me with evident pride, [that he] possessed a large penis and his testicles were grandes como huevos'—as large as eggs." Despite the physiological realities, the Acoma berdache believed herself (she was always referred to with the feminine pronoun) to possess the reproductive capacities of both male and female. Rising above the basic dualities that structured the world, she symbolized the coincidentia oppositorum, the joining of opposites that men created in ritual.[58]

Pre-menopausal women polluted male ritual and were thus excluded from active participation in all kiva-centered ceremonials. According to Gallegos, when men gathered to renew the universe or to recreate primordial time "only the men take part, the women never." The participants in these rituals "wore the masks and dress of both men and women even though they were all men," attested Don Esteban Clemente in 1660, even to the point of smearing the insides of their legs with rabbit blood to resemble menstrual discharge.[59]

Ritual female impersonators may not all have been berdaches, but the historical evidence does seem to indicate this. On the basis of the berdaches' role in Pueblo ritual we see again the male assertion that they controlled all aspects of human life. Women had power only over half of creation; through ritual men controlled its entirety—male and female—and were thus equal if not superior to women. Women obviously contested this claim.

The emphasis male ritual placed on village cooperation and social peace also explains in purely functional terms the meaning of the berdache. As sacred half-man/half-woman who conjoined all that was male and female, she was a living symbol of cosmic harmony. Castañeda witnessed a boy's initiation as a berdache in 1540 and described how the women endowed him with female clothing, turquoises, and bracelets:

> Then the dignitaries came in to make use of her one at a time, and after them all the others who cared to. From then on she was not to deny herself to any one, as she was paid a certain established amount for the service. And even though she might take a husband later on, she was not thereby free to deny herself to any one who offered her pay.

Alarcón added that the berdaches who dressed and behaved like women "could not have carnal relations with women at all, but they themselves could be used by all marriageable youths…. They receive no compensation for this work…although they were free to take from any house what they needed for their living." As noted earlier, bachelors were residentially segregated in kivas until they married, ostensibly to master male esoteric lore, but also to minimize conflicts between juniors and seniors over claims to female sexuality that adult married men enjoyed. Sex with a berdache served a personal erotic need and a religious (political) end. So long as bachelors were having sex with the half-man/half-woman, the social peace they represented was not beset with village conflicts between men over women. This may have been why the Spaniards called the berdaches *putos* (male whores). European prostitutes initiated young men to sexuality and gave married men a sexual outlet without disrupting family, marriage, or patrimony."[60]

These, then, were the contours of Pueblo Indian society in the sixteenth century. Each pueblo was an aggregation of sedentary horticulturists living in extended matrilineal households, supplementing their existence through hunting and warfare. Elders controlled the organization of production and, through the distribution of its fruits as gifts and ritual blessings, perpetuated the main inequalities of life; the inequality between juniors and seniors and between successful and unsuccessful seniors. The household and all the activities symbolically related to it belonged to women; the kivas and the pueblo's relationships with its gods was the province of men.

NOTES

The following abbreviated note citations are based on the manuscript sources and bibliography found in Ramón A. Gutiérrez, *When Jesus Came, the Corn Mothers Went Away: Marriage, Sexuality, and Power in New Mexico, 1500-1846* (Stanford University Press, 1991), 343–345, 389–415.

1. Several versions of Acoma Pueblo's origin myth exist. Here I have used Stirling's *Origin Myth of Acoma*, which is a transcription of a 1928 Bureau of American Ethnology taped interview with several Acoma Indians. The chief Acoma informant learned the origin myth as a youth during his initiation to the Koshari Society, a group of sacred clowns to whom all religious knowledge was entrusted. Other versions of the Acoma emergence myth can be found in White, *The Acoma Indians*; Boas, *Keresan Texts*; D. Ford, "A Creation Myth from Acoma"; J. Gunn, *Schat-Chen*; *PIR*, 242–48; Tyler, *Pueblo Gods and Myths*.

2. Several transliterations of katsina appear in ethnographic literature, including kachina, katcina, cachina, and catzina. The origins and significance of the katsina in Pueblo religion can be found in Dockstader, *The Katchina and the White Man*; Anderson, "The Pueblo Kachina Cult"; Bunzel, *Zuñi Katcinas*; Ellis, "A Pantheon of Kachinas"; Fewkes, "An interpretation of Katcina Worship"; Schaafsma and Schaafsma, "Pueblo Kachina Cult."

3. C. Lévi-Strauss, *Structural Anthropology* (New York, 1963), 220–21.

4. Eliade, *The Myth of the Eternal Return*. My understanding of the relationship between myth and history has been greatly influenced by Sahlins, *The Islands of History*, 56–60; Dumézil, *The Destiny of the Warrior*, 3–II; Vansina, *Oral Tradition as History*, 13–25; Eliade, *Patterns in Comparative Religion*, 388–409.

5. Stirling, *Origin Myth of Acoma*, 41–42. White, *The Acoma Indians*, 133–34.

6. My understanding of the politics of gift comes largely from Collier, *Marriage and Inequality*, 79–92; R. Ford, "Barter, Gift or Violence"; W. Jacobs, *Wilderness Politics and Gifts*; Mauss, *The Gift*; Sahlins, *Stone Age Economics*, 149–276; Whitehead, "Fertility and Exchange in New Guinea"; Meeker, Barlow, and Lipset, "Culture, Exchange, and Gender."

7. Collier, *Marriage and Inequality*, 103–5.

8. Stirling, *Origin Myth of Acoma*, 50–59.

9. *RNM*, 86; *PIR*, 43.

10. Collier, *Marriage and Inequality*, 71–141.

11. *NCE*, 174. *RNM*, 193–94. *NCE*, 183, 215.

12. Collier, *Marriage and Inequality*, 76.3

13. Parsons, "Hopi Mothers and Children," 100. *PIR*, 182. See also Sjö and Mor, *The Great Cosmic Mother*.

14. Niethammer, *Daughters of the Earth*, 11; Parsons, "Mothers and Children at Zuñi," 168; Haeberlin, *The Idea of Fertilization*; Collier, *Marriage and Inequality*, 131–33; Duberman, ed., "Documents in Hopi Indian Sexuality," 124.

15. Declaration of Marcelo Espinosa, 1601, *OD*, 636.

16. Eggan, *Social Organization of the Western Pueblos*, 231–32, 291–324; Benedict, *Patterns of Culture*, 75–76. *RNM*, 86. Fox, *Kinship and Marriage*, 90.

17. *NCE*, 256.

18. Qoyawayma, *No Turning Back*, 5; *RNM*, 85. On female domestic production, also see *NCE*, 158–59, 183, 252, 255; *RNM*, 85, 172.

19. The gifts women demanded for sex are mentioned numerous places. See *NCE*, 248; *RNM*, 206; *RBM*, 43–44; *HD* vol. 3, 149, 184; *AGN–INQ* 587–1: 19, 60, 64, 140.

20. Tyler, *Pueblo Gods and Myths*, 81; Hill, "Hermaphrodite and Transvestite in Navaho Culture"; Titiev, *Hopi Indians*, 153, 214–15. Titiev, *Old Oraibi*, 206; Hay, "The Hammond Report," 20. Ritual copulation is described in PIR, 566–67, 644, 805; Affidavits of Kuanwikvaya (1920), Steve Quonestewa (April 14, 1921), Quoyawyma (April 16, 1921), and L.R. McDonald (May 11, 1915) in the National Anthropological Archives, the Smithsonian Institution (Washington, D.C.). Bestiality, fellatio, and phallic clowning are reported in the affidavits of Siventiwa (1920), William H. Pfeifer (November 13, 1920), Blas Casaus (November 7, 1915), Otto Lomauitu (1920), and Emory A. Marks (December 11, 1920) deposited at the National Anthropological Archieves.

21. Eliade, *Patterns in Comparative Religion*, 239–64, 331–66. *PIR*, 428–31. Niethammer, *Daughters of the Earth*, 11.

22. Fewkes, "The Tusayan New-fire Ceremony," 447; Titiev, *Old Oraibi*, 164.

23. Titiev, *Hopi Indians*, 164–65; Voth, *The Oraibi Ceremony*, 32; Duberman, ed., "Documents in Hopi Sexuality," 108–13; *PIR*, 675–82.

24. Titiev, *Hopi Indians*, 166–67; Schlegel, "Male and Female in Hopi Thought and Action."

25. Sahlins, *Stone Age Economics*, 149–276; Whitehead, "Fertility and Exchange in New Guinea."

26. *MNM*, 257. Other scalp dances are described and analyzed in PIR, 624–25, 644–45; Bunzel, "Zuñi Ritual Poetry," 679; Parsons, *The Scalp Ceremonial of Zuñi.*

27. *PRI*, 350–51; White, *The Pueblo of Santo Domingo*, 144–48.

28. White, *New Material from Acoma*, , 336.

29. I thank Jane Collier for bringing this point to my attention. See also Yava, *Big Falling Snow*; and Talayesva, *Sun Chief.*

30. This spatial model is best described by Ortiz in *The Tewa World*, 11–28; Stubbs, *Bird's-Eye View of the Pueblos*; Tyler, *Pueblo Gods and Myths*, 169–79.

31. White, *The Acoma Indians*, 132. Stephen, *Hopi Journal*, vol. 2, 119on.

32. *RNM*, 101; *RBM*, 43; *RNM*, 193–94.

33. White, *Pueblo of Santa Ana*, 187; Parsons, *Hopi and Zuñi Ceremonialism*, 53; Schroeder, "Rio Grande Ethnohistory," 51.

34. These three categories of male political life come from Dumézil, *The Destiny of the Warrior* and *The Destiny of a King.*

35. *NCE*, 135. *PIR*, 169; Titiev, *Old Oraibi*, 131.

36. Bellah, "Religious Systems," 227–64; Benedict, *Patterns of Culture*, 54–55; Dozier, *Pueblo Indians of North America*, 151.

37. Bellah, "Religious Systems," 230. McCluskey, "The Astronomy of the Hopi Indians."

38. Tyler, *Pueblo Gods and Myths*, 219; *PIR*, 125.

39. Stirling, *Origin Myth of Acoma*, 97. Tyler, *Pueblo Gods and Myths*, 213.

40. Ibid. Those interested in the role that secrecy and the distribution of esoteric knowledge plays in creating and perpetuating inequality should consult Brandt, "On Secrecy and the Control of Knowledge," and "The Role of Secrecy in a Pueblo Society."

41. Nabokov, *Indian Running.*

42. Ellis, "Patterns of Aggression"; Woodbury, "A Reconsideration of Pueblo Warfare." Pueblo war societies have been extinct since the seventeeth century. To understand what Pueblo warrior societies may have been like, I studied warfare in other Indian tribes. See Hill, *Navaho Warfare*; Guernsey, "Notes on a Navajo War Dance"; Parsons, "Notes on a Navajo War Dance"; Bandelier, "On the Art of War and Mode of Warfare"; Ellis, "Patterns of Aggression"; Farmer, "Defensive Systems of the Southwest"; Hadlock, "Warfare Among the Northeastern Woodland Indians"; Mishkin, *Rank and Warfare Among the Plains Indians*; M. Smith, "The War Complex of the Plains Indians," and "American Indian Warfare"; Stewart, "Mohave Warfare."

43. *NCE*, 249; Bandelier, *Final Report of Investigations*, Part I, 69–70; *RBM*, 44; R. Smith, "Mexican and Anglo-Saxon Traffic in Scalps, Slaves, and Livestock," *West Texas Historical Association Year Book* (1960), 98–115. RMB, 239n. PIR, 467, 875, 923; J. Green, ed., *Zuñi: Selected Writing of Frank Hamilton Cushing* (Lincoln, 1979), passim.

44. Collier, *Marriage and Inequality*, 131–32. *NCE*, 184. Ibid., 175.

45. Fewkes, "A Few Tusayan Pictographs," 16–17; N. Judd, *The Material Culture of Pueblo Bonito*, 278. On phallic/serpentine symbolism see León, "El Culto del Falo"; Stoddard, "Phallic Symbols in America"; Lejeal, "Rites Phalliques."

46. *PIR*, 173. *RNM*, 99; *NCE*, 184, 258; *PIR*, 171. Katsina is a Hopi word meaning "respect spirit" (*ka*, respect, and *china*, spirit); the word is used here generically to refer to those cloud-beings known at Taos as *thlatsi* or *thliwa*, at Isleta as *wenin* or *thliwa*, at Jémez as *k'ats'ana* or *dysa*, and to the Tewa as *oxuhwa*. To Frederick Dockstader katsina means "life father" or "spirit father" (from *kachi*, life or spirit, and *na*, father). See Dockstader's *The Kachina and the White Man*, 9.

47. Tyler, *Pueblo Animals*, 32–35; Beaglehole, *Hopi Hunting*, 4–7; Underhill, *Ceremonial Patterns*, 30; Scully, *Pueblo*, 67.

48. Cushing, *Zuñi Fetishes*, 15.

49. Tyler, *Pueblo Animals*, 35–36. Beaglehole, *Hopi Hunting*, 6.

50. Driving animals into pits, into natural culs de sac, or over mesa tops were also common hunting techniques. Beaglehole, *Hopi Hunting*, 8.

51. White, *New Material from Acoma*, 336. Stirling, *Origin Myth of Acoma*, 24–25. Beaglehole, *Hopi Hunting*, 7, 11, 13. See also Bonnegjea, "Hunting Superstitions"; Hill, *Agriculture and Hunting Methods.*

52. Schlegel, "Socialization of a Hopi Girl," 453.

53. The illnesses and curses associated with various curing societies can be found in *PIR*, 189–92 and Titiev, *Old Oraibi*, 241. White, *The Acoma Indians*, 107–27; Underhill, *Ceremonial Patterns*, 38;

Tyler, *Pueblo Animals*, 184–202; Simmons, *Witchcraft in the Southwest*, 69–95; Parsons, "Witchcraft Among the Pueblos." It should be noted that although women could and still do become *chaianyi*, the Spanish friars and explorers never mentioned them as such. Rather, as shown in chapters 2 and 10, they thought of native women with religious or magical powers as witches.

Most pueblos today have clown societies. They probably existed in the sixteenth century but were not mentioned by the Europeans. I suspect that the Spanish chroniclers could not differentiate between the medicine men and their assistants, the clowns. On Pueblo clowning see Stirling, *Origin Myth of Acoma*, 33; Hieb, "Meaning and Mismeaning"; Erodes and Ortiz, *American Indian Myths and Legends*, 333–86.

54. Collier, *Marriage and Inequality*, 131–33.

55. These "men-women" were known to the Zuñi as *la'mana*, to the Tewa as *quetho*, and to the Navajo as *nadle*. They existed among the Keres (Acoma, Laguna, and Santa Ana) and Hopi, but I have not been able to locate their indigenous names. Parsons, "The Zuñi La'Mana"; S. Jacobs, "Comment"; Hill, "The Status of the Hermaphrodite"; Gifford, "Cultural Elements Distribution"; Fewkes, "A Few Tusayan Pictographs," AA, 5(1892), 11.

56. Male berdache status has been reported in 113 North American Indian Cultures; female berdache in only 30. The Navaho, Western Apache, and Utes are the only Southwestern Indian groups known to have female berdache. The berdache tradition is best studied in Callender and Kochems, "The North American Berdache"; S. Jacobs, "Berdache"; Williams, *The Spirit and the Flesh*. On female berdaches see Whitehead, "The Bow and the Burden Strap." Those interested in the cross-cultural meaning of homoeroticism and homosexuality will find the following works illuminating: Herdt, *Guardians of the Flute, Rituals of Manhood, and Ritualized Homosexuality in Melanesia*; Sergent, *Homosexuality in Greek Myth*; Boswell, *Christianity*; Ariès and Béjin, *Western Sexuality*; J. Trevisan, *Perverts in Paradise: Homosexuality in Brazil, from the Colonial Period to the Present* (New York, 1986); E. Blackwood, ed., *The Many Faces of Homosexuality*.

57. NCE, 130, 148. "Naufrahios de Alvar Núñez Cabeza de Vaca," quoted in Jonathan Katz, *Gay American History*, 285.

58. Fray Juan Agustín Morfi cited in Newcomb, *The Indians of Texas*, 74; Hammond, "The Disease of the Scythians." Ibid., 334–36. Eliade, *Mephistopheles and the Androgyne*, 78–124, and *Patterns in Comparative Religion*, 356–61, 419–25.

59. *RNM*, 99–100. Declaration of Don Esteban Clemente, 1660, AGN-INQ 587–1:123. Duberman, ed., "Documents in Hopi Indian Sexuality," 116. Hay, "The Hammond Report," 18.

60. *NCE*, 248. Ibid., 147–48.

A WORLD OF WONDERS

David D. Hall

Historians traditionally have presented the Puritan religion of seventeenth-century New Englanders as a rational and coherent intellectual system. In breaking with the superstitions of the past, and especially Catholicism, the Puritans apparently turned away from the "magic" of sacraments and sacred places. Recent work in colonial history, however, suggests that the colonists lived within a broader, older "world of wonders." Rather than initiating the world's disenchantment, seventeenth-century Puritans mixed together what we in "modern" times try to separate as Christianity, on the one hand, and as magical beliefs and practices, on the other.

In David Hall's rendering, the Europeans who settled North America brought with them a widespread belief in magic and the occult. Witchcraft, apparitions, and other unearthly phenomena as well as supernatural explanations of natural events such as comets, hailstorms, earthquakes, sudden deaths, and monster births pervaded New England culture. Unlike England, where the popular culture of the laity was frequently at odds with the "official" religion of the clergy, popular religion as described by Hall was accessible to everyone, providing a language that all groups shared. It is nothing new to assert that seventeenth-century New England was culturally homogeneous. What makes Hall's argument revisionist is his belief that this common culture did not derive from Puritan theology. Rather, what the clergy and educated laity held in common was a far more enchanted universe laced with the "debris" of other systems of thought, some older than Christianity.

Reprinted by permission from David D. Hall, "A World of Wonders: The Mentality of the Supernatural in Seventeenth-Century New England," in Hall and David Grayson Allen, eds., *Seventeenth Century New England* (Boston: The Colonial Society of Massachusetts, 1984), 239–274.

2

A WORLD OF WONDERS

The Mentality of the Supernatural in Seventeenth-Century New England

David D. Hall

THE PEOPLE of seventeenth-century New England lived in an enchanted universe. Theirs was a world of wonders. Ghosts came to people in the night, and trumpets blared, though no one saw from where the sound emerged. Nor could people see the lines of force that made a "long staff dance up and down in the chimney" of William Morse's house. In this enchanted world, the sky on a "clear day" could fill with "many companies of armed men in the air, clothed in light-colored garments, and the commander in sad [somber]." Many of the townsfolk of New Haven had seen a phantom ship sail regally into the harbor. An old man in Lynn had espied

> a strange black cloud in which after some space he saw a man in arms complete standing with his legs straddling and having a pike in his hands which he held across his breast…; after a while the man vanished in whose room appeared a spacious ship seeming under sail though she kept the same station.

Voices spoke from heaven, and little children uttered warnings. Bending over his son Joseph's cradle one evening, an astonished Samuel Sewall heard him say, "The French are coming."[1]

All of these events were "wonders" to the colonists, events betokening the presence of superhuman or supernatural forces. In seventeenth-century New England it was common to speak of the providence of God as "wonder-working."[2] Some wonders were like miracles in being demonstrations of God's power to suspend or interrupt the laws of nature. Others were natural events that God employed as portents or signals of impending change. The events that Cotton Mather described in *Wonders of the Invisible World* were the handiwork of Satan and his minions. A wonder could also be something unexpected or extraordinary, like a sudden death or freak coincidence.[3]

In the course of the seventeenth century, many of the colonists would experience a wonder and many others tell stories of them. Either way, these events aroused strong feelings. An earthquake in New England in 1638 had caused divers men (that had never known an Earthquake before) being at work in the fields, to cast down their working tools, and run with ghastly terrified looks, to the next company they could meet withall.[4]

Almost a century later, as an earthquake rocked Boston, the "young people" in Samuel Sewall's house "were quickly frighted out of the shaking clattering kitchen, and fled with weeping cries into" their father's bedroom, "where they made a fire, and abode there till morning." In responding to such "marvellous" events, people used words like "awful," "terrible" and "amazing" to describe what had happened.[5] Every wonder made visible and real the immense forces that impinged upon the order of the world. A wonder reaffirmed the insecurity of existence and the majesty of a supreme God.

This essay is about the wonder as the colonists would know and tell of it. At the outset, we may dispose of one false issue: the people in New England who heard voices and saw apparitions were not deluded fanatics or "primitive" in their mentality. The possibility of these experiences was widely affirmed as credible in the best science and religion of the early seventeenth century. We can never answer with complete satisfaction the question as to why some persons do see ghosts or witness apparitions. But for the people of seventeenth-century Europe and America, these were ordinary events that many persons encountered, and many more believed in.

This is an essay, therefore, about phenomena that occurred on both sides of the Atlantic, and among both Protestants and Catholics. We may speak of a lore of wonders, an accumulation of stock references and literary conventions that descended to the colonists from Scripture, antiquity, the early Church and the Middle Ages. People in the seventeenth century inherited a lore that stretched back to the Greeks and Romans. Chaucer had told of portents and prodigies in *The Canterbury Tales*, as had the author of *The Golden Legend*, a medieval collection of saints' lives. Whenever the colonists spoke or wrote of wonders, they drew freely on this lore; theirs was a borrowed language.

To speak of continuity is to raise two other questions: how did this lore pass to the colonists, and how did it consort with their doctrinal understanding of the universe? The key intermediaries in transmitting an old language to the colonists were the English printer-booksellers who published great quantities of wonder tales in the sixteenth and seventeenth centuries. They had allies in certain writers who put together collections of this lore to suit new purposes, like the emergence of Protestantism. Protestants drew freely on the lore of wonders, adapting it to indicate the merits of their cause. To this end Luther had retold the story of a "monster" fish found in the River Tiber, interpreting it as a portent of Rome's mistakes. And the wonder could serve to reinforce the concept of God's providence, a doctrine of importance to the early Reformers.

But what of all the "superstitions" that this lore reiterated? The language of the wonder was rich in motifs and assumptions that seem at odds with the mentality of the Puritans who colonized New England. In breaking with the past, and especially with Catholicism, the Puritan movement had turned against the "magic" of the sacraments and holy relics, of sacred places and saints' days. The religion of the colonists seems, in retrospect, to have forecast and initiated a "disenchantment" of the world.[6] The Puritan God was a God of order and reason, interpreted by learned men in the form of systematic theology. In such statements, Puritanism assumed the shape of a coherent world view, intellectually neat and tidy and swept clean of superstition.

Such, at least, is how we characteristically understand the religion of the colonists. But the lore of wonders as repeated and developed by the colonists cannot be reconciled with so static or so modernist an understanding. We may come instead to recognize that contradiction, or a kind of intellectual pluralism, was truer of the colonists than a uniform and systematic mode of thought. So too, we may come to recognize that these people were not hostile to a folklore that had roots in paganism. Indeed, the wonder tale would introduce them to a popular culture that drew on many sources and traditions. In reiterating these tales, the colonists would affirm their own participation in this wider, older culture.

The lore of wonders was popular culture in the sense of being accessible to everyone; it was a language that all groups in society shared, known not only to the "learned" but to ordinary folk as well. It was popular in being so pervasive, and in being tolerant of contradictions. A full history of this culture and its absorption into Protestantism would lead in several directions, including that of witchcraft. My purpose is more limited, to begin upon a history of this lore as it was received by the colonists, and to trace how it provided them with a mentality of the supernatural.

Portents and prodigies were routine events in English printed broadsides of the seventeenth century. "Strange news from Brotherton," announced a broadside ballad of 1648 that told of wheat that rained down from the sky. "A wonder of wonders" of 1663 concerned a drummer boy who moved invisibly about the town of Tidworth. In "Strange and true news from Westmoreland," a murder story ends with the devil pointing out the guilty person. Hundreds of such broadside ballads, stories told in verse and printed on a single sheet of paper, circulated in the England of Cromwell and the Stuarts. Newsheets, which began appearing with some regularity in the 1640's, carried tales of other marvels. Pamphlets of no more than eight or sixteen pages contained reports of children speaking preternaturally and offered *Strange and wonderful News…of certain dreadfull Apparitions*. The yearly almanacs weighted in with their accounts of mystic forces emanating from the stars and planets.[7]

The same prodigies and portents would recur again and again in broadside ballads, newsheets, chapbooks, and almanacs. Tales of witchcraft and the devil, of comets, hailstorms, monster births and apparitions—these were some of the most commonplace. "Murder will out," as supernatural forces intervened to indicate the guilty. The earth could open up and swallow persons who tell lies. "Many are the wonders which have lately happened," declared the anonymous author of *A miracle, of miracles*,

> as of sodaine and strange death upon perjured persons, strange sights in the Ayre, strange births on the Earth, Earthquakes, Commets, and fierie Impressions, with the execution of God himselfe from his holy fire in heaven, on the wretched man and his wife, at Holnhurst….

A single ballad spoke of blazing stars, monstrous births, a rainstorm of blood, lightning, rainbows, and the sound of great guns. Others told of dreams and prophecies that bore upon the future of kings and countries. Almanacs and other astrological compendia reported similar events: comets, eclipses, joined fetuses, infants speaking.[8]

All of these were cheap forms of print. Hawked by peddlars and hung up in stalls for everyone to see and gape at, they reached the barely literate and the lower orders as well as readers of more means and schooling. The stories they contained would also turn up in a very different kind of book that ran to several hundred pages. Big books—perhaps in the grand format of the folio—were too expensive to circulate in quantity and had authors who announced themselves as of the "learned." But these differences in form and audience did not extend into the contents. The lore of portents and prodigies appeared in books like Thomas Beard's *The Theatre of Gods Judgements* as well as in the cheapest pamphlet.

Thomas Beard was a learned man, a graduate of Cambridge who practiced schoolteaching and received ordination as a minister. Born in the early years of Elizabeth's reign, he published *The Theatre of Gods Judgements* in 1597. Three more editions followed, the last of these in 1648. That same year, Samuel Clarke, like Beard a graduate of Cambridge and a minister, brought out a rival collection: *A Mirrour or Looking-Glasse both for Saints and Sinners, Held forth in about two thousand Examples: Wherein is presented, as Gods Wonderful Mercies to the one, so his severe Judgments against the other.* Clarke's *Examples* (to call it by the title the colonists would use) went through five editions, the final one appearing in 1671. Clarke was a non-conformist after 1662, ejected from the Church of England because he would not recant his presbyterianism. The sequel to his book was William Turner's folio *Compleat History of the Most Remarkable Providences, Both of Judgement and Mercy, which have hapned in this Present Age* (1697). To this series should be added another Elizabethan work, Stephen Batman's The Doome warning all men to Judgmente: Wherein are contayned for the most parte all the straunge Prodigies hapned in the Worlde (1581). Ministers all, Batman, Beard, Clarke, and Turner had a secular competitor in the hack writer Nathaniel Crouch. His *Wonderful Prodigies of Judgment and Mercy*, discovered in above *Three Hundred Memorable Histories* (1682) was one of a string of works on prodigies and strange wonders that Crouch would publish in the 1680's under his pen name of Robert Burton.

As in the ballads and chapbooks, so in these books nature offered up innumerable signs of supernatural intervention:

> Now according to the variety and diversity of mens offences, the Lord in his most just and admirable judgment, useth diversity of punishments:…sometimes correcting them by storms and tempests, both by sea and land; other times by lightning, haile, and deluge of waters…and not seldome by remedilesse and sudden fires, heaven and earth, and all the elements being armed with an invincible force, to take vengeance upon such as traytors and rebels against God.

Earthquakes, multiple suns, strange lights in the sky, rainbows, sudden deaths, monstrous births—these were other frequent signs or signals.[9] Like the ballad writers, Beard and Batman reported esoteric, even violent, events: rats that ate a man, a crow whose dung struck someone dead, the agonies of martyrs. In one or another of these books, we hear of dreams and prophecies, of crimes detected by some form of sympathetic magic, of thieves who rot away, and of armed men in the sky.[10] Much too was made of Satan. He offered compacts to young men in need of money, while sometimes serving as God's agent for inflicting vengeance. Many tales revolved around the curse, "the devil take you," and its surprising consequences:

> Not long since a Cavalier in Salisbury in the middest of his health-drinking and carrousing in a Tavern, drank a health to the Devil, saying, That if the devil would not come, and pledge him, he would not believe that there was either God or devil: whereupon his companions strucken with

horror, hastened out of the room, and presently after hearing a hideous noise, and smelling a stinking savour, the Vintner ran up into the Chamber: and coming in, he missed his guest, and found the window broken, the Iron barre in it bowed, and all bloody, but the man was never heard of afterwards.

The devil might appear in several guises. Black bears, a favorite of the ballad writers, turned up again in stories told by Beard and Batman, as did black dogs.[11]

In telling of these wonders, the men who organized the great collections borrowed from the broadside and the chapbook; a ballad tale of a woman who sank into the ground was reported in Clarke's *Examples*, in Crouch's *Wonderful Prodigies*, and again in Turner's *Compleat History*.[12] This flow of stories meant that "learned" men accorded credibility to wonders as readily as any ballad writer. In this regard, the great folios were no more critical or selective than the cheapest forms of print. The one format was the work of learned men, the other of printers and their literary hacks. But the two shared a popular culture of portents and prodigies, a common lore that linked small books and great, the reader of the ballad and the reader of the folio.

This was a lore that other Europeans were collecting and reporting in the sixteenth and seventeenth centuries. Sixteenth-century German broadsides told of comets, multiple suns, monster births and armies in the air. A Lutheran who wrote an introduction to an encyclopedia of portents "attempted to define the spectrum of such 'wonder works,'" listing "signs, miracles, visions, prophecies, dreams, oracles, predictions, prodigies, divinations, omens, wonders, portents, presages, presentiments, monsters, impressions, marvels, spells, charms and incantations."[13] In Catholic France the *livrets bleus*, those inexpensive books that circulated widely in the seventeenth century, were dominated by accounts of apparitions, miracles, witchcraft, and possession. Some of these continental stories would reappear in England. Certain ballads were translated or adapted from a foreign source.[14] Thomas Beard described *The Theatre* as "translated from the French," and though his source remains unspecified, his book was parallelled by Simon Goulart's *Histories admirables et memorables de nostre temps*, of which there was an English translation in 1607.[15] On the Continent, as in the England of Beard and Clarke, the distinction between reading matter that was "learned" and reading that was "popular" did not apply to tales of wonders. Nor was this lore of more appeal to Catholics than to Protestants. Indeed it seemed to cut across the line between the pagan and the Christian worlds.

No better demonstration of this blending exists than the eclectic sources on which Beard, Clarke and their contemporaries drew. Aside from newsheets and ballads, whether English or imported, most of their material was culled from printed books that subsumed the sweep of western culture. The classical and early Christian sources included Vergil, Pliny, Plutarch, Seneca, Cicero, Josephus (a favorite), Gildas, Eusebius, and Bede. Then came the historians and chroniclers of the Middle Ages: Geoffrey of Monmouth, Voragine's *The Golden Legend*. The sixteenth and seventeenth centuries supplied a host of chronicles and encyclopedias: *The Mirrour of Magistrates*, the *Magdeburg Centuries*, and others by such writers as Hollingshead, Polydore Vergil, Conrad Lycosthenes, Sleiden, Camden, and Heylin. No source was more important to the English writers than John Foxe's Acts and Monuments, itself a résumé of narratives and chronicles extending back to Eusebius. A final source was that great wonder book, the Bible. Its narratives of visions, voices, strange deaths, and witches lent credence to such stories of a later date.[16]

In plundering this great mass of materials, Beard, Batman, and their successors made modest efforts to be critical. As Protestants, they followed Foxe's lead in dropping from their histories most of the visions, cures, and other miracles associated with the legends of the saints. But otherwise the English writers were willing to reprint the stories that descended to them from the Middle Ages and antiquity. No one questioned the legitimacy of Pliny's *Natural History* and its kin, to which, indeed, these writers conceded an unusual authority. The parting of the ways between the "ancients" and the "moderns" lay in the future. In conceding so much to their sources, whether classical or of the early Church or even of the Middle Ages, Beard and Clarke admitted to their pages a strange mixture of ideas and themes. This was a mixture that requires closer scrutiny, for the stories in these books were charged with several meanings.

Wonder stories were interesting in and of themselves; even now, events that seem to defy nature attract our curiosity. But in the seventeeth century, each portent carried a large burden of meaning. Much of this burden was compounded out of three main systems or traditions of ideas—apocalypticism, astrology, and the meteorology of the Greeks. Each of these systems was in decay or disrepute by the middle of the century, under challenge either from an alternative, more up-to-date science or from a growing disenchantment with prophetic visionaries. But even in decay these systems continued to give meaning to the wonder tales.

The most widely used of these traditions was the meteorology of the Greeks and Romans. In Aristotle's physics, meteorology referred to everything occurring in the region of the universe between the earth and moon. As a science it encompassed blazing stars, comets (deemed to circle earth below the moon), rainbows, lightning, and thunder as well as fanciful or misinterpreted phenomena like apparitions in the sky. After Aristotle, the key commentator on meteorology was Pliny, whose *Natural History* "embellished Aristotle's rational theory with many elements of wonder and even superstition." Pliny had become available in translation by the 1560's, and most other major Roman writers who spoke of meteors—Seneca, Plutarch, Vergil—had been made available in English by the early seventeenth century. But English readers learned of blazing stars and comets chiefly from translated versions of a dozen medieval and Renaissance encyclopedias, or from poetic versions such as *La Sepmaine* (1578), the work of a French Huguenot and poet du Bartas. His long poem, which proved immensely popular in English translation, melded Protestant didacticism with the lore of meteors as "prodigious signs."[17]

No less commonplace to most Elizabethans was astrology, the science of celestial bodies. Elizabethans learned their astrology from a medley of medieval and renaissance handbooks. These books taught a Christian version of the science, affirming, for example, that the stars and planets had no independent power but depended on the will of God. Astrology reached a wide audience via almanacs and their "prognostications" as keyed to planetary oppositions and conjunctions. Weather lore was another common vehicle of astrological ideas and images.[18]

A third intellectual tradition was apocalypticism. Several different strands converged to form this one tradition. The Scripture offered up a vision of the end in the Apocalypse. The Old and New Testaments told of persons who could prophesy the future on the basis of some vision, or perhaps by hearing voices: "If there be a prophet among you, I the Lord will make myself known unto him in a vision, and will speak to him in a dream" (Numbers

12:6). The legends of the saints were rich in visions, as were the lives of martyrs in Eusebius.[19] Geoffrey of Monmouth, a thirteenth-century English writer, invented prophecies that he ascribed to Merlin. These would survive into the seventeenth century in the company of other legendary sayings—of "Mother Shipton," of the Sybilline oracles, or of obscure Germans whose manuscript predictions were always being rediscovered.[20] With the coming of the Reformation, apocalypticism gained new vigor as Protestants connected their own movement to the cryptic references in Revelation. The feeling was pervasive that contemporary history manifested the great struggle between Christ and Antichrist, and that some cataclysmic alternation was impending. In his influential explication of the Book of Revelation, Joseph Mede reaffirmed the prophetic significance of voices, thunder, lightning, hail, eclipses, blazing stars, and the rise and fall of kings. Mede regarded all the seals and trumpets in Revelation as forecasting real historical events, and in working out the parallels he made it seem that the Apocalypse would not be long postponed.[21]

But the more crucial contribution of the Reformation was the doctrine of God's providence. The doctrine antedated Luther and Calvin. Chaucer's Knight had spoken of "Destiny, that Minister-General/Who executed on earth and over all/That providence which God has long foreseen," and the Psalmist sang of a God who stretched out his protection to the ends of the earth. Nonetheless, the doctrine had a fresh importance in the sixteenth century. In reaffirming the sovereignty of God, the Reformers also wished to understand their own emergence as prefigured in God's grand providential design. John Foxe, the martyrologist, made providence the animating principle of his great book. In its wake, Thomas Beard would reassure his readers that God was immediately and actively present in the world, the ultimate force behind everything that happened: "Is there any substance in this world that hath no cause of his subsisting...? Doth not every thunderclap constraine you to tremble at the blast of his voyce?" Nothing in this world occurred according to contingency or "blind chance." All of nature, all of history, displayed a regularity that men must marvel at, a regularity that witnessed to the "all-surpassing power of God's will." From time to time this "marvellous" order was interrupted by other acts of providence, for God had the power to suspend the laws of nature and work wonders that were even more impressive than the routine harmony of things. The providence of God was as manifest in the swift and unexpected as in the "constant" order of the world.[22]

Beard, Clarke, and Turner were aggressively Protestant in pointing out the significance of God's providence, especially as it affected evil-doers, papists, and persecutors of the Church. In doing so, they continued to rely on astrology, apocalypticism, and meteorology for motifs and evidence. No one viewed these systems as in contradiction with each other. Indeed they seemed to reinforce the patterns of a providential universe. Astrology taught men to regard the heavens as infused with law and order. The meteorology of the ancients rested on assumptions about natural law. Science, whether old or new, was still allied with religion,[23] and the synthesis of Christianity and classical culture remained intact. Then too, the sciences of Greece and Rome were rich in possibilities for disruption and disorder. The conjunction of two planets could send shock waves through the universe. Stars could wander out of their ordained paths, and storms arise as nature fell into imbalance. The world as pictured by astrologers and scientists was prone to violent eruptions. This sense of things was echoed in apocalypticism, and writers on the Apocalypse would cite comets and eclipses as signs of the portending end. Meanwhile Satan raged incessantly against God's kingdom, leading many into sin and tormenting seekers after truth. Sin, injustice, persecution—these disorders of the moral universe were mirrored in the conflict and disorder of the heavens. An angry God was the supreme agent of disruption. Astrologers, the Hebrew prophets, the oracles of Greece and Rome, all spoke alike of doom portended in the turmoil of the heavens and the earth. A teleological universe yielded incessant signals of God's providential plan and his impending judgments.

As emblem of God's providence in all of its variety, the wonder had a rich significance. Still more possibilities for meaning were provided by a set of themes that circulated widely in Elizabethan England. One of these was the theme of decay or dissolution. It was a commonplace assumption among Elizabethans that the world was running down and soon would be exhausted. Portents never seemed to hint at progress or improvement but at impending chaos.[24] Another theme was *De Causibus*, or the rise and fall of great men. In Beard as in books like the *Mirrour of Magistrates*, Elizabethans read of kings and princes, of men of greed and overreaching ambition, who seemed propelled by some inevitable force to fall from their high rank.[25] A third theme concerned evil as a power operating almost on its own. Evil was not distant or abstract but something always present in the flow of daily life. A book like Beard's, with its grand metaphor of "theatre," made good and evil the main actors in the drama of existence.[26] Yet another motif was fortune, its symbol a great wheel that swept some people up and others down.[27] A final theme was the interpenetration of the moral and the natural orders. Disruptions of the moral order had their echo in nature, and vice versa. This sympathy or correspondence was why Elizabethans assumed that corpses bled when touched by guilty persons. Hence too this correspondence meant that ills of the body, like sickness and death, betokened spiritual corruption. All of the natural world was permeated by forces of the spirit, be they forces working for good or for evil.[28]

The wonder books incorporated all these themes without concern for how they might seem contradictory. Fortune and providence were, after all, competing if not antithetical interpretations. But the wonder books were remarkably tolerant. They made room for decayed systems of belief; in their pages the pagan coexisted with the Christian, the old science of the Greeks with the new Protestant emphasis on providence. The "learned" may have preferred more distinctions, and a man like Thomas Hobbes found the whole body of this lore distasteful.[29] But in the first half of the seventeenth century, the lore of wonders remained generously eclectic both in its themes and in its audience. Everyone in Elizabethan England had some access to this lore. Writers such as Shakespeare and Milton availed themselves of references and motifs that also were the stock of ballad writers. Conventional, familiar, tolerant and open-ended, the lore of wonders was a language that everyone could speak and understand.

To trace the uses of this language for two or three examples is to trace them for the whole repertory of signs and signals. For Beard and his contemporaries, comets were perhaps the most widely publicized of all the meteors described in ancient science. It was a commonplace of Renaissance discussions to view comets as portending drastic change if not disaster—"drought, the pestilence, hunger, battels, the alteration of kingdomes, and common weales, and the traditions of men. Also windes, earthquakes, dearth, landflouds, and great heate to follow." Du Bartas summed up this wisdom in his *La Sepmaine*:

> There, with long bloody Hair, a Blazing Star Threatens the World with Famine, Plague & War:
> To Princes, death; to Kingdomes many crosses: To all Estates, Inevitable Losses....[30]

His idiom came straight from Pliny, who, in viewing comets as "a very terrible portent," had noted their appearance "during the civil disorder in the consulship of Octavius, and again during the war between Pompey and Caesar."[31]

Thunder and lightning were other portents that drew on ancient sources for their meaning. In Scripture, they were repeatedly the instruments of an avenging God: "Cast forth lightning, and scatter them: Shoot out thine arrows, and destroy them" (Psalm 144:6). The prophecies of St. John in Revelation evoked the "voice" of thunder, lightning, and earthquakes (8:5; 10:4). Pliny had viewed thunder bolts as "direful and accursed," associating them with many kinds of wonders such as prophecy. To writers of the Renaissance, lightning seemed especially to betoken destructive violence. But the prophetic context could be invoked in plays like Marlowe's *Tamburlaine*, where the hero saw himself as the scourge of "a God full of revenging wrath, From whom the thunder and the lightning breaks."[32]

As for apparitions in the sky, the would-be scientific description in writers such as Pliny yielded to interpretation of such sights as portents of impending conflict or defeat. Among Beard, Clarke, and their contemporaries, a much repeated apparition story concerned the fall of Jerusalem. Recounting the destruction of Jerusalem, Josephus had described at length "the strange signes and tokens that appeared" before the city's fall. "One while there was a comet in form of a fiery sword, which for a year together did hang over the city." There were voices, and a man who cried out, "Wo, wo unto Jerusalem." Iron chariots flew through the air, and an army became visible in the clouds. All of this seemed credible to Elizabethans, and no less so, as we shall see, to the people of New England.[33]

Apparitions were credible on the authority of Josephus and Pliny, but they also figured in the folk belief of the English people. Folk belief is not easily distinguished from popular culture in an age when both could circulate by word-of-mouth. Where such beliefs arose and how they were transmitted—and whether they were fragments of some "primitive" mentality—are questions that are difficult to answer. What remains clear is that the wonder books made room for folklore also: stories of the devil as black dog or bear, the legends of the saints and their "white magic," tales of fairies, ghosts, and apparitions, of "murder will out," of curses and their consequences.[34]

So many sources; so many possibilities for meaning! In their tolerance, the great collections ended up without a unifying order of their own. Clarke verged off into sensationalism. Ballads recounted fables of serpents and dragons. Writers such as Crouch felt free to invent stories—as if most ballads were not fiction to begin with.[35] This playfulness was nowhere more amusingly revealed than in a chapbook of the 1640's that mated the predictions of the legendary "Mother Shipton" with the prophecies of a radical Puritan. The new and the old lay side-by-side without apparent contradiction.[36]

But were the colonists this tolerant, or did they order and discriminate in keeping with their Puritanism?

The same wonder tales that Englishmen were buying circulated in the colonies, often via books imported from the London book trade. As a student at Harvard in the 1670's, Edward Taylor had access to a copy of Samuel Clarke's *Examples*, out of which he copied "An Account of ante-mortem visions of Mr. John Holland."[37] In sermons of the 1670's, Increase Mather quoted frequently from Clarke and Beard.[38] Imported broadsides made some of Beard's stories familiar to New England readers; the Boston printer, John Foster, published in 1679 a facsimile of a London broadside, *Divine Examples of Gods Severe*

Judgments against Sabbath-Breakers, a set of warning tales drawn mostly from *A Theatre of Gods Judgements*. Hezekiah Usher, a Boston bookseller, was importing copies of Nathaniel Crouch's *Wonderful Prodigies of Judgment and Mercy* in the 1680's,[39] and another of Crouch's books, *Delights for the Ingenious*, came into the hands of the children of the Goodwin family.[40] Many more such books and broadsides must have crossed the Atlantic in the seventeenth century, though leaving no specific trace of their presence.

In the absence of such evidence we may turn to books and pamphlets that the colonists were writing. Almanacs appeared each year as soon as the colonists had established a printing press. As in England, these local products included references to portents and wonders. The almanac for 1649 offered its readers a lengthy "prognostication" that played on the theme of earthquakes as a portent of impending catastrophe:

> Great Earthquakes frequently (as one relates)
> Forerun strange plagues, dearths, wars and change of states,
> Earths shaking fits by venemous vapours here,
> How is it that they hurt not, as elsewhere!

Like its European counterpart, the New England almanac contained cryptic clues to what the future held:

> The morning Kings may next ensuing year,
> With mighty Armies in the aire appear,
> By one mans means there shall be hither sent
> The Army, Citty, King and Parliament...
> A Child but newly born, shall then foretell
> Great changes in a winding-sheet; Farewell.[41]

The almanac for 1648 tucked portents and prodigies into a "Chronologicall Table" that later almanacs would update:

> Mr. Stoughton and all the souldiers returned home, none being slain.
> Mrs. Dier brought forth her horned-foure-talented monster.
> The great and generall Earth-quake.[42]

Soon enough, moreover, the colonists were writing commentaries on meteors. The first to appear was Samuel Danforth's *An Astronomical Description of the late Comet or Blazing Star... Together with a brief Theological Application thereof* (1665). The comets of 1680 and 1682 stirred the Reverend Increase Mather to publish *Heavens Alarm to the World... Wherein Is Shewed, That fearful Sights and Signs in Heaven are the Presages of great Calamities at hand* and *Kometographia or A Discourse Concerning Comets*. In 1684, Mather undertook a more ambitious project, a compendium that resembled Clarke's *Examples*. *An Essay for the Recording of Illustrious Providences* was at once a collection of wonder tales and a plea for greater efforts among the colonists to preserve such stories.

Reiterating the commonplaces of a literary tradition, these books—the almanacs, the works of meteorology—are proof of the transfer of culture. It should be noted that Danforth and Mather were learned men who had become aware of scientific challenges to

Aristotle's meteorology, challenges that jeopardized some aspects of the portent lore. Yet the two men put aside these alternatives to address a general audience, using an old language and familiar references, and insisting that "blazing stars" remained portents of God's providence.[43]

This message had wide credibility in seventeenth-century New England. We have some measure of its popularity in the record-keeping that went on. Certain public bodies, like the churches in Dorchester and Roxbury, incorporated references to "remarkable providences"—fires, storms, eclipses, victories, sudden deaths—into their records.[44] Each of the Puritan colonies summoned their people repeatedly to days of fasting and thanksgiving, and the calling of these days was cued to the perception of God's providence.[45] Early on, William Bradford, Edward Johnson, and John Winthrop wrote works of history that were richly providential in their narratives of how the colonists had overcome adversity and conflict. These books noted the usual array of signs and portents—eclipses, monster births, strange deaths and storms, miraculous deliverances and reversals—while telling also of more puzzling events, like the lights in the form of a man that were seen in Boston harbor, followed by a voice "calling out in a most dreadful manner, boy, boy, come away, come away."[46] Second- and third-generation historians would reiterate many of these stories, notably in Cotton Mather's *Magnalia Christi Americana* (1702).

All of this public record-keeping or public history was paralleled in private journals that functioned as individual "memorials" of "remarkable" providences."[47] The most extensive of these diaries were kept by John Hull, a Boston merchant and the mint master for Massachusetts Bay, and the magistrate Samuel Sewall, who was Hull's son-in-law. Hull seemed almost overwhelmed at times by the flow of prophetic signals, as in his entry for a year—1666—itself accorded apocalyptic significance because 666 was the mark of the beast (Revelation 13:18).

> At New Haven was distinctly and plainly heard the noise of guns, two, three, five at a time, a great part of the day, being only such noises in the air. The same day, at evening, a house at Northampton [was] fired by lightning; a part of the timber split; a man in it killed…At Narriganset, in Mr. Edward Hutchinson's flock of sheep, were several monsters. In July were very many noises heard by several towns on Long Island, from the sea, distinctly, of great guns and small, and drums.

Early on in Samuel Sewall's record-keeping, he responded strongly to an eclipse: "Morning proper fair, the weather exceedingly benign, but (to me) metaphoric, dismal, dark and portentous, some prodigie appearing in every corner of the skies." For more than fifty years he kept track of many kinds of portents, from thunder storms and rainbows to sudden deaths and disturbing sounds. A faithful buyer of each year's almanac, he inserted notes on deaths and weather portents in each monthly calendar.[48]

Hull and Sewall had witnessed many of the portents they took note of in their diaries; news of many others reached them secondhand. Travellers dropped by to tell of strange events, and Sewall heard of more from correspondents. A fierce hail storm that struck while he was having dinner with Cotton Mather led to an exchange of stories; Sewall remembered that a hail storm coincided with the Duke of Monmouth's ill-fated invasion of England in 1685, and Mather knew of other houses that had been struck by hail or lightning. The stories that reached Hull and Sewall were being told and listened to all over New England.[49]

This trade in stories is revealed with unique vividness in two places, a notebook Edward Taylor kept at Harvard and the correspondence passing in and out of Increase Mather's household. In his notebook Taylor recorded the story of "magical performances by a juggler." He had heard the story from Jonathan Mitchel, the minister in Cambridge, who in turn had learned it from Henry Dunster, the president of Harvard, "during recitation." Dunster had it from the Reverend John Wilson—and here the chain is interrupted. In his notebook Taylor wrote down the essence of another story passed along by word of mouth. A minister and Harvard president, Urian Oakes, had done the telling:

> A child that was born at Norwich last Bartholomew-Day...being in the nurses arms last Easterday...being about 30 weeks old spake these words (This is a hard world): the nurse when she had recovered herselfe a little from her trembling, & amazement at the Extraordinariness of the thing, said Why dear child! thou hast not known it: the child after a pause, replied, But it will be an hard world & you shall know it.

To this same notebook Taylor added his extracts out of Clarke's *Examples* and, from some other printed source, the prophetic scaffold speech of an Englishman executed in 1651.[50]

The traffic in wonder stories was crucial to the making of Increase Mather's *Essay for the Recording of Illustrious Providences*. In the early 1680's Mather was soliciting his fellow ministers for contributions to his impending book. John Higginson of Salem, an older man who came to Boston as a student in the 1630's, responded to this call for stories by sending him word of the Reverend Joshua Moodey's collection of annotated almanacs, "so that I doubt not but besides those [stories] he hath sent you, you may have many more from him. For instance,—he speaks of 26 men thereabouts, dying or cast away in their drunkennes which calls to mind some such case here."

The following year, having learned from Mather that he did not "confine" himself "to things done in N.E.," Higginson wrote out and dispatched two wonder stories attributed to "persons credible," and of events "I believe...to be certain." Both concerned the devil, the one a story of a book that acted strangely on its readers, the other of a man who covenanted with the devil to insinuate "that there was neither God nor Devil, no Heaven nor Hell." The informant who told Higginson of the magical book, a man no longer living, had been a ruling elder of the church in Salem. Long after the experience—it happened back in England—he could still remember that

> as he read in [the book], he was seized on by a strange kind [of] Horror, both of Body & minde, the hair of his head standing up, &c. Finding these effects severall times, he acquainted his master with it, who observing the same effects, they concluding it was a Conjuring Book, resolved to burn it, which they did. He that brought it, in the shape of a man, never coming to call for it, they concluded it was the Devil.

The other story Higginson had collected in his days as minister at Guilford "from a godly old man yet living."[51]

As Higginson predicted, Joshua Moodey had stories to pass on. One was of a house inhabited by evil spirits, as told by the man who lived there. All was relatively quiet now; "the last sight I have heard of," Moodey added, "was the carrying away of severall Axes in the night, notwithstanding they were layed up, yea, lockt up very safe." From a "sober woman" Moodey also had a story of a "monstrous birth" that he described at length, concluding with an offer to "goe up and discourse with the midwife" if Mather wanted more details.[52]

Meanwhile Mather had heard from several informants in Connecticut. The minister in Stamford, John Bishop, had written him some years earlier to answer his inquiries about "the noise of a great gun in the air." In his new letter, Bishop poured out a flood of stories:

> We have had of late, great stormes of rain & wind, & sometimes of thunder & lightning, whereby some execution hath been done by the Lord's holy Hand, though with sparing mercy to mankind. Mr. Jones his house at N[ew] H[aven] broken into, & strange work made in one room thereof especially, wherein one of his daughters had been a little before; & no hurt to any of the family, but the house only…. A little after which, at Norwalk, there were nine working oxen smitten dead in the woods, in a few rods space of ground, & after that, at Greenwich (a small town neer us, on the west side) on the 5 mo. 13, (when we had great thunder & lightning), there were seven swine & a dog smitten all dead, & so found the next morning, very near the dwelling house, where a family of children were alone (their parents not then at home) & no hurt to any of them, more then amazing fear.[53]

More such stories came to Mather from other hands—a narrative of Ann Cole's bewitchment, together with the story of a man who drank too much and died, accounts of providential rainstorms and remarkable deliverances, and of "two terrible strokes by thunder and lightning" that struck Marshfield in Plymouth Colony.[54]

From his brother, finally, came a letter of encouragement. Nathaniel Mather had moved to England in the early 1650's and remained there. But he remembered many of the stories he had listened to while growing up in Dorchester, or as a Harvard student:

> Mrs. Hibbons witchcrafts, & the discovery thereof, as also of H. Lake's wife, of Dorchester, whom, as I have heard, the devil drew in by appearing to her in the likeness, & acting the part of a child of hers then lately dead, on whom her heart was much set: as also another of a girl in Connecticut who was judged to dye a reall convert, tho she dyed for the same crime: Stories, as I heard them, as remarkable for some circumstances as most I have read. Mrs. Dyer's and Mrs. Hutchinson's monstrous births, & the remarkable death of the latter, with Mr. Wilson's prediction or threatning thereof, which, I remember, I heard of in New England.

Flowing from the memories of a man long since departed from New England, these stories reveal how much was passed along in conversation, and how rapidly a stock of native wonder tales had been accumulated.[55]

Most of these local stories had counterparts in stories told by Clarke and Beard or by the ballad writers. Many of these older stories passed among the colonists as well, enriching and legitimizing their own testimonies of the supernatural. We may speak again of all this lore as constituting a form of popular culture. Everyone knew this lore. Its circulation was not limited to print, as the Mather correspondence indicates so clearly. Nor was it something the rude multitude but not the learned could appreciate. When presidents of Harvard told wonder tales in class, when ministers retold stories of "magical" books and freakish bolts of lightning, we can be sure that we are dealing with a culture shared, with few exceptions, by all of the colonists. One other aspect of this culture deserves emphasis. Its cast was thoroughly traditional, employing the same mix of intellectual traditions, the same references and conventions, as the lore in Beard, Clarke, and the ballad writers.

Consider Danforth and Mather's descriptions of the comets they had witnessed. Like so many other commentators before them, Danforth and Mather relied on the meteorology of the ancients, as mediated via medieval and Renaissance encyclopedias. In proving that comets were "Portentous and Signal of great and notable Changes," Danforth drew upon du Bartas while citing, as parallels, events such as the death of Julius Caesar, which, according to tradition, had been prefigured by a comet.[56] Mather cited Josephus, Cicerco, du Bartas, Mede, and Scripture as authorities when preaching on the comet of 1680. The description he gave of a comet that appeared in 1527 was entirely derivative:

> On the eleventh day of August, a most terrifying Comet was seen, of an immense longitude, and bloody colour. The form of it, was like a mans arm holding an huge Sword in his hand with which he was ready to strike. Such terrour and horrour surprized the Spectators of this Prodigy, as that some died away with dread & amazement.[57]

So, too, the references in diaries and in histories to lightning and the phenomenon of three suns repeated elements of an old code of reference. All of the traditional associations between lightning, disorder and prophecy lay in the background of Sewall's frequent diary entries on thunder and lightning, Cotton Mather's *Brontologia Sacra: The Voice of the Glorious God in the Thunder*, and Samuel Arnold's description of a storm that struck the town of Marshfield, in which "the most dismal black cloud…that ever" anyone had seen had passed overhead, shooting forth its "arrows."[58] The phenomenon of three suns, remarked on in Shakespeare's works and by medieval chronicles as signalling the overthrow of kings, remained a "wonder" to Edward Johnson, who linked the "unwonted sights" of "two Parlii, or images of the Sun, and some other strange apparitions," with the "desperate opinion" of persons who in New England "would overthrow all the Ordinances of Christ."[59]

From medieval handbooks the colonists also borrowed the language of astrology. For them it was a Christian science; the stars were signs not causes. New England almanacs retained the old combination of weather lore and astrological prediction, as in an essay Israel Chauncey inserted in his almanac for 1663 on "The Natural Portents of Eclipses, according to Approved Authors."[60] Just as commonplace were the allusions to the consequences of certain planetary motions: "On October the third will be celebrated a famous conjunction of Saturn and Mars, and wherein they are deemed the two Malevolent and Infortunate Planets, the conjunction thereof (say Astrologers) Imports no good."[61] The mixture of astrology and political prediction that had flourished amid civil war in England also reached the colonies in 1690, when a printer newly disembarked from London published an abridged edition of John Holwell's fiercely anti-Tory, anti-Catholic *Catastrophe Mundi: or, Europe's Many Mutations Until the Year 1701.*[62]

Even more appealing to the colonists was the apocalyptic tradition. Visions, dreams, unseen voices—all these were almost everyday experiences, talked about in private and, remarkably, in books. Little children who spoke preternaturally were, as in the ballad literature, accorded special notice, as Taylor indicated by preserving the story of the child who told his nurse it was "an hard world." Nathaniel Morton reported an unseen "voice" that had alerted the beleaguered colonists at Plymouth to arson in their storehouse.[63] The Reverend Noadiah Russell heard of a man in Connecticut…who was taken with a sudden shivering after which he heard a voice saying that four dreadful judgments should come speedily upon the whole world viz: sword, famine, fire and sickness which should, without speedy reformation prevented, begin at New England.[64]

To interpret dreams as prophecy was to participate in a long-established tradition. John Winthrop, to whom a minister had told a dream of his, responded with another of his own:

[C]oming into his chamber, he found his wife…in bed, and three or four of their children lying by her, with most sweet and smiling countenances, with crowns upon their heads, and blue ribbons about their eyes. When he awaked, he told his wife his dream, and made this interpretation of it, that God would take of her children to make them fellow heirs with Christ in his kingdom.[65]

The *Magnalia Christi Americana*, a veritable encyclopedia of New England wonder tales, included many dreams and other acts of prophecying. The Reverend John Wilson had prophetic dreams as well as a "certain prophetical afflatus" that made his prayers affect or forecast the future. Another minister, John Eliot, was gifted with "forebodings of things that were to come," and a third, John Brock of Marblehead, could predict success for fishermen and locate missing boats![66]

Here we sense ourselves approaching folk belief. The wonder tales that passed among the colonists were openly folkloric in certain of their themes and motifs. Stephen Batman had incorporated the folk tradition of spectral, shape-shifting black dogs into *The Doome warning to Judgemente*.[67] A century later, people in New England testified that they had seen the devil in the shape of a black dog. William Barker, Jr., a confessing witch at Salem in 1692, had seen "the Shape of a black dog which looked Very Fercly Upon him" as "he was Goeing into the Woods one Evening" in search of cows. Sarah Carrier, enticed into witchcraft by members of her family, was promised "a black dog."[68] Many of the witnesses at Salem had been visited at night by apparitions of persons crying out for vengeance on their murderers. Such stories were a staple of folk legend and also of the ballad literature.[69] Another folk belief expressed at Salem was the power of white—or in this case, black—magic to keep persons dry in rainstorms. A witness had become suspicious of a visitor whose clothes showed no signs of passing through a storm on muddy roads. Many centuries before Salem witchcraft, the legend had grown up of a saint who remained dry in spite of rain. His was the power of white magic. In some fashion that defies analysis, the colonists were able to repeat this story, though modifying its details and making it a devil story.[70]

Where many of these strands converge—folklore, apocalypticism, white magic, the meteorology of Pliny and Aristotle—is in Increase Mather's *Essay for the Recording of Illustrious Providences*, because it built upon the wonder tales that people told as stories, the Essay has something of the quality of a folk narrative. Yet it is also a "learned" book. Between his own books—he owned the largest private library in New England—and those he found at Harvard, Mather could pillage most of western culture for his lore of portents. In keeping with its bookish sources, the Essay borrowed widely from the ancients and their mediators of the Renaissance. It borrowed also from the English collectors, especially Samuel Clarke and his *Examples*. And since Mather was committed to the mystery of the supernatural, he spent portions of the *Essay* arguing the validity of wonders against contemporary Europeans who were growing skeptical. As proof of the reality of witchcraft, he would repeat the story of the invisible drummer boy of Tidworth, taking it as true on the authority of the English minister and proto-scientist Joseph Glanville, though knowing that the story was denounced by others as a fable.[71]

The man on the receiving end of stories from his fellow clergy made use of some of them but not of others. The book bears signs of haste, as though his printer were impatient and his own control of what he wished to do imperfect. Chapter one told of "sea-deliverances," some of them native, others taken from an English book. In chapter two, a potpourri of stories, Mather reached back to King Philip's War for a captivity narrative and two related episodes; after telling of another "sea-deliverance," he opened up his Clarke's *Examples* and began to copy from it. In chapter three, on "Thunder and Lightning," he quoted from John Bishop's letter and added several other stories of lightning in New England. But the chapter ended with two German stories, some refernces to Scripture and several bits of pedantry. Chapters four, six, seven, and eight were meditations and general arguments on providence, using European sources. Chapter nine demonstrated how thin the line was between the wonder and the curiosity, for here he told of persons who were deaf and dumb but learned to speak.[72] Chapter ten, "Of remarkable tempests," covered hurricanes, whirlwinds, earthquakes, and floods; chapter eleven, "concerning remarkable judgements," related how the enemies of God—Quakers, drunkards, and other enemies of New England—had been punished. Mather added a letter from Connecticut as chapter twelve, and in chapter five drew together several stories of "things preternatural"—demons, apparitions, and evil spirits.

The many layers of the *Essay* included the esoteric. Like Beard and Clarke before him, Mather had an eye for the unusual event. Some of his stranger stories were borrowed from a manuscript, presumably of English origin, that he had inherited from John Davenport, the long-time minister of New Haven. From it he drew a Faust-type story of a young student who contracted with the devil for money. But the black magic of the devil yielded to the higher powers of a group of faithful ministers, whose prayers forced Satan

> to give up that contract; after some hours continuance in prayer, a cloud was seen to spread itself over them, and out of it the very contract signed with the poor creatures blood was dropped down amongst them.

From this manuscript Mather drew an even more sensational story of a minister who drank too much, went to a cockfight on the Lord's Day, and who, while "curses...were between his lips, God smote him dead in the twinkle of an eye. And though Juxon were but young...his carcase was immediately so corrupted as that the stench of it was insufferable."

From the same collection, finally, Mather copied out a "strange passage" concerning a man suspected of stealing sheep who swore his innocence and

> wished, that if he had stollen it, God would cause the horns of the sheep to grow upon him. This man was seen within these few days by a minister of great repute for piety, who saith, that the man has a horn growing out of one corner of his mouth, just like that of a sheep; from which he hath cut seventeen inches, and is forced to keep it tyed by a string to his ear, to prevent its growing up to his eye.

Here again we sense ourselves confronting folk belief. This story of the sheep's horn had its parallel or antecedent in a medieval legend of a man who stole and ate a sheep, and then found a sheep's ear growing out of his mouth. The story of a student who compacted with the devil had roots in legends of the saints and, more remotely, in lore of eastern cultures.[73]

How like it was for wonder tales to build on folk or pagan legends! With its mixture of motifs and sources, *An Essay for the Recording of Illustrious Providences* reaffirmed the traditional tolerance of the genre. The tolerance of the *Essay* was mirrored in broader patterns of response. As readers and book buyers, the colonists were caught up in the wonder tale as it appeared in Beard and Clarke. As storytellers, they repeated to each other a growing stock of local wonders. And in their almanacs and diaries they recorded the prodigies and portents that were the stuff of everyday experience—the voices and strange sounds, monster births and lightning bolts, apparitions in the sky and doings of the devil. In confirming the validity and significance of all of these phenomena, Mather's *Essay* summed up a popular culture that the colonists shared in common with most other Europeans. His book epitomized the transfer of old ways of thinking to the New World.

But still we need to ask what kind of world view was it that accepted the reality of evil spirits and of sheep's horns growing out of someone's mouth? The answer to this question lies elsewhere than in the theology of John Calvin or William Perkins. We are so accustomed to inflating the significance of Puritanism that we easily forget how much else impinged upon the making of beliefs among the colonists. Indeed, the historians who have commented on Mather's *Essay* have actively resisted its complexity. A century ago, the rational-minded Moses Coit Tyler was irritated by Mather's "palpable eagerness…to welcome, from any quarter of the earth or sea or sky, any messenger whatever, who may be seen hurrying toward Boston with his mouth full of marvels." Tyler deemed the stories in the book variously "tragic, or amusing, or disgusting, now and then merely stupid," and in one sweeping statement he condemned the book as "at once a laughable and an instructive memorial of the mental habits" of the colonists. Fifty years later, Kenneth Murdock tried to rescue the Essay, and by implication, Puritanism, by insisting that Mather was up-to-date in his science and in his efforts to weigh and judge the evidence for marvels. Dismissing this interpretation, Perry Miller politicized the book, while admitting that it "seems a collection of old-wives tales and atrocity stories, at best hilariously funny and at worse a parade of gullibility." This indifference to the texture of the Essay—Miller did acknowledge that its roots lay "in a venerable tradition, stretching back to the medieval exempla"—was symptomatic of a larger indifference to traditional belief and popular culture in early New England.[74] Center stage was wholly occupied by the complexities of Puritanism as an intellectual system, and if certain other beliefs, like witchcraft, lingered in the wings, they could safely be ignored since they were headed for extinction.

But the mental world of the colonists was not really fashioned in this manner. High or low, learned or unlearned, these people had absorbed a host of older beliefs. A modern critic who has written on Milton and science remarks that everyone in the early seventeenth century relied on a body of common knowledge that stemmed from Pliny, Aristotle, and the encyclopedists. This old lore was being challenged by new theories of the planets; yet like Mather and the colonists, Milton "was not ever seriously interested in a contest of cosmological theories." As a Christian and a Puritan, Milton believed that the universe was theocentric and teleological. He was also quite at home with a "popular science" that included astrology, finding "no incompatibility between" this science and the doctrines of free will and providence. This eclectic synthesis supported a view of the everyday world as hovering between anarchy and order. Decay and corruption were constant, and disorder in the moral sphere of things was echoed in the disorder of nature. Such a mixture of science and religion in Milton was formed out of intellectual, or popular, traditions that long antedated Puritanism.[75] It is not important to give dates or exact boundaries to these traditions. The point is rather that certain deeper layers of belief—call them folklore, call them "popular"—flowed into Milton's world view as into Increase Mather's.[76]

Armed with this insight, we come finally to understand that the mentality of the supernatural in seventeenth-century New England encompassed themes and motifs that owed little to formal theology or to Puritanism. The people of New England viewed the world about them as demonstrating pattern and order. This was the order of God's providence; their world, like Milton's, was theocentric. It was also teleological, its structure the grand scheme laid out in the Apocalypse, the war of Antichrist against the godly. The forces of evil were immensely strong and cunning, in such sort that the providential order could seem to be "overthrown and turned upside down, men speaking evill of good, and good of evill, accounting darkness light, and light darknesse."[77] Disorder was profound in other ways. The world was rife with violence—with wars and persecution, pestilence and famine, pride, greed and envy. A righteous God could strike with terrible swiftness, disrupting natural law to punish evildoers or afflict the godly. The devil too had powers to wreak havoc. Each kind of violence was attuned to every other, as were the forms of order. This correspondence enriched the meaning of portents and prodigies, making them more terrifying. The plan and order of the universe was, after all, not always visible or readily deciphered. If there were purpose and plan, there were also the marvellous, the inexplicable, and the wonderful:

> One providence seems to look this way, another providence seems to look that way, quite contrary one to another. Hence these works are marveilous. Yea, and that which does add to the wonderment, is, in that the works of God sometimes seem to run counter with his word: so that there is dark and amazing intricacie in the ways of providence.[78]

There was mystery at the heart of things. Death could strike at any moment, the devil could mislead, the earth begin to tremble. In dramatizing all these possibilities, the wonder tale evoked the radical contingency of a world so thoroughly infused with invisible forces.

This mentality of the supernatural reflects the syncreticism of the Christian tradition. Early in its history Christianity had come to terms with the pagan notion of the prodigy and with such systems as astrology. The mixture that resulted cannot arbitrarily be separated into distinct spheres, one "magical" or pagan, the other orthodox or Christian.[79] As one modern historian has noted, the early modern European was receptive to the wonder tale because he "believed that everybody, living or inanimate, was composed of matter and a spirit. This idea was shared by eminent minds right up to the scientific revolution in the seventeenth century; it underlay the neo-Platonic belief of the Renaissance in the souls of stars and justified the persistence of astrology." In this same period no one could "make a clear distinction between nature and supernature" or view the world as simply "ruled…by laws" and not "caprice."[80] This way of thinking made its way across the Atlantic with the colonists. Theirs too was a syncretic Christianity. In tolerating the wonder tale and all its underlying themes, the colonists demonstrated the capacity to abide contradiction and ambiguity. So too they demonstrated their attachment to an old mentality, a popular culture transmitted through the lore of wonders.

Before the century ended, this mentality began to fall apart. Witchcraft, prophecy, and portents came under attack from a coalition of scientists, freethinkers, and clergy (especially Anglicans) who wanted to discredit them as "superstitions." The world lost its enchantment as the realm of nature became separate from the realm of spirit. Comets lost their role as portents; a Harvard graduate of another generation spurned this old belief in an essay published in 1719. Wonder tales, and the mentality embedded in them, lived on but now more clearly in the form of fringe or lower-class beliefs.[81] No learned man dared take the point of view that Increase Mather had assumed in 1684. In its own day, the wonder tale united what became sundered in the eighteenth century. Living as we do on the further side of disenchantment, it is not easy to reenter a world where matter and spirit were interlinked, where "superstitions" remained credible. But therein lies the challenge of the wonder.

NOTES

The research that led to this essay was supported by the John Simon Guggenheim Memorial Foundation, the American Council of Learned Societies, the National Endowment for the Humanities (via the American Antiquarian Society), and Boston University. I am very grateful to these agencies for their support. I want also to thank Richard L. Bushman, Barbara Diefendorf, James Henretta, Keith Thomas, D. P. Walker, and Sam Bass Warner, Jr., for their comments on a previous version of this essay.

1. See footnote 6; George Lincoln Burr, ed., *Narratives of the Witchcraft Cases* (New York, 1914), 175; Increase Mather, *Remarkable Providences, illustrative of the earlier days of American colonisation* (London, 1856), 101, cited hereafter as *Essay*; "The Diaries of John Hull," American Antiquarian Society, *Transactions and Collections*, III (1897), 218; Cotton Mather, *Magnalia Christi Americana*, 2 vols. (Hartford, Conn., 1853–1854), I, 84; "The Diary of Noahdiah Russell," *New England Historical and Genealogical Register*, VII (1853), 53–54; Nathaniel Morton, *New-Englands Memoriall* (Cambridge, Mass., 1670), 52; *The Diary of Samuel Sewall*, M. Halsey Thomas, ed., 2 vols., (New York, 1973), I, 281.

2. Edward Johnson, *The Wonder-Working Providence of Sions Saviour*, ed. J. Franklin Jameson, *Original Narratives of Early American History* (New York, 1910); John Sherman, "To the Reader," in Cotton Mather, *Wonders of the Invisible World* (Boston, 1692).

3. Kitty Scoular, *Natural Magic: Studies in the Presentation of Nature in England Poetry from Spenser to Marvell* (Oxford, 1965), 5; Increase Mather, *The Latter Sign Discoursed of*, bound with *Kometographia* (Boston, 1682), second pagination, 7–11; Michael McKeon, *Politics and Poetry in Restoration England: The Case of Dryden's Annus Mirabilis* (Cambridge, Mass., 1975), 155–161.

4. Johnson, *Wonder-Working Providence*, ed. Jameson, 185.

5. *Letter-Book of Samuel Sewall*, 2 vols., Massachusetts Historical Society, *Collections*, 6th Ser., I–II (1886–1888), II, 229; *Diary of Samuel Sewall*, Thomas, ed., I, 369; II, 796.

6. Keith Thomas, *Religion and the Decline of Magic* (London). This complex, subtle book depicts seventeenth-century Protestants, and especially the more radical of the Puritans, as hostile to "magic"; and argues that the rural poor preferred the older beliefs that Puritans were opposing. But Thomas also provides much evidence of beliefs, e.g., astrology, that were not limited to the rural poor, and he is quite aware that Protestantism remained in touch with prophecy, exorcism, and even certain folk beliefs. My argument inevitably runs counter to the main emphasis of his book, but much of what I have to say is also present in his pages, and I am deeply indebted to the references he provides to sixteenth- and seventeenth-century sources.

7. Hyder Rollins, ed., *The Pack of Autolycus or Strange and Terrible News of Ghosts, Apparitions…as told in Broadside Ballads of the Years 1624–1693* (Cambridge, Mass., 1927), 36, 114, 162, and passim; Joseph Frank, *The Beginning of the English Newspaper 1620–1660* (Cambridge, Mass., 1961), 17; Bernard Capp, *English Almanacs 1500–1800* (Ithaca, N.Y., 1979), chap. 6; *Strange and wonderful News from Chippingnorton…Of certain dreadful Apparitions* [London, 1679].

8. Rollins, ed., *Pack of Autolycus*, 37, 62, 139, 82,

23; *A miracle, of miracles* [London, n.d.], 5; John Gadbury, *Natura Prodigiorum or, A discoure touching the nature of Prodigies* (London, 1660).

9. *The Theatre of Gods Judgements* (London, 1648), 409; Stephen Batman, *The Doome warning all men to the Iudgemente* (London, 1581), 317, 379, 390, 397.

10. Beard, *Theatre of Gods Judgements* 37, 48, 195; Batman, *Doome warning all men to the Iudgemente*, 403; [Nathaniel Crouch], *Admirable Curiosities, Rarities, & Wonders in England* (London, 1682), passim; Rollins, ed., *Pack of Autolycus*, 219. Here as elsewhere in this essay, the references could run into the hundreds in imitation of the dense texture of the great collections.

11. Samuel Clarke, *A Mirrour or Looking-Glasse both for Saints, and Sinners*, 2nd. ed., (London, 1654), 92–93; Beard, *Theatre of Gods Judgements*, Bk I, chapter 30; Rollins, ed., *Pack of Autolycus*, 75.

12. Rollins, ed., *Pack of Autolycus*, 62.

13. Miriam Chrisman, *Lay Culture, Learned Culture: Books and Social Change in Strasbourg 1480–1599* (New Haven, Conn., 1982), 257, 369ff; R. W. Scribner, *For the Sake of Simple Folk: Popular Propaganda for the German Reformation* (Cambridge, 1981), 125–127, 131, 184.

14. Rollins, ed., *Pack of Autolycus*, 81.

15. Simon Goulart, *Admirable and Memorable Histories containing the wonders of our time* (London, 1607). The original French edition appeared in 1547. Batman's *Doome* was largely a translation of Lycosthenes' *De prodigiis liber*.

16. The best guides (in English) to the lore of wonders are the literary historians whom I came to refer to as "the Shakespeareans," the men and women who have patrolled the sweep of English literary culture from Chaucer to Shakespeare and Milton, and who were very conscious of Shakespeare's roots in medieval and classical culture. A book of great practical utility, as my citations from it indicate, is S.K. Heninger, Jr., *A Handbook of Renaissance Meterology* (Durham, N.C., 1960), which opens with an important survey of the encyclopedias that codified and transmitted so much of the wonder lore. No less important is Kester Svendsen, *Milton and Science* (New York, 1969), with its superb discussion in Chapter 1 of "The Compendious Method of Natural Philosophy: Milton and the Encyclopedic Tradition." The notes and across references in Hyder Rollins's *Pack of Autolycus* remain the best guide to the print culture I describe briefly. Other studies of importance include: Don Cameron Allen, *The Star-Crossed Renaissance: The Quarrel about Astrology and Its Influence in England* (New York, 1966); Willard

Farnham, *The Medieval Heritage of Elizabethan Tragedy* (Berkeley, 1936); J. S. P. Tatlock, *The Scene of the Franklin's Tale Revisited* (London, 1914), and his *The Legendary History of Britain* (Berkeley and Los Angeles, 1950); Robert W. Hanning, *The Vision of History in Early Britain from Gildas to Geoffrey of Monmouth* (New York, 1966); Paul H. Kocher, *Science and Religion in Elizabethan England* (New York, 1969); George Lyman Kittredge, *The Old Farmer and His Almanac* (Boston, 1904); and Henry A. Kelly, *Divine Providence in the England of Shakespeare's Histories* (Cambridge, Mass., 1970). An exhaustive survey is Lynn Thorndike, *A History of Magic and Experimental Science*, 8 vols. (New York, 1923–1958), esp. vols. IV–VII.

17. Heninger, *Handbook of Renaissance Meterology*, 12, and chaps. 2–3.

18. Ibid., 30–32; Allen, *Star-Crossed Renaissance*, chap. 5; Capp, *English Almanacs*, chap.5.

19. Eusebius, *The Ancient ecclesiastical histories* (London 1619), 64, 80; Bede's *Ecclesiastical History of the English People*, Bertram Colgrave and R.A.B. Mynors, eds. (Oxford, 1969), 141, 361–363; G.R.Owst, *Literature and Pulpit in Medieval England* (Cambridge, 1937), 129–130.

20. Tatlock, *Legendary History of Britain*, chap. 17; Rupert Taylor, *The Political Prophecy in England* (New York, 1911); Thomas, *Religion and the Decline of Magic*, chap. 13.

21. Scribner, *For the Sake of Simple Folk*, 116–117, 140–147, 184; Katharine R. Firth, *The Apocalyptic Tradition in Reformation Britain, 1530–1645* (Oxford, 1979); Joseph Mede, *The Key of the Revelation, searched and demonstrated out of the Naturall and proper characters of the Visions* (London, 1643), Pt. 1, 88, 94.

22. Chaucer, *The Canterbury Tales*, trans. Nevill Coghill (Baltimore, 1952) 70; Peter Lake, *Moderate Puritans and the Elizabethan Church* (Cambridge, 1982), 119–120; Beard, *Theatre of Gods Judgements*, 88; Thomas, *Religion and the Decline of Magic*, chap. 4.

23. As Kocher proves at length in *Science and Religion in Elizabethan England*. The close ties between science and religion are evident in the letters that Cotton Mather sent to the Royal Society; many of them report events that previously had been described as "wonders" in his father's *Essay for the Recording of Illustrious Providences*. Cf. George L. Kittredge, "Cotton Mather's Scientific Communications to the Royal Society," American Antiquarian Society, *Proceedings*, N.S. XXVI (1916), 18–57.

24. Capp, *English Almanacs*, 165; Hershel Baker,

The Race of Time (Toronto, 1967) 57–63; Joseph J. Morgan, Jr., *Chaucer and the Theme of Mutability* (The Hague, 1961); Victor Harris, *All Coherence Gone* (Chicago, 1949), chaps. 4–5.

25. Farnham, *Medieval Heritage of Elizabethan Tragedy*, chap. 7; Scribner, *For the Sake of Simple Folk*, 117; Beard, *Theatre of Gods Judgements*, 80.

26. Michael MacDonald, *Mystical Bedlam: Madness, Anxiety, and Healing in Seventeenth-Century England* (Cambridge, 1981), 175, 202. "There hath ever been from the beginning an inveterate antipathy between Satan and his instruments, and the children of God." (Clarke, *Examples*, 35.)

27. Howard R. Patch, *The Goddess Fortuna in Medieval Literature* (Cambridge, Mass., 1927); J. G. A. Pocock, *The Machiavellian Moment: Florentine Political Thought and the Atlantic Republican Tradition* (Princeton, 1975), 349–350.

28. E. M. W. Tillyard, *The Elizabethan World Picture* (New York n.d.), chap. 7.

29. Thomas Hobbes, *Leviatan*, ed. Michael Oakeshott (Oxford, 1957), Pt. IV. Hobbes was almost sui generis; but there was widespread criticism in seventeeth-century England of astrology and apocalpticism, as well as an awareness that protents and prodigies were often manipulated for political benefit. This politicizing is evident in the flood of publications in 1679 and 1680, most of them anti-Catholic, anti-Stuart tracts in disguise, and in books like *Mirabilis Annus Secundus; Or, The Second Year of Prodigies. Being A true and impartial Collection of many strange Signes and Apparitions, which have this last Year been seen in the Heavens, and in the Earth, and in the Waters* (London, 1662), which, despite its title, is a radical Puritan onslaught against the restored monarchy. We are dealing with a series of contradictions, or better, of paradoxes: belief in portents, joined with skepticism about them; a conviction that some protents were not really significant, and that others were. For examples of this selectivity at work in the late sixteenth century, cf. L. H. Buell, "Elizabethan Portents: Superstition or Doctrine," in *Essays Critical and Historical Dedicated to Lily B. Campbell* (Berkeley and Los Angeles, 1950), 27–41.

30. Heninger, *Handbook of Renaissance Meterology*, 87–91; du Bartas, *La Sepmaine*, quoted on the reverse of the title page of Samuel Danforth, *An Astronomical Description of the late Comet or Blazing Star* (Cambridge, Mass., 1665).

31. Pliny, *Natural History*, trans. H. Rackham (Cambridge, Mass., 1949), I, 235 (Bk II.xxiii).

32. Ibid., I, 275 (Bk II.liii): Heninger, *Handbook of Renaissance Meteorology*, 72–87.

33. *The Famous amd Memorable Workers of Josephus…Faithfully Translated…by Thomas Lodge* (London, 1620), 738; Heninger, *Handbook of Renaissance Meteorology*, 91–94; Rollins, ed., *Pack of Autolycus*, 38.

34. Katherine M. Briggs, *The Anatomy of Puck: An Examination of Fairy Beliefs among Shakespeare's Contemporaries and Successors* (London, 1959); C. Grant Loomis, *White Magic: An Introduction to the Folklore of Christian Legend* (Cambridge, Mass., 1948); Kittredge, *Old Farmer and His Almanac*, chap. 6; T. F. Thiselton Dyer, *Folk Lore of Shakespear* (London, 1884).

35. As Rollins, ed., *Pack of Autolycus*, points out repeatedly.

36. *Twelve Strange Prophesies, besides Mother Shiptons. With the Predictions of John Saltmarsh* (London, 1648).

37. William P. Upham, "Remarks," *Massachusetts Historical Society, Proceedings*, 2d Ser., XIII (1899–1900), 126–127.

38. Increase Mather, *Wo to Drunkards* (Cambridge, Mass., 1673), 28; "The Diary of Increase Mather," *Massachusetts Historical Society, Proceedings*, 2d Ser., XIII (1899–1900), 345.

39. Worthington C. Ford, *The Boston Book Market, 1679–1700* (Boston, 1917), 149.

40. Mather, *Magnalia Christi Americana*, I, 205.

41. Kenneth B. Murdock, ed., *Handkerchiefs from Paul being Pious and Consolatory Verses of Puritan Massachusetts* (Cambridge, Mass., 1927), 109–111.

42. [Samuel Danforth], *An Almanack for the Year of Our Lord 1648* (Cambridge, Mass., 1648). Mary Dyer's monstrous birth was perhaps the first New England wonder to receive international attention. Cf. *Newes from New-England of A most strange and prodigious Birth* [London, 1642].

43. "My chief design, is to inform and edifie the ordinary sort of Readers. Yet considering that God hath made me a debter to the wise as well as to the weak, I have added some things of the nature, place, motion of Comets, which only such as have some skill in Astronomy can understand" ("To the Reader," in *Kometographia*).

44. *Records of the First Church at Dorchester in New England 1636–1734* (Boston, 1891); Roxbury Land and Church Records, Boston Record Commissioners, *Reports*, VI (Boston, 1881), 187–212.

45. William Deloss Love, Jr., *The Fast and Thanksgiving Days of New England* (Boston, 1895).

46. James Kendall Hosmer, ed., *Winthrop's Journal History of New England, 1630–1649*, 2 vols.

(New York, 1953 [orig. publ. New York, 1908]), II, 156.

47. A very large number of such journals or brief autobiographical sketches survive, and their authors include artisans and farmers as well as ministers and merchants. Two diaries kept by oridinary people are John Dane, "A Declaration of Remarkable Proudenses in the Corse of My Life," *New England Historical and Genealogical Register*, VIII (1854), 147–156; and Charles F. Adams, Jr., "Abstract of [John] Marshall's Diary," *Massachusetts Historical Society, Proceedings*, 2d Ser., I (1884–1885), 148–164, and its continuation, Samuel A. Green, "Remarks," ibid., 2d. Ser., XIV (1900–1901), 13–34.

48. *The Diaries of John Hull*, 217–218; *Diary of Samuel Sewall*, Thomas, ed. I, 12. I have analyzed this diary at greater length in "The Mental World of Samuel Sewall," *Massachusetts Historical Society, Proceedings*, XCII (1980), 21–44.

49. *Diary of Samuel Sewall*, Thomas, ed., I. 330–331.

50. Upham, "Remarks," 127–128. Taylor had access to one of the several versions of Christopher Love's scaffold speech; e.g., *The true and perfect Speech of Mr. Christopher Love* (London, 1651).

51. *Mather Papers*, 282–287.

52. Ibid., 360–362.

53. Ibid., 306–310.

54. Ibid. 466–481. The Marshfield episode, told in a letter from the Rev. Samuel Arnold, was later published by N. B. Shurtleff as *Thunder & Lightning; and Deaths at Marshfield in 1658 & 1666* (Boston, 1850).

55. *Mather Papers*, 58–59. The Mary Dyer story had long since passed into print in several places; cf. note 6, p. 258 above.

56. Danforth, *An Astronomical Description*, 16–21.

57. Mather, *Kometographia*, 96. Quoting again the familiar lines from du Bartas, *La Septhaine*, Mather also spoke approvingly of apparitions in the air. In keeping with tradition, the colonists were sensitive to the shape and direction of comets; cf. Johnson, *Wonder-Working Providence*, ed. Jameson, 40; *Mather Papers*, 312.

58. Mather, *Magnalia Christi Americana*, II, 363–372; Shurtleff, *Thunder & Lightning*. 13–15.

59. Johnson, *Wonder-Working Providence*, ed. Jameson, 243. Cf. "The Diaries of John Hull," 208; *Mather Papers*, 349; and for the tradition, Rollins, ed., *Pack of Autolycus*, 38; Batman, *Doome warning to Iudgemente*, 304.

60. Israel Chauncy, *An Almanack of the coelestial motions for...1663* (Cambridge, Mass., 1663).

61. Noadiah Russell, *Cambridge Ephemeris. An Almanac...for...1684* (Cambridge, Mass., 1684).

62. *Holwell's Predictions: of many remarkable things, which probably come to pass* (Cambridge, Mass., [1690]).

63. Morton, *New-Englands Memoriall*, 52.

64. "The Diary of Noahdiah Russell," 54. The references to such experiences were many; and I mean to write about them elsewhere, as the discussions of millennium and eschatology in New England Puritanism do not pay adequate (if any) attention to the everyday experience of prophecying. Anne Hutchinson was gifted with prophetic sight and visions; cf. David D. Hall, ed., *The Antinomian Controversy, 1636–1638: A Documentary History* (Middletown, Conn., 1968), 271–273.

65. Winthrop, *Journal*, I, 84, 121.

66. Mather, *Magnalia Christi Americana*, I, 314–316, 544; II, 37–38. As with visionary prophecying, I must pass by many other instances, as well as avoiding the stories provided by Beard, Clarke, and Turner.

67. The folklore of black dogs is summarized in Katharine M. Briggs, *British Folk Tales and Legends: A Sampler* (London, 1977), 115–120.

68. Paul Boyer and Stephen Nissenbaum, eds., *The Salem Witchcraft Papers*, 3 vols. (New York, 1977), I, 74, 202–203; III, 742; II, 568.

69. Ibid., I, 166, 246–247.

70. Ibid., II, 578. Cf. Loomis, *White Magic*, 39.

71. Joseph Glanville, *A Blow at Modern Sadducism in some Philosophical Considerations about Witchcraft*, 4th ed. (London, 1668); Rollins, ed., *Pack of Autolycus*, 115.

72. The same generosity is characteristic of Bread and Clarke, and has medieval precedents; Tatlock, *Legendary History of Britain*, 276–277.

73. Mather, *Essay*, "Introduction"; H.L.D. Ward, *Catalogue of Romances in the Department of Manuscripts in the British Museum*, 3 vols. (London, 1883–1910), I, 257, II, 595.

74. Moses Coit Tyler, *A History of American Literature during the Colonial Time*, rev. ed., 2 vols. (New York, 1897), II, 73; Kenneth B. Murdock, *Increase Mather: The Foremost American Puritan* (Cambridge, Mass., 1925), 170–174; Perry Miller, *The New England Mind: From Colony to Province* (Cambridge, Mass, 1953), 143; but for apparent approval of Murdock's arguments, cf. 180.

75. Svendsen, *Milton and Science*, 5, 44, 84.

76. In trying to account for attitudes toward the Negro in early America, Winthrop Jordan was driven to speaking of "deeper" attitudes that somehow formed and were perpetuated in Elizabethan culture:

Jordan, *White over Black: American Attitudes Toward the Negro, 1550–1812* (Baltimore, 1969), viii–ix, and chap. 1. My problem is akin to his, in that the popular culture I am describing was remarkably tenacious and encompassing, even though its exact sources and lines of influence cannot readily be specified.

77. Beard, *Theatre of Gods Judgements*, 2.

78. Increase Mather, *The Doctrine of Divine Providence Opened and Applyed* (Boston, 1684), 43, 30–32, 34, 81, 133; and for the figure of the wheel and the rise and fall of kings, cf. pp. 9, 16–17. The image of the wheel derives from Ezekiel 1:15–16, et seq.

79. As is suggested by Jon Butler, "Magic, Astrology, and the Early American Religious Heritage, 1600–1760," *American Historical Review*, LXXXIV (1979), 317–346, an essay that seems almost perverse in its refusal to acknowledge the syncreticism of seventeenth-century religion and the common interest of both clergy and laity in such "superstitions." The most important description of intellectual tolerance and syncreticism in seventeenth-century England is MacDonald, *Mystical Bedlam*, which in this regard serves to correct the impression that arises from Thomas, *Religion and the Decline of Magic*, of a clear line between the two.

Anthropologists struggle to define the difference between magic and religion; literary and cultural historians by and large agree in de-emphasizing the distinction. "Our hard and fast distinction between the natural and the supernatural was unknown in the middle ages; there was no line between jugglery… and magic, most people not knowing how either was performed; indeed any remarkable performance with a secular background…might be called a miracle." Tatlock, *Legendary History*, 362–363. "It is of course notoriously difficult…to say where religion becomes magic: the genuine Middle English charms (like many of their predecessors in Old English) use much religious imagery." Douglas Gray, *Themes and Images in the Medieval English Religious Lyric* (London, 1972), 34. See also Jean-Claude Schmitt, "Les Traditions Folkloriques dans la Culture Médiévale," *Archives de Sciences Sociales des Religions*, LII (1981), 5–20, a reference I owe to Keith Thomas.

80. Jean Delumeau, *Catholicism between Luther and Voltaire: A New View of the Counter-Reformation* (London, 1977), 63.

81. Thomas Robie], *A Letter to a Certain Gentleman, ec.* (Boston, 1719), 8; J.F.C. Harrison, *The Second Coming: Popular Millenarianism, 1780–1850* (London, 1979), chap. 3.

WAR AND CULTURE

Daniel K. Richter

In recent years, an older "clash of cultures" model for understanding Indian European relations has been replaced by the view that a "new world" was collectively created. The new model suggests that different Native American tribes and the diverse French, Dutch, English, and other European colonists in early America acted and interacted through a complex process of cultural accommodation and conflict. This perspective is helping us to see why and how the various peoples of early America acted in their own societies and with each other in cooperation, conflict, and often confusion.

As Daniel Richter's essay shows, Indians' motives for making war were quite different from those that led Europeans into combat. From the colonists' perspective, the importance that Indians gave to war confirmed their image as bloodthirsty savages. In contrast, Richter argues that the Iroquois went to war "for reasons rooted as much in internal social demands as in external disputes with their neighbors." For many Indian cultures the traditional institution known as the "mourning war," through which a dead person was replaced by capturing or adopting someone else, provided a means for maintaining the population and coping with death. As Richter explains, the Iroquois understood the need to restore their population in spiritual terms. When a person died, the power of the clan or nation was decreased in proportion to his or her individual spiritual power. During the last decades of the seventeenth century, the Iroquois faced the very real possibility of extinction through exposure to European diseases. Though the ravages of European disease and colonial warfare prevented the "mourning war" from fulfilling its intended purpose, throughout the late seventeenth century this traditional approach to war helped the Iroquois assuage the grief of mourners and address the loss of spiritual power in their ranks.

Adapted by permission from Daniel K. Richter, "War and Culture: The Iroquois Experience," *William and Mary Quarterly*, XL (1983) 528-559.

3

WAR AND CULTURE
The Iroquois Experience

Daniel K. Richter

THE CHARACTER of all these [Iroquois] Nations is warlike and cruel," wrote Jesuit missionary Paul Le Jeune in 1657. "The chief virtue of these poor Pagans being cruelty, just as mildness is that of Christians, they teach it to their children from their very cradles, and accustom them to the most atrocious carnage and the most barbarous spectacles."[1] Like most Europeans of his day, Le Jeune ignored his own countrymen's capacity for bloodlust and attributed the supposedly unique bellicosity of the Iroquois to their irreligion and uncivilized condition. Still, his observations contain a kernel of truth often overlooked by our more sympathetic eyes: in ways quite unfamiliar and largely unfathomable to Europeans, warfare was vitally important in the cultures of the seventeenth-century Iroquois and their neighbors. For generations of Euro-Americans, the significance that Indians attached to warfare seemed to substantiate images of bloodthirsty savages who waged war for mere sport. Only in recent decades have ethnohistorians discarded such shibboleths and begun to study Indian wars in the same economic and diplomatic frameworks long used by students of European conflicts. Almost necessarily, given the weight of past prejudice, their work has stressed similarities between Indian and European warfare.[2] Thus neither commonplace stereotypes nor scholarly efforts to combat them have left much room for serious consideration of the possibility that the non-state societies of aboriginal North America may have waged war for different—but no less rational and no more savage—purposes than did the nation-states of Europe.[3] This article explores that possibility through an analysis of the changing role of warfare in Iroquois culture during the first century after European contact.

The Iroquois Confederacy (composed, from west to east, of the Five Nations of the Seneca, Cayuga, Onondaga, Oneida, and Mohawk) frequently went to war for reasons rooted as much in internal social demands as in external disputes with their neighbors. The same observation could be made about countless European states, but the particular internal motives that often propelled the Iroquois and other northeastern Indians to make war have few parallels in Euro-American experience. In many Indian cultures a pattern known as the "mourning-war" was one means of restoring lost population, ensuring social continuity, and dealing with death.[4] A grasp of the changing role of this pattern in Iroquois culture is essential if the seventeenth- and early eighteenth-century campaigns of the Five Nations—and a vital aspect of the contact situation—are to be understood. "War is a necessary exercise for the Iroquois," explained missionary and ethnologist Joseph François Lafitau, "for, besides the usual motives which people have in declaring it against troublesome neighbours…, it is indispensable to them also because of one of their fundamental laws of being."[5]

I

Euro-Americans often noted that martial skills were highly valued in Indian societies and that, for young men, exploits on the warpath were important determinants of personal prestige. This was, some hyperbolized, particularly true of the Iroquois. "It is not for the Sake of Tribute…that they make War," Cadwallader Colden observed of the Five Nations, "but from the Notions of Glory, which they have ever most strongly imprinted on their Minds."[6] Participation in a war party was a benchmark episode in an Iroquois youth's development, and later success in battle increased the young man's stature in his clan and village. His prospects for an advantageous marriage, his chances for recognition as a village leader, and his hopes for eventual selection to a sachemship depended largely—though by no means entirely—on his skill on the warpath, his munificence in giving war feasts, and his ability to attract followers when organizing a raid.[7] Missionary-explorer Louis Hennepin exaggerated when he claimed that "those amongst the *Iroquoise* who are not given to War, are had in great Contempt, and pass for Lazy and Effeminate People," but warriors did in fact reap great social rewards.[8]

The plaudits offered to successful warriors suggest a deep cultural significance; societies usually reward warlike behavior not for its own sake but for the useful functions it performs.[9] Among the functions postulated in recent studies of non-state warfare is the maintenance of stable population levels. Usually this involves, in more or less obvious ways, a check on excessive population growth, but in some instances warfare can be, for the victors, a means to increase the group's numbers.[10] The traditional wars of the Five Nations served the latter purpose. The Iroquois conceptualized the process of population maintenance in terms of individual and collective spiritual power. When a person died, the power of his or her lineage, clan, and nation was diminished in proportion to his or her individual spiritual strength.[11] To replenish the depleted power the Iroquois conducted "requickening" ceremonies at which the deceased's name—and with it the social role and duties it represented—was transferred to a successor. Vacant positions in Iroquois families and villages were thus both literally and symbolically filled, and the continuity of Iroquois society was confirmed, while survivors were assured that the social role and spiritual strength embodied in the departed's name had not been lost.[12] Warfare was crucial to these customs, for when the deceased was a person of ordinary status and little authority the beneficiary of the requickening was often a war captive, who would be adopted "to help strengthen the familye in lew of their deceased Freind."[13] A father who has lost his son adopts a young prisoner in his place," explained an eighteenth-century commentator on Indian customs. "An orphan takes a father or mother; a widow a husband; one man takes a sister and another a brother."[14]

On a societal level, then, warfare helped the Iroquois to deal with deaths in their ranks. On a personal, emotional level it performed similar functions. The Iroquois believed that the grief inspired by a relative's death could, if uncontrolled, plunge survivors into depths of despair that robbed them of their reason and disposed them to fits of rage potentially harmful to themselves and the community. Accordingly, Iroquois culture directed mourners' emotions into ritualized channels. Members of the deceased's household, "after having the hair cut, smearing the face with earth or charcoal and gotten themselves up in the most frightful negligence," embarked on ten days of "deep mourning," during which "they remain at the back of their bunk, their face against the ground or turned towards the back of the platform, their head enveloped in their blanket which is the dirtiest and least clean rag that they have. They do not look at or speak to anyone except through necessity and in a low voice. They hold themselves excused from every duty of civility and courtesy."[15] For the next year the survivors engaged in less intense formalized grieving, beginning to resume their daily habits but continuing to disregard their personal appearance and many social amenities. While mourners thus channeled their emotions, others hastened to "cover up" the grief of the bereaved with condolence rituals, feasts, and presents (including the special variety of condolence gift often somewhat misleadingly described as *wergild*). These were designed to cleanse sorrowing hearts and to ease the return to normal life. Social and personal needs converged at the culmination of these ceremonies, the "requickening" of the deceased.[16]

But if the mourners' grief remained unassuaged, the ultimate socially sanctioned channel for their violent impulses was a raid to seek captives who, it was hoped, would ease their pain. The target of the mourning-war was usually a people traditionally defined as enemies; neither they nor anyone else need necessarily be held directly responsible for the death that provoked the attack, though most often the foe could be made to bear the blame.[17] Raids for captives could be either large-scale efforts organized on village, nation, or confederacy levels or, more often, attacks by small parties raised at the behest of female kin of the deceased. Members of the dead person's household, presumably lost in grief, did not usually participate directly. Instead, young men who were related by marriage to the bereaved women but who lived in other longhouses were obliged to form a raiding party or face the matrons' accusations of cowardice.[18] When the warriors returned with captured men, women, and children, mourners could select a prisoner for adoption in the place of the deceased or they could vent their rage in rituals of torture and execution.[19]

The rituals began with the return of the war party, which had sent word ahead of the number of captives seized. Most of the villagers, holding clubs, sticks, and other weapons, stood in two rows outside the village entrance to meet the prisoners. Men, but usually not women or young children, received heavy blows designed to inflict pain without serious injury. Then they were stripped and led to a raised platform in an open space inside the village, where old women led the community in further physical abuse, tearing out fingernails and poking sensitive body parts with sticks and firebrands.[20] After several hours, prisoners were allowed to rest and eat, and later they were made to dance for their captors while their fate was decided. Headmen apportioned them to grieving families, whose matrons then chose either to adopt or to execute them.[21] If those who were adopted made a sincere effort to please their new relatives and to assimilate into village society, they could expect a long life; if they displeased, they were quietly and uncermoniously killed.

A captive slated for ritual execution was usually also adopted and subsequently addressed appropriately as "uncle" or "nephew," but his status was marked by a distinctive red and black pattern of facial paint. During the next few days the doomed man gave his death feast, where his executioners saluted him and allowed him to recite his war honors. On the appointed day he was tied with a short rope to a stake, and villagers of both sexes and all ages took turns weilding firebrands and various red-hot objects to burn him systematically from the feet up. The tormentors behaved with religious solemnity and spoke in symbolic language of "caressing" their adopted relative with their firebrands. The victim was expected to endure his sufferings stoically and even to encourage his torturers, but this seems to have been ideal rather than typical behavior. If he too quickly began to swoon, his ordeal briefly ceased and he received food and drink and time to recover somewhat before the burning resumed. At length, before he expired, someone scalped him, another threw hot sand on his exposed skull, and finally a warrior dispatched him with a knife to the chest or a hatchet to the neck. Then the victim's flesh was stripped from his bones and thrown into cooking kettles, and the whole village feasted on his remains. This feast carried great religious significance for the Iroquois, but its full meaning is irretrievable; most European observers were too shocked to probe its implications.[22]

Mourners were not the only ones to benefit from the ceremonial torture and execution of captives. While grieving relatives vented their emotions, all of the villagers, by partaking in the humiliation of every prisoner and the torture of some, were able to participate directly in the defeat of their foes. Warfare thus dramatically promoted group cohesion and demonstrated to the Iroquois their superiority over their enemies. At the same time, youths learned valuable lessons in the behavior expected of warriors and in the way to die bravely should they ever be captured. Le Jeune's "barbarous spectacles" were a vital element in the ceremonial life of Iroquois communities.[23]

The social demands of the mourning-war shaped strategy and tactics in at least two ways. First, the essential measure of a war party's success was its ability to seize prisoners and bring them home alive. Capturing of enemies was preferred to killing them on the spot and taking their scalps, while none of the benefits European combatants derived from war—territorial expansion, economic gain, plunder of the defeated—outranked the seizure of prisoners.[24] When missionary Jérôme Lalemant disparaged Iroquoian warfare as "consisting of a few broken heads along the highways, or of some captives brought into the country to be burned and eaten there," he was more accurate than he knew.[25] The overriding importance of captive taking set Iroquois warfare dramatically apart from the Euro-American military experience. "We are not like you CHRISTIANS for when you have taken Prisoners of one another you send them home, by such means you can never rout one another," explained the Onondaga orator Teganissorens to Gov. Robert Hunter of New York in 1711.[26]

The centrality of captives to the business of war was clear in precombat rituals: imagery centered on a boiling war kettle; the war feast presaged the future cannibalistic rite; mourning women urged warriors to bring them prisoners to assuage their grief; and, if more than one village participated in the campaign, leaders agreed in advance on the share of captives that each town would receive.[27] As Iroquois warriors saw it, to forget the importance of captive taking or to ignore the rituals associated with it was to invite defeat. In 1642 missionary Isaac Jogues observed a ceremony he believed to be a sacrifice to Areskoui, the deity who presided over Iroquois wars. "At a solemn feast which they had made of two Bears, which they had offered to their demon, they had used this form of words: 'Aireskoi, thou dost right to punish us, and to give us no more captives' (they were speaking of the Algonquins, of whom that year they had not taken one…) 'because we have sinned by not eating the bodies of those whom thou last gavest us; but we promise thee to eat the first ones whom thou shalt give us, as we now do with these two Bears.'"[28]

A second tactical reflection of the social functions of warfare was a strong sanction against the loss of Iroquois lives in battle. A war party that, by European standards, seemed on the brink of triumph could be expected to retreat sorrowfully homeward if it suffered a few fatalities. For the Indians, such a campaign was no victory; casualties would subvert the purpose of warfare as a means of restocking the population.[29] In contrast to European beliefs that to perish in combat was acceptable and even honorable, Iroquois beliefs made death in battle a frightful prospect, though one that must be faced bravely if necessary. Slain warriors, like all who died violent deaths, were said to be excluded from the villages of the dead, doomed to spend a roving eternity seeking vengeance. As a result, their bodies were not interred in village cemeteries, lest their angry souls disturb the repose of others. Both in burial and in the afterlife, a warrior who fell in combat faced separation from his family and friends.[30]

Efforts to minimize fatalities accordingly underlay several tactics that contemporary Euro-Americans considered cowardly: fondness for ambushes and surprise attacks; unwillingness to fight when outnumbered; and avoidance of frontal assaults on fortified places. Defensive tactics showed a similar emphasis on precluding loss of life. Spies in enemy villages and an extensive network of scouts warned of invading war parties before they could harm Iroquois villagers. If intruders did enter Iroquoia, defenders attacked from ambush, but only if they felt confident of repulsing the enemy without too many losses of their own. The people retreated behind palisades or, if the enemy appeared too strong to resist, burned their own villages and fled—warriors included—into the woods or to neighboring villages. Houses and corn supplies thus might temporarily be lost, but unless the invaders achieved complete surprise, the lives and spiritual power of the people remained intact. In general, when the Iroquois were at a disadvantage, they preferred flight or an insincerely negotiated truce to the costly last stands that earned glory for European warriors.[31]

That kind of glory, and the warlike way of life it reflected, were not Iroquois ideals. Warfare was a specific response to the death of specific individuals at specific times, a sporadic affair characterized by seizing from traditional enemies a few captives who would replace the dead, literally or symbolically, and ease the pain of those who mourned. While war was not to be undertaken gladly or lightly, it was still "a necessary exercise for the Iroquois,"[32] for it was an integral part of individual and social mourning practices. When the Iroquois envisioned a day of no more wars, with their Great League of Peace extended to all peoples, they also envisioned an altenative to the mourning functions of warfare. That alternative was embodied in the proceedings of league councils and Iroquois peace negotiations with other peoples, which began with—and frequently consisted entirely of— condolence ceremonies and exchanges of presents designed to dry the tears, unstop the mouths, and clense the hearts of bereaved participants.[33] Only when grief was forgotten could war end and peace begin. In the century following the arrival of Europeans, grief could seldom be forgotten.

II

After the 1620s, when the Five Nations first made sustained contact with Europeans, the role of warfare in Iroquois culture changed dramatically. By 1675, European diseases, firearms, and trade had produced dangerous new patterns of conflict that threatened to derange the traditional functions of the mourning-war.

Before most Iroquois had ever seen a Dutchman or a Frenchman, they had felt the impact of the maladies the invaders inadvertently brought with them.[34] By the 1640s the number of

Iroquois (and of their Indian neighbors) had probably already been halved by epidemics of smallpox, measles, and other European "childhood diseases," to which Indian populations had no immunity.[35] The devastation continued through the century. A partial list of plagues that struck the Five Nations includes "a general malady" among the Mohawk in 1647; "a great mortality" among the Onondaga in 1656–1657; a smallpox epidemic among the Oneida, Onondaga, Cayuga, and Seneca in 1661–1663; "a kind of contagion" among the Seneca in 1668; "a fever of…malignant character" among the Mohawk in 1673; and "a general Influenza" among the Seneca in 1676.[36] As thousands died, ever-growing numbers of captive adoptees would be necessary if the Iroquois were even to begin to replace their losses; mourning-wars of unprecedented scale loomed ahead. Warfare would cease to be a sporadic and specific response to individual deaths and would become instead a constant and increasingly undifferentiated symptom of societies in demographic crisis.

At the same time, European firearms would make warfare unprecedentedly dangerous for both the Iroquois and their foes, and would undermine traditional Indian sanctions against battle fatalities. The introduction of guns, together with the replacement of flint arrowheads by more efficient iron, copper, and brass ones that could pierce traditional Indian wooden armor, greatly increased the chances of death in combat and led to major changes in Iroquois tactics. In the early seventeenth century Champlain had observed mostly ceremonial and relatively bloodless confrontations between large Indian armies, but with the advent of muskets—which Europeans had designed to be fired in volleys during just such battles— massed confrontations became, from the Indian perspective, suicidal folly. They were quickly abandoned in favor of a redoubled emphasis on small-scale raids and ambushes, in which Indians learned far sooner than Euro-Americans how to aim cumbersome muskets accurately at individual targets.[37] By the early 1640s the Mohawk were honing such skills with approximately three hundred guns acquired from the Dutch of Albany and from English sources. Soon the rest of the Five Nations followed the Mohawk example.[38]

Temporarily, the Iroquois' plentiful supply and skillful use of firearms gave them a considerable advantage over their Indian enemies: during the 1640s and 1650s the less well armed Huron and the poorly armed Neutral and Khionontateronon (Petun or Tobacco Nation) succumbed to Iroquois firepower. That advantage had largely disappeared by the 1660s and 1670s, however, as the Five Nations learned in their battles with such heavily armed foes as the Susquehannock. Once muskets came into general use in Indian warfare, several drawbacks became apparent: they were more sluggish than arrows to fire and much slower to reload; their noise lessened the capacity for surprise; and reliance on them left Indians dependent on Euro-Americans for ammunition, repairs, and replacements. But there could be no return to the days of bows and arrows and wooden armor. Few Iroquois war parties could now expect to escape mortal casualties.[39]

While European diseases and firearms intensified Indian conflicts and stretched the mourning-war tradition beyond previous limits, a third major aspect of European contact pushed Iroquois warfare in novel directions. Trade with Europeans made economic motives central to American Indian conflicts for the first time. Because iron tools, firearms, and other trade goods so quickly became essential to Indian economies, struggles for those items and for furs to barter for them lay behind numerous seventeenth-century wars. Between 1624 and 1628 the Iroquois gained unimpeded access to European commodities when Mohawk warriors drove the Mahican to the east of the Hudson River and secured an open route to the Dutch traders of Albany.[40] But obtaining the furs to exchange for the goods of Albany was a problem not so easily solved. By about 1640 the Five Nations perhaps had exhausted the beaver stock of their home hunting territories; more important, they could not find in relatively temperate Iroquoia the thick northern pelts prized by Euro-American traders.[41] A long, far-flung series of "beaver wars" ensued, in which the Five Nations battled the Algonquian nations of the Saint Lawrence River region, the Huron, the Khionontateronon, the Neutral, the Erie, and other western and northern peoples in a constant struggle over fur supplies. In those wars the Iroquois more frequently sought dead beavers than live ones: most of their raids were not part of a strategic plan to seize new hunting grounds but piratical attacks on enemy canoes carrying pelts to Montreal and Trois-Rivières.[42]

The beaver wars inexorably embroiled the Iroquois in conflict with the French of Canada. Franco-Iroquois hostilities dated from the era of Champlain, who consistently based his relations with Canada's natives upon promises to aid them in their traditional raids against the Five Nations. "I came to the conclusion," wrote Champlain in 1619, "that it was very necessary to assist them, both to engage them the more to love us, and also to provide the means of furthering my enterprises and explorations which apparently could only be carried out with their help."[43] The French commander and a few of his men participated in Indian campaigns against the Five Nations in 1609, 1610, and 1615, and encouraged countless other raids.[44] From the 1630s to the 1660s, conflict between the Five Nations and Canadian Indians intensified, and Iroquois war parties armed with guns frequently blockaded the Saint Lawrence and stopped the flow of furs to the French settlements. A state of open war, punctuated by short truces, consequently prevailed between New France and various of the Five Nations, particularly the Mohawk. The battles were almost exclusively economic and geopolitical—the Iroquois were not much interested in French captives—and in general the French suffered more than the Iroquois from the fighting.[45] Finally, in 1666, a French army invaded Iroquoia and burned the Mohawks' fortified villages, from which all had fled to safety except a few old men who chose to stay and die. In 1667, the Five Nations and the French made a peace that lasted for over a decade.[46]

While the fur trade introduced new economic goals, additional foes, and wider scope to Iroquois warfare, it did not crowd out older cultural motives. Instead, the mourning-war tradition, deaths from disease, dependence on firearms, and the trade in furs combined to produce a dangerous spiral: epidemics led to deadlier mourning-wars fought with firearms; the need for guns increased the demand for pelts to trade for them; the quest for furs provoked wars with other nations; and deaths in those conflicts began the mourning-war cycle anew. At each turn, fresh economic and demographic motives fed the spiral.

Accordingly, in the mid-seventeenth-century Iroquois wars, the quest for captives was at least as important as the quest for furs. Even in the archetypal beaver war, the Five Nations-Huron conflict, only an overriding—even desperate—demand for prisoners can explain much of Iroquois behavior. For nearly a decade after the dispersal of the Huron Confederacy in 1649, Iroquois war parties killed or took captive every starving (and certainly peltry-less) group of Huron refugees they could find. Meanwhile, Iroquois ambassadors and warriors alternately negotiated with, cajoled, and threatened the Huron remnants living at Quebec to make them join their captive relatives in Iroquoia. Through all this, Mohawks, Senecas, and Onondagas occasionally shed each other's blood in arguments over the human spoils. Ultimately, in 1657, with French acquiescence, most of the Huron refugees fled away from Quebec—the Arendaronon nation to the Onondaga country and the Attignawantan nation to the Mohawk country.[47]

Judging by the number of prisoners taken during the Five Nations' wars from the 1640s to the 1670s with their other Iroquoian neighbors—the Neutral, Khionontateronon, Erie, and Susquehannock—these conflicts stemmed from a similar mingling of captive-taking and fur trade motives. Like the Huron, each of those peoples shared with the Iroquois mixed horticultural and hunting and fishing economies, related languages, and similar beliefs, making them ideal candidates for adoption. But they could not satisfy the spiraling Iroquois demand for furs and captives; war parties from the Five Nations had to range ever farther in their quest. In a not atypical series of raids in 1661–1662, they struck the Abenaki of the New England region, the Algonquians of the subarctic, the Siouans of the Upper Mississippi area, and various Indians near Virginia, while continuing the struggle with enemies closer to home.[48] The results of the mid-century campaigns are recorded in the *Jesuit Relations*, whose pages are filled with descriptions of Iroquois torture and execution of captives and note enormous numbers of adoptions. The Five Nations had absorbed so many prisoners that in 1657 Le Jeune believed that "more Foreigners than natives of the country" resided in Iroquoia.[49] By the mid-1660s several missionaries estimated that two-thirds or more of the people in many Iroquois villages were adoptees.[50]

By 1675 a half-century of constantly escalating warfare had at best enabled the Iroquois to hold their own. Despite the beaver wars, the Five Nations still had few dependable sources of furs. In the early 1670s they hunted primarily on lands north of Lake Ontario, where armed clashes with Algonquian foes were likely, opportunities to steal peltries from them were abundant, and conflict with the French who claimed the territory was always possible.[51] Ironically, even the Franco-Iroquois peace of 1667 proved a mixed blessing for the Five Nations. Under the provisions of the treaty, Jesuit priests, who had hitherto labored in Iroquois villages only sporadically and at the risk of their lives, established missions in each of the Five Nations.[52] The Jesuits not only created Catholic converts but also generated strong Christian and traditionalist factions that brought unprecedented disquiet to Iroquois communities. Among the Onondaga, for example, the Christian sachem Garakontié's refusal to perform his duties in the traditional manner disrupted such important ceremonies as dream guessings, the roll call of the chiefs, and healing rituals.[53] And in 1671, traditionalist Mohawk women excluded at least one Catholic convert from her rightful seat on the council of matrons because of her faith.[54] Moreover, beginning in the late 1660s, missionaries encouraged increasing numbers of Catholic Iroquois—particularly Mohawks and Oneidas—to desert their homes for the mission villages of Canada; by the mid-1670s well over two hundred had departed.[55] A large proportion of those who left, however, were members of the Five Nations in name only. Many—perhaps most—were recently adopted Huron and other prisoners, an indication that the Iroquois were unable to assimilate effectively the mass of newcomers their mid-century wars had brought them.[56]

Problems in incorporating adoptees reflected a broader dilemma: by the late 1670s the mourning-war complex was crumbling. Warfare was failing to maintain a stable population; despite torrents of prisoners, gains from adoption were exceeded by losses from disease, combat, and migrations to Canada. Among the Mohawk—for whom more frequent contemporary population estimates exist than for the other nations of the confederacy—the number of warriors declined from 700 or 800 in the 1640s to approximately 300 in the late 1670s. Those figures imply that, even with a constant infusion of captive adoptees, Mohawk population fell by half during that period.[57] The Five Nations as a whole fared only slightly better. In the 1640s the confederacy, already drastically reduced in numbers, had counted over 10,000 people. By the 1670s there were perhaps only 8,600.[58] The mourning-war, then, was not discharging one of its primary functions.

Meanwhile, ancient customs regarding the treatment of prisoners were decaying as rituals degenerated into chaotic violence and sheer murderous rage displaced the orderly adoption of captives that the logic of the mourning-war demanded. In 1682 missionary Jean de Lamberville asserted that Iroquois warriors "killed and ate...on the spot" over six hundred enemies in a campaign in the Illinois country; if he was even half right, it is clear that something had gone horribly wrong in the practice of the mourning-war. The decay of important customs associated with traditional warfare is further indicated by Lamberville's account of the return of that war party with its surviving prisoners. A gauntlet ceremony at the main Onondaga village turned into a deadly attack, forcing headmen to struggle to protect the lives of the captives. A few hours later, drunken young men, "who observed[d] no usages or customs," broke into longhouses and tried to kill the prisoners whom the headmen had rescued. In vain leaders pleaded with their people to remember "that it was contrary to custom to ill-treat prisoners on their arrival, when They had not yet been given in the place of any person...and when their fate had been left Undecided by the victors."[59]

Nevertheless, despite the weakening of traditional restraints, in the 1670s Iroquois warfare still performed useful functions. It maintained a tenuous supply of furs to trade for essential European goods; it provided frequent campaigns to allow young men to show their valor; and it secured numerous captives to participate in the continual mourning rituals that the many Iroquois deaths demanded (though there could never be enough to restock the population absolutely). In the quarter-century after 1675, however, the scales would tip: by 1700 the Anglo-French struggle for control of the continent would make warfare as the Five Nations were practicing it dangerously dysfunctional for their societies.

III

By 1700 Iroquois warfare and culture had reached a turning point. Up to about 1675, despite the impact of disease, firearms, and the fur trade, warfare still performed functions that outweighed its costs. But thereafter the Anglo-French struggle for control of North America made war disastrous for the Five Nations. Conflict in the west, instead of securing fur supplies, was cutting them off, while lack of pelts to trade and wartime shortages of goods at Albany created serious economic hardship in Iroquoia.[60] Those problems paled, however, in comparison with the physical toll. All of the Iroquois nations except the Cayuga had seen their villages and crops destroyed by invading armies, and all five nations were greatly weakened by loss of members to captivity, to death in combat, or to famine and disease. By some estimates, between 1689 and 1698 the Iroquois lost half of their fighting strength. That figure is probably an exaggeration, but by 1700 perhaps 500 of the 2,000 warriors the Five Nations fielded in 1689 had been killed or captured or had deserted to the French missions and had not been replaced by younger warriors. A loss of well over 1,600 from a total population of approximately 8,600 seems a conservative estimate.[61]

At the turn of the century, therefore, the mourning-war was no longer even symbolically restocking the population. And, far from being socially integrative, the Five Nations' current war was splitting their communities asunder. The heavy death toll of previous decades had robbed them of many respected headmen and clan matrons to whom the people had looked for guidance and arbitration of disputes. As a group of young Mohawk warriors lamented in 1691 when they came to parley with the Catholic Iroquois settled near Montreal, "all those…who had sense are dead."[62] The power vacuum, war weariness, and the pressures of the imperial struggle combined to place at each other's throats those who believed that the Iroquois' best chance lay in a separate peace with the French and those who continued to rely on the English alliance. "The [Five] Nations are full of faction, the French having got a great interest among them," reported the Albany Commissioners for Indian Affairs in July 1700. At Onondaga, where, according to Governor Bellomont, the French had "full as many friends" as the English, the situation was particularly severe. Some sachems found themselves excluded from councils, and factions charged one another with using poison to remove adversaries from the scene. One pro-English Onondaga headman, Aquendero, had to take refuge near Albany, leaving his son near death and supposedly bewitched by opponents.[63] Their politics being ordered by an interlocking structure of lineages, clans, and moieties, the Iroquois found such factions, which cut across kinship lines, difficult if not impossible to handle. In the 1630s the Huron, whose political structure was similar, never could manage the novel factional alignments that resulted from the introduction of Christianity. That failure perhaps contributed to their demise at the hands of the Five Nations.[64] Now the Iroquois found themselves at a similar pass.

As the new century opened, however, Iroquois headmen were beginning to construct solutions to some of the problems facing their people. From 1699 to 1701 Iroquois ambassadors—in particular the influential Onondaga Teganissorens—threaded the thickets of domestic factionalism and shuttled between their country and the Euro-American colonies to negotiate what one scholar has termed "The Grand Settlement of 1701.[65] On August 4, 1701, at an immense gathering at Montreal, representatives of the Seneca, Cayuga, Onondaga, and Oneida, also speaking for the Mohawk, met Governor Callière and headmen of the Wyandot, Algonquin, Abenaki, Nipissing, Ottawa, Ojibwa, Sauk, Fox, Miami, Potawatomi, and other French allies. The participants ratified arrangements made during the previous year that provided for a general peace, established vague boundaries for western hunting territories (the Iroquois basically consented to remain east of Detroit), and eschewed armed conflict in favor of arbitration by the governor of New France. A few days later, the Iroquois and Callière reached more specific understandings concerning Iroquois access to Detroit and other French western trading posts. Mostly from the French standpoint, the Iroquois promised neutrality in future Anglo-French wars.[95]

On one level, this series of treaties represented an Iroquois defeat. The Five Nations had lost the war and, in agreeing to peace on terms largely dictated by Callière, had acknowledged their inability to prevail militarily over their French, and especially their Indian, enemies[67] Nevertheless, the Grand Settlement did secure for the Iroquois five important ends: escape from the devastating warfare of the 1690s; rights to hunting in the west; potentially profitable trade with western Indians passing through Iroquoia to sell furs at Albany; access to markets in New France and Pennsylvania as well as in New York; and the promise of noninvolvement in future imperial wars. The Grand Settlement thus brought to the Five Nations not only peace on their northern and western flanks but also a more stable economy based on guaranteed western hunting territories and access to multiple Euro-American markets. Henceforth, self-destructive warfare need no longer be the only means of ensuring Iroquois economic survival, and neither need inter-Indian beaver wars necessarily entrap the Five Nations in struggles between Euro-Americans.[68] In 1724, nearly a generation after the negotiation of the Grand Settlement, an Iroquois spokesman explained to a delegation from Massachusetts how the treaties, while limiting Iroquois diplomatic and military options, nevertheless proved beneficial. "Tho' the Hatchett lays by our side yet the way is open between this Place and Canada, and trade is free both going and coming," he answered when the New Englanders urged the Iroquois to attack New France. "If a War should break out and we should use the Hatchett that layes by our Side, those Paths which are now open wo[u]ld be stopped, and if we should make war it would not end in a few days as yours doth but it must last till one nation or the other is destroyed as it has been heretofore with us[.]... [W]e know what whipping and scourging is from the Governor of Canada.[69]

After the Grand Settlement, then, Iroquois leaders tried to abandon warfare as a means of dealing with the diplomatic problems generated by the Anglo-French imperial rivalry and the economic dilemmas of the fur trade. Through most of the first half of the eighteenth century the headmen pursued a policy of neutrality between the empires with a dexterity that the English almost never, and the French only seldom, comprehended. At the same time the Iroquois began to cement peaceful trading relationships with the western nations. Sporadic fighting continued in the western hunting grounds through the first decade and a half of the eighteenth century, as the parties to the 1701 Montreal treaty sorted out the boundaries of their territories and engaged in reciprocal raids for captives that were provoked by contact between Iroquois and western Indian hunters near French posts. Iroquois headmen quickly took advantage of Canadian arbitration when such quarrels arose, however, and they struggled to restrain young warriors from campaigning in the west.

In addition to its diplomatic benefits, the Grand Settlement of 1701 provided a partial solution to Iroquois factionalism. Iroquoian non-state political structures could not suppress factional cleavages entirely, and in the years after 1701 differences over relations with the French and the English still divided Iroquois communities, as each European power continued to encourage its friends. Interpreters such as the Canadian Louis-Thomas Chabert de Joncaire and the New Yorker Lawrence Claeson (or Claes) struggled to win the hearts of Iroquois villagers; each side gave presents to its supporters; and on several occasions English officials interfered with the selection of sachems in order to strengthen pro-English factions. As a result, fratricidal disputes still occasionally threatened to tear villages apart.[70] Still, in general, avoidance of exclusive alliances or major military conflict with either European power allowed Iroquois councils to keep factional strife within bounds. A new generation of headmen learned to maintain a rough equilibrium between pro-French and pro-English factions at home, as well as peaceful relations with French and English abroad. Central to that strategy was an intricate policy that tried to balance French against English fortified trading posts, Canadian against New York blacksmiths, and Jesuit against Anglican missionaries. Each supplied the Iroquois with coveted aspects of Euro-American culture—trade goods, technology, and spiritual power, respectively—but each also could be a focus of factional leadership and a tool of Euro-American domination. The Grand Settlement provided a way to lessen, though hardly eliminate, those dangers.[71]

The years following the Grand Settlement also witnessed the stabilization of Iroquois population. Though the numbers of the Iroquois continued to decline gradually, the forces that had so dramatically reduced them in the seventeenth century abated markedly after 1701. The first two decades of the seventeenth century brought only one major epidemic— smallpox in 1716–72 while the flow of Catholic converts to Canadian missions also slowed. The missions near Montreal had lost much of the utopian character that had previously attracted so many Iroquois converts.

By the early eighteenth century, drunkenness, crushing debts to traders, and insults from Euro-American neighbors were no less characteristic of Iroquois life in Canada than in Iroquoia, and the Jesuit priests serving the Canadian missions had become old, worn-out men who had long since abandoned dreams of turning Indians into Frenchmen.[73]

As the population drain from warfare, disease, and migration to mission villages moderated, peaceful assimilation of refugees from neighboring nations helped to replace those Iroquois who were lost. One French source even claimed, in 1716, that "the five Iroquois nations…are becoming more and more formidable through their great numbers."[74] Most notable among the newcomers were some 1,500 Tuscaroras who, after their defeat by the English and allied Indians of the Carolinas in 1713, migrated north to settle on lands located between the Onondaga and Oneida villages. They were adopted as the sixth nation of the Iroquois Confederacy about 1722. There are indications that the Tuscarora—who, according to William Andrews, Anglican missionary to the Mohawk, possessed "an Implacable hatred against Christians at Carolina"—contributed greatly to the spirit of independence and distrust of Europeans that guided the Six Nations on their middle course between the imperial powers. The Tuscarora, concluded Andrews, were "a great Occasion of Our Indians becoming so bad as they are, they now take all Occasions to find fault and quarrel, wanting to revolt."[75]

IV

The first two decades of the eighteenth century brought a shift away from those aspects of Iroquois warfare that had been most socially disruptive. As the Iroquois freed themselves of many, though by no means all, of the demographic, economic, and diplomatic pressures that had made seventeenth-century warfare so devastating, the mourning-war began to resume some of its traditional functions in Iroquois culture.

As the Five Nations made peace with their old western and northern foes, Iroquois mourning-war raids came to focus on enemies the Iroquois called "Flatheads"—a vague epithet for the Catawba and other tribes on the frontiers of Virginia and the Carolinas.[76] Iroquois and Flathead war parties had traded blows during the 1670s and 1680s, conflict had resumed about 1707, and after the arrival of the Tuscarora in the 1710s Iroquois raiding parties attacked the Flatheads regularly and almost exclusively.[77] The Catawba and other southeastern Indians sided with the Carolinians in the Tuscarora War of 1711–1713, bringing them into further conflict with warriors from the Five Nations, who fought alongside the Tuscarora.[78] After the Tuscarora moved north, Iroquois-Flathead warfare increased in intensity and lasted—despite several peace treaties—until the era of the American Revolution. This series of mourning-wars exasperated English officials from New York to the Carolinas, who could conceive no rational explanation for the conflicts except the intrigues of French envoys who delighted in stirring up trouble on English frontiers.[79]

Canadian authorities did indeed encourage Iroquois warriors with arms and presents. The French were happy for the chance to harass British settlements and to strike blows against Indians who troubled French inhabitants of New Orleans and the Mississippi Valley.[80] Yet the impetus for raiding the Flatheads lay with the Iroquois, not the French. At Onondaga in 1710, when emissaries from New York blamed French influence for the campaigns and presented a wampum belt calling for a halt to hostilities, a Seneca orator dismissed their arguments: "When I think of the Brave Warriours that hav[e] been slain by the Flatheads I can Govern my self no longer…. I reject your Belt for the Hatred I bear to the

Flatheads can never be forgotten."[81] The Flatheads were an ideal target for the mourning-wars demanded by Iroquois women and warriors, for with conflict channeled southward, warfare with northern and western nations that, in the past, had brought disaster could be avoided. In addition, war with the Flatheads placated both Canadian authorities and pro-French Iroquois factions, since the raids countered a pro-English trade policy with a military policy useful to the French. And, from the perspective of Iroquois-English relations, the southern campaigns posed few risks. New York officials alternately forbade and countenanced raids against southern Indians as the fortunes of frontier war in the Carolinas and the intrigues of intercolonial politics shifted. But even when the governors of the Carolinas, Virginia, Pennsylvania, and New York did agree on schemes to impose peace, experience with English military impotence had taught the Iroquois that the governors could do little to stop the conflict.[82]

While the diplomatic advantages were many, perhaps the most important aspect of the Iroquois-Flathead conflicts was the partial return they allowed to the traditional ways of the mourning-war. By the 1720s the Five Nations had not undone the ravages of the preceding century, yet they had largely extricated themselves from the socially disastrous wars of the fur trade and of the European empires. And though prisoners no longer flowed into Iroquois villages in the floods of the seventeenth century, the southern raids provided enough captives for occasional mourning and condolence rituals that dried Iroquois tears and reminded the Five Nations of their superiority over their enemies. In the same letter of 1716 in which missionary Andrews noted the growing independence of the Iroquois since the Tuscarora had settled among them and the southern wars had intensified, he also vividly described the reception recently given to captives of the Onondaga and Oneida.[83] Iroquois warfare was again binding Iroquois families and villages together.

NOTES

A preliminary version of this article was presented at the Institute's 41st Conference in Early American History at Millersville State College, Apr. 30–May 2, 1981, organized by Francis Bremer. For comments on various drafts the author thanks Aaron Berman, Elizabeth Capelle, Barbara Graymont, Francis Jennings, Sharon Mead, Diana Meisinger, Amy Mittelman, Linda Roth, Paula Rubel, Herbert Sloan, Alden Vaughan, Robert Venables, and Anthony Wallace.

1. Reuben Gold Thwaites, ed., *The Jesuit Relations and Allied Documents: Travels and Explorations of the Jesuit Missionaries in New France,* 1610–1791 (Cleveland, Ohio, 1896–1901), XLIII, 263, hereafter cited as *Jesuit Relations.*

2. See, for example, George T. Hunt, *The Wars of the Iroquois: A study in Intertribal Trade Relations* (Madison, Wis., 1940); W.W. Newcomb, Jr., "A Re-Examination of the Causes of Plains Warfare," *American Anthropologist,* N.S., LII (1950), 317–330; and Francis Jennings, *The Invasion of America: Indians, Colonialism, and the Cant of Conquest* (Chapel Hill, N.C., 1975), 146–170.

3. While anthropologists disagree about the precise distinctions between the wars of state-organized and non-state societies, they generally agree that battles for territorial conquest, economic monopoly, and subjugation or enslavement of conquered peoples are the product of the technological and organizational capacities of the state. For overviews of the literature see C. R. Hallpike, "Functionalist Interpretations of Primitive Warfare," *Man,* N.S., VIII (1973), 451–470; and Andrew Vayda, "Warfare in Ecological Perspective," *Annual Review of Ecology and Systematics,* V (1974), 183–193.

4. My use of the term *mourning-war* differs from that of Marian W. Smith in "American Indian Warfare," New York Academy of Sciences, *Transactions,* 2d Ser., XIII (1951), 348–365, which stresses the psychological and emotional functions of the mourning-war. As the following paragraphs seek to show, the psychology of the mourning-war was deeply rooted in Iroquois demography and social structure; my use of the term accordingly reflects a more holistic view of the cultural role of the mourning-war than does Smith's. On the dan-

gers of an excessively psychological explanation of Indian warfare see Jennings, *Invasion of America,* 159; but see also the convincing defense of Smith in Richard Drinnon, "Ravished Land," *Indian Historian,* IX (Fall 1976), 24–26.

5. Joseph Francois Lafitau, *Customs of the American Indians Compared with the Customs of Primitive Times,* ed. and trans. William N. Fenton and Elizabeth L. Moore (Toronto, 1974, 1977 [orig. publ. Paris, 1724]), II, 98–99.

6. Cadwallader Colden, *The History of the Five Indian Nations of Canada, Which Are Dependent on the Province of New-York in America, and Are the Barrier between the English and French in That Part of the World* (London, 1747), 4, hereafter cited as Colden, *History* (1747).

7. Gabriel Sagard, *The Long Journey to the Country of the Hurons,* ed. George M. Wrong and trans. H. H. Langton (Toronto, 1939 [orig. publ. Paris, 1632]), 151–152; *Jesuit Relations,* XLII, 139; William N. Fenton, ed., "The Hyde Manuscript: Captain William Hyde's Observations of the 5 Nations of Indians at New York, 1698," *American Scene Magazine,* VI (1965), [9]; Bruce G., Trigger, *The Children of Aataentsic: A History of the Huron People to 1660* (Montreal, 1976), I, 68–69, 145–147.

8. Hennepin, *A New Discovery of a Vast Country in America...,* 1st English ed. (London, 1698), II, 88.

9. Newcomb, "Re-Examination of Plains Warfare," *Am. Anthro.,* N.S., LII (1950), 320.

10. Andrew P. Vayda, "Expansion and Warfare among Swidden Agriculturalists," *Am. Anthro.,* N.S., LXIII (1961), 346–358; Anthony Leeds, "The Functions of War," in Jules Masserman, ed., *Violence and War, with Clinical Studies* (New York, 1963), 69–82; William Tulio Divale and Marvin Harris, "Population, Warfare, and the Male Supremacist Complex," *Am. Anthro.,* N.S., LXXVIII (1976), 521–538.

11. J.N.B. Hewitt, "Orenda and a Definition of Religion," *Am. Anthro.,* N.S., IV (1902), 33–46; Morris Wolf, *Iroquois Religion and Its Relation to Their Morals* (New York, 1919), 25–26; Alvin M. Josephy, Jr., *The Indian Heritage of America* (New York, 1968), 94; Ake Hultkrantz, *The Religions of the American Indians,* trans. Monica Setterwall (Berkeley, Calif., 1979), 12.

12. *Jesuit Relations,* XXIII, 165–169; Lafitau, *Customs of American Indians,* ed. and trans. Fenton and Moore, I, 71; B. H. Quain, "The Iroquois," in Margaret Mead, ed., *Cooperation and Competition among Primitive Peoples* (New York, 1937), 276–277.

13. Fenton, ed., "Hyde Manuscript," *Am. Scene Mag.,* VI (1965), [16].

14. Philip Mazzei, *Researches on the United States,* ed. and trans. Constance B. Sherman (Charlottesville, Va., 1976 [orig. publ. Paris, 1788]), 349. See also P[ierre] de Charlevoix, *Journal of a Voyage to North-America...*(London, 1761 [orig. publ. Paris, 1744]), I, 370–373, II, 33–34, and George S. Snyderman, "Behind the Tree of Peace: A Sociological Analysis of Iroquois Warfare," *Pennsylvania Archaeologist,* XVIII, nos. 3–4 (1948), 13–15.

15. Lafitau, *Customs of American Indians,* ed. and trans. Fenton and Moore, II, 241–245, quotation on p. 242.

16. *Jesuit Relations,* X, 273–275, XIX, 91, XLIII, 267–271, LX, 35–41. On wergild see Lewis H. Morgan, *League of the Ho-dé-no-sau-nee, or Iroquois* (Rochester, N.Y., 1851), 331–333, and Jennings, *Invasion of America,* 148–149. The parallel between Iroquois practice and the Germanic tradition of blood payments should not be stretched too far; Iroquois condolence presents were an integral part of the broader condolence process.

17. Smith, "American Indian Warfare," N.Y. Acad. Sci., *Trans,* 2d Ser., XIII (1951), 352–354; Anthony F.C. Wallace, *The Death and Rebirth of the Seneca* (New York, 1970), 101. It is within the context of the mourning-war that what are usually described as Indian wars for revenge or blood feuds should be understood. The revenge motive—no doubt strong in Iroquois warfare—was only part of the larger complex of behavior and belief comprehended in the mourning-war. It should also be noted that raids might be inspired by *any* death, not just those attributable to murder or warfare and for which revenge or other atonement, such as the giving of condolence presents, was necessary. Among Euro-American observers, only the perceptive Lafitau seems to have been aware of this possibility *(Customs of American Indians,* ed. and trans. Fenton and Moore, II, 98–102, 154). I have found no other explicit contemporary discussion of this phenomenon, but several accounts indicate the formation of war parties in response to deaths from disease or other nonviolent causes. See H. P. Biggar *et al.,* eds. and trans., *The Works of Samuel de Champlain* (Toronto, 1922–1936), II, 206–208, hereafter cited as *Works of Champlain; Jesuit Relations,* LXIV, 91; Jasper Dankers [Danckaerts] and Peter Sluyter, *Journal of a Voyage to New York and a Tour in Several of the American Colonies in 1679–80,* trans. and ed. Henry C. Murphy (Long Island Historical Society, *Memoirs,* I [Brooklyn, N.Y., 1867]), 277; and William M. Beauchamp, ed., *Moravian Journals Relating to Central New York, 1745–66*

(Syracuse, N.Y., 1916), 125–126, 183–186.

18. *Jesuit Relations*, X, 225–227; E.B. O'Callaghan *et al.*, eds., *Documents Relative to the Colonial History of the State of New-York*...(Albany, N.Y., 1856–1887), IV, 22, hereafter cited as N.-Y. *Col. Docs.*; Lafitau, *Customs of American Indians*, ed. and trans. Fenton and Moore, II, 99–103; Snyderman, "Behind the Tree of Peace," *Pa. Archaeol.*, XVIII, nos. 3–4 (1948), 15–20.

19. The following composite account is based on numerous contemporaneous reports of Iroquois treatment of captives. Among the more complete are *Jesuit Relations*, XXII, 251–267, XXXIX, 57–77, L, 59–63, LIV, 23–35; Gideon D. Scull, ed., *Voyages of Peter Esprit Radisson: Being an Account of His Travels and Experiences among the North American Indians, from 1652 to 1684* (Boston, 1885), 28–60; and James H. Coyne, ed. and trans., "Exploration of the Great Lakes, 1660–1670, by Dollier de Casson and de Bréhant de Galinée," Ontario Historical Society, *Papers and Records*, IV (1903), 31–35. See also the many other portrayals in *Jesuit Relations*; the discussions in Lafitau, *Customs of American Indians*, ed. and trans. Fenton and Moore, II, 148–172; Nathaniel Knowles, "The Torture of Captives by the Indians of Eastern North America," American Philisophical Society, *Proceedings*, LXXXII (1940), 181–190; and Wallace, *Death and Rebirth of the Seneca*, 103–107.

20. The gauntlet and the public humiliation and physical abuse of captives also served as initiation rites for prospective adoptees; see John Heckewelder, "An Account of the History, Manners, and Customs of the Indian Nations Who Once Inhabited Pennsylvania and the Neighbouring States," Am. Phil. Soc., *Transactions of the Historical and Literary Committee*, I (1819), 211–213. For a fuller discussion of Indian methods of indoctrinating adoptees see James Axtell, "The White Indians of Colonial America," *William and Mary Quarterly, 3d Ser.*, XXXII (1975), 55–88.

21. Usually only adult male captives were executed, and most women and children seem to have escaped physical abuse. Occasionally, however, the Iroquois did torture and execute women and children. See Scull, ed., *Voyages of Radisson*, 56, and *Jesuit Relations*, XXXIX, 219–221, XLII, 97–99, LI, 213, 231–233, LII, 79, 157–159, LIII, 253, LXII, 59, LXIV, 127–129, LXV, 33–39.

22. Several authors—from James Adair and Philip Mazzei in the 18th century to W. Arens in 1979—have denied that the Iroquois engaged in cannibalism (Adair, *The History of the American Indians*...[London, 1775], 209; Mazzei, *Researches*, ed. and trans. Sherman, 359; Arens, *The Man-Eating*

Myth: Anthropology & Anthropophagy [New York, 1979] 127–129). Arens is simply wrong, as Thomas S. Abler has shown in "Iroquois Cannibalism: Fact Not Fiction," Ethnohistory, XXVII (1980), 309–316. Adair and Mazzei, from the perspective of the late 18th century, were on firmer ground; by then the Five Nations apparently had abandoned anthropophagy. See Adolph B. Benson, ed., *Peter Kalm's Travels in North America* (New York, 1937), 694.

23. Robert L. Rands and Carroll L. Riley, "Diffusion and Discontinuous Distribution," *Am. Anthro.*, N.S., LX (1958), 284–289; Maurice R. Davie, *The Evolution of War: A Study of Its Role in Early Societies* (New Haven, Conn., 1929), 36–38; Hennepin, *New Discovery*, II, 92.

24. *Jesuit Relations*, LXII, 85–87, LXVII, 173; Knowles, "Torture of Captives," Am. Phil. Soc., *Procs.*, LXXXII (1940), 210–211.

25. *Jesuit Relations*, XIX, 81.

26. *N.Y. Col. Docs.*, V, 274.

27. *Works of Champlain*, IV, 330; Charlevoix, *Voyage to North-America*, I, 316–333.

28. *Jesuit Relations*, XXXIX, 221.

29. *Works of Champlain*, 73–74; *Jesuit Relations*, XXXII, 159.

30. *Jesuit Relations*, X, 145, XXXIX, 29–31; J.N.B. Hewitt, "The Iroquoian Concept of the Soul," *Journal of American Folk-Lore*, VIII (1895), 107–116.

31. *Sagard, Long Journey*, ed. Wrong and trans. Langton, 152–156; *Jesuit Relations*, XXII, 309–311, XXXII, 173–175, XXXIV, 197, LV, 79, LXVI, 273; Hennepin, *New Discovery*, II, 86–94; Patrick Mitchell Malone, "Indian and English Military Systems in New England in the Seventeenth Century" (Ph.D. diss., Brown University, 1971), 33–38.

32. Lafitau, *Customs of American Indians*, ed. and trans. Fenton and Moore, II, 98.

33. Paul A. W. Wallace, *The White Roots of Peace* (Philadelphia, 1946); A.F.C. Wallace, *Death and Rebirth of the Seneca*, 39–48, 93–98; William M. Beauchamp, *Civil, Religious and Mourning Councils and Ceremonies of Adoption of the New York Indians*, New York State Museum Bulletin 113 (Albany, N.Y., 1907). For a suggestive discussion of Indian definitions of peace see John Phillip Reid, *A Better Kind of Hatchel: Law, Trade, and Diplomacy in the Cherokee Nation during the Early Years of European Contact* (University Park, Pa., 1976), 9–17.

34. On the devastating impact of European diseases—some Indian populations may have declined by a factor of 20 to 1 within a century or so of contact—see the works surveyed in Russell Thornton, "American Indian Historical Demography: A Review Essay with Suggestions for Future Research,"

American Indian Culture and Research Journal, III, No. 1 (1979), 69–74.

35. Trigger, *Children of Aataentsic*, II, 602; Cornelius J. Jaenen, *Friend and Foe: Aspects of French Amerindian Cultural Contact in the Sixteenth and Seventeenth Centuries* (New York, 1976), 100. Most of the early Iroquois epidemics went unrecorded by Europeans, but major smallpox epidemics are documented for the Mohawk in 1634 and the Seneca in 1640–1641; see [Harmen Meyndertsz van den Bogaert], "Narrative of a Journey into the Mohawk and Oneida Country, 1634–1635," in J. Franklin Jameson, ed., *Narratives of New Netherland, 1609–1664* (New York, 1909), 140–141, and *Jesuit Relations*, XXI, 211.

36. *Jesuit Relations*, XXX, 273, XLIV, 43, XLVII, 193, 205, XLVIII, 79–83, L, 63, LIV, 79–81, LVII, 81–83, LX, 175.

37. *Works of Champlain*, II, 95–100; Malone, "Indian and English Military Systems," 179–200; Jennings, *Invasion of America*, 165–166. After the introduction of firearms the Iroquois continued to raise armies of several hundred to a thousand men, but they almost never engaged them in set battles. Large armies ensured safe travel to distant battle-grounds and occasionally intimidated outnumbered opponents, but when they neared their objective they usually broke into small raiding parties. See Daniel Gookin, "Historical Collections of the Indians in New England" (1674), Massachusetts Historical Society, *Collections*, I (1792), 162, and Cadwallader Colden, *The History of the Five Indian Nations Depending on the Province of New-York in America* (New York, 1727), 8–10, hereafter cited as Colden, *History* (1727).

38. *N.Y. Col. Docs.*, I, 150; "Journal of New Netherland, 1647," in Jameson, ed., *Narratives of New Netherland*, 274; *Jesuit Relations*, XXIV, 295; Carl P. Russell, *Guns on the Early Frontiers: A History of Firearms from Colonial Times through the Years of the Western Fur Trade* (Berkeley, Calif., 1957), 11–15, 62–66.

39. *Jesuit Relations*, XXVII, 71, XLV, 205–207; Elisabeth Tooker, "The Iroquois Defeat of the Huron: A Review of Causes," *Pa. Archaeol.*, XXXIII (1963), 115–123; Keith F. Otterbein, "Why the Iroquois Won: An Analysis of Iroquois Military Tactics," *Ethnohistory*, XI (1964), 56–63; John K. Mahon, "Anglo-American Methods of Indian Warfare, 1676–1794," *Mississippi Valley Historical Review*, XLV (1958), 255.

40. Bruce G. Trigger, "The Mohawk-Mahican War (1624–28): The Establishment of a Pattern," *Canadian Historical Review*, LII (1971), 276–286.

41. Harold A. Innis, *The Fur Trade in Canada: An Introduction to Canadian Economic History* (New Haven, Conn., 1930), 1–4, 32–33; Hunt, *Wars of the Iroquois*, 33–37; John Witthoft, "Ancestry of the Susquehannocks," in John Witthoft and W. Fred Kinsey III, eds., *Susquehannock Miscellany* (Harrisburg, Pa., 1959), 34–35; Thomas Elliot Norton, *The Fur Trade in Colonial New York, 1686–1776* (Madison, Wis., 1974), 9–15.

42. The classic account of the beaver wars is Hunt, *Wars of the Iroquois*, but three decades of subsequent scholarship have overturned many of that work's interpretations. See Allen W. Trelease, "The Iroquois and the Western Fur Trade: A Problem in Interpretation," MVHR, XLIX (1962), 32–51; Raoul Naroll, "The Causes of the Fourth Iroquois War," *Ethnohistory*, XVI (1969), 51–81; Allan Forbes, Jr., "Two and a Half Centuries of Conflict: The Iroquois and the Laurentian Wars," *Pa. Archaeol.*, XL, nos. 3–4 (1970), 1–20; William N. Fenton, "The Iroquois in History," in Eleanor Burke Leacock and Nancy Oestreich Lurie, eds., *North American Indians in Historical Perspective* (New York, 1971), 139–145; Karl H. Schlesier, "Epidemics and Indian Middlemen: Rethinking the Wars of the Iroquois, 1609–1653," *Ethnohistory*, XXIII (1976), 129–145; and Trigger, *Children of Aataentsic*, esp. II, 617–664.

43. *Works of Champlain*, III, 31–32; see also II, 118–119, 186–191, 246–285, III, 207–228.

44. *Ibid.*, II, 65–107, 120–138, III, 48–81.

45. *Jesuit Relations*, XXI–L, *passim*; Robert A. Goldstein, *French-Iroquois Diplomatic and Military Relations, 1609–1701* (The Hague, 1969), 62–99. The actual Canadian death toll in wars with the Iroquois before 1666 has recently been shown to have been quite low. Only 153 French were killed in raids while 143 were taken prisoner (perhaps 38 of those died in captivity); John A. Dickinson, "La guerre iroquoise et la mortalité en Nouvelle-France, 1608–1666," *Revue d'histoire de l'amerique francaise*, XXXVI (1982), 31–54. On 17th-century French captives of the Iroquois see Daniel K. Richter, "The Iroquois Melting Pot: Seventeenth-Century War Captives of the Five Nations" (paper presented at the Shelby Cullom Davis Center Conference on War and Society in Early America, Princeton University, March 11–12, 1983), 18–19.

46. *Jesuit Relations*, L, 127–147, 239; N.-Y. Col. *Docs.*, III, 121–127; A.J.F. van Laer, trans. and ed., *Correspondence of Jeremias van Rensselaer 1651–1674* (Albany, N.Y., 1932), 388.

47. *Jesuit Relations* XXXV, 183–205, XXXVI, 177–191, XLI, 43–65, XLIII, 115–125, 187–207, XLIV, 69–77, 165–167, 187–191; A.J.F. van Laer,

trans. and ed., *Minutes of the Court of Fort Orange and Beverwyck,* 1657–1660, II (Albany, N.Y., 1923), 45–48; Scull, ed., *Voyages of Radisson,* 93–119; Nicholas Perrot, "Memoir on the Manners, Customs, and Religion of the Savages of North America" (c. 1680–1718), in Emma Helen Blair, ed. and trans., *The Indian Tribes of the Upper Mississippi Valley and Region of the Great Lakes*...(Cleveland Ohio, 1911), I, 148–193.

48. *Jesuit Relations,* XLVII, 139–153

49. *Ibid.,* XLIII, 265.

50. *Ibid.,* XLV, 207, LI, 123, 187.

51. N.Y. *Col. Docs.,* IX, 80; Victor Konrad, "An Iroquois Frontier: The North Shore of Lake Ontario during the late Seventeenth Century," *Journal of Historical Geography,* VII (1981), 129–144.

52. *Jesuit Relations,* LI, 81–85, 167–257, LII, 53–55.

53. *Ibid.,* LV, 61–63, LVII, 133–141, LVIII, 211, LX, 187–195.

54. *Ibid.,* LIV, 281–283.

55. *Ibid,.* LVI, 29, LVIII, 247–253, LX, 145–147, LXI, 195–199, LXIII, 141–189.

56. *Ibid.,* LV, 33–37, LVIII, 75–77.

57. E.B. O'Callaghan, ed., *The Documentary History of the State New-York* octavo ed. (Albany, N.Y., 1849–1851), I, 12–14; *Jesuit Relations,* XXIV, 295. Reflecting the purposes of most Euro– Americans who made estimates of Indian population, figures are usually given in terms of the number of available fighting men. The limited data available for direct comparisons of estimates of Iroquois fighting strength with estimates of total population indicate that the ratio of one warrior for every four people proposed in Sherburne F. Cook, "Interracial Warfare and Population Decline among the New England Indians," *Ethnohistory,* XX (1973), 13, applies to the Five Nations. Compare the estimates of a total Mohawk population of 560–580 in William Andrews to the Secretary of the Society for the Propagation of the Gospel in Foreign Parts, Sept. 7, 1713, Oct. 17, 1715, Records of the Society for the Propagation of the Gospel, Letterbooks, Ser. A, VIII, 186, XI, 268–269, S.P.G. Archives, London (microfilm ed.), with the concurrent estimates of approximately 150 Mohawk warriors in Bernardus Freeman to the Secretary of S.P.G., May 28, 1712, *ibid.,* VII, 203; Peter Wraxall, *An Abridgement of the Indian Affairs....Transacted in the Colony of New York, from the Year 1678 to the Year 1751,* ed. Charles Howard McIlwain (Cambridge, Mass., 1915), 69: N.Y. *Col. Docs.,* V, 272; and Lawrence H. Leder, ed., *The Livingston Indian Records, 1666–1723* (Gettysburg, Pa., 1956), 220.

58. The estimates of 10,000 for the 1640s is from Trigger, *Children of Aataentsic,* 1,98; the figure of 8,600 for the 1670s is calculated from Wentworth Greenhalgh's 1677 estimate of 2,150 Iroquois warriors, in O'Callaghan, ed., *Documentary History,* I, 12–14. Compare the late 1670s estimate in Hennepin, *New Discovery,* II, 92–93, and see the tables of 17th- and 18th-century Iroquois warrior population in Snyderman, "Behind the Tree of Peace," *Pa. Archaeol.,* XVIII, nos. 3–4 (1948), 42; Bruce G. Trigger, ed., *Northeast,* in William C. Sturtevant, ed., *Handbook of North American Indians,* XV (Washington, D.C., 1978), 421; and Gunther Michelson, "Iroquois Population Statistics," *Man in the Northeast,* No. 14 (1977), 3–17. William Starna has recently suggested that all previous estimates for 1635 and earlier of Mohawk—and by implication Five Nations—population are drastically understated ("Mohawk Iroquois Populations: A Revision," *Ethnohistory,* XXVII [1980], 371–382).

59. *Jesuit Relations,* LXII, 71–95, quotation on 83.

60. Richard Aquila, "The Iroquois Restoration: A Study of Iroquois Power, Politics, and Relations with Indians and Whites, 1700–1744" (Ph.D. dissertation, Ohio State University, 1977), 16–29.

61. A 1698 report on New York's suffering during the War of the League of Augsburg states that there were 2,550 Iroquois warriors in 1689 and only 1,230 in 1698. The report probably contains some polemical overstatement: the first figure seems too high and the second too low. By comparison, 2,050 Iroquois warriors were estimated by Denonville in 1685, 1,400 by Bellomont in 1691, 1,750 by Bernardus Freeman in 1700, and 1,200 by a French cabinet paper in 1701 (*N.Y. Col. Docs.,* IV, 337, 768, IX, 281, 725; Freeman to the Secretary, May 28, 1712, Records of S.P.G., Letterbooks, Ser. A, VII, 203). If the figure of 1,750 warriors cited by Freeman—a minister who worked with the Mohawk—is correct, the total Iroquois population in 1700 was approximately 7,000, calculated by the ratio in note 57.

62. *Jesuit Relations,* LXIV, 59–61.

63. *N.Y. Col. Docs.,* IV, 648–661, 689–690.

64. Trigger, *Children of Aataentsic,* II, 709–724. See also the discussions of Indian factionalism in Robert F. Berkhofer, Jr., "The Political Context of a New Indian History," *Pacific Historical Review,* XL (1971), 373–380; and Edward H. Spicer, *Cycles of Conquest: The Impact of Spain. Mexico, and the United States on the Indians of the Southwest, 1533–1960* (Tucson, Ariz., 1962), 491–501.

65. Anthony F.C. Wallace, "Origins of Iroquois Neutrality: The Grand Settlement of 1701,"

Pennsylvania History, XXIV (1957), 223–235. The best reconstruction of the Iroquois diplomacy that led to the Grand Settlement is Richard L. Haan. "The Covenant Chain: Iroquois Diplomacy on the Niagara Frontier, 1697–1730" (Ph.D. diss., University of California, Santa Barbara, 1976), 64–147.

66. Bacqueville de La Potherie, *Histoire de l'Am130rique Septentrionale*, IV (Paris, 1722), *passim; N.Y. Col. Docs.*, IX, 715–725.

67. Leroy V. Eid, "The Ojibwa-Iroquois War. The War the Five Nations Did Not Win," *Ethnohistory*, XXVI (1979), 297–324.

68. Aquila, "Iroquois Restoration," 109–171; Richard Haan, "The Problem of Iroquois Neutrality: Suggestions for Revision," *Ethnohistory*, XXVII (1980), 317–330.

69. *N.Y. Col. Docs.*, V, 724–725.

70. *N.Y. Col. Doc.*, V, 545, 569, 632, IX, 816; Thomas Barclay to Robert Hunter, Jan. 26, 1713 (extract), Records of S.P.G., Letterbooks, Ser. A, VIII, 251–252. For examples of Claeson's and Joncaire's activities see Colden, "Continuation," 360–363, 432–434, and *N.Y. Col. Docs.*, V, 538, 562–569, IX, 759–765, 814, 876–903.

71. *N.Y. Col. Docs.*, V, 217–227; Colden, "Continuation," 408–409; Wraxall, *Abridgement of Indian Affairs*, ed. McIlwain, 79n–8on.

72. Andrews to the Secretary, Oct. 11, 1716, Records of S.P.G., Letterbooks, Ser. A, XII, 241; *N.Y. Col. Docs.*, V, 484–487, IX, 878.

73. *Jesuit Relations*, LXVI, 203–207, LXVII, 39–41; *N.Y. Col. Docs.*, IX 882–884; George F.G. Stanley, "The Policy of 'Francisation' as Applied to the Indians during the Ancien Regime," *Revue d'historie de l'amerique française*, II III (1949–1950), 333–348; Cornelius J. Jaenen, "The Frenchification and Evangelization of the Amerindians in the Seventeenth Century New France" (sic), *Canadian Catholic Historical Association, Study Sessions*, XXXV (1969), 57–71.

74. *Jesuit Relations*, LXVII, 27.

75. Andrews to the Secretary, Apr. 20, 1716, Apr. 23, 1717, Records of S.P.G. Letterbooks, Ser. A, XI, 319–320, XII, 310–312.

76. Henry R. Schoolcraft, *Notes on the Iroquois: Or, Contributions to the Statistics, Aboriginal History, Antiquities and General Ethnology of Western New York* (New York, 1846), 148–149; Fenton, "Iroquois in History," in Leacock and Lurie, eds., *North American Indians*, 147–148; Beauchamp, *History of New York Iroquois*, 139.

77. On Iroquois-Flathead conflicts before 1710 see of Colden, *History* (1727), 3071, and "Continuation," 361–363, and Wraxall, *Abridgement of Indian Affairs*, ed. McIlwain, 50–61. References to raids after 1710 in Colden, *N.Y. Col. Docs.*, and other sources are too numerous to cite here; a useful discussion is Aquila, "Iroquois Restoration," 294–346.

78. Wraxall, *Abridgement of Indian Affairs*, ed. McIlwain, 94–96; *N.Y. Col. Docs.*, V, 372–376, 382–388, 484–493; Verner W. Crane, *The Southern Frontier, 1670–1732* (Durham, N.C., 1928), 158–161.

79. *N.Y. Col Docs.* V, 542–545, 562–569, 635–640.

80. *Ibid.*, IX, 876–878, 884–885, 1085, 1097–1098.

81. Colden, "Continuation," 382–383, brackets in original.

82. For examples of shifting New York policies regarding the Iroquois southern campaigns see *N.-Y. Col. Docs.*, V, 446–464, 542–545, and Wraxall, *Abridgement of Indian Affairs*, ed. McIlwain, 123.

83. Andrews to the Secretary, Apr. 20, 1716, Records of S.P.G., Letterbooks, Ser. A., XI, 320.

AFRICAN AMERICANS, EXODUS, AND THE AMERICAN ISRAEL

Albert J. Raboteau

During the past two decades, research on African American religious beliefs and practices has challenged an older focus on the institutional and intellectual life of white, middle-class Protestantism. This research demonstrates that African religious life has been an integral part of American religious history. At the same time, an older scholarship that emphasized the deficiencies of black life, compared to the white middle-class ideal, has been overtaken by a new approach that, while underscoring the heavy toll of white racism, nevertheless stresses the capacity of African Americans to adapt creatively to their hostile environment. Perhaps more than any other scholar, Albert Raboteau has led this contemporary emergence of African American religious history. In the following essay, Raboteau demonstrates how African slaves found within European American Protestantism a theology of history that they adapted to help them make sense of their enslavement. In the Exodus story, in particular, African slaves found a narrative with broad implications for their own situation to which they gave a radically new meaning.

Reprinted by permission from Albert J. Raboteau, "African Americans, Exodus, and the American Israel," in *African American Christianity: Essays in History*, Paul E. Johnson, ed. (Berkeley: California, 1994), 1–17.

Canaan land is the land for me,
And let God's saints come in.
There was a wicked man,
He kept them children in Egypt land.
Canaan land is the land for me,
And let God's saints come in.
God did say to Moses one day,
Say, Moses, go to Egypt land,
And tell him to let my people go.
Canaan land is the land for me,
And let God's saints come in.

—Slave Spiritual

4

AFRICAN AMERICANS, EXODUS, AND THE AMERICAN ISRAEL

Albert J. Raboteau

IN THE ENCOUNTER with European Christianity in its Protestant form in North America, enslaved Africans and their descendants encountered something new: a fully articulated ritual relationship with the Supreme Being, who was pictured in the book that the Christians called the Bible not just as the Creator and Ruler of the Cosmos, but also as the God of History, a God who lifted up and cast down nations and peoples, a God whose sovereign will was directing all things toward an ultimate end, drawing good out of evil. As the transplanted Africans reflected upon the evil that had befallen them and their parents, they increasingly turned to the language, symbols, and worldview of the Christian holy book. There they found a theology of history that helped them to make sense of their enslavement. One story in particular caught their attention and fascinated them with its implications and potential applications to their own situation: the story of Exodus. What they did with that ancient story of the Near East is the topic of this essay. I begin by surveying the history of evangelization among the slaves in order to situate and define the Christianity that confronted them in North America. Then I describe what slaves and free blacks made of Christianity by focusing on their interpretation of the Exodus story, an interpretation which differed drastically, as we shall see, from that of white Americans.

CONVERSION

From the beginning of the Atlantic slave trade, Europeans claimed that the conversion of slaves to Christianity justified the enslavement of Africans. Yet the conversion of slaves was not a high priority for colonial planters. British colonists in North America proved especially indifferent, if not downright hostile, to the conversion of their slaves. At first, opposition was based on the suspicion that English law forbade the enslavement of Christians and so would require slaveholders to emancipate any slave who received baptism. Masters suspected that slaves would therefore seek to be baptized in order to gain freedom. These fears were quickly allayed by colonial legislation declaring that baptism did not alter slave status.

With the legal obstacles aside, slaveowners for the most part still demonstrated scant interest in converting their slaves. According to the common wisdom, Christianity spoiled slaves. Christian slaves thought too highly of themsleves, became impudent, and even turned rebellious. Moreover, Anglo-Americans were troubled by a deep-seated uneasiness at the prospect that slaves would claim Christian fellowship with white people. Africans were foreign; to convert them was to make them more like the English and therefore deserving of better treatment. In fact religion like language and skin color, constituted the colonists' identity. To Christianize black-skinned Africans, therefore, would confuse the distinctiveness of the races and threaten the social order based upon that distinctiveness. Finally, the labor, not the souls of the slaves, concerned most slaveholders. Peter Kalm, a Swedish traveler in America from 1748 to 1750, perceptively described the colonists' objections to religious instruction for slaves:

> It is…to be pitied, that the masters of these negroes in most of the English colonies take little care of their spiritual welfare, and let them live on in their Pagan darkness. There are even some, who would be very ill pleased at, and would by all means hinder their negroes from being instructed in the doctrines of Christianity; to this they are partly led by the conceit of its being shameful, to have a spiritual brother or sister among so despicable a people; partly by thinking that they should not be able to keep their negroes so meanly afterwards; and partly through fear of the negroes growing too proud, on seeing themselves upon a level with their masters in religious matters.[1]

A concerted attack on these obstacles to slave conversion was mounted by the Church of England in 1701 when it established the Society for the Propagation of the Gospel in Foreign Parts to support missionaries to the colonies. The first task was to convince masters that they had a duty to instruct their slaves in the truths of the gospel. In tract after tract, widely distributed in the colonies, officers of the Society stressed the compatibility of Christianity with slavery. Masters need not fear that religion would ruin their slaves. On the contrary, Christianity would make them better slaves by convincing them to obey their owners out of a sense of moral duty instead of out of fear. After all, Society pamphlets explained, Christianity does not upset the social order, but supports it: "Scripture, far from making an alteration in Civil Rights, expressly directs that every man abide in the condition wherein he is called, with great indifference of mind concerning outward circumstances."[2] To prove the point, they reiterated ad nauseam the verse from Ephesians (6:5): "Slaves be obedient to your masters." The missionaries thus denied that spiritual equality implied worldly equality; they restricted the egalitarian impulse of Christianity to the realm of the spirit. So, in effect, they built a religious foundation to support slavery. As the historian Winthrop Jordan aptly put it, "These clergymen had been forced by the circumstance of racial slavery in America into propagating the Gospel by presenting it as an attractive device for slave control."[3]

The success of missions to the slaves depended largely on circumstances beyond the missionaries' control: the proportion of African-born to Creole slaves, the geographic location and work patterns of the slaves, and the ratio of blacks to whites in a given locale. Blacks in the North and in the Chesapeake region of Maryland and Virginia, for example, experienced more frequent and closer contact with whites than did those of the lowland coasts of South Carolina and Georgia, where large gangs of African slaves toiled on isolated rice plantations with only limited and infrequent exposure to whites or their religion. Even if a missionary gained regular access to slaves, the slaves did not invariably accept the Christian gospel. Some rejected it, according to missionary accounts, because of "the Fondness they have for their old Heathenish Rites, and the strong Prejudice they must have against Teachers from among those, whom they serve so unwillingly."[4] Others accepted Christianity because they hoped—colonial legislation and missionary pronouncements notwithstanding—that baptism would raise their status and ensure eventual freedom for their children, if not for themselves. One missionary in South Carolina required slaves seeking baptism to swear an oath that they did not request the sacrament out of a desire for freedom.[5] (Apparently he missed the irony.) Missionaries complained that, even after instruction and baptism, slaves still mixed Christian beliefs with the traditional practices of their African homelands.

Discouraging though the prospects were, colonial clergymen had established a few successful missions among the slaves by the early eighteenth century. When the Bishop of London distributed a list of questions in 1724 requiring ministers to describe their work among the slaves, several respondents reported impressive numbers of baptisms. The great majority, however, stated vague intentions instead of concrete achievements. During the first 120 years of black slavery in British North America, Christianity made little headway in the slave population.

Slaves were first converted in large numbers in the wake of the religious revivals that periodically swept parts of the colonies beginning in the 1740s. Accounts by George Whitefield, Gilbert Tennent, Jonathan Edwards, and other revivalists made special mention of the fact that blacks were flocking to hear the message of salvation in hitherto unseen numbers. Not only were free blacks and slaves attending revivals, but they were also taking active part in the services as exhorters and preachers. For a variety of reasons Evangelical revivalists succeeded where Anglican missionaries had failed. Whereas the Anglicans had depended upon a slow process of indoctrination, the evangelicals preached the immediate experience of conversion as the primary requirement for baptism, thereby making Christianity more quickly accessible. Because of the centrality of the conversion experience in their piety, evangelicals also tended to de-emphasize instruction and downplay learning as prerequisites of Christian life. As a result, all classes of society were welcome to participate actively in prayer meetings and revival services, in which the poor, the illiterate, and even the enslaved prayed, exhorted, and preached.

After the Revolution, revival fervor continued to flare up sporadically in the South. More and more slaves converted to Christianity under the dramatic preaching of evangelical revivalists, especially Methodists and Baptists. The emotionalism of the revivals encouraged the outward expression of religious feeling, and the sight of black and white converts weeping, shouting, fainting, and moving in ecstatic trance became a familiar, if sensationalized, feature of the sacramental and camp meeting seasons. In this heated atmosphere slaves found a form of Christian worship that resembled the religious celebrations of their African heritage. The analogy between African and evangelical styles of worship enabled the slaves to reinterpret the new religion by reference to the old, and so made this brand of Christianity seem less foreign than that of the more liturgically sedate Church of England.

The rise of the evangelical denominations, particularly the Methodists and the Baptists, threatened the established Anglican church in the South. Because they appealed to the "lower sort," the evangelicals suffered persecution at the hands of the Anglican authorities. Baptist preachers were jailed, their services were disrupted, and they were even roughed up by rowdies such as those in Virginia who thought it humorous to immerse the Baptists in mud. They were thought of as different in an unsettling sort of way. "There was a company of them in the back part of our town, and an outlandish set of people they certainly were," remarked one woman to the early Baptist historian David Benedict. "You yourself would say so if you had seen them.... You could hardly find one among them but was deformed in some way or other."[6] The evangelicals seemed to threaten the social as well as the religious order by accepting slaves into their societies. An anti-Baptist petition warned the Virginia assembly in 1777 that "there have been nightly meetings of slaves to receive the instruction of these teachers without the consent of their masters, which have produced very bad consequences."[7]

In the 1780s the evangelicals' implied challenge to the social order became explicit. Methodist conferences in 1780, in 1783, and again in 1784 strongly condemned slavery and tried "to extirpate this abomination," first from the ministry and then from the membership as a whole, by passing increasingly stringent regulations against slave-owning, slave-buying, and slave-selling.[8] Several Baptist leaders freed their slaves, and in 1789 the General Committee of Virginia Baptists condemned slavery as "a violent deprivation of the rights of nature."[9] In the South, these antislavery moves met with strong, immediate, and, as the leadership quickly realized, irreversible opposition. In 1785, the Baltimore Conference of the Methodist Church suspended the rules passed in 1784 by the Methodist General Conference. Methodist leader Thomas Coke explained, "We thought it prudent to suspend the minute concerning slavery, on account of the great opposition that had been given it, our work being in too infantile a state to push things to extremity." Local Baptist associations in Virginia responded to the General Committee's attack on slavery by declaring that the subject was "so abstruse" that no religious society had the right to concern itself with the issue; instead, each individual should be left "to act at discretion in order to keep a good conscience before God, as far as the laws of our land will admit."[10] As for the slaves, the goal of the Church should be the amelioration of their treatment, not their emancipation.

Thus, the evangelical challenge to slavery in the late eighteenth century failed. The intransigence of slavery once again set the limits of the Christian egalitarian impulse, just as it had in colonial days for the Anglican mission. Rapid growth of the Baptist and Methodist churches forced an ineluctable accommodation to slaveholding principles rather than the overthrow of slavery. At the beginning of the nineteenth century, Robert Semple, another Baptist historian, described the change that came over the "outlandish" Baptists after 1790: "Their preachers became much more correct in their manner of preaching. A great many odd tones, disgusting whoops and awkward gestures were disused.... Their zeal was less mixed with enthusiasm, and their piety became more rational. They were much more numerous, and, of course, in the eyes of the world, more respectable. Besides, they were joined by persons of much greater weight in civil society; their congregations became more numerous.... This could not but influence their manners and spirit more or less."[11] Though both Methodists and Baptists rapidly retreated from antislavery pronouncements, their struggle with the established order and their uneasiness about slavery gave slaves, at least initially, the impression that they were "friendly toward freedom." For a short time, revivalist evangelicalism breached the wall that colonial missionaries had built between spiritual and temporal equality. Converting slaves to Christianity could have implications beyond the spiritual, a possibility slaves were eager to explore.

Methodists and Baptists backed away from these implications in the 1790s, but they had already taken a momentous step, and it proved irreversible. The spread of Baptist and Methodist evangelicalism between 1770 and 1820 changed the religious complexion of the South by bringing unprecedented numbers of slaves into membership in the church and by introducing even larger numbers to at least the rudiments of Christianity. During the antebellum decades, Christianity diffused throughout the slave quarters, though most slaves did not hold membership in regular churches. Those slaves who did attend church generally attended with whites, but some—in greater numbers than historians have realized—attended separate black churches, even in the antebellum South.

Thanks to the willingness of the evangelical churches to license black men to exhort and preach, during the 1770s and 1780s a significant group of black preachers had begun to pastor their own people. Mainly Baptist, since the congregational independence of the Baptists gave them more leeway to preach than any other denomination, the black preachers exercised a ministry that was mostly informal and extra-ecclesial. It would be difficult to overestimate the importance of these early black preachers for the development of an African-American Christianity. In effect, they mediated between Christianity and the experience of the slaves (and free blacks), interpreting the stories, symbols, and events of the Bible to fit the day-to-day lives of those held in bondage. And whites—try as they might—could not control this interpretation or determine its "accuracy." Slave preachers, exhorters, and church-appointed watchmen instructed their fellow slaves, nurtured their religious development, and brought them to conversion—in some cases without any active involvement of white missionaries or masters whatsoever. By nurturing Christian communities among slaves and free blacks, the pioneer black preachers began to build an independent black church.

We tend to identify the development of the independent black church with free blacks in the North, but the spirit of religious independence also created separate black churches in the South. Several "African" churches, as they were called, sprang up before 1800. Some of these black congregations were independent to the extent that they called their own pastors and officers, joined local associations with white churches, and sent their own delegates to associational meetings. However, this early independence of black preachers and churches was curtailed during the antebellum period when, in reaction to slave conspiracies, all gatherings of blacks for whatever purpose were viewed with alarm. For slaves to participate in the organization, leadership, and governance of church structures was perceived as dangerous. Nevertheless, unlikely as it may seem, black churches continued to grow in size and number in the slave South. Though nominally controlled by whites, these separate congregations were frequently led by black ministers, some free and some slaves. Often the black congregations outnumbered the largest white churches in the local church associations. Although never numerous in the South, the separate black churches were extremely important, if limited, institutional expressions of black religious independence from white control.

In the North, the abolition of slavery after the Revolution gave black congregations and clergy much more leeway to assert control over their religious lives. Federal and state disestablishment of religion created an environment of voluntarism in which church organization flourished. Between 1790 and 1820, black Episcopalians, Methodists, Baptists, and Presbyterians founded churches, exercised congregational control where possible, and struggled with white elders, bishops, and associations to gain autonomy. Among the first to succeed in doing so was Bethel African Methodist Episcopal Church in Philadelphia. Founded in 1794 by Richard Allen, a former slave who had become a licensed Methodist preacher, Bethel was organized after discriminatory treatment drove black Methodists to abandon St. George's, the white church they had supported for years. When the white elders of St. George's tried to take control of the Bethel church property, the black congregation went to court to retain their rights to the church they had built themselves. They won.

Conflicts elsewhere between black Methodists and white elders prompted Allen to call for a convention of African Methodists to meet in Philadelphia in 1816. There, delegates organized an independent black denomination, the African Methodist Episcopal (A.M.E.) Church, and elected Richard Allen as its first bishop. Two other African Methodist denominations had organized by 1821. Though the black Methodists were the first to take independent control of their church property, finances, and governance on the denominational level, northern blacks in other churches also demonstrated their spirit of independence. In all denominations, the black churches formed the institutional core for the development of free black communities. Moreover, they gave black Christians the opportunity to articulate publicly their own vision of Christianity, which stood in eloquent testimony to the existence of two Christian Americas.

Of course, independent religious institutions were out of the question for the vast majority of black Americans, who were suffering the system of slavery in the southern states. If they attended church at all, they did so with whites or under white supervision. Nevertheless, slaves developed their own, extra-ecclesial "invisible institution" of religious life. In the slave quarters and brush arbors, they held their own religious meetings, where they interpreted Christianity according to their experience. Conversely, they also interpreted their experience by means of the myths, stories, and symbols of Christianity. They were even willing to risk severe punishment to attend forbidden prayer meetings in order to worship God free of white control. A former slave, Lucretia Alexander, explained why:

> The preacher came and…he'd just say, "Serve your masters. Don't steal your master's turkey. Don't steal your master's chickens. Don't steal your master's hawgs. Don't steal your master's meat. Do whatsomever your master tell you to do." Same old thing all the time. My father would have church in dwelling houses and they had to whisper…. Sometimes they would have church at his house. That would be when they want a real meetin' with some real preachin'…. They used to sing their songs in a whisper. That was a prayer meeting from house to house…once or twice a week.[12]

Inevitably the slaves' Christianity contradicted that of their masters. For the slaves knew that no matter how sincerely religious the slaveowners might be, their Christianity was compatible with slavery, and the slaves' was not. The division went deep; it extended to the fundamental interpretation of the Bible. The dichotomy between the faiths of black and white Christians was described by a white Methodist minister who pastored a black congregation in Charleston, South Carolina, in 1862:

> There were near fourteen hundred colored communications…. [Their] service was always thronged—galleries, lower floor, chancel, pulpit, steps and all…. The preacher could not complain of any deadly space between himself and his congregation. He was positively breast up to his people, with no possible loss of…rapport. Though ignorant of it at the time, he remembers now the cause of the enthusiasm under his deliverances [about] the "law of liberty" and "freedom from Egyptian bondage." What was figurative they interpreted literally. He thought of but one ending of the war; they quite another. He remembers the sixty-eighth Psalm as affording numerous texts for their delectation, e.g., "Let God arise, let his enemies be

scattered"; His "march through the wilderness"; "The Chariots of God are twenty thousand"; "The hill of God is as the hill of Basham"; and especially, "Though ye have lain among the pots, yet shall ye be as the wings of a dove covered with silver, and her feathers with yellow gold." ...It is mortifying now to think that his comprehension was not equal to the African intellect. All he thought about was relief from the servitude of sin, and freedom from the bondage of the devil.... But they interpreted it literally in the good time coming, which of course could not but make their ebony complexion attractive, very.[13]

What the preacher is describing is the end of a long process, spanning almost two hundred and fifty years, by which slaves came to accept the gospel of Christianity. But the slaves did not simply become Christians; they fashioned Christianity to fit their own peculiar experience of enslavement in America. The preacher, like many white Christians before and since, thought there was no distance between him and "his people," no possible loss of rapport. He learned belatedly that the chasm was wide and deep. As one freedman succinctly stated, "We couldn't tell NO PREACHER NEBER how we suffer all dese long years. He know'd nothin' 'bout we."[14]

EXODUS

No single symbol captures more clearly the distinctiveness of Afro-American Christianity than the symbol of Exodus. From the earliest days of colonization, white Christians had represented their journey across the Atlantic to America as the exodus of a New Israel from the bondage of Egypt into the Promised Land of milk and honey. For black Christians, the imagery was reversed: the Middle Passage had brought them to Egypt land, where they suffered bondage under a new Pharaoh. White Christians saw themselves as the New Israel; slaves identified themselves as the Old. This is, as Vincent Harding remarked, one of the abiding and tragic ironies of our history: the nation's claim to be the New Israel was contradicted by the Old Israel still enslaved in her midst.[15]

American preachers, politicians, and other orators found in the story of Exodus a rich source of metaphors to explicate the unfolding history of the nation. Each section of the narrative—the bondage in Egypt, the rescue at the Red Sea, the wandering in the wilderness, and the entrance into the Promised Land—provided a typological map to reconnoiter the moral terrain of American society. John Winthrop, the leader of the great Puritan expedition to Massachusetts Bay, set the pattern in his famous "A Modell of Christian Charity" sermon composed on his ship in 1630. Having elaborated the convental obligations that the settlers had contracted with God, echoing the Sinai convenant of Israel with Yahweh, Winthrop concluded his discourse with a close paraphrase of Moses' farewell instruction to Israel (Deuteronomy 30):

Beloved there is now sett before use life, and good, deathe and evill in that wee are Commaunded this day to love the Lord our God, and to love one another, to walke in his wayes and to keepe his Commaundements and his Ordinance, and his lawes, and the Articles of our Covenant with him that wee may live and be multiplied, and that the Lord our God may blesse us in the land whither we goe to poses it: But if our heartes shall turne away soe that wee will not obey, but shall be seduced and worship...other Gods, our pleasures, and proffitts, and serve them; it is propounded unto this day, wee shall surely perishe out of the good Land whither wee passe over this vast Sea to possesse it....[16]

Notice the particular application that Winthrop draws from the Exodus story: possession of the land is contingent upon observing the moral obligations of the covenant with God. It is a mark of the greatness of Winthrop's address that the obligations he emphasizes are justice, mercy, affection, meekness, gentleness, patience, generosity, and unity—not the qualities usually associated with taking or keeping possession of a land. Later and lesser sermons would extol much more active and aggressive virtues for the nation to observe.

Already in Winthrop's address there is an explicit notion of reciprocity between God's Will and America's Destiny: God has made a contract with us; if we live up to our part of the bargain, so will He. This pattern of reciprocity between Divine Providence and American Destiny had tremendous hortative power, which Puritan preachers exploited to the full over the next century and more in the jeremiad. In sermon after sermon, a succession of New England divines deciphered droughts, epidemics, Indian attacks, and other misfortunes as tokens of God's displeasure over the sins of the nation. Unless listeners took the opportunity to humble themselves, repent, and reform, they might expect much more of the same.

Implicit in this relationship of reciprocity there lay a danger: the danger of converting God's Will into America's Density. Winthrop was too good a Puritan to succumb to this temptation. Protected by his belief in the total sovereignty of God, he knew that the relationship between God's Will and human action was one-sided and that the proper human attitude was trust in God, not confidence in man. God's Will was the measure of America's deeds, not vice versa. Of course, no American preacher or politician would have disagreed, but as time went on the salient features of the American Exodus story changed. As the actual experience of migration with all its fear and tenuousness receded, Americans tended to lose sight of their radical dependence upon God and to celebrate their own achievements as a nation.

We can catch sight of the change by comparing the tone of Winthrop's "A Modell of Christian Charity" with the mood of an election sermon entitled "The United States Elevated to Glory and Honor," preached by Ezra Stiles in 1783. Flush with excitement over the success of the Revolution, Stiles dwelled at length on the unfolding destiny of the new nation. Quoting, like Winthrop, from the book of Deuteronomy, Stiles struck a celebratory rather a hortatory note:

> "And to make thee high above all nations which he hath made, in praise, and in name, and in honour; and that thou mayest be an holy people unto the Lord thy God…." I have assumed [this] text as introductory to a discourse upon the political welfare of God's American Israel, and as allusively prophetic of the future prosperity and splendour of the United States. Already does the new constellation of the United States begin to realize this glory. It has already risen to an acknowledged sovereignty among the republicks and kingdoms of the world. And we have reason to hope, and I believe to expect, that God has still greater blessings in store for this vine which his own right hand hate planted, to make us "high among the nations in praise, and in name, and in honour."[17]

Stiles went on at great length to identify the reasons for his optimism about America's present and future preeminence, including the fact that "in our civil constitutions, those impediments are removed which obstruct the progress of society towards perfection."[18] It's a long away from Winthrop's caution to Stiles' confidence, from an "Errand in the Wilderness" to "progress towards perfection." In Stiles' election sermon we can perceive

God's New Israel becoming the Redeemer Nation. The destiny of the New Israel was to reach the pinnacle of perfection and to carry liberty and the gospel around the globe.

In tandem with this exaggerated vision of America's Destiny went an exaggerated vision of human capacity. In an increasingly confident and prosperous nation, it was difficult to avoid shifting the emphasis from divine sovereignty to human ability. Historian Conrad Cherry has succinctly summarized the change in perception of America's destiny: "Believing that she had escaped the wickedness of the Old World and the guilt of the past, God's New Israel would find it all too easy to ignore her vices and all too difficult to admit a loss of innocence."[19]

Among the realities this optimistic vision ignored was the presence of another, darker Israel:

> America, America, foul and indelible is thy stain! Dark and dismal is the cloud that hangs over thee, for thy cruel wrongs and injuries to the fallen sons of Africa. The blood of her murdered ones cries to heaven for vengeance against Thee.... You may kill, tyrannize, and oppress as much as you choose, until cry shall come up before the throne of God; for I am firmly persuaded, that he will not suffer you to quell the proud, fearless and undaunted spirits of the Africans forever; for in his own time, he is able to plead our cause against you, and to pour out upon you the ten plagues of Egypt.[20]

So wrote Maria Stewart, a free black reform activist in Boston, in 1831. Her words were addressed to an America that projected itself as the probable site of the coming Millennium, Christ's thousand-year reign of peace and justice. From the perspective of slaves, and of free blacks like Maria Stewart, America was Egypt, and as long as she continued to enslave and oppress Black Israel, her destiny was in jeopardy. America stood under the judgment of God, and unless she repented, the death and destruction visited upon Biblical Egypt would be repeated here. The retribution envisaged was quite literal, as Mary Livermore, a white governess, discovered when she overheard a prayer uttered by Aggy, the slave housekeeper, whose daughter had just been brutally whipped by her master:

> Thar's a day a comin'! Thar's a day a comin'.... I hear de rumblin' ob de chariots! I see de flashin' ob de guns! White folks' blood is a-runnin' on de ground like a riber, an' de dead's heaped up dat high!... Oh, Lor'! hasten de day when de blows, an' de bruises, an' de aches, an' de pains, shall come to de white folks, an' de buzzards shall eat 'em as dey's dead in de streets. Oh, Lor'! roll on de chariots, an' gib de black people rest an' peace.[21]

Nor did slaves share the exaggerated optimism of white Americans about human ability. Trapped in a system from which there seemed little, if any, possibility of deliverance by human actions, they emphasized trusting in the Lord instead of trusting in man. Sermon after sermon and prayer after prayer echoed the words that Moses spoke on the banks of the Red Sea: "Stand still and see the salvation of the Lord." Although the leaders of the three principal slave revolts—Gabriel Prosser in 1800, Denmark Vesey in 1822, and Nat Turner in 1831—all depended upon the Bible to justify and motivate rebellion, the Exodus story was used mainly to nurture internal resistance, not external revolution among the slaves.

The story of Exodus contradicted the claim made by white Christians that God intended Africans to be slaves. It seemed to prove that slavery was against God's will and that slavery would inevitably end, although the when and the how remained hidden in Divine Providence. Christian slaves thus applied the Exodus story, whose end they knew, to their own experience of slavery, which had not yet ended, and so gave meaning and purpose to lives threatened by senseless and demeaning brutality. Exodus functioned as an archetypal myth for the slaves. The sacred history of God's liberation of his people would be or was being reenacted in the American South. A white Union Army chaplain working among freedmen in Decatur, Alabama, commented disapprovingly on the slaves' fascination with Exodus: "There is no part of the Bible with which they are so familiar as the story of the deliverance of Israel. Moses is their *ideal* of all that is high, and noble, and perfect, in man. I think they have been accustomed to regard Christ not so much in the light of a *spiritual* Deliverer, as that of a second Moses who would eventually lead *them* out of their prison-house of bondage."[22]

Thus, in the story of Israel's exodus from Egypt, the slaves envisioned a future radically different from their present. In times of despair, they remembered Exodus and found hope enough to endure the enormity of their suffering. As a slave named Polly eloquently explained to her mistress, "We poor creatures have need to believe in God, for if God Almighty will not be good to us some day, why were we born? When I heard of his delivering his people from bondage, I know it means the poor Africans."[23]

By appropriating the story of Exodus as their own story, black Christians articulated their own sense of peoplehood. Exodus symbolized their common history and common destiny. It would be hard to exaggerate the intensity of their identification with the children of Israel. A.M.E. pastor William Paul Quinn demonstrated how literal the metaphor of Exodus could become when he exhorted black Christians, "Let us comfort and encourage one another, and keep singing and shouting, great is the Holy One of Israel in the midst of us. Come thou Great Deliverer, once more awake thine almighty arm, and set thy African captives free."[24] As Quinn's exhortation reveals, it was prayer and worship that made the identification seem so real. Sermons, prayers, and songs recreated in the imagination of successive generations the travail and triumph of Israel. Exodus became dramatically real, especially in the songs and prayer meetings of the slaves, who reenacted the story as they shuffled in the ring dance they called "the shout". In the ecstasy of worship, time and distance collapsed, and the slaves literally became the children of Israel. With the Hebrews, they traveled dry-shod through the Red Sea; they, too, saw Pharaoh's army "get drownded"; they stood beside Moses on Mount Pisgah and gazed out over the Promised Land; they crossed Jordan under Joshua and marched with him around the walls of Jericho. Their prayers for deliverance resonated with the experiential power of these liturgical dramas.

Identification with Israel, then, gave the slaves a communal identity as a special, divinely favored people. This identity stood in stark contrast with racist propaganda, which depicted them as inferior to whites, as destined by nature and providence to the status of slaves. Exodus, the Promised Land, and Canaan were inextricably linked in the slaves' minds with the idea of freedom. Canaan referred not only to the condition of freedom but also to the territory of freedom—the North or Canada. As Frederick Douglass recalled, "A keen observer might have detected in our repeated singing of 'O Canaan, sweet Canaan,/I am bound for the land of Canaan,' something more than a hope of reaching heaven. We meant to reach the *North*, and the North was our Canaan."[25] Slave owners, too, were well aware that the Exodus story could be a source of unflattering and even subversive analogies. It took no genius to identify Pharaoh's army in the slave song "My army cross ober, My army cross ober/O Pharaoh's army drownded."

The slaves' faith that God would free them just as he had freed Israel of old was validated by Emancipation. "Shout the glad tidings o're Egypt's dark sea/Jehovah has triumphed, his people are free!" the ex-slaves sang in celebration of freedom. But it did not take long for the freedmen to realize that Canaan Land still lay somewhere in the distance. "There must be no looking back to Egypt," a band of refugee slaves behind Union lines were instructed by a slave preacher in 1862. "Israel passed forty years in the wildnerness, because of their unbelief. What if we cannot see right off the green fields of Canaan, Moses could not. He could not even see how to cross the Red Sea. If we would have greater freedom of body, we must free ourselves from the shackles of sin.... We must snap the chain of Satan, and educate ourselves and our children."[26]

But as time went on and slavery was succeeded by other forms of racial oppression, black Americans seemed trapped in the wilderness no matter how hard they tried to escape. Former slave Charles Davenport voiced the despair of many when he recalled, "De preachers would exhort us dat us was de chillen o' Israel in de wilderness an' de Lord done sent us to take dis land o' milk and honey. But how us gwine-a take land what's already been took?"[27] When race relations reached a new low in the 1880s and 1890s, several black leaders turned to Africa as the black Promised Land. Proponents of emigration, such as Henry McNeal Turner, urged Afro-Americans to abandon the American wilderness for an African Zion. Few black Americans, however, heeded the call to emigrate to Africa; most continued to search for their Promised Land here. And as decade succeeded decade they repeated the story of Exodus. which for so many years had kept their hopes alive. It was, then, a very old and evocative tradition that Martin Luther King, Jr., echoed in his last sermon:

> We've got some difficult days ahead. But it really doesn't matter with me now. Because I've been to the mountaintop. Like anybody I would like to live a long life. Longevity has its place. But I'm not concerned about that now. I just want to do God's will. And He's allowed me to go up to the mountain. And I've seen the Promised Land. And I may not get there with you. But I want you to know tonight that we as a people will get to the Promised land.[28]

A period of over three hundred years stretches between John Winthrop's vision of an American Promised Land and that of Martin Luther King. The people whom Winthrop addressed long ago took possession of their Promised Land; the people whom King addressed still wait to enter theirs. For three centuries, white and black Americans have dwelt in the same land. For at least two of those centuries, they have shared the same religion. And yet, during all those years, their national and religious identities have been radically opposed. It need not have been so. After all, Winthrop's version of Exodus and King's were not so far apart. Both men understood that charity is the charter that gives title to the Promised Land. Both taught that mercy, gentleness, and justice are the terms for occupancy. Both believed that the conditions of the contract had been set by God, not by man. At times in our history, the two visions have nearly coincided, as they did in the antislavery stance of the early evangelicals, or in the abolitionist movement, or in Lincoln's profound realization that Americans were an "almost chosen people," or in the civil rights movement of our own era. Yet, despite these moments of coherence, the meaning of the Exodus story for America has remained fundamentally ambiguous. Is America Israel, or is she Egypt?

NOTES

1. Peter Kalm, *Travels into North America*, 2d ed. (London: 1772), reprinted in vol. 13 of *A General Collection of the Best and Most Interesting Voyages and Travels*, ed. John Pinkerton (London: 1812), 503.

2. Thomas Secker, Bishop of London, *A Sermon Preached before the Incorporated Society for the Propagation of the Gospel in Foreign Parts...February* 20, 1740–1 (London: 1741), reprinted in Frank J. Klingberg, *Anglican Humanitarianism in Colonial New York* (Philadelphia: Church Historical Society, 1940), 223.

3. Winthrop D. Jordan, *White over Black: American Attitudes toward the Negro, 1550–1812* (Baltimore, Md.: Penguin, 1969), 191.

4. Secker, "A Sermon Preached," 217.

5. Edgard Legare Pennington, *Thomas Bray's Associates and Their Work among the Negroes* (Worcester, Mass.: American Antiquarian Society, 1939), 25.

6. David Benedict, *Fifty Years among the Baptists* (New York: Sheldon & Company, 1860), 93–94.

7. Charles F. James, ed., *Documentary History of the Struggle for Religious Liberty in Virginia* (Lynchburg, Va.: J. P. Bell, 1900), 84–85.

8. Donald G. Mathews, *Slavery and Methodism: A Chapter in American Morality, 1780–1845* (Princeton, N.J.: 1965), 293–99.

9. David Barrow, *Circular Letter* (Norfolk, Va.: [1798]), 4–5; Robert B. Semple, *A History of the Rise and Progress of the Baptists in Virginia, ed. George W. Beale (Philadelphia: American Baptist Publication Society, 1894), 105*.

10. *Francis Asbury, The Journal and Letters of Francis Asbury*, ed. Elmer T. Clark, J. Manning Potts, and Jacob S. Payton, 3 vols. (Nashville, Tenn.: Abingdon, 1958), 2: 284; Wesley M. Gewehr, *The Great Awakening in Virginia, 1740–1790* (Durham, N.C.: Duke University Press, 1930), 240–41, 244–48.

11. Semple, *History of Baptists in Virginia* 59.

12. George P. Rawick, ed., *The American Slave: A Composite Autobiography*, 19 vols. (Westport, Conn.: Greenwood, 1972), vol. 8, *Arkansas Narratives*, pt. 1, p. 35.

13. Abel McGee Chreitzberg, *Early Methodism in the Carolinas* (Nashville, Tenn.: Publishing House of the M[ethodist] E[piscopal] C[hurch], South, 1897), 158–59.

14. Austa Melinda French, *Slavery in South Carolina and the Ex-Slaves; or, The Port Royal Mission* (New York: W.M. French, 1862), 127.

15. Vincent Harding, "The Uses of the Afro-American Past," in *The Religious Situation, 1969*, ed. Donald R. Cutter (Boston: Beacon, 1969), 829–40.

16. John Winthrop, "A Modell of Christian Charity," in *Winthrop Papers* (Boston: Massachusetts Historical Society, 1931), 2: 282–84, 292–95. Reprinted in Conrad Cherry, *God's New Israel: Religious Interpretations of American Destiny* (Englewood Cliffs, N.J.: Prentice-Hall, 1971), 43.

17. Ezra Stiles, "The United States Elevated to Glory and Honor," in *A Sermon Preached before Gov. Jonathan Trumbull and the General Assembly...May 8th, 1783*, 2d. ed. (Worcester, Mass.: Isaiah Thomas, 1785), 5–9, 58–75, 88–92, 95–98. Reprinted in Cherry, *God's New Israel*, 82–84.

18. Ibid., in Cherry, *God's New Israel*, 84.

19. Cherry, *God's New Israel*, 66.

20. Marilyn Richardson, ed., *Maria W. Stewart, America's First Black Woman Political Writer: Essays and Speeches* (Bloomington: Indiana University Press, 1987), 39–40.

21. Mary A. Livermore, *My Story of the War: A Woman's Narrative of Four Years Personal Experience...* (Hartford, Conn.: A. D. Worthington, 1889), 260–61.

22. William G. Kephart to L. Tappan, May 9, 1864, American Missionary Association Archives, Decatur, Ala., Reel 2; also in *American Missionary 8*, no. 7 (July 1864), 179.

23. As cited in diary entry of 12 December 1857 by her mistress: Barbara Leigh Smith Bodichon, *An American Diary, 1857–1858*, ed. Joseph W. Reed, Jr. (London: Routledge & Kegan Paul, 1972), 65.

24. W. Paul Quinn, *The Sword of Truth Going "Forth Conquering and to Conquer"; The Origin, Horrors, and Results of Slavery Faithfully and Minutely Described...* (1834); reprinted in *Early Negro Writing, 1760–1837*, ed. Dorothy Porter (Boston: Beacon, 1971), 635.

25. Frederick Douglass, *Life and Times of Frederick Douglass: Written by Himself* (1892; reprint, New York: Crowell-Collier, 1969) 159–60.

26. *American Missionary* 6, no. 2 (February 1862): 33.

27. Norman R. Yetman, ed., *Voices from Slavery* (New York: Holt, Rinehart and Winston, 1970), 75.

28. Martin Luther King, Jr., sermon of April 3, 1968, delivered at Mason Temple, Memphis, Tenn., reprinted in *A Testament of Hope: The Essential Writings of Martin Luther King, Jr.*, ed. James Melvin Washington (San Francisco: Harper & Row, 1986), 286.

PART TWO

REVOLUTION AND
SOCIAL CHANGE
1750–1865

THE SOCIAL ORIGINS OF NATIONALISM

David G. Hackett

During the Revolutionary War a new devotion to the American nation was born. Anticipated by colonial sermons that heralded the guiding providence of God in the New World and enacted through Fourth of July rituals that celebrated the nation's birth, what many have called America's "civil religion" brought the peoples of the thirteen colonies into a new national unity that transcended local political and religious ties. This sanctified nationalism has its own Bible (Declaration of Independence), symbols (the Flag, Liberty Bell), ministers (elected officials), shrines (Statue of Liberty, World War Memorials), rituals (Fourth of July, Thanksgiving), and saints (Washington, Lincoln, Martin Luther King). We often hear its words of civic faith in presidential speeches and at times of national crisis when patriotic voices grow strong.

Though many affirm the existence of this ideology that relates the American nation to God, throughout United States history its meaning has been understood in a number of ways. At the time of the Revolution many believed that to be an American was to be opposed to England, though some saw it differently. By the early nineteenth century some felt that patriotism meant to support economic productivity, yet others dissented. Similar debates continue to the present day. Much of the previous scholarship on America's "civil religion" has focused on the ideas put forth in sermons and presidential addresses. The following article, instead, pays attention to the social divisions within one newly American community in order to shed light on the origins and multiple meanings of this devotion to the nation.

Adapted by permission from David G. Hackett, "The Social Origins of Nationalism: Albany, New York, 1754–1835," *Journal of Social History* 21(1988): 660–682.

5

THE SOCIAL ORIGINS
OF NATIONALISM

Albany, New York, 1754–1835

David G. Hackett

FOR SOME TIME NOW, American historians have attempted to explain the emergence of a new devotion to the nation during and after the Revolution. The recent scholarship of intellectual historians has explored the political and religious aspects of this nascent nationalism. On one hand, Bernard Bailyn's examination of political pamphlets has demonstrated that colonial political leaders worked over several decades to adapt British Whig political culture to the colonies so that individual liberty and property became central tenets of the emerging cause.[1] On the other hand, Nathan Hatch's analysis of the political content of sermons has shown how New England's ministers extended the canopy of religious meaning so that republican ideas became sacred.[2] Edmund Morgan has called the resulting nationalism "the strongest force binding Americans of the Revolutionary generation together."[3] This conviction concerning the force of early American nationalism is particularly strong among those historians who emphasize the consensus achieved by the rebelling colonists; yet it is also shared by those who emphasize conflict among the colonists. Gordon Wood's analysis of political debates between 1776 and 1787 underscored this conflict within consensus approach by demonstrating that Americans used a shared language and a common conceptual framework to debate very real political differences.[4]

Several attempts have been made to consider these differences in the light of social history. For example, Eric Foner's study of Tom Paine placed its subject in relation to the crowds and mechanics of Philadelphia. Foner demonstrated the ways in which Paine's vivid cries for "liberty" and "revolution" spoke to and for people who sought individual rights in a future egalitarian society.[5] In contrast, Rowland Berthoff and John Murrin have linked similar Revolutionary rhetoric to the conservative interests of a ruling elite who retained control over a hierarchical social structure well into the nineteenth century. Berthoff and Murrin's belief that "Revolutionary ideology powerfully stimulated a nostalgic attachment to a seventeenth century simplicity"[6] suggests that at least in some places appeals for "liberty" and "revolution" signaled a desire to restore an older communal ideal. Taken together these studies indicate that, while the national ideology of the Revolutionary generation was widely shared, particular communities and even sub-groups within those communities understood its tenets differently.[7]

One explanation for the different reasons advanced by Revolutionary era Americans for supporting the new nation is the different experiences of social change undergone by the inhabitants of late eighteenth century cities and towns. A number of investigators have suggested that such trends as population growth, commercialization, and social differentiation, experienced first in the seaboard cities, upset the equilibrium of an older system of social relations and turned these urban centers into crucibles of revolutionary agitation.[8] It was in these cities, Gary Nash has argued, that "Almost all the alterations associated with the advent of capitalist society happened first…and radiated outwards to the smaller towns, villages, and farms of the hinterland.[9] These commercial centers may well have predicted the future, yet only one in twenty colonists lived in them in 1775. On the eve of the Revolution most Americans lived in villages and towns where religion was as significant as either politics or the economy in shaping the life and values of the new nation. This was particularly true, Patricia Bonomi has posited, in those northern towns that had a "settled character and compactness."[10] In these communities an older communal ideology prevailed. We know a great deal about the encompassing role of religious life in the villages and towns of the earlier colonial period.[11] We are coming to know more about the emergence of revolutionary agitation among the working people in the larger cities.[12] What we do not know is the social origins of the new devotion to the nation that emerged in those towns that still clung to their older communal ideal in the face of mounting social changes before and after the Revolution. A portrayal of one such town may help us discover how many new Americans understood their new commitment to the nation.

This essay will attempt to clarify the social meaning and practical significance of the new national ideology for at least some early Americans by linking the changing social order of Albany, New York with the birth and development of its new commitment to America. Unlike the port city of New York, where, by the beginning of the eighteenth century, a larger, more heterogeneous population facilitated religious toleration and ethnic competition in trade, the frontier isolation of Albany, with its smaller and overwhelmingly Dutch population, fostered the preeminence of the Dutch Calvinist church and ethnic control over local trade. Moreover, in contrast to many New England towns, where the dispersal of land led to contending sectional interests, Albanians were not farmers. Rather, as a village of traders and artisans living within the protection of a three-quarter mile palisade wall, they continued to rely upon their older way of life until and after the Revolution. During the 1760's, however, recent English and Scotch-Irish immigrants challenged the economic and political control held by the Dutch and the pervasive influence of their church.

This study argues that the new national ideology provided Albanians with a new basis for unity that, in turn, became a vehicle for challenging that unity as social and economic conditions changed. The immediate cause for the emergence of a new commitment to the nation among Albany's ethnically diverse inhabitants was the need to create political unity in response to the threat of British invasion. At the beginning of the Revolution, a common political identity as Americans supplanted Dutch ethnicity as the basis for local political unity. Following the Revolution, an inter-ethnic federation of community leaders sanctified this new union through Fourth of July rituals in which they enacted and articulated the new civil faith. A common identity as Christians, therefore, supplanted Dutch church membership as the moral foundation for community order. This new identity as Americans and Christians did not immediately draw the town's people out of their communal orientations. As late as 1820, Albanians were divided among recognizably Dutch, English,

Scotch-Irish, and Yankee cultural groups. Still the new ideological unity did link them to other local communities who together formed a nation. Similarly, while the new devotion to the nation did not check the social trends that were creating tensions in the community, it did provide Anti-Federalists and Dutch church elders with a common moral and political language.

After the completion of the Erie Canal in 1825, pronounced divisions over the meaning of the nation began to appear. Prior to that time, and despite signs of conflict between artisans and the old elite, devotion to the nation had meant first and foremost a commitment to the political unity of Albany's diverse ethnic groups against a foreign enemy. This new basis for unity only marginally affected the hierarchical structure implicit in the earlier Dutch communalism. As the war fervor died down, however, accelerating mobility and the extension of the market undermined the social order of denominationalism as the basis for community stability. Calvinist church membership shrank to an elite and largely female minority. Merchant-elders were voted out of the Common Council. They were replaced by political leaders more notable for their common economic interests than ties of religion and kin. The new leaders shifted the meaning of nationalism from the political unity of different cultural groups to support of economic productivity. Manufacturers invoked American "Liberty" to justify economic growth. In contrast, journeymen employed the language of the new republic to secure better working conditions. As Albany's economy expanded, therefore, manufacturers and journeymen advanced antagonistic visions of the American future.

Four periods of this social and cultural process require analysis: first, religion and politics in Dutch Albany prior to 1754; second, the social changes that divided the city in the 1760's; third, the emergence of a new political and religious unity during and after the Revolution; and finally, the changing meaning of nationalism in the early nineteenth century.

I. RELIGION AND POLITICS PRIOR TO 1754

Prior to the Revolution, Albany was a Dutch colony set apart from America's early European settlements on the northern periphery of the known colonial world. The townspeople divided themselves into merchant and artisan family networks that extended through the economic, political, and religious spheres of their life.[13] The local merchant families were also members of the Common Council responsible for their community's political welfare. In addition, as elders of the church, they supervised the spiritual well-being of their communicants.[14] The Albany artisans constituted a largely separate network of families subject to the political and spritual authority of the merchants. This organic, hierarchical social organization intermingled civil and religious authority. Members of the same merchant families served as the community's temporal and spiritual leaders.

Albany's Dutch Reformed Church supplied the moral ties that bound the community's social order. The church building's site in the middle of the intersection of the town's two main streets was a powerful symbol of the centrality of religion in social life. Church records for the years prior to 1750 show that more than 70% of the inhabitants were members of the church.[15] Throughout the colonial period, the deacons of the church took responsibility for all of the community's poor. The Heidelberg Catechism, the fundamental text of Dutch Calvinism, was both the basis for Sunday sermons and the primary text used in educating the young.[16] The moral logic of this catechism made the community's leaders responsible to

God for the town's spiritual welfare and the people responsible to these leaders for their behavior.[17]

This covenant between elders and congregation was similar to the civil bond between Common Council members and citizens. Both relationships derived their moral power from a Calvinist theology that envisioned the closest possible cooperation between the political and religious spheres.[18] Merchant kinship provided that close cooperation in Albany. The members of the town's extended merchant families ruled both the town and the church. This relationship exemplified a decisive characteristic of Calvin's theology and Albany's church-town relations: if confusion were to break out in one realm, it was bound to affect the other. Thus, it was the duty of the Common Council to enforce the doctrine of the church with worldly power. Throughout the bulk of the colonial period, Albany's political and religious leaders carried out these sacred duties by resisting English efforts to control the Dutch economy and to impose their Anglican church.

II. ETHNIC DIVERSITY AND ECONOMIC POLARIZATION IN THE 1760's

The impact of the French and Indian War changed this way of life. Skirmishes between British and French forces over control of northern New York had, by 1754, made Albany the last physically secure community on the northern frontier. Refugees fled to the safety of the town's fortified walls, increasing the population from 1,800 to more than 3,000. The following winter as many as 1,400 officers and soldiers were moved into the already doubly occupied Dutch homes. During the winter of 1756, Albany's tightly circumscribed world comprised seventy-five acres filled with 355 households, and a teeming population of more than 4,000 natives, refugees, and soldiers.[19] Previously sporadic intrusions into the Dutch way of life had become constant. The Dutch responded with their minister's expression of moral outrage and a selective enforcement of local laws.[20] In 1760, the army marched triumphantly northward only to be replaced by a nettlesome invasion of "foreign" settlers.

Following the French and Indian War, Albany's economy changed. Indians were pushed farther away from the town, allowing for an increase in regional settlement. The old frontier trading post became a regional shipment center for settlers' produce and supplies. English and Scotch-Irish immigrants settled in the city. A handful of English merchants competed with the Dutch. Many more new immigrants took up artisan trades. A 1766 city tax list reveals that the local non-Dutch minority amounted to 36% of the town's population and a majority of the city's poor.[21] In sum, the new immigrants created a polarization of rich and poor, merchants and artisans, old Dutch natives and new "strangers," which, in turn, placed new demands on the city's traditional political system.

This was more than simply a growth in population and a polarization of wealth. It was also a matter of increasing numbers of English and Scotch-Irish immigrants becoming dependent upon the wealth of that small minority of their countrymen who were successful, the long dominant Dutch families, or the Common Council to maintain their lives. It was therefore a matter of deeply divided interests as some offered while others asked for housing, money, and employment. This "foreign" minority's growing dependence, separate interests, and disproportionately high representation among the town's poor, considered in the context of a predominantly Dutch town where the longterm inhabitants maintained a monopoly over the local sources of power, were the unmistakable ingredients of political conflict.[22] It is not too surprising, therefore, that as Albany's population and economy changed, so did its politics. Wealthy Dutch merchants, who were also leaders of their church, still dominated the Common Council. But now they were joined by a few recent non-Dutch immigrants and descendants of British soldiers formerly stationed at the fort. Rather than relying upon the traditional requirements of social rank and wealth as prerequisites of political leadership, these "foreign" insurgents turned to the support of a popular following.

Abraham Yates, a former sheriff and grandson of a British soldier who settled in the town, was the leader of these rebels.[23] His new approach to politics may well have been motivated by what he read in the tracts of the early eighteenth century radical Whigs while working in a local lawyer's office, his experiences of British military abuse during their occupation of the city, or his resentment toward the ruling Dutch families for using their influence to force him and two followers out of their Common Council seats. Together these influences contributed to his seeing local politics as a practical struggle for those of the "common sort" to secure for themselves the economic and political opportunities denied by the "aristocrats." Moreover, this local experience determined his later attitude toward national questions.

Yates became New York's most influential and articulate Anti-Federalist. During the Revolution he was chairman of the Committee of the Provincial Convention which drafted New York's revolutionary constitution in 1777. He also became a state Senator under the new government. His papers, published and unpublished, may well constitute the largest corpus produced by any Anti-Federalist in the nation.[24] James Hutson has portrayed the Anti-Federalists as actually having political ideas similar to those of Federalists, in that they concurred with their opponents on most of the principles of political theory. The primary difference was that the Anti-Federalists feared the abuse of power by government.[25] Abraham Yates exemplified this attitude. His argument against the Federal Constitution contained repeated attacks upon British imperialism and Dutch aristocracy. Against these evil forces Yates employed a host of Biblical analogies, suggesting a malevolent lust for power, and punctuated his argument with references to Montesquieu, Franklin, Adams and other Enlightenment thinkers. All this was intended to portray the Federalist's Constitution as but one more sad example of aristocracy's effort "to get the Power out of the Hands of the People."[26] For Abraham Yates and his Albany followers, fighting for American liberty meant fighting for freedom from British imperialism and Dutch aristocracy.

In contrast, the members of the Dutch church may well have looked upon all of these developments as signs of a growing evil that threatened the very existence of their traditional world. Despite the changes the community was undergoing in its economic, social, and political life, throughout the 1760's and on into the 1780's the religious life of the Dutch continued. Richard Pointer has argued against the widely held assumption that religious life in New York was largely suspended during the War. Even though many churches were indeed closed and church property damaged, Pointer has found that a surprisingly large number of churches continued to function.[27] This was particularly true in Albany where the Anglican Church was closed and the fledgling Presbyterian and Methodist congregations suspended operation, yet the regular rhythm of Sunday services at the Dutch church persisted. Even though English language and manners gradually spread throughout the community, it was more than twenty years before an English-speaking minister was called to the Church to assist the Dutch minister, Domine Westerlo. This indicates not only that the Dutch language continued to be easily understood by the congregation, but also that the Dutch townspeople were accustomed to using it in their homes. Westerlo's nickname,

"Pope," given to him derisively by British outsiders, suggests their perception of the control he maintained over his congregation. At least until the 1780's, the Albany Dutch remained a coherent and dominant group within the expanding local population.[28]

As the Dutch watched their formerly good, simple, consensual world give way to an evil, complex, and diverse society, confused by conflicting interests, they may well have seized the Revolution as an opportunity to revolt against the persistent intrusions of an aggressive British overlord.[29] Throughout the colonial period the town's British authorities and Dutch majority had skirmished over British influence within the town. The occupation by British soldiers during the French and Indian War had led to moral outrage by the Dutch minister as well as to political and economic action against sustained British intrusions into the Dutch way of life. As old habits and ways of thought became less applicable to the new circumstances, the traditional Dutch may well have welcomed the Revolution as an opportunity to restore traditional order to their town. Moreover, the departure of British merchants during the Revolution gave them reason to believe they had succeeded.[30] Perhaps for reasons of revolt then, rather than of revolution, Albany's Dutch merchant leaders joined leaders from the town's British and Scotch-Irish ethnic groups to confront their common imperial enemy.

III. POLITICAL UNITY AND A NEW CIVIL FAITH

The external threat of war forced the divided townspeople to find a new basis for political unity. When Albany's property holders were asked to elect representatives to a Committee of Correspondence to direct the local war effort, they revealed the persistence of their traditional habits by electing mostly church elders. Abraham Yates was elected, but he was joined by more than a dozen men who served at one time as leaders within their Dutch, Anglican,[31] and Presbyterian churches. Each of these congregations maintained a distinction between merchants and artisans in their selection of religious leaders. As war approached, this inter-ethnic Committee dominated by merchant elders directed its efforts to weeding out the enemy supporters in their midst.

To identify these Tories, the Committee of Correspondence created an oath of allegiance that articulated a new basis for community membership. Those few British merchants and Dutch sympathizers who refused to sign were shunned by the townspeople, then jailed, and finally banished if they still did not sign. This oath changed the traditional basis of community membership from Dutch ethnicity and Reformed Church membership to American citizenship and belief in God. Its critical passage included the following:

> PERSUADED that the salvation of the Rights and Liberties of America depends under God on the firm Union of its Inhabitants.... We the Freemen, Freeholders and Inhabitants of the City and County of Albany...Do in the most Solemn Manner resolve never to become Slaves; and do associate under all the Ties of Religion, and Love to our Country.[32]

Every inhabitant was called upon to reach beyond local and ethnically based political and religious bonds to affirm their common national and religious ties.

Following the Revolution, new civil rituals[33] sanctified the bonds of this new union. The primary carriers of Albany's new commitment to political unity were the members of the Common Council who were also leaders of the community's Dutch, Presbyterian, and Anglican churches. Most of these men had served together on the Committee of

Correspondence or in the local militia during the war. They were repeatedly elected to the Common Council by a similarly heterogeneous population which also held in common the experience of the Revolution. As supporters of the nation, Albany's leaders came together as Americans and Christians, not as Albanians or members of particular churches. Together they believed in the "liberty of America" and the need to unite under the leadership of God.

Every Fourth of July one of the town's ministers sanctified these sentiments in a sermon that articulated their leaders' new faith in the nation. In the first Fourth of July sermon published in Albany,[34] the Dutch minister John Barent Johnson drew an analogy between God's liberation of Israel and the role God played in America's struggle for independence.[35]

> As Jehovah not only broke the chains and secured the liberty of his ancient people, but also gave them a name among nations; so we can call to mind his providential interference in those measures which led to the establishment of our Independence.[36]

America was the promised land for Albany's European settlers. God had led his people to establish a new nation. Through this "wonderful interposition of the God of Battles, in our behalf," Johnson continued, a "purer" form of church participation became possible through the separation of church and state. No longer was Christianity's beauty to be "tarnished, and its purity polluted by an illegitimate connexion with the state. God's liberation of America freed Americans as a people and as Christians. As Americans, they were free from British colonial rule; as Christians, they were free to worship according to the precepts of God and the dictates of their own conscience. To maintain this "two-fold liberty," Johnson warned, Albany's heterogeneous people had to come together as a "firm and united band of brothers…and inculcate the principle of UNION as the rock of our political salvation. To do this they needed to "cultivate wisdom and practice religion" for this was the "best security and essential support of republican governments."[37] In conclusion, the Dutch minister declared that Americans now needed to carry out actively God's will on earth. During the two decades after the Revolution, the ministers of Albany's leading churches emphasized this pressing need for political unity that needed the support of denominational worship and the active participation of Americans in carrying out the will of God.

Johnson's sermon, and others like it, provided a religious context within which Albany's leaders could come to terms with their new political reality. On the local level, the struggle to secure America's liberty had meant a struggle for a no longer homogeneous community to find a new basis for unity. In colonial Dutch Albany's Calvinist theocracy, God's will had meant resisting all efforts to change the community's traditional way of life. The town's political leaders had worked closely with their brother church elders to resist competition from "foreign" merchants and the imposition of an Anglican church. The political liberation of America, however, brought a reversal in these traditional values. As God had led Americans to Independence, so too had he led Albanians to embrace one another in political unity. A common identity as Americans and Christians replaced Dutch ethnicity and Reformed Church membership as the moral foundation for community order. After the war, the traditional alliance between Common Council members and church elders continued. The community leaders, however, were no longer from the same ethnic background nor did they worship at the same church.

Even more striking is the contrast between the attitude of the earlier Dutch and that of the post-war leaders toward the establishment of new churches. Rather than resist efforts that further dissolved the community's Dutch homogeneity, the new Common Council members saw the establishment of new churches as the best means of promoting the common religious bonds of an increasingly diverse population. Between 1780 and 1800 the Common Council willingly gave city land for the construction of new Presbyterian, Methodist, and Dutch church buildings.[38] Moreover, Common Council members and religious leaders were prominent in their contributions to the financial support of denominations other than their own.[39] Unlike the town's traditional leaders who had resisted all threats to the homogeneity of their people and the monopoly of their single established church, the advocates of Albany's new civil faith encouraged the political unity of ethnically diverse people and supported the establishment of new churches.

It was out of these social circumstances that Albany's new commitment to the nation was born. A once tightly-knit community was overcome by a wave of new immigrants who precipitated a local political crisis. This crisis was temporarily resolved during the Revolutionary War and its aftermath when the basis of community membership was redefined to include people of different ethnic backgrounds and churches. After the Revolution, the responsibility for the welfare of the whole community passed from the church to the town. When the Dutch moved their house of worship away from the onslaught of Yankee wagons passing through the center of town on their way west, this also signaled the withdrawal of their care for every community member. By the end of the century, the traditionally Dutch responsibility for the community's poor was taken over by a sub-committee of the Common Council known as the Overseers of the Poor. The town, now more than and distinct from the Dutch community, became responsible for the welfare of the community as a whole. Thus, in lieu of the identification of the political sphere with a particular church, the new nationalism provided unity in Albany by incorporating traditional religious functions into a newly separated political sphere and by broadening the moral basis of unity to include multiple denominations.

IV. THE CHANGING MEANING OF NATIONALISM
IN THE EARLY NINETEENTH CENTURY

As the war fervor died down, accelerating mobility and the extension of the market undermined the social order of denominationalism as the basis for community stability. As early as the 1790's, Albany's inhabitants daily witnessed the arrival of several hundred westward bound New Englanders on their way to the newly secure farmlands of upstate New York. Two-thirds of those who remained long enough to be counted on the 1790 census were gone by 1800. More than a thousand of the Dutch townspeople and a thousand more "strangers" who had lived in the town during the revolution also migrated west.[40] Between 1790 and 1820 Albany's population increased from 3,490 to 12,630 with the Dutch accounting for no more than 5% of the inhabitants in 1820.[41] During the five years following the completion of the Erie Canal in 1825 the population increased by more than half, yet only one in five workingmen remained in the community.[42] A new Yankee merchant and manufacturing elite rode to prosperity on this wave of western migration. Yankee shops and stores lined the main streets, warehouses dominated the riverfront, and factories developed on the outskirts of town. By 1830 most of the town's newcomers were transient laborers and journeymen. Prior to the Revolution, the Dutch had lived within a tightly knit, relatively static society; after the Revolution, the town's Americans passed through a bewildering era of acceleratng mobility and economic expansion.

As a local solution for transcending particular ethnic and religious differences that might otherwise divide society, the unity of Albanians as Americans and Christians was sufficient to carry them through the Revolution. This new national identity did not alter fundamentally the way the inhabitants conducted their collective lives. It did not immediately draw the townspeople out of their Dutch, English, Scotch-Irish, and Yankee communal orientations. Moreover, the merchant-elders' commitment to the liberty of America did not imply any change in the community's hierarchical social structure. Well into the second decade of the new century the inhabitants affirmed these sentiments by electing their church elders, now members of the Federalist Party, to the Common Council.

Some of the townspeople, however, continued to understand American liberty as an endorsement of human equality. Following the war, Anti-Federalist immigrants and artisans, led by those who had begun their assault on the Dutch "aristocracy" in the 1760's, engaged in an increasingly bitter feud with the town's leaders. In 1788, they went so far as to disrupt the city's parade in celebration of New York's approval of the Federal Constitution.[43] These tensions surfaced again in 1805 in a quarrel over a central symbol of the nation. During the summer of that year, the Federalist Common Council members sought to remove the reading of the Declaration of Independence during Fourth of July services. They argued that the Declaration should not be read because it contained "disrespectful language" that would only further harm America's relations with Great Britain.[44] Opposing these Federalists were the town's mechanics, a growing community of Yankee skilled tradesmen whose influence expanded with the extension of the market.[45] "Liberty," the mechanics held, "is the equalization of civil privileges.[46] For those opposed to rule by the elite, the decision not to solemnly read the Declarations' endorsement of human equality was a denial of the very meaning of America. In the end, the Declaration was read and the Mechanics' Society did march in the annual parade.[47] Yet the consensus that had carried Americans through the Revolution continued to erode.

By the second decade of the nineteenth century Albany's communal and hierarchical society, based on the confluence of religious and political authority, was giving way in the face of growing economic, social, and political change. In 1817, the largest and most influential churches were the two Dutch and three Yankee congregations, all of which subscribed to the principles of Calvinism. These assemblies of merchants, master craftsmen, and their families accounted for nearly two-thirds of the town's church members.[48] Moreover, they accounted for more than two-thirds of all church members in the top two deciles of the 1817 tax list.[49] Yet, in that same year, less than half of the names of Albany's taxpayers can be found on all of the available church membership lists. Though the unchurched were found in every economic bracket, they most noticeably accounted for nearly seventy-five percent of the taxpayers with incomes below the community median. Men in this lower bracket worked primarily as journeymen and laborers. At the same time that church members and non-church members were dividing along economic lines, women were flocking to the churches. In 1817, women accounted for more than two-thirds of the new Second Dutch and First Presbyterian church members.[50] In sum, Calvinist church membership, which traditionally bound together all members of the community, was limited to an elite and increasingly female minority. By 1827 Albany's population doubled, yet the number of Calvinist congregations remained the same.

At the same time that the influence of the older congregations was declining in society, their leaders were being voted out of the Common Council. During the second and third decades of the nineteenth century, the merchant-elder elite lost control over city politics to a variety of newcomers who were less involved in church life and more interested in economic productivity. Between 1810 and 1816, twenty-nine of the town's thirty-six aldermen (81%) were members of either the Dutch, Episcopal or Presbyterian congregations. Eighteen (50%) were at some point in their lives ordained by their churches as deacons, elders, or trustees responsible to God for the moral behavior of their fellow Christians. A new need to appeal to the popular will, mandated by the 1820 state law that removed the property requirement for white male suffrage, hastened the decline of religious leaders on the Common Council. After 1820, the majority of Albany's voters were not church members and, as attested by their voting patterns, less willing to follow the political guidance of church elders. Between 1823 and 1830 less than half of the members of the Common Council elected by these voters were members of the elite congregations (45%) and only about half of these (24%) were church leaders. In consequence, political decisions were no longer made by the consensus of elders responsible to God but by politicians who offered conflicting interpretations of the popular will. Moreover, these newly elected officials could no longer be easily grouped by culture and kin. Rather, what marked them were their common economic interests as attorneys, merchants, master craftsmen, and allies of local banking establishments.

As the influence of the traditional church elders waned, new political leaders shifted the meaning of commitment to the nation from the political unity of different cultural groups to single-minded support for economic productivity. New attitudes toward the poor and in support of manufacturing were expressed by the Common Council, reflecting a growing interest in cost-effective management and increased production.[51] These new leaders employed patriotism to bolster entrepreneurial activity. Their Heroes and Great Men were no longer carved from Revolutionary War lore but from the tales of a growing and expanding society. Eulogists of these now fallen leaders exalted their spirit of innovation and enterprise rather than their ability to unite the nation. De Witt Clinton was the first of Albany's new American heroes.

Albanians revered Clinton in a manner rivaled only by the reverence paid to George Washington. Nephew of the state's first governor and son of a major general in the Revolutionary War, Clinton led the successful post-war effort of the Republican party to replace the Federalist aristocrats with new men committed to economic growth and development of the arts and sciences. As governor, he was universally acclaimed for accomplishing the construction of the Erie Canal. Even his detractors agreed that his lifelong ambition had been to promote the permanent prosperity of the state. The governor's death in 1827 brought forth unprecedented public mourning. As one citizen lamented:

> Since the day that the FATHER OF HIS COUNTRY was gathered to the tomb of his fathers the public expression of regret for a public loss was never more deep toned or emphatic than when DeWitt Clinton died.[52]

Numerous eulogies soon poured forth. They all sought to articulate the meaning of his life by describing Clinton as a transcendent figure, one who was "raised up by Providence to aid in the fulfillment of its grand designs.[53]

If Clinton had been an instrument of God, then God's design was for a nation of "useful" people to apply their skills to greater productivity. The revered Governor's name became synonymous with nearly every progressive new departure in the life of the town.[54] The first boat to pass through the Erie Canal was called the DeWitt Clinton. The first train to enter the city's gates was christened the same. The DeWitt Clinton Stove Works, and even DeWitt Clinton Fay, son of a trustee of the leading evangelical church, testify to the spirit of innovation and enterprise associated with his name. By the 1820's, Albany's official heroes were the town's economic leaders for whom patriotism meant a commitment to economic growth.

Economic expansion, however, forced changes in the social relations between workingmen and their employers that inevitably rendered suspect the unifying appeal of patriotic productivity. Under the traditional handicraft system prevalent prior to 1800, the master craftsman and his journeymen lived and worked together. Work, relaxation, and family life took place in the same place and among the same people; relations between master and workers moved easily from the shop to the home. The early nineteenth century growth in the scale of production altered these relations. Masters began to move away from their shops to live on affluent residential streets, leaving their workmen to find living space in boardinghouses on busy commercial streets. As the market continued to expand, these craftsmen-turned-entrepreneurs increased the speed, size, and regularity of manufacturing, while hiring transient workers with whom they shared no more than economic relations. As a result, journeymen in the 1829's experienced harsher conditions and more obvious forms of exploitation than had workers in the same trades at the beginning of the century. As the same time, as they lived, worked, and talked with each other, journeymen began to develop a sense of themselves that set them apart from their employers.[55] By the late 1820's, Albany's single society of master craftsmen and journeymen, the Mechanics' Society, had dissolved, and in its place were created separate journeymen societies and similarly exclusive societies of master craftsmen. For a large portion of the town's early nineteenth century Americans, the businessmen's new celebration of productivity appeared to come at their own expense.

The beliefs and forms of social organization of Albany's journeymen first emerged in the years following the canal's completion and their sequestration into working class neighborhoods. The immediate reason for the town's first labor strike in May 1826 was the carpenters' demand for higher wages. Though the results of this strike are not known, it is apparent that over the next several years the carpenters continued to attack the increased competition among master builders that undercut the carpenter's ability to earn a "just wage." To counter this trend they sought to establish "permanent prices for piece and day work" so that they would no longer be "dupes of our own usefulness."[56] By the 1830's, they had formed their own Journeyman Carpenters' Association.

The journeymen carpenters' demand for more money was a symptom of a deeper, more troubling, and internally contradictory concern over the erosion of communal bonds between master and worker. When the Journeyman Painters' Society met in 1831, they made this plea to their employers:

> There is not that degree of reciprocal feeling between the journeyman and his employer which should exist and is highly necessary to both.... Unity is the answer. Let the master declare the journeyman's rights and their own inseparable.[57]

Sounding like traditional artisans, dependant on the leadership and care of their masters, the journeymen only asked that their employers "do justice to themselves to set a price adequate to their labor." Then, in contrast, they asserted their independence by invoking their newly earned freedom as Americans independent from the subtle economic enslavement practiced by their employers.

> Woe to the power who dares to presume to rob us of the sacred name of freemen—and yet while we risk our lives and fortunes to protect our liberties from foreign invasion and despotic power from abroad. Yet will we nurse the canker in our own bosom which will sooner or later poison or corrode our whole system and render us the fit subjects for tyrants and despots to trample upon.

Like traditional artisans, the journeyman painters were willing to let their masters decide "among themselves" what should be their "just wage." At the same time, they asserted their independence from their employers by phrasing their demand in patriotic terms. "He who deserts his own cause," they concluded, "also deserts his country.[58]

This use of republican ideals to protest the exploitation of journeymen by their employers and the use of these same ideals by enterpreneurs to promote economic growth were signs of what became a widespread practice of refashioning the ideology of the nation to serve a variety of ends. Ideas like liberty, freedom, and love of country were used by all of the town's interest groups to come to terms with profound changes in the nature of society. By the early 1830's, evangelical preachers had commandeered the Fourth of July rites to advance their millennial vision of national reform. They, in turn, were attacked by workingmen who saw individual rights as the focus of the day's activities. Other voices joined in the fray.[59] The language of nationalism was broadly shared, yet its meaning was differently understood.

By the early 1830's Albany's society was neither united by religious revivals nor divided by class conflict but an arena of rapid geographic mobility. Unlike the revival city of Rochester, where Paul Johnson found a community-wide conversion to evangelical Christianity providing a new basis for social order,[60] Albany's revivals did not unite the community. Only 26% of the men listed on the 1830 census were members of churches during the town's 1828-1835 revival period.[61] Though the number of churches doubled and by 1835 the majority of the town's Christians were evangelicals, 72% of these congregants were women.[62] In contrast to Johnson's Rochester, Albany's churches were less central to the social order while women became a moral force within every congregation.[63] If a renewal of Christian fervor did not unite Albanians neither did class conflict tear them apart. Unlike New York City in the 1830's, where Sean Wilentz found widespread journeymen revolts and radical attacks on private property,[64] Albany's working-men were particularly cautious in asserting their rights. Proclaiming themselves "neither infidels nor agrarians...but rather honest men seeking their rights,"[65] the town's workers stopped short of prolonged strikes and articulate critiques of capitalist wage labor. More apparent than either Christian unity of class conflict was a rapid rate of mobility into and out of Albany. In just five years following the completion of the canal, the town's population increased by more than half while less than a third of the job holders listed in the 1825 city directory can be found in the directory for 1830.[66] This pervasive unsettlement underscored a widespread uncertainty over the direction and ordering of the new society.

At least by the early 1830's the revolutionary power of nationalism as a catalyst for converting diversity into unity had weakened. As a local solution for transcending particular ethnic and religious differences at the time of the Revolution, the new ideology had broadened the basis for community membership to include all Americans and Christians. Yet this new basis for unity had little effect on the hierarchical structure implicit in the earlier Dutch communalism. As accelerating mobility and economic expansion undermined the social order of denominationalism in the early nineteenth century, the broad call to unity as Americans and Christians gave way to competing visions of unity based on economic productivity and equal rights. New political leaders, more notably linked by economic interests than bonds of religion and family, employed the language of the republic to bolster economic growth. Journeymen used the same ideology to press for their individual rights. Despite their disagreement over the meaning of its words, both employers and employees shared with nearly all of Albany's inhabitants a commitment to republican ideology. This common vocabulary could not prevent the class conflicts of the 1860's but it may have run deeply enough to slow their emergence.[67] In a sense, Albanians still had not faced the local conflicts that the Revolution averted. Their understanding of those conflicts, however, would continue to be shaped by the images and symbols of their new commitment to the nation.

NOTES

1. Bernard Bailyn, *The Ideological Origins of the American Revolution* (Cambridge, MA, 1967). Bailyn's *The Origins of American Politics* (New York, 1968) supplements the original argument. Several scholars have expanded on and contended with Bailyn's position. For a discussion, see Robert E. Shalhope, "Toward a Republican Synthesis: The Emergence of an Understanding of Republicanism in American Historiography," *William and Mary Quarterly* 29 (January 1972): 49–80.

2. Nathan O. Hatch, *The Sacred Cause of Liberty* (New Haven, 1977). Historians and sociologists of American religion have converged on this overlapping of religion and politics often to argue about the implications of Robert Bellah's "civil religion" concept. Robert N. Bellah, "Civil Religion in American," *Daedalus* 96 (Winter, 1967): 1–21. For a discussion of the range and application of Bellah's concept, see Russell E. Richey and Donald G. Jones; eds., *American Civil Religion* (New York, 1974). John F. Wilson persuasively argues against Bellah's claim that a "well-institutionalized" civil religion actually exists by demonstrating the difficulty of finding its social correlates, John F. Wilson, *Public Religion in American Culture* (Philadelphia, 1979).

3. Edmund S. Morgan, "Conflict and Consensus in the American Revolution," in *Essays on the American Revolution*, ed. Stephen G. Kurtz and James H. Hutson (Chapel Hill, 1973), 303.

4. Gordon S. Wood, *The Creation of the American Republic, 1776–1787* (Chapel Hill, 1969).

5. Eric Foner, *Tom Paine and Revolutionary America* (New York, 1976).

6. Rowland Berthoff and John Murrin, "Feudalism, Communalism, and the Yeoman Freeholder," in Kurtz and Hutson, *Essays on the American Revolution*, 263.

7. The enduring potential for conflict within this larger consensus is discussed by Morgan in "Conflict and Consensus," 307–309. In a similar vein, John F. Wilson suggests that there is "an open set or cluster of meanings central to American culture." This approach makes it possible to deal with empirical observations that there are sub-cultures within American society for whom words like "liberty" have different meanings. Wilson, *Public Religion*, 117.

8. Kenneth A. Lockridge, "Social Change and the Meaning of the American Revolution," *Journal of Social History* 6 (Summer 1973): 415–432; James Henretta, "Economic Development and Social Structure in Colonial Boston," *William and Mary Quarterly* 3d ser. 28 (July 1971): 375–412; Gary B. Nash, "Urban Wealth and Poverty in Pre-Revolutionary America," *Journal of Interdisciplinary History* 6 (1975–1976): 545–584.

9. Gary B. Nash, *The Urban Crucible: Social Change, Political Consciousness, and the Origins of the American Revolution* (Cambridge, MA, 1979), vii.

10. Patricia U. Bonomi, *Under the Cope of Heaven: Religion, Society, and Politics in Colonial America* (New York, 1986), 5.

11. See the bibliographic essay in Kenneth A. Lockridge, *A New England Town: The First Hundred Years*, enlarged ed. (New York, 1985), 193–212.

12. In addition to Nash, *Urban Crucible*, see Dirk Hoerder's study of Massachusetts' crowds,

Crowd Action in Revolutionary Massachusetts, 1765–1780 (New York, 1977). Pauline Maier analyzes in the relationship between those crowds and their leaders in, *From Resistance to Revolution: Colonial Radicals and the Development of American Opposition to Great Britain,* 1765–1776 (New York, 1972); and *The Old Revolutionaries: Political Lives in the Age of Samuel Adams* (New York, 1980). Richard Alan Ryerson examines the development of the radical committees of Philadelphia and how committee members took and transformed power in *The Revolution Is Now Begun: The Radical Committees of Philadelphia,* 1765–1776 (Philadelphia, 1978).

13. Unlike New England, where Calvinism came in its Puritan form as an effort to create the pure church of God on earth, Dutch Calvinism came to New Netherland only after the West India Company determined that settlement was necessary in order to turn a profit. Nevertheless, a mixture of economic and religious motives characterized the European settlement of both regions. Bernard Bailyn has described the decidedly mercantile mentality of Bostonians as early as the 1630's, *The New England Merchants in the Seventeenth Century* (Cambridge, 1955). Kenneth Lockridge has pointed to the increased importance of economic factors in the decline of the New England town, *A New England Town.* In contrast, the initial Dutch interest in trade meant that the Reformed Church came to Albany more than twenty years after the arrival of the first immigrants. Once established, however, the Church continued to provide a basis for meaning and order among Albany's merchants and artisans long after its contemporary Puritan congregations in New England's agrarian villages had succumbed to dissension and pluralism.

14. Members of politically influential merchant families similarly predominate among the names of church elders. These names are listed in the "Deacon's Account Book 1647–1715" and "Pew Records 1719–1770," in Joel Munsell, ed., *Collections on the History of Albany* (Albany, 1865–1872) 1:2–56, 57–80; Consistory Minutes 1790–1815, Papers of the Dutch Reformed Church, First Dutch Reformed Church, Albany, New York; and scattered through both Joel Munsell, ed., *Annals of Albany* (Albany, 1850–1860) and Hugh Hastings, ed., *Ecclesiastical Records of the State of New York* (Albany, 1901).

15. Beginning with the British takeover of New Netherland in 1664 and at least until 1742, the number of non-Dutch Albany residents increased to no more than 25% of the inhabitants. "1742 Freeholders List," in Munsell, Annals, 2:282–283. Nearly all Dutch residents for this period are listed in Louis Duermyer,

ed., *Records of the Reformed Dutch Church of Albany,* New York 1683–1809 (Baltimore, 1978).

16. To control the content of sermons, the Netherland's Church divided the catechism into fifty-two sections and instructed that a different section form the content of the sermon for each successive Sunday of the year. See E.T. Corwin, ed., *A Digest of Synodical Legislation* (New York, 1906). The minister used this same catechism to teach Christian principles to the community's children. Two of Albany's colonial Reformed ministers wrote and published catechisms for children. See *Codman Hyslop, Albany: Dutch, English, and American* (Albany, 1936), 85. Moreover, estate inventories of Albany's Dutch householders reveal that the catechism and the Bible, and little other reading material, were present in their homes. These inventories are available at the Albany Institute of History and Art.

17. The catechism stated that, because of Adam's defiance of God, all people were "conceived and born in sin." To escape this state, people not only had to believe in the salvation offered by Jesus, they also had to receive from God an experince of "assured confidence" which was "freely given by God, merely of grace only for the sake of Christ's merit." In Albany, the elders of the church apparently had received this grace. Merchants were always chosen to be elders by their relatives who had served as elders before them. As religious leaders favored by God, these men were responsible to God for the community's moral welfare. See "The Heidelberg Catechism," in *The Psalms of David with Hymns and Spiritual Songs also the Catechism, Compendium. Confession of Faith and Liturgy of the Reformed Church of the Netherlands* (Albany, 1791), 352, 355.

18. Dutch Calvinists believed that humanity was divided between Christendom and infidels and that, in time, God would reunite humanity under the authority of Christ. Until that time, however, God ruled the whole world, not just Christendom. Since God employed both civil and religious authorities to carry out his rule, the Calvinists believed that between the two there must be the closest imaginable cooperation. John Calvin, *Institutes of the Christian Religion,* (Grand Rapids, 1957), 4. 1. 1–8. For an overview of the Dutch understanding of religion and politics in Netherland, see George L. Smith, *Religion and Trade in New Netherland* (Ithaca, 1973).

19. "A list of the Inhabitants of the City of Albany in America with the Number of Troops they can Quarter...made in November 1756," Loudon Papers, Huntington Library, San Marino, California.

20. The minister led the leaders of the Dutch congregation in denouncing the "lax morals and

second hand manners" of the British officers. Through their minister, the Dutch particularly warned against attendance at the plays presented by the British officers whose false renderings of reality "were themselves a lie." Anne Grant, *Memoirs of An American Lady* (London 1808), 292–303. Against the Dutch selective enforcement of local laws, one British merchant complained: "they picked out the Strangers from one end of Albany to the other with much discretion and Judgt. but the persons that might readily be suspected of the right breed they passed over."

21. "1766 City Tax List," Box 10, Schuyler Papers, New York City Public Library. This list includes the names of 470 Albany inhabitants. Only 18 of the top 100 taxpayers were not of Dutch origin. In contrast, 54 of the bottom 100 taxpayers were non-Dutch immigrants. David A. Armour, "The Merchants of Albany, New York, 1683–1781," (Ph. D. dissertation, Northwestern University, 1965), 261–263.

22. The emergence of political conflict in this way was first suggested to me by Lockridge, "Social Change."

23. Before the Revolution, Abraham Yates practiced law, mended shoes, and played a political role in the city (member of the Common Council for various terms 1754–73) and county (sheriff of Albany County, 1754–59). Much of the information for the following discussion of Abraham Yates and the origins of popular politics in Albany is taken from Stefan Bielinski, *Abraham Yates and the New Political Order in Revolutionary New York* (Albany, 1975).

24. See Staughton Lynd, "Abraham Yates's History of the Movement for the United States Constitution," *William and Mary Quarterly* 3d ser., 20 (April 1963): 224, 226.

25. James H. Hutson, "Country, Court, and Constitution: Antifederalism and the Historians," *William and Mary Quarterly* 3d ser., 38 (1981): 337–368.

26. Abraham Yates as quoted in Lynd, "Abraham Yates," 228.

27. Richard W. Pointer, "Religious Life in New York During the Revolutionary War," *New York History* 66 (October 1985): 358–373.

28. Throughout the war, the Dutch minister gathered the majority of the community into the large stone church that continued to stand at the center of town. The pew records show that during the 1760's and 1770's nearly all of the town's Dutch inhabitants held seats in the church. "Seatings," in Munsell, *Collections* 1:57–80. When General Burgoyne's army approached the city, special services were held for the entire community to pray for deliv-

erance from the British army. Kenney, *Gansevoorts,* 105–106.

29. This traditional response of medieval Netherlanders to intrusions by rulers of their region is traced to the responses of the Albany Dutch to their British rulers by Alice Kenney. See Kenney, "The Dutch Patricians of Colonial Albany," *New York History* 49 (July 1968): 249–283.

30. The departure of nearly all of the new British merchants is confirmed through a variety of sources: "A Church of England Record," in Papers of Sir William Johnson (Albany: State University of New York, 1921–1965) 8:221; Rev. Joseph Hooper, *History of St. Peter's Church* (Albany, 1900), 125; "1779 City Tax List," Gerrit Y. Lansing Papers, New York State Library; Victory H. Paltsits, ed., *Minutes of the Commission for Detecting and Defeating Conspiracies in the State of New York: Albany County Sessions 1778–1781,* 3 vols. (Albany, 1909–1910). For further discussion, see Alice P. Kenney, "The Albany Dutch: Loyalists and Patriots," *New York History* 42 (July 1961): 331–350.

31. Despite anti-British sentiment which led to the closing of St. Peter's Episcopal Church during the war, some of the lay leaders of that church were longterm community residents. They obviously were trusted by the Dutch who united with them to oppose external aggression. For a history of St. Peter's Church during these years, see Rev. Joseph Hooper, *A History of St. Peter's Church in the City of Albany* (Albany, 1900).

32. James Sullivan, ed., *The Minutes of the Albany Committee of Correspondence 1775–1778* (Albany, 1923), 1:3.

33. Annual Fourth of July rituals brought to the fore and reaffirmed the community's common American and religious ties. These day-long rites combined the form of the traditional military parade and dinner toasts to the king on his birthday with an inter-ethnic church service. The church in which this liturgy took place varied from year to year. Usually more than one local clergyman presided, and a regular order of worship, including a reading of the Declaration of Independence followed by a sermon, was invariably followed. That evening, in a custom formerly used to honor the king on his birthday, the members of the Common Council and the most respectable citizens attended a dinner during which patriotic toasts were given. *Albany Gazette,* July 1799.

34. Prior to the Revolution none of the sermons of Albany's ministers was published. A small, homogeneous community where face-to-face contacts and the pervasive principles of the Heidelberg Catechism predominated had little need to socialize its people to

moral ideas known by all since childhood. Unlike the larger and more heterogeneous New York, where sermons were published as early as the 1720's, Albany's ministers only began to publish their sermons after the Revolution when the town's population approximated the size and ethnic heterogeneity of mid-eighteenth century New York City. Moreover, the emergence of printing offices in town coincided with a newly perceived need, as these printers stated, "to promote civil and religious liberty" and to advance the "knowledge and instruction" of the people. *Albany Gazette,* 25 November 1771. By articulating the new basis for political and religious unity, the Fourth of July sermons served these ends.

35. The well known Puritan theme of America as the "New Israel" is discussed in Robert Bellah, *The Broken Covenant: American Civil Religion in Time of Trial* (New York, 1975), 1–35.

36. John Barent Johnson. *The Dealings of God with Israel and America* (Albany, 1798), 14–15.

37. Ibid., 14–18.

38. City of Albany, "Common Council Minutes," 1780–1800, New York State Library Albany, New York.

39. "1786 Subscription List." First Reformed Church of Albany; "1793 Subscription List," First Presbyterian Church of Albany; "1788–1799 Subscription List," St. Peter's Episcopal Church, Albany, New York.

40. U.S. Department of Commerce, Bureau of Census, *Heads of Families of the First Census of the United States Taken in 1790: New York* (Washington, D.C., 1908); U.S. Department of Commerce, Bureau of Census, *Heads of Families of the Second Census of the United States Taken in 1800* (Washington, D.C., 1908).

41. 1790 Census, United States Department of Commerce, Bureau of Census, *U.S. Census, Fourth, 1820: New York* (Washington, D.C.: U.S. Census Bureau, n.d.); the percentage of Dutch descendants in the 1820 city population was determined from the federal census of that year by William Esmond Rowley, "Albany: A Tale of Two Cities 1820–1880" (Ph.D. diss., Harvard University, 1967).

42. The population in 1825 was 15,971. State of New York, State Census: 1825 (Albany, 1826). In 1830 the population was 24,209. United States Department of Commerce, Bureau of the Census, U.S. Census, Fifth, 1830. New York (Washington, D.C., 1832). The rate of mobility for workingmen (journeymen and laborers) was determined through a comparison of the names in the 1825 and 1830 city directories. T.V. Cuyler, ed., *Albany City Directory for 1825* (Albany 1825); Cammeyer and Gaw, eds.,

Albany City Directory, 1830–1831 (Albany 1830).

43. "Celebration of the Adoption of the Federal Constitution, 1788," in Munsell, *Annals* 1:228–235.

44. *Albany Register,* 18 June 1805.

45. These largely Yankee skilled tradesmen formed themselves into a society in 1793. "Albany Mechanics' Society," in Munsell, *Annals* 7:240–244.

46. *Albany Register,* 10 August 1805.

47. *Albany Register,* 5 July 1805.

48. This is based on the complete and partial membership lists of nine of the eleven churches existing in Albany in 1817. The elite churches accounted for 65% of Albany's adult male church members. First Methodist, First Baptist and First Lutheran accounted for the rest. There are no membership lists available for the small Catholic and Associate Reformed Presbyterian congregations. All church records are located in their respective churches unless otherwise noted. Membership List, 1816–1836, First Dutch Reformed Church; List of Communicants, 1815–1840, Second Dutch Reformed Church, New York State Library; Register of Communicants, 1795–1840, First Presbyterian Church; List of Communicants, 1816–1870, Second Presbyterian Church, New York State Library; List of Officers and Elders, 1817–1855 and "List of Associate Reformed Church Members 1810–1813 Who Joined Third Church," Third Presbyterian Church, New York State Library; List of Communicants, 1821–1834, St. Peter's Episcopal Church, New York State Library; Marriage and Baptism Records, 1806–1830, List of Officers, 1793–1830, and Annual Membership Statistics, 1793–1840, First Methodist Church; Record Book (including communicants list), 1811–1840, First Baptist Church, American Baptist Archives, Colgate-Rochester Divinity School, Rochester, New York; List of Communicants, 1786–1835, First Lutheran Church, New York State Library.

49. City Tax List, 1817, Albany County Records Office, Albany, N.Y.

50. List of Communicants, 1815–1840, Second Dutch Reformed Church; Register of Communicants, 1795–1840, First Presbyterian Church. By 1836, the available membership lists show, women accounted for two-thirds of both the old Calvinist congregations and the new Methodist, Baptist, and New School Presbyterian Evangelical congregations. For an explanation of the growing numbers of women joining churches in nearby Utica during this period see chapter eight in this book, Mary P. Ryan, "A Woman's Awakening: Evangelical Religion and the Families of Utica, New York 1800–1840."

51. The Common Council Minutes show that

citizens' complaints regarding the noise and pollution of manufacturing establishments were often disregarded for the greater good of productivity. See for example, Common Council Minutes, 7 January 1828, New York State Library, Albany, New York.

52. James R. Manley, *An Eulogium on DeWitt Clinton* (New York, 1828).

53. Citizen of Albany, *Tribute to the Memory of DeWitt Clinton* (Albany, 1828).

54. In September 1985, Paul E. Johnson suggested to me this relationship between Clinton's name and "progress" in New York.

55. This well known transformation of the social relations of production is presented in detail by Paul E. Johnson, *A Shopkeepers Millenium: Society and Revivals in Rochester, New York 1817–1837* (New York, 1976), 37–61.

56. *Farmers', Mechanics', and Workingman's Advocate, Advocate*, 2 February 1831.

57. Ibid., 1 January 1831.

58. Ibid.

59. In 1832, for example, the local Scottish Associate Reformed minister delivered a sermon that stubbornly denied the authority of the Constitution over the theocracy ordained by god. James Renwick Willson, *Prince Messiah's Claims to Dominion Over All Governments and the Disregard of His Authority by the United States in the Federal Constitution* (Albany, 1832).

60. Johnson, *Shopkeeper's Millennium* 95–115.

61. 1830 Census; In 1836 there were twenty-two churches in Albany. No membership information is available for seven of these churches. These include the African Methodist, African Baptist, Third Methodist, Fourth Methodist, Associate Reformed, Friends, and Catholic churches.

62. Largely female congregations were as much the rule for the old and established First and Second Presbyterian congregations as they were for the young and growing Methodist churches. And this occurred without any imbalance in the number of men and women in the community. 1830 Census.

63. For a helpful critique of Johnson's argument and an assessment of the variety of roles played by women of different backgrounds in Rochester's revivals see Nancy A. Hewitt, *Women's Activism and Social Change, Rochester, New York, 1822–1872* (Ithaca, 1984).

64. Sean Wilentz, *Chants Democratic, New York City and the Rise of the American Working Class, 1788–1850* (New York, 1984) 145–218.

65. Rowley, "Two Cities," 117.

66. 1825 State Census and 1830 Federal Census; *Albany City Directory for* 1825 and *Albany City Directory*, 1830–1831.

67. For a helpful discussion of the force of "community consciousness" in Albany's response to industrialization, see Brian Greenburg, *Worker and Community: Response to Industralization in a Nineteenth Century American City, Albany, New York 1850–1884* (Albany, 1985).

THE DIALECTIC OF DOUBLE-CONSCIOUSNESS
IN BLACK AMERICAN FREEDOM CELEBRATIONS

William B. Gravely

During the past two decades a number of scholars have argued that racism did not emerge with slavery but rather with the Revolution, when Africans and their descendants were incorporated into a new society in which they lacked the rights of equality that were given to white people. Racism explained why some people could be denied the liberty that the Declaration of Independence guaranteed to all of the new nation's citizens as a matter of self-evident natural law. By labeling African Americans as an inferior race, European Americans resolved the contradiction between slavery and equality; African Americans, in contrast, called for resolution through an end to slavery.

Between the Revolution and the Civil War the "double-consciousness" of being African and being American became an issue for free blacks in the Northern states. Unlike the slaves in the South, Northern blacks were supposedly "free." Yet they remained shackled by a complex set of racial ideas, which evolved over the nineteenth century until they were systematically "proven" by late-nineteenth-century "scientific" depictions of African people's less evolved and immutable physical traits. In William Gravely's analysis, the black American freedom celebrations that emerged in the early nineteenth century ritualized this dialectic of "double-consciousness" in Northern free black experience. Not surprisingly, many blacks rejected the patriotic nationalism that regularly marked the celebration of the Fourth of July. Instead, through their participation in the commemoration of specific events in the African pilgrimage in the New World, the freedom celebrations gave roots to black peoples' emerging African American identity.

Reprinted by permission from William B. Gravely, "The Dialectic of Double-Consciousness in Black American Freedom Celebrations, 1808–1863," *Journal of Negro History* (Winter 1982), 302–317.

6

THE DIALECTIC OF DOUBLE-CONSCIOUSNESS IN BLACK AMERICAN FREEDOM CELEBRATIONS, 1808–1863

William B. Gravely

IN A CELEBRATED PASSAGE in *The Souls of Black Folk*, W.E.B. DuBois characterized black American existence in terms of "a peculiar sensation" of "double-consciousness." "One ever feels his two-ness," he wrote, "—an American, a Negro; two souls, two thoughts, two unreconciled strivings; two warring ideals in one dark body, whose dogged strength alone keeps it from being torn asunder. The history of the American Negro is the history of this strife...."[1]

In the period from the Revolution to the Civil War the "double-consciousness" of being black and being American, of which DuBois spoke, came into sharp focus for free blacks in the Northern states. Residing in a racially-based, slaveholding republic, their national identity was perenially challenged. The prevailing sentiment of the white majority, North and South, proclaimed the United States a white man's country. From individual incidents of discrimination to "black laws" which proscribed all "quasi-free Negroes," as John Hope Franklin terms the caste, that sentiment was dramatically reinforced.[2]

For some free blacks—especially after new reminders of American racism like the Fugitive Slave Law of 1850 or the Dred Scott decision of the Supreme Court seven years later—the dilemma of "double-consciousness" grew into an irreconcilable and unbearable paradox. Emigration became a way to resolve the dilemma—as a dream, if not always a reality.[3] More often, however, free blacks maintained a dialectical existence—black and American—and created a culture of alternative institutions which reflected both aspects of the dialectic. They made a viable community life by building schools and churches, forming literary societies and library companies, and organizing voluntary associations for mutual assistance and benevolence. They joined vigilance committees which aided fugitive slaves and convened protest meetings to counter racial injustice locally and nationally. By their presence and their persistence, Northern free blacks contradicted the white vision of America and in its place articulated and lived out an image of the country which could accommodate the dialectic—being black and being American.[4]

Their freedom celebrations ritualized the dialectic of "double-consciousness" in Northern free black experience, and interpreted it in oration and song. Begun to commemorate three specific events in the black pilgrimage in the New World, the freedom celebration told a story of peoplehood and gave roots to an emerging black identity "within the embrace of American nationality."[5]

The tradition of black freedom celebrations predated general emancipation by more than a half century.[6] Of the three most important holidays of black freedom before 1863, the first was New Year's Day, commemorating the abolition of the foreign slave trade by England, Denmark and the United States. On January 1, 1808 free blacks in two cities where their numbers were greatest—New York and Philadelphia—gathered to salute the occasion.[7]

The program for the day in New York set a pattern that was duplicated in subsequent New Year's Day festivals, as well as in other freedom celebrations later in the century. The morning service at the African church (historic Mother Zion Church) opened with "A solemn address to Almighty God," offered by Abraham Thompson, an African Methodist Episcopal Zion minister. A choir under the direction of William Hamilton, who would be the speaker in 1809 and in 1815, then sang "an appropriate anthem," otherwise unidentified. Henry Sipkins, who gave an oration the next year, read the congressional act of abolition and made a brief introductory statement. He was followed by Peter Williams, Jr., a twenty-one year old student preparing for the ministry in the Protestant Episcopal church, who delivered the formal address of the day. After a congregational hymn, Thomas Miller, Sr. (a Methodist local preacher) concluded the exercises with another prayer. In the afternoon there was a similar order of service, mixing prayer with song and highlighting a sermon by James Varick, who later became the first A. M. E. Zion bishop in America.[8]

For at least eight years blacks in New York kept New Year's Day in this manner. In Philadelphia, the practice continued as late as 1830.[9] Boston's smaller free black community also commemorated the end of the foreign slave trade between 1808 and 1822, but on July 14. The date for the anniversary was selected "for convenience, merely," an official explanation stated, but it also acknowledged "the abolition of *slavery* in [the] Commonwealth [of Massachusetts]."[10]

As far as current evidence indicates, other black communities did not keep New Year's Day as a holiday of freedom. Nor is it entirely clear when and why the celebration ceased. One possible factor, as Benjamin Quarles has suggested, was a loss of enthusiasm for commemorating the end of the foreign slave trade, since there were wholesale violations of the law.[11] The growing domestic traffic in slaves probably had an impact as well, undermining the earlier optimism of January First orators that the proscription of the foreign trade spelled the end of slavery. In Boston, at least, the end of the celebrations was attributed to white opposition and ridicule and the apparent inability of the political authorities to protect blacks, especially as they marched through the city streets on the holiday.[12]

Despite the decline of New Year's Day as a freedom holiday, until the Emancipation Proclamation of 1863 marked January First with even greater significance, the tradition of celebrations remained vital. The end of slavery in New York on July 4, 1827 spawned a new black holiday.[13] For the next eight years, New York State Abolition Day was commemorated in five states. There are records of eighteen separate celebrations, beginning with the original observance in eight locations. In four of these places (New York City, Baltimore, Cooperstown, New York and Fredericksburg, Virginia), Independence Day, the actual date on which the legislation abolishing slavery took effect, was used. For a second celebration in New York City, however, and for festivities in Albany, Rochester and New Haven, blacks chose the next day for the commemoration. The desire for a separate black holiday favored the fifth, though there was considerable debate at the time over which day to set aside.[14]

Like the January First celebration, most July Fifth festivals were held in black churches. At the same time they included more outdoor activities. Parades became typical, though not without a hot dispute concerning whether public processions were appropriate or not.[15] Other symbolic acts—the firing of gun salutes, the display of banners and community dinners with formal toasts—expressed the mood of jubilation for this summer holiday. The entire celebration at Rochester in 1827 was out of doors, culminating in an address in the Public Square by the fugitive slave, Austin Steward.[16]

New York Abolition Day was observed in some localities as late as 1859, but it was kept the most consistently between 1827 and 1834.[17] As in the case of the New Year's freedom celebration, July Fifth was replaced in the tradition by a new event, the emancipation of 670,000 bondsmen and bondswomen in the British West Indies in 1834. In recognition of their freedom, August First became the most widely commemorated and most enduring of the antebellum freedom holidays in America.[18]

The new abolitionism of the 1830's encouraged a broader white participation in the annual August First observances than was true of the two earlier holidays.[19] Blacks often joined with whites to celebrate, but they also continued separate exercises, yet without prohibiting whites from attending. The decision to hold separate celebrations was prompted by the sentiment which the A. M. E. Zion pastor, Jehiel C. Beman, expressed in 1843. "He insisted that the colored man, as he was the injured party, could alone *feel* on this occasion," the *Liberator* reported. "Freely acknowledging all the sympathies of our white friends, he considered they *could not*, having never been placed in the same circumstances with the colored people, *feel* as they do in celebrating this great event."[20]

Dating from 1834 through 1862, there are nearly 150 recorded black observances of West Indies Emancipation Day in the United States.[21] Geographically, those August First gatherings produced by blacks represented fifty-seven different places in thirteen states. According to newspaper accounts there were additional celebrations by fugitive slaves in London (1851, 1853) and by black American expatriates in Liberia (1859) and in Canada (1852, 1854–55, 1857, 1859–60).[22]

The format for August First festivities also expanded beyond the pattern of the two earlier celebrations. Some crowds, numbering as many as 7,000 people, could only be accommodated out of doors.[23] For that reason, and because the ceremonies took on a less restrictive religious atmosphere, fewer celebrations occurred in black churches. The growing number of organizations which wished to display their banners and the benefit of the summer climate made processions routine. Some, with local black militia companies and brass bands, added a martial atmosphere to the parade.[24] Since the celebration lasted most of the day and when the weather was favorable, outdoor picnics and community dinners provided the necessary refreshments. The early black historian, William C. Nell, amusingly described one such "feast" at which "about eighty ladies and gentlemen 'proclaimed liberty' to their masticating machinery, and manifested quite an industrious spirit while engaged in discussing the fare of various kinds with which the table was bountifully supplied."[25] Teetotal reformers at some dinners attested to their convictions either by using lemonade or cold water for toasts or by sponsoring separate Temperance Festivals on August First.[26] Black groups in Albany (1836), Boston (1838), Detroit (1854) and Cincinnati (1855) spent part of the holiday on steamboat excursions, earning, in the initial instance, a rebuke from other celebrants in Catskill, New York.[27]

As early as 1846, August First activities featured an Emancipation Ball, at which "the light fantastic toe was kept in motion till 'break of dawn,'" according to one account. The ball in Geneva, New York's Temperance House was restrained—"comfortable and quiet"—but more sober-minded blacks still objected, without success, to the innovation of dancing on August First. The practice spread, so that in 1853 Rochester's celebration witnessed "the 'mazy dance.'" Two years later, the San Francisco correspondent to the leading black weekly commented that dancing "was evidently more enjoyed than anything else" on the holiday. Unapprovingly, he noted that "with a majority of the colored people of this city, [it] is the acme of human happiness."[28]

Other commentators were more indulgent of the need for "a day of freedom," as Frederick Douglass put it in 1859, "when every man may seek his happiness in his own way, and without any very marked concern for the ordinary rules of decorum." With "no Fourth of July here, on which to display banners, burn powder, ring bells, dance and drink whiskey," Douglass added on another occasion, blacks turned to "the First of August." As always, he admitted, there were "a few…who carried this 4th of Julyism a little too far."[29] Describing the New Bedford, Massachusetts celebration of 1851, William C. Nell pronounced, with similar tolerance, "prayer or speech, song or dance" as "acceptable garlands, hung on the altar of Freedom."[30]

With West Indies Emancipation Day the freedom celebration reached its zenith before the Civil War. The three freedom holidays—January First, July Fifth and August First—did not, of course, exhaust the possibilities of public ritualization of the black experience.[31] Nor did all blacks support the celebrations or acknowledge the three holidays. Some objected to commemorating West Indies emancipation, since it compensated slaveholders as well as gave blacks their freedom. "Let us seek some day in which some enslaved black man in our land swelled beyond the measure of his chains and won liberty or death," exclaimed J. McCune Smith, a medical graduate of the University of Glasgow, who had, by 1856, become disaffected with the August First tradition. He nominated the date of Denmark Vesey's death in South Carolina in 1822, after his plot against slavery was uncovered, or the date of Nat Turner's rebellion in Virginia in 1831.[32] The Cleveland correspondent for the *Weekly Anglo-African* (New York) recommended Turner's birthday or the date of the downfall of slavery in Haiti.[33] Other blacks complained that the freedom holidays wasted time and money.[34] By the 1850's, however, the appeal of the freedom celebration had grown beyond the point that individual dissent could effectively challenge its continuity. Long before the observance of the abolition of slavery in the District of Columbia in 1862 or of a national emancipation day, it had become an institution in Northern free black life.[35]

In its development over fifty years certain features of the form of the freedom celebration remained constant, despite the improvisation and innovation that accompanied the commemoration of the holidays. That form had its roots in the black church's style of worship, using choirs, congregational singing, prayers, readings and sermons. In the freedom festivals the sermons became formal orations and the readings were taken as frequently from legislative acts related to the observance or from the Declaration of Independence as from the Bible.[36] Some of the church's music was sung as part of the celebration, as when one August First concluded with a sacred concert, but it was characteristic to perform new compositions especially written for the occasion or to sing "those soul-stirring freedom songs" that were familiar in anti-slavery circles.[37] The basic liturgical unit, which joined the spoken word, with the sung word, the word of prayer and the written word, remained much the same.[38]

Likewise, there was, from the first, an explicit rationale stated for the functions and meanings of the annual rituals which the freedom celebrations became. Unquestionably, the desire to "remember, with gratitude and rejoicing, the day of deliverance to so many of our long-abused race," as Frederick Douglass observed, was an initial purpose for keeping the freedom holiday.[39] The same logic governed the recommendation by Absalom Jones, the first black Episcopal priest in America, that "the day of the abolition of the slave trade in our country, be set apart in every year, as a day of publick thanksgiving."[40]

The celebrative nature of the freedom holiday did not obscure a second reason for public commemoration—to remember those who were still enslaved. "The cheerless condition of our southern brethren," as Joseph Sidney described it in 1809, sharply contrasted with the "day of festivity."[41] Because "our brethren in this land are in slavery still," Solomon R. Alexander announced at Boston in 1840, "we come…to show how we feel for [them], and to show our opposers that we feel how much their redemption depends on us."[42] Such a mood of empathy was not difficult to evoke. The audiences were full of those, the *Colored American* reported of Newark's observance in 1839, "who had once wore [sic] the galling yoke of slavery." On the platform that day were two who had escaped bondage, Samuel R. Ward and James W. C. Pennington.[43] When they, or other fugitives like Douglass, Jermain W. Loguen, William Wells Brown, or Lunsford Lane, spoke of slavery to black gatherings, they lent an experiential depth that no white abolitionist could manage. Hence, Loguen affected his Geneva, New York audience when he "revered the memory of a mother, who was black as she could cleverly be made," as did Douglass when he said, "While I am addressing you, four of my own dear sisters and one brother are enduring the frightful horrors of American slavery."[44]

These two complementary motives for the freedom celebrations drew on the countervailing feelings of joy and sorrow, of despair and hope. As Austin Steward stated in 1827, "we will rejoice, though sobs interrupt the songs of our rejoicing, and tears mingle in the cup we pledge to Freedom."[45] But there was still another reason to keep the "annual jubilee."[46] It was, to quote a committee of the Banneker Institute of Philadelphia in 1858, an occasion which "keeps before the minds of the American people *their* duty to the millions of slaves upon the Southern plantations, and, coming right in the wake of the 4th of July, gives abolitionists a fine opportunity to expose the hollow-heartedness of American liberty and Christianity, and to offset the buncombe speeches made upon our national anniversary."[47]

The culminating factor to keep alive the tradition of freedom celebrations was their function in expressing a feeling of community among free blacks. "They bring our people together," Douglass remarked in 1857, "and enable us to see and commune with each other to mutual profit."[48] The elaborate planning for the anniversaries already indicated a high degree of community spirit, but the orators appealed for ever greater unity and for common courses of action by free blacks. They admonished blacks to identify with each other, to use every advantage for social and intellectual improvement, to uphold high standards of conduct in order not to provoke charges of immorality or irresponsibility upon the race.[49] As a fourth reason, then, the freedom holidays imparted a sense of the collectivity, to which the speakers gave historical roots.

"It has always been, and still is, customary for nations to set apart some day, or days in the year," Amos Gerry Beman observed in 1839, "when their orators recount the glory of their ancesters." The Congregationalist pastor bemoaned the fact that blacks, "as a people," had "no such day to celebrate."[50] Ironically, in the same address Beman demonstrated how First of August functioned to fill the void. When he surveyed in rough outline an historical tradition for Africans in America, he was engaged, as were most orators before and after him, in the process of telling the black American story.

At Philadelphia's original celebration, Absalom Jones recognized that the meaning of the event being commemorated depended on an historical consciousness and the sense of belonging to a tradition. Citing the example of the people of Israel, whose Passover liturgy required every Jew to think of himself as having come forth from Egyptian bondage, Jones contended, "Let the history of the sufferings of our brethren and of their deliverance descend by this means to our children, to the remotest generations."[51] In spite of Jones' allusion to the Hebrew exodus, the freedom celebration's orators seldom directly compared the black and the Jewish experiences.[52] Their consciousness of belonging to a distinct people rather depended on two interlocking images, of Africa and of a racially based enslavement against which the struggle for freedom was fought in the New World.[53] Even Jones recognized as much when he admonished, "It becomes us, publickly and privately, to acknowledge, that an African slave, ready to perish, was our father or our grandfather."[54]

The idea of Africa as a single reality, and of a psychic tie with it as the source of black peoplehood, appeared in the earliest of the freedom addresses.[55] Peter Williams' oration of 1808 identified him as "A Descendent of Africa," even though he was born in this country and actually referred to himself later in the speech "as an American."[56] A year later Henry Sipkins spoke of Africa as "our parent-country," a phrase similar to William Hamilton's allusion in 1815, "the country of our parents."[57] To Russell Parrott, Africa was "the native land of our fathers" while to George Lawrence it was "the mother country."[58] Moreover, when black spokesmen on January First addressed their compatriots, they commonly employed designations that linked them with Africa.[59]

Besides this collective identity with Africa, the earliest speeches contained romanticized pictures of the continent prior to the coming of the white European. It was, according to Hamilton in 1809, "the country of our forefathers [which] might truly be called paradise."[60] The speech by Sipkins the same year depicted a state of perfection in portraying Africa. "It exhibits the most blissful regions," he declared, "productive of all the necessaries and even luxuries of life, almost independent of the arm of husbandry. Its innocent inhabitants regardless of, or unacquainted with the concerns of busy life, enjoyed with uninterrupted pleasure the state in which, by the beneficient hand of nature, they were placed."[61]

The Fifth of July celebrations continued to emphasize African origins and employed equivalent titles to refer to blacks. The term "Ethiopian" was freely heard at Cincinnati's commemoration in 1831, and the poetic phrase "Afric's sons" or "sons of Afric" occurred in two separate speeches in 1827.[62] One toast offered in 1828 paid tribute to "the fair daughters of Africa," while another saluted "Our Colored Brethren throughout the universe."[63]

While the theme of African identity dominated the oratory of the first two freedom holidays, the dialectic of "double-consciousness" still remained. The same speakers who ritualized African origins also reiterated the advantages of being born in America. As early as 1808 Peter Williams claimed the revolutionary heritage of the republic for himself, referring to "the sons of 76" whose "inspired voice" gave mankind the "noble sentiments" of the Declaration of Independence.[64] Because the "black bore his part" in two wars with the British, Russell Parrott did not hesitate to commend "the pure love of country."[65] On the one hand, George Lawrence complained, "Many are the miseries of our exiled race in this land," but on the other, he praised "the land in which we live" because it gave the "opportunity rapidly to advance the prosperity of liberty."[66]

Up to the time of West Indies emancipation, therefore, the characteristic form of black "double-consciousness" in the freedom celebration was an explicit "Afri- American" identity, as New Haven's Peter Osborne termed it.[67] In the oratory of August First the dialectic shifted in emphasis from African origins to the crucible of American slavery. The speakers paid less attention to the people's beginnings and made fewer references to an African past. They concentrated instead on how American slavery originated and on the struggle for freedom in America. They demonstrated that as a people they were committed to the liberation of blacks in slavery. In the process they affirmed that they had American as well as African roots, that the full meaning of the black saga, encompassing both sides of the dialectic, summed up the cultural transformation of Africans into "colored Americans."[68]

The corporate consciousness among Northern free blacks, which all the freedom celebrations assumed as well as fostered, expressed itself assertively in the texts of the oratory of all three holidays of black freedom. The addresses, taken as a whole, confronted and challenged white racial ideologies in religious and political guises. The freedom orators found that it was necessary from the first to oppose the "reproach," as Adam Carman put it in 1811, that branded blacks "an inferior species of human beings," who were "incapable of reason and virtue."[69] In a continuing polemic against white racism the connection to an African past had, they discovered, strategic uses as well as deep resonances of collective meaning. On January First and July Fifth, they called upon the glories of the ancient Egyptian and Ethiopian civilizations to disprove the charge, to quote William Hamilton in 1809, "that we have not produced any poets, mathematicians, or any to excel in any science whatever."[70] With obvious pride, Owen B. Nickens told an Ohio audience that Africa was "the birthplace and cradle of the arts and sciences."[71] Likewise, William Miller contended that the Bible and classical history confirmed each other in acclaiming "that the first learned nation, was a nation of blacks."[72]

The major difficulty with proclaiming the greatness of the African past was the necessity to explain the fall of the race from its originally elevated status in learning and culture. That problem, and the need to refute the religious pro-slavery outlook which pervaded white American theology and church life,[73] required a consideration of the ultimate cause of black bondage, that led, in turn, to the issue of theodicy—how to reconcile the suffering of Africans with a belief in divine benevolence. The orators did not turn away from the issue.

"Ye peaceful people, what have ye done, to merit this?" Russell Parrot burst forth with the agonizing question.[74] Portraying "the middle passage," black Baptist Nathaniel Paul asked the ocean and the "winds" why they aided the process of enslavement. Then he inquired how God could "look on with the calm indifference of an unconcerned spectator" when "a portion" of his "own creatures" were "reduced to a state of mere vassalage and misery."[75] The fact of black suffering prompted William Miller to lament his existence like the biblical figure, Job, by cursing the day of his birth and the time of conception. Yet, among all freedom orators, only Miller was willing to risk saying that God was punishing Africans for their sins. "Our progenitors, after arriving at the plentitude of prosperity, and the pinnacle of national greatness," he explained, "forgot Jehovah's benignity, and dared to defy his wrath." Applying a literalist view to the prophecies of Isaiah concerning Egypt and Ethiopia, he found them "astonishingly fulfilled, even to a very late period, upon the unhappy Africans."[76] By contrast, all other speakers maintained the tensions within the problem of theodicy, confirming the divine intention for and origination of human freedom while reflecting, without a final explanation, upon the mystery of evil and the destructive potential in human nature.

The consensus in the oratory supported a belief that the nature and will of God was benevolent and that justice would ultimately reign in history. "The fugitive blacksmith," James W. C. Pennington claimed "God's agency in our behalf," even as Frederick Douglass described "the spirit of God commanding the devil of slavery to go out of the British West Indies."[77] They shared the sentiment of Presbyterian preacher and editor, Samuel Cornish, who confessed "the cause of the oppressed" as "the cause of God."[78] It was God's nature, Absalom Jones preached, to intervene "in behalf of oppressed and distressed nations, as the deliverer of the innocent, and of those who call upon his name." Nonetheless, Jones confided to his Philadelphia congregation, "it has always been a mystery, why the impartial Father of the human race should have permitted the transportation of so many millions of our fellow creatures to this country, to endure all the miseries of slavery."[79]

Although there were a few blacks who thought that God's designs might encompass slavery as a means to christianize, civilize and restore modern Africa to her original greatness,[80] the more basic tendency in the oratory left the final explanation for the oppression of blacks unresolved in the mystery of divine providence. Holding on to the hope for ultimate vindication while disavowing any "attempt to justify the cruelty, the avarice and injustice of those who dragged our forefathers from their native land," Joseph Sidney told his audience, "God's ways are not as our ways, nor his thoughts as our thoughts."[81] Any other alternative was unthinkable. To denounce God seemed to surrender the transcendent basis for moral judgment, and to sanction slavery as divinely ordained required that blacks agree with the "blasphemy" of their "enemies" who maintained, William Hamilton explained, "*God hath made [us] to be slaves.*"[82]

When the orators sought to explain the human cause of slavery, they had less difficulty. Some said it lay in "the desire of gain" or in the "heart of avarice."[83] Others, like Russell Parrott, pondered the connection between "the commencement of the sufferings of the Africans, and the discovery of the new world; which, to one portion of the human family, has afforded such advantages, to the unfortunate African, has been the source of the greatest misery."[84] Anticipating the theme of his Famous "Address to the Slaves" four years later, Henry Highland Garnet told the Troy, New York celebration of 1839, "Let the time come when the traders in human flesh cannot fill their pockets with the wages of those who have reaped down their fields, and the system will fly as upon the wings of the wind."[85] An inability to account for the divine purpose in slavery, thus, did not relieve "the oppressors" who were "culpable for their savage treatment to the unoffending Africans," as William Miller stated it.[86]

The final mystery was, therefore, less theodicy than anthropodicy, less the inexplicable character of God than of man, and more particularly of white Europeans and Americans who were "destitute of those generous and noble sentiments that dictated our emancipation," as Russell Parrott charged.[87] In the end, however, William Hamilton could not even fathom the human source of the scourge of slavery. "We stand confounded," he remarked in 1809, "that there could be found any...so lost to their nature and the fine feelings of man, as to commit, unprovokedly commit, such acts of cruelty on an unoffending part of the human family." Six years later, recounting the barbarities associated with slavery, he concluded sarcastically, "If these are some of the marks of superiority, may heaven in mercy always keep us inferior."[88]

The problems of theodicy and anthropodicy had a counterpart in the conflict over how to reconcile a commitment to democratic ideals as found in American republicanism with the reality of slavery and racial prejudice. Early and often in the freedom celebrations, orators invoked the Declaration of Independence and its principles of freedom and equality in a valiant attempt to salvage the democratic faith from proslavery, racist perversion.

The great American contradiction as "a slaveholding Republic,"[89] black spokesmen made clear, did not come after the beginning of the nation. It predated, coexisted with and endured after the revolution. "While the siren song of liberty and equality was sang [sic] through the land," William Hamilton observed in 1809, "the groans of the oppressed made the music very discordant, and…America's fame was very much tarnished thereby."[90] On July Fifth, 1827 Nathaniel Paul mused over the "palpable inconsistencies" of America. He queried how slavery could "ever have found a place in this otherwise happiest of all countries—a country, the very soil which is said to be consecrated to liberty, and its fruits the equal rights of man."[91]

The paradox from the beginning of the nation was nowhere more exposed than in the career of the author of the Declaration of Independence, Thomas Jefferson. In his speech of January 1, 1814, Joseph Sidney, a federalist in politics, inquired "Is the great idol of democracy our friend?" Responding negatively, Sidney accused the "Virginian Junto" of disrespecting "the rights of our African brethren; several hundreds of whom he keeps as slaves on his plantation."[92] In a New York Abolitian Day address, a year after Jefferson's death, William Hamilton described him as "an ambidexter philosopher." Recalling the ex-president's comments about black inferiority in his *Notes on Virginia*, Hamilton asked how it was possible to reconcile the egalitarian claims of the Declaration with an argument "that *one class of men are not equal to another.*" Then, he went on, "Suppose that such philosopher should keep around him a number of slaves, and at the *same* time should tell you, that God hath no attribute to favour the cause of the master in case of an insurrection of the slaves."[93] The implication was clear. Jefferson's dilemma was, in microcosm, the national contradiction.

Not surprisingly, many blacks rejected the mainstream tradition of patriotic nationalism which regularly marked the celebration of the Fourth of July. It would be, David Nickens argued in 1832, "a mock pretence" and "a want of sound understanding" for blacks to acknowledge a day which "causes millions of our sable race to groan under the galling yoke of bondage."[94] On August First in Newark, seven years later, James W. C. Pennington agreed. "We cannot rejoice in an event in which our case is made an exception;" he proclaimed, and "we cannot exult in what is termed the blessing of the nation, when this blessing is positively denied to one sixth of the community."[95]

To reject "all the unmeaning twaddle of Fourth of July orators,"[96] in William Watkins' words, did not mean that Northern free blacks had conceded to those who denied them American citizenship or ignored their plight and the contradiction which is posed to the democratic dream. They did dissent, radically, from a version of the nation which, through racism, had all but destroyed that dream, but they simultaneously and fervently affirmed an alternative vision of America. In it, new heroes replaced the founding fathers. Praising the charter members of the New York State Manumission Society, William Hamilton advised his listeners that "the names of WASHINGTON and JEFFERSON should not be pronounced *in the hearing of your children* until they learned who were the true defenders of American liberty."[97]

The black counter-version of the national story, however, included more than white heroes. Referring to Crispus Attucks, August First speakers noted "that the first blood spilt for independence in this country was by a colored man."[98] The "fathers" in the black story were still the descendants of African slaves, but the emphasis was on the struggle in America, instead of the people's beginnings. They were black patriots in America's wars and those who resisted bondage, like Nat Turner, the insurrectionists in New York in 1741 and the fugitives whose escapes attested that they belonged to "a people determined to be free."[99]

As a vocal and determined minority, Northern free blacks did not choose to be known as "colored Americans" from a grovelling mentality or self-deprecating need for white acceptance.[100] That designation, which replaced the more self-conscious African terminology by the 1830's, was a bold challenge thrown against a society which had cynically accommodated itself to human bondage and created a social system of racial caste. The black declaration of American faith was not a request "for sympathy" or "favors at the hand of [the] country," but a pressing "demand" for essential "rights," which, because they were given "by the Creator," as William Wells Brown contended in 1858, "they cannot be taken from us by any Congress or Legislature."[101]

The new "colored American" form of "double-consciousness" required an identity with "the millions...quivering in the rice swamp, or the cottonfield, beneath the oppressor's lash," as William Watkins put it, "for we are one people."[102] It encompassed the defiance of Charles L. Remond, who told the New Bedford August First observance in 1858, "that he was prepared to spit upon the [Dred Scott] decision of Judge [Roger D.] Taney," and that he was willing to be branded "a traitor to the government and the Union, so long as his rights were denied him for no fault of his."[103] It provoked the determination by free blacks, in the words of a committee in New York on August 1, 1836, to "fill every continent and island with the story of the WRONGS done to our brethren, by the *Christian, church-going, psalm-singing, long prayer-making, lynching, tar and feathering, man-roasting, human-flesh-dealers of America!*" and "to *preach* the DECLARATION OF INDEPENDENCE, till it begins to be put in PRACTICE."[104] Finally, it included a consistent opposition to colonization and emigration because blacks were, as Abraham D. Shadd stated it in 1840, "Americans in common with others." Peter Osborne agreed, when he told a July Fifth assembly, "this is our native country" and "our forefathers planted trees" in it "for us, and we intend to stay and eat the fruit."[105]

From the same perspective, George Downing spoke against the emigrationist sentiment among blacks following the Dred Scott decision. "We have," he confirmed, "a hopeful, and I will add, an inseparable providential identity with this country; with its institutions—with the ideas connected with its formation, which were the uplifting of man—universal brotherhood." Then, formulating a remarkable statement of national mission with reference to the black experience, Downing declared: "We, the descendents, to a great extent, of those most unjustly held in bondage [have become] the most fit subjects to be selected to work out in perfection the realization of a great principle, *the fraternal unity of man.* THIS IS AMERICA'S MISSION. We suffer in the interim; but we can, as is abundantly proven, endure. We can and do hope."[106]

With Downing's assertion the last step in the evolution of antebellum free black "double-consciousness" had been taken. The stage was set, in Frederick Douglass' words in the summer of 1861, "for an event which shall be for us, and the world, more than West Indies Emancipation; and that would be the emancipation of every slave in America."[107] In this sense the freedom celebrations had all along been a "harbinger of American emancipation," as William C. Nell expressed it in 1840—a ritualization of free blacks of their own freedom, however proscribed, and a dramatic expression of hope for "a national jubilee." "America will yet become," Nell told his Boston audience, "what she is now on paper—'The asylum for the free and home of the oppressed.'"[108]

Identifying both with the slave and with what the New England convention of August 1, 1859 called "our own loved but guilty land," Northern free blacks were prepared to see the forthcoming Civil War, with all its ambiguities, in terms of the struggle for black freedom.[109] The same points of contact—with the emancipated slave and with the democratic faith for which they had assumed a unique custody—carried them into the era of Reconstruction with the conviction that being black was a distinctive way of being American.

NOTES

The author acknowledges the support of the University of Denver and the National Endowment for the Humanities which aided the research for this study.

1. W.E.B. DuBois, *The Souls of Black Folk in Three Negro Classics*, intro. by John Hope Franklin (New York, 1965), 215. The passage originally appeared in "Strivings of the Negro People," *Atlantic Monthly*, 80 (1897), 194–95.

2. John Hope Franklin, *From Slavery to Freedom*, 3d. ed. (New York, 1967), 220. See also Leon F. Litwack, *North of Slavery: The Negro in the Free States 1790–1860* (Chicago, 1961).

3. Floyd J. Miller, *The Search for a Black Nationality: Black Colonization and Emigration 1787–1863* (Urbana, Ill., 1975).

4. Leonard I. Sweet, *Black Images of America 1784–1870* (New York, 1976), 5–6, 89, 147. See also Jane H. and William H. Pease, *They Who Would Be Free: Blacks' Search for freedom, 1830–1861* (New York, 1974).

5. Paul C. Nagel, *This Sacred Trust: American Nationality 1798–1889* (New York, 1971), xii. This suggestive study, however, makes no references to blacks.

6. William H. Wiggins has done an impressive study of the folk tradition of emancipation celebrations beginning in 1863. See his dissertation, "'Free at Last!': A study of Afro-American Emancipation Day Celebrations" (University of Indiana, 1974) and his essay, "'Lift Every Voice': A Study of Afro-American Emancipation Celebrations," in Roger D. Abrahams and John F. Szwed, eds., *Discovering Afro-America* (Leiden, 1975), 46–57.

7. In 1810 there were 9,823 blacks in New York City and 40,350 the state. The same census reported 23,287 blacks in Pennsylvania with the largest concentration in Philadelphia. Leo H. Hirsch, "The Negro and New York, 1783–1865," *Journal of Negro History*, 16 (1931), 415; *Negro Population in the United States 1790–1915* (New York, 1968 reprint-ed.), 45.

The following black and abolitionist newspapers and periodicals were consulted in this study: *Aliened American* (Cleveland); *Anglo-African Magazine* (New York City); *Anti-Slavery Bugle* (Salem, Ohio); *Colored American* (New York City): *Christian Recorder* (Philadelphia); *Douglass' Monthly* (Rochester, New York); *Emancipator* (New York City); *Frederick Douglass' Paper* (Rochester, New York); *Freedom's Journal* (New York City); *Genius of Universal Enamcipation* (various places of publication); *Herald of Freedom* (Concord, New Hampshire); *The Liberator* (Boston): *Mirror of the Times* (San Francisco); *National Anti-Slavery Standard* (New York City) *National Enquirer and Constitutional Advocate of Universal Liberty* (Philadelphia); *National Principia* (New York City); *National Reformer* (Philadelphia); *Northern Star and Freeman's Advocate* (Albany, New York): *Palladium of Liberty* (Columbus, Ohio); *Pennsylvania Freeman* (Philadelphia); *Provincial Freeman* (Toronto): *Repository of Religion and Literaure, And of Science and Art* (Indianapolis and Baltimore); *Rights of All* (New York City): *Union Missionary* (New York City); *Union Missionary Herald* (Hartford, Connecticut); *Weekly Anglo-African* (New York).

8. The Program was printed in Peter Williams, Jr., *An Oration on the Abolition of the Slave Trade: Delivered in the African Church, in the City of New-York, January 1, 1808* (New York, 1808), unnumbered p. 3. Daniel Coker listed a sermon by

"Rev. James Varrick" on this occasion, but without indicating its published status. See *A Dialogue Between a Virginian and an African Minister* (Balitmore, 1810), 40–42 as reprinted in Dorothy Porter, ed., *Negro Protest Pamphlets* (New York, 1969).

9. Benjamin Quarles erroneously states that New York Negroes ceased the celebrations within three years. See *Black Abolitionists* (New York, 1969), 119. From the thirteen celebrations in New York and six in Philadelphia, for which there is primary evidence, fifteen orations have survived in published form.

10. Thomas Gray, *A Sermon Delivery in Boston Before the African Society. On the 14th day of July, 1818: The Anniversary of the Abolition of the Slave Trade* (Boston, 1818), unnumbered p. 2. Orations by four other white guest speakers, all area clergymen (Jedidiah Morse, Paul Dean, Thaddeus M. Harris, John S. J. Gardiner), survive from the Boston celebrations of 1808, 1810, 1819, 1822. All were sponsored by the African Society of Boston, a black organization formed in 1796. See Dorothy Porter, ed., *Early Negro Writing 1760–1837* (Boston, 1971), 9–12.

11. *Black Abolitionists*, 119.

12. For a retrospective account of Boston's July 145th celebrations, see *The Liberator*, August 13, 1847. There are in the Boston Public Library five broadsides which were published as satirical attacks by whites from 1816 through 1825 (the latter date is an estimate).

13. By statute the state legislature of New York began to abolish slavery by gradual means in 1799. After July 4, 1827 no other persons could be born into or subjected to slavery who were not finishing out defined terms of servitude. It was still legal for non-resident slaveholders to bring their chattels into the state for periods not exceeding nine months. Arthur Zilversmit, *The First Emancipation: The Abolition of Slavery in the North* (Chicago, 1967), 180–82, 208–14.

14. *Freedom's Journal*, April 20, June 22, 29, July 6, 13, 20, 27, 1827.

15. Samuel Cornish and John Russwurn, editors of the first black newspaper, opposed parades, as did the national Negro convention of 1834. *Ibid.*, April 27, June 29, July 13, 1827; July 18, August 1, 15, 1828; *Minutes of the Fourth Annual Convention, for the Improvement of the Free People of Colour, in the United States, Held by Adjournments in the Asbury Church. New-York, From the 2d to the 12th of June Inclusive* (New York, 1834), 14, as reprinted in Howard Holman Bell, ed., *Minutes of the Proceedings of the National Negro Conventions 1830–1864* (New York, 1969).

16. *Freedom's Journal*, July 27, 1827. Steward gave the locations as "Johnson's Square" in his autobiography, which contains a full text of his speech: *Twenty-two Years a Slave, and Forty Years a Freeman* (Rochester, 1857), 150–63.

17. Quarles claims that the emancipation day observance "lasted only three or four years," and that "it was resurected for a single time" in 1856 in Auburn, New York. (*Frederick Douglass' Paper*, July 18, 1856 as cited in *Black Abolitionists*, 121, 274.) I have no evidence of celebrations between 1834 and 1856, although William C. Nell wrote in 1859 of the continued recognition of July Fifth while acknowledging that it was a declining practice "for many reasons." That same year William J. Watkins delivered the oration for festivities at Jefferson, New York which included the firing of 100 guns and the performance of the Mannsville Saze Horn Band. *Weekly Anglo-African*, June 9, 23, 30, 1859.

18. The originasl abolition law of August 1, 1834 retained an apprenticeship system which functioned as another kind of forced labor until finally outlawed by Parliament, effective August 1, 1838. Some black celebrations dated from the former; others from the latter date. The figure 670,000 revises the older general estimate of 800,000 and is based on recent scholarship. Stiv Jakobsson, *Am I Not a Man and a Brother? British Missions and the Abolition of the Slave Trade and Slavery in West Africa and the West Indies 1786–1838* (Uppsala, 1972), 511–14, 572–76; W. L. Mathieson, *British Slavery and Its Abolition* (London, 1926), 230ff., 243–46, 300–06.

19. The American Anti-Slavery Society recommended that all abolitionists keep August First. *Liberator*, July 18, 1835.

20. *Ibid.*, August 11, 1843.

21. This number does not include more than a hundred other celebrations during the same period which were organized by white abolitionists and which featured racially mixed audiences and black speakers on the program.

22. *Liberator, Sept. 1, 1851; Aug. 20, 1852; Aug. 26, 1859; Aug. 23, 1861; Frederick Douglass' Paper, Aug. 11, 1854; Provincial Freeman, Aug. 5, 19, 1854; Aug. 2, 1855; Aug. 15, 1857; National Anti-Slavery Standard, Aug. 20, 1853; Aug. 19, 1854; Aug. 13, 1859; Weekly Anglo-African, Oct. 15, 1859.*

23. Some of the larger crowds were at New Bedford, Mass.: 7000 in 1855; Staten Island, N.Y.: 500 in 1855; Urbana, Ohio; 5000 in 1856; Canadaigua, N.Y.: 4000 in 1847.

24. For some of the names of military companies and bands, see *Liberator*, Sept. 1, 1843; Aug. 7, 1846; Aug. 15, 1851; Aug. 19, 1853; *Frederick*

Douglass' Paper, Aug. 12, 1853; *National Anti-Slavery Standard*, Aug. 11, 1855.

25. *Liberator*, Aug. 14, 1840.

26. *Ibid.*, Aug. 10, 1838; July 26, 1839; *Colored American*, Aug. 31, 1839; Aug. 15, 1840; *National Enquirer and Constitutional Advocate of Universal Liberty*, Aug. 31, 1836; *Pennsylvania Freeman*, Aug. 15, 1839.

27. *Liberator*, Aug. 10, 1838; July 27, 1855; *Emancipator*, Aug. 11, 1836; *Frederick Douglass' Paper*, Aug. 11, 1854.

28. *National Anti-Slavery* Aug. 20, 1846; Aug. 13, 1859; *Frederick Douglass' Paper*, Aug. 21, 1851; Aug. 5, 1853; Sept. 28, 1855; *Liberator*, Aug. 26, 1859.

29. *Douglass' Monthly*, 2 (1859), 113; 3 (1860), 323.

30. *Liberator*, Aug. 15, 1851.

31. In a few instances Northern free blacks turned traditional Independence Day and Thanksgiving observances into protests against the inconsistencies of white America. In at least one other state, New Jersey, they kept state emancipation day (September 5) though with what frequency it is not clear. In 1825 blacks in Baltimore commemorated Haytien independence. Two new celebrations evolved in the 1850's. One in Massachusetts on March 15 beginning in 1858 honored Crispus Attucks' death in the pre-Revolutionary Boston Massacre. After 1851 in and around Syracuse, N.Y. Jerry Rescue Day was an anniversary in October, marking the successful revolt to free, by force, a fugitive slave. Northern blacks also conducted memorial services for and sometimes kept the anniversaries of the deaths of prominent leaders of the race and anti-slavery heroes. Public ceremonies of certain black Masonic orders performed some of the same functions as the freedom celebration.

32. *Frederick Douglass' Paper*, Aug. 16, 1856 as quoted in Quaries, *Black Abolitionists*, 128, 275. Even though Smith had earlier participated in August First celebrations, he argued, "we, the colored people, should do something ourselves worthy of celebration, and not be everlastingly celebrating the deeds of a race by which we are despised." Frederick Douglass answered him by citing examples of black resistance as having forced, through "outbreaks and violence," the end of slavery in the West Indies. Philip S. Foner, ed., *The Life and Writings of Frederick Douglass* (New York, n.d.), II, 434, 439. Martin Delany, a leading black emigrationist, made the same point at a First of August observance in Liberia in 1859. See *Liberia Herald*, as quoted in *Weekly Anglo-African*, Oct. 15, 1859.

33. *Weekly Anglo-African*, Aug. 6, 1859.

34. See Andrew B. Slater's complaint in *Frederick Douglass' Paper*, Apr. 8, 1853.

35. *National Principia*, May 27, 1862; *Douglass' Monthly*, 5 (1862) 676, 769–70, 796–97; *Christian Recorder*, Jan. 3, 17, 1863; James M. McPherson, *The Negro's Civil War* (New York, 1965), 48–52.

36. For examples of the order of service for freedom celebrations, see William Hamilton, *An Address to the New York African Society, for Mutual Relief, Delivered in the Universalist Church, January 2, 1809* (New York, 1809) in Porter, *Early Negro Writing*, 33–34; Adam Carman, *An Oration Delivered at the Fourth Anniversary of the Abolition of the Slave Trade, in the Methodist Episcopal Church, in Second-Street, New York, January 1, 1811 (New York, 1811)*, 4–5; Joseph Sidney, *An Oration, Commemorative of the Abolition of the Slave Trade in the United States; Delivered in the African Asbury Church, in the City of New-York, on the First of January, 1814* (New York, 1814), 16; Russel Parrott, *An Oration of the Abolition of the Slave Trade, Delivered on First of January, 1812 at the African Church of St. Thomas* (Philadelphia, 1812), unnumbered p. 1; *Liberator*, Aug. 20, 1834; July 27, 1855; *National Anti-Slavery Standard*, Aug. 1, 1844; *Frederick Douglass' Paper*, Aug. 12, 1853; *Weekly Anglo-African*, July 30, 1859.

37. Examples of texts of songs are in Carman, *Oration* (1811), 21–23; Sidney, *Oration* (1814), 13–15; Absalom Jones, *A Thanksgiving Sermon, Preached January 1, 1808, In St. Thomas', or the African Episcopal Church, Philadelphia: On Account of the Abolition of the African Slave Trade, On That Day, by the Congress of the United States* (Philadelphia, 1808), 5–6; Nathaniel Paul, *An Address, Delivered on the Celebration of the Abolition of Slavery, In the State of New-York, July 5, 1827* (Albany, 1827) in Porter, Negro Protest Pamphlets, 24; Liberator, Nov. 21, 1835; July 26, Aug. 16, 23, 1839; July 22, Aug. 19, 1842; Aug. 4, 11, 1843; Aug. 1, 8, 1845; Aug. 19, 1853; Aug. 19, 1859; *National Anti-Slavery Standard*, Sept. 11, 1851; Aug. 13, 1853; *Weekly Anglo-African*, Aug. 6, 1859; June 2, 1860; *Colored American*, Aug. 5, 1837; Aug. 18, 25, 1838; Aug. 24, Sept. 28, 1839; *Frederick Douglass' Paper*, Aug. 10, 1855.

38. In a remarkable address before the American Academy of Religion in Atlanta in 1971, Vincent Harding contended: "We are a people of the spoken word, we are a people of the danced word, we are a people of the sung word, we are a people of the musical word." From a tape-recording of "The Afro-American Experience as a Source of Salvation History."

39. *National Anti-Slavery Standard*, Aug. 19, 1847.

40. Jones, *Sermon*, 19.

41. *Sidney, An Oration Commemorative of the Abolition of the Slave Trade in the United States; Delivered before the Wilberforce Philanthropic Association, in the City of New York on the Second of January, 1809* (New York, 1809) in Porter, *Early Negro Writing*, 358.

42. *Liberator*, Aug. 24, 1839.

43. *Colored American*, Aug. 24, 1839.

44. *Geneva Courier in Frederick Douglass' Paper*, Aug. 21, 1851; Foner, *Works of Douglass*, I, 328; *Liberator*, Aug. 8, 1845.

45. Sidney, *Oration* (1809) in Porter, *Early Negro Writing*, 358; Steward, *Twenty-two Years a Slave*, 157.

46. Sidney, *Oration* (1814), 5.

47. American Negro Historical Society Papers, Leon Gardiner Collection, Pennsylvania Historical Society, file 5G, folio 9.

48. Foner, *Works of Douglass*, II, 433.

49. Jones, *Sermon*, 17–18; Williams, *Oration* (1808), 26; Steward, *Twenty-two Years a Slave*, 158–61; Paul, *Address (1827), 18–21 and An Address, Delivered at Troy, on the Celebration of the Abolition of Slavery, in the State of New-York, July 6, 1829.— Second Anniversary* (Albany, 1829), 13–16; Amos Gerry Beman, *Address Delivered at the Celebration of the West India Emancipation, in Davis' Hall, Hudson, N.Y., on Monday; August 2, 1847* (Troy, 1847), 15–16; *Colred American*, Aug. 22, Sept. 26, Oct. 3, 1840. The emphasis on morality and self-improvement, common to free black literature of the period, leads Frederick Cooper to make an erroneous distinction between abolitionism and civil rights on the one hand, and social uplift on the other. He fails to see that in a racist society, self-improvement and success can be one form of asserting equal rights. See "Elevating the Race: The Social Thought of Black Leaders, 1827–50," *American Quarterly*, 24 (1972), 604–25 and Sweet's caveat in *Black Images*, 129–30, n. 12 (which is in contrast with comments on 108).

50. *Colored American*, Sept. 26, 1840; James W.C. Pennington, *An Address Delivered at Newark, N.J. at the First Anniversary of West India Emancipation, August 1, 1839* (Newark, 1839), 9.

51. Jones, *Sermon*, 19–20; Paul, *Address* (1827), 3.

52. Other direct allusions, besides Jones' references, are in *Liberator*, Aug. 11, 1843; *Frederick Douglass' Paper*, Aug. 4, 1854; Steward, *Twenty-two Years a Slave*, 156–57.

53. On Africa as "a religious image," see Charles H. Long, "Perspectives for a Study of Afro-American Religion in the United States," *History of Religions*, 11 (1971), 56–58.

54. Jones, *Sermon*, 17.

55. On the tendency to view the African continent as a unitary image, see Sterling Stuckey, *The Ideological Origins of Black Nationalism* (Boston 1972), 1–2, n. 1.

56. Williams, *Oration* (1808), 1, 21; Parrott, *Oration* (1812), 3; Sipkins, *An Oration on the Abolition of the Slave Trade; Delivered in the African Church, in the City of New York, January 2, 1809* (New York, 1809) in Porter, *Early Negro Writing*, 365.

57. Williams, *Oration* (1808), 9; Sipkins, Oration *Oration* (1809) in Porter, *Early Negro Writing*, 367; William Hamilton, *An Oration, on the Abolition of the Slave Trade, Delivered in the Episcopal Asbury African Church, in Elizabeth-St. New York, January 2, 1815* (New York, 1815) in Porter, *Early Negro Writing*, 391.

58. Parrott, Oration (1812), 6; George Lawrence, *Oration on the Abolition of the Slave Trade, Delivered on the First Day of January, 1813, in the African Methodist Episcopal Church* (New York, 813) in Porter, *Early Negro Writing*, 375–76.

59. Examples are "Africans," "beloved Africans," "descendants of Africans," "descendants of African forefathers," "African brethren," and "natives of Africa. "William Miller, *A Sermon on the Abolition of the Slave Trade: Delivered in the African Church, New-York, on the First of January, 1810* (New York, 1810), 3; Russell Parrott, *An Oration of the Abolition of the Slave Trade. Delivered on the First of January, 1814. At the African Church of St. Thomas* (Philadelphia, 1814) in Porter, *Early Negro Writing*, 384; Sidney, *Oration* (1814), 6; Lawrence, *Oration* (1813) and Sipkins, *Oration* (1809) in Porter, *Early Negro Writing*, 371, 375, 380; Williams, *Oration* (1808), 11, 18–19; Jones, *Sermon*, 15.

60. Hamilton, *Address* (1809) in Porter, *Early Negro Writing*, 35.

61. Williams, *Oration* (1808), 12–13; Sipkins, *Oration* (1809); Lawrence, *Oration* (1813); Parrott, *Oration* (1814) and Hamilton. *Oration* (1815) in Porter, *Early Negro Writing*, 367–68, 376–77, 384ff., 391–94.

62. *Liberator*, July 30, 1831; Paul, *Address* (1827), 21; William Hamilton, *An Oration Delivered in the African Zion Church, on the Fourth of July, 1827, in Commemoration of the Abolition of Domestic Slavery in This State* (New York, 1827), 5.

63. *Liberator*, July 30, 1831; *Freedom's Journal*, July 11, 1828.

64. Williams, *Oration* (1808), 21; Hamilton, *Address (1809) in Porter, Early Negro Writing*, 39; Russell Parrott, *An Address, on the Abolition of the Slave-Trade, Delivered before the Different African Benevolent Societies. On the 1st of January, 1816*

(Philadelphia, 1816), 12.

65. Parrott, *Oration* (1814) in Porter, *Early Negro Writing*, 390.

66. Lawrence, *Oration* (1813) in Porter, *Early Negro Writing*, 379, 382.

67. *Liberator*, Dec. 1, 1832.

68. Charles Long has contended that "the history of the names by which [the black] community has chosen to call itself...can be seen as a religious history." See "Perspectives for a Study of Afro-American Religion in the United States," 60–61.

69. Carman, *Oration* (1811), 18.

70. Hamilton, *Address* (1809), in Porter, *Early Negro Writing*, 36.

71. *Liberator*, July 30, 1831.

72. Miller, *Sermon*, 4.

73. H. Shelton's Smith's study of southern religion and race is set in a national context, especially in the antebellum era. See *In His Image, But... Racism in Southern Religion* 1790–1910 (Durham, 1972).

74. Parrott, *Oration* (1812), 6.

75. Paul, *Address* (1827), 10–11.

76. Miller, *Sermon*, 5–6. Timothy Smith treats Miller as a representative black preacher who dealt with the problem of suffering and evil, but he neglects to notice the implications of Miller's literalism for attributing collective guilt upon Africans. See "Slavery and Theology in the Emergence of Black Christian Consciousness in Nineteenth-Century America," *Church History*, 41 (1972), 501–02.

77. James W. C. Pennington, *The Reasonableness of the Abolition of Slavery at the South, a Legitimate Inference from the Success of British Emancipation. An Address, Delivered at Hartford, Conn., on the First of August, 1856* (Hartford, 1856), 14, 16, 18; Foner, *Works of Douglass*, II, 27; Williams, *Oration* (1808), 11, 20; Miller, *Sermon*, 3; Paul, *Address* (1827), 3, 5, 8, 18; Paul, *Address* (1829), 4; Sidney, *Oration* (1814), 6, 9; Parrott *Oration* (1812), 7; Sidney, *Oration* (1809), Sipkins, *Oration* (1809), Lawrence, *Oration* (1813), and Parrott, *Oration* (1814) in Porter, *Early Negro Writing*, 362–63, 366, 372, 375, 387; *Frederick Douglass' Paper*, August 5, 1853. See also Sweet, *Black Images of America*, 70–71.

78. *Colored American*, July 28, Aug. 11, 1838; *Frederick Douglass' Paper*, Aug. 18, 1854.

79. Jones, *Sermon*, 10–11, 18.

80. *Liberator*, July 30, 1831; Miller, *Sermon*, 13–14; Parrott, *Oration* (1812), 10; Parrott, *Oration* (1814) in Porter, *Early Negro Writing*, 390; Paul, *Address* (1826), 22.

81. Sidney, *Oration* (1814), 11.

82. Hamilton, *Oration* 11; Paul, *Address* (1829), 7, 11.

83. Williams, *Oration* (1808), 12, 17; Sipkins, *Oration* (1809) and Hamilton, *Oration* (1815) in Porter, *Early Negro Writing*, 367, 395; Foner, *Works of Douglass*, II, 431–32.

84. Parrott, *Oration* (1814) in Porter, *Early Negro Writing*, 384.

85. Henry Highland Garnet, "An Oration Delivered Before the Citizens of Troy, N.Y. *On the First of August*, 1839," *National Reformer*, 1 (Oct., 1839), 156. Garnet's "Address to the United States of America" in 1843 is available in several reprint editions and anthologies like Ruth Miller, ed. *Black American Literature 1760–Present* (Beverly Hills, Cal., 1971), 129–37.

86. Miller, *Sermon*, 8.

87. Parrott, *Address* (1816), 3.

88. Hamilton, *Address* (1809) and *Oration* (1815) in Porter, *Early Negro Writing*, 35, 398.

89. Foner, *Works of Douglass*, I, 324. See August Meier, "Frederick Douglass' Vision of America: A Case-Study in Nineteenth-Century Negro Protest," in Harold M. Hyman and Leonard W. Levy, eds., *Freedom and Reform*(New York, 1967), 127–48.

90. Hamilton, *Address* (1809) in Porter, *Early Negro Writing*, 39.

91. Paul, *Address* (1827), 11–12.

92. Sidney, *Oration* (1814), 7–8; Sidney, *Oration* (1809) and Hamilton, *Oration* (1815) in Porter, *Early Negro Writing*, 361–62, 399.

93. Hamilton, *Oration* (1827), 12.

94. *Liberator*, Aug. 11, 1832.

95. Pennington, *Address* (1839), 10; Foner, *Works of Douglass*, II, 181–205; *Liberator*, Dec. 1, 1832.

96. *Frederick Douglass' Paper*. Aug. 10. 1855.

97. Hamilton, *Oration* (1827), 8.

98. *Liberator* as quoted in *Colored American*. Aug. 31, 1839.

99. *Liberator*, Aug. 14, 1840; Aug. 13, 1858; *Frederick Douglass' Paper*, Aug. 26, 1853; *Weekly Anglo-African*, Aug. 20, 1859; Foner, *Works of Douglass*, I, 328; II, 437–39.

100. *Weekly Anglo-African*, Aug. 6, 1859; *Liberator*. Aug. 14, 1840; Aug. 19, 1842; Aug. 15, 1851; Aug. 19, 1853; Aug. 13, 1858; Pennington, *Address* (1839), 9–10, 12.

101. *Liberator*, Aug. 13, 1858; *Frederick Douglass' Paper*, Aug. 26, 1853.

102. *Frederick Douglass' Paper*, Aug. 10, 1855.

103. *Liberator*, Aug. 13, 1858.

104. *Address in Commemoration of the Great Jubilee, Of the 1st of August, 1834* (n.p. [New York?], n.d. [1836]) issued by "Committee of Arrangements: Samuel E. Cornish, Theodore S.

Wright, Henry Sipkins, Thomas Downing, Thomas Van Ransalaer," 2–3.

105. *Colored American*, Aug. 22, 1840; *Liberator*, Dec. 1, 1832. On the resurgence of emigrationist views among blacks in the 1850's, see Hollis R. Lynch, "Pan-Negro Nationalism in the New World, Before 1862," in August Meier and Elliott Rudwick, eds., *The Making of Black America* (New York, 1969), I, 42–65.

106. *Liberator*, Aug. 15, 1859.

107. *Douglass' Monthly* IV (1861), 500.

108. *Liberator*, Aug. 14, 1840.

109. *Weekly Anglo-African*, Aug. 6, 1859.

FROM "MIDDLE GROUND" TO "UNDERGROUND"

Joel W. Martin

Despite the fact that most histories of American religion exclude Native Americans from all but the beginning of their narratives, throughout American history Native American religious traditions continued not only to exist but to improvise and adapt to the new European American culture. As Joel Martin demonstrates, during the period of the early Republic the emergence of the southeastern Indians' cultural "underground" signalled a new phase in European-Indian cultural interaction. Prior to the Revolution, the southeastern Indians in the interior had created a "middle ground" of contact with the English and the French through which they were able to accommodate the new European ways within their traditional patterns of life. In ways reminiscent of the "mourning wars" described by Daniel Richter, Native Americans intensified their traditional rituals in response to European challenges. By the beginning of the 1800s, however, the systematic exploitation characteristic of complete colonization was well underway. Now Native Americans not only reacted against their captors, they also created new traditions and adapted old ones in the new world created by colonization. What Joel Martin calls the Indians' cultural "underground" represented a "hidden set of beliefs and practices that reinforced their identity as Indians and strengthened their will to survive and resist." As Martin emphasizes, these innovative responses to European colonizing were neither reactionary nor non-traditional; instead, they provided a resource for the continual reformulation of beliefs and ritual practices to meet new circumstances.

Reprinted by permission from Joel W. Martin, "From 'Middle Ground' to 'Underground': Southeastern Indians and the Early Republic," in *Native Americans and the Early Republic*, Ronald Hoffman and Frederick Hoxie, eds. (Charlottesville: University of Virginia, 1996).

7 ❧

FROM "MIDDLE GROUND" TO "UNDERGROUND"

Southeastern Indians and the Early Republic

Joel W. Martin

DURING THE PERIOD of the early Republic, unprecedented numbers of white settlers invaded the southeastern interior and introduced a new order hostile to the existence of Indians in the region. Southeastern Indians responded with a variety of strategies. Some emigrated. A small and highly visible elite turned toward white ways and became commercial planters and slave owners. A much larger number pursued alternative paths designed to prevent the extinction of their cultures. As residents of homelands being occupied by a hostile, alien force, this group relied increasingly upon a kind of cultural "underground," a hidden set of beliefs and practices that reinforced their identity as Indians and strengthened their will to survive and resist. This essay unearths the "underground" developed by Cherokees and Muskogee Creeks.

The necessity for a cultural "underground" emerged earlier among the Cherokees, a people who, unlike the Creeks, were defeated militarily during the American Revolution. Before the American Revolution, Cherokees, like other large groups of southeastern Indians in the interior, had succeeded fairly well in requiring the English to accommodate indigenous cultural and political expectations. Cherokee men and women traded frequently and successfully with the English. While Cherokee men traded deerskins, human captives, and horses for guns, paint, rum, mirrors, looking glasses, and many other items that they adapted to their own ends, Cherokee women traded food, herbs, and cane baskets for clothes, money, bread, and butter. Cherokee women formed sexual liaisons with English traders, and gave birth to and raised métis children who later played a very important role in Cherokee society. In sum, Cherokee men and women had handled cross-cultural contact and exchange very successfully. They had accommodated material, economic, social, and political changes within traditional patterns and routines.[1]

If it required several generations of English and Cherokee efforts to build this "middle ground," a set of relationships, interactions and altered identities, it took only a single generation to destroy it.[2] Two wars did the fatal damage. During the first, the Cherokee-Carolina war of 1759–1761, white troops burned many Cherokee towns and destroyed their stores of corn and beans. This caused Cherokees to reappraise their relationship with Carolinians. After the war, the Cherokees curtailed their economic contact and political engagement with Carolinians.[3] Meanwhile, Carolinians also devalued trade with Cherokees, their former enemies. During the 1760s, English refugees from Indian attacks in Virginia settled in great numbers in Carolina's backcountry. They had no tolerance for Indians or those who traded with them. They ostracized and attacked traders. Intercultural exchange, the main bridge between Carolinians and Cherokees, was dismantled as new forms of cultural and racial hatred became the norm. How the Cherokees responded to this new situation was shaped in large measure by their decentralized form of governance.[4]

Throughout the eighteenth century, Cherokee villages operated with considerable autonomy. While the Cherokees seemed closer than other southeastern Indians to creating a centralized and coercive political organization at a national level, no state existed. Cherokees gave their primary loyalties to individual villages. Villages had a great say in shaping their relations with the rest of the world. Influenced by regionalism, local leadership, unique historical experiences, and a host of other variables, villages frequently adopted divergent stances toward the English. Within any given village, no individual leader or governing body could coerce people to obey their decisions. Headmen might decide to promote neutrality, but villagers might decide for war.[5]

During the 1760s and 70s, Cherokee headmen ceded great quantities of land to the English to cover trade debts. Not surprisingly, Cherokees who disliked these cessions did not hesistate to express themselves.[6] The most bitter opposition came from young Cherokee men. Treaties signed in 1771, 1775, and 1777 ceded millions of acres of Cherokee lands north of the Cumberland river, including prime hunting lands. Young Cherokee men said additional loss of territory would be fatal to the Cherokee people. To give them their hunting lands would force a change in Cherokee subsistence, a shift away from hunting and toward raising livestock. Such a change was equated with cultural death by a Cherokee leader named Dragging Canoe. "It seemed to be the intention of the white people to destroy them from being a people," he said, emphasizing how whites nearly surrounded Cherokees.[7] Young Cherokee men did not want to rely upon domesticated animals for subsistence. The Maker had given tame animals to whites, and wild ones to Indians. Not wanting to be penned up like hogs by encircling white settlers, they determined to maintain open access to traditional hunting grounds. During the mid-1770s followers of Dragging Canoe went on the offensive. They left their respective villages and formed Chickamauga, a new settlement on the Tennessee river.[8]

Chickamauga people maligned those Cherokees who did not join them with the hated name of "Virginians," and called themselves *Ani-yuníwiya*, or "real people."[9] Because they opposed white domination, emphasized the cultural division between whites and Indians, and rejected certain aspects of European civilization, we might call them "nativists." Yet, that label is too simplistic and it is pejorative.[10] The Chickamaugans showed considerable openness to cultural pluralism. They fostered direct ties to other indigenous groups and to the British in Pensacola. Chickamauga's inhabitants included Cherokees, Cherokee métis, Muskogees, and British loyalists. In 1776, the Chickamaugans attacked the Virginians who had settled in the Watauga Valley. During subsequent years, many bloody exchanges followed.[11]

Most Cherokees did not join the Chickamaugans. Nevertheless, they were caught up in the warfare of the American Revolution. During the summer of 1776, thousands of Whig troops invaded Cherokee country. Motivated by the rhetoric of genocide and enslavement, they destroyed Cherokee habitations, orchards, and crops. Several subsequent campaigns attested to the determination of whites to destroy the Cherokee people. While they did not succeed in this goal, whites did destroy the middle ground once and for all. By 1777, the old patterns of mutual accommodation were gone. Whites no longer showed Cherokees respect, and Cherokees could not forget how whites had stained their hands with the blood of Cherokee women and children.[12]

After their defeat in the American Revolution, most Cherokees in the Carolinas adopted a strategy of non-militant separatism. They developed a cultural "underground," a set of practices and beliefs that reinforced linguistic, cultural, ethical, and religious boundaries between themselves and whites. If they could not preserve physical distance and political independence, they could at least bolster symbolic distinctions in many areas of life and protect the core of their identity. For instance, Cherokees fluent in English pretended they did not understand it when addressed by Americans. As they had long done, Cherokees continued to keep their sacred rituals secret. Additionally, it may have been around this time that they began performing a dance that satirized negative traits associated with whites. Among themselves, Cherokees danced the Booger dance, in which masked Cherokee men pretended to be Europeans: "awkward, ridiculous, lewd, and menacing."[13]

Just as the dance dramatized the difference between whites and Indians, myths describing the separate creation of human races became widely popular among the Cherokees. Originating among Indian prophets in the eighteenth century, the theory of racial polygenesis held that "red" people were fundamentally different from "white" people. Some Cherokees were proponents of the theory as early as 1799. In 1811, a Cherokee prophet promoted a small revitalization movement saying the following: "You yourselves can see that the white people are entirely different beings from us; we are made of red clay; they, out of white sand." Evidently, by that time at a popular level Cherokees had come to assume that the difference between whites and Indians to be ontological: sacred and permanent.[14]

On a less metaphysical plane, many post-Revolutionary Cherokees created distance between themselves and whites by relying increasingly upon métis individuals to serve as cultural intermediaries. These individuals were perfectly poised to play such a role. Bicultural progeny of English fathers and Cherokee mothers, they owned a disproportionate number of slaves and increasingly modeled their lifestyle on that of white planters. At a time when many Cherokees were trying to differentiate themselves symbolically from whites, these individuals were identifying more openly with white ways. Their role as cultural brokers was crucial for several decades.[15]

The métis elite accepted Protestant missionaries into their midst, became producers of crops and livestock for white markets, and eventually reorganized the Cherokee polity by forming a constitutional government (1827).[16] During the 1820s, the Cherokee elite attracted national praise. Anglo writers heralded their agrarian, mercantile, religious, and social achievements. In his *Remarks on the Practicability of Indian Reform* (1828), Isaac McCoy, eager to convince policy-makers and church officials that Indians could be civilized, pointed to the Cherokee countryside.

> Numerous flocks of sheep, goats, and swine, cover the vallies and hills.... The natives carry on a considerable trade with the adjoining States.... Apple and peach orchards are quite common, and gardens are cultivated.... Butter and cheese are seen on Cherokee tables. There are many publick roads in the nation, and houses of entertainment kept by natives. Numerous flourishing villages are seen in every section of the country.... The population is rapidly increasing.... Some

of the most influential characters are members of the church, and live consistently with their professions. Schools are increasing every year; learning is encouraged and rewarded. The female character is elevated and duly respected.[17]

McCoy concluded that the Cherokees as a whole were "a *civilized* people." Another commentator agreed, saying that the "Cherokees have the aspect, and the elements, at least, of a regular, civilized, Christian nation."[18] The Cherokees, it was implied, were exceptional Indians.

But when white commentators like McCoy described Cherokee society, they were really only describing the lifestyle and values of the Cherokee elite. As one missionary admitted, he worked primarily with "persons who speak both languages; as half-breeds, whites brought up in the nation, or married into Indian families, or otherwise dependent on them. This class of people have always been *the connecting link* between the Indians and the whites."[19] Dependent upon this class of mediators, whites inevitably knew the members of that class better than they knew the majority of Cherokees with whom they had less direct contact. This state of affairs may have been precisely the one ordinary Cherokees desired. Métis mediators provided them with a very useful and effective screen behind which they could continue to lead traditional lives beyond the gaze of whites. In effect, Cherokees used the métis to connect them to and shield them from a dominant public order organized around threatening values.

A comparison of elite and non-elite responses to Christianity underscores the difference between the two groups. During the 1820s, Cherokees were missionized more than any group of interior Indians. Four denominations (Presbyterian, Moravian, Baptist, and Methodist) vied for converts. In 1827 these denominations supported eight Indian schools and seventy-one teachers who directly affected the lives of two hundred Cherokee boys and girls. Nevertheless, in 1830, these denominations could only claim 1300 members out of total Cherokee population exceeding 15,000. Within the pool of converts, one would find almost all of the members of the Cherokee elite.[20]

Ninety percent of the Cherokee people did not have significant contact with Christian missionaries. Among the ten percent of Cherokees who were exposed directly to Christianity, many were persuaded by arguments circulating among the Cherokees against the alien religion. An epistemological argument held that Christians' stories were "mere legendary tales." An ontological argument reasoned that because "the Cherokees were a different race from the whites," they could have "no concern in the white people's religion." And an ethical argument, after observing how Christians acted, concluded that Christians were hypocrites. Rather than adopt the new religion, they continued to tell sacred stories, participate in rituals, and practice values cherished by their ancestors. Even among the small number of Cherokees who attended Christian services regularly, most refused to entirely forsake their traditional practices.[21]

The great majority of Cherokees did not convert to Christianity, attend school, hold elected office, run houses of entertainment, own slaves, or publish newspapers.[22] Literacy, another aspect of "civilization" embraced by the elite, also elicited negative responses from ordinary Cherokees. Cherokees and other southeastern Indians experienced literacy as an essential part of white domination. Literacy was associated primarily with missionaries, government agents, treaty negotiators, land speculators, and powerful traders. Literacy was linked to people who routinely denigrated Cherokee religion, tried to control Cherokee politics, and defrauded Cherokees of their lands. Given these associations, it is not surprising that most Cherokees did not try to learn to read and write. As one of their myths revealed, they felt that literacy, like Christianity, belonged exclusively to white people. According to the myth, in the beginning, the Maker had given the book to the Indian, the real or genuine man. When the Indian was not paying attention, however, the tricky white man stole the book. As a consequence of that primordial theft, the white man has since had an easy life, and the Indian has been compelled to gain his subsistence by hunting.[23]

All of this changed when Sequoyah, the son of a European man and a Cherokee woman, created in 1821 a syllabary, a set of written symbols representing the basic sounds of the Cherokee language.[24] The syllabary was a cultural hybrid. It was European in form (the symbols were written and read) and Cherokee in content (the symbols represented the spoken Cherokee language). But if we would appreciate fully Sequoyah's achievement we need to go beyond noting its bi-cultural roots. Sequoyah's syllabary precipitated a movement of significant cultural renewal in the early 1820s among common Cherokee men and women.[25]

When Sequoyah through his syllabary made literacy in Cherokee possible, Cherokee men and women thought initially he had done something magical. Because they associated literacy with a use of power for destructive purposes, they thought Sequoyah's efforts were delirious or idiotic.[26] Soon, however, Sequoyah convinced them through public demonstrations that he had done nothing magical or crazy, that anyone could learn to write the Cherokee language. Cherokees realized that here was new power that could be employed to preserve the core of Cherokee identity. From that point on, they showed zeal in learning and teaching the syllabary. White observers were astounded at how the new mode of writing caught on. In 1824, they reported that "the Knowledge of Mr. Guess's Alphabet is spreading through the nation like fire among the leaves." By 1825, the majority of Cherokees had learned the system, and "letters in Cherokee were passing in all directions."[27] With every letter written, non-elite Cherokees strengthened their own culture and implicitly refuted white claims to superiority. White culture was no more sacred than was the culture of the Cherokees. Or to put it another way, Cherokee culture was no less sacred than that of whites. By taking the tools and symbols associated with the invading culture and turning them to counter-colonial purposes, Sequoyah produced a written language that served as "virtually a code to sustain the traditional community *beyond the perception* of the authorities, red or white." Sequoyah had given non-elite Cherokees a valuable way to nurture and preserve Cherokee identity during the very period when whites were invading their lands in unprecedented numbers. Though in theory whatever was written was public and could be read by whites literate in Cherokee, in practice the overwhelming majority of letters were never seen by whites. In effect, this kind of literacy nurtured, without betraying, the Cherokee underground, the set of beliefs and practices, cultural values and affiliations, that defined the Cherokees as a distinct people.[28]

Literate or not, all Cherokees, including the elite, could not prevent the invasion of their land by thousands of outsiders. Whichever strategy of resistance or accommodation they employed, they were unable to overcome the fundamental power relations shaping their world during the period of the early Republic. Whites entered their land by the thousands during the Gold Rush of 1829; Georgia extinguished Cherokee sovereignty June 1, 1830; whites stole Cherokee property with impunity and drove Cherokees from their farms. In 1838, the great majority of Cherokees (sixteen thousand people) were forced to remove west in a murderous march that cost the people thousands of lives.[29] Two years earlier, their native neighbors to the south, the Muskogees, had been compelled to travel their own "Trail of Tears."[30] In essence, both southeastern peoples were forced to leave their ancestral homes by whites who wanted Indian lands for cotton culture.

If Muskogee and Cherokee experiences of dispossession and removal in the 1830s seem very similar, their earlier experiences with the white invasion were distinct in some very important ways. Geography was key. Because the Muskogees were much farther away from Carolina's backcountry and because their trade was essential to backcountry Georgia, the Muskogees, unlike the Cherokees, were not targeted for massive intercultural violence during the 1760s or during the American Revolution. Muskogee towns survived the entire eighteenth century without being attacked by Europeans or Euro-Americans, a very remarkable record for the eastern half of North America.

Nevertheless, if they successfully avoided the wars with whites that hurt Cherokees so badly, the Muskogees had faced some tough challenges during the eighteenth century. Beginning in the 1760s, Augusta merchants and traders had dramatically expanded the rum trade to the Muskogees. Over the next five decades, this trade increased the Muskogees' economic dependency, encouraged violence among villagers, promoted overhunting, precipitated an ecological crisis, and increased intertribal conflicts.[31] Eventually, the trade would provide whites with the means to force large cessions of land, cessions which would in turn inspire a movement of violent resistance among the Muskogees, the Redstick revolt of 1812–14. Only then did the Muskogees experience the kind of crushing military invasion that the Cherokees had faced decades earlier. This difference in timing is very significant. It underscores the fact that the stories of Cherokee and Muskogee resistance are not identical. Rather, these stories converge and diverge in ways that warrant closer examination.[32]

Before the Redstick revolt, most Muskogees avoided massive conflicts by employing a rich range of small-scale modes of resistance. While less spectacular than the Redstick movement, these forms of resistance were very important throughout the period of the early Republic, a time when domination was on the rise, but not yet complete. Many elementary forms of resistance were performed in secret, in the woods, under the cover of darkness, or in a state of intoxication. During the 1790s, for example, as white encroachment made hunting on the Georgia-Muskogee frontier more difficult and dangerous, "gangs" of young Muskogee men began stealing whites' horses and slaves, and selling them to complicit traders in Tennessee and Florida. Young men explicitly justified their acts as retaliation for white encroachment. When white hunting parties poached their game, the Muskogees responded by killing the settlers' cattle. In a few instances, they murdered individual whites, took women and children captive, plundered the stores of traders, and burned settlers' farm buildings and houses. When white authorities demanded justice, headmen said they were powerless to provide it. They blamed the unruliness of young men whose "mischief" they could not prevent. Furthermore, many of the accused men said they had committed their crimes while drunk and therefore were not accountable.[33]

Muskogees found creative ways to frustrate dominating whites. Proselytized by Moravian missionaries, they dissembled and said they already knew everything about the Savior. Lectured by the United States agent on the merits of patrilineal kinship patterns or commercial agriculture, they turned silent or pretended they could not understand. Advised to cede land at treaty conferences, they recalled the great quantity of lands already lost, reminded U.S. officials of the promises of previous Presidents, invoked the ways of their own ancestors, and pled the future needs of their progeny. Acts of theft, arson, and murder; the strategic use of flattery, equivocation, procrastination, lies, and dissimulation; careful appeals to high moral principles or the exonerating circumstance of intoxication—these were but a few of ways Muskogees resisted white aggression and settler incursions without risking everything in a direct conflict.[34]

What is striking is that many of these less dramatic and small-scale modes, because they were performed in secret or involved purposeful obfuscation, allowed Muskogees and other southeastern Indians to express deep-seated resentments while keeping the well-springs of resistance "underground," partially hidden from whites and collaborating Indians. Unfortunately for us, this had the additional effect of insuring that the full depth and range of the Muskogees' responses to domination would not be clearly recorded in the historical documents. Because most of these documents were written by whites who were kept partially in the dark, it is difficult to establish precisely the Muskogees' true feelings, motivations, ideas, and rationales. In anthropologist James Scott's terms, the documents do a good job of showing us the "public transcript," the ways Muskogees and other southeastern Indians acted in the presence of power. The documents do a much less satisfactory job of revealing the "hidden transcript," the discourses, gestures, rituals, and symbols southeastern Indians cultivated among themselves to justify, promote, and perpetuate resistance.[35] Like other scholars who deal with documents produced in situations of domination, we find there are no transparent windows into the consciousness of the oppressed.[36] This lack, however, should not lead to skepticism or agnosticism. If not exactly transparent, some windows nonetheless exist. The Redstick revolt is such a window. Because the Redsticks risked everything and dared to resist openly, their movement provides historians with one of our best glimpses at the hidden transcript developed by southeastern Indians resisting domination.

Like the Chickamaugan movement, the Redstick movement attracted people who were angry with their headmen for authorizing massive land cessions to whites. Intended to cover debts incurred in the deerskin trade, these cessions signaled for Muskogees a profound change in Indian-white relations. Everything hinged on the interpretation and handling of debt. Essential to the everyday transactions of the deerskin trade, debt for generations had signified ties between individual hunters and traders. Hunters went into debt to obtain what they needed for a season's hunt and to supply their kin with goods. They negotiated with traders whom they knew personally. In the new system, debt was abstracted from personal relationships and made into a commodity that could itself be traded on the market. The debts owed small traders were purchased at discount by the largest trading firm in the region, Panton, Leslie and Company—later John Forbes and Company. This firm then aggregated the debts of entire communities of hunters, indeed of all Muskogee hunters, to produce one astronomical lump sum which the firm charged against the Muskogee people. By 1803, the firm claimed the Muskogees owed $113,000.[37]

This extraordinary debt would have been impossible for the firm to collect, if not for the cooperation of the United States. Such cooperation was novel. In previous years, hostility and competition had characterized the relations of United States officials and Pensacola merchants. In 1793, for instance, William Panton of Pensacola encouraged the Muskogees to resist the advance of the Georgians through whatever means possible, including violence. United States officials said Panton "would rather see the whole state of Georgians in flames, and women and children massacred by the savages, than lose one hundred deer skins."[38] By

1803, Panton was dead, and the interests of the United States and the Pensacola merchants coincided. During the first decade of the nineteenth century, United States agents compelled Muskogee headmen to cede millions of acres of land to the United States. In exchange for the land, the United States paid off some of the Indians' aggregate debt. Thus, thousands of small, face-to-face exchanges between traders and hunters were transmuted by a multinational company and an expanding nation-state into massive land cessions that affected an entire people. These cessions signaled the end of play-off politics, expanded United States sovereignty, took from the Muskogee people many of their best hunting grounds, and undermined the deerskin trade, the central economic basis of the middle ground.[39]

This example shows how Americans, working with Pensacola merchants, exploited an established practice, the giving of credit, for new ends antithetical to the existence of the middle ground itself. A similar tale of ex post facto transmutation can be told by examining what happened to the institution of alliance chiefs after the departure of the French and defeat of the British. During the 1790s and 1800s, intercultural diplomacy did not work as it had in the past. Earlier alliance chiefs like Malatchi had struggled to find a compromise between European demands and the expectations of his people. Later alliance chiefs did the same thing, but now the white side of the balance weighed far more heavily upon them. The Americans, too numerous and too strong, no longer needed to listen to or compromise with their Indian interlocutors. Chiefs found themselves compelled to execute or legitimize policies that signified not mutual accommodation, but U.S. domination. They were required to sign treaties permanently ceding massive quantities of land, to authorize the building of roads through their people's territories, and to enforce justice against their own peoples even when this meant violating sacred cultural values. Some chiefs such as Hopoithle Miko of Tallassee refused to comply, and tried to set up alternative governments. Others chiefs such as Tustunnuggee Thlucco (Big Warrior) of Tuckabatchee promised to comply, but dissimulated in speech or procrastinated in action. Still others such as William McIntosh of Coweta profited personally from their mediating role and adopted the lifestyle of white settlers or planters. Was a chief like McIntosh a true intermediary or a colonial collaborator? It was becoming hard to tell.[40]

As Americans and complicit Indians corrupted the institutions that supported cross-cultural exchange and mutual accommodation, and as white populations increased and settled closer to the Indians of the interior southeast, white authorities and intellectuals developed a coherent narrative that legitimated and depoliticized these great changes. According to this narrative, the United States was the great benefactor of southeastern Indians, and if Indians could only make a few adjustments, they would be much happier. The old system of gift-giving was dead, the rules of the market applied now, and cessions were necessary to pay trade debts. Although these cessions deprived the Muskogees and other Indians of ancestral game lands, hunters need not despair. They could cease "savagery" to become commercial agriculturalists and raise livestock. Men should stay home, accumulate property, and pass it on to their children. Chiefs should police their people and enforce white justice. All would benefit. Whites would gain and use the land to its full potential, and Indians would become civilized. The plan of civilization, as represented to the Muskogees by U.S. Agent Benjamin Hawkins, was for the Muskogees' own good.[41]

Muskogees did not have to obey the U.S. agent, but they had to listen to him and show respect. Because Hawkins controlled the federal annuities paid to Muskogees, could materially reward and punish villagers, and increasingly monopolized the execution of justice in Muskogee country, he could enter Muskogee villages with impunity and presume to tell the Muskogees how they had to change. His influence signaled that a new set of power relations was shaping Indian-white encounters. The United States, and for that matter individual states such as Georgia, possessed vastly more economic and military power than the Muskogee people. By the turn of the century, Muskogees could no longer compel cultural, political, or economic reciprocity.

As Muskogees experienced the rise of domination and witnessed its effects on subsistence, commerce, politics, and intercultural relations, they created their own narratives to explain what was happening. Just as whites told stories, proposed plans, and developed institutions to impose their will, Muskogees told stories, created movements, and developed practices to resist the loss of territory, economic dependency, political domination, and cultural imperialism. Usually this subversive cultural activity went on out of the sight of whites, in the southeastern "underground." However, in the Redstick revolt it came into almost full view when thousands of Muskogees decided to revolt against the United States. Because Muskogee resistance took a massive and open form in the Redstick prophetic movement, study of this movement provides one of our best documented glimpses of the otherwise hidden transcript of southeastern Indians.

When the New Madrid earthquake violently shook their lands in 1811–1812, Muskogees cast about for a meaningful and useful interpretation of the unprecedented events.[42] In shaping their interpretations, the Muskogee people, unlike whites, did not turn to the Book for guidance.[43] As a Muskogee man put it, "white people have the old book from God. We Indians do not have it and are unable to read it."[44] Even so, he averred, his people still possessed insight into the order of things. "The Indians know it without a book; they dream much of God, and therefore they know it." Instead of turning to Scriptures, Muskogees turned to their spiritual leaders, their shamans. Inspired shamans trembled and convulsed as if vibrated by an earthquake or seized by a spirit. These shamans or "shakers" traveled to and from the spirit worlds.[45] They declared a charismatic event revelatory of sacred forces was at work, and interpreted historical events and the earthquake through the template of Muskogean religious myth.

Muskogees imagined the cosmos divided into three primordial worlds: the Upper World, This World, and the Lower World. Just as the Sun and Moon illumined the earth, manifested order in their movements and helped demarcate temporal boundaries, the Upper World released the powers of perfection, order, permanence, clarity, periodicity. Pitted against the Upper World and releasing exactly contrary powers was the Lower World, the realm of reversals, madness, creativity, fertility, chaos. In the Lower World, there lived a major class of sacred beings. It was not taken lightly, for it included the most dangerous spirit beings. Foremost among these was the Tie-Snake, a primeval dragon-like antlered monster snake. Although most Europeans denied the existence of Tie-Snakes, some traders like James Adair were not sure. Adair accepted southeastern Indians' accounts of snakes "of a more enormous size than is mentioned in history" that could bewitch their prey with their eyes and tongues, change color, and dazzle spectators with "piercing rays of light that blaze from their foreheads."[46] Muskogees strongly affirmed the reality of these creatures. According to Muskogees, these great snakes could stretch themselves across the channel and practically dam the stream. During the early nineteenth century in Muskogee, the Tie-Snake was closely associated with a particularly dangerous rocky stretch of the Chattahoochee river and could often be seen there. "It had the appearance, when floating on the water, of a large number of barrels strung together, end to end, and could, almost at any time, be seen catching its prey by folding its helpless victims in the coils or 'tie' of its tail and instantly destroying life by a deadly hug."[47] In addition to making water travel dangerous, these Snakes brought numerous sicknesses to humans. Merely looking at the creature could cause insanity or death. And yet, it was very difficult for a human not to look, for the Tie-Snake was strangely beautiful. Dreadfully alluring, its body was armored with crystalline scales that shined iridescently, its forehead crowned with an extraordinarily bright crystal. Highly prized as aids in divination, these dazzling scales and crystals could only be obtained by a shaman purified for contact with the dangerous powers of the Lower World.

In 1812, a Muskogee shaman Captain Sam Isaacs related to Upper Muskogees his vision of "diving down to the bottom of the river and laying there and traveling about for many days and nights receiving instruction and information from an enormous and friendly serpent that dwells there and was acquainted with future events and all other things necessary for a man to know in this life."[48] As Captain Isaacs revealed, it was the powerful Tie-Snake who recklessly shook the earth and unleashed a new force for recreating the world. Based upon this vision, the special knowledge and power that it provided him, and his familiarity with Tecumseh and the Shawnee prophets, Isaacs acquired the veneration of several hundred people.[49] As the movement grew, however, a younger group of shamans came to the fore. Borrowing from the fiery tales of apocalypse told by runaway Afro-Christian slaves, they said the Upper World power known as the Maker of Breath was about to destroy the present colonial order. This prophecy of cosmological upheaval provided the metaphors, symbols, and values that justified revolt against seemingly insurmountable odds. By identifying with these cosmic forces, the Muskogee rebels gained courage and felt they could purge their land of colonizers. Allied with the Shawnees and other Indians, they would "make the land clear of the Americans or lose their lives."[50]

Just as the Muskogees interpreted earthly events through the symbolic template of sacred stories, so they acted politically in a way directly patterned after rituals of purification and world renewal. Homologies between rituals and revolutionary acts were strong. When they attacked an enemy town, the shamans said it would fall on the eighth day, for eight was a sacred number. Eight days was also the length of time it took the Muskogees to perform their most important collective ceremony, the *póskita* or Busk, an annual ritual celebrating the primordial origins of corn and the rebirth of the social order. Muskogee rebels performed a dance borrowed from the Shawnees to symbolize solidarity with other Indians and their utter determination to resist white civilization's hegemonic power. If this meant attacking collaborating Muskogees or coercing people to join their movement, the Redsticks were willing to do so. "The declaration of the prophets [was] to destroy every thing received from the Americans, all the Chiefs and their adherents who are friendly to the customs and ways of the white people." They were directed by the prophets "to kill any of their own People if they do not take up the war Club."[51] The rebels ritually assassinated collaborating chiefs and targeted Hawkins and his assistants for execution. They waged war on cattle. Central to the subsistence base of invading settlers, cattle symbolized white civilization itself. The Muskogee rebels agreed with their Chickamaugan predecessors. These tame animals were the very antithesis of the wild animals given to real Indians by the Maker of Breath. As they had always done in traditional initiation ceremonies, the rebels withdrew to the woods, fasted, consumed purifying beverages, and danced. Through these and many other acts, Muskogee rebels turned an upside-down world right side up. With prophetic declarations, new dances, purification ceremonies, wars on certain animals and people, humorous inversionary gestures, the Muskogee rebels rejected domination and showed that they were indeed the masters of the land and all of its symbols.[52]

As historian Gregory Dowd notes in his study of earlier Indian revolts, prophetic messages spread very fast in Indian country.[53] One of the main ways prophecies were disseminated was through rumors. As scholars of anti-colonial movements have shown, rumors can elaborate, distort, and exaggerate information regarding events of vital importance, can spread with incredible speed, and can give voice to popular utopian longings. Rumors have no identifiable authors, so people can spread them while disavowing responsibility for their contents and effects. Rumors circulated rapidly in the southeastern underground. After the New Madrid earthquake, among the Muskogees "flying tales daily multiplied and were exaggerated in all parts of the [Muskogee] nation, told and received as truth by every one.... [These] Tales had no Father for they were said to be told by first one and then another and nobody could ascertain who, but the relators were at a distance in general and hard to be detected." In many of these "flying, fatherless tales," Tecumseh, the great Shawnee leader of pan-tribalism, figured prominently. Indeed, according to some of the popular narratives, Tecumseh had stomped his foot and caused the earth to shake. In others, Tecumseh did not cause the earthquakes, but he prophesied how the Lower World would release awesome power, collapse the old order and allow a new one to emerge. Responding to these rumors and other stories, seven to nine thousand Muskogees revolted against the United States.[54]

An equal number did not revolt. Why not? If several thousand Muskogees living on the Chattahoochee (Lower Muskogees) did not take up the red club, it does not mean that they were not religious or even less religious than the Redsticks. People can share the same religion, but interpret its implications differently. They can cherish the same myths and rituals, and still come to blows. When the Redsticks called for revolt, the Lower Muskogees listened, hesitated, and decided against joining their more militant cousins. They felt there were better ways to resist white domination. Since Lower Muskogees lived very close to Georgians, they feared they would suffer catastrophic losses, if they joined the revolt. But fear was not the only factor shaping their response. By 1811, Lower Muskogees had already dealt with the major economic and social challenges caused by the loss of their ancestral hunting lands. Like their Cherokee neighbors, they had shifted their secondary subsistence cycle away from hunting towards the raising of livestock and the trading of agricultural products. Women gained greater direct access to the market. Old men also benefited. A Coweta chief said he had "more pleasure...in carding and dying his cotton and making his clothing [with a loom] than he ever had in his young days hunting. 'I am old...and as such according to our old ways useless but according to the new way more useful than ever.'"[55] As for the young men, the Lower Muskogees most directly affected by the loss of hunting lands, many of them had emigrated, relocating in northern Florida. A region where settlers were rare and game was plentiful, northern Florida had served as a kind of escape valve for generations of Lower Muskogees frustrated with white encroachment. As a consequence, in 1811, among Lower Muskogees living on the Chattahoochee, there was no critical mass of angry young men determined to keep the traditional hunting grounds free of whites. Excepting the ethnically distinct town of Yuchis, Lower Muskogee towns determined to side with the Georgians against the Upper Muskogees. They expected to be amply rewarded for this alliance.[56]

Neither the Upper or Lower Muskogees saw their expectations fulfilled. The Redsticks were devastated utterly by their war with the United States. The Lower Muskogees, although the allies of the victorious United States, were forced by Andrew Jackson to cede millions of acres of their land. After the war, the influx of white settlers accelerated. Nevertheless, Upper and Lower Muskogees continued to resist. Muskogees had employed a wide range of subtle and not so subtle forms of resistance before the Redstick movement. They did so afterwards as well, and learned much from the Cherokees. In the decades following the Redstick war, Muskogees increasingly relied upon métis individuals, including educated Cherokees, to serve as cultural intermediaries. Cherokee métis involved themselves quite visibily in Muskogee affairs during the 1820s. For instance, in 1826, John Ridge and David Vann provided counsel and served as secretaries to Muskogee headmen during treaty negotiations with the United States.[57]

There is also evidence that Muskogees, like Cherokees, made special efforts to hide their culture of the sacred from Anglo scrutiny. For instance, during the 1820s, the Tuckabatchees would not let any white person see their ancient copper plates, sacred items displayed during that town's Busk ceremony. Although Lee Compere, a Baptist missionary, lived among the Tuckabatchees from 1822 to 1828, he "would never get to see them.... The Indians were reluctant to talk about them." Compere did succeed in persuading Tustunnuggee Thlucco to relate some of the Muskogees' sacred history, including how they had defeated the indigenous inhabitants of the southeast. However, when Compere made an insensitive comparison between this ancient story of conquest and the ongoing Anglo-American invasion, the chief turned silent. Compere had crossed the line. "From that time I could never after induce him or any of the other chiefs to give me any more of their history."[58]

In addition to hiding their most sacred relics and keeping much of their oral tradition secret, Muskogees tried to protect their ceremonies from white civilization. They created new rules governing the consumption of alcohol and the use of manufactured goods during the Busk. In some towns, both were banned. At least in one square ground, it was "considered as a desecration for an Indian to allow himself to be touched by even the dress of a white man, until the ceremony of purification is complete."[59] This could have been the case earlier, but the fact that the rule was enforced in 1835 reveals an active concern to protect sacred ceremonies from white meddling.

In addition to protecting their own religion, Muskogees tried to check the influence of the Christian religion in their country. Most chiefs would not permit preaching in their towns. When Compere (through a Muskogee interpreter named John Davis) began conversing on the Gospel in the square ground of Tuckabatchee, the men ignored him and concentrated on cutting sticks and rubbing their pipes. On another occasion, they protested that they were too old to learn such things, and "did not want to hear them." In another town, Muskogees told Compere to avoid the square altogether as many Indians were intoxicated and would cause trouble.[60]

Not surprisingly, Compere's mission was not very successful. Except for Davis, he converted almost no "full-bloods." He simply did not have access to the Muskogees' inner lives. They kept their sacred life secret, as an incident in the spring of 1828 revealed. When clearing land for cultivation, Compere killed a hickory, unwittingly violating a Muskogee rule of propriety. A Muskogee woman informed him that he had "broke in upon some of the secrets of the Indians' superstition...which is that the Indians consider such trees when they happen to be found in the Townfield as sacred to the Great Spirit." Informed of his error, Compere was "not very sorry." Aware that he was being kept in the dark about major aspects of Muskogee life, Compere was pleased the accident had happened. It had served as "the means of dragging out a secret which I might never have learned without."[61] Muskogees simply did not trust Compere. Not surprisingly, the mission failed. Within a few years, the Muskogees were forcibly removed from Alabama.

In the decades prior to removal, Muskogees and Cherokees alike had experienced the invasion of their lands by missionaries, miners, government agents, settlers, and slaves. Although they had occasionally responded with violence, much more common were the everyday non-violent means they used to protect their feelings, rituals, identities, and cultures. Confronted with hostile whites in their midst, Muskogees and Cherokees consciously kept important things, values, beliefs, practices, and ideas secret. They developed alternative stories and myths to explain the origins of the diverse races, performed rituals and dances that celebrated their identities as Indians, and carefully controlled whites' access to their interior lives. By developing and hiding an underground cultural life, they retained their sense of their separate identity even as their land was being invaded.

To be sure, sometimes the Cherokees and Muskogees used violent means to repel whites, most spectacularly in the Chickamaugan and Redstick revolts. Even these revolts, however, were linked to the southeastern underground. The revolts simply concentrated in a vivid, explicit manner what was already present in a more diffuse, less visible way among the Cherokees and Muskogees. In the revolts, symbols, practices, and narratives emphasizing Indian distinctiveness were underscored, exaggerated, dramatized, and, most important, made public. Like geysers, the violent character of the Chickamauga and Redstick revolts attracted a lot of attention from shocked whites. But also like geysers, these revolts owed their existence to larger underground currents flowing out of sight. If the revolts deserve attention, surely deserving equal or greater attention is the cultural underground that made them possible. Southeastern Indians found much of value there: powerful symbols of a separate Indian identity, opportunities to vent frustrations, and a rich repertoire of strategies to resist domination. Although purposefully hidden by its creators and long overlooked by historians, the southeastern Indians' underground should be unearthed at last and ignored no longer, for it exercised significant influence during the period of the early republic.

NOTES

This essay benefited from comments by Mary Young, Frederick Hoxie, Peter Wood, Stephen Aron, and James Merrell.

1. James Merrell, "'Our Bond of Peace': Patterns of Intercultural Exchange in the Carolina Piedmont, 1650–1750," in *Powhatan's Mantle*, 198–204; Gary Goodwin, *Cherokees in Transition: A Study of Changing Culture and Environment Prior to 1775* (Chicago: University of Chicago Press, 1977), 94; Marvin Thomas Hatley, "The Dividing Paths: The Encounters of the Cherokees and the South Carolinians in the Southern Mountains, 1670–1785," (Ph.D. diss., Duke University, 1989), 96,103, 137, 139, 144, 146, 156.

2. Richard White, *The Middle Ground Indians, Empires, and Republics in the Great Lakes Region,* 1650–1815 (New York: Cambridge University Press, 1991), x, 38–40, 79, 84–90, 114–115, 179–180, 175, 202, 312–313.

3. John R. Alden, *John Stuart and the Southern Colonial Frontier* (Ann Arbor: University of Michigan Press, 1944), 208, 298–301; Hatley, "The Dividing Paths," 606–621.

4. David Cockran, *The Cherokee Frontier, 1540–1783* (Norman: University of Oklahoma Press, 1962), 194, 256–65; Hatley, "The Dividing Paths," 391, 395–396, 443, 456–464, 483–484, 533, 535, 538, 539, 54, 560.

5. Duane Champagne, *Social Order and Political Change: Constitutional Governments among the Cherokee, The Choctaw, The Chickasaw, and the Creek* (Stanford: Stanford University Press, 1992),

25, 28, 39, 57–59, 74–77.

6. Alden, *Southern Frontier*, 187, 208, 298, 303; Louis DeVorsey, *The Indian Boundary in the Southern Colonies, 1763–1775* (Chapel Hill: University of North Carolina Press, 1966), 102, 116, 126, 128, 133, 135; Duane H. King, "Long Island of the Holston: Sacred Cherokee Ground," *Journal of Cherokee Studies* (Fall 1976): 113–127. Hatley, "The Dividing Paths," 606–621, 627, 658–661.

7. Henry Stuart, "Account of his Proceedings with the Indians, Pensacola, August 25, 1776," [PRO, CO 5/7, 333–378], in William L. Saunders, ed., *The Colonial Records of North Carolina, 1662–1776* (10 vols., Raleigh, 1886–1890), X, 764.

8. Samuel Coles Williams, ed., *Adair's History of the American Indians*,(Johnson City, Tennessee: The Watauga Press, 1930), 138–139; DeVorsey, *Indian Boundary*, 74–85; Hatley, "The Dividing Paths," 631–642, 648–672. .

9. James Paul Pate, "The Chickamauga: A Forgotten Segment of Indian Resistance on the Southern Frontier," Ph.D. dissertation, Mississippi State University, 1969, 81; John Brown, *Old Frontiers: The Story of the Cherokee Indians from Earliest Times to the Date of Their Removal to the West, 1838* (Kingsport, TN: Southern Publishers, Inc., 1938), 165–167.

10. "Nativism" has negative connotations. Contemporary scholars associate nativism with closed-mindedness, ethnocentrism, racist attitudes, and a surrender of reason. See the way the word is used in current abstracts in *Dissertation Abstracts International, A, Humanities and Social Sciences* (Ann Arbor: University Microfilms International, 1991), *passim.*

11. Gregory Evans Dowd, *A Spirited Resistance: The North American Struggle for Unity, 1745–1815* (Baltimore: The Johns Hopkins University Press, 1992), 48–56.

12. For the 1776 intercolonial expedition and its consequences, see James H. O'Donnell, *Southern Indians in the American Revolution* (Knoxville: University of Tennessee Press, 1973), 34–69, 118–119; Hatley, "The Dividing Paths," 571, 573, 578, 674, 675. For the rhetoric of genocide and enslavement, ibid., 567, 570, 582, 593, 648, 665. For the end of the Cherokee middle ground, ibid., 684, 718.

13. For the Booger Dance and secret rituals, see Frank G. Speck and Leonard Broom, *Cherokee Dance and Drama* (Berkeley: University of California Press, 1951), 36–39; Raymond D. Fogelson and Amelia B. Walker, "Self and Other in Cherokee Booger Dances," *Journal of Cherokee Studies* 5 (Fall 1980): 88–102; Hatley, "The Dividing Paths," 680–695, 698–699, 702–706.

14. For stories of separate creation and distinct destinies, see Bishop Edmund De Schweinitz, ed. and trans., "The Narrative of Marie Le Roy and Barbara Leiniger," in *Pennsylvania Archives* 7 (1878); James Mooney, *The Ghost-Dance Religion and Wounded Knee* (Dover Publications, New Publications, 1973), 677; William G. McLoughlin, *Cherokees and Missionaries, 1789–1839* (New Haven: Yale University Press, 1984), 91, 97; ; McLoughlin, *The Cherokee Ghost Dance: Essays on the Southeastern Indians, 1789–1861* (Macon, GA: Mercer University Press, 1984), 253–260; Gregory Evans Dowd, *A Spirited Resistance: The North American Indian Struggle for Unity, 1745–1815* (Baltimore: Johns Hopkins University Press, 1992), 21, 63.

15. For métis mediators, see Ronald N. Satz, "Cherokee Traditionalism, Protestant Evangelism, and the Trail of Tears, Part II," *Tennessee Historical Quarterly* XLIV (Winter 1985): 380–402; Hatley, "The Dividing Paths," 695–697. For métis slaveowning, see Theda Perdue, *Slavery and the Evolution of Cherokee Society, 1540–1866* (Knoxville: University of Tennessee Press, 1979), 57–60.

16. See William G. McLoughlin, "Who Civilized the Cherokees?," *Journal of Cherokee Studies* 1988 (13): 55–81; Douglas C. Wilms, "Cherokee Acculturation and Changing Land Use Practices," *Chronicles of Oklahoma* 1978 56(3): 331–343; Marguerite McFadden, "The Saga of "Rich Joe" Vann," *Chronicles of Oklahoma* 1983 61(1): 68–79; Michelle Daniel, "From Blood Feud to Jury System: The Metamorphosis of Cherokee Law from 1750 to 1840," *American Indian Quarterly* 1987 11(2): 97–125. Cherokee slaveowners, like Muskogees, were usually lenient when compared to whites. See Theda Perdue, "Cherokee Planters, Black Slaves, and African Colonization," *Chronicles of Oklahoma* 1982 60(3): 322–331; William G. McLoughlin, *Cherokee Renascence in the New Republic* (Princeton: Princeton University Press, 1986); Duane Champagne, *Social Order and Political Change: Constitutional Governments Among the Cherokee, the Choctaw, the Chickasaw, and the Creek* (Stanford: Stanford University Press, 1992).

17. Isaac McCoy, *The Practicability of Indian Reform, Embracing Their Colonization* (Boston: Lincoln and Edmands, 1827), 27–28.

18. Review of *The Practicability of Indian Reform, Embracing Their Colonization,* in *The American Baptist Magazine* 137 (May, 1828), 151. See also, William G. McLoughlin, *Cherokee Renascence in the New Republic* (Princeton: Princeton University Press, 1986), 277–301.

19. Letter from Evan Jones, May 1, 1828, *American Baptist Magazine* 139 (July, 1828), 213 [emphasis mine].

20. "Official Statement of Indian Schools," *The American Baptist Magazine* 134 (February, 1828), 64; McLoughlin, *Cherokees and Missionaries*, 175.

21. For mere legends and hypocrites, see *The American Baptist Magazine* 132 (December 1827) 364. For a different race, see *The American Baptist Magazine*,100 (April, 1825), 111. For majority participation in a traditional rite (a new year ceremony), see *The American Baptist Magazine* 141 (September, 1828), 269. For simultaneous participation in Christianity and traditional religion, see Isaac Proctor to Jeremiah Evarts, December 11, 1827, American Board of Commissioners for Foreign Missions, Houghton Library, Harvard University [henceforth: ABCFM].

22. Journal of Lee Compere, postscript, March 1828, American Indian Correspondence, American Baptist Foreign Mission Societies, Records, 1817–1959, American Baptist Historical Society, Rochester, New York.

23. The myth is related in Grant Foreman, *Sequoyah* (Norman: University of Oklahoma Press, 1938), 21. Another version of the myth, recorded by a Moravian in 1815, is reprinted in Clemens de Baillou, "A Contribution to the Mythology and Conceptual World of the Cherokee Indians," *Ethnohistory* 8 (1961): 100–102. See also Hatley, "The Dividing Paths," 698–99.

24. See Albert V. Goodpasture, "The Paternity of Sequoya, The Inventor of the Cherokee Alphabet," *The Chronicles of Oklahoma* 1 (January, 1921): 121–130; Samuel C. Williams, "The Father of Sequoyah: Nathaniel Gist," *The Chronicles of Oklahoma* 15 (March, 1937): 3–20; William G. McLoughlin, *Cherokees and Missionaries*, 183.

25. See McLoughlin, *Renascence*, 350–354. During a conversation in July, 1991 in Lexington, Kentucky, Theda Perdue directed my attention to this subject.

26. "Invention of the Cherokee Alphabet," August, 13, 1828, the *Cherokee Phoenix*; see also the comments of Samuel Lorenzo Knapp, quoted in Foreman, 24–25.

27. McLoughlin, *Renascence*, 352–353. For knowledge of the alphabet, William Chamberlain's Journal, October 22, 1824, ABCFM; for letters in Cherokee, Isaac Proctor to Jeremiah Evarts, January 25, 1825, ABCFM.

28. McLoughlin, *Cherokees and Missionaries*, 185–186 [emphasis mine].

29. Harold David Williams, "The North Georgia Gold Rush" (Ph.D. dissertation, Auburn University, 1988); Mary Young, "Racism in Red and Black: Indians and Other Free People of Color in Georgia Law, Politics, and Removal Policy," *Georgia Historical Quarterly* 73 (Fall 1988): 492–518; Russell Thornton, "The Demography of the Trail of Tears Period: A New Estimate of Cherokee Population Losses," in *Cherokee Removal: Before and After*, ed. William L. Anderson (Athens: University of Georgia Press, 1991); David Kleit, "Living Under the Threat and Promise of Removal: Conflict and Cooperation in the Cherokee Country During the 1830s," unpublished paper presented at the 1993 Conference of the Society for Historians of the Early American Republic, July 22, 1993, Chapel Hill, North Carolina.

30. Mary Elizabeth Young, *Redskins, Ruffleshirts, and Rednecks: Indian Allotments in Alabama and Mississippi, 1830–1860* (Norman: University of Oklahoma Press, 1961); idem, "Tribal Reorganization in the Southeast, 1800–1842," 59–82; Marvin L. Ellis, III, "The Indian Fires Go Out: Removing the Creeks From Georgia and Alabama, 1825–1837," (M.A. thesis, Auburn University, 1982).

31. Williams, ed., *Adair's History*, 35; Edmond Atkin, *Indians of the Southern Colonial Frontier: The Edmond Atkin Report and Plan of 1755*, ed. by Wilbur Jacobs (Columbia, S.C., 1954), 35; William Bartram, *Travels Through North and South Carolina, Georgia, East and West Florida, The Cherokee Country, The Extensive Territories of the Muscogulges, or Creek Confederacy, and The Country of the Chactaws* (1791, rpt. New York: Penguin, 1988), 53–62; David Taitt, "Journal of David Taitt's Travels from Pensacola, West Florida, to and through the Country of the Upper and Lower Creeks, 1772," in *Travels in the American Colonies*, edited by Newton D. Mereness (New York: Macmillan Company, 1916), 507, 513, 524–525; Joel W. Martin, *Sacred Revolt: The Muskogees' Struggle for a New World* (Boston: Beacon Press, 1991), 65–69; Samuel J. Wells, "Rum, Skins, and Powder: A Choctaw Interpreter and The Treaty of Mount Dexter," *Chronicles of Oklahoma* 1983–84 61(4): 422–428; Blue Clark, "Chickasaw Colonization in Oklahoma," *Chronicles of Oklahoma* 1976 54(1): 44–59; White, *Roots of Dependency*, 69–92, 122.

32. Peter H. Wood, "The Changing Population of the Colonial South: An Overview by Race and Region, 1685–1790," 35–103, in *Powhatan's Mantle*, ed. Peter H. Wood, Gregory A. Waselkov, and Thomas M. Hatley, es59–60; Martin, *Sacred Revolt*, 46–113.

33. For stealing horses, abducting slaves, and killing cattle, see Timothy Barnard to Gov. George Hanley, January 18, 1789, May 27, 1789, November 6,

1789, Unpublished Letters, 86, 94, 98; Timothy Barnard to James Seagrove, July 13, 1792, April 19, 1793, June 20, 1793, Unpublished Letters, 120, 149, 174; Timothy Barnard to Major Henry Gaither, March 4, 1793, Unpublished Letters, 130; Daniel Stewart to General Gunn, November 2, 1796, Creek Indian Letters, Talks, and Treaties, 1705–1839, 420, Department of Archives and History of the State of Georgia, Atlanta, Georgia. For white traders dealing in stolen horses, see "A talk delivered by Mr. Barnard to the Indians assembled at the Cussetahs," March 22, 1793, Unpublished Letters, 132; Timothy Barnard to Major Henry Gaither, April 20, 1793, Unpublished Letters, 154; "A talk from the Big Warrior of the Cussetahs," May 2, 1793, Unpublished Letters, 164. For white poaching of Indian game and plundering of Indian property, see Timothy Barnard to James Seagrove, March 26, 1793, Unpublished Letters, 136; Proceedings of the Court of Enquiry, July 22, 1794, Creek Indian Letters, 387–390. For murder of individual whites, see Timothy Barnard to James Seagrove, May 10, 1792, Unpublished Letters, 116; Timothy Bernard to James Seagrove, April 9, 1793, Unpublished Letters, 142. For captives, see Timothy Barnard to James Seagrove, June 20, 1793, Unpublished Letters, 172. For the plunder of traders' stores, see Timothy Barnard to Major Henry Gaither, April 10, 1793, Unpublished Letters, 143. For intoxication as exonerating circumstance, "Journal of Thomas Bosomworth," August 25, 1752, 286.

34. For dissimulation with missionaries, see Carl Mauelshagen and Gerald H. Davis, trans., *Partners in the Lord's Work: The Diary of Two Moravian Missionaries in the Creek Indian Country*, Research Paper Number 21 (Atlanta: Georgia State College, 1969), 22; see also 30, 72. For silence and feigned ignorance, see Hawkins, *Letters, Journals, and Writings*, I: 47–48. For negotiating strategies, see ibid., II: 562; James F. Doster, *The Creek Indians and Their Florida Lands, 1740–1823* (New York: Garland Publishing, 1974), II: 16; Hoboheilthlee Micco [Hopoithle Miko] to the President of the United States, May 15, 1811, Letters Received by the Office of the Secretary of War on Indian Affairs, 1800–1823, Microcopy #M271 Roll #1 Frame 554, U.S. National Archives, Washington.

35. See James C. Scott, *Domination and the Arts of Resistance: Hidden Transcripts* (New Haven: Yale University Press, 1990). Scott defines the "*public transcript* as a shorthand way of describing the open interaction between subordinates and those who dominate" (2). Hidden transcripts, in contrast, are not expressed so openly. On the one hand, "every subordinate group creates, out of its ordeal, a 'hidden transcript' that represents a critique of power spoken behind the back of the dominant." On the other, "the powerful, for their part, also develop a hidden transcript representing the practices and claims of their rule that cannot be openly avowed" (xii).

36. See *Subaltern Studies: Writings on South Asian History and Society, III*, ed. Ranajit Guha (Oxford: Oxford University Press, 1984); Gayatri Spivak, "Subaltern Studies: Deconstructing Historiography," 197–221, in *In Other Worlds: Essays in Cultural Politics* (New York: Methuen, 1987); Ranahit Guha and Gayatri Chakravorty Spivak, eds., *Selected Subaltern Studies* (New York: Oxford University Press, 1988).

37. William Simpson, August 20, 1803, Letters Received by Sec. of War, Indian Affairs, 1800–1823, Microfilm M-271, Reel 1, NARG 75; William S. Coker and Thomas D. Watson, *Indian Traders of the Southeastern Spanish Borderlands, Panton, Leslie and Company and John Forbes and Company, 1783–1847* (University of West Florida Press: Pensacola, 1986), 228.

38. Timothy Barnard to James Seagrove, July 2, 1793, Unpublished Letters of Timothy Barnard, 1784–1820, 188, Department of Archives and History of the State of Georgia, Atlanta, Georgia.

39. For U.S. collection efforts, see Hawkins, *Letters, Journals and Writings*, 476, 483, 505, 526–527, Coker and Watson, *Indian Traders of the Southeastern Spanish Borderlands*, 227–30, 243–72; Florette Henri, *The Southern Indians and Benjamin Hawkins, 1796–1816* (Norman: University of Oklahoma Press, 1986), 219–220, 244–253; White, *Roots of Dependency*, 95–96; Samuel J. Wells, "Federal Indian Policy: From Accommodation to Removal," 181–213, in *The Choctaw Before Removal*, es186–87, 208n17.

40. Hassig, "Internal Conflict in the Creek War of 1813–1814," 256; Waselkov and Wood, "The Creek War of 1813–1814," 7; Hawkins, *Letters, Writings and Journals*, 631–632, 632–634; Frank Lawrence Owsley, Jr., *The Struggle for the Gulf Borderlands: The Creek War and the Battle of New Orleans, 1812–1815* (Gainesville: University Presses of Florida, 1981), 15–16. See also Douglas Barber, "Council Government and the Genesis of the Creek War," *Alabama Review* 1985 (3): 163–174; Martin, *Sacred Revolt*, 125.

41. Martin, *Sacred Revolt*, 87–113; Henri, *The Southern Indians*, 83–111.

42. Halbert and Ball, *The Creek War*, 71. Geologists refer to this event as the New Madrid earthquake and estimate that it would have measured 8.2 on the Richter scale, thus making it the largest such event to have occurred in North America

in the last several centuries. See Moravian Mission Diary entry, Springplace, Georgia, February 10, 1811, Moravian Archives, Winston-Salem, North Carolina, quoted in McLoughlin, *The Cherokee Ghost Dance*, Appendix E, 142; Francis Howard to Dr. Porter, Jefferson, Georgia, February 14, 1812, "Creek Indian Letters, Talks and Treaties,1782–1839," ed. Louise Frederick Hays, Georgia Department of Archives and History, Atlanta, Georgia; Mauelshagen and Davis, trans. and eds., *Partners in the Lord's Work*, 68; Moravian Mission Diary entry, Springplace, Georgia, December 17, 1811, Moravian Archives, Winston-Salem, North Carolina, quoted in McLoughlin, *The Cherokee Ghost Dance*, Appendix E, 143; R. A. Eppley, *Earthquake History of the United States, Part I* (Washington: Government Printing Office, 1965), 67–68; Yamaguchi, "Macon County, Alabama," 197; *Niles Weekly Register*, Jan. 4, 1812.

43. Homi Bhabha theorizes the problematic of the Book in the colonial context in his articles, "Signs Taken for Wonders: Questions of Ambivalence and Authority under a Tree Outside Delhi, May 1817," *Critical Inquiry* 12 (1985), 144–165; and idem, "Of Mimicry and Man: The Ambivalence of Colonial Discourse," *October* 28 (1984), 125–133; See also Peter Worsley, *The Trumpet Shall Sound*, 241.

44. Mauelshagen and Davis, trans. and eds., *Partners in the Lords' Work*, 53.

45. The following discussion of shamans is based upon Bartram, *Travels*, 390; Jean Bernard-Bossu, *Travels*, 149; Wiliams, *Adair's History*, 90; Swanton, "Creek Ethnographic and Vocabulary Notes"; idem, *The Indians of the Southeastern United States*, 774; Wright, *Creeks and Seminoles*, 157–159; Waselkov and Wood, "The Creek War of 1813–1814," 4.

46. Williams, ed., *Adair's History*, 250 [237].

47. F. L. Cherry, "History of Opelika," *The Alabama Historical Quarterly* Vol. 15, No. 2 (1953): 184; See also, Charles Hudson, "Uktena: A Cherokee Anomalous Monster," *Journal of Cherokee Studies* 3/2 (Spring 1978): 62–75; Raymond D. Fogelson, "Windigo Goes South: Stoneclad among the Cherokees," in *Manlike Monsters on Trial: Early Records and Modern Evidence*, eds. Marjorie M. Halpin and Michael M. Ames (Vancouver: University of British Columbia Press, 1980): 132–151.

48. Nunez, "Creek Nativism," 149.

49. Isaacs had visited Tecumseh in the northwest. According to Woodward, Isaacs was a Muskogee from the town of "Coowersortda [Coosaudee]" (*Woodward's Reminiscences*, 36–37).

50. John Innerarity to James Innerarity, July 27, 1813, Creek Indian Letters, 797. For a much fuller

development of the different shamans' interpretations, see Martin, *Sacred Revolt*, 114–149.

51. Hawkins, *Letters, Journals and Writings*, 652. "Testimony of James Moore," July 13, 1813, Creek Indian Letters, 785. For Redstick coercion, see Hawkins, *Letters, Journal and Writings*, 666, 669, 673.

52. "Report of Alexander Cornells, interpreter, to Colonel Hawkins," June 22, 1813, *American State Papers: Indian Affairs* (Washington: Gales and Seaton, 1832), I, 845–846; Hawkins, *Letters, Journals and Writings*, II: 641; Frank Lawrence Owsley, Jr., *The Struggle for the Gulf Borderlands: The Creek War and the Battle of New Orleans, 1812–1815* (Gainesville: University Presses of Florida, 1981), 17; Martin, *Sacred Revolt*, 114–149.

53. Dowd, *A Spirited Resistance*, 34, 138.

54. Nunez, "Creek Nativism," 146. For the importance of rumor in anti-colonial movements, see Kenelm Burridge, *New Heaven, New Earth: A Study of Millenarian Activities* (New York: Schocken Books, 1969), 106–107; Shahid Amin, "Gandhi as Mahatma: Gorakhpur District, Eastern UP, 1921–22," 1–61, in *Subaltern Studies: Writings on South Asian History and Society, III*, ed. Ranajit Guha (Oxford: Oxford University Press, 1984); James Scott, *Domination and the Arts of Resistance*, 144–148.

55. Hawkins, *Letters, Journals and Writings*, 562.

56. Ibid., 612, 636, 646, 648, 650–51, 654–57, 664, 666, 672. For the migration of Lower Muskogees to Florida, see William C. Sturtevant, "Creek Into Seminole," In *North American Indians in Historical Perspective*, ed. Eleanor Burke Leacock and Nancy Oestreich Lurie (New York: Random House, 1971); Bartram, *Travels*, 181–182. For descriptions of ample game in Florida, see ibid., 165, 170, 172.

57. McLoughlin, *Cherokee Renascence*, 372–375; Edwin C. McReynolds, *Oklahoma: A History of the Sooner State* (Norman: University of Oklahoma Press, 1954),122–23.

58. Notes Furnished A. J. Pickett by the Rev. Lee Compere of Mississippi relating to the Creek Indians among whom he lived as a Missionary, Albert J. Pickett Papers, Notes upon the History of Alabama, section 24, Alabama Department of Archives and History, Montgomery, Alabama.

59. For "considered as a desecration," John Howard Payne, "The Green-Corn Dance," *Continental Monthly*, Vol. 1 (1862), 24.

60. For ignoring, protesting, and delaying, *The American Baptist Magazine* 125 (May 1827): 143–146.

61. Journal of Lee Compere, April 25, 1828, American Indian Correspondence.

A WOMEN'S AWAKENING

Mary P. Ryan

For more than two decades, scholars in the field of women's studies have been working to establish the importance of women's experience in place of the assumption that men adequately represent the human norm. In the area of American religious history most of this new scholarship has focussed on the nineteenth century, a time when women became the great majority of all Protestant church members. As a number of studies have demonstrated, this shift in church membership was prefigured by the early nineteenth-century separation of the home from the workplace during the early phase of industrialization. Men increasingly worked away from home, stayed away from churches, and were identified with a public world of economics and politics; women took control of the household, joined churches, and through their increasingly narrow role as nurturing mothers held sway over a private sphere of children, religion, and morality. Gradually what historians have come to call "woman's sphere," a female dominated household world of piety and domesticity began to emerge.

In "A Women's Awakening," Mary Ryan traces the origins of this change in women's consciousness through the social history of the early nineteenth-century revivals in Utica, New York. The women who converted to the new evangelical faith and created the women's societies that formed around the revivals were the force behind Utica's "awakening." Unlike previous interpretations of the Second Great Awakening as a rite of youthful independence, Ryan argues that the evangelism of mothers led legions of young men and women into the churches. By standing out from the revival crowd and experiencing its egalitarian spirit, women's consciousness was raised. At the same time, these women participated in creating a narrowly maternal role for themselves by helping one another find ways of inculcating morality in their children. Ironically, as the Yale historian Nancy Cott has observed, nineteenth-century evangelical Protestant women were both "bound down" to their children within the home and "bound together" in their women's societies where they gained for themselves a greater autonomy.

Reprinted by permission from Mary P. Ryan, "A Woman's Awakening: Evangelical Religion and the Families of Utica, New York, 1800–1840," *American Quarterly* 30 (1978): 602–623.

8

A WOMEN'S AWAKENING

Evangelical Religion and the Families
of Utica, New York, 1800–1840

Mary P. Ryan

WRITING MORE THAN A QUARTER CENTURY AGO, Whitney Cross observed that women "should dominate a history of enthusiastic movements, for their influence was paramount."[1] Although Cross retreated from the question of the relationship between sex and revivalism, his history of religion and reform in western New York state was riddled with evocative references to women. The women of the "Burned-Over District" still stand in the sidelines of antebellum history ready to play a variety of roles. First of all, there is woman as convert, piously, at times hysterically, approaching the anxious seat. Then there is her more audacious sister, perhaps her alter ego, who grasped for social power under cover of religious enthusiasm as she led men in private prayer or even preached. Finally, hidden in the history of American revivalism, is woman; the power behind the pulpit, the minister's financial and moral support, the convert's evangelizing wife or mother.

A trail of anecdotes leads out of this literature into the eastern section of the Burned-Over District, to the county of Oneida and its bustling regional marketplace, the town of Utica. The grand master of antebellum revivalism, Charles Finney, experienced childhood, courtship, and conversion in Oneida County. More to the point, Finney's career as an evangelist began with a tour of Oneida funded by the Female Missionary Society of the Western District. The direct antecedent of this organization had been established in 1806 at a tiny trading post in the frontier township of Whitestown, the village of Utica. For nearly 20 years the women of Utica carefully prepared the soil, planted and nourished the seeds for Finney's renowned evangelical harvest of 1825 and 1826. Utica, then, is an appropriate place to begin writing the women's history of the Burned-Over District.[2]

Utica and its environs, like other bounded localities, also provides the specific population and a concrete and manageable body of records through which to identify the precise roles women played in the Second Great Awakening. The names of converts were inscribed in the registries of four local churches: the First Presbyterian Church of Utica; its parent church, the First Presbyterian Society of Whitestown, located in the adjacent town of Whitesboro; its offshoot, the Second Presbyerian Church; and one of its denominational rivals, the Whitesboro Baptist Church. Each of these lists of church members was arranged according to the date when a parishioner formally professed his or her faith. Admissions to all churches clustered in a similar chronological pattern with each peak of new entries matching the dates of revivals designated by contemporary observers. Altogether, these lists yield a revival population consisting of over 1,400 men and women who proclaimed their salvation during the years 1814, 1819, 1826, 1830 to 1832, and 1838. The distribution of Christian names within this population indicates that women were in the majority during each revival and at every church. The proportion of female converts ranged from a low of approximately 52 percent in the Whitesboro Baptist Church in 1814 to a high of around 72 percent during the revival that occurred in the same church in 1838. All these proportions were above the sex ratio of the population at large: women constituted slightly less than 50 percent of the combined population of Utica and Whitestown at the beginning of the revival cycle and accounted for only 51.3 percent by 1838. Within the membership of each church, however, women outnumbered men by a larger margin, accounting for 62 to 65 percent of the total admissions. The ratio of females to males occasionally fell below this percentage during seasons of revival. In other words, most revivals, and particularly those of the 1820s and 1830s, saw a relative increase in the proportion of male church members and hence, an actual diminution of the female majority (see Table 1 and 4).[3]

In addition to sex ratios, these simple church lists contain other demographic evidence: kin relationships as signaled by common surnames. The church records of Utica and Whitesboro are meshed with these suggestions of kin ties (see Tables 1 and 2).[4] Depending on which church or revival year is considered, from 17 to 54 percent of the converts professed their faith in the company of relatives. The same records suggest significant differences between men and women: on the one hand the majority of men, as opposed to only one third of the women, assumed full church membership during the same revival period as did persons of the opposite sex and same surname; on the other hand, approximately half the female converts, compared to 41 percent of the males, made their appearance in the church lists unaccompanied by relatives of either sex.

These data evoke at least two hypotheses about the position of women in Utica's evangelical history. First of all, the proportion of solitary female converts suggests that by joining a church independently of relatives many women exercised a degree of religious autonomy during seasons of revival. A second hypothesis can be shakily constructed around the propensity of men to profess their faith in the company of female kin. This statistic could be read as an indication that the male converts were led into the churches by pious wives, mothers, and sisters. This intriguing hypothetical relationship is given further credence by the analysis of the larger kin networks that laced the church membership. Approximately 30 percent of the revival converts were preceded into full church membership by persons who shared their surname. The first family member to enter the church was twice as likely to be female than male. It would follow that women, in addition to constituting the majority of revival converts, were also instrumental in a host of other conversions among their kin of both sexes.

To test these hypotheses requires reference to the records that specify the kin relations that may underlie common surnames. Unfortunately, the volatile communities of antebellum New York are unlikely places in which to find reliable sets of vital statistics. The First Presbyterian Church of Utica compiled the only extensive series of marriage and baptismal records for the revival period. These parish records provide information about the 476 men and women who flocked into the church during the revival seasons. Upon initial examination, these records seem unpromising; more than 60 percent of the men and

Table 1. PERCENTAGE OF CONVERTS BY SEX AND BY SURNAME

Year of Revival	Utica First Presbyterian			Whitesboro Presbyterian			Utica Second Presbyterian			Whitesboro Baptist		
	N*	% Female	% with same surname	N*	% Female	% with same surname	N*	% Female	% with same surname	N*	% Female	% with same surname
1814	65	69.2	41.5	45	69.6	36.9	—	—	—	44	52.3	52.2
1819	90	67.9	27.7	65	56.9	54.5	—	—	—	70	70.0	44.2
1826	123	59.3	35.1	134	67.1	26.9	53	71.6	30.0	87	63.2	40.2
1830	121	58.6	29.7	110	55.4	44.8	236	59.3	31.0	—	—	—
1838	57	56.1	42.1	—	—	—	76	69.7	17.0	82	71.9	46.0

*Total Number of Converts

Table 2. FAMILY PRECEDENTS OF CONVERSION 1800 TO 1838

	Utica First Presbyterian N = 456 %	Whitesboro Presbyterian N = 354 %	Whitesboro Baptist N = 201 %
Converts related to church members	29.7	29.3	30.0
Cases in which males are the first professors	20.7	15.3	29.5
Cases in which females are the first professors	48.3	61.2	43.1
Cases in which couples are the first professors	37.0	23.5	36.2

women admitted to the First Presbyterian church during the revivals left no trace in the birth and marriage records. There is no indication that they underwent baptism, married, or had their children christened in the same church in which they first professed their faith. Thus their age, marital status, and kin associations remain unknown. This poorly documented majority can be described only through a series of negative inferences.

In most cases these elusive church members left the First Presbyterian Church shortly after their revival experiences: fully 30 percent of the converts requested official letters of dismissal within five years of their conversions. Countless others must have left the church more hastily and without this formality. Although women registered their intention of leaving the church less frequently than men, more than a quarter of them had also removed from the place of their conversion within five years (see Table 3).[5] Thus it is safe to draw one conclusion about this historically silent majority: they were, at least in the short run, a peripatetic lot with shallow roots in church and community.

There is reason to suppose that the bulk of revival converts was not only mobile but also young and of relatively low social status. Evidence of youth is convincing in the case of male converts. The low enumeration of converts in city directories compiled soon after the revivals cannot be attributed entirely to mobility. It is also plausible that large numbers of converts failed to meet the qualification for inclusion in the directory, namely, being a head of household. Conversely, when the compilers of the directories changed their policy and began to include young men 17 years of age and over regardless of family status, the number of identifiable converts tended to increase. For example, 44 percent of the male converts of 1838 appeared in that year's directory and were identified as boarders. Almost 65 percent of the male converts whose names appeared in the directory at all exhibited the status of boarder, one which often connoted not only youth but also deracination from the conjugal family.[6] There is little reason to believe that female converts differed markedly from males in age or family status. The absence of almost 60 percent of the female converts from the

Table 3. INDICES OF MOBILITY, AGE AND STATUS FOR UTICA FIRST PRESBYTERIAN CONVERTS

Year of revival	N	% in Church Records	% Dismissed within 5 years	% in Directory	% (of Males) Boarders
1814	65	48	8	14 (1817)	—
1819	90	38	31	9 (1817)	—
1826	123	34	35	17 (1828)	—
1830	121	25	38	22 (1832)	28
1838	57	44	25	24 (1838)	44

records either of marriage or of the parents of newly baptized infants suggests that few of them were adult married women.[7]

The inference that large numbers of Utica's converts were young and single was repeatedly affirmed by contemporary observers. Ministers sympathetic to the revivals admitted that only a choice minority of their converts ranked among the community's respectable heads of households. The opponents of revivalism unleashed apocalyptic rhetoric as they described the age and social status of Finney's recruits. The conservative ministers of Oneida County penned a pastoral letter in 1827 which indicted the leaders of the recent revival for "disregard of the distinctions of age and station," and charged the converts with acts of rebellion against patriarchal authority. A typical crime, the ministers alleged, was to address a church elder as follows: "You old, grey headed sinner, you deserved to have been in hell long ago."[8]

The religious history of Oneida county contains hints of evangelical disregard for the distinctions of sex as well as age. From the town of Paris, located a few miles south of Utica, came a defense of female preaching in the incendiary tones of Deborah Peirce. The author demanded that sinful males "remove the yoke from my sisters' necks," and challenged timid women to "rise up ye careless daughters," and give public testimony for Christ.[9] Another inspired and daring woman toured the environs of Utica preaching against the practice of infant baptism. Martha Howell's evangelism elicited a jeremiad and the accolade Jezebel from James Carnahan, Utica's first Presbyterian minister. Yet a Baptist defender of Martha Howell pointed out that on at least one occasion a woman had spoken before a promiscuous audience in the Reverend Carnahan's own meetinghouse.[10]

These examples of bold female piety were concentrated in rural areas during the first decade of the nineteenth century and were typical of the relatively youthful Baptist and Methodist sects. As such they may be more a symptom of frontier leniency than an example of beneficent evangelical policy toward women. The revivals themselves occasioned only a minor expansion of woman's public role, her right to pray aloud and speak out during religious services. There is evidence that women exercised even this limited new freedom with constraint. In a report favorable to revivals, a committee of the Oneida Presbytery observed; "We have also had various small circles for prayer, as well as stated and public prayer-meetings, and in the former females, in some cases, though more seldom than we could wish, have taken part."[11] In short there is little direct evidence that the young women who swelled Utica's church rolls during the Second Great Awakening were in open and militant defiance of male authority.

Table 4. INDICES OF HOUSEHOLD AND FAMILY CHANGE

Year of Census	Mean Household Size	Child/ Sex Ratio*	% Boarders Woman Ratio**	(in Directory Listings)
1800 (Whitestown Township)	6.19	108.2	2,091	—
1810 (Whitestown Township)	6.22	107.8	2,018	—
1820 (Utica)	6.24	105.6	1,387	—
1830 (Utica)	6.48	103.1	1,008	28 (1835)
1840 (Utica)	6.82	96.9	885	30 (1845)

* Men per 100 women.

** Children aged 0-9 per 1,000 women aged 15–49.

These young women, and men, who passed so quickly and quietly through the evangelical history of Utica left little direct evidence of the motivations surrounding conversion. The personal meaning of conversion can only be illuminated by speculative references to the social world encountered during a sojourn in Utica between 1814 and 1838. The strongest reaction inspired by this time and place was probably a heady sense of change, bustle, and impermanence. The military post known as Fort Schulyer during the Revolution had become a village of some 3,000 inhabitants by 1817. Stimulated by the completion of the Erie Canal in 1825, the town of Utica had grown to a city of four times that population before 1840. Stores, workshops, banks, insurance companies, shipping offices, and law firms proliferated as quickly as the population and apace with the evangelical harvest. In sum, Utica was the archetypal commercial town, the bustling marketplace for a maturing agricultural economy. The sheer volatility and newness of this way of life and making a living might well have augured uncertain futures for Utica's young of either sex.

Young Uticans, however, were spared the direct experience of industrialization and the accompanying challenge to traditional sex roles that beset their neighbors in Whitestown. The influx of young women into the cotton mills of this nearby village had made the men of Whitestown a minority group by the 1820s. Utica's men, by contrast, were nearly equal to women numerically until the advent of the city's first textile factories in 1845. Their preindustrial city offered young Uticans an expanding range of occupations and opportunities, which male converts seemed to have exploited to the fullest. Men entered the revival rolls from the ranks of merchants, shopkeepers, artisans, professionals, white collar workers, and clerks. The lowly class of common laborers, however, contributed only two converts to the entire revival roster. The city directory also recorded a twofold increase in female occupations during the revival era. Yet females still accounted for a mere 3.3 percent of the directory's entries in 1835. The limited ranks of female occupations, chiefly milliners, dressmakers, washerwomen, and teachers, sent only two women, both seamstresses, into the revivals of the First Presbyterian Church. Thus, whatever economic uncertainty might have propelled women to the anxious seat remained hidden in the homes and home economics of the busy city.[12]

Although the majority of the women of Utica remained in the households of shopkeepers and artisans, the advances of a market economy encroached upon their roles. First, the domestic manufacturers that once occupied so much of a woman's time were almost nonexistent in Utica. The entire town produced only 2,500 yards of homespun in 1835, or slightly more than a yard per household. The products of home gardens and dairies were also miniscule within the city limits, at a time when newspapers advertised everything from flour to candles to crockery, all for sale in cash. Utica's market economy was also absorbing the female roles of shopkeeper's assistant and artisan's helper. The cash revenues that accrued to the petty bourgeoisie could pay the wages of a growing number of clerks and hired laborers, all of whom were male. Finally an increasing number of the town's women were removed from the source of their families' livelihood. As early as 1817 approximately 14 percent of entries in the village directory listed separate addresses for home and workplace. Twenty years later this measure of the disintegration of the home economy combined with an extraordinarily high rate of boarding. According to the city directory of 1837-38 a full 28 percent of the entries identified boarders, men and women who resided apart from their kin and remote from their place of work.[13]

The structure of the family as well as the work force changed during the revival era. Although mean household size remained at the same high level (more than six resident members), household composition was changing in important ways. The practice of boarding brought the brittle monetary relations of commercial capitalism into the household itself. Moreover, the proliferation of boarders and boarding houses coincided with a decline in Utica's birth rate. Extrapolating from the federal census of 1820, there were 1,390 children between the ages of zero and ten for every thousand women of childbearing age. This crude measure of fertility had declined to 885, or by 36 percent, at the time of the 1840 census (see Table 4). This drop in the child-woman ratio is due in part to an increase in the proportion of young adult women in the city's population. These unmarried females, rather than shunning motherhood, had simply not yet begun the reproductive period of their life cycles. Nonetheless, the overall role of Utica's women in reproduction, as well as production, declined during the revival period.

Referring to a similar social setting, Nancy Cott has demonstrated how such changes in the history of the family and the economy worked a particular hardship on America's daughters.[14] Cott has argued that the young women who experienced or anticipated changes in their social and economic roles early in the nineteenth century might assuage their anxieties and affirm a modern identity in the act of religious conversion. This interpretation may constitute the best possible explanation for the behavior of the youthful and anonymous majority of Utica's converts. Such inferences do not, however, fully differentiate women's experience from that of the many men who converted at the same time and place. Nor do they account for the dense network of kin ties that riddled church membership lists, often linking male to female in one evangelical process. The kinship of conversion is particularly significant because it invites a revision of the frequent understanding of antebellum revivalism as exemplary of youthful, independent, and individualistic Jacksonian America.

Only an examination of the select minority of converts who left evidence of kin ties in

Utica can yield a more satisfying description of the relation between women and revivalism. Thus the remainder of this analysis is based on the experience of the 160 men and women who left more substantial testimony in the records of Utica's First Presbyterian Church. They may or may not be representative of the bulk of converts who made a minor appearance in the annals of local churches. Nonetheless, the minority commands attention both in its own right and because its more durable church ties insured a greater capacity to affect the course of evangelism itself. Many of these converts, however, made but a single appearance in the vital records—at the time of their marriage, their baptism, or their children's christening. Thus any conclusions based solely on these fragmentary records are heuristic—rare and suggestive tracks through an uncharted historical landscape.

In the case of Utica's first revival, that of 1814, these tracks lead in a specific direction: toward a religious awakening among Utica's parents. Although less than half of those men and women who professed their faith in the 1814 revival left any trace in the vital records, 65 percent of these (or almost a third of all converts) left evidence of being married and 23 percent of them baptized an infant child within a year of their conversion. In addition more than a dozen older children were promptly brought forward to be christened by their newly converted parents. All these relationships reappeared with the second revival in 1819. The subsequent revivals seem to follow naturally upon these first two, as progeny came to supplant parentage as the predominant family status of converts. Despite an increase in the proportion of mobile and independent converts during and after the revival of 1826, approximately 20 percent of the new communicants can be identified as the children of church members. Many of the parents in question had presented these very children for baptism in the full flush of their own conversion in 1814 or 1819. By 1838 more than 40 percent of the converts could be identified as the offspring of this firmly entrenched first generation. In some cases the lineage of conversion had passed unbroken through each stage of the revival cycle. Seventy converts, 15 percent of the total, had a relative who joined the church during a previous or subsequent revival (see Table 5).

Thus beneath the febrile evangelism of Utica's First Presbyterian Church there lay a solid infrastructure, the family cycle of the church's first generation. During the revivals of the 1810s Utica's first settlers took the opportunity to plant religious roots in the frontier soil. These revivals of 1814 and 1819 also coincided with the highest marriage and birth rates in the church's history. The revivals of the 1820s and 1830s can then be attributed to the echo effect of this high birth rate, as the children of the prolific first generation came of age, grew in grace, and professed their faith in the church of their parents. In short, the family pattern of the revivals is in part a reflection of the peculiar demographic history of the First Presbyterian Church.

The family cycle is a partial but hardly sufficient explanation of either revivalism or the conversion of Utica's second generation. Certainly the Presbyterian ministry did not rely on demography as a means of salvation. In fact, they were preoccupied with admonishing Oneida's parents of their obligation to guide their offspring into the church. The theologians of Oneida County steered a treacherous path through Calvinist dogma and simultaneously conducted pamphlet and sermon warfare against the local Baptists—all in defense of infant baptism and the Abrahamic covenant interpreted as a kind of birthright of salvation for their progeny. Every human agency, both pastoral and parental, was mobilized to bring the children of the frontier into full church membership. The Synod of Utica instructed pastors to preach every November on "the privileges and obligations of the Abrahamic covenant,

Table 5. PARENT/CHILD CONVERSIONS FOR UTICA FIRST PRESBYTERIAN CHURCH

Year of Revival	N	Number of Converts in Vital Records	Infants baptized within year	Children of Church members
1814	65	31	15	0
1819	90	33	7	0
1826	123	41	1	25
1830	121	30	1	22
1838	57	25	0	24
Total	456	160	24	71

presenting distinctly the duty of pious parents to dedicate their infant children to God in baptism." The annual sermon should also remind parents of their "responsibilities in connection with their [children's] religious training and the precious grounds of expectation and confidence that, if found faithful, saving blessings would follow." This rather Antinomian interpretation of the lineage of salvation was reinforced by the revival of 1826, which brought so many of the children of the first generation to the ranks of the elect. The report of the clergymen of Oneida on the Finney revival closed with this lesson: "One great end of the baptism of households is that parents and ministers and church may be impressed with the obligation of bringing [their children] up in the nurture and admonition of the Lord." Oneida County was littered with pamphlets, sermons, and ecclesiastical resolutions testifying to this same religious imperative, devising practical ways to guide a section and generation toward salvation and full allegiance to the church of their parents.[15]

This same literature, addressed to "heads of households" or "parents," did not acknowledge the conscientious guardians of this religious inheritance, the mothers. A review of the records of Utica's First Presbyterian Church exposes the female agency of the Second Great Awakening with striking clarity. At the time of the first revival women constituted 70 percent of the church population. The mothers, in other words, first planted the families' religious roots on the frontier. Women certainly claimed a maternal role in the first revival, for 12 percent of all the converts of 1814 appear to have been pregnant when they professed their faith. Mothers, unaccompanied by their mates, also accounted for approximately 70 percent of the baptisms that followed in the wake of revivals in 1814 and 1819.[16] Nancy Lynde exemplified this maternal fervor. Within two years of her conversion in 1814, she had given six children to the Lord in baptism. The church records referred to the children's father, who was not a member of the congregation, by the perfunctory title of Mr. Lynde. This family failed to appear in the village's first directory, compiled in 1817.

Yet in some later revival, perhaps somewhere to the west, the children of Nancy Lynde may have swelled the membership of another evangelical church. At any rate many of Nancy Lynde's peers who remained in Utica enrolled their children in the church during the sequence of revivals that began in 1826. Of those children of church members who dominated the revival of 1838, for example, more than 60 percent professed the faith of their mothers, but not their fathers.[17] These later revivals brought some of Utica's mothers a pious sense of achievement, when after years of prayer and instruction their children pledged their souls to Christ. Harriet Dana must have felt this satisfaction when her son John joined the ranks of the saved in 1826, and again with the belated conversion in 1838 of her son James Dwight Dana, who would soon acquire a national reputation as a Yale professor of natural science. Mrs. Dana's own conversion had occurred in July of 1814, at the zenith of Utica's first revival. She was most likely pregnant at the time; her son James was baptized the following September, his brother John two years thereafter. The religious biographies of an additional eight children are outside the purview of Utica's church records and beyond the time span of the revival cycle.

Another episode in the private revival of Harriet Dana is worthy of note, however. In 1826 James Dana, Senior, joined the church in which his wife had been ensconced for a dozen years. This conjugal dimension of the kinship of conversion was not unusual. In the revival occasioned by Finney's appearance in Utica, for example, seven husbands followed their wives into full church membership after many years of recalcitrance. This trend continued in the revivals that followed, much to the delight of the local ministry, ever eager to snare a head of household. One church history written 40 years after the event recalled with special pride the conversion in 1838 of Mr. John H. Ostrom, lawyer, bank officer, and prominent Utica politician. The author failed to mention that Ostrom's wife, then the young Mary Walker (notable church member and community leader in her own right) had converted in a revival that occurred almost a quarter-century earlier.[18]

Another example illustrates the matrilineage that runs through the history of revivalism in the Utica Presbyterian Church. This story of domestic evangelism began with the conversion of Sophia Bagg, who professed her faith on July 7, 1814, in the company of seven women and two men. Her daughter Emma was baptized the following September; the baptismal covenant was recited for her son Michael 14 months later; and two more sons were christened before 1820. When Finney arrived in Utica, Emma Bagg was at least 11 years old and promptly entered the church. A Mary Ann Bagg who was examined for admission to the church at about the same time may have been another of Sophia's daughters whose baptism was not recorded in the church records. At any rate the family of Sophia Bagg figured prominently in the revival of 1826, for in that year Moses Bagg, the wealthy and respected son of one of Utica's very first entrepreneurs, joined his wife and children in church membership. Moses Bagg was one of those "gentlemen of property and standing" who helped to organize Utica's anti-abolitionist riot in 1835.[19] Amid the uproar of the 1830s the Bagg family continued quietly to play out the family cycle of revivals. Moses Junior ranked among the converts of 1831, and his brother Egbert enrolled in the church in 1838. The Bagg family may be atypical only in social stability, public prominence, and the consequent wealth of historical documentation. Perhaps countless anonymous women left a similar legacy of conversions across the frontier or in poorly documented evangelical denominations, the Baptist and the Methodist.

Nor do the church records reveal the more extended kinship ties that underpinned the revival. Utica supplies one anecdote illustrating this wider network of revivalism and at the same time suggests the modes of evangelism peculiar to women. The central female character in this religious homily generally appears in the church's history under the name of Mrs. C or Aunt Clark. During the revival of 1825 and 1826 Mrs. C was visited by a nephew, a student at nearby Hamilton College. The nephew in question came from conservative Calvinist stock and looked with disdain upon the vulgar evangelist Charles Finney, a friend and temporary neighbor of his aunt. Thus Aunt Clark resorted to a pious deception to entice her young kinsman to a revival meeting at the Utica Presbyterian

Table 6. LINKS BETWEEN REVIVALS AND WOMEN'S ORGANIZATIONS

Year of Revival	N*	Number of Female Converts	Converts in Female Missionary Society	Converts in Maternal Association	Mothers of Converts in Female Missionary Society	Mothers of Converts in Maternal Association
1814	65	45	23	3	0	0
1819	90	57	13	4	0	0
1826	123	73	1	4	18	16
1830	121	71	4	3	7	21
1838	57	32	0	1	6	18
Total	456	278	41	15	31	55

*Utica First Presbyterian Church only.

Church. She persuaded him to attend a morning service on the pretense that Finney would not be preaching until later in the day. Once in the church and in the presence of the despised preacher, the young man realized that he was caught in a trap of woman's making. He recalled it this way: "When we came to the pew door [Aunt Clark] motioned me to go in and followed with several ladies and shut me in." When he attempted a second escape his pious and wily aunt whispered in his ear, "You'll break my heart if you go!" A woman's role in the conversion that ensued would have remained forever unrecorded were it not that the convert in question was none other than Theodore Dwight Weld.[20] The famed abolitionist's aunt was Sophia Clark, whose many accomplishments included the enrollment of at least three children among the revival converts.

Such anecdotes would have to be compounded hundreds of times in order to demonstrate a causal rather than a coincidental relationship between women's revival fervor and the subsequent conversion of their kin. Obtaining such proof would entail an exhaustive and probably futile search through women's diaries and letters for confessions of bringing extreme evangelical pressure to bear upon members of their families. This exercise is not entirely necessary in Utica, where women's role in the revival was not confined to her private efforts. Rather, it was conducted publicly and collectively within two women's organizations, the Female Missionary Society and the Maternal Association. Both these organizations left membership lists, the first for the year 1814, the second dating from 1840 but including the names of deceased members. Despite the sporadic and incomplete nature of these records almost one third of the revival converts can be traced to one of these documents, either directly or through their mothers (see Table 6). For example, Harriet Dana, Mary Walker Ostrom, Sophia Bagg, and Sophia Clark all subscribed to one or both of these organizations.

During the earliest revivals the strongest connection was between female converts and the Missionary Society. More than one third of the women who professed their faith in the revival of 1814 can be found among the members of the Female Missionary Society. In the 1820s and 1830s the links between women and revivalism were more often forged by mothers of converts enrolled in the Maternal Association. By 1838 over 30 percent of the converts had mothers in the Maternal Association alone. Neither missionary societies nor maternal associations were unique to Utica or to the Presbyterian Church. The city's

Table 7. SOCIAL CHARACTERISTICS OF MEMBERS OF WOMEN'S ORGANIZATIONS

Class Composition	Female Missionary Society (N = 55) %	Maternal Association (N = 65) %	Total Directory Listings	
			1817 %	1828 %
Merchants and Merchant Manufacturers	31	25	19	10
Professionals and White Collar	33	18	14	12
Artisans	16	35	40	42
Shopkeepers and Farmers	11	14	8	13
Laborers	—	—	15	14
Widows	7	5	4	6
Female Occupations	2	3	2	3

Baptists, for example, established analogues to both these women's groups. Within these associations—the female contribution to the "new measures" of the Second Great Awakening—the historian can see women weaving the social and familial ties that ran through the revival.

Female missionary activity actually predated the formal organization of both the church and the village of Utica. In 1806 women associated with the First Religious Society of Whitestown met at the nucleus of stores and houses that would become the city of Utica and formed themselves into the Female Charitable Society. These women, who had assembled at the home of Sophia Clark, pledged a small annual contribution toward the support of missionary tours of the New York frontier. By 1824 this women's organization had evolved into the Female Missionary Society of the Western District, which spawned over 70 auxiliaries and contributed more than $1,200 annually for the support of eleven missionaries. The treasurer's report for 1824 revealed that $192 from the Society's coffers had gone to an untried young preacher named Charles Finney.[21]

The organizational and financial sophistication of this woman's organization invites comparison with the trading network built up by Utica's merchant capitalists. In fact the missionary society's officers almost mimic these entrepreneurs. The Female Charitable Society appeared under the heading of "Corporations" in the Utica Almanack for 1810,[22] in the company of a glass factory, a cotton factory, and a bank, as well as the village corporation. Throughout their history and in the style of businessmen the Female Missionary Society elected presidents, vice presidents, and trustees; met in formal meetings; and kept accounts.

The ties between female missionaries and male merchants were more substantial than such analogies. In fact 31 percent of the members of the missionary society were married to "merchants." The men who went by this title in the city directory were rarely shopkeepers but rather substantial retail and wholesale dealers involved in the regional market, men like James and Jerimiah Van Rensselaer, import merchants and scions of the New York aristocracy, or Samuel Stocking, shoe merchant and manufacturer who would amass one of

Utica's largest fortunes. The wives of professional men had almost equal representation in the Missionary Society, and the wives of attorneys contributed almost one third of the membership (see Table 7).[23] Notable among these women were Ann Breese and Sophia Clark, who along with Susan and Adaline Van Rensselaer and Phoebe Stocking served as officers of the Society. By contrast, few wives of artisans, the largest occupational group in Utica, found berths among the officers or membership of the Female Missionary Society. Involvement in the missionary society seems characteristic of the sexual division of labor within Utica's more prominent merchant and professional families. By joining the Female Missionary Society women of the upper class publicly assumed the moral and religious responsibilities of their mercantile households. By efficiently and visibly fulfilling such social obligations these women enhanced the status of their busy mates.

At the same time these groups expanded woman's social role, and in a sphere that was organizationally independent of the male head of the household. Accordingly, another related social characteristic of the members of the Female Missionary Society is as significant as their husbands' class standing. Analysis of the city directories indicates that 66 percent of these women were married to men who maintained a business address detached from their place of residence. This percentage, which is too large to be attributed to a single class within the society's membership, compares with a figure of only 14 percent for the total population listed in the city directory (see Table 7). In other words, the members of the Female Missionary Society differed from the other women of Utica in that they had experienced the removal of basic economic activities from the household to the shops and offices of Genesee Street, hub of Utica's commercial life. It might follow that involvement in religious benevolence filled the consequent vacuum in women's everyday life. To put it another way, participation in the Female Missionary Society might be one way of exercising the first breath of freedom from the duties and restrictions of a patriarchal home economy.

The alternative roles and activities that these women devised for themselves within the missionary society were more social than domestic. That is not to say that the society's officers eschewed heartrending appeals to women's domestic sensibilities. Their circular for 1819 begged the women of western New York to "imagine a pious mother, surrounded with a numerous family—none of them give evidence of possessing an interest in Christ."[24] Yet, although this image may have reflected the personal sentiments of many of the society's members, it led rhetorically to some remote frontier town where a paid agent might save unknown children from damnation. The Female Missionary Society presented itself primarily as the financial support of male missionaries who wrought the conversion of other women's children. This approach typified the early female benevolence that subordinated personal domestic relations to a wider ranging, more highly rationalized, more hierarchical, and more characteristically masculine mode of organization. In 1827 the Female Missionary Society was absorbed into a masculine organization. In that year the society voted to accept an invitation to consolidate with their recently founded male counterpart, the Western Domestic Missionary Society. In the process many of these enterprising women forfeited evangelical leadership to their own husbands. Before this abdication, however, the members of the female missionary society saw their homes, their churches, and the surrounding countryside set ablaze with the evangelical fervor of 1825 and 1826.

The demise of the Female Missionary Society did not mark the retirement of Utica women from the battle for souls. Three years earlier eight members of the First Presbyterian Church, including the ubiquitous Sophia Clark, had formed one of the first Maternal

Associations outside New England. Utica's Maternal Association shared the evangelical purpose of its sister organization and contributed financially to the education of missionaries. Yet most of the association's energy focused in a novel direction. The constitution pledged each member to perform religious and parental duties—praying for each of her children daily, attending meetings every other Wednesday, renewing her child's baptismal covenant regularly, reading systematically through the literature of Christian childrearing, setting a pious example to her offspring at all times, and, finally, spending the anniversary of each child's birth in prayer and fasting. With the formation of the Maternal Association, the evangelical energies of Utica's women seemed to change course. The current that once gushed forth from Utica to inundate countless villages of the Western District was now diverted toward the homes of individual women, where it nurtured grace in the souls of their own children and kindled private family revivals.[25]

This transition from the Female Missionary Society to the Maternal Association hardly occurred in a single movement. Only six of the women associated with the revivals held membership in both organizations. These women represented the pioneer generation; all were converted before 1820 and half of them came from lawyer families. Yet the professional classes were poorly represented in the membership of the Maternal Association. In fact they were outnumbered by the wives of common mechanics. Women of the artisan class accounted for 35 percent of the association's identifiable members and assumed the dominant position granted to merchants' wives within the Missionary Society (see Table 7). The class composition of the Maternal Association reflected the social structure of Utica in the canal era, when the city's economy was geared to small-scale artisan production for the local farm market.

The presence of these representatives of Utica's middling sort introduced some distinctive domestic concerns and relations into the Maternal Association. Consider, for example, the case of the Merrill family, four of whose members (Harriet, Lucina, Maria, and Julia) enrolled in the Maternal Association of the First Presbyterian Church. All these women were linked by marriage to a family of artisan printers and bookbinders. The clan's partriarch, Bildad Merrill, Sr., constructed an extended family economy out of such materials as a series of business partnerships among his sons, brothers, and nephews, and two strategic marital alliances with the family of his first business partner, Talcott Camp. The women who married into this family network inhabited an intricate and difficult domestic environment. In 1834, for example, Julia Merrill appeared before the session meeting of the First Presbyterian Church to charge her mother-in-law, Nancy Camp Merrill, with acts of personal abuse. The trial that ensued brought several of Julia's in-laws to her defense and exposed a frenetic and embittered household to historical scrutiny.

Julia Merrill's home, inhabited by four small children and replete with visiting neighbors, relatives, and customers, was further cluttered by two boarders, her father-in-law and his cranky wife. Nancy Merrill's animosity toward her daughter-in-law became unbearable when the elder Mrs. Merrill, to use Julia's phrase, "Took hold of me with violence." Such domestic contention could not but interfere with the pious mother's fulfillment of her maternal responsibilities. Julia Merrill herself testified that "My little children have often asked why Gramma talked so to me and why mamma cried so."[26] The turmoil in this household may have been rare among Utica's families. Yet there is reason to believe that many members of the Maternal Association inhabited equally complex if more harmonious households. Only 45 percent of the members of the Maternal Association, as opposed to 66 percent of the Missionary Society's members, resided in homes that were separated from the husband's place of work (see Table 7). These women, like Julia Merrill, were likely to reside and work in households that retained many of the economic functions of the "little commonwealth." For many women of the Maternal Association, then, the demands of what they called "Christian Motherhood" came as an addition to the "arduous duties" that continued to characterize the households of Utica's middling sort.

A busy mistress of one of these households, recently awakened to her responsibility for her child's salvation, would seek out a special kind of organization. Accordingly, the founders of the Maternal Association eschewed the elaborate system of officers, trustees, and corporate charters that typified the Female Missionary Society. They resorted instead to the cooperative style exemplified by Article Six of the Association's charter. It stipulated that each mother should "suggest to her sister members such hints as her own experience may furnish, or circumstances seem to render necessary."[27] The Maternal Association may have formalized a longstanding network of neighborly advice and consultation, yet the articulation of common maternal responsibilities and the intention of fulfilling them in such a systematic fashion marked a crucial historical twist both in woman's roles and the methods of evangelism.

The casual organizational structure of the Maternal Association resembles the female prayer groups that Charles Finney discovered in Utica in 1825. The First Presbyterian Church had employed this "new measure" as early as 1822, and there were rumors of a quickening of grace within the woman's prayer group during the same year.[28] The idea for a maternal association probably emerged in one of these religious circles as women shared their anxiety about their children's souls.

It is easy to discern the Maternal Association's history coincided with the opening of the Erie Canal, the doubling of the city's population, and the accompanying proliferation of grog shops, boarding houses, and brothels. Neither the social elite represented by the Female Missionary Society nor relics of the New England social order such as the Presbyterian church trials could successfully oversee public morality. By turning their religious fervor as well as methods of childhood education on their own offspring, the women of the Maternal Association hoped to reinforce the Abrahamic Covenant against the assaults of a secular and individualistic culture. The revivals of 1826, 1831, and 1838 seemed to proclaim their enterprise a success. Known members of the Maternal Association saw at least 55 of their children enter the church during these years.

Toward the end of the revival cycle, Maternal Associations evangelized as much on behalf of their own institutions as for the church itself. In 1833 the Presbyterian Maternal Association voted to establish a magazine that would circulate advice to mothers throughout central New York. The early issues of *The Mother's Magazine* depicted women guiding children and husbands toward salvation. Yet ministers and revival churches that once mediated the kin relations of conversion rarely appeared in these accounts. In fact, the typical reference to clergymen was a polite rebuke for their failure to foster Maternal Associations within their congregations. The Maternal Association seemed to be outgrowing the need for ministers and revivals. In 1835 the female editor of *The Mother's Magazine* put it this way: "The Church has had her seasons of refreshing and her returns of decay; but here in the circle of mothers, it is felt that the Holy Spirit condescends to *dwell*. It seems his blessed 'rest.'"[29] In other words mothers may have ultimately surplanted ministers as the agents of religious conversion and of its functional equivalent, the Christian socialization of children.

More to the point, the experience of a small group of mothers in upstate New York suggests an alternative interpretation of antebellum revivalism. Propelled by the fervor of their own conversions and strengthened by the female institutions that grew up around revivals, Utica women conducted a systematic evangelical campaign. As wives and mothers, and earlier as the trustees of an extensive missionary organization, women's contribution to revivalism did not stop with their own conversions. It exceeded their numbers in the revival population as it expanded to gather in converts of both sexes and spread throughout the revival cycle. The success of this woman's evangelism contradicts the interpretation of the Second Great Awakening as a rite of youthful independence. Quite the contrary, maternal evangelism in particular led scores of young men and women to an active, intensive, and deeply personal affirmation of the faith of their parents. The proliferation of such conversions among the sons and daughters of the middling sort moderated nineteenth-century individualism as it demonstrated the internalization of parental values. Simultaneously, the women who orchestrated the domestic revivals played a central part in creating a narrowly maternal role and image for their sex, with all its attendant contradictions. Thus, if the case of Utica, New York, at all represents the hundreds of communities enbroiled in antebellum revivalism, then women were more than the majority of the converts, more even than the private guardians of America's souls. The combination and consequence of all these roles left the imprint of a women's awakening on American society as well as on American religion.

NOTES

I would like to thank Paul Johnson, Louise Knauer, and Kathryn Kish Sklar for their helpful criticism of an earlier draft of this paper.

1. Whitney R. Cross, *The Burned-Over District: The Social and Intellectual History of Enthusiastic Religion in Western New York*, 1800 to 1850 (Ithaca: Cornell Univ. Press, 1950), 84.

2. Charles Finney, *Memoirs of Reverend Charles G. Finney* (New York, 1876), chaps. 1 and 2; "Records of the Female Charitable Society of Whitestown," MS, The Whitestown Collection, Oneida Historical Society, Utica, N.Y. (hereafter OHS).

3. The records of the First Presbyterian, Utica, and the First Presbyterian, Whitesboro were transcribed from the original by the New York Genealogical and Biographical Society in 1920, edited by Royden Woodward Vosburgh; these typescripts along with the original records from the Second Presbyterian Church and the Whitesboro Baptist Church are found at the Oneida Historical Society and the Utica Public Library. Church records unavailable for the local Methodist Congregation, which reportedly played a small role in Utica's revivals. The records of Trinity Episcopal Church revealed no significant increase in membership during revival years. Sex ratios were calculated from published summaries of the Federal Census, 1800–1840.

4. Of the total number of converts 49.9 percent of the females entered the church alone, 17.6 percent in the company of relatives of the same sex, and 32.5 percent with relatives of the opposite sex; the comparable figures for males are 41.2 percent, 5.5 percent and 53.3 percent.

5. The church records list formal professions of faith made several months after the peak of the revival and exclude professions made in a second church. As such they may underestimate the mobility of converts.

6. Of the 13 known boarders who converted in 1830, 7 resided with persons of a different surname whereas 8 of the 11 boarders were in this position in 1838.

7. See Tables 3 and 5.

8. "Pastoral Letter of the Ministers of the Oneida Association to the Churches under their Care on the Subject of Revivals of Religion" (Utica, 1827), 13–14.

9. Deborah Peirce, "A Scriptural Vindication of Female Preaching, Prophesying, or Exhortation" (n.d., n.p.), OHS.

10. James Carnahan, "Christianity Defended Against the Cavils of Infidels and the Weakness of Enthusiasts" (Utica, 1808), 29; Elias Lee, "A Letter to the Rev. James Carnahan, Pastor of the Presbyterian Churches in Utica and Whitesborough Being a

Defense of Martha Howell and the Baptists Against the Misrepresentations and Aspersions of that Gentleman" (Utica, 1808), 22.

11. "A Narrative of the Revival of Religion in the County of Oneida, Paticularly in the Bounds of the Presbytery of Oneida" (Utica, 1826), 26.

12. Calculations based on: *Census for 1820* (Washington, 1821); *Census of the State of New York for 1835* (Albany, 1836); Manuscript Schedules of the Federal Census for 1840; *Utica City Directory,* 1817, 1837–38. Too few of Utica's converts were traceable in the city directories to provide a precise description of their class backgrounds. For an excellent portrait of male converts, see Paul Johnson, "A Shop Keepers' Millennium: Society and Revivals in Rochester, N. Y., 1815–1837," (Ph.D. diss. UCLA, 1975).

13. Calculations based on *Census of the State of New York for 1835; Utica City Directory,* 1817, 1837–38.

14. Nancy F. Cott, "Young Women in the Second Great Awakening in New England," *Feminist Studies,* 3 (Fall 1975), 14–29.

15. P. H. Fowler, *Historical Sketch of Presbyterianism Within the Bounds of the Synod of Central New York* (Utica, 1844), 110; *Narrative of the Revival,* 54.

16. The Baptismal Records of the First Presbyterian Church reveal that 8 converts of 1814 baptized infant children within nine months of their profession of faith. Of the 28 children of recent converts baptized in 1814 and 1819, 15 had mothers among converts, 11 had 2 parents converting, and only 2 children had merely a father in full church membership.

17. During this revival 24 children of church members converted; 16 of them were preceded into the church by a mother alone, 5 by two parents, and 3 by a father alone.

18. Fowler, 222.

19. See Leonard L. Richards, *Gentlemen of Property and Standing: Anti-Abolitionist Mobs in Jacksonian America* (New York: Oxford Univ. Press, 1970).

20. Charles Beecher, ed., *Autobiography, Correspondence, Etc., of Lyman Beecher, D.D.* (New York, 1865), 2: 310–12.

21. "Minutes of the Whitestown Female Charitable Society," Oct. 21, 1806, MS., OHS; "Constitution of the Female Missionary Society of Oneida" (Utica, 1814); "First Annual Report of the Trustees of the Female Missionary Society of the Western District" (Utica, 1817); "Eighth Annual Report of the Trustees of the Female Missionary Society of the Western District," (Utica, 1824), 19, 20, 24.

22. *Utica Almanack* (Utica, 1810), n.p.

23. The term "shopkeepers" refers to such business designations as "grocery," "drug store," or "hardware store," and conveys fewer pretensions of economic stature than the self-proclaimed title of "merchant."

24. "The Third Annual Report of the Trustees of The Female Missionary Society of the Western District" (Utica, 1819), 26.

25. "Constitution of the 'Material Association of Utica' Adopted June 30, 1824," printed copy, New York State Library, Albany.

26. "Records of the Session Meetings of the First Presbyterian Church," MS, The First Presbyterian Church, Utica, Vol. 11, Nov. 10–Nov. 28, 1834. The Merrill family history was reconstructed from church records, the city directories, and Moses Bagg, Jr., *Pioneers of Utica* (Utica, 1877).

27. "Constitution of the Maternal Association."

28. Session Records, 1, Apr. 1822; 11, July 10, 1822.

29. *The Mother's Magazine,* Jan. 1833, 4–5; June 1833.

THE GENESIS OF MORMONISM

Jan Shipps

The Mormon religion traces its origins to the revelations received by Joseph Smith, Jr., in upstate New York during the religious ferment of the early nineteenth century. Smith's vision of God and Christ, the Angel Moroni's appearances to him, and his discovery of buried golden plates containing lost books of holy scriptures represent the intrusion of sacred power into secular history for Mormons. The subsequent story of persecution, martyrdom of the Prophet Smith, and exodus to the promised land of Salt Lake City enriches the meaning of this sacred history. Unlike previous interpretations that have explained away Mormonism as an idiosyncratic Christian sect, Jan Shipps argues that Mormonism did not seek to reform Protestant Christianity. Rather, utilizing a comparative approach to religion and the insights of cultural anthropologists and theoretical sociologists, Shipps holds that the emergence of Mormonism is best seen as the birth of a new religion.

Reprinted by permission from Jan Shipps, "History as Text," in her *Mormonism: The Story of a New Religious Tradition* (University of Illinois, 1985), 41–65.

9

THE GENESIS OF MORMONISM
The Story of a New Religious Tradition

Jan Shipps

WHEN GOD'S IN HIS HEAVEN and all's right with the world, the nature of divinity is not debatable. The nature of humanity is also settled and the proper divine-human connection is firmly established. An ordered and harmonious universe rests on a complex body of right relationships between humankind and the natural world, on the one hand, and among all manner of persons, on the other. While the pattern of these relationships is rarely articulated, it is universally understood because it follows naturally from cultural conceptions of reality that—in circular fashion—depend on a culture's particular conceptions of divinity, humanity, and the natural world. If things are at sixes and sevens, however, as they are during periods of crisis, dislocation, and change, the equilibrium of assumed agreement that created and supported culture is disturbed. Disordered status relationships develop as novel ways evolve to organize and conduct the business of society under stress. Order and harmony dissipate; tradition disintegrates; only confusion remains.

When answers to questions arising out of concern about property and place are worked out so that the rights and responsibilities of persons in society are clearly specified, order reestablishes itself, harmonizing old and new to make everything right with the world again, although in a far different, much more legalistic atmosphere. But describing the precise character of the network of right relationships on which a culture depends and spelling out the rights and responsibilities attending those relationships is extremely difficult. For that reason, attempts at such articulation often founder on the variability of human beings and the complexity of the changed state of affairs. If that happens, if the rights and responsibilities attending proper relationships cannot be effectively clarified, then confusion veers over toward chaos, a cultural situation that is not so much to be defined as a time in which fundamental questions have no answers as one in which every sort of question—important and unimportant—has too many answers, all of them tentative and subject to modification.

Enough is known about the origins of most of the world's religions to make it clear that this kind of cultural chaos was a precondition for the coming forth of the prophets and enlightened ones whose words and deeds became the focus of the movements that developed into major religious traditions. Yet similarity in the contexts in which these religions came into being is not always noted in general historical and theological surveys of the religions of Judaism, Hinduism, Buddhism, Confucianism, Christianity, and Islam. In fact, so much attention is normally concentrated on the leaders and early followers that it is often hard to discern the corresponding cultural patterns that nourished the different movements. Consequently, the voices of Moses, Gotama, Jesus, Muhammad, and the others may appear to have been heard at random, in circumstances having nothing in common. Actually, however, these voices were all first heard in troubled times and places in which new peoples, new ideas, or new methods of organizing political and economic life had so severely disturbed the traditional network of right relationships that chaotic situations obviously existed.

Moreover, in addition to originating in cultural conditions that had much in common, all these religions accomplished essentially the same thing as they developed. They transformed cultures that were dangerously close to being without form and void into ordered universes. In a manner never easy to determine precisely, the inhabitants of the several cultures under stress came to accept the messages spoken or written by the prophets or enlightened ones as absolutely reliable information that, by extension, could answer all imaginable questions and provide solutions to problems that had appeared insoluble. When the voice of a new religious leader became authoritative for a community, the darkness that had been on the face of the deep gradually disappeared. Chaos was banished; order and harmony were restored.

The perspective provided by the thousands of years since the occurrence of the founding events of the world's major religions makes it easy to identify this characteristic movement from chaos to order. But since the mystery of antiquity shrouds their times of beginnings and since most extant accounts of their histories bear heavy theological burdens, not much is known about what really happened as these religions were established. Details are lacking even about the development of Christianity and Islam, the two youngest world religions. Through close study of artifacts and careful consideration of surviving written documents from the standpoint of both linguistics and literary form, scholars are trying to extend existing knowledge about the process by which cultures were restructured and regained equilibrium as new religions acquired followers and started to be regarded by whole populations as sources of ultimate authority. But the serious problem of missing information presents an immense challenge to students of the history of pre-exilic Israel, for example, or early Hinduism, Buddhism, Christianity, and so on.

Students of Mormonism are not similarly confronted by the challenge of missing information. Because this movement started in the United States in the late 1820s and early 1830s, it is not difficult to establish the extent of cultural confusion, occasioned by dislocation and change that infected the milieu into which it came. In addition, there is evidence aplenty about the Mormons themselves since, as religious duty requires, they have been prodigious record-keepers from the very beginning, preserving for their posterity full accounts of what happened to them personally and what happened to the movement corporately. But if it seems, at first blush, that all this firsthand evidence would make describing the beginnings of Mormonism so simple that its story could readily serve as a modern analogue that could shed light on how the older religions started and became established, this is not exactly the case.

While neither temporal distance nor lack of evidence hamper the recovery of the Mormon story, conflicting data are a serious problem. In addition to primary and secondary accounts written by Latter-day Saints who were there when things occurred and by Saints who became a part of the movement somewhat later, but who heard the principals tell the story of what happened, the genesis of Mormonism is described in a large number of contemporary accounts written by persons who had moved into and then back out of close association with the Saints and by persons who merely observed the movement from the outside. As a result, rather than one story, there are several stories of Mormon beginnings from which to choose.

Alternative narratives about Joseph Smith and the coming forth of the Book of Mormon evolved from these conflicting sources. One of them is about ancient records engraved on metal plates translated by a young man chosen by God for the task, and the other describes a work of nineteenth-century fiction somehow produced by a ne'er-do-well member of a disreputable farm family living on the fringes of society in western New York. This is the place to consider the amazing persistence across time of both this elemental component of the Mormon faith-story and its antithesis. Since the days of its first telling, intense efforts have been made to explain the Mormon story away by citing contemporary reports of the unsavory character of Joseph Smith and his entire family, and by compiling a wealth of commonsense information about obvious Book of Mormon parallels to other nineteenth-century accounts tying the American Indian to Israel's lost tribes; also by pointing out the book's descriptions of situations, incidents, characters, and theology suspiciously like those within its so-called translator's ken, and its echoes of Masonic lore, its Isaiah passages, and its bountiful anachronism supply. But while new accounts ringing the changes on the anti-Mormon version of Smith's story have continued to appear, at what sometimes seem regular intervals since Alexander Campbell first analyzed the Book of Mormon in the *Millennial Harbinger* in 1831, and Eber D. Howe published *Mormonism Unvailed* in 1834, the prophet's testimony endures, unchanged in any particular, a stumbling block to scientific history and foolishness to many.

Thus, the story of Mormon beginnings appears to be an exception to the normal modern expectation that natural explanation based on objective evidence will be more persuasive than supernatural explanation growing from subjective accounts. Like the gospels that include the story of the resurrection of Jesus without supporting it with objective evidence obtained from persons outside the incipient Christian community, the Mormon story includes an account of the translation of the Book of Mormon supported only by the testimony of members of the incipient LDS community. In both of these instances, the story of a tradition's beginnings rests on a paradoxical event that has proved anomalous enough to sustain the weight of supernatural explanation across a long period of time. Furthermore, in the Christian tradition, the story of the resurrection of Jesus in the flesh has not only been kept alive within the community of faith, but it has been brought to life again and again outside it. So, likewise, the LDS account of the translation of sacred records by one who became a prophet has been preserved within Mormonism and also has over and over again proved persuasive to individuals outside the community, notwithstanding the commonsense arguments that, in an open and public manner, have repeatedly called into question the supernatural explanation that undergirds the Mormon story.

Parallels between Christianity and Mormonism are not limited to their both having been introduced into contexts of cultural crisis and both having faith-stories that rest on paradoxical events. Before others can be pointed out, however, explicit distinctions need to be made among the several terms generally used to refer to communities of faith gathered under different circumstances for different reasons. *For the purposes of this discussion*, the most economical and unambiguous means of making such distinctions is developing definitions that all refer to the usual categories or dimensions—mythological, doctrinal, ritual/liturgical, ethical, social/institutional, and experiential—that scholars have developed over the years to facilitate discussion of religion.[1] Here, however, these dimensions need to be ranked so that the most significant is the mythological rather than the experiential (the classification very often receiving greatest emphasis in studies of specific religious traditions, because it is the one that includes the reports of direct encounters with the sacred that are turned into the founding stories of new religious movements), the doctrinal (the area so often stressed in apologetic works), or the social/institutional (the dimension that was the main focus of both the sociological and historical study of religion for many years and the one that remains the primary focus of much of the sociological study of the topic). Moreover, besides elevating the mythological dimension to primacy in this instance, it is extremely important to keep in mind that when it is used in religious studies, mythological does not refer to fairy tales, fables, and other forms of patent untruth. It refers to *story*, to accounts of beginnings (dramatizing how the world came to be) and endings (holding out possibilities both of devastation and renewal), of sin and redemption, of heroes, heroines, and life lived out in the larger-than-life "olden days" when divinity is said to have dealt with humanity face to face, providing a foundation for culture.

Because the word *religion* is so general that it is difficult to use in a definite or precise sense, *religious tradition* will here be used as the umbrella category that will cover (i) all the corporate bodies and (2) individuals unattached to corporate bodies in whose systems of belief a particular story is central. Because Abraham's story and Israel's history are central to the mythological dimension of more than one tradition in Western religion, a distinction will be made here between the Jews, whose belief system rests on this story essentially as it is recorded in the Old Testament, and other traditions whose belief systems center on the same story plus significant additions or alterations. By this means the elements in the so-called Judeo-Christian tradition will be precipitated out, since the account of the resurrection of Jesus and the report of his everlasting existence at the right hand of God make it impossible to fit the Christian Messiah into any of the categories by which Old Testament figures are classified. As the Christian story is neither simply a reinterpretation nor continuation of the Hebraic-Judaic story, so the Mormon story departs significantly from the story of Abraham and the histories of Israel and Christianity as those stories are understood by Christians and Jews.

This departure started with the Book of Mormon. But even as it reiterated the Judeo-Christian story in a different framework, that work served as a conduit to bring Christianity's mythological base into the New World more or less directly. Other LDS additions and modifications are much more consequential. Alterations to the story that came in Joseph Smith's revelations, especially the Book of Moses, and his translations of the Bible and the Book of Abraham—this last accomplished by means of inspiration using an Egyptian papyrus as text—are the truly important counters to charges that the Mormon story is merely an idiosyncratic interpretation of the Christian story.

Church, denomination, sect, and *cult* are the other widely used technical terms that refer to communities of faith. In a study in which establishing classifications for the various LDS communities is one of the principal goals, their use is indispensable. Yet these are vexing terms in which subjective rankings stubbornly inhere. For that reason, it must be understood at the outset that when they are used in this study no value load is attached. Descriptions of faith communities as churches or denominations are usually interpreted as expressions of respect, while descriptions of the same communities as sects or cults are generally thought to be expressions of disrespect, with *cult* being the more pejorative term, but that is not the case here.

A long tradition of the study of religion in society has produced a body of well-developed and fully articulated theory which makes useful distinctions among these four terms, with particular regard for the social and psychological makeup of the different communities and for the manner in which churches, denominations, sects, and cults are related to the sources of power in their cultures. Much use is made of these illuminating distinctions in the following chapters (where appropriate reference is made to the works of the sociologists and anthropologists who worked these distinctions out), but this particular study places more emphasis on the distinctions that grow out of considering religion's mythological dimension.

Therefore, the term *church* will be used to refer specifically to institutions that assume direct responsibility for the whole of a tradition's story: for proclaiming it, keeping it alive through liturgy and ritual, and transmitting it from one generation to another; for preserving the story's integrity through canonization and systematic doctrinal statement; and for drawing from it patterns, examples, and principles that will insure the arrangement of a network of right relationships within the community, will prescribe the proper relationships to maintain with the world outside, and will serve as the basis for an ethical code. *Denomination* also refers to an institution, one that is by and large a subdivision of a church, the more inclusive term. Denominations likewise bear responsibility for a tradition's story, but as a result of their various histories, the different denominations within a tradition preserve the story in distinctive ways, emphasizing some things and neglecting others. *Sect* refers to a group that coalesces around a leader or leaders who find themselves in disagreement with ecclesiastical authorities over matters that manifest themselves as concern about ritual and liturgy, institutional structure, the pattern of relationships within and without the community, or the nature of authentic spiritual experience, but are matters ultimately rooted in disagreement over interpretation of a tradition's story and the implications following therefrom. *Cult*, by contrast, refers to a group that coalesces around a leader who mounts a challenge to the fundamental integrity of a tradition's story by adding to it, subtracting from it, or by changing it in some more radical way than merely setting out a new interpretation of the events and happenings in the existing story.

Churches and denominations resemble each other, especially in that—more inclusive than exclusive—they serve as unifying agents in culture. By telling and retelling their tradition's story, they perpetuate a common symbolic universe that strengthens the life of the community. But unlike churches and denominations that are more or less contiguous with culture, sects and cults separate themselves from the community, create alternative symbolic universes, and erect and maintain virtually impenetrable boundaries between inside and outside. The two are socially similar in the makeup of their membership, in their appeal to the disinherited (whether relatively or absolutely deprived), and in their tendency to become millenarian/millennial movements. Yet sects and cults stand in opposition to the world on different grounds. However much they are alike in the way their activities turn out to sanction simultaneously the social, political, and economic aspirations of those who join and question prevailing cultural assumptions about power and prestige, it is important to remember that a sect grows out of disagreement over how a tradition's story ought to be understood, i.e. over interpretation, while a cult's antagonistic stance rests on acceptance of a story changed in essentials, not just by means of interpretation. Notwithstanding its quarrel with denomination or church over the correct understanding of a tradition's story, a sect remains under the same categorical umbrella as its adversaries. But the same cannot be said about a cult. If it survives and grows, the altered story eventually becomes central to a new system of belief that serves as the foundation of a new religious tradition.

As recently as the decades of the 1960s and 1970s, history again proved the truth of the maxim that when cultural confusion starts to tilt toward chaos, prophets and enlightened ones appear on every hand. Insufficient time has elapsed to allow knowledgeable assessment of the potential staying power of any of the new methods of reaching blissful states, new means of assuring redemption, or new candidates to messianic leadership that attracted such amazing numbers of followers ten or twenty years ago. But looking back to this recent period of frenetic religious novelty is instructive, because it provides a valuable comparative perspective from which to view the proliferation of unusual, different, and sometimes bizarre religious movements in the United States in the period of the early republic, from 1800 to 1860. For that matter, the comparison can likewise be extended backward in time to the volatile religious situation in Palestine at the turn of the ages. Just as Sun Myung Moon was not the first or even the twenty-first person to claim a divinely issued leadership mandate in the contemporary world, Joseph Smith was not the first or even the twenty-first American prophet of his day, any more than Jesus was the first or even the twenty-first Jewish prophet to claim a divine calling in inter-testamental times.

The babble of voices of potential prophets and the concatenation of religious claims during these three periods led to the development of more faith communities than it is now possible to count. Yet of that enormous number, a very select few developed into significant religious movements, and most of those were sectarian groups—Pharasaic Jews, for example, Seventh-day Adventists, Christian Scientists, or the so-called Jesus Freaks—who gradually found comfortable places for their interpretations of their traditions' stories within the religious traditions that spawned them. Of the cultic movements whose members accepted radically revised or fundamentally altered versions of the faith-stories regnant in their cultures, only Christianity and Mormonism are now full-scale religious traditions. How and why did these two movements take hold and develop into religious traditions while many other movements of essentially the same character lost followers and failed to last more than a decade or two?

When this question is posed to persons within a faith community, their response to the *why* part of the compound query often refers—directly or indirectly—to the will of the divine; their answers to the *how* part are then advanced in light of an ontological argument that uses the movement's survival and growth as evidence that it is "of God" and that, therefore, the ultimate explanation of its survival and growth is that it was God's will. As reassuring as such reasoning is within the community of faith and as useful as it is as a missionary tool, it finally convinces only those who are within (and those who are ready to move into) the faith circle. And yet, because this matter of why and how one religious movement flourishes while a virtually identical counterpart does not is so perplexing to persons interested in religion as phenomenon that there is no shortage of alternative explanations or bodies of theory to fit them in.

Still another theory that would make it possible to predict whether, out of the multiplicity of religious movements on the contemporary scene, Scientology, say, or Transcendental Meditation will be around 500 years from now is not being proposed here. Instead, in an important sense, Mormonism is being used here as a case study that falls generally into the ongoing wide-ranging exploration of the important question of what it is that makes one movement thrive while others wither and die. More specifically, an examination of Mormonism from this perspective fits into efforts currently under way to investigate the *process* by which religious movements survive and grow. But unlike many social science analyses that focus on a triad composed of (I) the cultural situation, (2) potential converts, and (3) leaders and their claims, this one concentrates on what went on within the movement itself as Mormonism moved along the rigorous and treacherous path from cult to religious tradition.

Religion in nineteenth-century America was like a collage made up of a huge number of diverse materials put together in a pattern that made sense to the artist but that still appeared to many observers to be a jumble and little more. The one common element that pulled American religion together was the religious history of Europe. Despite the Reformation and a good deal of less formidable sectarian splintering, the story of European Christianity provided a thread that, while it did not bind American religion together internally, did connect all the separate parts to the Apostolic era. European religious history was even shared by the Jews, who, as descendants of the people shamefully treated for something their ancestors had reputedly done to Jesus, were also bound, unhappily, to New Testament times. Latter-day Saints, however, were not tied to the ministry of Jesus and the world of the early church through the history of Christianity in Europe. Theirs was a different past.

Actually, the very first Mormons did not merely have a past that differed from the past of other nineteenth-century Americans; they had no recent past at all. Just as the outcome of the American Revolution had left the former English colonies without a usable political history, by designating all existing churches—not just the Roman Catholic variety—as corrupt abominations growing out of a "Great Apostasy" that began in the days of the ancient apostles, the Book of Mormon left the Saints with an enormous 1,400- to 1,800-year lacuna in their religious history. This huge hiatus meant that parallels between their experiences and experiences described in the Bible came so naturally to the Saints that, as immensely egotistical as it now sounds, even Sidney Rigdon's observation that his agonizing imprisonment in Liberty Jail was comparable to the sufferings of Jesus is not terribly surprising, since the LDS pantheon of saints and martyrs did not include Joan of Arc, Savonarola, and the "inhabitants" of Foxe's *Acts and Monuments*, from which a more appropriate comparative referent might have been found. Yet the profound historylessness of early Mormonism cannot be satisfactorily explained entirely in terms of the Saints' conscious rejection of the institutional history of Christianity.

Something more fundamental had happened, and, although it involves dealing in abstractions to some extent, comprehending what it was is so critical to this study that it needs to be spelled out one step at a time:

1.   History, the story of the past, is linear. It moves from step A to step B, from promise to consummation, from prophecy to fulfillment.
2.   Since it was at one and the same time prophecy (a book that said it was an ancient record prophesying that a book would come forth) and (as the book that had come

forth) fulfillment of that prophecy, the coming forth of the Book of Mormon effected a break in the very fabric of history.

3.   This interruption of history's presumably inexorably linear movement wiped clean the slate on which the story of the past had been written, making a place for the story of a past that led directly up to "the new dispensation of the fulness of times" whose events would be recorded there.

4.   Standing on the threshold of a new age, the first Mormons were, then, suspended between an unusable past and an uncertain future, returned as it were to a primordial state.

5.   But as their future unfolded, the activities the Saints engaged in—reestablishing the covenant, gathering the Lord's elect, separating Israel from the Gentiles, organizing the church, preaching the gospel, building up the kingdom—took on such a familiar cast that it is plain to see that they moved out of the primordial present into the future by replicating the past.

6.   This replication was not conscious ritual re-creation of events, but rather experiential "living through" of sacred events in a new age.

7.   Although it seemed strange and even dangerous in the modern world of nineteenth-century America, this activity allowed the Saints to recover their own past, their own salvation history, which, despite its similarity to words and acts, places and events in the biblical stories of Israel's history and the history of Christianity, was the *heilsgeschichte* of neither Christian nor Jew.

Analyzed in this fashion, this process may sound more complicated than it really was. People who base their understanding of reality on a new set of religious claims often (perhaps always) come to the conclusion that the past is utterly irrelevant in view of an imminent *eschaton*. In truth, however, the past is a matter of fundamental importance to new religious movements. The assertions on which they rest inevitably alter the prevailing understanding of what has gone before, creating situations in which past and future must both be made new. Believing that Jesus fulfilled Mosaic law and Hebrew prophecy with his life and death, early Christians, for example, could no longer share a vision of the past with other Jews. They were as much constrained to create a usable past for themselves in the years between 50 and 150 C.E. as were the Mormons between 1830 and 1930.

Actually, Christianity and Mormonism both rest finally on claims that in them Hebrew prophecy has been fulfilled. Jesus was said to be Messiah, the king who would rule Zion in righteousness, whose coming Isaiah had foretold. The Book of Mormon was said to be the "stick of Joseph in the hand of Ephraim" of which Ezekiel spoke as he described the coming of the undivided Kingdom of God. By recognizing this structural parallel, and by paying close attention to what happened as the early Christian saints appropriated a vision of Israel's past that could be ritually re-created to serve as meaningful background to the Christian story, it is possible to discern the pattern of reappropriation that allowed the Latter-day Saints to take as their own a vision of the past of both Israel and Christianity that now serves both directly and through ritual re-creation as meaningful background to the Mormon story.

While the difficulty of reconstructing exactly how things happened nearly 2,000 years ago frustrates the development of an elaborate theoretical model that could be rigorously tested, it is clear that in early Christianity, the pattern of recovery included four principal activities: *reiteration* of Israel's story, with heavy emphasis on the means by which the life and death of Jesus fulfilled Hebrew law and prophecy; theological *reinterpretation*, based on consideration of the meaning of the story in light of what was seen as the eschatological event of the ages, the resurrection of Christ; actual *recapitulation* of key events of the story in a new setting; and appropriate *ritual re-creation* of the story in a Christian context. Furthermore, it is also clear that through these acts of appropriation, Christianity transformed Israel's past so that it seemed as alien to the Jews as did the developing Christian tradition whose belief system was supported not only by the proclamation of a resurrected messiah, but also by a particular vision of Israel's history that gave meaning to the life and death of Jesus. In the nineteenth century the Mormons were engaged in similar activities, out of which emerged a similar result. This time, however, reiteration, reinterpretation, recapitulation, and ritual re-creation of the significant events in Israel's past *and* the significant events in the story of early Christianity were both required.

Just as the early Mormons tended to be persons who were well versed in the Judeo-Christian scriptures, and hence sufficiently familiar with both the story and prophecy to be sensitive to the claims that were set forth in the Book of Mormon, so it was that the first Christians were persons who not only knew what had happened to Israel before their time, but knew prophecy intimately enough to appreciate all the fine points of the declaration that Jesus was the long-anticipated Messiah. For that reason, and since the Hebrew Bible served as the basic Christian scripture, it is very likely that the sort of reiteration of Israel's story preserved in Chapter 7 of the Book of Acts occurred repeatedly in the initial stages of the formation of the Christian community.[2] The Book of Hebrews is perhaps the most explicit example of theological reinterpretation of key portions of the Old Testament story in the Christian canon. But the entire New Testament makes it obvious that, in addition to repetition of the assertion that Hebrew prophecy had been fulfilled, reinterpretation of Israel's story was an integral part of what was going on.

The community's recapitulation of the salvation history of the Hebrews must be recaptured mainly through its reflection in the construction of the gospels, which means that it is hard to determine precisely whether this (perhaps necessary) phenomenon preceded, accompanied (as is probable), or followed theological reinterpretation. Also difficult to determine with any precision is where Christianity's ritual re-creation of Israel's story entered the developmental sequence. Notwithstanding when they started, however, Christianity's activities of recapitulation and ritual recreation are evident in the way that, as retold, the life of Jesus played out Israel's story once again. John the Baptist was clothed in Elijah's raiment, for example, and the miraculous circumstances surrounding his conception and birth practically parallel the story of the conception and birth of Samuel; Mary and Joseph carried Jesus down into Egypt, where the children of Israel once sojourned; the crossing of the Red Sea was symbolically repeated in the baptism of Jesus; the days He spent in the wilderness numbered forty as did the years the Israelites spent in the wilderness; like the tribes of Israel, the disciples Jesus led numbered twelve; He went up into a mountain, from which He dispensed the law; and so on. More directly, Christianity's recapitulation of Israel's story is revealed in the account of what went on at Pentecost. And while its incorporation into the community's ritual and liturigical life leaves the impression that the Eucharist recalls only the Lord's Supper, it is possible that, even though the communal meals in early Christian times probably were not consciously conducted as Passover meals, they were nevertheless recapitulations of events connected with the Exodus, the Passover, and God's miraculous provision of manna to the Israelites in the wilderness.

So delineated, the activities by which the early Christians appropriated Israel's past, made it an integral part of their ritual and liturgical life, and used it as the foundation for the development of a new religious tradition appear more spontaneous than calculated, more open than esoteric, more transparent than opaque. Because the LDS reiteration of the Hebrew-Christian story was inaugurated with the Book of Mormon, because its theological reinterpretation came through Joseph Smith's revelations and translations as well as through the sermons of Joseph Smith and Brigham Young and the sermons and writings of such persons as Orson and Parley Pratt, because the Saints were obliged to recapitulate the significant events in the stories of Israel and Christianity virtually simultaneously, and because the ritual re-creations of such extremely critical parts of the story as creation and redemption were introduced in the LDS temple ordinances that are not in the public domain, the process by which Mormonism recovered its salvation history from the Hebrew-Christian story is not nearly so open and transparent. For those reasons, despite the availability of an enormous body of primary source material, early Mormonism has proved to be almost impervious to objective study.

The Christian structural parallel suggests, however, a means of ordering the data that clarifies the picture of the reiteration and reinterpretation of Christianity's mythological dimension that was at the heart of early Mormonism. More important, the Christian pattern illuminates Mormon history by suggesting that Mormonism's ritual re-creation of the stories of Israel and Christianity rests not only on theological reinterpretation, but on a recapitulation of biblical events much more complex than scholars have heretofore recognized. When Russell Mortensen and William Mulder pulled together their extremely useful collection of source documents, published under the title *Among the Mormons* in 1958, they designated the sections of the book "Genesis," "Exodus," "Lamentations and Judges," and "Psalms," for example.[3] But as they made no effort in the editorial matter to argue that the Mormons had actually replicated these scriptural accounts, it is clear that the titles were simply descriptive labels suggesting a connection between the nineteenth-century Mormon experience and the events described in the Bible. This connection has also been noted by virtually every person who has ever attempted a narrative reconstruction of the Mormon past. But the extent to which the Saints recapitulated the Hebrew-Christian story by living it through again does not really reveal itself in chronological accounts of LDS history.

Linear recounting divides the first sixty years of Mormon history into chronological units that reveal an almost unrelieved movement from east to west in the United States and a consistent pattern of growth despite unceasing opposition. It describes important LDS doctrinal and institutional developments and concentrates heavily on the conflict between Mormonism and the national government, as well as the governments of the several states in which the Saints settled for a time. Told in this fashion, the story begins with Joseph Smith's First Vision in 1820, proceeds to the publication of the Book of Mormon, the organization of the church, and its subsequent removal from western New York to Kirtland, Ohio. The construction of the Kirtland temple, economic and political troubles in the Old Northwest, and Mormon settlement in Independence, Missouri, make up the second chronological segment. The Missouri period, which concludes with a Mormon war in which the Saints are driven back across the Mississippi River, dramatizes Mormon-Gentile conflict and points out fundamental differences in the character of the sociopolitical organization of Mormon and non-Mormon society. Accounts of the Nauvoo years following the Missouri episode stress this *Gemeinschaft-Gesellschaft* distinction, the introduction of plural marriage into Mormonism, and the murders in 1844 of Joseph and Hyrum Smith that bring the first linear unit of Mormonism to an end. The struggle for possession of the "mantle of the prophet" which led to an atomization of the movement opens Mormonism's second chronological unit. From that point forward there are several Mormon histories, not just one. But all the others are ordinarily treated as footnotes to the more dramatic story of the Saints' journey to the intermountain region and their establishing the State of Deseret there.

Narratives of the pioneer period are dominated by the Mormon War of 1857, the continuing practice of polygamy, the struggle for political hegemony between the Latter-day Saints and the representatives of the federal government, the "Raid," in which polygamous Saints were driven into hiding in order to escape imprisonment, and the "Manifesto," in which the president of the LDS Church acknowledged Mormon acquiescence to the government's demand for a cessation of the practice of plural marriage. Emphasis is placed on Brigham Young and other Mormon leaders, on the Saints' achievements in making the desert "blossom as a rose," on the sophisticated political and economic organization of the community, the systematizing of LDS doctrine, the efficient bureaucratic structure of the church, and so on.

While it is all fascinating, it is by and large an exterior story rather than an interior one. Nevertheless, whether it has been set out as a mass of undigested information in need of analysis or analyzed with great skill by scholars trained to apply the canons of professional/scientific history to the records the Saints left behind, most Mormon history has been written in this mode. As a result, although many details need to be filled in, the main outlines of the institutional history of Mormonism are well known, and the story of the interrelationships between Mormonism and American culture is reasonably clear. But exoteric history does not always provide satisfactory answers to questions about the essential differences between the Mormonism of the early period and modern Mormonism, or to queries about how each of the several forms of Mormonism differs from all the others. The answers to these and many other questions about the LDS past are related to Mormonism's recapitulation of the biblical stories of God's chosen people.

This recapitulation process started with the discovery of a book whose contents told Saints in the nineteenth century what had happened to the people of God who came to America before them in much the same way that the priests' discovery in the recesses of the temple of a book said to have been written by Moses told the people in King Josiah's reign about those who came to Israel before them. Then the process moved forward through a series of "reprises" of events in the Hebrew-Christian story. But because the Saints had both to appropriate Israel's story and *re*appropriate Christianity's appropriation of the same story, the process did not involve linear movement through the story from beginning to end. Hence, the "restoration" of the Aaronic (Levitical) priesthood in 1829 was followed in less than a year by the organization of a "Church of Jesus Christ." A temple modeled on the pre-exilic temple of Solomon's day was constructed in Kirtland, but in the initial ceremonies conducted there, the Christian ordinance of washing of the feet was introduced. More directly integrating old and new was an 1836 vision in which Joseph Smith and Oliver Cowdery, who had separated themselves from the congregation in the temple by retiring behind the veils surrounding the pulpit, were visited by "the Lord." The eyes of their understanding were opened, and they saw this personage, who spoke with a voice that "was as the sound of the rushing of great waters, even the voice of Jehovah," and yet one who—in accepting the temple as a place in which he would manifest himself to his people—identified himself by saying, "I am the first and the last; I am he who liveth, I am he who was slain; I am your advocate with the Father." In that same visionary episode, recalling Matthew: 17, the prophet and his Second Counselor were visited by Moses, Elijah, and Elias, who committed into LDS hands the keys to the gathering of Israel and the "new dispensation of the fullness of times."[4]

The Saints started to build a City of God that would be the jewel of a literal kingdom organized on the Hebrew model. But when the Mormon kingdom was buffeted with troubles as dreadful as any with which ancient Israel had to contend, opinion among the Saints divided, as in the olden days, about whether God would continue to act inside history or outside it. Apocalyptic expectation likewise integrated the experiences of the Israelites and early Christians with Mormon experience, since no matter whether they looked back to the Book of Daniel or to Revelation, Saints came to believe that they were living in the world's "winding-up scene."

For complex reasons related to the fact that the Nauvoo experience was a recapitulation of the so-called Patriarchal Age for only a part of the Mormon population, Joseph Smith's murder was not generally perceived as a reprise of the crucifixion. He sealed his testimony with his blood, as Brigham Young said, but the result did not unify Mormonism. Instead, the prophet's death ushered in divisions in Mormonism that are as dramatic and potentially as long-standing as the sundering of Israel's northern and southern tribes, because the murder brought the recapitulation process to an abrupt halt in the experience of one part of the community, while the same murder exponentially intensified it in the other part. For the former, Mormonism ever afterward took on the character of primitive Christianity that it had had in the very beginning. For the latter, the prophet's observation that he was "going as a lamb to slaughter" apparently suggested suffering servant more than crucified messiah, Israel more than early Christianity, since his death turned these Latter-day Saints away from New Testament stories to an even more elaborate and direct reprise of Old Testament times.

Historical accounts of the corporate movement of the Saints from Nauvoo to the Great Basin are rarely written without mentioning that the Saints who followed Brigham Young westward resolved themselves into a Camp of Israel organized into companies with captains of hundreds, fifties, and tens over them, as had the ancient Israelites during their journey from Egypt to the Promised Land in Palestine. But the real extent of the Exodus-like character of the Saints' journey from Illinois to the Great Salt Lake Valley is only fully disclosed when it is remembered that an ice bridge over the Mississippi River facilitated the Mormon departure from Nauvoo. It is neither so wide nor so deep as the Red Sea, but at Nauvoo the river is more than a mile broad, and "running ice" had made crossing difficult in the days before the main body of Mormons was ready to leave. The fact that many Saints walked across the river without getting their feet wet is enough to serve as a means of separating the Mormon trek from all the other pioneer companies who left for the west from St. Louis, Quincy, and the other cities and towns along the river's edge, especially as more than one group of starving and desperate Saints reported miracles in which quail and a manna-like substance called honey-dew kept them from perishing. Moreover, even as it continued in some ways for virtually forty years, while Saints from across the world traveled through the wilderness to the valleys of the intermountain region, this LDS exodus led directly to the building up of a latter-day Zion in the tops of the mountains, a kingdom with a religious leader at its political helm and a temple at its center.

Full and complete records of the Mormon pioneer period contain so many references to the extensive use of militant "kingdom language" in the sermons and public statements of Joseph Smith, Brigham Young, Heber C. Kimball, Jedediah Grant, and other LDS leaders that some scholars are convinced that nineteenth-century Saints were engaged in a quest for empire. Others disagree, interpreting the often-used "kingdom language" as a metaphor, mere repetitive allusion to passages of scripture that refer to the Kingdom of God. A wide-ranging and sometimes rancorous scholarly debate that turns on whether references to the kingdom should be understood metaphorically or taken literally has developed in recent years. Recognition of the Exodus-like character of the Mormon trek and the kingdom-like character of Utah Mormonism during the pioneer period (note this narrowing from Mormonism, in general, to Utah Mormonism) will not entirely settle this issue, but it will make it obvious that, as recapitulations of episodes in Hebrew history, these events took on an experiential character appropriately described as metaphorical only if metaphor is understood as something more than literary device.

In *Metaphors We Live By*, linguists George Lakoff and Mark Johnson provide a persuasive demonstration of their thesis that "our ordinary conceptual system, in terms of which we both think and act, is fundamentally metaphorical in nature."[5] Their demonstration is helpful here, for the River Jordan flowed north from Utah Lake into the Great Salt Lake, rather than south through the Waters of Merom and the Sea of Galilee to the Dead Sea, but it still coursed through Zion. Brigham Young was not king—after 1858 he was not even governor—but he might as well have been, since Latter-day Saints actually, if not officially, lived in a literal LDS kingdom over which an ecclesiastical establishment presided for nearly fifty years. Thus this delineation of the Mormon replication of the Hebrew-Christian past tends to support the contention that scholars across the years have underestimated the importance of the political kingdom of God.

At the same time, this manner of interpreting the historical data calls into question the intimate connection that most scholars posit between the patriarchal order of marriage (polygamy) and the LDS political kingdom. As printed in section 132 of the Doctrine and Covenants of the Church of Jesus Christ of Latter-day Saints, the Mormon prophet's revelation about plural marriage is dated 12 July 1843. This date seems to place the inauguration of plural marriage in the same time period as Smith's organization of a Mormon political kingdom. But it is ever more obvious that the revelation is given an 1843 date because it was first written down at that time. In reality, along with the introduction of the temple ordinances and the ordination of Joseph Smith, Sr., as patriarch (which led directly to the custom of conferring patriarchal blessings), plural marriage entered Mormonism in Kirtland. All were part of a latter-day recapitulation of the ancient Patriarchal Age, which, in the Bible, is separated from the kingdom-building of David and Solomon by a great span of years and which, in Mormonism, is analytically distinct from the creation of the political kingdom of God. This means that a literal plurality of wives was one of the main elements figuring in the Saints' recapitulation of the stories of Abraham, Isaac, Jacob, and Joseph, while the LDS experience of living in a kingdom that the Saints themselves controlled politically recapitulated the stories of David and Solomon, kings of Israel during a much later era.

By indicating that the prophet made separate inquiries about the plural marriages of Abraham, Isaac, and Jacob, on the one hand, and those of Moses, David, and Solomon, on the other, the opening verse of the revelation about the plurality of wives suggests that Joseph Smith was aware of the differences that existed between these two periods in Hebrew history. But Smith's distinction was not communicated to his followers. It was even missed by the scribe to whom the revelation was dictated, William Clayton, whose diary account says that the revelation showed "the designs in Moses, Abraham, David, and Solomon having many wives and concubines & c."[6] And the distinction apparently was not later recognized, even after 1852, when the revelation was finally published. Although the Latter-day Saints did not fully realize at the time that they were living through reprises of the ages of the Hebrew patriarchs and kings simultaneously, the distinction is nevertheless significant in the context of this study because it highlights the non-linearity and complexity of the recapitulation process.

The subliminal, often involuntary nature of the process is revealed in the final Utah-Mormon reprise of Hebrew history: exile. Equally outraged by evidence that the patriarchal order of marriage was a reality and that an unofficial yet actual Kingdom of God was organized, non-Mormons mounted an all-out campaign in the late 1880s to stop the practice of polygamy and destroy the political kingdom. Seen from a Mormon perspective, the "Raid" was a Gentile threat to turn to ashes all the Saints' accomplishments in building cities for habitation and making the barren land fruitful. An army of "greedy politicians," intent on dismantling the political kingdom, and an army of federal marshals, intent on casting polygamists into prison, drove Mormons from their homes and made Zion desolate. Some of the patriarchs hid in the mountains, others sought asylum in Mexico or Canada, but when the Corporation of the Church of Jesus Christ of Latter-day Saints was dissolved and its property (including the nearly completed temple in Salt Lake City) confiscated, the Saints acceded to the superior strength of the Gentile government. Appropriately, as befits the end of exile, the Saints were allowed to return to their homes and everyday pursuits on the condition that they would give up marital plurality and that their kingdom would thereafter take on the political status of client state.

As was the death of Joseph Smith in 1844, the end of the practice of plural marriage was an event of overriding importance in Mormonism. Before LDS Church President Wilford Woodruff's Manifesto was issued and accepted as authoritative by the Saints, Mormonism was one thing; afterward, Mormonism was something else. Unlike Smith's martyrdom, however, the demise of plural marriage was not an inexplicable event that was sudden and unforeseen. The issuing of the Manifesto was preceded by years of struggle with the larger culture over what was permissible in the United States insofar as the organization of the Mormon kingdom and the behavior of the Saints was concerned. For that reason, chronological narrations of Mormon history must always explain this event in terms of cause and effect. In the context of this work, however, the matter of whether the Manifesto was the result of divine revelation or whether it was an extreme instance of religion accommodating itself to the world is far less important than the fact that the promulgation of this document and the informal political accords that accompanied its appearance brought the Mormon recapitulation of the Hebrew-Christian story to a close. With Zion and Babylon come to terms, the past was filled up. Complete.

Henceforth that past would be continually reiterated and sometimes reinterpreted. But its replication would come in the form of ritual re-creation, which differs fundamentally from recapitulation in that in ritual re-creation the Saints consciously and purposely played out the story of what had once happened to Israel in order to call up to modern memory the times when God tested, or tried, or was good to his chosen people. With temples and priesthood in place and sacred ordinances ever ready to signal renewal of divine-human covenants, the necessity of recapitulation, of living through the particular events of Hebrew-Christian history, disappeared. But the story of Mormonism's recapitulation of that past stayed very much alive as it moved out of experiential reality into Mormon history.

As temple ceremonies kept ancient times and the covenants of the new dispensation alive in Latter-day Saint minds, so festival, pilgrimage, and the recital of the stories of the nineteenth-century past preserved the vitality of the pioneer period. Moreover, because that history recapitulated more ancient pasts, it opened out to reveal Mormonism's reappropriation of Christianity's appropriation of Hebrew history and, especially in the case of the Saints who went to the Great Basin, its own direct appropriation of Israel's story. In "The Ritualization of Mormon History," an important article published in the *Utah Historical Quarterly* in 1975, Davis Bitton described the rapidity and "cumulative intensity" with which the Saints ritualized their past.[7] But there is still more to be said about this process, because it not only allowed the Saints to take hold of their own past, it also gave them a tenacious hold on the reality of the biblical story. For example, even as Mormonism continued to the activity of recapitulation, an annual 24 July festival developed. Each year the Saints reenacted the fulfillment event of the LDS exodus, reentering the Salt Lake Valley with appropriate ceremony, thus symbolically reentering not only the Great Basin but also the Promised Land. Episodes in the Mormon past that reflected other sacred events, such as temple buildings or the journey through the wilderness, also called the Saints to pilgrimage, making eventual historical restoration inevitable at Kirtland, Nauvoo, Mt. Pisgah, and all the many other sites where LDS pioneer events took place. More important, because the nineteenth-century Saints had engaged in reestablishing the covenant, organizing the church, preaching the gospel, living the patriarchal order of marriage, and building up the kingdom—in short, in replicating sacred story—Mormon history itself took on a sacred character.

As a result, Mormonism's salvation history begins with the story of Abraham, the beginning point of the salvation histories of Judaism and Christianity, but it extends across the LDS experience in the pioneer period. It happened in the here and now, in the United States less than two centuries ago. And yet the story of the LDS past is in many ways as much a "historical product of a visionary tradition" as is the Bible, a work in which, according to literary critic Northrop Frye, religious and historical saga is continuously reshaped. Specifically, in *Fearful Symmetry* Frye writes that "the Gospels consolidate [the] vision of the [Old Testament] Messiah into the vision of Jesus, who has the same name as Joshua, and the proof of the events in Jesus' life, as recorded in the Gospels, is referred not to contemporary evidence but to what the Old Testament prophets had said would be true of the Messiah."[8] The modern critical mind makes reference to the biblical accounts rather than contemporary evidence well-nigh impossible in the scholarly reconstruction of the Mormon past. Yet in its popular recital within Mormonism, the same pattern of referring to biblical prophecy operates in Mormon history.

The framework of interpretation in this work makes it possible to see, then, that accounts of Mormon history that reflect the experience of the Saints themselves consolidate and reshape the vision of Old and New Testaments in much the same way that accounts of the experience of the early Christian community consolidated and reshaped Israel's story. Moreover, it is equally true that as early Christianity's experience gave it a unique understanding of the gospel of the God of Abraham, so Mormonism's pioneer experience figures more prominently than has been recognized in the development of the Latter-day Saints' unique understanding of the "principles of the gospel." While Mormonism's transition from cultic movement to religious tradition follows the pattern by which other traditions made the transition, its unique understanding of "the gospel," which rests on its history as well as its theology, turns the story of Mormonism into a story that has meaning for all persons interested in religion as generic phenomenon.

NOTES

1. Ninian Smart, *Worldviews: Crosscultural Explorations of Human Beliefs* (New York: Charles Scribner's Sons, 1983) is a recent volume which devotes separate chapters to these dimensions of religion.

2. Such reviews of a new tradition's past serve, to a great degree, as creedal statements.

3. Mortensen and Mulder, *Among the Mormons* (New York: Alfred A. Knopf, 1958) is a collection of documents about the Saints written by non-Mormons. Its content tells the LDS story from the outside and thus could not have captured the same sense of replication as documents written by the Mormons themselves.

4. The Doctrine and Covenants text indicates that Moses, Elijah, and Elias appeared to Smith and Cowdery. Since *Elias* is simply the Greek form of the name Elijah, it is not clear whether the reference refers to two or to three biblical figures.

5. Lakoff and Johnson, *Metaphors We Live By* (Chicago: University of Chicago Press, 1980).

6. James B. Allen, "One Man's Nauvoo: William Clayton's Experience in Mormon, Illinois," *Journal of Mormon History* 6 (1979): 52.

7. Davis Bitton, "The Ritualization of Mormon History," *Utah Historical Quarterly* 43 (Winter 1975): 67–85.

8. Frye, *Fearful Symmetry*, p. 317.

"BELIEVER I KNOW"

Charles Joyner

Charles Joyner believes that what is original about African American Christianity "lies neither in its African elements nor in its Christian elements, but in its unique and creative synthesis of both." Joyner reminds us that the slaves did not simply become Christians; instead, they imaginatively fashioned their faith from the available cultural resources. In the following essay, Joyner enters the inner world of the slaves who lived on the South Carolina and Georgia low-country plantations during the antebellum period in order to explore the transformation of their diverse African cultures into an emerging African American Christianity. Joyner notes that most mature low-country slaves came directly from different ethnic groups in Africa and the Carribean and were aware of their roots. He argues that to underestimate the retention and adaptation of those African behavior patterns most meaningful to these slaves is to deprive them of their past. Yet to overestimate the African contribution to African American Christianity is to take from the slaves their creativity. Rather, the emergence of African American Christianity is an evolving story that includes both the retention of African traditions as well as innovative adaptations to American Christianity.

Reprinted by permission from Charles Joyner, "'Believer I Know': The Emergence of African American Christianity" in *African American Christianity: Essays in History*, Paul E. Johnson, ed. (Berkeley: California, 1994), 18–46.

Suffering produces endurance,
endurance produces character,
and character produces hope.

—Romans 5: 3–4

Glory Hallelujah
Believer I know
I done cross Jurden
Believer I know

—Georgia slave song sung by Katie Brown

10 🌺

"BELIEVER I KNOW"

The Emergence of African American Christianity

Charles Joyner

THE LITTLE SHIP with its human cargo sailed up the Altamaha river. Major Pierce Butler had purchased a large number of Africans for his Georgia plantation in 1803. When the vessel arrived at Butler's Island, the Major's plantation manager informed him, "You have no people that can talk with them but they are so smart your young Wenches are Speculating very high for husbands."[1] In the new physical and social environment of the lowcountry, African men and women of various ethnic groups mixed in ways that did not occur in Africa. Similarly, the varied African cultures were increasingly fused in combinations that did not exist in Africa. A new culture, predominantly African in origin, but different from any *particular* African culture, began to take shape.

During the formative years of African American culture, most of the mature slaves on many South Carolina and Georgia lowcountry plantations came either directly from Africa or from the Caribbean. According to a Georgia slave, "Doze Africans alluz call one annudduh 'countryman'.... Dey know ef dey come frum duh same tribe by duh mahk dey hab. Some hab a long mahk an some hab a roun un. Udduhs weah eahring in duh eah. Some weahs it in duh lef eah an doze from anudduh tribe weahs it in duh right eah."[2]

There was a great mixture of African ethnic groups in the lowcountry, but African ethnic distinctions continued to be made among the slaves as long as slavery lasted. Coromantees from the Gold Coast were said to be ferocious and unforgiving, but hardy and therefore favored as field hands. Congos and Angolas were alleged to be handsome and docile, but weak and predisposed to run away. And Ibos from the Niger Delta were considered sickly, melancholy, and suicidal. On any given morning in a lowcountry rice field, an enslaved African would meet more Africans from more ethnic groups than he or she would have encountered in a lifetime in Africa.[3]

To underestimate the Africanity of African American Christianity is to rob the slaves of their heritage. But to overestimate the Africanity of African American Christianity is to rob the slaves of their creativity. Africans were creative in Africa; they did not cease to be creative as involuntary settlers in America. The African American Christianity that developed was neither a dark version of the Christianity preached by slaveholders nor a continuation of African religion disguised as Christianity. The story of the emergence of African American

Christianity is a story of an emergent African American culture as well as of residual African cultures, a story of innovation as well as of tradition, a story of change as well as of continuity.

MUSLIM SLAVES

The old man always wore a fez and a long coat, just as he would have done in Africa. He was the driver on Thomas Spalding's Sapelo Island plantation, near Darien, Georgia. A Georgia rice planter's daughter who visited the Spalding plantation in the 1850s wrote of the old man and his family many years later: "They were all tall and well-formed, with good features. They conversed with us in English, but in talking among themselves they used a foreign tongue that no one else understood.... These Negroes held themselves aloof from the others as if they were conscious of their own superiority." The old man's name was Bilali Mohomet, and he was the great-grandfather of Katie Brown and Shadrach Hall. According to Shad, Bilali and his wife "pray at sun-up and face duh sun on duh knees an bow tuh it tree times, kneelin on a lill mat." Katie added, "Dey wuz bery puhticluh bout duh time dey pray an dey ber regluh bout duh hour. Wen duh sun come up, wen it straight obuh head and wen it set, das duh time dey pray. Dey bow tuh duh sun an hab lill mat tuh kneel on. Duh beads is on a long string. Bilali he pull bead an he say, 'Belambi, Hakabara, Mahamadu.' Phoebe she say, 'Ameen, Ameen.'" When Bilali died, he was buried with his prayer rug and his Quiran. Many former Gullah slaves remembered their ancestors praying in the Muslim fashion.[4]

Bilali and other Muslim slaves on the Georgia coast carefully observed Muslim fasts and feast days. Katie Brown recalled the Muslim rice cakes made by her grandmother: "She make funny flat cake she call 'saraka'. She make um same day ebry yeah, an it big day. Wen dey finish, she call us in, all duh chillun, an put in hans lill flat cake an we eats it. Yes'm, I membuh how she make it. She wash rice, an po off all duh watuh. She let wet rice sit all night, an in mawnin rice is all swell. She tak dat rice an put it in wooden mawtuh, an beat it tuh paste wid wooden pestle. She add honey, sometime shuguh, an make it in flat cake wid uh hans. 'Saraka' she call um." Shad Hall remembered that his grandmother made the pieces of saraka into dumplings. Katie Brown said her grandmother rolled the rice paste into balls "the size of small fowls' eggs" and set them aside to harden. When the saraka was ready, the children were lined up so that the grandmother could make certain their hands were clean. Any child whose hands were not clean had to go wash them. The other children had to wait until everyone was ready. As she handed each child some of the saraka, the grandmother would say either "Saraka dee" or "Ah-me, Ah-me."[5]

It is important to note that Christianity enjoyed no religious monopoly among Gullah slaves. Christianity had to compete in a religiously diverse environment. African-born slaves, for instance, often maintained their traditional religious outlooks. "At the time I first went to Carolina, there were a great many African slaves in the country," recalled fugitive slave Charles Ball. "Many of them believed there were several gods; some of whom were good, and others evil." Other African-born slaves embraced Islam. There was a considerable Muslim presence in the Georgia and South Carolina lowcountry. "I knew several who must have been, from what I have since learned, Mohammedans," Ball noted. "There was one man on this plantation who prayed five times every day, always turning his face to the east." It has been estimated that as many as twenty percent of the enslaved Africans in America embraced Islam. There is evidence that Muslim slaves in coastal Georgia deliberately sought marriage partners of the same faith as late as the second generation. On some lowcountry plantations, Muslim slaves were given a ration of beef instead of pork.[6]

THE SLAVEHOLDERS' MISSION TO THE SLAVES

The Reverend Charles Colcock Jones stood in his Savannah pulpit and, in his ringing voice, delivered an eloquent sermon urging slaveholders to instruct their slaves in the principles of the Christian religion. Not only would religious instruction save the slaves' souls, he said, but it would also create "a greater subordination" among the slaves and teach them "respect and obedience [to] all those whom God in his providence has placed in authority over them." The Reverend Jones was not only pastor of Savannah's First Presbyterian Church but also the master of three rice plantations and more than one hundred slaves in Liberty County, Georgia. While he seemed genuinely concerned for the salvation of his slaves' souls, there is no question that he consciously and deliberately used religion as an instrument of discipline and control. A faithful servant, Jones believed, was more profitable than an unfaithful servant. So he attempted to tailor Christianity to keep bondsmen reconciled to their bondage. Jones and similarly inclined slaveholders wanted their slaves delivered from "savage heathenism" to the true light of the Christian gospel, preferably of the Episcopal or Presbyterian persuasion.[7]

Early low-country planters were reluctant to tolerate missionary efforts among their slaves. "There has always been a strong repugnance amongst the planters, against their slaves becoming members of any religious society," Charles Ball wrote in 1837. "They fear the slaves, by attending the meetings and listening to the preachers, may imbibe the morality they teach, the notions of equality and liberty, maintained in the gospel." Planters doubted that preachers could be depended upon to defend the Peculiar Institution. "The abolition measures have excited such a spirit of jealousy and suspicion that some planters will not listen to the introduction of religion on their places," wrote a Charleston clergyman in 1836. Gradually, however, at least some ministers won the trust of the slaveholders and began missionary work among the slaves. Henry Brown, a former slave near Charleston, recalled that his master's slaves "went to meeting two nights a week and on Sunday they went to Church, where they had a white preacher Dr. Rose hired to preach to them."

Masters came more and more to believe that religion sustained rather than threatened slavery, and slave churchgoing came to seem less and less threatening. By the 1830s, lowcountry masters were giving increased attention to controlling the *content* of slave religion. A Georgia planter's daughter remembered her father's efforts to evangelize his slaves. "There was Sabbath School each Sunday afternoon, under the big live oaks," she recalled. "My Father would read from the Bible and we would tell simple stories to the children and many grownups, who came with them."[8] In 1837 the Reverend Jones published a *catechism* especially for slaves. One section was devoted to "Duties of Masters and Servants." In it Jones, too fastidious to call a slave a slave, addressed a series of questions to the "servants":

Q.   What are the Servants to count their Masters worthy of?
A.   All honour.
Q.   How are they to try to please their Masters?
A.   Please them well in all things, not answering again.
Q.   Is it right for a Servant when commanded to do anything to be sullen and slow, and answering his master again?

A.   No.

Q.   But suppose the Master is hard to please, and threatens and punishes more than he ought, what is the Servant to do?

A.   Do his best to please him.

Q.   Are Servants at liberty to tell lies and deceive their Masters?

A.   No.

Q.   If servants will faithfully do their duty and Serve God in their stations as Servants, will they be respected of men, and blessed and honoured of God, as well as others?

A.   Yes.[9]

Slaveholders supported religious instruction partly out of sincere Christian concern for the salvation of the slaves. On his deathbed one Charleston master instructed his children, "I wish you also to give all the indulgence you possibly can to the negroes in going to Church, and making them repeat their questions, for this reason that if neglected we will have to answer for the loss of their souls." The Christianity disseminated by slaveholders, however, was very selective, emphasizing obedience in the here and now as much as salvation in the hereafter. The slaves were going to get religion whether their masters liked it or not, many masters reasoned, so making religion safe for slavery became a matter of high priority. South Carolina planter Robert F. W. Allston described his slaves as "attentive to religious instruction, and greatly improved in intelligence and morals, in domestic relations, etc.... Indeed, the degree of intelligence which as a class they are acquiring is worthy of deep consideration." If the planters evidence a genuine concern for their slaves' spiritual welfare, they also recognized that religion was a more subtle, more humane, and more effective means of control than the whip.[10]

There are incessant references in the Jones family correspondence to the spiritual as well as physical welfare of the slaves. Sandy Maybank, then working as the head carpenter at Montevideo plantation in coastal Georgia, received a letter from the man who claimed to own him. "I trust," Charles Colcock Jones wrote to Maybank, "that you are holding on to your high profession of the Gospel of our Lord and Saviour Jesus Christ at all times, and constantly watch and pray." "You know our life and health are in His hands," Jones constantly counseled his driver Catoe, "and it is a great comfort to me to have a good hope that you love Him, and do put all your trust in our Lord and Saviour Jesus Christ, who is a precious Saviour to us in life and in death." And Jones was quite pleased when Catoe sent back such replies as "Your people all seem to be doing very well. They attend praise and go to church regularly whenever there is preaching in reach." Another Jones driver, Andrew, wrote, "About a month ago Revd Mr Law administered the sacraments in Sunbury and among several black people that joined the church was my daughter Dinah, and I trust that she may practice what she professes, for as Mas John says it is no light thing to be a christian, for we may play with the lightning and the rattle snake, but dont trifle with Almighty God 'lest he tear you to pieces in his anger and then be never to deliver you.'"[11]

To suggest that lowcountry slaveholders cynically reduced Christianity to patience, humility, and the fear of sin, or that they were more concerned with the discipline of slaves than with the salvation of souls, would be untrue to history. "In our philosophy, right is the highest expediency," James Henley Thornwell insisted, "and obedience to God the firmest security of communities as well as individuals. We have not sought the protection of our property in the debasement of our species; we have not maintained our own interests in this world, by the deliberate sacrifice of the eternal interests of the thousands who look to us for the way to salvation." Nevertheless, it would also be untrue to history not to point out that much of the slaveholders' missionary motivation was their understanding that preaching had a significant effect on slave discipline. Ministers went out of their way to appease the slaveholders by approaching slave religion with the utmost discretion. Masters knew that so long as the slaves were listening to a trusted white preacher, they could not (at least for the moment) be listening to a subversive black one.[12]

Some slaveholders opposed the religious education of slaves as useless. Certainly not all slaveholders believed that slave religion would promote slave control. One reason for doubt was their belief in black Christians' excessive propensity for backsliding. In fact, black Christians were no more and no less immune to backsliding than were white Christians, even with the constant religious instruction that was the stock-in-trade of such slaveholders as the Reverend Charles Colcock Jones. Others maintained that the slaves were not fully human creatures and were therefore incapable of reasoning and of learning the truths of the Christian religion. Still others feared the intense emotionalism preferred by the slaves as the appropriate form of worship. The Reverend Jones encountered considerable opposition from his fellow slaveholders until he was able to prove to their satisfaction that he favored only quiet and sedate worship services. Others, such as the Georgia slaveholders Pierce Butler and James Hamilton Couper, were simply indifferent to the religious education of their slaves. At Couper's showplace Georgia plantation, Swedish visitor Fredericka Bremer tried to teach a gathering of the slave children to recite the Lord's Prayer. "The children grinned, laughed, showed their white teeth," she said, "and evinced very plainly that none of them knew what that wonderful prayer meant nor that they had a Father in heaven."[13]

White preachers had to face the dilemma that their Christianity was—at least potentially—subversive of slavery. During the 1834 South Carolina legislative debate over the prohibition on teaching slaves to read and write, Whitemarsh Seabrook noted that anyone who wanted slaves to read the *entire* Bible belonged in "a room in the Lunatic Asylum." To be fair, the ministers were more than mere sycophants of cynical slaveholders. They did not select only the texts that promoted order and discipline among the slaves. But they could not fail to realize that while Christianity promoted order among the slaves, it also contained the seeds of disorder. They certainly would not preach to their congregations that Pharoah had enslaved the children of Israel and had held them in bondage in Egypt, that the Lord had then visited plagues on the slaveholders, or that Moses had led the slaves in a mass escape out of bondage in Egypt to the Promised Land.[14]

If the white ministers shied away from scriptural passages with clear analogies to the condition of the slaves, they did preach the equality of all in the sight of God and the equality of human sinfulness. The Reverend James Henley Thornwell put it thus:

> It is a publick testimony to our faith, that the Negro is of one blood with ourselves—that he has sinned as we have, and that he has an equal interest with us in the great redemption. Science, falsely so-called, may attempt to exclude him from the brotherhood of humanity. Men may be seeking eminence and distinction by arguments which link them with the brute; but the instinctive impulses of our nature, combined with the plainest declarations of the word of God, lead us to recognize in his form and lineaments—in his moral, religious, and intellectual nature—the same humanity in which we glory as the image of God. We are not ashamed to call him our brother.

Christianity, such ministers preached, imposed obligations not just on the slaves but on their earthly masters as well. Both master and slave on this earth would be held to the same account before the heavenly Master. As the Bible taught servants to obey their masters, these ministers preached, so it required masters to rule their servants wisely, and it required the rich to use their riches to do good.[15]

Thus was the slaveholders' theological dilemma posed: as Christians, they were committed to the religious instruction of their slaves, but the religion preached to the slaves also called the masters to account. Masters were as subject as slaves were to the requirements of Christianity. The idea of equality before God created a problem of role boundaries and emphasized tensions and anomalies within the institution of slavery that could not easily be ignored. Governor Robert F. W. Allston believed that the "best inducement to keep the slaves both Christian and quiescent" was "example on our part; next a just, consistent, systematic administration of domestic government."[16]

SLAVE WORSHIP

The preacher began softly and conversationally, his voice cool and level. But slowly and gradually he built toward a more pronounced, more powerful rhythm. The slaves in the congregation did not receive his words passively. As the rhythm rose and fell, they became participants as well. The congregational response was essential to worship, a religious requirement. Just as in Africa, such antiphony exemplified the solidarity of the community even as the sermon called forth the profoundest expression of the individual: neither I-Thou nor I-you, but the sacred link between the individual and the social body. The slaves *had* to talk back to the sermon. The preacher had not come to give his own opinions; he had come to preach the word of God to a people who refused to be passive and uncritical receptors. "Amen!" "Yes, Lord!" "Yes, Jesus!" "Yes! Yes!" Feet began to pat. Under the influence of congregational response, the preacher built steadily.

> An dem buckra dat beat dem nigger onjestly an onmusefully, jes kase de po nigger cant help e self, dems de meanest buckra ob all, an berry much like de sheep-killin dog dat cowud to take sumpn dat cant help e self.

"Preach the sermon!" someone shouted. "Yes, Lord!" "Yes, Jesus!" "Yes!" The preacher began to pace back and forth, raising his hands. Someone began to hum a mournful air, and the humming spread through the congregation. The slaves' bodies rocked, their heads nodded, their hands clapped, and their feet stamped a steady rhythm, pushing the preacher onward.

> Dat berry ting dat de nigger cant fend e self an helpless, mek de gentleman buckra berry pashunt an slow to punish dem nigger.

The preacher told them to put all their faith in the Lord. The Lord would deliver them from the House of Bondage as He had delivered the children of Israel from bondage in Egypt. The preacher also likened his flock of slave Christians to a flock of sheep.

> An de berry fack dat de Lawd sheep is po helpless ting, mek de Lawd pity an lub we mo, an mek we pen pun Him an cry fur Him in de time ob trouble an danejur. An dat wha de Lawd want, fur we feel we own weakness an trust in Him strenk. De mudder lub de morest de chile dats de

weakest an dat need um de morest, and so wud de Sabeyur an e lettle wuns dat pend only pun Him.

As he moved his congregation toward a crescendo of exaltation, the preacher broke into a chant. The response was no longer confined to antiphonal amens but also included shouts and cries, the clapping of hands and the stamping of feet, and the indescribable sounds of religious transcendence. The congregation worshiped with soul and body in unison. Relying heavily on tone, gesture, and rhythm, the preacher preached a sermon defiant enough to release pent-up frustrations among the slave community, although neither so incendiary as to stir hopeless revolts nor so blatant as to bring down the wrath of the masters upon their heads. But expressing even such mild sentiments could be dangerous. Who could tell when slaves might begin to ask the Lord not merely to deliver them in the next world, but to aid them in casting off the shackles of those who claimed to own them in this one?[17]

Slave preachers achieved renown in the slave community as "men of words." They delivered sermons and prayers with memorable Biblical imagery, imagery that seemed especially relevant to the slaves' own situations. "We're down here, Lord," they preached, "chewin' on dry bones an' swallerin' bitter pills!" The slaves could identify with Moses leading the children of Israel out of enslavement in Egypt after the Lord had visited seven years of plagues upon the slaveholders. They could identify with the crucified Jesus, suffering through his time on the cross, as the slave preacher chanted:

> They led him from hall to hall!
> They whipped him all night long!
> They nailed him to the cross!
> Don't y'u hear how the hammer ring?

It is not difficult to understand why the slaves preferred their own preachers to the emotionless and self-serving platitudes of the white missionaries.[18]

To Christian slaves, the slave preachers were men of status. "My pa was a preacher why I become a Christian so early," testified one. "He used to tell us of hell an' how hot it is. I was so afraid of hell 'till I was always tryin' to do the right thing so I couldn't go to that terrible place." The slave preachers' continuing importance as men of words exemplified another adaptation of African traditions to African American Christianity. The linguistic inventiveness of the slave preachers was related to the ancient concept of *nommo*: the properly spoken word that results in appropriate action. Utilizing ritualized language and behavior as symbolic action, they transformed religious ritual through transcendental ecstasy into structured meaning, renewing and recycling the energies of the slave community. Such "gifted" men, straddling the sacred and secular worlds, were believed to exercise sacred powers within the secular domain. They often mediated between the slaves' Christian beliefs and the workaday world of the low country. The role they played as arbiters in settling disputes among the slaves was itself a product of their African heritage of the involvement of religion in everyday life. Through such mediation the preachers not only promoted social order but also played a major role in solidifying a sense of community among the slaves. In addition, as strong cultural personalities whose identities did not depend upon their positions as slaves, they served younger slaves as important role models.[19]

Slave preachers also sowed the seeds of discontent. The slaves' spiritual life was largely hidden from white observation. Often the slave preachers held services apart from the whites and without their knowledge. The major slave insurrections of the Old South—those of Gabriel Prosser, Nat Turner, and Denmark Vesey—were planned under the cover of such religious associations. According to Charleston's official account of the Vesey plot, "among the conspirators a majority of them belonged to the African church," a recently formed Methodist church described as "composed wholly of persons of color and almost entirely of blacks." The importance of the slaves' religion thus rested upon its capacity to serve them as a source not only of cultural values but also of an understanding of themselves, of their world, and of the relations between themselves and their world. It served them, in other words, both as a model *for* behavior and as a model *of* behavior. The power of African American Christianity in supporting the social values of Gullah slaves rested upon its ability to make plain a world in which those values, as well as the forces opposing them, were primal elements.[20]

THE SPIRITUALS

The theological orientation of African American Christianity is strikingly revealed in African American spirituals collected in South Carolina in the 1860s. Because the spirituals were transmitted orally, it may be assumed that whatever did not correspond to the slaves' shared religious and poetic sensibilities was eliminated. Deriving their raw materials from Biblical passages, nature, work patterns, and other songs, slave poets often used material objects as poetic devices in the spirituals to amplify their artistry with the resonance of hidden meanings. In the spirituals, for instance, gates symbolically lead to a new and better life. "Children Do Linger," for instance, promises a reunion in the next world when "we'll meet at Zion Gateway." Gates imply passage into the new life for some, but exclusion for others. Not everyone will be allowed through the gates of heaven. In the spiritual "Heaven Bell A-Ringing," the slaves sang, "I run to de gate, but the gate shut fast." In this verse the anonymous slave poet voices the despair of the downtrodden sinner with little hope, a downtrodden sinner barred from entry into heaven. The same theme echoes through yet another spiritual, "Bell Da Ring." Sinners are excluded from the new life, for "the gates are all shut, when de bell done ring."[21]

Streets and roads undergo poetic transformation into symbols of deliverance in the spirituals. Streets are used to suggest that if one walks and lives in the right path, one will find redemption and success: "If you walk de golden street and you join de golden band / Sing glory be to my Emanuel," the slaves sang in "King Emanuel." One who lives on or walks down the golden street is on the path to deliverance. But the verses, by beginning with "if" clauses, also imply that not everyone will walk down the golden street or join the golden band. Roads fulfill a similar poetic function in the spirituals. Singers announce that they are traveling down the right road, the golden road—set apart from common, ordinary roads—because "I know de road, Heaven bell a'ring, I know de road." But roads in the spirituals are not always as "golden" as streets. Sometimes roads are ordeals, expressing the slaves' belief that one must travel the dark and stormy road of life—full of trials, tribulations, and temptations—if one hopes to reach the golden road to heaven. The road is long ("O walk Jordan long road") and hard ("Road so stormy, Bell da ring"). But the spirituals offer hope to the sinner, reminding believers that the golden road is farther along, beyond the misery of life in bondage ("If you look up de road you see Fader Mosey, join the Angel Band"). If the road is long and dark, "Sister Dolly light the lamp, and the lamp light the road." The road is long and hard, but it leads to Paradise ("I'se been on de road into heaven, My Lord!").[22]

A road itself implies movement, and the slaves always seem to be on the move in the spirituals. In "I Wish I Been Dere," the singer's family has died, and the singer expresses the desire to go with them to Heaven. "I wish I been dere to climb Jacob's ladder." The ascending motion of the spiritual was transcendent to slaves held down too long. The ladder, usually depicted as the Biblical Jacob's ladder, is another poetic transformation in the spirituals. It symbolizes social, economic, or religious climbing. To ascend the ladder is to reach a higher and better level of existence. The line "I wish I been dere to climb Jacob's ladder" reflects the slaves' aspirations to climb to a better place.[23]

Slave poets use ships, boats, and arks in the lowcountry spirituals to symbolize the transfer of people or souls from one place to another over impassable terrain. The Sea Island rowing song "Michael Row the Boat Ashore" utilizes this poetic transformation several times: "Michael row the boat ashore, Hallelujah.... Michael boat a music boat.... Sister help for trim dat boat.... Michael haul the boat ashore, then you'll hear the horn they blow." The boat that carries the souls of men and women into heaven is recalled in such lines as "When de ship is out a-sailin, Hallelujah" and "O brudder will you meet us when de ship is out a-sailin?"[24]

Whereas many spirituals express a desire for change symbolized by traveling roads or climbing ladders, "Fare Ye Well" expresses a feeling that a new life must begin by sweeping the old life clean ("Jesus gib me a little broom, for to sweep 'em clean"). Brooms symbolize the power to become new and better by the act of cleansing, therefore leading the slave upward and forward toward God and a good life.[25]

Through the spirituals slaves were striving to climb higher, to get to a better place, to find a happier life. One way they might fulfill their desire for accomplishment was to build something with their own hands, something they could call their own. The act of building appealed to the slaves. When they sang "Build a house in Paradise / Build it widout a hammer or a nail," they added another dimension to their desire to build houses of their own. A house built without hammer or nail is more than just a house; it is transformed into something miraculous. The hammer and the nail recall Jesus on the cross. And the spiritual assured the slaves that there are many mansions in heaven built not with hammers and nails but with faith.[26]

All of these poetic transformations symbolize deliverance, the passage of souls from this world into the next. Believers either cross through the gates of heaven, enter heaven by sweeping their souls clean with a broom, ride in a boat to heaven, or enter heaven by passing over the streets and roads of righteousness. For some slaves, at least, these devices must also have symbolized the end of slavery and their passage into freedom.[27]

SPIRIT POSSESSION

African American Christianity emerged from the fragmentation of a unified African religious outlook into separate streams in America. Fragmentation and re-formation were especially marked among the Gullah-speaking slaves of the South Carolina and Georgia lowcountry. One stream of inherited African cosmology included polytheism, the concept of rebirth, and spirit possession in religious ritual. In the South Carolina and Georgia lowcountry, far from the African context of their sacred cosmos, the slaves worshiped their new Christian God with the kind of expressive behavior their African heritage taught them was appropriate for an important deity: a high degree of spiritualism in worship, including the use of chants and bodily movement to rhythmic accompaniment, leading to trances and spirit possession. The phenomenon of spirit possession, one of the most significant features in African religion (especially pronounced among the Bantu, the Yoruba, and the Fante-Ashanti), was reinterpreted in Christian terms to become a central feature of expressive behavior in African American Christianity and a necessary part of the conversion experience. Conversion was the climax of a spiritual journey called "seeking." A prolonged period of praying "in the wilderness" induced an ecstatic trance without which conversion was not considered authentic. On Sapelo Island, Georgia, Katie Brown sang:

> The way to get to Heaven
> Believer I know
> Go in the wil'erness
> Believer I know
> Cry Lord have mercy
> Believer I know
> Cry Lord have mercy
> Believer I know
> Glory Hallelujah
> Believer I know
> I done cross Jorden
> Believer I know

Not until one had actually experienced spirit possession was one accepted as a church member; those who had not experienced it were still regarded as sinners.[28]

Slave Christians often held secret meetings at night to pray, to sing, and to "shout." "Shouting" was not the same as yelling or making a loud noise. "Shouting" denoted bodily movements accompanied by singing, handclapping, and foot-stomping. As late as the 1930s, the folklorist John A. Lomax reported that in Murrells Inlet, South Carolina, he had seen "young girls dive through the air and fall headlong on the hard floor in defiance of bruised flesh and broken bones. The men were more careful of bodily injuries, seemingly content to 'hold' the riotous females temporarily under the influence of the words of the minister." White observers often mistook shouting for dancing. In shouting, however, the feet were not supposed to cross each other or to leave the floor; such acts would be dancing, and dancing was regarded as sinful. Frederika Bremer reported having heard that "the Methodist missionaries, who are the most influential and effective teachers and preachers among the negroes, are very angry with them for their love of dancing and music, and declare them to be sinful." Such hostility seemed to her "a very unwise proceeding on the part of the preachers. Are not all God's gifts good, and may they not be made use of in His honor?...I would, instead, let them have sacred dances, and let them sing to them joyful songs of praise in the beautiful air, beneath the blossoming trees. Did not King David dance and sing in pious rapture before the ark of God?" Exemplifying the creative adaptation of the West African ring "dance," which was performed to complex drum rhythms, the shout consisted of body motions performed to the accompaniment of spirituals. Slaves improvised a substitute for the drums, with polyrhythmic hand-clapping and foot-stomping. While slave Christians often deprecated dancing, they shouted with great enthusiasm.[29]

When slave Christians gathered for praise meetings at one another's quarters, the soaring rhetoric of the prayers, the antiphonal singing, and the ecstatic shouts provided a release for pent-up emotions. For the slaves, religious services constituted not a relationship between a performer and an audience but a mutual performance. Just as the spirituals were marked by the strong call-and-response antiphony of African music, so prayers and sermons were punctuated by congregational responses.[30]

HAGS, HAUNTS, AND PLAT EYES

Her hair was plaited and tightly wrapped with white twine. Her garments hung loosely about her gaunt frame. Her name was Addie, and she came out of slavery times. Her windowless cabin had but one room. Her table consisted of a board and four sticks, her china of clam shells. A blue milk-of-magnesia bottle served as a flower vase. But in this cabin Addie had reared fourteen grandchildren and great-grandchildren. In her yard redbirds visited, sunflowers turned their faces to the sun, and crape myrtles displayed their colorful finery. Wild plum trees hugged the sides of her house, and green corn waved a bright promise in the fields beyond. In March of 1936, Addie sat on the porch of her cabin at Murrells Inlet, South Carolina, with Genevieve Willcox Chandler, a fieldworker for the Federal Writers Project, spinning out her memories of life in bondage. Addie's nose crinkled with the effort to put her life into words, to leave behind her testimony so that future generations could know what the slaves had been forced to live through. She was asked about "plat eyes," the most hideous and most malevolent of the occult spirits of the Georgia and South Carolina coast, evil spirits that changed shapes at will in order to lure victims into danger and rob them of their sanity. "De ole folks is talk bout Plat Eye," Addie recalled.

Dey say dey takes shape ob all kind da critter—dawg, cat, hawg, mule, varmint and I is hear tell ob Plat Eye takin form ob gator. I ain see dem scusing wan lettle time. You know dat leetle swamply place hind de Parsonage? Well, wan time—I hab meh bloom on me [was in her prime] een dem days....En I bawg tru dat deep white sand en I passes de grabe yard entrance en I leabes de open en enters dem dahk woods whey de moss wabe low en brush een yuh face. En I been tink bout Plat Eye. De min come tuh me it wuz good time tuh meet um.

   Den I bresh dem weepin moss aside en I trabble de wet mud een meh bare feets en my shoe been tie tuh meh girdle string. En wen I been come tuh de foot lawg...a cootuh [small turtle] slide offen de lawg at meh feets. En, clare tuh Gawd, I been fuh look up at dat cootuh en den I turn meh eye up en der wuz a cat—black cat wid he eye lak balls ob fire en he back all arch up en he tail twissin en er switchin en he hair stan on end. E move backward front ob me cross dat cypress lawg. En he been big. E been large ez meh leetle yearlin ox.

   En I talk tuh 'em en try fuh draw close. En I say tuh um, "I ain fuh feah nuttin! Ain no ghos'! Ain no hant! Ain no Plat Eye! Ain no nuttin'!" En I'se try fuh sing,

     E carry me tru many ob danger
     Because he fus lubb me.
     E guard gainst hant en Plat Eye
     Because he fus lubb me.

En dat Plat Eye ain gib me back meh word. E mobe forward en he tail swish en swish same lak big moccasin tail wen e lash de rushes.

   En de mind come to me, "Chile ob Gawd, doan you show no fear!" En I is brace up. En meh short handle leetle clam rake been een meh han', en I sing,

     Gawd will take care ob me.

> Walkin' tru many of dangers,
> Gawd will take care ob me.

En den de min [mind] come tuh me, "De Lawd heps dem wut heps deyself!" En I raise up meh rake en I come right cross dat critter head.

Ef dat had uh been a real cat, I'd uh pin um tuh dat lawg. Meh rake been bury deep, en de lawg hold um. En I clare tuh Gawd, e up en prance right under meh feets, dem eyes burnin holes een me en e tail swish, swish lak ole Sooky tail wen de flies bad.

En I gits mad. I fuh struggle wid meh rake en de lawg loosen e grip en I fuh pray, "Gib Addie strenth, O Gawd!" En down I come straight tru dat critter middle...But dat critter ain feel meh lick.

En I'se rassel lak Jacob wid de angel. I been strong en hab meh bloom on me. It ain 'vail nuttin. No man! Mr. Plat Eye jes ez pert en frisky as fore he been hit. En I 'buse um en I cuss um en I say, "You debbil! Clare mah path!" En if dat critter didn't paw de air en jus rise up dat big bamboo vine an me fuh hit um ebry jump!

So, I tink, "Sinner, lebel dat lawg." De min' come to me, "Chile ob Gawd, trabbel de woods path!" En I tuhn back en I hit dat path. En I ain been tarry en jes ez I wuz gibbin Gawd de praise fuh delivuh me, DERE DAT CAT! Dis time he big ez meh middle size ox en he eye been BLAZE!

En I lam [strike at] en I lam. En dat rake handle been wire en been nail on. En jus ez I mek meh las' lam, dat critter rise up for my eyes en dis time e been big ez cousin Andrew full grown ox. En he vanish up dat ole box pine ez yuh quits de deep woods.

I ain b'lieve een Plat Eye 'twell den, but I min's meh step since dem days. En wen I trabbles de deep woods whey de moss wabe low...en de firefly flickuh, I'se ready fuh um.

Uncle Murphy, e witch doctuh en e been tell me how fuh fend um off. Gunpowder en sulphur. Dey is say Plat Eye can't stan' dem smell mix. Dat man full ob knowledge. E mus hab Gawd min' een um. So I totes meh powder en sulphur en I carries meh stick een meh han en I puts meh truss een Gawd.[31]

Addie's plat eye narrative illustrates a second stream of African cosmology, a stream that proved less compatible with African American Christianity than rebirth and spirit possession. Many slaves in the South Carolina and Georgia lowcountry continued to embrace African supernatural beliefs that were not incorporated into African American Christianity but instead persisted in a kind of parallel stream. Addie's defense against plat eyes, in its ingenious blend of creativity, tradition, and common sense, may be seen as a metaphor for the emergence of African American Christianity.[32]

"Hags"—or "boo hags"—were one example of these supernatural beliefs. Hags were the disembodied spirits of witches or "conjure men" who were believed to leave their skins behind in order to fly through the air and give people nightmares, or "ride" them. Especially bothersome creatures, hags were believed able to fly through the air to midnight rendezvous, and to sail through keyholes by placing the bone of a black cat in their mouths. It was said that hags could bewitch people merely by looking at them. Even accusations of cannibalism attached to those suspected of witchcraft. Old Grace, an elderly slave on St. Simons Island, was rumored by her neighbors to be a hag. Local children were warned to stay away from her cabin because she allegedly boasted that she had eaten children in her native land. Slaves could take precautions, however, to keep hags from riding them: "conjure balls" (hair balls filled with roots, herbs, and other substances) were sometimes successful in keeping them at bay. But the only certain preventive was to eliminate the hag. That could best be done by the traditional African method of salting and peppering the skin while she had left it behind to go out "hagging."[33]

"Haunts"—the spirits of the dead—returned from time to time to trouble the living, in a modified version of the Congo *zumbi* or the Haitian *zombi*. The process of dying, according to West African belief, was not complete for up to five years. The spirits of the ancestors—the living dead—were the closest link between the world of the living and the world of the spirits, because they straddled both worlds.[34]

Haunts were most likely to appear at certain times, such as during a full moon or on Friday nights when the moon was young, although they were believed also to show themselves in broad daylight at certain places. Some believed that haunts rose up in every graveyard on the stroke of twelve; one haunt—the spirit of the oldest dead—would stay behind to guard the vacated graves while the others roamed the roads and entered houses. At slave funerals, efforts were made to contain the spirits of the ancestors; the living sought to prevent the dead from remaining behind as malign spirits.[35]

CONJURATION

Many features of African religion thus either converged or coexisted with Christianity. A third stream of African cosmology maintained a subterranean existence outside of and inimical to African American Christianity. This element of slave religion continues to be largely unknown and at least partly unknowable. Documentation of voodoo, or hoodoo (as African conjuration was called in the New World), is inevitably scanty, as such magical shamanism was practiced clandestinely. Still, sufficient evidence remains to testify to the existence of an underground stream of magical shamanism, not only throughout the slavery period, but long beyond.[36]

Illness was regarded as supernatural in origin; thus it was necessary, through sorcery, to summon the spirits of the dead to offer advice or to perform cures. Voodoo, or hoodoo, could be used for either protective or malevolent purposes: it could cure an illness, kill an enemy, or secure someone's love. All misfortune, including (presumably) slavery, was regarded as the result of magical shamanism. The only way a slave could gain protection from sorcery was by stronger countersorcery. With some variation, voodoo was known throughout the slave societies of the New World.[37]

The survival of African sorcery seems to have been most pronounced in the South Carolina and Georgia lowcountry, where slaves were concentrated in significant numbers. Voodoo grew with the arrival of slaves from the West Indies or directly from Africa, who adapted African snake cults to a new environment. High in the African pantheon, the snake god of the Ewe, Fon, Bantu, Dahomey, Ouidah, and Yoruba symbolized the cosmic energy of nature, the dealer of fortune or misfortune. The African names for the voodoo gods were lost; their personalities converged with those of Judeo-Christian prophets and saints, demons and devils. They continued to comfort believers and to wreak havoc on the wicked. Only the snake god's sorcerers could invoke his protective power. Snakeskins were prominent in initiation rituals. Snake charming was featured in some rites. All sorts of supernatural might were attributed to serpents in the snake lore of lowcountry slaves.[38]

Voodoo in the lowcountry never approached the complexities of Haitian Vodun; nevertheless, it achieved a distinctive character above the level of simple, unorganized sorcery. Gullah slaves took their physical or personal problems more often to local conjurers—the priests of the old religion—than to their masters. Such conjurers often enjoyed considerable power within the slave community, even among some of the Christians. They were spoken of with great awe, and some were considered invulnerable. No feat of black magic was considered beyond their ability to perform. Conjurers gained and held their influence over the slaves by various methods and especially by fear. Their patrons relied upon them both for protection and relief from spells and for casting spells upon their enemies.[39]

The sorcerer's spells could be benign as well as malign. If conjurers were considered the source of most misfortunes, they were also held in high esteem as healers. The positive role played by the sorcerers in treating slave illnesses demonstrates the role religion played in every aspect of life among the slaves. Voodoo allowed the slaves the exalted feeling of direct contact with the supernatural in attempting to cope with their ailments.[40]

Not all Gullah slaves believed in magical shamanism; the sorcerers neither commanded universal adherence nor approached the political power of the priests of Obeah, Myalism, or Vodun in the West Indies. Most Christian slaves—if they did not summarily reject the appeal of sorcery—considered the shaman's powers to be evil, hostile to the spirit of Christianity. Nevertheless, conjurers exercised an extraordinary influence over the lives of other slaves that they could have neither gained nor maintained if they had not fulfilled a real function. Even if they are often considered frauds and extortionists, sorcerers served their fellow slaves in times of suffering. They were interpreters of those unobservable spirits whose activities directed everyday life; they were awesome beings whose supernatural powers could be enlisted in the redress of grievances. Gullah Jack, one of the organizers of the Denmark Vesey plot, enlisted his occult powers in the cause of the slave revolt. Sorcerers in the lowcountry bridged for Gullah slaves the precarious life of servitude in this world and the mysteries of the spirit world. They turned human behavior into a perceived cosmic order and projected images of that order onto the plane of the slaves' everyday experience. They created a buffer against mental and emotional submission for the slaves who believed in them. Many—perhaps most—of the slaves abandoned shamanistic traditions, but those who held on tenaciously to their beliefs helped to preserve and extend an autonomous African heritage, making an important contribution to community and survival.[41]

THE CREATIVITY OF SLAVE CHRISTIANITY

Thus the once-unified religious cosmology fragmented. Adherence to the various components was by no means uniform. Some Gullah slaves abandoned belief in all forms of non-Christian supernaturalism; many selectively adhered to some beliefs and abandoned others. Some undoubtedly continued African religious practices under cover of Christianity. What may have appeared to the slaveholders to be the Christian cross may well have referred, in the mind of a given slave, to the Yoruba belief in sacred crossroads or the Kongo symbol for the four points of the sun. How easily Christianity might be interpreted in the same "primitive" terms that Western scholars apply to African religions is pointed up by Zora Neale Hurston in a letter she wrote, with mock naïveté, to her anthropological mentor, Franz Boas:

> Is it safe for me to say that baptism is an extension of water worship as a part of pantheism just as the sacrament is an extension of cannibalism? Isn[']t the use of candles in the Catholic chu[r]ch a relic of fire worship? Are not all the uses of fire upon the altars the same thing? Is not the christian ritual rather one of attenuated nature-worship, in the fire, water, and blood?

Might not the frequently mentioned fire of the Holy Ghost not be an unconscious fire worship. May it not be a deification of fire?"[42]

Despite a large number of "survivals" of African cultural patterns, what is most obvious from a truly Afrocentric perspective is the creativity of slave culture in the lowcountry. Most of the slaves' culture was neither "retained" from Africa nor "adopted" from white slaveholders. Rather, it was created by the slaves from a convergence of various African cultural patterns, white cultural influence, and the necessities demanded by new environment.[43]

The religion created by enslaved Africans shaped as much as it reflected their worldview. The Christianity of African Americans reveals both their mental picture of the unalterable shape of reality and their deepest, most comprehensive concepts of cosmic order. For them, religion functioned to portray their ethical and aesthetic preferences as normative—given the imposed conditions of reality—while it also supported such preferences by invoking deeply felt ethical and aesthetic beliefs as evidence of their truth. The African contribution to African American Christianity was enormous. The slaves did not simply adopt the God and the faith of the white missionaries. In establishing a spiritual life for themselves, they reinterpreted the elements of Christianity in terms of deep-rooted African religious concerns. Africa was not culturally homogeneous, nor did it bequeath to its exiles in the African diaspora a legacy of static survivals. In fact, religious expression in Africa was diverse, and borrowings among ethnic groups were common. Rising above the variety of beliefs and practices, however, was a shared bond—a concept of the sacred cosmos in which virtually all experience was religious, from the naming of children to planting, hunting, and fishing practices. Underlying the various African cultures were shared cognitive (or "grammatical") orientations—mental rules governing appropriate behavior—that profoundly affected the slaves' adoption, adaptation, and application of Christianity.[44] The originality of African American Christianity, then, lies neither in its African elements nor in its Christian elements, but in its unique and creative synthesis of both. Examination of the selective Christianity evangelized to the slaves may provide some perspective on the process by which lowcountry slaves mixed both elements and adapted both to the realities of slave life.

Despite unusually strong continuities of Islam and of traditional African religions, most Gullah slaves embraced Christianity. In their praise meetings, in their ecstatic prayers and exuberant shouts, and especially in their transcendent spirituals, they found a source of strength and endurance that enabled them to triumph over the collective tragedy of enslavement.

NOTES

Part of this essay was written while the author was an associate of the W.E.B. Du Bois Institute for Afro-American Research at Harvard University. The support of the Du Bois Institute is gratefully acknowledged. Earlier versions of this paper were presented in the New Christianities series at the University of Utah and in the symposium on the History of African American Christianity at the Harvard Divinity School, Cambridge, Mass., December 8–9, 1989. I am grateful to Randall Burkett, Ronald Coleman, Robert L. Hall, Paul Johnson, Albert Raboteau, Margaret Washington, and David Wills for their helpful comments.

1. Roswell King to Pierce Butler, May 13, 1803, quoted in Malcolm Bell, Jr., *Major Butler's Legacy: Five Generations of a Slaveholding Family* (Athens: University of Georgia Press, 1987), 132.

2. Interviews with Robert Pinckney,

Wilmington Island, and Ryna Johnson, St. Simons Island, in Savannah Unit, Federal Writers Project [eds.], *Drums and Shadows: Survival Studies among the Georgia Coastal Negroes* (Athens: University of Georgia Press, 1940; reprint, 1987), 106, 176. Cf. Daniel C. Littlefield, *Rice and Slaves: Ethnicity and the Slave Trade in Colonial South Carolina* (Baton Rouge: Louisiana State University Press, 1981).

3. One of the most controversial topics in the controversial literature of American slavery is the nature and origin—the intellectual and spiritual sources—of the religion of the slaves. One school of thought, deriving from the work of the black sociologist E. Franklin Frazier, emphasizes the influence of white culture upon enslaved Africans. Some leading contemporary scholars of slavery emphasize that the values and practices of white Christians penetrated deeply into black Christianity, and the black church became perhaps the most important agency in "Americanizing" enslaved Africans and their descendants. See John Boles, *Black Southerners, 1619–1869* (Lexington: University of Kentucky Press, 1983), 153–68; John Boles, ed., *Masters and Slaves in the House of the Lord* (Lexington: University of Kentucky Press, 1988); and John Blassingme *The Slave Community: Plantation Life in the Antebellum South*, 2d ed. (New York: Oxford University Press, 1979), 98. An opposite school of thought, emphasizing the "Africanity" of slave religion, derves from the work of the white anthropologist Melville J. Herskovits. Sterling Stuckey, for example, argues that the Christianity of the slaves was "shot through with African values." A leading contemporary spokesman for Africanity, Stuckey interprets the culture of the African diaspora using African rather than European ideals. "By operating under cover of Christianity," Stuckey writes, "vital aspects of Africanity, which were considered eccentric in movement, sound, or symbolism, could more easily be practiced openly." As Stuckey sees it, slave Christianity was simply "a protective exterior beneath which more complex, less familiar (to outsiders) religious principles and practices were operative." Writing from an Afrocentric critical perspective, Stuckey insists that the distinctive attributes of slave Christianity were outward and visible manifestations of inward and invisible African cognitive orientations, reflecting "a religious outlook toward which the master class might otherwise be hostile." What John Blassingame describes as "the 'Americanization' of the bondsman" Stuckey calls the "Africanization of Christianity." See Sterling Stuckey, *Slave Culture: Nationalist Theory and the Foundations of Black America* (New York: Oxford University Press, 1987), 35–36, 54, 57. Cf. Blassingame, *Slave*

Community, 98. A third school of thought, exemplified by Mechal Sobel, sees the emergence of slave religion as a convergence of European and African religious values. In her study of the colonial Chesapeake, Sobel contends that stressing the relative autonomy of slave culture overlooks the cultural interaction of Africans and Europeans. Enslaved Africans, she argues, adopted Christian eschatology, while their white neighbors adopted African practices of spirit possession and the African sense of life as a spiritual pilgrimage. Thus, not only was black culture shaped by exposure to white culture, but emergent forms of white culture were also shaped by close association with bearers of African tradition. See Mechal Sobel, *The World They Made Together: Black and White Values in Eighteenth-Century Virginia* (Princeton, N.J.: Princeton University Press, 1987), esp. 11, 137, 221, 233. To acknowledge the convergence of African and European elements in African American Christianity, however, is not to imply that Europe and Africa always converged in relatively equal proportions. In such places as the South Carolina and Georgia lowcountry, enslaved Africans and their descendants constituted 80 to 90 percent of the population for most of the eighteenth and nineteenth centuries. In such places, African cultural influences necessarily out-weighed European ones.

4. Georgia Bryan Conrad, "Reminiscences of a Southern Woman," *Southern Workman* 30 (1901): 13; see also her *Reminiscences of a Southern Woman* (Hampton, Va.: [1901]). Interview with Shad Hall, Sapelo Island, Georgia, in Savannah Writers Project, *Drums and Shadows*, 166; interview with Katie Brown, Sapelo Island, Georgia, ibid, 161. The name is transcribed Bi-la-li, Bu Allah, or Ben Ali in various sources. See also Clyde Ahmad Winters, "Afro-American Muslims from Slavery to Freedom," *Islamic Studies* 17 (1978), 187–90; Alan D. Austin, *African Muslims in Antebellum America* (New York: Garland, 1984).

5. Katie Brown, in Savannah Writers Project, *Drums and Shadows*, 162; Katie Brown, quoted in Lydia Parrish, *Slave Songs of the Georgia Sea Islands* (New York: Creative Age Press, 1942; reprint, Athens: University of Georgia Press, 1991), 27; Shad Hall, in Savannah Writers Project, *Drums and Shadows*, 166.

6. Charles Ball, *Slavery in the United States: A Narrative of the Life and Adventures of Charles Ball, A Black Man, Who Lived Forty Years in Maryland, South Carolina and Georgia, as a Slave* (New York: John Taylor, 1835), 164–65; Ball Family Papers, South Carolina Library, University of South Carolina, Columbia. According to Sterling Stuckey, "the great bulk of the slaves were scarcely touched by

Christianity": *Slave Culture*, 37–38.

7. Charles Colcock Jones, *Suggestions on the Religious Instruction of the Negroes in the Southern States* (Philadelphia: Presbyterian Board of Publication, 1847), quoted in Robert S. Starobin, ed., *Blacks in Bondage: Letters of American Slaves* (New York: New Viewpoints, 1974), 42.

8. Ball, *Slavery in the United States*, 164–65, 201–3; Rev. Edward Thomas to Rt. Rev. R. W. Whittingham, March 10, 1836, quoted in Eugene D. Genovese, *Roll, Jordan, Roll: The World the Slaves Made* (New York: Pantheon, 1974), 187; Paul Trapier, *The Religious Instruction of the Black Population: The Gospel To Be Given to Our Servants* (Charleston, S.C.: 1847), 14; Henry Brown, Charleston, interviewed by Jessie A. Butler, in *The American Slave: A Composite Autobiography*, ed. George P. Rawick (Westport, Conn.: Greenwood, 1972), vol. 2, sec. 1, 120; Sarah Hodgson Torian, ed., "Antebellum and War Memories of Mrs. Telfair Hodgson, "*Georgia Historical Quarterly* 27 (1943): 351. Cf. William W. Freehling, *Prelude to Civil War* (New York: Harper and Row, 1966), 336–37; Luther P. Jackson, "Religious Instruction of Negroes, 1830–1860, With Special Reference to South Carolina," *Journal of Negro History* 15(1930): 72–114.

9. Charles Colcock Jones, *A Catechism of Scripture, Doctrine and Practice for Families and Sabbath Schools. Designed Also for the Oral Instruction of Colored Persons* (Savannah and New York: Observer Office Press, 1844), 127–30, quoted in Bell, *Major Butler's Legacy*, 152–63.

10. John Rogers, "My Dear Children," April 5, 1842, quoted in Genovese, *Roll, Jordan, Roll*, 190; Robert F. W. Allston, quoted by Ulrich B. Phillips, "Racial Problems, Adjustments, and Disturbances," in *The South in the Building of the Nation*, ed. Julian A.C. Chandler, Franklin L. Riley, James C. Ballagh, John Bell Henneman, Edwin Mims, Thomas E. Watson, Samuel Chiles Mitchell, and Walter Lynwood Fleming, (Richmond, Va.: Southern Historical Publishing Society, 1909–12), 4: 210.

11. Charles Colcock Jones to Sandy Maybank, quoted in Starobin, *Blacks in Bondage*, 42; Charles Colcock Jones to Catoe, January 28, 1831, ibid., 44; Catoe to Charles Colcock Jones, September 3, 1852, ibid., 48; Andrew to Charles Colcock Jones, September 10, 1852, ibid., 51–52.

12. James Henley Thornwell, *The Rights and Duties of the Masters: A Sermon Preached at the Dedication of a Church Erected in Charleston, S.C. for the Benefit and Instruction of the Colored Population* (Charleston, S.C.: Walker and James, 1850), 11; *Public Proceedings Relating to Calvary Church and the Religious Instruction of Slaves* (Charleston, S.C.: Walker and James, 1805), 19.

13. Frederika Bremer, *Homes in the New World: Impressions of America* (New York: Harper, 1853), 1:491.

14. Whitemarsh Seabrook, quoted in Freehling, *Prelude to Civil War*, 335; Whitemarsh Seabrook, *Essay on the Management of Slaves* (Charleston, S.C.: Miller and Brown, 1834), 15, 28–30. On the revolutionary potential of African American Christianity, see Orville Vernon Burton, *In My Father's House Are Many Mansions: Family and Community in Edgefield, South Carolina* (Chapel Hill: University of North Carolina Press, 1985), 152–58.

15. Thornwell, *Rights and Duties of Masters*, 11; Alexander Glennie, *Sermons Preached on Plantations to Congregations of Slaves* (Charleston, S.C.: 1844), 1–5, 21–27. Cf. John Blassingame, *The Slave Community: Plantation Life in the Anti-Bellum South* (New York: Oxford University Press, 1972), 170.

16. Robert F.W. Allston, *Essay on Sea Coast Crops* (Charleston, S.C.: A.E. Miller, 1854), 41. On the problem of role boundaries in culture, see Mary Douglas, *Purity and Danger: An Analysis of Concepts of Pollution* (London: Praeger, 1966), 143.

17. This is a composite of descriptions of slave religious services in Bremer, *Homes in the New World*, 1: 289–90; William Wyndham Malet, *An Errand to the South in the Summer of 1862* (London: Richard Bentley, 1863), 49–50, 74; Laurence Oliphant, *Patriots and Filibusters; or Incidents of Political and Exploratory Travel* (Edinburgh: Blackwood, 1860), 140–41; Sir Charles Lyell, *A Second Visit to the United States of America* (London: John Murray, 1849), 1: 269–70, 2: 213–14; A. M. H. Christensen, "Spirituals and Shouts of the Southern Negroes," *Journal of American Folk-Lore* 7 (1894): 154–55; H. G. Spaulding, "Under the Palmetto," *Continental Monthly* 4 (1863): 196–200; Daniel E. Huger Smith, "A Plantation Boyhood," in *A Carolina Rice Planation of the Fifies* ed. Alice R. Hugher Smith and Herbert Ravenel Sass (New York: William Morrow, 1936), 75; C. Vann Woodward, ed., *Mary Chestnut's Civil War* (New Haven, Conn.: Yale University Press, 1981), 213–14; and John G. Williams, *De Ole Plantation: Elder Coteney's Sermons* (Charleston, S.C.: Walker, Evans, and Coggswell, 1895), 2–11. The text is quoted from Williams, *De Ole Plantation*, 40. I recorded a similar African American religious service at New Bethel Baptist Church on Sandy Island, S.C., January 16, 1972. William Faulkner includes a literary description of such a service in the "Dilsey" section of *The Sound and the Fury* (New York: Jonathan Cape and

Harrison Smith, 1929). See also analyses of African American preaching styles in W. E. B. Du Bois, "Religion of the Southern Negro," *New World 9* (1900); Grace Sims Holt, "Stylin' Outta the Black Pulpit," in *Rappin' and Stylin' Out*, ed. Thomas Kochman (Urbana: University of Illinois Press, 1972), 189–95; Le Roi Jones, *Blues People: Negro Music in White America* (New York: William Morrow, 1963), 45–46; Henry H. Mitchell, *Black Preaching* (Philadelphia: J. B. Lippincott, 1970); Bruce A Rosenburg, *The Art of the American Folk Preacher* (New York: Oxford University Press, 1970), 7, 10, 14, 17, 40, 47, 51, 115–16; Gerald L. Davis, *I Got the Word in Me and I can Preach It, You Known* (Philadelphia: University of Pennsylvania Press, 1987); W. D. Weatherford, *American Churches and the Negro: An Historical Study from early Slave Days to the Present* (Boston: Christopher Publishing House, 1957), 114–15; Carter G. Woodson, *History of the Negro Church* (Washington, D.C.: Association for the Study of Negro Life and History, 1921), 41; Clarence E. Walker, *A Rock in a Weary Land: The African Methodist Episcopal Church during the Civil War and Reconstruction* (Baton Rouge: Louisiana State University Press, 1982), 61. On the status of the slave preachers in the slave community, see John W. Blassingame, "Status and Social Structure in the Slave Community," in *The Afro-American Slaves: Community or Chaos*, ed. Randall M. Miller (Malabar, Fla.: Robert Krieger, 1981), 114, 120–21. *Buckra* means white person.

18. Parrish, *Slave Songs*, 166.

19. Henry Brown interview in Rawick, *The American Slave*, vol. 2, sec. 1, 126. Cf. Albert J. Raboteau, Jr., *Slave Religion: The "Invisible Institution" in the Antebellum South* (New York: Oxford University Press, 1978), 136–37; Roger Bastide *African Civilisations in the New World*, trans. Peter Green (New York: Harper and Row, 1971), 92. On the social position of the preacher in the slave community, see Blassingame, "Status and Social Structure," 114, 120–21. On the social position of the man of words elsewhere in the African diaspora, see Roger D. Abrahams, *The Man of Words in the West Indies* (Baltimore, Md.: Johns Hopkins University Press, 1983). On the social position of the man of words in African societies, see S. A. Babalola, *The Content and Form of Yoruba Ijala* (Oxford: Clarendon Press, 1966), 40–55; Dan Ben-Amos, *Sweet Words: Storytelling Events in Benin* (philadelphia: Institute for the Study of Human Issues, 1975), and his "Two Benin Storytellers," in Richard M. Dorson, ed., *African Folklore* (Garden City, N.Y.: Doubleday, 1972), 103–14; Ruth Finnegan, *Limba*

Stories and Storytelling (Oxford: Clarendon Press, 1966), 64–85; and Judith Irvine, "Caste and Communication in a Woloj Village" (Ph.D. dissertation, University of Pennsylvania, 1973). For a discussion of the "phenomenon of mid-transition"—of one who straddles sacred and secular worlds—see Victor W. Turner, *The Forest of Symbols: Aspects of Ndembu Ritual* (Ithaca, N.Y.: Cornell University Press, 1967), 110; and Victor W. Turner, ed., *Celebration: Studies in Festivity and Ritual* (Washington, D.C.: Smithsonian Institution, 1982). See also Kenneth Burke, *Language as Symbolic Action: Essays in Life, Literature, and Method* (Berkely and Los Angeles: University of California Press, 1971), 391; and Peter Berger and Thomas Luckmann, *The Social Construction of Reality: A Treatise in the Sociology of Knowledge* (Garden City, N.Y.: Doubleday, 1966), 47–49.

20. Lionel H. Kennedy and Thomas Parker, *An Official Report of the Trials of Sundry Negroes Charged with an Attempt to Raise an Insurrection in the State of South Carolina* (Charleston, S.C.: James R. Schenk, 1822), 14–15, 50, 54, 61. Other contemporary accounts include Edwin C. Holland, *A Refutation of the Calumines against Southern and Western States: An Account of the Late Intended Insurrection among a Portion of the Blacks of this City*, 3d ed. (Charleston, S.C.: A. E. Miller, 1822) 22–23, 30; [James Hamilton, Jr.], *Narrative of the Conspiracy and Intended Insurrection among a Portion of the Blacks in the State of South Carolina in the Year 1822* (Boston: Joseph W. Ingram, 1822); and [Thomas Pinckney,] *Reflections, Occasioned by the Late Disturbances in Charleston* (Charleston, S.C.: A. E. Miller, 1822). There is a manuscript trial transcript in [Thomas Bennett], Governor's Message No. 2, November 2, 1822, Governor's Papers, South Carolina Department of Archives and History, Columbia. Book-length secondary accounts of the Vesey plot include John Lofton, *Denmark Vesey's Revolt: The Slave Plot that Lit a Fuse to Fort Sumter* (Kent, Ohio: Kent State University Press, 1983); and Robert S. Starobin, ed., *Insurrection in South Carolina: The Slave Conspiracy of 1822* (Englewood Cliffs, N.J.: Prentice-Hall, 1970). Cf. Clifford Geertz, *The Interpretation of Cultures* (New York: Basic Books, 1973), 123–31.

21. William Francis Allen, Charles P. Ware, and Lucy McKim Garrison, eds., *Slave Songs of the United States* (Boston: A. Simpson, 1867), 51, 55, 20, 34. Cf. John Lovell, Jr., *Black Song: The Forge and The Flame. The Story of How the Afro-American Spiritual Was Hammered Out* (New York: Macmillan, 1972), 244–50.

22. Allen, Ware, and Garrison, *Slave Songs of the U.S.*, 6, 13, 26, 28, 34, 39, 42, 50, 63, 66, 75, 81.

23. Ibid., 67, 29.

24. Ibid., 23, 50–51.

25. Ibid., 93.

26. Ibid., 68, 29.

27. Charles Joyner, *Folk Song in South Carolina* (Columbia, S.C.: University of South Carolina Press, 1971), 62–95.

28. Katie Brown, in Parish, *Slave Songs*, 131–32; Chalmers S. Murray, "Edisto's Ghosts Fond of Whiskey," Chalmers S. Murray Papers, South Carolina Historical Society, Charleston (hereinafter abbreviated SCHS). Cf. Julia Peterkin, *Green Thursday* (New York: Alfred A. Knopf, 1924), 94–101; and Roland Steiner, "Seeking Jesus," *Journal of American Folklore* 14 (1901): 672. For comparative examples of the convergence of African spirit possession with Christianity in African American cultures, see Erika Bourguignon's "Ritual Dissociation and Possession Belief in Caribbean Negro Religion," in Norman E. Whitten, Jr., and John F. Szwed, eds., *Afro-American Anthropology: Contemporary Perspectives* (New York: Free Press, 1970), 87–101; Elsa Goveia, *Slave Society in the British Leeward Islands at the End of the Eighteenth Century* (New Haven, Conn.: Yale University Press, 1965), 247–48; Edward Brathwaite, *The Development of Creole Society in Jamaica, 1770–1820* (Oxford: Clarendon Press, 1971), 219; George E. Simpson, "'Batismal,' 'Mourning,' and 'Building' Ceremonies of the Shouters of Trinidad," *Journal of American Folklore* 79 (1965): 537–50; and George E. Simpson, *The Shango Cult in Trinidad* (San Juan, P.R.: Institute of Caribbean Studies, 1965), 155.

29. John A. Lomax, *Field Notes 1935–1937*, John A. Lomax Papers, Archive of Folk Culture, Library of Congress; Bremer, *Homes in the New World*, 1: 290; Chalmers S. Murray, "Tom-Toms Sound for Edisto Rites," in Murray Papers, SCHS; Smith, "A Plantation Boyhood," 75–76; Charlotte Forten, "Life on the Sea Islands," *Atlantic Monthly* 13 (1864): 593–94, and *The Journal of Charlotte L. Forten*, ed. Ray L. Billington (New York: Dryden Press, 1953), 153, 184, 190, 205; Allen, Ware, and Garrison, *Slave Songs of the U.S.*, xiv; Thomas Wentworth Higginson, "Negro Spirituals," *Atlantic Monthly* 19 (1867): 685–94, and his *Army Life in a Black Regiment* (Boston, 1870), 197–98; Elizabeth Ware Pearson, ed., *Letters from Port Royal* (Boston: W. B. Clarke, 1906), 22–28; Rupert S. Holland, ed., *Letters and Diary of Laura M. Towne: Written from the Sea Islands of South Carolina, 1862–1884* (Chambridge, Mass.: 1912), 20–23; Society for the Preservation of Spirituals, *The Carolina Low Country* (New York: William Morrow, 1931), 198–201; Zora Neale Hurston, "Shouting," in Nancy Cunard, ed., *Negro: An Anthology* (London: Wishart, 1934), 49–50; Willie Lee Rose, *Rehearsal for Reconstruction: The Port Royal Experiment* (Indianapolis, Ind.: Bobbs-Merrill, 1964), 91. The symbolic significance of drums to both blacks and whites is illustrated in Edward G. Mason, "A Visit to South Carolina in 1860," *Atlantic Monthly* 53 (1884): 244. The importance of shouting in African American Christianity is underlined by an exchange between a Gullah preacher and a white folklorist in 1936. After a field trip to All Saints Parish in the South Carolina low country, John A. Lomax wrote in his field notes, "Once I asked the Reverend Aaron Pinnacle of Heavens Gate Church, South Carolina, why he deliberately attempted in his sermons to influence his congregation to 'shout'…. The Reverend Pinnacle, coal black [illegible] replied without hesitation: 'If I did not preach shoutin' sermons, my congregation would pay me nothing.' Even in religious matters, the economic factor is dominant. We can't get away from it." See Lomax, Field Notes, 1935–1937, Lomax Papers, Library of Congress.

30. Trapier, *Religious Instruction*, 4; Almira Coffin to Mrs. J. G. Osgood, May 10, 1851, in J. Harold Easterby, ed., "South Carolina through New England Eyes: Almira Coffin's Visit to the Low Country in 1851," *South Carolina Historical Magazine* 45 (1944): 131.

31. "Truss Gawd or Ad's Plat Eye," collected by Genevieve Willcox Chandler, Murrells Inlet, South Carolina, WPA Manuscript Collection, South Caroliniana Library (hereafter, SCL), University of South Carolina, Columbia. "Memories of an Island," 90–94; "Conjure Horses Have Passed," "Edisto Treasure Tales Unfruitful," and "Negroes Plagued by Edisto Ghosts," in Murray Papers, SCHS; John Bennett Papers, MS vol., 60, 63–64, SCHS; Ben Washington, Eulonia, Georgia, in Savannah Writers Project, *Drums and Shadows*, 136; Peterkin, *Green Thursday*, 77–78. Cf. Henry C. Davis, "Negro Folk-Lore in South Carolina," *Journal of American Folklore* 27 (1914), 248; Newbell Niles Puckett, *Folk Beliefs of the Southern Negro* (Chapel Hill: University of North Carolina, 1926), 130; and Ambrose E. Gonzales, *The Black Border: Gullah Stories of the Carolina Coast* (Columbia, S. C.: The State Company, 1922), 33.

32. MS vol. 10–17, 61–76, 103–104, 112, in Bennett Papers, SCHS; "Boo-Hags," "Conjer-Horsed," and "Edisto Reveres Old Time Magic," in Murray Papers, SCHS. Cf. Davis, "Negro

Folk-Lore," 247; Puckett, *Folk Beliefs*, 147; William R. Bascom, "Acculturation among the Gullah Negroes," *American Anthropologist* 43 (1941): 49. In Josephine Pinckney's novel *Great Mischief* (New York: Viking Press, 1948), a retelling of the Faust legend, a nineteenth-century Charleston apothecary becomes enmeshed in black magic and is lured to his doom by a charming hag. For a comparative perspective, see Bastide, *African Civilisations*, 108–10. For an African derivation, see E. E. Evans-Pritchard, *Theories of Primitive Religion* (Oxford: Clarendon Press, 1965), 17.

33. MS vol. 10–17, 61, 76, 103, 112, in Bennett Papers, SCHS; "Conjer Horses Have Passed," "Edisto's Ghosts Fond of Whiskey," and "Edisto Reveres Old Time Magic," in Murray Papers, SCHS. Cf. Bascom, "Acculturation among Gullah Negroes," 49; F. C. Bartlett, *Psychology and Primitive Culture* (New York: Macmillan, 1923), 63, 110, 117–18.

34. Jack Wilson, Old Fort, Georgia, in Savannah Writers Project, *Drums and Shadows*, 7; Shad Hall, Sapelo Island, Georgia, ibid., 167.

35. Solbert Butler, Hampton County, interviewed by Phoebe Faucette, in Rawick, *The American Slave*, vol. 2, sec. 1, 161–65; Isaiah Butler, Hampton County, interviewed by Phoebe Faucette, ibid., vol. 2, sec. 1, 160; MS vol. in Bennett Papers, SCHS; "Gullahs Nearer to Spirit World," "Edisto Negroes Close to Spirits," and "Voodoo Gods Yet Alive on Islands," in Murray Papers, SCHS. Cf. Bstide, *African Civilisations*, 108–10.

36. "Voodoo Survivals Traced on Edisto," "Tom-Toms Sound for Edisto Rites," and "Edisto Reveres Old Time Magic," in Murray Papers, SCHS; James R. Sparkman, "The Negro," in Sparkman Family Papers, SCL. For a similar portrayal of the fragmentation of African religion in Jamaica, see Bastide, *African Civilisations*, 103. That all three streams should be considered aspects of slave religion is suggested by Anthony F.C. Wallace's definition of religion as "that kind of behavior which can be classified as belief and ritual concerned with supernatural beings, powers, and forces" in his *Religion: An Anthropological View* (New York: Random House, 1966), 5; and by Mary Douglas, in her *Edward Evans-Pritchard* (New York: Viking, 1980), 25–26.

37. MS vol., 18–24, 39A, 81–87, 158 in Bennett Papers, SCHS; "Voodoo Gods Yet Alive on Island," "Voodoo Survivals Traced on Edisto," and "Memories of an Island," 193–96, in Murray Papers, SCHS. Cf. George Eaton Simpson, "The Shango Cult in Nigeria and Trinidad," *American Anthropologist* 54 (1962): 1204–29, and his *Shango Cult in Trinidad*,

Harold Courlander, *The Dream and the Hoe: The Life and Lore of the Haitian People* (Berkeley and Los Angeles: University of California Press, 1960); Alfred Metraux, *Voodoo in Haiti*, trans. Hugo Charteris (New York: Oxford University Press, 1959); Melville J. Herskovits, *Life in a Haitian Valley* (New York: Alfred A. Knopf, 1937); John Mbiti, *African Religions and Philosophy* (Garden City, N.Y.: Doubleday, 19&9), 83; Bastide, *African Civilisations* 59–60, 101–3; Martha Beckwith, "Some Religious Cults in Jamaica," *American Journal of Psychology* 34 (1923): 32–45; Donald Hogg, "The Convince Cult in Jamaica," in Sidney Mintz, ed., *Papers in Caribbean Anthropology (New Haven, Conn.: Yale University, Department of Anthropology, 1960)*; George Eaton Simpson, *"Jamaica Revivalist Cults," Social and Economic Studies* 5 (1956): 321–42; Puckett, *Folk Beliefs*, 167–310; E. Horace Fitchett, "Superstitions in South Carolina," *Crisis* 43 (1936): 360–71; Monica Shuler, "Afro-American Slave Culture," in Michael Craton, ed., *Roots and Branches: Current Directions in Slave Studies* (Toronto, Ontario: Pergamon Press, 1979), 129–37.

38. "Voodoo Gods Yet Alive On Islands," "Edisto Overrun by Rattlesnakes," "Voodoo Survivals Traced on Edisto," and "Conjer-Men Keep Den of Reptiles," in Murray Papers, SCHS: *Account of the late Intended Insurrection*, 23 Cf. Davis, "Negro Folk-Lore in South Carolina," 245; Benjamin A. Botkin, "Folk-Say and Folk-Lore," in William T. Couch, ed., *Culture in the South* (Chapel Hill: University of North Carolina Press, 1934), 590; Batside, *African Civilizations*, 134–47; Paul D. Escott, *Slavery Remembered: A Record of Twentieth-Century Slave Narratives* (Chapel Hill: University of North Carolina Press, 1979), 105; Genovese, *Roll Jordon, Roll* 220; John Blassingame, *The Slave Community*, 41; Zora Neale Hurston, *Mules and Men* (Philadelphia: J.B. Lippincott, 1935), 247, and her "Hoodoo in America," *Journal of American Folklore* 44 (1931), 317–417; Leonora Herron and Alice Bacon, "Conjuring and Conjure-Doctors," *Southern Workman* 24 (1895): 118. Julia Peterkin's novels of African American folk life in South Carolina are veritable catalogs of such folk beliefs: see, e.g., *Black April* (Indianapolis, Ind.: Bobbs-Merrill, 1927), 147–48, 245, and *Bright Skin* (Indianapolis, Ind.: Bobbs-Merrill, 1932), 59.

39. Kennedy and Parker, *Official Report*, 15–16, 78; "Memories of an Island," 108, 193–97, and "Edisto Reveres Old Time Magic," in Murray Papers, SCHS; MS vol., 18–24, and "Edisto Negroes Close to Spirits" in Bennett Papers, SCHS. Cf. Davis, "Negro Folk-Lore," 245–48; Fitchett, "Superstitions," 360–71; Puckett *Folk Beliefs*, 200; Herron and Bacon,

"Conjuring and Conjure-Doctors," 193–94; Blassingame, *Slave Community*, 109; Gilbert Osofsky, ed., *Puttin' On Ole Massa* (New York: Harper and Row, 1969), 37; Du Bois, "Religion of the Southern Negro," 618; W.E.B. Du Bois, *The Souls of Black Folk* (Chicago: A.C. McClurg, 1903), 144; "Lizard in the Head," collected by Genevieve Willcox Chandler, WPA Manuscript Collection, SCL; Peterkin, *Green Thursday*, 158–63, *Black April*, 123, and *Bright Skin*, 114.

40. "Edisto Reveres Old Time Magic," in Murray Papers, SCHS. Cf. Peterkin, *Black April*, 7; Julia F. Morton, *Folk Remedies of the Low Country* (Miami, Fla.: E.A. Seaman, 1974), Davis, "Negro Folk-Lore," 247; Wayland D. Hand, *Popular Beliefs and Superstitions from North Carolina* (Durham, N.C.: Duke University Press, 1961), 858–62; Roland Steiner, "Breziel Robinson Possessed of Two Spirits," *Journal of American Folklore* 13 (1900), 226–28; Charles W. Chesnutt, "Superstitions and Folklore of the South," *Modern Culture* 13 (1901), 231–35; Herron and Bacon, "Conjuring and Conjure-Doctors," 210–11. The distrust of white medicine is well portrayed in Peterkin, *Black April*, 71, 275, 281–83. For a comparative perspective, see Metraux, *Voodoo in Haiti*.

41. Isaiah Butler, Hampton County, interviewed by Phoebe Faucette, in Rawick, *American Slave*, vol. 2, sec. 1, 160; "Edisto Negroes Close to Spirits," in Murray Papers, SCHS; Kennedy and Parker, *Official Report*, 76.

42. Zora Neale Hurston, Eau Gallie, Florida, to Franz Boas, New York, April 21, 1929, in Zora Neale Hurston Papers, American Philosophical Society Library, Philadelphia, Pa. I am grateful to Amy Horowitz for bringing this letter to my attention. A quilter on Johns Island, South Carolina, explained to folklorist Mary Arnold Twinning in the 1970s that the cross in her quilt pattern was not a Christian cross. Instead, "it represented danger, evil, and bad feelings." See Mary Arnold Twinning, "An Examination of African Retentions in the Folk Culture of the South Carolina and Georgia Sea Islands" (Ph.D. dissertation, Indiana University, 1977), 188. Cf. Peterkin, *Bright Skin*, 51; Leland Ferguson, "The Cross Is a Magic Sign: Marks on Pottery from Colonial South Carolina," paper presented at "Digging the Afro-American Past: A Research Conference on Historical Archaeology and the Black Experience," (University of Mississippi, May 18, 1989).

43. I have elsewhere described this process of convergence as the *creolization* of slave culture. See Charles Joyner, *Down by the Riverside: A South Carolina Slave Community* (Urbana: University of Illinois Press, 1984); my "The Creolization of Slave Folklife: All Saints Parish, South Carolina, as a Test Case," *Historical Reflections/Reflexions Historiques* (Waterloo, Ontario) 6 (1979): 435–53; and my "Creolization," *Encyclopedia of Southern Culture*, ed. William R. Ferris and Charles Reagan Wilson (Chapel Hill: University of North Carolina Press, 1989), 147–49.

44. Cf. Geertz, *Interpretation of Cultures*, 89–90; 119; Darryl Forde, ed., *African Worlds: Studies in the Cosmological Ideas and Social Values of African Peoples* (London: Oxford University Press, 1954); Meyer Fortes, *Oedipus and Job in West African Religion* (Cambridge: Cambridge University Press, 195:); Geoffrey Parindeer Parrinder, *African Traditional Religion* (Westport, Conn.: Greenwood Press, 1962); William R. Bascom, *Ifa Divination: Communication between Gods and Men in West Africa* (Bloomington: Indiana University Press, 1969); E. E. Evans-Pritchard, *Nuer Religion* (Oxford: Clarendon Press, 1956), and his *Witchcraft, Oracles, and Magic among the Azande* (Oxford: Clarendon Press, 1937); W. E. Abraham, *The Mind of Africa* (Chicago: University of Chicago Press, 1962), chap. 2; R. S. Rattray, *Religion and Art in Ashanti* (Oxford: Clarendon Press, 1926); Mbiti, *African Religions and Philosophy*, chap. 3; Melville J. Herskovits and Frances S. Herskovits, *An Outline of Dahomean Religious Belief* (Menasha, Wisc.: American Anthropological Association, 1933); Martha Warren Beckwith, *Black Roadways: A Study of Jamaican Folk Life* (Chapel Hill: University of North Carolina Press, 1929), chaps. 2,6; Dominique Zahan, *The Religion, Spirituality, and Thought of Traditional Africa*, trans. Kate E. Martin and Lawrence M. Martin (Chicago: University of Chicago Press, 1979); Mechal Sobel, *Trabelin' On: The Slave Journey to an Afro-Baptist Faith* (Westport, Conn.: Greenwood Press, 1979). The importance of a continuing Yoruba and Ashanti influence and declining Bantu religious influence in African American religion, despite Bantu demographic dominance in the New World, is discussed in Bastide, *African Civilizations*, 104–15.

CALIFORNIA DREAMS

Tamar Frankiel

Most Protestants in the Western United States are well aware that the religious life of their churches is not quite the same as the Protestantism east of the Rockies. Tamar Frankiel is among the first historians of religion to take these western regional differences seriously. In contrast with the evangelical Protestants who dominated religious life in the East, the New Englanders who emigrated to California in the mid-nineteenth century were a minority population amid an established Spanish Mexican Roman Catholic culture and a small, largely dispersed Native American community. Then came the gold rush and a dizzying array of Europeans and Asians as well as American blacks, Catholics, and Jews poured into the region. The hope of immigrant New England ministers to press the image of their homeland onto California gradually turned into a resigned acceptance of the new ethnic and cultural pluralism. Yet out of this new situation, the sons and daughters of eastern Protestant immigrants developed their own cultural identity.

Central to this identity was the belief that Californians were a generous, genteel, and open-minded people. Frankiel traces the origins of this myth to the social experience of democratic values and generosity during the gold rush; an idealized memory of the pre-Anglo Californios—the Spanish Mexican landowners—who lived an hospitable and leisurely lifestyle; and an easygoing tolerance and resistance to institutional constraints which gave rise to the mystical emphases in California Protestantism. The popular tradition blended together these experiences into a myth of a different kind of society than the New England world of their Protestant forebearers. Though the myth conflicted with the reality, it stood in stark contrast with the Puritan ideal of hard work that still dominated Protestant images of the good life back East.

Reprinted by permission from Tamar Frankiel, "California Dreams" in her *California's Spiritual Frontiers: Religious Alternatives in Anglo-Protestantism, 1850-1910* (Berkeley: University of California Press, 1988), 1–17.

11

CALIFORNIA DREAMS

Tamar Frankiel

WHEN THE NEWS of the discovery of gold in California reached the East, thousands of young men, singly or in companies, boarded ships for Panama and westward or set out on the arduous cross-country journey. These were the famous Forty-Niners. Not far behind them were Protestant ministers, acting as missionaries to those who had left civilization and religion behind. The young men were starry-eyed about the riches that awaited them in the gold mines; they hoped to make their fortune and return home unbelievably wealthy. The missionaries were starry-eyed too, not so much for wealth (though some did try their hands at mining) as for the opportunity of spreading Christianity and civilization to the far reaches of the continent. Like the circuit riders and the frontier pastors who had been migrating west for decades, the California ministers felt that they carried their treasure—Christianity—with them; and they wanted to make sure that it became firmly established in their new location.

New England ministers cherished the idea of remaking California in the image of their homeland. Their tradition had taught them to see New England as a great Puritan city on a hill, toward which all the world would look for an example of a perfect civilization. By replanting their faith—now a considerably modified version of their ancestors' religion—they hoped to establish California as a center of civilization as well. Joseph A. Benton, the "father of California Congregationalism," expressed the sentiments of many New Englanders:

> We are here, in the Providence of God, to establish and mature...the same institutions—to rear and perfect the same fabric of government—to extend the sphere of the same civil rights and social order—to diffuse the blessings of the same benign and holy faith—and to hallow in memory and observe the same secular and religious festivals, as have been the strength, and glory, and beauty of the land of our Fathers and the places of our birth.

Benton envisioned a California cultivated like New England, with marshes drained, farm houses dotting the valleys, and blossoming flowers in what seemed to him the arid waste around San Francisco Bay. When that vision was fulfilled, he believed, then everyone would come to California: "The world's centre will have changed.—This will be the land of pilgrimage, and no man will be thought to have seen the world till he has visited California!"[1] William Pond, another Congregationalist minister, prophesied that "the time was surely coming when not New York but California would be the 'empire state' in our Union—no one with open eyes can doubt it."[2]

Nor were the powerful New England Congregationalists the only ones to have a dramatic vision of California and its future. James Woods, a pioneer Presbyterian of the Old School, echoed Benton's and Pond's perceptions of the significance of California:

> *Unparalleled in the history of the world is the march of progress in California.*...Instead of being a remote, and almost unknown, and uncared for portion of the globe, with but a few scattering and degenerate sons of Spain, and a few enterprising adventurers, and a few tribes of wretchedly degraded Indians, it now in the short space of two years has become a central spot of earth, where almost all nations of the world have their representatives congregated.[3]

S.D. Simonds, a Methodist minister, proclaimed that "California is the New World of the Nineteenth Century, and her influence will be lasting as her majestic mountains…and more precious than the gold of her quartz and placers."[4] Similarly, Darius Stokes, a leading black minister of the African Methodist Episcopal church, spoke of California as destined to be the next great "world emporium." He warned, however, that the churches must ensure the progress of religion and morals, especially freedom from oppression for blacks, along with the temporal and material achievements of the age.[5] Another Methodist, Lorenzo Waugh, as he settled in Petaluma, extolled California as a new Eden[6]—and quickly set about organizing a temperance crusade.

None of the ministers, of course, saw California as perfect; it had to be made Christian. Many worried about the temptations that stemmed from the focus on gold and wealth and from the fast-paced life of adventurers. Others were concerned about California's cosmopolitanism and the lack of unity among the population.[7] On the whole, however, ministers came to the Golden State with high hopes and a strong drive to make California a fine Christian state. An essay in the *Congregational Quarterly* of 1861 argued that the New England influence would turn the trick:

> A single family of genuine Puritan substance…is a germ, around which a whole flood of miscellaneous population will take form…the innate validity of this element molds the rising communities of the West, and unconsciously fashions all after the ideas with which it comes charged.[8]

Laymen also thought it likely that California would be transformed into a replica of the East. A farmer writing to the *American Agriculturist* in 1849 declared, apparently with some ambivalence, that "California will soon be California no longer. The hordes of emigrants and adventurers…will speedily convert this wild, cattle-breeding, lasso-throwing, idle, bigoted, bull-baiting race, into an industrious, shrewd, trafficking Protestant set of thorough-going Yankees."[9]

What did it mean for Anglo-Protestants of the nineteenth century to be making California a Christian state like Massachusetts or some other place east of the Mississippi? The ministers possessed a fairly clear image of themselves and their role in such an enterprise: they were shapers of society; the churches were its pillars.[10] Leaders of each denomination saw themselves as cooperating with others, but they did not necessarily view themselves as parts of a grand alliance. The Presbyterians and Congregationalists cooperated most closely, as they had in the eastern states. For seventeen years one major newspaper served them both—the *Pacific*, sponsored by the Congregational churches—which claimed it was "the organ of no Sect or Party."[11] By 1868, however, the Presbyterians had decided to publish their own paper, the *Occident*, which clearly supported their denominational "sentiments and aims" while maintaining harmonious relations with other Christians.[12] The Methodist paper, the *California Christian Advocate*, never wanted to be other than Methodist, stating clearly in its first issue, "We cannot claim to be Union." The Methodists held that each denomination ought to be itself, and believed that differences "in names, and modes, and governments, and beliefs" would not necessarily lead to strife among Christians.[13]

A gentle and courteous denominationalism, rather than a united front, was the implicit rule. Writers for the popular Protestant media did not generally refer to themselves as evangelicals, but simply as Christians. Some of the ministers brought this attitude with them from the East; they knew of the efforts at union and the difficulties that had been encountered. Anglo-Protestant opinion at midcentury generally favored acceptance of differences within the framework of a general common purpose. By 1867, the *California Christian Advocate* could cite with approval Henry Ward Beecher (a Congregationalist) to the effect that harmony among differences was the state most desired.[14] Each denomination had a fairly clear sense of itself. The Methodists' peculiar mission, said Bishop E. Thompson in his speech to the California Conference in 1867, was to awaken spiritual life and lead "to the high places of religious experience" while encouraging a life of self-denial and constant prayer.[15] The Presbyterian *Occident* saw its church's purpose as helping to build society and strengthen the churches.[16] The Baptists saw themselves as enforcing a clear standard of church discipline and doctrine as well as general social morality.[17] Moreover, the situation in California reinforced this attitude. Bishop Thompson summed it up:

> The Pacific coast is the theological equator. As early as the last century, the Latin and Greek churches met in the valley of the Sonoma…. Monotheism in its four forms; Judaism, in its orthodox and heterodox schools; Christianity, in its Latin, Greek, and Protestant churches; Deism,… from that of the devout and considerate Herbert, to that of the blaspheming Paine; Polytheism, in its different shapes; and defiant Mormonism, with its polygamous practices and cruel spirit, meet here. Hence, we should be especially on our guard, doctrinally…we are in danger of, first, liberalism, then indifferentism, finally skepticism…. The Christian faith should be clearly defined; and while its minor points are but little insisted on, its *essential* doctrines and full experience should be steadily, fully, and uncompromisingly, though charitably, maintained.[18]

The pluralism of California made it essential for each denomination to have a clear sense of itself, to oppose "Romanists," Mormons, and other suspect groups, and at the same time to be charitable, as Christians, toward other denominations.

In daily life, the role of the Protestant ministers was to guide the people in devotion and morality. They would raise up churches where the Word would be preached. The people would not only attend services, but also keep Sunday apart as a day of worship. They would pray daily, alone and with their families. The population in general would abstain from vice, especially liquor, gambling, and worse sins. People would respect order and government while guarding against corruption and bad influences. Church members would organize to correct social abuses, help the needy, and support missionaries to bring into the fold those who had not received the gospel. They would be educated in secular knowledge in common schools and religious colleges, which would also inculcate a Christian spirit at all levels.

That kind of society was, of course, an ideal seldom realized even in the East. Anglo-Protestant ministers did not seem daunted, however, by any differences they found in their new environment. They set about creating the institutions and movements that they believed would be pillars of California society as they had been of the eastern branch of the Protestant empire. Churches were the most obvious of these institutions, and the buildings rose rapidly. In 1850, only two years after the great migration began, Protestant churches in California had "sittings," that is, seats in the churches, for twelve thousand people, or 13 percent of the population. San Francisco, though it had the greatest proportion of non-Protestants, boasted twenty-two Protestant churches by 1852, and many of these by 1860 had attracted well-known ministers from the East. Whether church membership matched the growth in buildings and ministers' salaries is another question; unfortunately, membership figures are not available for the early years. Nevertheless the clergy clearly had some support, both for churches and for the other staple of Anglo-Protestant culture, the printed word. Every denomination established one or more newspapers, and by 1860 the largest, the *Pacific*, had a circulation of four thousand, while the *California Christian Advocate* was sent to nearly two thousand in the state.[19]

Other activities soon followed the building of churches. Anglo-Protestant concern for social and moral order found expression in a crusade, beginning in 1851, for a strong state Sabbath law. By 1855 the legislature passed a mild law banning noisy amusements, and by 1858 a stricter law was approved, forbidding businesses to be open on Sunday. Other reform organizations were created to propagandize against liquor, gambling, and prostitution, and to aid sailors and orphans. Temperance was one of the more popular causes: Lorenzo Waugh's Bands of Hope, established to involve young people in the anti-liquor movement, spread throughout the towns of California. Ministers were instrumental in convincing San Franciscans to set up free elementary schools, and they themselves frequently established high schools (the first public high school was not founded until 1875). Denominations founded seminaries—Baptist, Congregational, Methodist, Presbyterian—and eventually some created colleges: the College of California (later the University of California, Berkeley) was founded by New England Congregationalists and Presbyterians, and the University of the Pacific by the Methodists. In all, sixty church-sponsored schools were founded between 1850 and 1874.[20]

Finally, the Anglo-Protestant clergy often appointed themselves watchmen over government. When in 1856 conflict erupted in San Francisco over alleged government corruption, ministers generally supported the Vigilance Committee, a businessmen's organization that took the law into its own hands, claiming to restore order and honest government. Whether support of the vigilantes was the most honorable of causes is debatable, but the alliance with the mercantile community clearly showed that Protestant ministers had become part of the network of social power in early California.[21]

Josiah Royce, a Harvard philosopher and California native, recalled that in those early years community spirit was at least as well represented by the churches as by the saloons.

That may say more for the saloons than the churches. But early California has so often been portrayed as wild country, dominated by men lusting for pleasure and wealth, that we should consider the force of Royce's observations. "There was from the first," he wrote, "the characteristic American feeling prevalent that churches were a good and sober element in the social order, and that one wanted them to prosper, whether one took a private and personal interest in any of them or not."[22]

Yet the end of that statement presents the other side of the coin. Royce portrays a society where people wanted churches to support order and community spirit, but did not always take a "private and personal" interest in them. Royce believed, indeed, that many church members who would have been devout back East were quite "cold" in California; they had a "distrust toward enthusiasm." His observations agree with evidence from other sources; enthusiastic religion did not succeed, and people often did not make strong personal commitments to the churches. Camp meetings with their more emotional religious style did not fare as well in California as on earlier frontiers; nor did urban revivalists. Californians participated in the nationwide "lay revival" of 1858, but comment on the movement is infrequent in the annals of the time.[23] Ministers' complaints must be taken with a grain of salt, but many of their comments support this general impression. Presbyterian pastor Albert Williams bemoaned the fact, not that people ignored religion entirely, but that less than half the "professors of religion" (in other words, those who had been converted) would admit it openly.[24] Another minister observed in 1880 that the secular press in California, unlike the Eastern press, seldom reported religious news.[25] People gave freely of their wealth, but expended their personal energy on other things.

Thus even as church membership grew, there was little of what Royce called "enthusiasm." By 1871 the *Pacific Methodist*, the organ of the Southern Methodist church, had acknowledged that "business Christianity"—that is, the support of the church as an institution—was as good as or better than contemplative and joyous campmeeting Christianity.[26] Such a remark is as startling in its context as the famous turnaround of Lyman Beecher, who, after fighting tooth and nail to keep the Congregational church established, decided after defeat that voluntarism was better. In California, though, society was electing "business Christianity" and condemning enthusiasm. If a prominent person took an unusual religious position, he was open to ridicule. For example, when the well-known editor Mr. Owen of the *San Jose Mercury* joined the Disciples of Christ, the *Petaluma Crescent*, far away at the opposite end of the Bay, declared him a "Campbellite" and heaped scorn on him:

> We expect soon to hear of his cultivating a pig-tail and preaching Confucius and rats, or else advocating Mohammedanism in San Jose. But the world should be lenient with Owen; he is as crazy on religion as a bedbug that has filled itself from the body of a benzine-saturated individual.[27]

We may reasonably suspect some personal animosity between the two editors. Still, if one's neighbors were watching so closely for signs of religious eccentricity, there must have been considerable pressure to be reserved about one's religious interests and commitments.

Ministers often blamed this situation on competition from secular and material pursuits. As Baptist minister O.C. Wheeler wrote, it was extremely difficult "to get a man to look through a lump of gold into eternity."[28] Secular entertainments made matters worse; one minister reported that his revival camp meeting had to compete with a circus. Mexican fiestas and bullfights were often held on Sundays; gambling houses and saloons were often the only places where single men might meet women. Methodist street preacher William Taylor believed that despite people's open and generous temperaments, California was still "the hardest country in the world in which to get sinners converted to God."[29]

Do secularism and materialism provide an adequate explanation for Californians' reluctance to get involved in the churches? California was an unusual society in many ways; gold was not the only factor. The population, for example, in 1850 was made up almost entirely of men (about 90 percent), and most of them were between the ages of twenty and forty years. By 1860 more women had arrived, but it was not until after 1870 that the sexes approached equality in numbers. Most men came to California with the intention of leaving soon; they were called "argonauts," from their eagerness to gather the golden fleece and return home. Few had economic security; many had sold all their possessions to finance the trip west. Some, especially from New England, had come in "companies" that provided temporary economic and social support. But early California in general was not a stable society of householders and their families; rather, it was a collection of independent individuals trying to become self-made men.[30]

Cultural variety was much greater than on earlier frontiers. California already had an established culture, the Spanish-Mexican one that had begun some seventy years before. Native Americans, largely assimilated or dispersed, made up a small part of the population. When the gold rush began, people from many different backgrounds flocked to the region, and not only from the United States. Besides American Jews, Catholics, blacks, and white Protestants, there were men from France, Germany, England, Ireland, and other parts of Europe, plus a large population of Orientals, mostly Chinese. Protestants were a minority, and they did not have the advantages of earlier settlement, a firm attachment to the land, or special connections, which might have made them more resistant to the unsettled life and new wealth of the region. By about 1870 California began to look more like the rest of the country in its ethnic balance, but between 1850 and 1870 the gold region and its cities, including San Francisco, were among the most cosmopolitan areas in the world.[31]

As a state, an organized society, California was barely formed. In contrast to earlier additions to the Union, which tended to grow gradually before being admitted to statehood, California became one of the United States while still in its infancy as a society. Laws of property and juries to settle disputes had to be created on the spot during gold rush times. Mining camps were flourishing towns one year and ghost towns the next. Those who decided to settle on the land were likely to be involved for years in disputes over former Mexican holdings and competing claims to the land. The land and its settlements were unstable; community, law, and tradition had to be created virtually from scratch. That was not the case on earlier frontiers, where families generally traveled west together, where the next frontier adjoined the former, and where there was immediate permanent settlement. Californians, on the contrary, were intensely aware of the distance from their former homes and families and of the difference in the lives they had to live. They were thrown back on their own resources time and again. They gained a reputation for independence and were proud of it.[32]

This was not the sort of society that Anglo-Protestant ministers had grown up in and been trained to serve. As Kenneth Janzen has argued, the New England tradition demanded a culturally homogeneous, theologically versed, responsible body of householders. Kevin

Starr has observed, similarly, that the radically new situation of California simply could not be regulated by the forms and procedures of a New England parish[33]—or, we might add, an Ohio village or Virginia plantation. Methodists and Baptists might seem to be better suited, as they were on other frontiers, to a loosely structured society than were the Congregationalists and Presbyterians; they did not require such high standards of theological education, and they were flexible in licensing preachers and serving new congregations. But in place of education they expected higher "enthusiasm." They, too, assumed a society of householders with relatively stable occupations, a society with mutual obligations, interlocking interests, ties of tradition, and bonds of affection.

Even the theologies of the Anglo-Protestant churches presumed the social elements they had left behind in the East. If a minister was conservative, he preached a strongly orthodox doctrine of sin and guilt, which meant that a person had to repent and be forgiven and saved through Christ's sacrificial atonement, or else be damned. This theology was based on a legal model—a sinner was like a guilty criminal—which assumed clear obligations and definitions of right and wrong. But Californians had no commonly accepted obligations: laws were in flux, different groups had different customs, and any moral code could appear to be merely a private opinion.

On the other hand, a more liberal minister might de-emphasize guilt and damnation, preaching instead the love of God in Christ. In the mid-nineteenth century liberal ministers would usually liken Jesus to an intimate friend or loving parent, especially a mother who would give her all in loving self-sacrifice for her child. God's love was like a mother's love; in response, a person should turn to God, or "rest in the arms of Jesus." The model of divine-human relations here is the ideal family, which Californians no longer had. The social context—thousands of independent, striving, mostly single men—was not suited to the theology that was heard even in the more liberal churches.[34]

Anglo-Protestant thought, then, was something of an anomaly; yet in such a structureless society, churches were one of the few sources, or at least reminders, of morality and order. Thus people supported them, though without "enthusiasm."[35] But we still have not explained the lack of susceptibility of Californians to revivalist religion. It may be true that Californians had left home and mother, society and legal traditions; but had they also left behind their emotions? Would we not expect that out of revivalism, which so often prospers in a society in flux, a new tradition of emotional religion might have emerged?

Under other circumstances, that might have happened. But Californians of the 1850-1870 period had learned to associate religious or political enthusiasms with factionalism, sectarianism, divisiveness, and even violence. Most of the men in California had been born in the East or Midwest between 1810 and 1830. They grew up during or shortly after the Second Great Awakening, the greatest period of religious excitement in the United States since colonial times. In its aftermath reform crusades, utopian ideas, and new sects mushroomed all over the Northeast, and religious schisms appeared in the South as well. Religious enthusiasm ofter resulted in acrimonious debates within and among churches and reformers, or persecution of fringe groups like the Mormons. One of the worst examples within mainstream Protestantism was the debate, which sometimes erupted in mob violence, between radical abolitionists and anti-abolitionists in the North; the abolitionists were directly influenced by revivals and religious enthusiasm.

Politics was also heating up during the same period, with popular heroes like Andrew Jackson and popular issues like the movement against the Bank of the United States creating enormous political excitement. Then, in the 1830s, there emerged the specter of civil war. In 1832 South Carolina precipitated the nullification crisis, which could have led to secession and war. After that, the nation's leaders were preoccupied with the struggle to preserve the Union. By the 1850s many people were advocating stricter social control and were accusing any enthusiasts, whether political or religious, of being extremists or fanatics.

Under any circumstances it would have been natural for men in their twenties and early thirties to rebel against the tendencies of their parents—in this case to turn away from religious enthusiasm. That reaction would be even more pronounced under the threat of war, and still more in a section of society that was highly disorganized. It is in this light that we can understand the slogan of the San Francisco Vigilance Committee of 1856: "No creed. No party. No sectional issues." It meant: no religion, no politics, no war. Unity in the nation and social order in California seemed to depend on controlling factors—especially emotional enthusiasms—that could give rise to factionalism and divisiveness. Furthermore, Californians were familiar with another kind of emotional derangement: one of the early institutions of the state was the insane asylum at Stockton. While many stories about its inhabitants implied that the lust for wealth had driven them crazy, there were occasional accounts of an overzealous religious person or false Messiah who ended up there.[36] In every realm, from the national to the local to the mental, order was too fragile to allow the exploration of deep religious emotions. The lack of religious enthusiasm in Protestant California was an intense response to the sense of fragmentation in American society in the period.[37]

Lower levels of emotionalism went hand in hand with the gentle denominationalism espoused, as we noted earlier, by the clergy. Most denominations showed declining interests in tests of orthodoxy, while their parishioners showed a growing indifference to actual church membership. There was a brief spate of heresy trials; but interdenominational fighting among Protestants was rare. By 1869 the Presbyterian *Occident* observed that denominational differences were no longer a reason for churches to attack one another. While criticizing the Unitarians for having no binding creed and the Universalitists for abandoning certain biblical doctrines, the *Occident* also declared that soon all the denominations would say simply, "We are Christians."[38] Unity and tolerence were becoming the watchwords of California religious attitudes, and would remain so for many decades to come.

Thus far the religious experience of the Californians whom Anglo-Protestant ministers hoped to reach appears merely negative. There was no enthusiasm, no sectarianism, little commitment to religious institutions. Churches were supported only for instrumental reasons, such as their support of social order; ultimately there was a resigned tolerance, since nothing else was possible. But in fact the immigrants from the East, sons and daughters of old Protestants, were developing their own sense of identity, their own mythology, outside the traditional churches. Clerics saw no unity among the people, no common bonds. (As the Rev. Albert Williams asked, "Can settled, fixed purposes coexist with the manifold interests, aims, and projects of communities without any seeming bond of union?"[39] From his eastern Protestant perspective, the answer would be no.) But Californians considered themselves a unique community despite their diversity. Years later Royce observed, "How swiftly, in that country, the Californians of the early days seized upon every suggestion that could give a sense of the unique importance of their new provincial life." They tended, he said, "to idealize whatever tended to make [their] community, and all its affairs, seem unique, beloved, and deeply founded upon some significant natural basis."[40] Indeed, the attempt to forge an identity out of California experience led eventually to the development, among a significant number of white Protestant Californians, of an alternative to the Anglo-Protestant religious tradition.

Before identifying that alternative, however, we must understand better how ordinary Californians viewed themselves in those first crucial years. One of the unique elements they idealized was their recent social experience—the gold rush itself. In descriptions of those times we find repeatedly an exaltation of democratic values, generosity and sharing during hard times, and noncompetitiveness. We know that in fact there was a great deal of competition, claim-jumping, theft, and outlawry in the mining areas, but people preferred to remember the brighter side. They cherished the fact—which must at first have been a shock—that they could not tell a person's status or occupation by his dress or appearance.[41] People of all backgrounds mingled together: a former attorney and a factory worker, a grocer and a medical doctor, would all be knee-deep in mud, panning gold from the same stream. Further, the ups and downs of gold rush economics meant that people could be enormously wealthy and liberal with handouts, or find themselves struggling to make a meal together. James Woods recalled being overwhelmed by a "donation party" for his family, in which goods were piled high around his home by generous neighbors; while miners remembered sharing bits of food they had scrounged to make a holiday dinner.[42] Such stories helped create images of democratic values, generosity, shared joys and hardships, and generally the plentitude of California itself.

Some Californians also cherished an idealized memory of the pre-Anglo past. Legends of the Californios—the Spanish-Mexican landowners—supported the mythical image of the gold rush. The Californios, it was said, were known far and wide for their generosity and hospitality. They supposedly lived a life of leisure, not unlike the genteel Southern plantation owner, but without the negative side of slavery. Later, white Californians romanticized the mission era, when, it was said, gentle Franciscan fathers tenderly took degraded Indians under their wings. Ultimately California took on the coloring of an exotic Mediterranean country, a perfect Greece or Italy. Such images ignored large chunks of reality: the destruction of Native American cultures, evidence of violence and poverty among Californios, the impact of urban economics on the region after Anglos arrived. But the legends in many ways were more powerful, reinforcing the idea of a society gentle and genteel, open and hospitable, intimately related to the land and the climate. Kevin Starr has suggested that the image of California as Mediterranean "encouraged new attitudes toward work and leisure and what was important to live for. As a metaphor, it stood for a culture anxious to foster an alternative to the industrial ethic."[43] Of course, the very people who created that metaphor were deeply implicated in urban industrial and commercial society. Yet the metaphor indicates that some of them, at least, yearned for a different way of life, even more than did their eastern countrymen.

Together with generosity and gentility went that open-minded tolerance mentioned earlier, which gradually became a universalistic belief that all religions were different aspects of a fundamental truth. Not only other Protestants were tolerated: any tradition could be viewed as a sincere attempt to find God or as a source of universal wisdom. This attitude grew very strong in the latter part of the nineteenth century; but even in the early years it is evident in Protestant attitudes toward Roman Catholics and Asians. There were, of course, many Protestant clerical pronouncements against "Romanism"; but at the popular level there was far less tension between Protestants and Catholics then there had been in the East. Some prejudice emerged in the 1850s during the Vigilante episodes of San Francisco, when mostly Protestant merchants allied against Irish Catholic elements they believed to be corrupt. For generations, too, there was discrimination against Mexicans. The latter, however, was clearly a racial rather than a religious prejudice; although the Catholic church was sometimes criticized for not educating the Spanish-speaking well enough, both Indian and Hispanic Mexicans were generally regarded as lower-class citizens because of racial qualities rather than religious heritage. On the positive side, many Protestants sent their children to Catholic schools, because in the early years they were often far better staffed. This encouraged more positive interaction and lessened the friction between the two groups.

Asians, especially the Chinese, suffered from prejudice and out-right persecution, especially during times of economic depression or high rates of immigration. At these times Chinese competed with Americans as a cheap source of labor in the mines or in building the railroads. During intense periods of persecution and legislation against the Chinese, everything about their religion and culture came in for criticism. They were regarded as idol-worshippers and as conceited people who believed their civilization was the highest in the world.[44] Many Protestants, however, while viewing the Chinese as rather strange, also saw them as bearers of a great, ancient tradition. As early as 1852 the *Pacific* announced in a surprised tone that the Chinese were showing themselves to be self-respecting human beings who cared about justice and morality and deserved to be treated justly and humanely.[45] One Protestant clergyman, the Rev. A.W. Loomis, wrote a book on Confucianism that was favorably reviewed by the *Occident* and frequently mentioned in clerical circles with high praise; while the Rev. William Speer expended great efforts to convince California Protestants that the Chinese and American empires could interact to their mutual benefit. Thus the clergy encouraged an openness that never appeared in their writings on Roman Catholicism. Of course, Protestants still regarded Chinese and other Pacific peoples as targets for missionary work;[46] but at least among the educated populace an interest in understanding other peoples sowed the seeds of positive attitudes toward other traditions.

Many white Californians of Anglo-Protestant background were developing a new picture of themselves as expansive, open, social beings, unique in their potential for development, searching for the best and truest as they moved vigorously into the future. They found in their natural environment a reflection of those same traits. The pages of California's magazines for the first half-century and more were filled with glorious descriptions of a wondrous, grand, and healthy environment. The Geysers (a natural hot springs), Yosemite, the Pacific coast, the southern deserts—nature in California seemed unique, and each new scene seemed to demand that a person experience life more fully. Methodists holding their camp meeting conferences in the countryside appreciated that, as S.D. Simonds put it, the meetings could bring together such congenial spirits, "the lovers of God and the lovers of nature."[47] Even New Englanders, on occasion, forgot their urge to remake California into Massachusetts and admired the distinctive beauty of the state. One article in the *New Englander* of 1858 argued against civilizing California too much:

> Culture improves nothing. California was finished as a world of beauty, before civilization appeared. The magnificent valleys opened wide and clean. The scattered oaks stood in majesty, here and there, and took away the nakedness. Civilization comes, cuts down the oaks for firewood, fences off the plains into squares, covers them with grain or stubble, scatters wild

mustard over them, it may be, and converts them into a weedy looking desolation.... There is never to be a lawn, or a neat grassy slope, as with us, because there is no proper turf.[48]

Some were so awed by the natural wonders that they made the land an allegory for their spiritual understanding. The *Occident* in 1868 printed a sermon, preached by Henry M. Scudder after his vacation in the Sierras, that was essentially a meditation on the life of the soul as like a mountain stream.[49] Even the most conservative churchmen sometimes translated the beauties of California into religious terms—or, one might equally well argue, allowed their religious sensibilities to be transformed by their California experience. One of the most remarkable examples comes from the *California Sketches* of O.P. Fitzgerald, a Southern Methodist pastor. He ends the book with a poem he wrote in the Russian River Valley, describing what was virtually a mystical experience of viewing Mount St. Helen at sunrise. Seeing the light at the top and orange-tinted clouds beneath the summit, he proclaimed its "glory supernal," and went on:

> O glory yet greater! The white, silent mountain,
> Transfigured with sunrise, flames out in the light
> That beams on its face from its far-distant fountain,
> And bathes in full splendor its East-looking height.
>
> My soul, in that moment so rapt and so holy,
> Was transfigured with nature and felt the deep spell;
> My spirit, entranced, bent meekly and lowly
> With rapture that only an angel could tell.
>
> When the night mists of time around me are flying,
> When the shadows of death gather round me apace,
> O Jesus, my Sun, shine on me when dying,
> Transfigure my soul with the light of thy face![50]

Fitzgerald, experiencing nature as transformative, prayed that Jesus might bring such transformation at the moment of death, like a sunrise for the soul on the way to the life beyond the grave. In that kind of experience Fitzgerald, though an orthodox Protestant pastor, was a forerunner of the many Californians who would turn to nature as a spiritual resource and mode of understanding the divine.

Thus many Protestants in California experienced some transformation, through nature or their new society or both. Some saw their society as the epitome of democracy; others felt themselves to be natural aristocrats—without any slaves or oppressed workers. Some saw their new home as a land of plenty, while still others felt transported into other dimensions by the sight of a sunset over the Pacific. All these experiences blended in the popular tradition, as Californians described themselves to each other and to their acquaintances back home. Even while building an urban industrial society, they were creating a myth of their state as a very different kind of society—a leisured, elegant life in glorious natural surroundings, a non-competitive society without hierarchy, whose people, through the bounty of the land and the generosity of all, were supplied with everything they needed, both physically and spiritually.

However fantastic the myth, in light of reality, it is in striking conflict too with traditional Anglo-Protestant images of the good life. Midcentury Protestants back East were still dedicated to the Puritan ideal of hard work, with economic reward as a blessing from God, not a natural gift of the land. They accepted, implicitly, if not explicitly, the necessity of fair competition and the ideal of material progress. A leisurely society would seem merely a collection of idlers. The Mediterranean image might cause a Yankee to shudder, for it could mean Catholic oppression or Southern decadence. As for nature, the beauties of God's creation were private experiences confirming God's wisdom and goodness; one could not build on them a public consciousness and a sound Christian civilization.[51] Protestant ministers might understand some of the yearnings that were emerging among many new Californians, but they were not likely to sympathize deeply with all the new experiences their fellow statesmen cherished. They offered, with pride, the image of an orderly, morally conscious, democratic society, and invited other Californians to participate in building it. For the most part they could not integrate into this image the unique California dreams that were emerging from the people's reflection on their own experience.

NOTES

1. Joseph A. Benton, *California As She Was: As She Is: As She Is to Be* (San Francisco, 1850), 5, 12. Kenneth L. Janzen, in "The Transformation of the New England Tradition in California, 1849–1860" (Ph.D. thesis, Claremont Graduate School, 1964), uses Benton as the prime example of the New England mind. For an Episcopal bishop's version of the transformation hoped for from civilized cultivation of the land, see William Ingraham Kip, *A California Pilgrimage* (Fresno, Calif., 1921), 26.

2. William C. Pond, *Gospel Pioneering: Reminiscences of Early Congregationalism in California* 1833–1920 (Oberlin, Ohio, 1921).

3. James A. Woods, *A Sermon at the Dedication of the Presbyterian Church of Stockton, California, May 5, 1850* (Barre: Patriot Press, 1851), 14. Woods added the hope that now, through California, Christianity could shed its light on China and "Hindostan." The Pacific orientation recurs throughout California literature, but its effects on religion are small in the early period. As we will see, a few Protestant ministers, notably the Reverends A.W. Loomis and William Speer, tried to pass on to their fellow Protestants an appreciation of Chinese culture while at the same time trying to convert the Chinese to Christianity.

4. *California Christian Advocate*, October 10, 1851.

5. Darius Stokes, *A Lecture Upon the Moral and Religious Elevation of the People of California* (San Francisco, 1853), delivered June, 1853, at the AME Church, Sacramento. Compare Mifflin Wister Gibbs, another black minister, who claimed to see in the American expansion into California the exemplary fulfillment of moral law (*Shadow and Light: An Autobiography* [Washington, D.C., 1902]). In this kind of imperial consciousness, black Protestants were in accord with their white counterparts. They also had to struggle, however, for their own rights in a California that was as discriminatory as most northern states at this time. See Douglas Henry Daniels, *Pioneer Urbanites* (Philadelphia: Temple University Press, 1980).

6. Lorenzo Waugh, *Autobiography*, 3rd edition (San Francisco: S. P. Taylor & Co., 1885), 194–95, 217–19. Waugh came to California in part because of a vision in 1851 of a beautiful valley, which he claimed to recognize when he arrived in Petaluma. This is the same Waugh who was a famous midwestern circuit rider and Indian missionary. For similar glorification of California, see J.C. Simmons, *My Trip to the Orient* (San Francisco: Whitaker and Ray, 1902), 182: "Of all the lands I have seen, there is none to compare with America, and in America, none to compare with California."

7. William Taylor, a Methodist street preacher and later a famous bishop, saw San Francisco as "the Sebastopol of his Satanic majesty" (referring not to California's town of that name, but to the seige of the Russian city Sebastopol). See Taylor's *Seven Years Street Preaching in San Francisco* (New York, 1856), 342; and Douglas Anderson, "Give Up Strong Drink, Go to Work, and Become a Man: William Taylor in Gold Rush San Francisco," paper presented at the American Academy of Religion, Western Region, March 1982. For other concerns about the temptations of California, see the *Pacific* and the *California Christian Advocate* in their early years. As late as 1868

the *Occident* was complaining about the lack of home influence, of respect for reputation, and of watchful neighbors to keep society's morals in order. On the lack of unity, see Albert Williams, *A Pioneer Pastorate and Times* (San Francisco: Wallace & Hassett, 1879), 193. For an excellent description of the subtle differences in ministers' attitudes and aims, see Kevin Starr, *Americans and the California Dream 1850–1915* (New York: Oxford University Press, 1973), especially 87–97; see also Richard Lyle Power, "A Crusade to Extend Yankee Culture," *New England Quarterly* 13 (1940): 638–53; and the comments on manifest destiny by Colin B. Goodykoontz, "Protestant Home Missions and Education in the Trans-Mississippi West, 1835–1860," in *The Trans-Mississippi West*, edited by James F. Willard and Colin B. Goodykoontz (Boulder: University of Colorado, 1930).

8. Quoted in Power, "Crusade," 645.

9. Ibid., 647.

10. S.D. Simonds, in the *California Christian Advocate* of July 1, 1852, was proud that the first ceremonial cornerstone laying he had seen was at a church in Sacramento, suggesting that churches were indeed the pillars of society.

11. *Pacific*, August 1, 1851, 1.

12. *Occident*, January 4, 1868, 2.

13. *California Christian Advocate*, October 10, 1851, 1.

14. Ibid., August 22, 1867, 2.

15. Ibid., November 7, 1867, 1.

16. *Occident*, January 4, 1868, 1.

17. *Evangel*, January 29 and February 6, 1874.

18. *California Christian Advocate*, November 7, 1867, 1.

19. For accounts of various aspects of California religious enterprises, see Starr, *California Dream*, chapter 3; William Hanchett, "The Question of Religion and the Taming of California, 1849–1854," *California Historical Society Quarterly* 32 (1953): 49–56, 119–44; William Warren Ferrier, "The Origins and Growth of the Protestant Church on the Pacific Coast," in *Religious Progress on the Pacific Slope*, edited by Charles Sumner Nash and John Wright Buckham (Boston: Pilgrim Press, 1917); Norton Wesley, "'Like a Thousand Preachers Flying': Religious Newspapers on the Pacific Coast to 1865," *California Historical Society Quarterly* 56 (1977): 194–209; Charles S. Greene, *Magazine Publishing in California* (San Francisco: Library Association of California, 1898). Denominational histories include Sandford Fleming, *God's Gold: The Story of Baptist Beginnings in California, 1849–60* (Philadelphia: Judson Press, 1949); C. V. Anthony, *Fifty Years of*

Methodism (San Francisco: Methodist Book Concern, 1901); Arnold Crompton, *Unitarianism on the Pacific Coast: The First Sixty Years* (Boston: Beacon Press, 1957); Clifford M. Drury, "The Beginnings of the Presbyterian Church on the Pacific Coast," *Pacific Historical Review* 9 (June 1940): 195–204, and *The Centennial of the Synod of California* (Presbyterian Synod, 1951); Janzen, "Transformation"; Floyd Looney, *History of California Southern Baptists* (Fresno, Calif., 1954); E.B. Ware, *History of the Disciples of Christ in California* (Healdsburg, Calif., 1916); W.B. West, Jr., "Origin and Growth of the Churches of Christ in California" (M.A. thesis, University of Southern California, 1936). See also Kenneth Wilson Moore, "Areas of Impact of Protestantism upon the Cultural Development of Northern California, 1850–1870" (M.A. thesis, Pacific School of Religion, 1970). It is no accident that most of these studies deal with the first ten to twenty years of California Protestantism; after that time much of the energy of church leaders goes into maintaining what they have built and dealing with the challenges of other groups.

20. On schools, see Clifford M. Drury, "Church-Sponsored Schools in Early California," *Pacific Historian* 20 (1976): 158–66; on Sabbatarian agitation, William Hanchett, "The Blue Law Gospel in Gold Rush California," *Pacific Historical Review* 24 (1955): 361–68, and below, Chapter 4.

21. The Vigilantes appear in any basic California history; for their connection with evangelical Protestantism, see Starr, *California Dream*, 106. Starr argues that the mercantile establishment controlled the whole enterprise and that the ministers simply allowed themselves and their pulpits to be used because the Vigilantes represented their fantasies of cleansing regeneration. Such an extreme interpretation is unnecessary; it is likely that the Protestant leadership for the most part shared the same social and moral values as the merchants. Most preferred not to see that Vigilantes were sometimes perpetrating evils as great as their opponents were.

22. Josiah Royce, *California: From the Conquest in 1846 to the Second Vigilance Committee in San Francisco: A Study of American Character* (New York: Alfred A. Knopf, 1948), 316–17. There is considerable evidence supporting Royce's contention that people wanted churches to prosper, in the first ten or fifteen years of the American period in California. Despite clerical complaints about an unsympathetic press, the early papers, especially those outside San Francisco, urged the importance of religion without favoring denominations as such. See, for example, the *Petaluma Journal* and the *Sonoma County Journal*

(Santa Rosa), both of which extolled the spiritual influences of home and mother and carried occasional reports of camp meetings or revivals in the churches. In the mining country, when the *Placerville Herald* in 1853 published "The Miner's Ten Commandments," reminding the men especially of the duty of Sabbath observance, the paper sold triple editions. See also Rodman Paul, *Mining Frontiers of the Far West* 1848–1880 (New York: Holt, Rinehart & Winston, 1963), 46, 164–65. Even in San Francisco, the *Herald* was kind enough to report in 1856 that religion there would compare well with that in any northern city (cited in Fleming, *God's Gold*, 118). It is true, however, that the secular papers declined over the years in their promotion of, or kind words for, specific religious activities.

23. Denominational and general secular histories of California usually do not mention the 1858 revival; an exception is Fleming in *God's Gold*. Starr, *California Dream*, reports simply that "a religious revival followed the upheavals" of 1856 (p. 95), thus linking it to the Vigilantes. Revivals in general were far less popular than on earlier frontiers. Anthony's *Methodism* mentions a few traveling evangelists, notably Maggie Van Cott and A.B. Earle (Earle's were holiness revivals); Pond, in *Gospel Pioneering*, also refers to an Earle revival in Petaluma in 1866. Anthony mentions that the Methodists did not do well at union (that is, interdenominational) meetings. For a treatment of later mass revivals held by D. L. Moody, see Douglas F. Anderson, "'You Californians': San Francisco Evangelicalism, Regional Religious Identity, and the Revivalism of D. L. Moody," *Fides et Historia* 15 (Spring/Summer 1983): 44–66.

24. Williams, *Pioneer Pastorate*, 158.

25. Philo F. Phelps, *The Relief Signal in the Hour of Need*, sermon at First Presbyterian Church (San Francisco, 1880).

26. *Pacific Methodist*, December 21, 1871.

27. *Petaluma Daily Crescent*, December 11, 1870, 2.

28. "Selected Letters of Osgood Church Wheeler," edited by Sandford Fleming, *California Historical Society Quarterly* 27 (1948): 9–18, 123–31, 229–36, 301–9; letter of August 1, 1849. A similar observation was made in later years by Presbyterian minister Robert Mackenzie, reviewing the history of his denomination in California: the pressure of material things was always so great that it took a great effort to make people pay attention to the cause of the kingdom of God (in *Californian Illustrated* [April 1892]: 441). Charles A. Farley, a Unitarian minister, wrote that in California "a nation has liter-

ally been born in a day; a nation the strangest and most miscellaneous ever brought together...animated primarily, it must be confessed, by...a passion for money." See "The Moral Aspect of California: A Thanksgiving Sermon of 1850," introduction by Clifford M. Drury, *California Historical Society Quarterly* 19 (1940): 302.

29. William Taylor, *Seven Years*, 342.

30. For some description see Paul, *Mining Frontiers*, and Earl Pomeroy, *The Pacific Slope: A History of California, Oregon, Washington, Idaho, Utah, and Nevada* (New York: Alfred A. Knopf, 1966). Dorothy O. Johansen has argued persuasively that California immigrants were self-selected to be of a different temperament than other westward migrants who went, at roughly the same time, to Oregon. Because of different kinds of promotion and publicity, the Oregon fever of 1842 had attracted more sober, conservative, and "respectable" people; California attracted the risk-takers. See "A Working Hypothesis for the Study of Migrations," *Pacific Historical Review* 36 (1967): 1–12.

31. The cosmopolitan character of early California is treated in Pomeroy, *Pacific Slope*, 160–62; Moses Rischin, "Immigration, Migration, and Minorities in California," in *Essays and Assays: California History Reappraised*, edited by George H. Knoles (California Historical Society, Ward Ritchie Press, 1973); and Doris Marion Wright, "The Making of Cosmopolitan California, 1840–1870: An Analysis of Immigration," *California Historical Society Quarterly* 19 (1940), 20 (1941).

32. See, for example, the comments on Californians' independence in religion in Ella M. Robinson, *Lighter of Gospel Fires, John N. Loughborough* (Mountain View, Calif.: Pacific Press, 1954), 129. The struggles to organize the state, its legal system, and its government, as well as the battles over land titles, are recounted in any good general history of the state.

33. Janzen, "Transformation," chapter 3; Starr, *California Dream*, 106.

34. Contemporary men's experience was not emphasized in midcentury Anglo-Protestantism; as many recent studies have noted, this was the period of "feminization" in American religion. See especially Ann Douglas, *The Feminization of American Culture* (New York: Alfred A. Knopf, 1977); and Sandra S. Sizer [Frankiel], *Gospel Hymns and Social Religion: The Rhetoric of Nineteenth-Century Revivalism* (Philadelphia: Temple University Press, 1978), chapter 4. The 1857–58 "businessmen's revival" might be seen as an early attempt to reclaim Christianity for men, but it was not until the Moody

revivals with their young men's meetings, and even more Billy Sunday with his sportsman's appeal, that we find specific attention to the male side.

35. Horace Bushnell, on a visit to California in 1856, exhorted Californians to support the churches precisely because they were guardians of order. This was, of course, the disturbing Vigilante period. See Bushnell's *Society and Religion: A Sermon for California* (San Francisco, 1856).

36. On the insanity issue, see the discussion in Crerar Douglas, "The Gold Rush and the Kingdom of God: The Rev. James Woods' Cure of Souls," in *The American West and the Religious Experience*, edited by William M. Kramer (Los Angeles: Will Kramer, 1975).

37. John Higham has argued persuasively that the midcentury years marked a transition from expansiveness to control in his *From Boundlessness to Consolidation: The Transformation of American Culture* (Ann Arbor, Mich.: William L. Clements Library, 1969). In religion, one can certainly observe that movement from open, highly emotional revivals to sentimentalism in Henry Ward Beecher and Dwight L. Moody. I have traced some of this trend in my *Gospel Hymns.* Lawrence Foster has identified similar dynamics in the areas of family and sexuality, in his *Religion and Sexuality: Three American Communal Experiments of the Nineteenth Century* (New York: Oxford University Press, 1981). California, for the reasons of social history I have already presented, was a special case of this broader trend.

38. On interdenominational cooperation in the early years, see *California Christian Advocate*, April 23, 1868, and Kip, *California Pilgrimage*, 27–28. Janzen argues as a primary thesis that the California situation led to Congregationalists becoming nondenominational in ideology; Fleming's *God's Gold* shows the Baptist contrast. The quotation is from the *Occident*, February 13, 1869, 85.

39. Williams, *Pioneer Pastorate*, 119, 193.

40. Josiah Royce, *Race Questions, provincialism, and Other American Problems* (New York: Macmillan, 1908), 70.

41. For one example among many, see William Ingraham Kip, *Early Days of My Episcopate* (New York: Thomas Whittaker, 1892).

42. James A. Woods, *Recollections of Pioneer Work in California* (San Francisco: Joseph Winterburn, 1878), 47; Joseph J. McCloskey in *Christmas in the Gold Fields*, 1849 (San Francisco: California Historical Society, 1959).

43. Starr, *California Dream*, 413; his entire discussion, pp. 374–423, is highly illuminating.

44. See the *California Christian Advocate*, October 17, 1867, for comments on how the Chinese were showing fewer of these bad traits after having been in America.

45. *Pacific*, May 7, 1852.

46. It seems that some clergymen were wont to engage in self-deception about the effects of missions to Asians—or at least to exaggerate them. For example, the *Evangel* (Baptist) printed a letter from a missionary to Japan claiming not only that many Japanese were now looking to Western culture and religion for inspiration but also that "all feel that Bhudisha [*sic*] is a cham" (January 29, 1874). They also assumed, as hinted in the *California Christian Advocate* article cited above, n. 44, that a decrease in the Asian peoples' presumed negative traits meant a greater openness to Christianity.

47. *California Christian Advocate*, October 10, 1851.

48. *New Englander* 60 (1858): 157.

49. *Occident*, February I, 1868.

50. O.P. Fitzgerald, *California Sketches* (Nashville, Tenn.: Methodist Episcopal Church, South, 1896), 208.

51. There were, of course, Eastern churchmen who were known for their responsiveness to and sermons upon the beauties of nature and the inner meaning of nature. Some were in the dissident liberal tradition, like Theodore Parker and Ralph Waldo Emerson; others were closer to the mainstream, like Henry Ward Beecher. Emerson, of course, became the inspiration for many who were spiritually drawn to nature as well as for people in the alternative metaphysical traditions.

PART THREE

THE MODERN WORLD
1865–1945

THE RELIGION OF THE LOST CAUSE

Charles Reagan Wilson

Students of southern history know that the South's separate cultural identity did not die after the Civil War. Charles Reagan Wilson identifies how this southern civil religion, represented by a fusion of evangelical Protestantism and southern white culture, emerged after 1865 in response to the need for defeated southerners to nurture their distinct spiritual and cultural values. After the Civil War, southern preachers portrayed Dixie as a godly society violated by marauding Yankees. The Southern military leaders (especially Robert E. Lee, Jefferson Davis, and "Stonewall" Jackson) were depicted as prophets and martyrs whose Christian virtues and military valor were signal traits of the southern character. In southern churches stained glass windows depicting Confederate sacrifices evoked thoughts of the suffering Christ, museums housed "sacred relics," and battlefields were dedicated as the people sang religious hymns. Of course this sanctification of southern society posed a difficult theological problem. Preachers never quite resolved why the righteous South had fallen to the infidel Yankees. Instead they gave solace to their people by recalling how, like Christ crucified, the South could be defeated while its ideals lived on. By remembering the Civil War as a holy cause and mythologizing their past, Wilson argues, southerners "tried to overcome their existential worries and to live with their tragic sense of life."

Reprinted by permission from Charles Reagan Wilson, "The Religion of the Lost Cause: Ritual and Organization of the Southern Civil Religion, 1865-1920," *The Journal of Southern History* XLVI, no. 2 (May 1980): 219–238.

12

THE RELIGION OF THE LOST CAUSE

Ritual and Organization of the Southern
Civil Religion, 1865–1920

Charles Reagan Wilson

SCHOLARS HAVE LONG NOTED the importance of religion in the South. The predominant evangelical Protestantism and the distinct regional church structures have been key factors in a "southern identity" separate from that of the North. Historians of southern religion have noted the close ties between religion and southern culture itself. Denominational studies have pointed out the role of the churches in acquiescing to the area's racial orthodoxy and in imposing a conservative, moralistic tone on the South since the late nineteenth century, while other works have posited the existence of two cultures in Dixie, one of Christian and one of southern values. At times, it is clear, the churches have been in "cultural captivity," rather than maintaining a judgmental distance, to southern values. The ties between religion and culture in the South have actually been even closer than has so far been suggested. In the years after the Civil War a pervasive southern civil religion emerged. This common religion of the South, which grew out of Confederate defeat in the Civil War, had an identifiable mythology, ritual, and organization. C. Vann Woodward noted long ago that the southern experience of defeat in the Civil War nurtured a tragic sense of life in the region, but historians have overlooked the fact that this profound understanding has been expressed in a civil religion which blended Christian and southern values.[1]

The religion of the Lost Cause originated in the antebellum period. By 1860 a religious culture had been established, wherein a religious outlook and tone permeated southern society. The popular sects (Methodists, Baptists, and Presbyterians) provided a sense of community in the individualistic rural areas, which helped to nurture a southern identity. At a time when northern religion was becoming increasingly diverse, the southern churches remained orthodox in theology and, above all, evangelical in orientation. Despite a conversion-centered theology, ministers played a key role in defending the status quo, and by 1845 the Methodists and the Baptists had split from their northern counterparts, supplying an institutionalized foundation for the belief in southern distinctiveness. The proslavery argument leaned more heavily on the Bible and Christian ministers than on anything else, thus tying churches and culture close together. Because of the religious culture, southern life seemed so Christian to the clerics that they saw threats to their society as challenges to the last bastion of Christian civilization in America.

During the Civil War religion played a vital role in the Confederacy. Preachers nourished Confederate morale, served as chaplains to the southern armies, and directed the intense revivals in the Confederate ranks. As a result of the wartime experience the religious culture became even more deeply engrained in the South. Preachers who had been soliders or chaplains became the celebrants of the Lost Cause religion after the war. By 1865 conditions existed for the emergence of an institutionalized common religion that would grow out of the antebellum-wartime religious culture.[2]

Judged by historical and anthropological criteria, the civil religion that emerged in the postbellum South was an authentic expression of religion. The South faced problems after the Civil War which were cultural but also religious—the problems of providing meaning to life and society amid the baffling failure of fundamental beliefs, offering comfort to those suffering poverty and disillusionment, and encouraging a sense of belonging in the shattered southern community. Anthropologist Anthony F. C. Wallace argues that religion originates "in situations of social and cultural stress," and for postbellum southerners such traditional religious issues as the nature of suffering, evil, and the seeming irrationality of life had a disturbing relevance. Scholars stress that the existence of a sacred symbol system and its embodiment in ritual define religion. As Clifford Geertz has said, the religious response to the threat of disorder in existence is the creation of symbols "of such a genuine order of the world which will account for, and even celebrate, the perceived ambiguities, puzzles, and paradoxes in human experience." These symbols create "long-lasting moods and motivations," which lead men to act on their religious feelings. Mythology, in other words, is not enough to launch a religion. Ritual is crucial because, as Geertz has said, it is "out of the context of concrete acts of religious observance that religious conviction emerges on the human plane." As Wallace concisely expresses it, "The primary phenomenon of religion is ritual." Not all rituals, to be sure, are religious. The crucial factors are rhetoric and intent: whether the language and motivation of a ritual are religious. The constant application of Biblical archetypes to the Confederacy and the interpretation of the Civil War experience in cosmic terms indicated the religious importance of the Lost Cause.[3]

The southern civil religion assumes added meaning when compared to the American civil religion. Sociologist Robert Neelly Bellah's 1967 article on the civil religion and his subsequent work have focused scholarly discussion on the common religion of the American people. Bellah argued that "an elaborate and well-institutionalized civil religion" existed that was "clearly differentiated" from the denominations. He defined "civil religion" as the "religious dimension" of a "people through which it interprets its historical experience in the light of transcendent reality." Like Sidney Earl Mead, Bellah saw it as essentially prophetic, judging the behavior of the nation against transcendent values. Will Herberg has suggested that the civil religion has been a folk religion, a common religion emerging out of the life of the folk. He argues that it grew out of a long social and historical experience that established a heterogeneous society. The civil religion came to be the American Way of Life, a set of beliefs that were accepted and revered by Protestants, Catholics, and Jews. "Democracy" has been the fundamental concept of this civil religion. Scholars have identified the sources of the American public faith in the Enlightenment tradition and in the secularized Puritan and Revivalist traditions. It clearly was born during the American Revolution, but the American civil religion was reborn, with the new theme of sacrifice and renewal, in the Civil War.[4]

In the post-Civil War South the antebellum religious culture evolved into a southern civil religion, differing from the national faith. A set of values arose that could be designated a Southern Way of Life. Dixie's value system differed from that which Herberg discussed— southerners undoubtedly were less optimistic, less liberal, less democratic, less tolerant, and more homogeneously Protestant. In their religion southerners stressed "democracy" less than the conservative concepts of moral virtue and an orderly society. Though the whole course of southern history provided the background, the southern civil religion actually emerged from the Civil War experience. Just as the revolution of 1776 caused Americans to see their historical experience in transcedent terms, so the Confederate experience led southerners to a profound self-examination. They understood that the results of the war had clearly given them a history distinct from the northern one. Southerners thus focused the mythic, ritualistic, and organizational dimensions of their civil religion around the Confederacy. Moreover, the Enlightenment tradition played virtually no role in the religion of the Lost Cause, but the emotionally intense, dynamic Revivalist tradition and the secularized legacy of idealistic, moralistic Puritanism did shape it.

As a result of emerging from a heterogeneous, immigrant society, the American civil religion was especially significant in providing a sense of belonging to the uprooted immigrants. As a result of its origins in Confederate defeat, the southern civil religion offered confused southerners a sense of meaning, an identity in a precarious but distinct culture. One central issue of the American public faith has been the relationship between church and state, but, since the Confederate quest for political nationhood failed, the southern civil religion has been less concerned with that question than with the cultural issue of identity.

The mythology of the American civil religion taught that Americans are a chosen people, destined to play a special role in the world as representatives of freedom and equality. The religion of the Lost Cause rested on a mythology that focused on the Confederacy. It was a creation myth, the story of the attempt to create a southern nation. According to the mythmakers a pantheon of southern heroes, portrayed as the highest products of the Old South civilization, had appeared during the Civil War to battle the forces of evil as symbolized by the Yankees. The myth enacted the Christian story of Christ's suffering and death with the Confederacy at the sacred center. But in the southern myth the Christian drama of suffering and salvation was incomplete. The Confederacy lost a holy war, and there was no resurrection.[5]

As Mircea Eliade has said, "it is not enough to *know* the origin myth, one must *recite* it...." While other southern myths could be seen in literature, politics, or economics, the Confederate myth reached its true fulfillment after the Civil War in a ritualistic structure of activities that represented a religious commemoration and celebration of the Confederacy. One part of the ritualistic liturgy focused on the religious figures of the Lost Cause. Southern Protestant churches have been sparse in iconography, but the southern civil religion was rich in images. Southern ministers and other rhetoricians portrayed Robert Edward Lee, Thomas Jonathan ("Stonewall") Jackson, Jefferson Davis, and many other wartime heroes as religious saints and martyrs.[6] They were said to epitomize the best of Christian and southern values. Their images pervaded the South, and they were especially aimed at children. In the first two decades of this century local chapters of the United Daughters of the Confederacy undertook successfully to blanket southern schools with portraits of Lee and Davis. Lee's birthday, January 19, became a holiday throughout Dixie, and ceremonies honoring him frequently occurred in the schools.[7]

An explicit link between Confederate images and religious values was made in the stained-glass windows placed in churches to commemorate Confederate sacrifices. One of the earliest of these was a window placed in Trinity Church, Portsmouth, Virginia, in April 1868, while Federal troops still occupied the city. The window portrayed a Biblical Rachel weeping at a tomb, on which appeared the names of the members of the congregation who had died during the war. In Mississippi, Biloxi's Church of the Redeemer, "the Westminister of the South," was particularly prominent in this endeavor at the turn of the century. St. Paul's Episcopal Church in Richmond, which had been the wartime congregation of many Confederate leaders, established a Lee Memorial Window, which used an Egyptian scene to connect the Confederacy with the stories of the Old Testament. Even a Negro Presbyterian church in Roanoke, Virginia, dedicated a Stonewall Jackson memorial window. The pastor had been a pupil in Jackson's Sunday school in prewar Lexington, Virginia.[8]

Wartime artifacts also had a sacred aura. Bibles that had been touched by the Cause were especially holy. The United Daughters of the Confederacy kept under lock and key the Bible used when Jefferson Davis was sworn in as President of the Confederacy. More poignantly, a faded, torn overcoat belonging to a young Confederate martyr named Sam Davis was discovered in 1897, and when shown to a United Daughters of the Confederacy meeting the response was, said an observer, first "sacred silence" and then weeping. Presbyterian preacher James Isaac Vance noted that, "like Elijah's mantle of old, the spirit of the mighty dwells within it." Museums were sanctuaries containing such sacred relics. The Confederate Museum in Richmond, which had been the White House of the Confederacy, included a room for each seceding state. These rooms had medals, flags, uniforms, and weapons from the Confederacy, and the Solid South Room displayed the Great Seal of the Confederate States.[9]

The southern civil religion had its reverent images and its sacred artifacts, and it also had its hymns. One group of hymns sung at postwar Confederate gatherings was made up of Christian songs straight from the hymnal. "Nearer My God to Thee," "Abide with Me," and "Praise God from Whom All Blessings Flow" were popular, but the favorite was "How Firm a Foundation." Another group of Confederate sacred songs was created by putting new words to old melodies. The spirit of "That Old-Time Religion" was preserved when someone retitled it "We Are Old-Time Confederates." J.B. Stinson composed new verses for the melody of "When the Roll is Called Up Yonder I'll Be There." A change from the original lyric was the phrase "let's be there," rather than "I'll be there," indicating a more communal redemption in the Lost Cause version. The song used Confederates as evangelical models of behavior: "On that mistless, lonely morning when the saved of Christ shall rise,/In the Father's many-mansioned home to share;/Where our Lee and Jackson call to us [sic] their homes beyond the skies,/When the roll is called up yonder, let's be there."[10] Of special significance was the hymn "Let Us Pass Over the River, and Rest Under the Shade of the Trees," which was officially adopted by the Southern Methodist Church. The words in the title were the last words spoken by the dying Stonewall Jackson. Two other hymns, "Stonewall Jackson's Requiem" and "Stonewall Jackson's Way," made a similar appeal. At some ceremonial occasions choirs from local churches sang hymns. In 1907 southerners organized the United Confederate Choirs of America, and soon the young belles from Dixie, clad in Confederate gray uniforms, were a popular presence at ritual events.[11]

These liturgical ingredients appeared during the ritualistic expressions of the Lost Cause. In the years immediately after the war southern anguish at Confederate defeat was most apparent during the special days appointed by the denominations or the states for humiliation, fasting, prayer, or thanksgiving. These special days could be occasions for jeremiads calling prodigals back to the church, prophesying future battles, or stressing submission to God's mysterious providence in the face of seemingly unwarranted suffering.[12] Southerners, however, usually ignored the national Thanksgiving Day, complaining that northerners used the day to exploit the war issue and to wave the bloody shirt. D. Shaver, the editor of the *Christian Index*, a Baptist newspaper in Atlanta, noted in 1869 that such days too often evoked in the Yankee "the smell (if they do not wake the thirst) of blood." He characterized the northern Christian's behavior on Thanksgiving Day as like that of a Pharisee of old who stood "pilloried through the ages as venting a self-complacent but empty piety." Southerners did celebrate thanksgiving days designated by their denominations, but in general the days of humiliation, fasting, and prayer were more appropriate to the immediate postwar southern mood.[13]

Southern reverence for dead heroes could be seen in the activities of yet another ritual event—Confederate Memorial Day. Southern legend has it that the custom of decorating the graves of soldiers arose in Georgia in 1866 when Mrs. Charles J. Williams, a Confederate widow, published an appeal to southerners to set apart a day "to be handed down through time as a religious custom of the South to wreathe the graves of our martyred dead with flowers." Like true Confederates, southern states could not at first agree among themselves as to which day to honor, but by 1916 ten states had designated June 3, Jefferson Davis's birthday, as Memorial Day. Women played a key role in this ritual since they were in charge of decorating the graves with flowers and of organizing the day's events. It was a holy day, "the Sabbath of the South." One southern woman compared her sisters to the Biblical Mary and Martha, who "last at the cross and first at the grave brought their offerings of love...." Another southern woman noted that the aroma of flowers on Memorial Day was "like incense burning in golden censers to the memory of the saints."[14]

A third ritual was the funeral of a wartime hero. The veterans attending the funerals dressed in their gray uniforms, served as active or honorary pallbearers, and provided a military ceremony. Everything was done according to the "Confederate Veteran's Burial Ritual," which emphasized that the soldier was going to "an honorable grave." "He fought a good fight," said the ritual, "and has left a record of which we, his surviving comrades, are proud, and which is a heritage of glory to his family and their descendants for all time to come." These ceremonies reiterated what southerners heard elsewhere—that despite defeat the Confederate experience proved that they were a noble, virtuous people. Moreover, the Confederate funeral included the display of the Confederate flag, the central symbol of the southern identity. Often, it was dramatically placed over the hero's casket just before the box was lowered into the ground, while at other times the folded battle flag was removed from the coffin and placed at the head of the grave. Even after southerners began again to honor the American flag, they continued to cherish the Stars and Bars as well.[15]

The dedication of monuments to the Confederate heroes was the fourth ritualistic expression of the Lost Cause. In 1914 the *Confederate Veteran* magazine revealed that over a thousand monuments existed in the South, and by that time many battlefields had been set aside as pilgrimage sites with holy shrines. Preachers converted the innumerable statues dotting the southern countryside into religious objects, almost idols, that quite blatantly taught Christian religious and moral lessons. "Our cause is with God" and "In hope of a joyful resurrection" were among the most directly religious inscriptions on monuments, but they were not atypical ones. El Dorado, Arkansas, erected a marble drinking fountain to the Confederacy, and its publicity statement said—in a phrase culled from countless hymns and sermons on the sacrificial Jesus—that the water in it symbolized "the loving stream of blood" that was shed by the southern soldiers. Drinkers from the fount were thus symbolically baptized in Confederate blood. The dedication of such monuments became more elaborate as the years went on. Perhaps the greatest monument dedication came in 1907, when an estimated 200,000 people gathered in Richmond for the dedication of a statue to Jefferson Davis on Monument Boulevard. Richmond was the Mecca of the Lost Cause, and Monument Boulevard was the sacred road to it containing statues of Lee, James Ewell Brown ("Jeb") Stuart, George Washington, and Stonewall Jackson, as well as Davis.[16]

Rituals similar to these existed as part of the American civil religion. In both instances, they were, to use Claude Lévi-Strauss's categories, partly commemorative rites that re-created the mythical time of the past and partly mourning rites that converted dead heroes into revered ancestors. Both civil religions confronted the precariousness and instability of collective life. They were ways for communities to help their citizens meet their individual fears of death. As sociologist William Lloyd Warner has said: "Whenever the living think about the deaths of others they necessarily express some of their own concern about their own extinction." By the continuance of the community, the citizens in it achieve a measure of immortality. For southerners the need for such a symbolic life was even greater than for northerners. Union soldiers sacrificed, but at least the success of their cause seemed to validate their deaths. Postwar southerners feared that the defeat of the Confederacy had jeopardized their continued existence as a distinctively southern people. By participating in the Lost Cause rituals southerners tried to show that the Confederate sacrifices had not been in vain. Similar rituals existed to honor the Grand Army of the Republic, but the crucial point was that southern rituals began from a very different starting point and had a different symbolic content. Thus, within the United States there was a functioning civil religion not dedicated to honoring the American nation.[17]

The permanence of the Lost Cause religion could be seen in its structural-functional aspect. Three institutions directed its operations, furnishing ongoing leadership and institutional encouragement. One organizational focus was the Confederate veterans' groups. Local associations of veterans existed in the 1870s and 1880s, but southerners took a step forward in this activity with the establishment of the United Confederate Veterans in New Orleans in 1889. The heirs of the Lost Cause formed another group in 1896, the United Sons of Confederate Veterans, which supplied still more energy for the movement. The local chapters of these organizations held frequent meetings, which were an important social activity for southerners, especially those in rural areas. They also had their sacred elements, mostly in the rhetoric used in orations. The highlight of the year for the veterans was the annual regionwide reunion, which was held in a major southern city. It was one of the most highly publicized events in the South. Railroads ran special trains, and the cities gave lavish welcomes to the grizzled old men and their entourage of splendidly dressed young women sponsored by the local chapters. Tens of thousands of people flocked into the chosen city each year to relive the past for a few days. The earliest reunions were boisterous gatherings, but that spirit did not subdue an equally religious tone, especially as the veterans aged. In 1899 the reunion was in Charleston, and a city reporter noted that the veterans were lighthearted at times but that they also were as devout as any pilgrim going "to the tomb of the prophet, or Christian knight to the walls of Jerusalem."[18]

Each day of the reunion began with a prayer, which usually reminded the aging Confederates that religion was at the heart of the Confederate heritage. Presbyterian clergyman Peyton H. Hogue, in a prayer at the tenth reunion in 1900, was not subtle in suggesting his view of the typical Confederate's afterlife. He prayed that those present "may meet in that Heavenly Home where Lee, Jackson and all the Heroes who have gone before are waiting to welcome us there."[19] A hymn was usually sung after the invocation. One favorite was the "Doxology," which ended with the explicitly Christian reference, "Praise Father, Son, and Holy Ghost." A memorial service was held each year at a local church as part of the official reunion program, and it was here that the most direct connections were made between Christianity and the Confederacy. At the 1920 reunion, for example, the Baptist cleric B. A. Owen compared the memorial service to the Christian sacrament, the Holy Communion. In the Communion service, he said, "our hearts are focused upon Calvary's cross and the dying Lamb of God," and in the Confederate sacrament "we hold sweet converse with the spirits of departed comrades." In order to coordinate their work at memorial services and elsewhere the ministers of the Lost Cause organized a Chaplains' Association before the Atlanta reunion in 1898.[20]

The Nashville reunion of 1897 was probably the single most religiously oriented Confederate meeting. The veterans met that year at the downtown Union Gospel Tabernacle, later known as Ryman Auditorium, the home of southern music's Grand Old Opry. A new balcony was added to the tabernacle for the 1897 convention, and it was dedicated as a Confederate memorial. Sitting on hard church pews facing the altar and the permanent baptismal font, the veterans had a rollicking but reverent time in 1897 in the sweltering summer heat of the poorly ventilated tabernacle. Each reunion ended with a long parade, and the 1897 procession was one of the most memorable. The reviewing stand was set up on the campus of the Methodists' Vanderbilt University, where the old veterans paused before continuing their march. The reunion coincided with Tennessee's centennial celebration and included the unveiling in Nashville's new Centennial Park of the Parthenon, the replica of the ancient Greek temple, and a mammoth statue to the goddess Athena. The Confederate parade ended in Centennial Park, and as the old soldiers entered the grounds the bells from a nearby tower chimed the old hymn, "Shall We Gather at the River?" Apparently unintentionally, the ceremony evoked comparisons with the annual Panathenaic procession in ancient Athens from the lower agora to the Acropolis, and then to the Parthenon, the temple of Athena.[21]

If religion pervaded the United Confederate Veterans, it saturated the United Daughters of the Confederacy. The importance of Christianity to the Daughters could be seen in the approved ritual for their meetings. It began with an invocation by the president: "Daughters of the Confederacy, this day we are gathered together, in the sight of God, to strengthen the bonds that unite us in a common cause; to renew the vows of loyalty to our sacred principles; to do homage unto the memory of our gallant Confederate soldiers, and to perpetuate the fame of their noble deeds into the third and fourth generations. To this end we invoke the aid of our Lord." The members responded, "From the end of the Earth will I cry unto Thee, when my heart is overwhelmed; lead me to the rock that is higher than I." After similar chanted exchanges, the hymn "How Firm a Foundation" was sung, followed by the reading of a prayer composed by Episcopal bishop Ellison Capers of South Carolina, who had been a Confederate general before entering the ministry. After the prayer the president then read the Lord's Prayer, and the meeting or convention began its official business.[22]

The Daughters provided an unmatched crusading zeal to the religion of the Lost Cause. The members rarely doubted that God was on their side. Cornelia Branch Stone entitled her 1912 pamphlet on Confederate history a *U. D. C. Catechism for Children,* a title that suggested the assumed sacred quality of its contents. The Daughters took an especially aggressive role in preserving the records of the southern past. These were sacred documents that were viewed by the women in a fundamentalist perspective. Mrs. M. D. Farris of Texas urged the organization in 1912 to guard its records and archives, "even as the children of Israel did the Ark of the Covenant."[23]

The Christian churches formed the second organizational focus for the southern civil religion. The postwar development of the religion of the Lost Cause was intimately related to developments in the churches themselves. Before the war an evangelical consensus had been achieved in the South, but it had not been institutionalized. Not until after the war did church membership become pervasive. The evangelical denominations that profited from this enormous expansion of what Samuel S. Hill, Jr., calls a "single-option religious culture" taught an inward, conversion-centered religion. Fundamental beliefs on such matters as sin, guilt, grace, judgment, the reality of heaven and hell, and the loving Jesus were agreed upon by all without regard to denominational boundaries. The concept of a civil religion at first glance seems contrary to this inward theology, but the southern churches were not so otherwordly as to ignore society entirely. A southern social gospel existed, as did successful attempts to establish moral reform through state coercion. The combination of a societal interest and the dynamic growth of an evangelical Protestantism was not antithetical to the development of a civil religion.[24]

Unlike the American civil religion, the religion of the Lost Cause did not entirely stand apart from the Christian denominations. They taught similar religious-moral values, and the southern heroes had been directly touched by Christianity. The God invoked in the Lost Cause was a distinctly Biblical, transcendent God. Prayers at veterans' gatherings appealed for the blessings of, in John William Jones's words, the "God of Israel, God of the centuries, God of our forefathers, God of Jefferson Davis and Sidney Johnston and Robert E. Lee, and Stonewall Jackson, God of the Southern Confederacy." Prayers invariably ended in some variation of "We ask it all in the name and for the sake of Christ our dear Redeemer." At the 1907 veterans' reunion the Reverend Randolph Harrison McKim, like other preachers before and after him, invoked the third person of the Christian godhead, praying for "the blessing of the Holy Ghost in our hearts." The references to Christ and the Holy Ghost clearly differentiated the southern civil religion from the more deistic American civil religion. The latter's ceremonies rarely included such Christian references because of potential alienation of Jews, who were but a small percentage of the southern population. In the South, in short, the civil religion and Christianity openly supported each other.[25]

Certainly, the most blatant connections between Christianity and the Confederacy were made during Confederate rituals. Though they praised their society and its customs, it is clear that in their normal Christian services southerners did not worship the Confederacy. Nevertheless, southern religious journals, books, and even pulpits were the sources of Lost Cause sentiments. Church buildings were the most frequently used sites for Memorial Day activities, funerals of veterans, and memorial observances when prominent Confederates died. Such gatherings were interdenominational, with pastors from different religious bodies participating. A spirit of interdenominationalism had existed in the wartime Confederate armies, and it survived in the postbellum South in the ceremonies of the Lost Cause. The overwhelmingly Protestant character of southern religion facilitated the growth of an ecumenical Lost Cause religion. It, in turn, furthered Protestant ecumenism. Although predominantly Protestant, southern religion was not manifested in any one denomination but was ecclesiastically fragmented. The Lost Cause offered a forum for ministers and laymen from differing churches to participate in a common spiritual activity. References to particular denominational beliefs were occasionally made, but since southerners shared so many of the same doctrines there was a basis for cooperation.[26] Moreover, despite the Protestant orientation of the Lost Cause, Catholics and Jews were not excluded from it. Members of these faiths joined the Confederate groups, and rabbis and priests occasionally appeared at Lost Cause events. Undoubtedly, with some discomfort, Catholics and Jews accepted the Protestant tinge of the southern civil religion and made their own contributions to it.[27]

The southern churches proved to be important institutions for the dissemination of the Lost Cause. Despite the opposition of some clerics, on Sunday morning November 27, 1884, congregations across the South contributed to a well-promoted special collection to finance a Robert E. Lee monument in Richmond. The denominational papers approvingly published appeals of Confederate organizations for support, editorially endorse Lost Cause fund raising, recommended Confederate writings, and praised the Lost Cause itself. The Confederate periodicals, in turn, printed stories about Christianity seemingly unrelated to the usual focus on the Civil War. Richmond was the center of Lost Cause activity, and the city was also a religious publishing center. The Episcopalians, Baptists, Methodists, and Presbyterians all published periodicals there, and the Southern Presbyterian Publishing House was located in the Confederate capital. Nashville was a religious publishing center as well, and it had the same Confederate-Christian mixture. The *Confederate Veteran* magazine, the most important organ of the Lost Cause after 1890, had its offices in and was published by the Publishing House of the Southern Methodist Church in the city.[28]

The close connection between the churches and the Confederate organizations could be seen in terms of the central experience of southern Protestantism—evangelism. Confederate heroes were popular choices to appear at southern revivals. The most influential southern evangelist, iconoclastic Georgia Methodist Samuel Porter ("Sam") Jones, was a master at having Confederates testify to the power of Christianity in their lives, preferably its inspirational effect on the battlefield. At the same time, a significant feature of the religious rhetoric of the reunions was the insistence on a response by the veterans. The invitation to follow Christ, which was made during the memorial services, was also an invitation to follow once again Robert E. Lee, Stonewall Jackson, and Jefferson Davis. Some reunions thus resembled vast revivals, with tens of thousands of listerners hearing ministers remind them of the imminence of death for the aged veterans and of the need to ensure everlasting life.[29]

The third organizational embodiment of the Lost Cause, the educational system, directed the effort to pass the Lost Cause religion on to future generations. Confederate veterans and their widows and daughters dominated the schools, serving as teachers and administrators, and they had no reticence in teaching the southern tradition. The year 1907 was especially observed in the southern schools. It was the centennial of General Lee's birth, and state boards of education issued pamphlets providing guidelines to encourage appropriate celebrations in the schools. In addition, the latter-day Confederates were sought to maintain a prosouthern interpretation of the Civil War in the textbooks used in southern schools. The United Daughters of the Confederacy directed this endeavor, pressuring school boards to adopt textbooks from an approved list compiled by the organization. The same concern motivated the later southern Fundamentalists who campaigned to keep the doctrine of evolution out of textbooks. The most direct Christian-Confederate connections were not in the public schools but in the private academies, particularly in the denominational schools. Typical of these were the Episcopal High School of Alexandria, Virginia, and the Stonewall Jackson Institute, a Presbyterian female academy, in Abingdon, Virginia. Confederate leaders like Lee and Jackson were the explicit models of behavior for the students, and the ex-Confederate teachers served as living models of virtue. The students wore Confederate-style uniforms and drilled on campus, and the advertisements for these religious schools played upon the Confederate theme to attract young people. The United Daughters of the Confederacy supported the Stonewall Jackson Institute by financing scholarships to the school.[30]

Two colleges existed as major institutional shrines of the Lost Cause. The first was the University of the South, an Episcopal college located like an isolated retreat in the mountains at Sewanee, Tennessee. Bishop Leonidas Polk, who would later die at the Battle of Pine Mountain in Georgia while serving as a brigadier general, founded the school in the sectionally divisive 1850s, conceiving of it in part as a place to educate young southerners in regional as well as Christian values. The nascent institution was all but destroyed during the Civil War, but Bishop Charles Todd Quintard, himself a Confederate chaplain and active member of postwar Confederate veterans' groups, resurrected it. The most potent Lost Cause influence came from the faculty he assembled. They were "a body of noble men," said Sarah Barnwell Elliott, daughter of Bishop Stephen Elliott, in 1909, "with the training, education, and traditions of the Old South and whose like we shall never see again." They included William Porcher DuBose, a captain in Lee's Army of Northern Virginia and later a respected theologian; Major George Rainsford Fairbanks of the Army of Tennessee; Brigadier General Francis Asbury Shoup of Florida; Brigadier General Josiah Gorgas, the Confederacy's chief of ordnance; and General Edmund Kirby Smith, commander of the Trans-Mississippi Department of the Confederate armies, who had the honor of being known as the last general to surrender. Women also contributed to the inculcation of Lost Cause religious values. The University of the South gave free tuition to the children of Confederate widows who boarded college students. The Sewanee matrons purposely chose names to connect their homes to the South; thus, one could find a Palmetto Hall, a Magnolia Hall, and an Alabama Hall. They re-created and fostered the culture of the Old South that had produced the heroes of the war.[31]

Sewanee was also an institutional center for Lost Cause orations, dedications, and other rituals. These events adapted Lost Cause themes to the student audience. When Lee died in 1870, for example, the Episcopal bishop of Louisiana, Joseph Pere Bell Wilmer, preached a sermon on the general's moral and religious virtues for the edification of the students. Moreover, when one of the heroes on campus died, regional attention concentrated on Sewanee, prompting the appearance of the ritualistic trappings of the civil religion. Confederate monuments and plaques still dot the campus, serving as devotional points on the holy ground.[32]

Washington and Lee University reflected a different aspect of the southern civil religion than that at the University of the South. Located at Lexington in the Virginia valley, it was more Virginian in its Confederate orientation, and its Christian influence was predominantly Presbyterian. Stonewall Jackson had taught in Lexington at the Virginia

Military Institute before the war, and the town provided recruits for his famed Stonewall Brigade. Washington College itself, like Sewanee, suffered during the war, but the choice in 1865 of Robert E. Lee to head the school gave it a new start and a new fame as a center of the Lost Cause. In a sermon, Baptist preacher Edwin Theodore Winkler described the sacred atmosphere of the campus in evocative phrases: "Lexington is the parable of the great Virginia soldiers. In that quiet scholastic retreat, in that city set upon a hill and crowned with martial trophies, they, being dead, yet speak."[33]

The presence of prominent Confederates was again the key factor in fostering a Lost Cause aura in Lexington. Among the residents of the town were Colonel William Preston Johnston, son of the martyred General Albert Sidney Johnston; Colonel William Nelson, chief ordnance officer for Stonewall Jackson's command; John Letcher, wartime governor of Virginia; Confederate Judge John White Brockenbrough; General Francis Henney Smith, superintendent of Virginia Military Institute; Colonel John Mercer Brooke, builder of the *Merrimac*; Commander Matthew Fontaine Maury, famed geographer who taught at the institute; and Brigadier General William Nelson Pendleton, rector of the Grace Memorial Episcopal Church, where Lee worshipped. The Lost Cause religious orientation came most directly from the influence of one man—Lee. A deeply religious man himself, he encouraged spiritual activities, including revivalism, at his school. He helped launch the town's Young Men's Christian Association, supervised the erection of a chapel on campus, organized daily interdenominational devotionals conducted by the town's pastors, and invited preachers from across the South to deliver baccalaureate sermons.[34]

As at Sewanee, Lexington was a focus for orations, dedications, and funerals. The chapel was one of the most holy of all Lost Cause shrines. Lee was buried there in a limestone mausoleum, and the site was marked by a recumbent statue of white marble resting on a sarcophagus. The unveiling of the monument on June 23, 1883, was a media event throughout the South. In 1907, the year of the centennial of Lee's birth, the entire region looked to Lexington for the major commemoration of the birth. Stonewall Jackson was also buried in the town, in the cemetery of the Presbyterian church. Lexington came to be so full of Lost Cause shrines that one could take an organized walking tour, which bore some resemblance to a medieval processional of the Stations of the Cross.[35]

All these rituals and institutions dealt with a profound problem. The southern civil religion emerged because defeat in the Civil War had created the spiritual and psychological need for southerners to reaffirm their identity, an identity which came to have outright religious dimensions. Each Lost Cause ritual and organization was tangible evidence that southerners had made a religion out of their history. As with all ritualistic repetition of archetypal actions, southerners in their institutionalized Lost Cause religion were trying symbolically to overcome history. By repetition of ritual, they recreated the mythical times of their noble ancestors and paid tribute to them.[36] Despite the bafflement and frustration of defeat, southerners showed that the time of the myth's creation still had meaning for them. The Confederate veteran was a living incarnation of an idea that southerners tried to defend at the cultural level after Confederate defeat had made political success impossible. Every time a Confederate veteran died, every time flowers were placed on graves on Southern Memorial Day, southerners relived and confronted the death of the Confederacy. The religion of the Lost Cause was a cult of the dead, which dealt with essential religious concerns. Having lost what they considered to be a holy war, southerners had to face suffering, doubt, guilt, a recognition of what seemed to be evil triumphant, and above all death. Through the ritualistic and organizational activities of their civil religion southerners tried to overcome their existential worries and to live with their tragic sense of life.

NOTES

1. Kenneth K. Bailey, *Southern White Protestantism in the Twentieth Century* (New York and other cities, 1964); Rufus B. Spain, *At Ease in Zion: Social History of of Southern Baptists, 1865–1900* (Nashville, 1967); Hunter D. Farish, *The Circuit Rider Dismounts: A Social History of Southern Methodism, 1865–1900* (Richmond, 1938); Ernest T. Thompson, *Presbyterians in the South* (3 vols., Richmond, 1963–1974); Samuel S. Hill, Jr., *Southern Churches in Crisis* (New York and other cities, 1966); Hill et al., *Religion and the Solid South* (Nashville and New York, 1972); John L. Eighmy, *Churches in Cultural Captivity: A History of the Social Attitudes of Southern Baptists* (Knoxville, 1972); H. Shelton Smith, *In His Image, But ...: Racism in Southern Religion, 1780–1910* (Durham, N.C., 1972); Woodward, *The Burden of Southern History* (Baton Rouge, 1960), especially Chap. I.

2. Hill, *Southern Churches*, 12–14, 52, 56–59; John B. Boles, *The Great Revival, 1787–1805: The Origins of the Southern Evangelical Mind* (Lexington, Ky., 1972); Boles, *Religion in Antebellum Kentucky* (Lexington, Ky., 1976), 123–45; Dickson D. Bruce, Jr., "Religion, Society and Culture in the Old South: A Comparative View," *American Quarterly*, XXVI (October 1974), 399–416; Donald G. Mathews, *Religion in the Old South* (Chicago and London, 1977). For the wartime role of the churches there is no synthesis, but see James W. Silver, *Confederate Morale and Church Propaganda* (Tuscaloosa, Ala., 1957); Herman Norton, *Rebel Religion: The Story of Confederate Chaplains* (St. Louis, 1961); John Shepard, Jr., "Religion in the Army of Northern Virginia," *North Carolina Historical Review*, XXV (July 1948), 341–76; and the special issue of *Civil War History*, VI (December 1960).

3. Wallace, *Religion: An Anthropological View* (New York, 1966), 30 (first quotation), 102 (fifth quotation); Geertz, "Religion as a Cultural System," in Michael Banton, ed., *Anthropological Approaches to the Study of Religion* (New York, 1966), 4 (third quotation), 8–12, 14, 23 (second quotation), 28 (fourth quotation). See also Andrew M. Greeley, *The Denominational Society: A Sociological Approach to Religion in America* (Glenview, Ill., 1972), 28, and Mircea Eliade, Myth and Reality (New York and Evanston, 1963), 8, 17–18.

4. Bellah, "Civil Religion in America," in Russell E. Richey and Donald G. Jones, eds.,

American Civil Religion (New York and other cities, 1974), 21–44 (first two quotations on p. 21); Bellah, *The Broken Covenant: American Civil Religion in Time of Trial* (New York, 1975), 3 (last two quotations); Mead, "The 'Nation with the Soul of a Church,'" in Richey and Jones, eds., *American Civil Religion*, 45–75; Herberg, "America's Civil Religion: What It Is and Whence It Comes," ibid. 76–88; Herberg, *Protestant Catholic Jew: An Essay in American Religious Sociology* (Garden City, N.Y., 1955); Catherine L. Albanese, *Sons of the Fathers: The Civil Religion of the American Revolution* (Philadelphia, 1976); James H. Moorhead, *American Apocalypse: Yankee Protestants and the Civil War, 1860–1869* (New Haven, 1978).

5. For the political, economic, intellectual, and literary aspects of the Lost Cause myth see Rollin G. Osterweis, *The Myth of the Lost Cause, 1865–1900* (Hamden, Conn., 1973); Daniel Aaron, *The Unwritten War: American Writers and the Civil War* (New York, 1973); Paul M. Gaston, *The New South Creed: A Study in Southern Mythmaking* (New York, 1970); Richard M. Weaver, *The Southern Tradition at Bay: A History of Postbellum Thought* (New Rochelle, N.Y., 1968): Richard B. Harwell, "The Confederate Heritage," in Louis D. Rubin, Jr., and James J. Kilpatrick, eds., *The Lasting South: Fourteen Southerners Look at Their Home* (Chicago, 1957), 16–27; William B. Hesseltine, *Confederate Leaders in the New South* (Baton Rouge, 1950); Susan S. Durant, "The Gently Furled Banner: The Development of the Myth of the Lost Cause, 1865–1900" (Ph. D. dissertation, University of North Carolina, 1972); and Sharon E. Hannum, "Confederate Cavaliers: The Myth in War and Defeat" (Ph.D. dissertation, Rice University, 1965).

6. Eliade, *Myth and Reality*, 17; "Robert E. Lee," and "Innocence Vindicated," Atlanta *Christian Index*, October 20, 1870, p. 162; August 23, 1866, p. 135; "Robert E. Lee," Richmond *Southern Churchman*, January 19, 1907, p. 2; T. V. Moore, "Memorial Discourse on the Death of General Robert E. Lee," and "Jefferson Davis," in Nashville *Christian Advocate*, November 5, 1870, p. 2; December 12, 1889, p. 8; and James P. Smith, "Jackson's Religious Character: An Address at Lexington, Va.," Southern Historical Society, *Papers*, XIIII (September 1920), 67 75. The *Papers* will be cited hereinafter as SHSP.

7. United Daughters of the Confederacy,

*Minutes of the Fourteenth Annual Convention...*1907 (Opelika, Ala., 1908), 6; ibid, 1915 (Charlotte, N. C., n.d.), 357; "The South's Tribute to General Lee," *Confederate Veteran*, XXII (February 1914), 62. The minutes of conventions of the United Daughters of the Confederacy will hereinafter be cited as UDC, *Minutes* along with the proper years. The *Confederate Veteran* will hereinafter be cited as CV.

8. "The Memorial Window in Trinity Church, Portsmouth, Va., to the Confederate Dead of Its Congregation," SHSP, XIX (January 1891), 207 12; "Pegram Battalion Association," ibid., XVI (January–December 1888), 194–206; J. William Jones, "The Career of General Jackson," ibid., XXXV (January–December 1907), 97; "A Memorial Chapel at Fort Domelson," CV, V (September 1897), 461; Elizabeth W. Weddell, *St. Paul's Church, Richmond, Virginia...* (2 vols., Richmond, 1931), 1, frontispiece, 224–25.

9. CV, VIII (November 1900), 468; "Sermons Before the Reunion," *ibid.*, V (July 1897), 351 (quotation); ibid., XXII (May 1914), 194; Herbert and Marjorie Katz, *Museums, U.S.A.: A History and Guide* (Garden City, N. Y., 1965), 181.

10. United Confederate Veterans (hereinafter UCV), *Minutes of the Ninth Annual Meeting and Reunion ... 1899* (New Orleans, 1900), 17, 32; UCV, *Minutes of the Twenty–first Annual Meeting and Reunion ... 1911* (New Orleans, n.d.), 111; UCV, *Minutes of the Nineteenth Annual Meeting and Reunion ... 1909* (New Orleans, n.d.), 64; UDC, *Minutes ... 1912* (Jackson, Tenn., n.d.), 321, 407; UDC, *Minutes ... 1914* (Raleigh, N. C., 1915), 406; UDC, *Ritual of the United Daughters of the Confederacy* (Austin, Texas, n.d.); "Burial of Margaret Davis Hayes," CV, XVII (December 1909), 612; "Old Time Confederates," ibid., VIII (July 1900), 298; Joseph M. Brown, "Dixie," ibid., XII (March 1904), 134; "Memorial Ode," ibid., IX (December 1901), 567.

11. CV, IX (April 1901), 147; UDC, *Minutes ... 1909* (Opelika, Ala., 1909), 56. See also C. H. Scott, "The Hymn of Robert E. Lee," SHSP, N.S., II (September 1915), 322; A. W. Kercheval, "The Burial of Lieutenant–General Jackson: A Dirge," *New Eclectic*, V (November 1869), 611; "The Ohio Division," CV, XXVI (August 1918), 368; Harold B. Simpson, *Hood's Texas Brigade in Reunion and Memory* (Hillsboro, Texas, 1974), 76; "The Confederate Choir No. 1," CV, XV (April 1907), 154–55; "United Confederate Choirs of America," ibid., XV (July 1907), 304; "Stonewall Jackson's Way," ibid., XXV (November 1917), 528–29; "Our Confederate Veterans," ibid., V (August 1897), 439; ibid., VI (November 1898), cover.

12. Southern Presbyterian General Assembly, *Minutes of the General Assembly of the Presbyterian Church in the United States* (Columbia, S. C., 1867), 137; Stephen Elliott, "Forty-fifth Sermon: On the State Fast-day," in Elliott, *Sermons by the Right Reverend Stephen Elliott...* (New York, 1867), 497, 505, 507; "Day of Fasting, Humiliation and Prayer," Atlanta *Christian Index*, March 9, 1865, p. 3.

13. "Thanksgiving Day: Its Afterclaps," Atlanta *Christian Index*, December 16, 1869, p. 2. See also "Day of Thanksgiving," Columbia (S. C.) *Southern Presbyterian*, November 14, 1872, p. 2; "The Two Proclamations," Atlanta *Christian Index*, November 22, 1866, p. 1; and Elliott's sermon "On the National Thanksgiving day," in Elliott, *Sermons*, 514–15.

14. James H. M'Neilly, "Jefferson Davis: Gentleman, Patriot, Christian," CV, XXIV (June 1916), 248; "Our Memorial Day," ibid., XXII (May 1914), 195; Lizzie Rutherford Chapter, UDC, *A History of the Origin of Memorial Day ...* (Columbus, Ga, 1898), 24 (first quotation); Mrs. A. M'D. Wilson, "Memorial Day," CV, XVII (April 1919), 156 (second and third quotations); UDC, *Minutes... 1901* (Nashville, 1902), 112.

15. UCV, Texas Division, James J. A. Barker Camp, No. 1555, *Burial Ritual* (n.p., n.d.); "Burial Ritual for Veterans," CV, III (February 1895), 43 (first and second quotations); "Burial Ritual. Suitable for Confederates Everywhere," ibid., XVII (May 1909), 214; Arthur B. Kinsolving, *Texas George: The Life of George Herbert Kinsolving ...* (Milwaukee and London, 1932), 130; "Rev. Romulus Morris Tuttle," CV, XII (June 1904), 296–97; and "Summer Archibald Cunningham," ibid., XXII (January 1914), 6–8.

16. "The Monumental Spirit of the South," CV, XXII (August 1914), 344; Confederate Monumental Association, *Tennessee Confederate Memorial* (Nashville, n.d.); 44; "Dedicatory Prayer of Monument," CV, IX (January 1901), 38; "Confederate Monument at San Antonio," ibid., VII (September 1899), 399 (first quotation); "Confederate Monument at Bolivar, Tenn.," ibid., VIII (August 1900), 353 (second quotation); "Fourth Report of Monumental Committee," UCV, *Minutes of the Twenty-first Annual Meeting and Reunion*, 52; ?? *Historic Southern Monuments: Representative Memorials of the Heroic Dead of the Southern Confederacy* (Washington and New York, 1911), 53–54 (third quotation), 133, 265, 426–27; UCV, *Minutes of the Seventeenth Annual Meeting and Reunion 1907 ??*

17. Warner, *The Living and the Dead: A Study of the Symbolic Life of Americans* (New Haven, 1959),

280. See also Claude Levi-Strauss, *The Savage Mind* (Chicago, 1962), 236–37; Warner, "An American Sacred Ceremony," in Richey and Jones, eds., *American Civil Religion*, 89–111; Catherine Albanese, "Requiem for Memorial Day: Dissent in the Redeemer Nation," *American Quarterly*, XXVI (October 1974), 386–98; Conrad Cherry, "Two American Sacred Ceremonies: Their Implications for the Study of Religion in America," ibid., XXI (Winter 1969), 739–54.

18. For background on the veterans groups see William W. White, *The Confederate Veteran* (Tuscaloosa, Ala., 1962). The reporter's quotation was in UCV, *Minutes of the Ninth Annual Meeting and Reunion*, 8.

19. UCV, *Minutes of the Tenth Annual Meeting and Reunion…1900* (New Orleans, 1902), 70 (quotation). For examples of this revealing theme in other forums see UCV, *Minutes of the Twelfth Annual Meeting and Reunion…1902* (New Orleans, n.d.), 10; "The Confederate Dead of Mississippi: Prayer," SHSP, XVIII (January–December 1890), 297; "The Monument to General Robert E. Lee: The Prayer," ibid., XVII (January–December 1889), 301–302.

20. For hymns at the reunions see UCV, *Minutes of the Seventh Annual Meeting and Reunion… 1897* (New Orleans, 1898), 15; UCV, *Minutes of the Tenth Annual Meeting and Reunion*, 40; UCV, *Minutes of the Thirteenth Annual Meeting and Reunion… 1903* (New Orleans, n.d.), 50. For the memorial services see UCV, *Minutes of the Tenth Annual Meeting and Reunion*, 95–101; UCV, *Minutes of the Seventeenth Annual Meeting and Reunion*, 110; UCV, *Minutes of the Thirtieth Annual Meeting and Reunion… 1920* (New Orleans, n.d.), 41 ??

21. "The Reunion: The Seventh Annual Convention of the U. D. C.," CV, V (July 1897), 338–39; ibid., V (June 1897), 243; "Comment on Nashville Reunion," ibid., V (September 1897), 463; "About the Nashville Reunion," CV, V (August 1897), 427–28.

22. UDC, *Ritual of the United Daughters of the Confederacy* (Austin, Texas, n.d.), 1–2 (quotations); UDC, *Minutes… 1905* (Nashville, 1906), 265–66. Local women's groups in 1900 formed an organization similar to the U. D. C., the Confederated Memorial Associations of the South. See *History of the Confederated Memorial Associations of the South* (New Orleans, 1904), 32–34.

23. *Poppenheim, History, 1–12; Some, U. D. C. Catechism for Children* (n.p., 1912); UDC, *Minutes… 1912*, p. 398.

24. Hill et al., *Religion and the Solid South*, 18–19, 26–28, 36–37 (quotation on p. 37); Hill, *Southern Churches*, xvii, 18, 201; Bailey, *Southern White Protestantism*, 2–3.

25. "Chaplain Jones' Prayer," UCV, *Minutes of the Eighteenth Annual Meeting and Reunion… 1908* (New Orleans, n.d.), 49–50(first quotation); UCV, *Minutes of the Twentieth Annual Meeting and Reunion… 1910* (New Orleans, n.d.), 53–54, 121; "Prayer," UCV, *Minutes of the Seventeenth Annual Meeting and Reunion… 1907*, 64 (third quotation). See also "The Confederate Dead in Stonewall Cemetery, Winchester, Va." SHSP. XXII (January–December 1894), 42; ?? Hoge's Prayer," ibid., 352–53; "Confederate Dead of Florida…," ibid., XXVII (January–December 1899), 112. The failure to make specifically Christian references is noted by Bellah, "Civil Religion in America," and Martin E. Marty, "Two Kinds of Two Kinds of Civil Religion," in Richey and Jones, eds., *American Civil Religion*, 23, 28, 148; and by Conrad Cherry, *God's New Israel: Religious Interpretations of American Destiny* (Englewood Cliffs, N. J., 1971), 9–10.

26. For examples of the interdenominational character of the Lost Cause see John L. Johnson, *Autobiographical Notes* (Boulder, Colo., 1958), 279; Moses D. Hogue to Peyton Hogue, May 22, 1891; January 20, 1893, Moses Drury Hogue Papers (Historical Foundation of the Presbyterian and Reformed Churches, Montreat, N.C.); "Gordon Memorial Service at Nashville," CV, XII (June 1904), 293; J. William Jones, *The Davis Memorial Volume; or, Our Dead President, Jefferson Davis, and the World's Tribute to His Memory* (Waco, Texas, 1890), 590–91, 595, 598.

27. For examples of Catholic and Jewish involvement in the Lost Cause see "Monument to Father Ryan in Mobile," CV, XXI (October 1913), 489–90; "The Reunion," ibid., V (July 1897), 340–41; "Address of Rabbi J. K. Gutheim," SHSP, X (June 1882), 248–50; "Sir Moses Ezekiel," CV, XXV (May 1917), 235–36.

28. Thomas I., Connelly, *The Marble Man: Robert E. Lee and His Image in American Society* (New York, 1977), 45; "Appeal to the South," *Atlanta Christian Index*, February 28, 1884, p, 4; CV, V (July 1897), 359; Edward P. Humphrey, "Moses and the Critics," *Southern Bivouac*, N.S., I (August 1885), 134–39; "Bishop John James Tigert," CV, XV (January 1907), 25; ibid., V (August 1897), 401.

29. Laura M. Jones and Walt Holcomb, *The Life and Sayings of Sam P. Jones…* (Atlanta, 1907), 142–48, 447–48; George C. Rankin, *The Story of My Life…* (Nashville and Dallas, 1912), 227; J. William Jones, *Personal Reminiscences, Anecdotes and Letters of Gen. Robert E. Lee* (New York, 1874), 333; UCV, *Minutes of*

the Tenth Annual Meeting and Reunion, 102 104, 108.

30. A. D. Mayo, "The Woman's Movement in the South," *New England Magazine*, N.S., V (October 1891), 257; White, *Confederate Veteran*, 59–60; UDC, *Minutes...* 1901 (Nashville, 1902), 127–28; J. William Jones, *School History of the United States* (Baltimore, 1896): Arthur B. Kinsolving, *The Story of a Southern School: The Episcopal High School of Virginia* (Baltimore, 1922), 79–80, 102, 132; C. D. Walker, "A Living Monument," CV, VIII (July 1900), 334; advertisement for Stonewall Jackson Institute, *ibid.*, XII (July 1904), back cover; *ibid.*, XXV (July 1917), back cover; UDC, *Minutes...* 1915 (Charlotte, N.C., n.d.), 142.

31. Arthur B. Chitty, "Heir of Hopes: Historical Summary of the University of the South," *Historical Magazine of the Protestant Episcopal Church*, XXIII (September 1954), 258–60; Chitty, *Reconstruction at Sewanee: The Founding of the University of the South and Its First Administration, 1857–1872* (Sewanee, Tenn., 1954), 45, 54–55, 73, 83; George R. Fairbanks, *History of the University of the South at Sewanee, Tennessee* (Jacksonville, Fla., 1905), 38–59, 70, 394; Richard Wilmer, *In Memoriam: A Sermon in Commemoration of the Life and Labors of the Rt. Rev. Stephen Elliott...* (Mobile, 1867), 13–14; Elliott, *An Appeal for Southern Books and Relics for the Library of the University of the South* (Sewanee, 1921), no pagination (quotation); Moultrie Guerry, *Men Who Made Sewanee* (Sewanee, Tenn., 1932), 73 89, 92, 49–71; Queenie W. Washington, "Memories,"; Louise Finley, "Magnolia Hall"; and Monte Cooper, "Miss Sada," in Lily Baker et al., eds., *Sewanee* (Sewanee, Tenn., 1932), 61 63, 100 101, 142–43.

32. Wilmer, *Gen'l Robert E. Lee: An Address Delivered Before the Students of the University of the South, October 15, 1870* (Nashville, 1872), 5, 9–12;

"Funeral of Gen. E. Kirby–Smith," CE I (April 1893), 100 101; "Monument of Gen. E. A. Shoup," *ibid.*, XI (July 1904), ??

33. The Winkler quotation is in Jones, *Personal Reminiscences*, 130–31. See also Henry A. White, *The Scotch-Irish University of the South: Washington and Lee* (Lexington, Va.?; 1890), 21–22; W. G. Bean, *The Liberty Hall Volunteers: Stonewall's College Boys* (Charlottesville, Va., 1964); Walter C. Preston, *Lee, West Point and Lexington* (Yellow Springs, Ohio, 1934), 48–51, 53–57; Ollinger Crenshaw, *General Lee's College: The Rise and Growth of Washington and Lee University* (New York, 1969), 152–54.

34. Franklin L. Riley, ed., *General Robert E. Lee After Appomattox* (New York, 1922), 19–20, 22–23, 62; Marshall W. Fishwick, "Robert E. Lee Churchman," *Historical Magazine of the Protestant Episcopal Church*, XXX (December 1961), 251–58, 260–63; Archibald T. Robertson, *Life and Letters of John Albert Broadus* (Philadelphia, 1910), 224–26; Francis H. Smith, *The Virginia Military Institute, Its Building and Rebuiding* (Lynchburg, Va., 1912); and Susan P. Lee, *Memoris of William Nelson Pendleton* (Philadelphia, 1893), 422–38.

35. *Ceremonies Connected with the Inauguration of the Mausoleum and the Unveiling of the Recumbent Figure of General Robert Edward Lee at Washington and Lee University, Lexington, Va., June 28, 1883* (Richmond, 1883); Thomas N. Page, *The Old South: Essays Social and Political* (New York, 1894), 3, 51-54; Crenshaw, *General Lee's College*, 282-89; Charles F. Adams, *Lee's Centennial: An Address* (Boston, 1907), 2, 6, 8, 14, 57; "The Old Virginia Town, Lexington," CV, I (April 1893), 108.

36. Mircea Eliade, *Patterns in Comparative Religion* (New York, 1958), 216–35.

THE EASTER PARADE

Leigh Eric Schmidt

At least since the beginning of the nineteenth century, Christianity has been deeply involved in the American commercial culture. This relationship has only recently been carefully examined. In the following essay, Leigh Schmidt considers the "complementary yet contested relationship" between Christianity and commercial culture when the relationship became particularly apparent in the late nineteenth century. At that time the commercialization of religious holidays suggested both the pervasive influence of Christianity on American culture and a profound transformation of Christian symbols from earlier ideals of self-denial to a new gospel of prosperity. Schmidt investigates the growth of this "devout consumption" through the elaborate displays of Easter flowers and the parade of Easter fashions both inside and outside of churches. Though the churches helped to create this new Easter, critics saw the growing commercialism as a cultural contest over the very meaning of Christianity. This was a struggle that pitted Christ against culture, religious hopes of heavenly salvation against secular desires for earthly pleasure. "But the critics," Schmidt observes, "rarely fathomed the complexity of the drama that so disturbed them."

Reprinted by permission from Leigh Eric Schmidt, "The Easter Parade: Piety, Fashion, and Display," *Religion and American Culture* 4:2 (Summer 1994): 135–164.

13 ❧

THE EASTER PARADE
Piety, Fashion, and Display

Leigh Eric Schmidt

IRVING BERLIN'S POPULAR MUSICAL of 1948, *Easter Parade*, starring Fred Astaire and Judy Garland, opens with a wonderful shopping scene. It is the day before Easter, 1911. Astaire's character, Don Hewes, sings and dances his way along the streets of New York past a dry-goods store and through millinery, florist, and toy shops. "Me, oh, my," he sings, "there's a lot to buy. There is shopping I must do. Happy Easter to you." In the millinery store saleswomen model elaborate Easter bonnets and mellifluously offer their wares: "Here's a hat that you must take home. Happy Easter…. This was made for the hat parade on the well-known avenue. This one's nice and it's worth the price. Happy Easter to you." Everywhere Hewes goes he buys things—a bonnet, a large pot of lilies, a toy bunny. By the time he leaves the florist, he has purchased so many gifts that he is followed by three attendants who help carry all the packages. Don Hewes is a consumer on a spree, and Easter is the occasion for it.[1]

With a boyish exuberance, Hewes prepares for Easter by shopping. His efforts are aimed not at readying himself for church or sacrament but at insuring that his companion will make a fine appearance in New York's fashion parade. The opening chorus chirrups this theme: "In your Easter bonnet with all the frills upon it, you'll be the grandest lady in the Easter parade. I'll be all in clover, and when they look you over, I'll be the proudest fellow in the Easter parade." Fulfillment consists of having his consort admired with envious gazes. When Hewes and his new dance partner, a humble show girl who doubles as a barmaid, actually encounter the promenade the next day, she is overawed." I can't believe I'm really here," she gasps. "You know, I used to read about the Easter parade in New York, and then I'd look at the pictures of the women in their lovely clothes and dream that maybe someday I'd …" Her voice trails off in wonder and dreamy aspiration. The only religious image in the film appears in the last scene when the Easter parade has returned for another year. A Gothic church looms as a dim backdrop for the fancily dressed couples who stroll by in a streaming concourse of affluence.

The film is not primarily about Easter, of course, but about Astaire and Garland and their marvelous dancing and singing. But the movie and Berlin's popular theme song are illuminating texts about the American Easter all the same. From at least the 1880's through the 1950's, this dress parade was one of the primary cultural expressions of Easter in the United States, one of the fundamental ways that the occasion was identified and celebrated. The holy day blossomed in the late nineteenth century into a cultural rite of spring with elaborate floral decorations, new clothes, fancy millinery, chocolate bunnies, greeting cards, and other gifts. The movie, like the Easter parade itself, embodied an expansive public faith in American abundance, a gospel of wealth, self-gratification, and prosperity: "Everything seems to come your way," the chorus lilts, "Happy Easter!"

In his recent novel *Operation Shylock*, Philip Roth celebrates Irving Berlin's *Easter Parade* for its creative de-Christianization of the festival, for its promotion of a "scholockified Christianity" in which the bonnet overthrows the cross.[2] But, in many ways, Berlin was merely offering a catchy, hummable benediction for the fashionable modern festival that American Christians had been busily creating for themselves over the previous century. This consumer-oriented Easter actually had deep religious wellsprings, and the juxtapositions of Christian devotion and lavish display were as richly polychromatic as the holiday flowers and fashions themselves. Fathoming the growing significance attached to church decoration in the second half of the nineteenth century is of first importance in making sense of this modern Easter. These religious patterns of embellishment, in turn, fed commercial holiday displays and spectacles of Easter merchandising. Lushly adorned churches provided the backdrop for finely appareled congregants and for the efflorescence of the Easter parade in New York City and elsewhere. All along, this Easter fanfare elicited sharp criticism from devotees of simplicity and plainness; that is, from those who were alienated from this faith of comfortable materialism, an estrangement that was often etched in sharply gendered terms. A complementary yet contested relationship between American Christianity and the modern consumer culture became increasingly evident in the second half of the nineteenth century, and that conjunction found performance in the Easter festival.

THE ART OF CHURCH DECORATION AND THE ART OF WINDOW DISPLAY

The Gothic church that flickers in the last frames of *Easter Parade* stands very much in the background, perhaps a nostalgic image—distant, unobtrusive, evanescent. Yet, to understand the development of the Easter parade as a cultural and religious event, this neo-Gothic edifice and others like it have to be brought into the foreground. Churches such as Trinity Episcopal Church, St. Patrick's Cathedral, and St. Thomas's Episcopal Church in New York City, with their rich Gothic ornament, are central, not peripheral, to this story. The elaborate decorations that these splendid urban churches created for ecclesiastical festivals such as Christmas and Easter are crucial for fathoming the emergence of a fashionable Easter in the second half of the nineteenth century. The newly cultivated art of church decoration, in turn, helped inspire inventive window trimmers and interior designers in their creation of holiday spectacles for merchandising purposes.

Easter, even more than Christmas, remained under a Puritan and evangelical cloud in the antebellum United States. Though various denominations all along preserved the holiday—most prominently Episcopalians, Roman Catholics, Lutherans, and Moravians—their celebrations were, until mid-century, localistic, parochial, and disparate. The festival became a well-nigh ubiquitous cultural event only in the decades after 1860 as low-church Protestant resistance or indifference gave way to approbation and as Episcopalian, Roman Catholic, and new immigrant observances became ever more prominent. Middle-class Victorians, fascinated with the recovery of fading holiday traditions and the cultivation of new home-centered festivities, discovered lush possibilities in this spring rite. The *New York Herald*, in a report on "Eastertide" in 1881, proclaimed that "A few years ago and Easter as a holiday was scarcely thought of, except by the devout; now all are eager to join in the celebration." Between about 1860 and 1890, Easter took distinctive religious and cultural shape as an American holiday.[3]

In an 1863 article on Easter, *Harper's New Monthly Magazine* suggested the growing embrace of the feast in American culture. "It is one of the obvious marks of our American religion," the article related, "that we are noticing more habitually and affectionately the ancient days and seasons of the Christian Church." Easter, following Christmas's rising popularity, showed "unmistakable signs that it is fast gaining upon the religious affection and public regard of our people." "We have carefully noted the gradual increase of observance of the day," the journal continued, "and can remember when it was a somewhat memorable thing for a minister, not Catholic or Episcopal, to preach an Easter sermon." What the magazine found most revealing of "this new love for Easter," however, was the increasing use of elaborate floral decorations for the festival. "Easter flowers are making their way into churches of all persuasions," the magazine applauded. "One of our chief Presbyterian churches near by decked its communion-table and pulpit with flowers for the third time this Easter season." The writer praised Easter floral displays for their artistic taste and devotional symbolism their "ministry of the beautiful." The splendor of Easter flowers embodied the new compelling allure of the festival.[4]

In lauding Easter flowers, the *Harper's* piece was celebrating the expanding art of church decoration. As a liturgical movement, this art effloresced in England and the United States in the middle decades of the nineteenth century. An outgrowth of the ritualist or Catholic turn within Anglican and Episcopalian circles, the new forms of church decoration meshed with the Gothic revival in Victorian church architecture and ornament. English writers such as William A. Barrett and Ernest Geldart led the way in formalizing the rubrics of modern church decoration in a number of handbooks that helped foster and guide the burgeoning art on both sides of the Atlantic. These writers codified a new aesthetic for church adornment, nostalgically medieval and Gothic in its vision but decidedly Victorian and modern in its elaboration. They cultivated what T.J. Jackson Lears has called "the religion of beauty"—a devotional love of liturgical drama, material symbolism, polychromatic color, sumptuous music, and graceful ornament. They wanted to fill the churches, as one handbook attested, with "sermons in stones, in glass, in wood, in flowers, and fruits, and leaves."[5]

Much of this ritual adornment focused on the high holy days of Christmas and Easter. Festooning the interior of churches with evergreens, flowers, vines, mosses, berries, leaves, wreaths, illuminated texts, emblems, tracery, and other devices became holiday staples. Indeed, such festal decorations reached modish proportions among Victorian churchgoers. "Few fashions," Edward L. Cutts commented in 1868 in the third edition of his handbook on church decoration, "have made such rapid progress within the last few years as the improved fashion of Decorating our Churches with evergreens and flowers for the great Church festivals." By 1882, another leading advocate of the "new fashion," Ernest Geldart, could remark that "it requires an effort of memory to recall the days when, save a few ill-set sprigs of holly at Christmas, none of these things were known."[6]

Christmas initially led the way in church decoration, but Easter soon came to rival, if not surpass, the winter feast for special adornment. Ernest R. Suffling commented on Easter's ascent in his manual *Church Festival Decorations*:

> Decorating the church at Easter, which a generation ago was but feebly carried out, has now
> become a recognized and general institution, and at no season of the year is it more appropriate.
> The joy of our hearts at the Resurrection of our Saviour—the seal of the completion of His
> work on earth—must surely be even greater than on the festival of His birth. The festival,
> coming as it does in early spring, is best commemorated by the use of as many flowers as
> possible.[7]

Weaving garlands around pillars, covering fonts and reading desks with fresh blooms,
hanging wreaths from arches and rails, erecting floral crosses on the altar or communion
table, filling windowsills with bouquets, setting up vine-covered trellises, and creating
pyramids of lilies—in short, putting flowers everywhere—became an Easter vogue of
dazzling proportions.

One way to render specific the rising importance of floral decorations at Easter is through
diaries. The journal of Henry Dana Ward, rector of St. Jude's Episcopal Church in New York
City, survives for the years 1850 to 1857, and it suggests the budding interest in Easter
flowers. He mentioned no special floral displays for his Easter services from 1850 to 1854,
but, in 1855, he noted that "the recess behind the Table was furnished with three pots of
flowers in full bloom and the Font with the same in partial bloom." Ward thought that the
flowers, all "Egyptian lilies," were pretty and pleasing, adding to the solemnity of the service.
Of these decorations, as well as new coverings for the communion table and the pulpit, he
took comfort that "no one was offended by these small novelties." He also made clear that his
forays into festal decoration were tame compared to those of some other Episcopal churches.
Visiting an afternoon Easter service at Trinity in 1857, he found the ritualism and
decorations excessive: "They make *too much* of a good thing—chant the Anthems to death—
and make a show of flowers on the Font & the reading Desk."[8] Decades before "the concept
of show invaded the domain of culture" in the form of showplaces, showrooms, and fashion
shows, churches like Trinity were cultivating a festive, luxuriant, and dramatic religious
world through the increasingly ornate art of church decoration.[9] This sense of Easter
decorations as a show or spectacle would become all the more evident in the decades after
the Civil War.

The diary of a young man who worked as a clerk at Tiffany's in New York City in the early
1870's suggests the dramatic impression that Easter decorations made. For Easter 1873, he
went to a morning service at Christ Church and an afternoon service at St. Stephen's, both of
which he found "magnificent," if fearfully crowded. The two churches, "well trimmed with
beautiful flowers," were stunning in their decorations. He continued:

> At Christs Church the burning star they had Christmas was over the alter [*sic*] besides the
> decorations of flowers. At St Stephens was arranged in the same manner—gas jets[.] Over the
> alter [*sic*] (as if it was there without anything to keep it there) was suspended a cross and above
> over it a crown. The effect was very good[,] the flaming of the gas making it so brilliant.[10]

The decorations clearly made a lasting impression on this young man (here at Easter he still
remembers the blazing star from the previous Christmas). Indeed, he seemed far more
overawed by the decorations that he saw in New York's Episcopal and Catholic churches

than anything he came across in New York's stores. For theatrical effect, the stores in the 1870's still had much to learn from the churches.

The special floral decorations for Easter received particular attention in women's diaries. An active Baptist laywoman in New York City, Sarah Todd, commented in her diary on a visit to an Episcopal church for an Easter service in 1867: "Being Easter Sunday the Church was handsomely dressed with flowers." Likewise, in her diary, New Yorker Elizabeth Merchant often made note of the Easter display of flowers: "Our church was beautifully dressed with flowers," she wrote of Easter 1883; "The church was lovely with flowers," she recalled of Easter worship in 1886; "Flowers perfectly beautiful & Mr Brooks splendid," she eulogized of two Easter services at Trinity Episcopal that she and her son enjoyed in 1887. Another New York woman made similar notations about Easter in her diary, writing in 1888: "Easter Day, Communion Sunday. Flowers in church. Alice & I took the children to the Church to see the flowers." Decorations seen, as much as sermons heard or eucharistic elements received, stood out in the memories that these women recorded. Perhaps for women especially, who often took charge of these floral displays, Easter in the churches became preeminently a time of flowers.[11]

The implications and consequences of the new fascination with Easter decorations were manifold. Certainly, and perhaps quintessentially, this art constituted an important new medium for religious expression. The decorations were devotional; their "double purpose" was to glorify God and edify wayfaring Christians. At Trinity Episcopal in 1861, the *New York Sun* reported, the Easter floral decorations were "in fine taste": "Flowers suggestive of the fundamental doctrines of Christianity composed the ornaments, and were so grouped as to indicate the cardinal truths of religion. In the centre of the altar was a floral globe mounted by a cross, and expressive of the redemption of the world." Floral decorations, testifying to the promise of new life, became for Victorians one of the dominant ways of communicating the Christian message of resurrection. To make certain that the devotional significance of the decorations remained clear, the churches often prominently displayed illuminated scriptual texts, usually drawn in intricate Gothic lettering. Arches and altars, chancels and choirs, brimmed with monumental affirmations: "He is risen"; "I am the Resurrection and the Life"; "Now is Christ risen from the dead, the first-fruits of them that slept"; "O death, where is thy sting? O grave, where is thy victory?" Easter decorations were a form of popular piety that evoked the ancient coalescence of the rebirth of spring and the resurrection of Christ.[12]

In their devotional dimensions, Easter decorations also suggested a sentimental and domestic version of Christian piety. Easter, *Harper's* said, was "winning our household feeling as well as our religious respect"; it served as a liturgical affirmation of the eternality of "family affections," as a celebration of "the great sentiment of home love." This domestic tenor was evident in the increasing overlap of church and home decorations: lilies, floral crosses, and distinctive Easter bouquets, for example, all ornamented Victorian altars and parlors alike. The decorative result was to join the church and the home in a shared, overarching design—"the House Beautiful."[13] Moreover, flowers suggested how Easter was becoming preeminently "the festival of sacred remembrance." Easter blooms, lilies especially, were presented in the churches as personal memorials for "departed kindred and friends"; they were hopeful, powerful tokens of the restored wholeness of familial circles. Indeed, the new love of Easter flowers was at one level the liturgical counterpart to Elizabeth Stuart Phelps's Victorian best-seller *The Gates Ajar*—a sentimental, consoling portrayal of heaven in terms of home, family, and friends: The new Easter helped reinforce the Victorian predilection for picturing heaven more as a place of human relationships and domestic reunions than as a God-centered realm of divine praise, light, and glory.[14]

The new passion for floral decoration clearly carried consequences that were not only devotional and domestic. For one thing, issues of competition and emulation crept into the Easter displays. The handbooks warned against the tendencies toward extravagance and rivalry: "Never try to beat the record," Ernest Geldart instructed. "Pray don't let it be your ambition that prompts you to 'beat' anything you have ever done, and above all, don't try to beat your neighbour's efforts." Admonitions notwithstanding, competition became an acknowledged undercurrent in holiday decoration. Who would have the most beautiful and extensive floral displays? Who would have the most inspiring music, the most solemn, dramatic, and crowded services? As the *New York Herald* observed in 1881, "The Catholics and Episcopalians are, of course, the foremost in the observance of the season, but other denominations are not far behind, and all vie with each other to make their house the most attractive to the worshipper." In America's free-market religious culture, church decoration became another way of attracting parishioners and gaining attention. Less ritualistic denominations—Presbyterians, Methodists, and even Baptists—learned to emulate Episcopalian and Catholic forms of holiday celebration in order to hold the allegiance of their people at these seasons of the year. Thorstein Veblen was wrong to view the "devout consumption" of the churches in the 1890's—their increasingly elaborate "ceremonial paraphernalia"—simply in terms of "status" and "conspicuous waste" (such an interpretation was irredeemably monochromatic and reductionistic). But he was right to see competition and emulation as component parts of Victorian church furnishing and decoration.[15]

Another unintended consequence of holiday church decoration was how it fostered modishness and exoticism. In 1867, the *New York Herald,* in commenting on the "elaborate floral decorations" for Easter at St. John the Baptist Episcopal Church, noted that the display included "one of the only three genuine palms known to exist in the United States." Similarly, the *Herald's* 1873 report on the Easter decorations in the Church of the Divine Paternity struck the same chord of rarity: "Surmounting the reredos was a magnificent cross made of lilies, on either side of which were two recumbent beds of roses. The altar was profusely covered with the rarest of exotics." Ernest Suffling, summarizing this trend toward floral exoticism—if not colonialist rampage—observed that where a few "indigenous evergreens" had formerly satisfied the church decorator, now "we ransack the whole world, for our grasses, flowers, and palms, or fruits and mosses." There was little that was traditional, antimodern, or medieval, the *New York Sun* declared, in searching out "rare evergreens," "choice tropicals," or "calla lilies of remarkable size and beauty, sent hermetically sealed from California." Style, taste, abundance, and novelty—the very values of the burgeoning consumer culture—became defining features of Easter decorations in the churches. The fashionable Easter given expression in the Easter parade and in turn-of-the-century department stores had its roots in the religious culture, which itself was becoming progressively more consumerist in its modes of celebration. At Easter, devout consumption fed its more worldly counterpart.[16]

A final, portentous consequence of the new art of church decoration was that it provided a model or repertory for holiday displays outside the churches in the marketplace. With Easter, even more than with Christmas, the commercial culture built its enterprise very directly on the religious culture—on Christian patterns of decoration, display, and celebration. Church music, flowers, ornaments, banners, and other decorations all found their way into show windows and interior displays in late-nineteenth- and early twentieth-century department stores. Easter decorations were clearly very attractive for commercial appropriation; their associations with the church, with women and the home, with fashion and affluence, were all useful connections for merchandising. With multiple layers of meaning, Easter emblems, popularized through church decoration, provided retailers with rich and redolent symbols. More broadly, the art of church decoration offered a useful aesthetic for the art of store decoration. Church decorators, like their commercial counterparts after them, stressed the power of visual representation, the importance of harmonizing form and color, the careful planning of designs, and the expressive potentialities of lighting and glass. Church decorators also provided a principle of innovation, regularly experimenting with new decorative materials and warning against "sameness," "feeble repetition," and "distasteful monotony" in beautifying the sanctuary. This outlook intermeshed with the mounting desire of window trimmers and store decorators to bring seasonal variety and originality to their display of goods. Thus, in surprising and hitherto little seen ways, the art of church decoration helped generate what William Leach has called "the display aesthetic" that came to characterize the modern consumer culture.[17]

Irving Berlin's *Easter Parade* in itself suggests the migration of church decoration into the marketplace: Don Hewes passes the show window of a dry-goods store that is trimmed with Easter lilies, as is the interior of the millinery shop he patronizes. The transformation of church decorations into store embellishments was evident as early as the 1880's and 1890's. "Make a gala week of the week before Easter," the *Dry Goods Chronicle* exhorted in 1898. "Tog your store out until it shines with the Easter spirit.... Blossom with the Easter lily, give your store a dress in keeping with this Easter festival." This kind of advice was regularly put into practice. "The store is in harmony with the occasion," Wanamaker's Easter catalog boasted in 1893; "Easter Symbols are everywhere in the decorations.... Easter merchandise is all over the store." By the turn of the century, such Easter displays and embellishments had become standard trade preparations: lavish store decorations were considered essential for imparting and evoking the Easter spirit and for attracting holiday shoppers.[18]

All along, trimming a store for Easter meant a profusion of seasonal folk symbols such as rabbits, chicks, and eggs. It also meant a surplus of Christian iconography—miniature churches, choirs, pipe organs, stained glass, crosses, lilies, religious banners, and devotional mottoes. The *American Advertiser* offered this description of a "delicate and pleasing" Easter window in a Chicago jewelry store in 1890:

> The window floor was covered with white jewelers' cotton in sheets, looking pure as snow. A cross of similar material and whiteness was slightly raised above the level of the window-floor, in the middle rear part of the window. On each side of the window was a calla lily blossom, the flower being cut short off below the bloom. Inside the lily, like a drop of purest dew, sparkled a diamond—just one on each lily. The cross was slightly twined with smilax, which also bordered the back of the window. A white rose was scattered here and there, and on the cross and on the white window floor were displayed a few gems and trinkets,—not enough to distract the attention or give the appearance of crowding.... Taken altogether the display was the perfection of good taste and artistic skill.

The cross and lilies, staples of church decoration, became mainstays of the window dresser's art—repeated centerpieces for the display of goods, whether millinery, greeting cards, or even groceries. In this case, jewelry and other items were actually attached to the lilies and the cross, making their linkage direct and tangible.[19]

Designs for show windows also played upon the sentimental, domestic dimensions of Victorian Easter piety. One window trimmer bragged in 1896 of a crowd-stopping Easter display that proved pleasing to patrons and proprietor alike. Entitled "Gates Ajar," the window was trimmed from floor to ceiling "with spotless white silk handkerchiefs entwined with ferns and smilax from the millinery stock and plants from the hot-house." The focal point of the window was "a flight of five steps, at the head of which was a large double gate, partially opened, so as to show one large figure in white silk and pretty little cherubs (dolls with wings of gold and silver paper) as if in the act of flying." This show-window glimpse of silky white seraphs and everlasting life dovetailed with the alluring domestic heaven depicted in Elizabeth Stuart Phelps's *Gates Ajar* and its sequels. In *The Feminization of American Culture*, Ann Douglas wryly comments that reading Phelps' novels about heaven with all their luminous detail about domestic furnishings and possessions "is somewhat like window-shopping outside the fanciest stores on Fifth Avenue." Window trimmers and store decorators had the same intuition. In their appropriation of Phelps's themes, they made explicit the otherwise implicit interconnections between this domestic piety and consumerist ideals.[20]

Store decorations for Easter were often more elaborate than such relatively modest show windows and sometimes rivaled the churches in what one window trimmer called "cathedral effect[s]." This decorative intricacy was epitomized in the Easter adornment in Wanamaker's in Philadelphia. As was the case at Christmas, Wanamaker's Grand Court was transformed at Easter into a religious spectacle. Statues of angels, thousands of lilies and ferns, displays of ornate ecclesiastical vestments, religious banners and tapestries, and mottoes proclaiming "He is Risen!" and "Alleluia!" all found place in Wanamaker's during the Easter season in the early decades of this century. The store's grandest Easter spectacle, however, was the annual display, beginning in the mid-1920's, of two monumental canvases by the Hungarian artist Michael de Munkacsy—one painting (20' 8" by 13' 6"), entitled *Christ before Pilate*, and the other (23' 4" by 14' 2"), entitled *Christ on Calvary*. Painted respectively in 1881 and 1884, these works had been widely exhibited and heralded in this country and had achieved international repute in their day as grand masterpieces. Purchased by John Wanamaker as favored treasures for his own impressive collection of art, the paintings were eventually put on display in the Grand Court each year during Lent and Easter. The exhibition of paintings with this level of acclaim was something that the churches could rarely match or duplicate. Easter displays like these brought into sharp relief the dynamic interplay of art, piety, and commerce in the American marketplace. Easter in Wanamaker's epitomized the translation of the Gothic revival and the art of church decoration into a commercial idiom.[21]

Discerning the meaning and significance of the varied Christian emblems that found their way into show windows and department stores is no easy task. What did religious symbols—such as the cross, lilies, church replicas, or the Agnus Dei—come to symbolize when placed within the context of Easter displays? In the ersatz, artful, and cunning world of the marketplace, the meanings of symbols were particularly unstable, uncertain, and slippery. Perhaps such religious emblems became quite literally so much window dressing, that is, artificial, distracting, and illusory fluff, little more than splashes of color and attractive packaging, a vapid and insincere mimicry of liturgical art. Certainly, the employment of religious symbols as merchandising icons carried an undeniable artifice and doubleness, a sharp edge of deception. In their intramural discussions of display techniques, window trimmers were often quite candid about their purposes. L. Frank Baum, who started in the fantasy world of show windows before moving on to the *Wizard of Oz*, commented matter-of-factly on the place of the cross in Easter displays: "The cross is the principal emblem of Easter and is used in connection with many displays, being suitable for any line of merchandise. To be most effective it should be a floral cross." The essential object in window dressing was, after all, to sell goods, and religious symbols, as with all display props, were used self-consciously to maximize this effect. Creatively negotiating the borderland between commerce and Christianity was part of the window trimmer's calling, and these Easter icons were, at one level, simply another trick of the trade.[22]

But these displays represented more than commercial artifice. The widespread infusion of religious symbols into the marketplace also suggested the deep hold of Christianity on the culture and indicated anew how "adaptable" American religion was to "popular commercial forms."[23] Far from eschewing Christian emblems, retailers seized the opportunity to consecrate their stores through holiday decorations. Often enough, churchgoing merchants employed these emblems straightforwardly to evoke and affirm the old-time piety; certainly John Wanamaker, YMCA leader and Sunday school titan, understood his cathedral-like decorations and his in-store choir concerts in religious terms. The density of spiritual referents was, after all, what made these symbols so powerful; it is also, of course, what made them so useful. Still, the manipulation, misappropriation, or displacement of Christian symbols was rarely the issue for merchants or customers: in these displays, Christian hopes and consumerist dreams regularly merged into a cohesive cultural whole. Rather than shunting aside the church, the department stores (and the emergent mass culture that these institutions represented) accorded Christianity considerable cultural authority during the holidays. And, in some ways, merchants seemed to be doing exactly what liberal Protestant pundits had been calling for; namely, the wholesale sacralization of the marketplace. Social gospeller George Herron exhorted "the Christian business men of America" to "make the marketplace as sacred as the church." "You can draw the world's trades and traffics within the onsweep of Christ's redemptive purpose," Herron insisted. Wanamaker and other merchants like him were seen by many Protestants as the consummate consecrators of wealth and the market. In the "one undivided Kingdom of God," commerce and Christianity would harmoniously support one another. The turn-of-the-century celebrations of Christmas and Easter in the department stores were the festivals of that liberal cultural faith. Indeed, in some ways, they represented a re-visioning in modern Protestant guise of the "festive marketplace" of the Middle Ages and the Renaissance in which church celebration met the "brimming-over abundance of the fair."[24]

This seemingly happy convergence of Christianity and consumption suggested in itself, however, a profound transformation in the meaning of Christian symbols. The stores all too clearly presented a new prosperity gospel that was far removed from traditional Christian emphases on self-abnegation. "When I survey the wondrous cross on which the Prince of glory died," Isaac Watts had versified in the eighteenth century in lines his Victorian heirs still sang, "My richest gain I count but loss, and pour contempt on all my pride.... All the vain things that charm me most, I sacrifice them to his blood." Surveying the wondrous cross within a show window or a department store effectively shifted the foundations of this crucicentric piety from self-denial to self-fulfillment. The very context in which these symbols appeared suggested a substantial revision of the faith—a new image of piety at peace with plenty and at home in the new "dream world" of mass consumption. This was no small subversion. Traditional Christian symbols of self-abnegation had come to legitimate luxury, elegance, and indulgence. The cross itself had become one of the charms of the merchandiser's art, its religious power absorbed into the new magic of modern commodities and advertising.[25]

PIETY, FASHION, AND A SPRING PROMENADE

The vogue for Easter flowers and church decoration intertwined with other Easter fashions—those in clothing and millinery. Of an Easter service at Christ Church, an Episcopal congregation on Fifth Avenue, the *New York Herald* wrote in 1873: "More than one-half of the congregation were ladies, who displayed all the gorgeous and marvelous articles of dress which Dame Fashion has submitted to be the ruling idea of Spring, and the appearance of the body of the church thus vied in effect and magnificence with the pleasant and tasteful array of flowers which decorated the chancel." In a similar vein, a reporter compared "the costumes of the ladies" at St. Patrick's Cathedral for Easter 1871 with "a parterre of flowers." Since spring millinery fashions actually tended to include various flora and fauna, such comparisons were not mere similes. Fashions in flowers and dress, indeed, interpenetrated one another. In 1897, for example, the *New York Times* reported that violets were in greater demand than any other Easter flower "because the violet, in all its various shades, is the predominating color in dress." The very development of the Easter parade along Fifth Avenue was in part connected with the popularity of visiting the different churches to see their elaborate floral decorations. "Many will go to church to-day to see the flowers," the *New York Times* observed in 1889, "and not a few are accustomed to join the parade on Fifth-avenue from church to church, just to look at the beautiful productions of nature." The Victorian love of Easter flowers and church decoration blossomed naturally into the famous promenade of fashions.[26]

Having new clothes for Easter or dressing up in special ways for the festival was never simply about modern fashions or modern forms of consumption and display. The practice had deep roots, or at least resonances, in European religious traditions and folk customs at Easter. Sacred times—baptisms, weddings, funerals, fasts, and feasts—warranted special forms of dress, material markers of holiness and celebration. Uncommon or distinctive garb for Easter, as with the Sunday best of the sabbatarian or the special vestments of priests, had long communicated the solemnity, sacrality, and seriousness of the occasion. The special raiment might be as simple as wearing new gloves, ribbons, or stockings or as stunning as dressing wholly in white. Conventions were localistic and diverse, but the overarching point was captured in an Irish adage: "For Christmas, food and drink; for Easter, new clothes." A frequently recited maxim from Poor Robin distilled such holiday expectations into a couplet:

> At Easter let your clothes be new,
> Or else be sure you will it rue.

This old English saying itself became part of the Victorian memory about Easter, a selective slice of Easter folklore that helped people situate their own interest in new attire for the holiday within the comforting framework of tradition. As the *New York Herald* noted in

1855, "There is an old proverb that if on Easter Sunday some part of your dress is not new you will have no good fortune that year."[27]

The parade of Easter fashions in New York City emerged as a distinct religious and cultural event in the 1870's and 1880's, and the Easter services of the churches were at the center of it. An account in 1873 in the *New York Herald* of "the throngs of people" going to and from church suggested the parade's incipient form:

> They were a gaily dressed crowd of worshippers, and the female portion of it seemed to have come out *en masse* in fresh apparel, and dazzled the eye with their exhibition of shade and color in the multitudinous and variegated hues of their garments. Fifth avenue, from Tenth street to the Central Park, from ten o'clock in the morning till late in the afternoon, was one long procession of men and women, whose attire and bearing betokened refinement, wealth and prosperity, and nearly all these were worshippers of some denomination or another, as the crowds that poured in and out of the various religious edifices along the line of the avenue amply testified.

By the end of the 1870's, the "fashionable promenade" was more clearly defined in terms of the early afternoon, ensuing at the conclusion of the morning church services: "In the afternoon," the *Herald* reported in 1879, "Fifth avenue was a brilliant sight when the thronging congregations of the various churches poured out upon the sidewalks and leisurely journeyed homeward." *Le beau monde* flowed out of the churches into a vast concourse of style, affluence, and luxury.[28]

In the 1880's, the afternoon promenade of Easter churchgoers became all the more "the great fashion show of the year." By 1890, the procession had achieved standing as a recognized marvel on New York's calendar of festivities and had taken on its enduring designation as *the Easter parade.* As the *New York Times* reported in 1890, "It was the great Easter Sunday parade, which has become such an established institution in New York that the curious flock to Fifth-avenue almost as numerously and enthusiastically as they do to see a circus parade." A spectacle of new spring fashions, prismatic colors, Easter bouquets and corsages, elaborate and ever-changing millinery, New York's "great Easter parade" was an occasion for people "to see and be seen." By the mid-1890's, day-trippers from New Jersey and Long Island as well as other visitors flocked to the Fifth Avenue pageant to survey the fashions and to join in the promenade. Thus having begun as a procession of fashionable and privileged churchgoers, the parade quickly became a jostling, crowded scene—"a kaleidoscope of humanity that changed incessantly and presented a new picture with every change."[29]

The emergence of the Easter parade presented a choice opportunity for dry-goods and millinery establishments. Surprisingly, however, retailers were not overly quick to push the promotional connection between Easter and seasonal fashions. While Christmas was already garnering the advertising attention of New York's emergent dry-goods palaces in the 1840's and 1850's as well as attracting the humbug of smaller shopkeepers even earlier, Easter went unnoticed. Spring openings were a merchandising staple for New York firms by the mid-nineteenth century, yet no advertising efforts were fabricated to link spring bonnets or other spring fashions explicitly to Easter. In the 1850's and 1860's, newspaper advertisements for seasonal apparel remained the same before and after Easter. Through the mid-1870's, few, if any, attempts were made to create a specific market for the holiday, even though the connection between Easter and new spring styles was already apparent in New York's most fashionable churches. Only in the late 1870's did New York's merchants begin to exploit the growing religious linkage between Easter and fashion. According to Ralph M. Hower, Macy's first began to promote goods specifically for Easter in its newspaper advertising in 1878, and this coincides with the early efforts of other retailers. For example, in the *New York Sun* in 1878, E. Ridley & Sons advertised "Trimmed Bonnets and Round Hats, Manufactured for Easter," and Lord & Taylor made a similar pitch. In the 1880's, almost all the leading department stores would join in this kind of advertising, thus bringing spring fashions and the Easter festival into explicit and deepening alliance.[30]

By the 1890's, promotion of Easter within the dry-goods industry was in full swing. There was no bigger event in the trade's calendar. "Easter is pre-eminently the festival of the dry goods trade," the *Dry Goods Economist* concluded in 1894. "Much of the success of the year's business hangs upon the demand experienced during the weeks just preceding Easter." Retailers did all they could to stoke the desire for Easter fashions. "Everything is done during these days to influence the shopper to buy," the *Dry Goods Economist* observed of the Easter season in 1894. "Windows are trimmed with all the art at the dresser's command and with as much study as the Royal Academician gives to a magnificent painting." Merchants had clearly come to see their role in the Easter festival as more than one of simply responding to a demand for seasonal goods. Instead, their goal was to expand the market, to deepen and widen these holiday customs. "Women may be induced to think more and more of something special for Easter by telling insinuations judiciously put in your advertising," the *Dry Goods Chronicle* theorized in 1898. "Women may be induced to forego the satisfying of some actual need in order to gratify an Easter fancy, provided you prod their vanity with suggestive advertising and supplement it with a fetching store display." As was the case with so many other dimensions of the expanding consumer culture, women were condescendingly cast as the arch-consumers at Easter and received most of the attention in its promotion. If merchants had been slow to get on the Easter band-wagon in the 1860's and 1870's, they were among its loudest trumpeters and trombonists by the 1890's. Through their tireless promotions, they helped define Easter as "a time for 'dress parade' and 'full feather.'"[31]

A spectacle of vast proportions, the Easter parade was assuredly a multivalent ritual, a multilayered cultural performance. For the devout, the season's new clothes were part of a synthesis of piety and material culture. As the gray of winter and the darkness of Lent and Good Friday gave way to the rebirth of spring and the Resurrection, the sumptuous hues of Easter fashions reflected these transitions. New Yorker Elizabeth Orr suggested this interplay of themes in her diary entry about Easter in 1871:

> Easter Sunday came in bright and beautiful[,] has been one of the most beautiful Spring days I ever experienced. Every one seemed to be influenced by the weather, bright happy faces. Most every one out in their holiday clothes gotten up for the occasion. Dr Eddy gave us one of his good discourses on the reserection [sic] of Christ and his followers. Oh that I may be one of that number! 'Am I his or Am I not' should be a question with us. I know and feel my sinfulness, and he came to save just such a sinner. I repent every day, and trust I am forgiven. Oh that happy day when we will have no more sin to repent of, but constantly [be] in the presence of our Lord and Master.[32]

In her recollections of the day's activities, the beautiful spring weather led naturally to promenading in holiday clothes, which connected seamlessly, in turn, with pious reflections on sin, repentance, and resurrection. Easter devotion was part of a rich mix or jumble of experiences in which impressions of clothes and sunshine and smiles flitted alongside the ringing words of the pastor's sermon.

Elizabeth Merchant's diary entries for Easter displayed the same sort of tangled synthesis of seasonal rejoicing, new clothes, and resurrection. The Saturday before Easter in 1881 she noted: "Went to town looking for Easter cards & buying myself a dress...with linings &c. [T]hen went to Bible class & heard a lovely lecture from Dr. Hall on the resurrection." In another passage she waxed eloquent on the interconnections between the new life of Easter and the vernal revival:

> Oh! Such a perfect day! trees budding birds singing—grass is green & sky so beautiful with its fleecy clouds. All the air full of sweet Spring sounds. I long to be out Enjoying every Moment at this season of so much beauty. There is an immense Robin red breast hopping and flying over the lawn! Oh God will the resurrection of our frail bodies be glorious like this waking of nature from the cold death of Winter?

Elizabeth Merchant readily combined the simple satisfactions of Easter shopping with the deeper mysteries of Christianity and nature. The same overlay of experiences was captured in Clara Pardee's clipped entry for Easter 1883: "A lovely Easter day—Out to church & walked up 5th Ave. Crowds of people—spring hats." Marjorie Reynolds was similarly terse in her notes about Easter in 1912: "Robed in new white corduroy. To the Brick [Church] with Oliver & a bunch of flowers. I don't know [what] I enjoyed more...a packed church...beautiful music & a good sermon...on the Av. afterwards w[ith] O[liver] & Mr. M[iddle] up to 59th St." The clear reconfiguring of Easter by the burgeoning consumer culture did not necessarily lessen the feast's religious power; instead it added to its sensuous richness and complexity. In these women's diaries, there was no necessary movement away from salvation to self-fulfillment, no hard-and-fast opposition between Christian soteriology and cosmopolitan display. For religious and cultural critics, it would prove all too easy to associate the feminized domains of church decoration and Easter fashion with vanity and immodesty (one trade writer tellingly spoke of the "masculine contempt" for dress and millinery). In these women's jottings, however, church and parade, fashion and festival, coalesced into an undivided whole.[33]

As Irving Berlin's movie suggests, not all the spring promenaders and curious onlookers cared about this synthesis of piety and materiality. As with any festival, a wide range of motivations and expectations animated those in attendance. Thousands and eventually hundreds of thousands clogged New York's fashionable thoroughfares for the Easter parade, and people took their bearings from various sources, sometimes divergent, often overlapping. Some went forth from the churches on errands of benevolence, making their way to hospitals and orphanages with flowers to brighten up the holiday for others. Others were abroad mostly to court and flirt and ogle; almost all were seeking diversion and entertainment of one kind or another. Not a few came out to work the milling crowds: thieves and pickpockets with fleet hands, hucksters and hawkers with various wares. At the same time, many of Veblen's leisure class graced the avenue, showcasing their status, urbanity, and importance, perhaps most interested in the occasion as a theater of social prestige. Also, many who were frankly indifferent to religion joined in the procession—those, as the *New York Herald* groused in 1890, who had heard "no Easter benediction" and whose holiday glow "came from a brandy cocktail with a dash of absinthe in it." In all, the parade presented a pluralistic mélange of characters who processed to various rhythms.[34]

Certainly among the loudest drummers was fashion: lovers of new spring apparel and millinery, devotees of the latest style and vogue, peopled Fifth Avenue. The Easter parade, as Irving Berlin's movie highlighted, was indeed a celebration of the consumer culture—its capitalistic abundance, its unfettered choices, its constantly changing styles. If there was ever a holiday spectacle that apotheosized the American Way of Life, this was it. New York's dress parade was a tableau of American prosperity. Eventually, it even came to be seen as a parable about the bounties of American enterprise that contrasted sharply with the failures of Soviet communism. "Fifth Avenue on Easter Sunday," a *New York Times* columnist wrote in 1949, "would probably irritate Stalin more than he is already exasperated with the United States.... It will take a long series of five-year plans before the Soviet woman can buy a dress, a hat or a pair of shoes for anything near the price a New York working girl paid for her Easter outfit."[35] In 1955, the *Saturday Evening Post* was even more blunt about the parade's cultural meaning: New York's springtime pageant stood as "a reflection of the American Dream—that a person is as good as the clothes, car and home he is able to buy." In this writer's reckoning, the church's celebration of Easter was "incidental" to this wider public affirmation of American abundance and prosperity. The Easter parade's essential trademark was, to be sure, a gospel of wealth.[36]

Still, the parade remained all along a polysemous event, hardly reducible to a surface of fashion, respectability, and buttoned-up conventionality. Beneath its consumerist credo were carnivalesque tinges reminiscent of old Easter Monday traditions of mummery, which, as at New Year's, included outlandish costumes and boisterous conviviality. (How else but in terms of the fantastical and improvisational could one explain the large hat worn by one woman in 1953 that contained both a replica of the Last Supper and a live bird in a cage?) In many ways, the Easter parade was an unstructured, boundless, liminal event; there was "no apparent beginning, ending, organization or purpose." People flowed in and out of it—something of a leisurely free-for-all where fashionable promenaders, idle spectators, and publicity mongers merged into a closely commingled throng. The Easter parade may have begun in the 1870's as a parade of refinement—a middle- and upper-class staging of gentility, a sort of ritual primer for immigrants and the working class on the accoutrements of respectability—but by the turn of the century it had far more of the crowded, unpredictable energy of a street fair in which both Lenten and bourgeois strictures often melted into Easter laughter. Certainly, the residual form of the parade that survives today in New York City is more masked frolic than fashion show.[37]

The creative, playful possibilities were also seen in the role women assumed in this public performance. With their elaborate dresses and millinery, they took center stage. In a culture in which men and their civic associations had long dominated formal street parades and in a culture in which rowdy male youths had long made carnivalesque festivity and masking their special domain, the Easter parade was decidedly different. In contrast to the home-centered celebrations that so often prevailed among middle-class Victorian women and in contrast to the commonly minimal role of women as spectators on the edges of civic ceremony, Easter was about women in public procession. Whereas most nineteenth-century parades revolved quite literally around the *man* in the street, the Easter parade turned this convention on its head. Also, women's parading in Easter millinery served as a subversion of Pauline (and evangelical Protestant) views about head-coverings as emblematic of female modesty and meekness. The new world of Easter millinery was, in part, about the assertion of the self; about a world of mirrors and studied appearances ("You cannot have too many mirrors," one book on the art of millinery advised); about self-transformation through bewitching lines, fabrics, and colors; about the fashioning of the self in a parade of protean styles.[38]

Among the most far-reaching consequences of New York's dress parade was that it became a cultural model for spin-off observances around the country. Parallel events cropped up in other major cities, such as Philadelphia and Boston, and appeared in smaller towns as well. The cultural diffusion of New York's great Easter procession became especially evident in satellite resorts such as Coney Island, Asbury Park, and Atlantic City, where the entrepreneurs of commercialized leisure reproduced facsimiles for their own purposes. In these places the Easter parade was transformed into an excursion, a tourist attraction. At Coney Island in 1925, for example, the *New York Herald* reported that the local chamber of commerce had organized, with the help of several manufacturers, "a fashion show and Easter parade." To augment the proceedings the promoters had hired fifty show girls to parade in bathing suits; the crowds were overwhelming. No less hucksterish were the proceedings at Atlantic City, where, by the 1920's, the Easter parade was attracting annual crowds of 200,000 and more. Like Coney Island, Atlantic City was an excursionist's wonderland, and the parade there presented a kaleidoscopic scene of lolling, laughing pleasure-seekers—a Boardwalk carnival of costuming and consumption. Easter, like other American holidays, became a vacation. Begun in an outflow of the churches, the Easter parade climaxed in an amusement for that ultimate consumer, the tourist.[39]

RAINING ON THE EASTER PARADE: PROTEST, SUBVERSION, AND DISQUIET

All the display and fashion of the modern American Easter bewildered various people and inspired recurrent cultural criticism. Distressed commentators presented a wide range of intellectual perspectives from social gospel principles about economic justice to bedrock Puritan and republican convictions about simplicity and plainness. Above all, critics saw this as a cultural contest over the very meaning of Easter. Could the age-old Christian message of redemptive sacrifice and resurrection at the heart of Holy Week shine through the modern fanfare of style, novelty, and affluence? It was a struggle in ritual, liturgy, and performance to define what the values of the nation were and what Christianity demanded of its adherents. Seen from the perspective of the long history of the church, the struggle embodied perennial strains between Christ and culture, God and mammon. Viewed from the narrower span of American religious history, the conflict evoked familiar tensions between Puritan theocentrism and Yankee anthropocentrism, between otherwordly hopes of redemption and consumer dreams of material abundance, and between republican notions of male virtue and the corresponding fears of effeminacy and foppery.

Critics worried regularly over Easter extravagance. This "vaunting of personal possessions" in a parade of fashions abraded deep-seated cultural values of simplicity, frugality, and self-denial. If waning in the face of the expanding consumer culture, these principles continued to hold considerable allegiance, and concerns over Easter fashions brought these cultural tensions into sharp relief, perhaps particularly so since, as a religious event, Easter was expected to undergrid, not subvert, the traditional values of thrift and moderation. Challenges to Easter indulgence took various forms. One Nazarene minister in Illinois in 1930, for example, gained notice with a bit of evangelical showmanship: he protested the predilection for turning Easter into "a fashion show" and a time of luxury by leading worship "attired in overalls." Likewise a Methodist minister in New Jersey in 1956 made the same point by wearing old clothes to conduct his Easter service. The worldliness of the Easter parade, the swaggering of "supreme ego, self-interest, [and] self-conceit," the searing contrast between Jesus' suffering and humiliation on the road to Calvary and the modern "fanfaronade of women in silks and furs" jarred a writer for the *Christian Century* in 1932. Two decades later another contributor to the same weekly wondered at the Fifth Avenue procession in which all seemed to cry "Look at me!" To its critics, the Easter parade was seen as a giant spectacle of vain self-assertion.[40]

Commentary on the American Easter sometimes cut deep to fundamental issues of social and economic justice. Like the Christmas rush, Easter preparations put huge burdens on workers to meet the surging demand for holiday goods and to satisfy the throng of holiday shoppers. Edwin Markham, poet of the social gospel whose "The Man with the Hoe" (1899) launched him to fame as a prophet against dehumanizing labor, spotlighted the crushing hardships of the holiday seasons in a series of blistering, reform-minded essays on child labor. Fired in part by his understanding of Jesus as a socialistic and progressivist visionary, Markham laid into "this generation of the colossal factory and the multitudinous store and the teeming tenement-house," all of which darkened even the joys of Christmas and Easter. "To thousands of those who depend on…the fashion-plate for light and leading," he blasted, "Easter means only a time of changing styles—a date on which to display new spring gowns and bonnets—a sort of national millinery opening. But to the workers in the shadow,…it means only a blind rush and tug of work that makes this solemn festival a time of dread and weariness. They might truly say in tears, 'They have taken away my Lord, and I know not where they have laid him.'"[41]

Markham aimed his sharpest attacks at sweatshops where children labored late into the night at piecework wages over artificial flowers for milinery to satisfy "the season's rush." He estimated that three-quarters of those making this production in New York City, the center of the industry, were children under age fourteen. "There is no other Easter preparation," he concluded, "where children are so cruelly overworked as in the making of artificial flowers." These "vampire blossoms" robbed children of education, health, and play:

> I lately visited a factory where a group of girls were making artificial roses. They were working ten hours a day, some of them getting only a dollar and a half a week…. Swiftly, rhythmically, the ever-flying fingers darted through the motions, keeping time to the unheard but clamorous metronome of need. Many of the girls had inflamed eyes…. The faces were dulled, the gaze was listless. Here was another illustration of the tragedy in our civilization—the work that deadens the worker.

The sweatshop exploitation of women and children, raised to feverish levels during the holiday rush, was, to Markham, "the tragedy behind the flaunting festoons of our Easter Vanity Fair."[42]

With stinging directness, Markham raked the muck on Easter fashions. Writing with a second-person bluntness that indicated again the gendered nature of this contest, he blasted: "Perhaps, last Easter, you, my lady, wore one of those pretty things of lace and chiffon trimmed with shining beads and made at midnight by your starved-down sister."[43] Like Washington Gladden, Walter Rauschenbusch, and other social reformers, Markham pressed the middle class to see their complicity in the suffering of the urban poor, to recognize that their choices as consumers were deeply interwoven with issues of economic justice, and to understand that their festive indulgence intensified city sweatshops and tenements. But since, in the gendering of consumption, women were seen as the chief devotees of fashion and novelty, these attacks were always directed far more at women than men. In raining on the Easter parade, critics inevitably aimed their sharpest barbs at the supposed vanity and folly of women.

Issues of social justice were also raised within the Easter parade itself as New York's colossal spectacle became the occasion for turning grievance into ritual. Protesters exploited the carnivalesque or fantastical potentialities within the procession to create a platform for various causes. During the Great Depression, groups of the unemployed, for example, paraded in "battered top hats, lumberjack coats, frayed trousers and broken shoes." If their social commentary was not clear enough, some carried placards or banners: "ONE FIFTH AVENUE GOWN EQUALS A YEAR OF RELIEF." Inverting the fashionableness and capitalistic excesses of New York's Easter procession was often used as a tool for labor and socialist protests. The Easter parade as an embodiment of American complacency and abundance called forth protesters and critics who used it as occasion to question the very values that underpinned this rite of spring. The meanings of the festival were thus never univocal, but contested and challenged, always subject to inversion and antithesis. The very modishness of the Easter parade provided the wedge for critics to open up issues of economic fairness and social justice-the lever by which to turn the whole ritual upside down.[44]

It is important, though, to see that these cultural contests over the meaning of Easter were never simply a matter of polarities: anxious critics versus unabashed celebrants; clear-eyed prophets versus profit-seeking merchants; ascetics versus sybarites. When people faced consumerist tensions in their own celebrations of Easter, they resolved them variously or simply lived with them. For example, the Reverend Morgan Dix, rector at Trinity Episcopal Church in New York, a parish as fond as any of elaborate floral decorations and the display of Easter finery, found himself wondering in 1880 if festal ornamentation had become too extravagant. Was the church turning into "a hot-house"? One writer in 1883 considered Easter floral adornments in the churches attractive and appropriate, but still questioned whether the churches had, "even without intention, become but poor imitations of the theatre in their efforts at exhibition." The writer praised "simple" floral decorations but rejected costly ones which displayed a "foolish pride and a selfish ambition to out-do all others." Some suggested that Easter flowers should be distributed after church to the poor; still others recommended foregoing them and giving the money to charity. Unresolved tensions, ambiguities, and contradictions were evident also in Edwin Markham's career. At once critic of the "multitude of baubles" and "unmeaning trinkets" of the commercialized Easter—the "flimsy cards," the "glass eggs," the "paste chickens," the "plaster rabbits"—Markham turned around and happily sold his verses for sentiments on greeting cards. Not even the sharpest critics were exempt from the tensions that they highlighted.[45]

Some experienced these polarities and sought self-consciously to harmonize them. Reflecting on the Easter parade in 1905, a writer in *Harper's* recognized the tensions that many felt between mere "outward adornment" and the religious meaning of the festival. "I have known," he reported, "women to say that they avoided springing new frocks on an admiring world on Easter Sunday because they did not wish to intrude so trivial a thing as millinery upon a religious festival of such deep significance." But it "seems to me," he said, "that if one gets the right point of view, all the outward tokens of Easter are harmonious with the inner spiritual meanings of it." The flowers and clothes had sacramental importance; they were "outward manifestations" of Easter's religious solemnity and significance. One minister, writing in 1910, summarized both the tensions and their potential resolution:

> One dislikes the element of fashionable frivolity which has come to mark some people's keeping of the Easter feast; but, apart from that, as the city shops and streets break out into fragrant and beautiful bloom, one realizes the close kinship between heavenly and spiritual things and things material and earthly.

All along this was the core concern—how to mediate piety and materiality, flesh and spirit, faith and riches, the inward and the outward in a world of proliferating goods.[46]

Easter, even more than Christmas, disclosed the role of the churches in the rise of consumer-oriented celebrations. The enlarging scope of "devout consumption" was seen in the elaborate displays of Easter flowers and other church decorations. The conflux of consumption and Christianity was nowhere more evident than in the streaming parade of Easter fashions as stylish celebrants poured into and out of the churches. Even as the churches helped facilitate this new Easter, cultivating a modern synthesis of piety and display, some critics demonstrated considerable wariness about where this alliance between Christian celebration and the consumer culture was headed. They foresaw the dim outlines of Irving Berlin's *Easter Parade* or Philip Roth's "schlockified Christianity" in which the holiday became a synonym for shopping and abundance, a ritual display of consumerist plenty. But the critics rarely fathomed the complexity of the drama that so disturbed them. They failed to see the hybridized commingling of faith and fashion, renewal and laughter, piety and improvisation that paraded before them.

NOTES

1. These and subsequent quotations have been transcribed from the movie itself, which is widely available on video cassette. I have also consulted a copy of the screenplay at the Lilly Library, Indiana University.

2. Philip Roth, *Operation Shylock: A Confession* (New York: Simon and Schuster, 1993), 157.

3. *New York Herald*, April 16, 1881, 5. Existing secondary literature focuses more on the holiday's folk beliefs and customs than on historical shifts or modern reconfigurations of the festival. See Theodore Caplow and Margaret Holmes Williamson, "Decoding Middletown's Easter Bunny: A Study in American Iconography," *Semiotica* 32 (1980): 221–32; Nada Gray, *Holidays: Victorian Women Celebrate in Pennsylvania* (University Park: Pennsylvania State University Press, 1983), 54–67;

Elizabeth Clarke Kieffer, "Easter Customs of Lancaster County," *Papers of the Lancaster Historical Society* 52 (1948): 49–68; Venetia Newall, *An Egg at Easter: A Folklore Study* (Bloomington: Indiana University Press, 1971); and Alfred L. Shoemaker, *Eastertide in Pennsylvania: A Folk Cultural Study* (Kutztown: Pennsylvania Folklife Society, 1960). For a notable exception, see James H. Barnett, "The Easter Festival: A Study in Cultural Change," *American Sociological Review* 14 (1949): 62–70.

4. "Easter Flowers," *Harper's New Monthly magazine* 27 (July 1863): 189–94.

5. T.J. Jackson Lears, *No Place of Grace: Antimodernism and the Transformation of American Culture, 1880–1920* (New York: Pantheon, 1981), 183–215; Ernest Geldart, ed., *The Art of Garnishing Churches at Christmas and Other Times: A Manual*

of Directions (London: Cox Sons, Buckley and Co., 1882), 12. See also William A. Barrett, *Flowers and Festivals: Or, Directions for the Floral Decoration of Churches* (New York: Pott and Amery, 1868).

6. Edward L. Cutts, *An Essay on the Christmas Decoration of Churches: With an Appendix on the Mode of Decorating Churches for Easter, the School Feast, Harvest Thanksgiving, Confirmation, a Marriage, and a Baptism*, 3rd ed. (London: Horace Cox, 1868), 12; Geldart, ed., *Art of Garnishing Churches*, 11.

7. Ernest R. Suffling, *Church Festival Decorations: Being Full Directions for Garnishing Churches for Christmas, Easter, Whitsuntide, and Harvest*, 2d ed. (New York: Charles Scribner's Sons, 1907), 74.

8. Henry Dana Ward, "Diary," April 8, 1855; March 23, 1856; April 12, 1857, New York Public Library, Rare Books and Manuscripts.

9. On this invasion, see William R. Leach, "Transformations in a Culture of Consumption: Women and Department Stores, 1890–1925," *Journal of American History* 71 (1984):325.

10. Unidentified Author, "Dairy, 1872–1873," April 13, 1873, New York Historical Society, Manuscripts.

11. Sarah Anne Todd, "Diary," April 21, 1867, New York Historical Society, Manuscripts; Elizabeth W. Merchant, "Diary," March 25, 1883; April 25, 1886; April 10, 1887, New York Public Library, Rare Books and Manuscripts; Mrs. George Richards, "Diary," April 1, 1888, New York Historical Society, Manuscripts. For the initiative of women in church decoration, see, for example, "How Some Churches Looked Last Easter," *Ladies' Home Journal* 21 (March 1904):32–33.

12. Geldart, ed., *Art of Garnishing Churches*, 12, 44; *New York Sun*, April 1, 1861, 2; Suffling, *Church Festival Decorations*, 85–86.

13. "Easter Flowers," 190; Suffling, *Church Festival Decorations*, 2. On this domestic and sentimental piety, see Ann Douglas, *The Feminization of American Culture* (New York: Knopf, 1977); and Colleen McDannell, *The Christian Home in Victorian America*, 1840–1900 (Bloomington: Indiana University Press, 1986).

14. "Easter Flowers," 190. On Phelps's novel and "the new domestic heaven," see Douglas, *Feminization of American Culture*, 214–15, 223–26.

15. Ernest Geldart, *A Manual of Church Decoration and Symbolism Containing Directions and Advice to Those Who Desire Worthily to Deck the Church at the Various Seasons of the Year* (Oxford: A. R. Mowbray and Co., 1899), 17–18; *New York Herald*,

April 16, 1881, 5; Thorstein Veblen, *The Theory of the Leisure Class: An Economic Study of Institutions* (New York: Macmillan, 1899; repr., New York: Random House, 1934), 119, 307–9. On the narrow limits of Veblen's model, see T.J. Jackson Lears, "Beyond Veblen: Rethinking Consumer Culture in America," in *Consuming Visions: Accumulation and Display of Goods in America, 1880–1920*, ed. Simon J. Bronner (New York: Norton, 1989), 73–97.

16. *New York Herald*, April 21, 1867, 4; April 14, 1873, 4; Suffling, *Church Festival Decorations, 32–33*; *New York Sun*, April 22, 1878, 3. Here I am playing off Lears's argument in *No Place of Grace* about the antimodernism in Anglo-Catholic aesthetics. As Lears suggests, this antimodernist, medievalist stance often had modernist, therapeutic consequences. This was at no point clearer than in the Victorian elaboration of the art of church decoration.

17. Geldart, ed., *Art of Garnishing Churches*, 12, 19; William Leach, "Strategists of Display and the Production of Desire," in Bronner, ed., *Consuming Visions*, 104. Leach's conclusions about this "display aesthetic" are offered in expanded and far more critical form in his *Land of Desire: Merchants, Power, and the Rise of a New American Culture* (New York: Pantheon, 1993).

18. *Dry Goods Chronicle*, March 26, 1898, 19; John Wanamaker (Philadelphia), "Easter, 1893," Dry Goods Scrapbook, Bella Landauer Collection, New York Historical Society.

19. "News from the Cities," *American Advertiser* 4 (April 1890): unpag. For other examples, see [Charles A. Tracy], *The Art of Decorating Show Windows and Interiors*, 3rd ed. (Chicago: Merchants Record Co., 1906), 199–206, 314–15; Alfred G. Bauer, *The Art of Window Dressing for Grocers* (Chicago:Sprague, Warner & Company, [1902]), 30–32; "Robinson Window," *Greeting Card* 8 (March 1936): 28; "Lilies, a Cross, Lighted Candles," *Greeting Card* 5 (March 1933): 5; and "The Cross Was Illuminated," *Greeting Card* 5 (March 1933), 8.

20. Robert A. Childs, "*The Thoughful Thinker*" *on Window-Dressing and Advertising Together with Wholesome Advice for Those in Business and Those about to Start* (Syracuse: United States Window Trimmers' Bureau, [1896], 21; Douglas, *Feminization of American Culture*, 225.

21. Tracy, *Art of Decorating Show Windows*, 315. For Wanamaker's Easter displays, see box 11B, folders 10 and 23; box 12D, folder 2, Wanamaker Collection, Historical Society of Pennsylvania, Philadelphia. On the paintings of Michael de Munkacsy, see box 55, folder 14; box 63, folder 3, Wanamaker Collection. See also Leach, *Land of*

Desire, 213–14, 222–23.

22. L. Frank Baum, *The Art of Decorating Dry Goods Windows and Interiors* (Chicago: Tile Show Window Publishing Co., 1900), unpag. intro., 181, 185. On Baum, see Leach, *Land of Desire*, 55–61.

23. This is R. Laurence Moore's conclusion about the varied blendings of Protestant values with commercial amusements and popular literature in the first half of the nineteenth century. See Moore, "Religion, Secularization, and the Shaping of the Culture Industry in Antebellum American," *American Quarterly* 41 (1989):236

24. George D. Herron, *The Message of Jesus to Men of Wealth* (New York: Fleming H. Revell Co., 1891), 29–31. The "one undivided Kingdom of God" is a phrase from Washington Gladden, *Things New and Old in Discourses of Christian Truth and Life* (Columbus, Ohio: A. H. Smythe, 1883), 260. On the "festive marketplace," see the classic evocation in Mikhail Bakhtin, *Rabelais and His World*, trans. Helene Iswolsky (Cambridge, Mass.: M.I.T. Press, 1968), 19, 92. For Wanamaker as the consummate sacralizer of prosperity, see "The Power of Consecrated Wealth: John Wanamaker—What the Rich Can Do," *Christian Recorder*, March 15, 1877, 4–5. On liberal Protestantism and the consumer ethos, see Susan Curtis, *A Consuming Faith: The Social Gospel and Modern American Culture* (Baltimore: Johns Hopkins University Press, 1991).

25. For the Watts hymn within the context of a Victorian Easter service, see Jennie M. Bingham, *Easter Voices* (New York: Hunt and Eaton, 1891), 2. On the consumer culture as a dream world, see Rosalind H. Williams, *Dream Worlds: Mass Consumption in Late Nineteenth-Century France* (Berkeley: University of California Press, 1982). On the new therapeutic gospel, see especially T.J. Jackson Lears, "From Salvation to Self-Realization: Advertising and the Therapeutic Roots of the Consumer Culture, 1880–1930," in *The Culture of Consumption: Critical Essays in American History, 1880–1980*, ed. Richard Wightman Fox and T.J. Jackson Lears (New York: Pantheon, 1983), 3–38. On the wider absorption of religious symbols into modern advertising, see Roland Marchand, *Advertising the American Dream: Making Way for Modernity, 1920–1940* (Berkeley: University of California Press, 1985), 264–84.

27. For the Irish adage, see Francis X. Weiser, *The Easter Book* (New York: Harcourt, Brace and Co., 1954), 159–61. For Poor Robin's maxim, see John Brand and W. Carew Hazlitt, *Popular Antiquities of Great Britain: Comprising Notices of the Moveable and Immoveable Feasts, Customs, Superstitions and Amusements Past and Present*, 3 vols. (London: John Russell Smith, 1870), 1:93. On Easter clothes, see A. R. Wright, *British Calendar Customs: England*, 3 vols., ed. T. E. Lones (London: The Folk-Lore Society, 1936–1940), 1:101; and Shoemaker, *Eastertide in Pennsylvania*, 24. For the *Herald's* version of the proverb, see *New York Herald*, April 8, 1855, 1.

28. *New York Herald*, April 14, 1873, 4; April 14, 1879, 8.

29. *New York Herald*, April 26, 1886, 8; *New York Times*, April 7, 1890, 2.

30. Ralph M. Hower, *History of Macy's of New York, 1858–1919: Chapters in the Evolution of the Department Store* (Cambridge: Harvard University Press, 1943), 170, 451n.37; *New York Sun*, April 17, 1878, 4; April 16, 1878, 4. It is important to underline that my analysis of Easter's commercialization is confined to the United States. It is likely that merchants in Paris or London, where the growth of the consumer culture was somewhat ahead of the United States and where Easter traditions were far less encumbered by low-church Protestant sentiments, were significantly in advance of their American counterparts. For a hint of this, see Neil McKendrick, John Brewer, and J. H. Plumb, *The Birth of a Consumer Society: The Commercialization of Eighteenth-Century England* (Bloomington: Indiana University Press, 1982), 74.

31. *Dry Goods Economist*, March 24, 1894, 36, 37; *Dry Goods Chronicle*, March 26, 1898, 19; *Dry Goods Economist* March 18, 1893, 55.

32. Elizabeth Schuneman Orr, "Diary," April 9, 1871, New York Public Library, Rare Books and Manuscripts.

33. Merchant, "Diary," April 16, 1881; April 21, 1867; Clara Burton Pardee, "Diary," March 25, 1883, New York Historical Society, Manuscripts; Majorie R. Reynolds, "Diary," April 7, 1912, New York Historical Society, Manuscripts; "New York Millinery," *Millinery Trade Review* 7 (April 1882):56.

34. *New York Herald*, April 7, 1890, 3.

35. Anne O'Hare McCormick, quoted in "The Easter Parade," *Time*, April 25, 1949, 19.

36. Rufus Jarman, "Manhattan's Easter Madness," *Saturday Evening Post*, April 9, 1955, 103.

37. Ibid. On Easter conviviality and costuming, see Shoemaker, *Eastertide in Pennsylvania*, 43–45; and Bakhtin, *Rabelais and His World*, 78–79, 146. For the woman's outlandish hat, see *New York Times*, April 6, 1953, 14.

38. Anna Ben Yusuf, *The Art of Millinery* (New York: Millinery Trade Publishing Co., 1909), 227. On the male domination of nineteenth-century parades and public ceremonies as well as the efforts of

women to gain a foothold in these rituals, see Mary P. Ryan, *Women in Public: Between Banners and Ballots, 1825–1880* (Baltimore: Johns Hopkins University Press, 1990), 19–57; and Susan G. Davis, *Parades and Power: Street Theatre in Nineteenth-Century Philadelphia* (Philadelphia: Temple University Press, 1985; repr., Berkeley: University of California Press, 1986), 47, 149, 157, 190.

39. *New York Herald*, April 13, 1925, 3. For representative accounts of Easter parades in the resorts, see *New York Times*, April 16, 1906, 9; John Steevens, "The Charm of Eastertide at Atlantic City," *Harper's Weekly*, April 18, 1908, 20–22; *New York Times*, April 20, 1908, 3; *New York Herald*, April 8, 1912, 4; and *New York Times*, April 22, 1935, 11. On Coney Island and Atlantic City, see respectively, John F. Kasson, *Amusing the Million: Coney Island at the Turn of the Century* (New York: Hill and Wang, 1978); and Charles E. Funnell, *By the Beautiful Sea: The Rise and High Times of That Great American Resort* (New York: Alfred A. Knopf, 1975), esp. 46, 89. Barnett noted in 1949 of New York's Easter parade: "The pattern appears to be diffusing as an *American* practice." See Barnett, "Easter Festival," 69.

40. *New York Times*, April 23, 1946, 25; April 19, 1930, 9; April 2, 1956, 14; Raymond Kresensky, "Easter Parade," *Christian Century*, March 23, 1932, 384–85; Dorothy Lee Richardson, "Easter Sunday, Fifth Avenue," *Christian Century*, April 28, 1954, 511.

41. Edwin Markham, "The Blight on the Easter Lilies," *Cosmopolitan* 42 (April 1907): 667–68. Markham's essays on child labor were collected in *Children in Bondage* (New York: Hearst's International, 1914).

42. "Blight on the Easter Lilies," 670–73.

43. Ibid., 669.

44. *New York Times*, March 28, 1932, 1; Jarman, "Manhattan's Easter Madness," 104.

45. *New York Times*, March 28, 1880, 2; "Proper Observance of Easter," *Concert Quarterly* 1 (March 1883): 1; *New York Times*, March 18, 1894, 18; Markham, "Blight on the Easter Lilies," 668; Louis Filler, *The Unknown Edwin Markham: His Mystery and Its Significance* (Yellow Springs, Ohio: Antioch Press, 1966), 140.

46. E. S. Martin, "New York's Easter Parade," *Harper's Weekly*, April 22, 1905, 567; William C. Doane, *The Book of Easter* (New York: Macmillan, 1910), vii.

THE DEBATE OVER MIXED SEATING IN THE AMERICAN SYNAGOGUE

Jonathan D. Sarna

A new generation of scholars is employing innovative methods to uncover the "inner" history of American Jews. Until recently, American historians have either paid little attention to Jewish religious history or focused their attention on the "external" history of Jewish interaction with American society. The new scholarship, in contrast, enters into the world of the synagogue and the experiences of ordinary people in order to tell the story of American Jewish religious life.

In the following essay, Jonathan Sarna demonstrates that throughout most of American Jewish religious history debates over separate (male and female) seating and mixed (family) seating were visible expressions of a host of more deep-seated differences over Jewish social and religious values. The issue first emerged in the Reform congregations of the nineteenth century, divided Reform from Orthodox in the early twentieth century, and remains a division between Conservatism and Orthodoxy in the contemporary period. Those congregations that advocated the end to separate seating of women in the gallery and men on the ground floor justified this change in traditional practices on the multiple grounds of family unity, women's equality, improved decorum, modernization, and keeping young people involved in religious life. For opponents the same changes signaled assimilation, Christianization, violation of Jewish law, and the abandonment of tradition. By closely attending to this seemingly mundane issue, Sarna provides insight into both the changing American synagogue and the changing relationship between Jewish religious life and the surrounding American society.

Adapted by permission from Jonathan D. Sarna, "The Debate Over Mixed Seating in the American Synagogue," in Jack Wertheimer, ed., *The American Synagogue: A Sanctuary Transformed* (New York: Cambridge University Press, 1987), 363–393.

14

THE DEBATE OVER MIXED SEATING IN THE AMERICAN SYNAGOGUE

Jonathan D. Sarna

"PUES HAVE NEVER YET FOUND AN HISTORIAN," John M. Neale complained, when he undertook to survey the subject of church seating for the Cambridge Camden Society in 1842.[1] To a large extent, the same situation prevails today in connection with "pues" in the American synagogue. Although it is common knowledge that American synagogue seating patterns have changed greatly over time—sometimes following acrimonious, even violent disputes—the subject as a whole remains unstudied, seemingly too arcane for historians to bother with.[2] Seating patterns, however, actually reflect down-to-earth social realities, and are richly deserving of study. Behind wearisome debates over how sanctuary seats should be arranged and allocated lie fundamental disagreements over the kinds of social and religious values that the synagogue should project and the relationship between the synagogue and the larger society that surrounds it. As we shall see, where people sit reveals much about what they believe.

The necessarily limited study of seating patterns that follows focuses only on the most important and controversial seating innovation in the American synagogue: mixed (family) seating. Other innovations—seats that no longer face east,[3] pulpits moved from center to front,[4] free (unassigned) seating, closed-off pew ends, and the like—require separate treatment. As we shall see, mixed seating is a ramified and multifaceted issue that clearly reflects the impact of American values on synagogue life, for it pits family unity, sexual equality, and modernity against the accepted Jewish legal (*halachic*) practice of sexual separation in prayer. Discussions surrounding this innovation form part of a larger Jewish debate over Americanization, and should really be viewed in the overall context of ritual reform.[5] By itself, however, the seating issue has taken on a symbolic quality. It serves not only as a focus on the changing nature of the American synagogue, but also on the changing nature of the larger society—American and Jewish—in which the synagogue is set.

I

The extent to which men and women were separated in the synagogues of antiquity has been disputed. There can, however, be no doubt that separate seating of one form or another characterized Jewish worship from early medieval times onward. The idea that men and women should worship apart prevailed in many Christian churches no less than in synagogues—although the latter more frequently demanded a physical barrier between the sexes—and separate seating remained standard practice in much of Europe down to the contemporary period.

In 1845, the Reform Congregation of Berlin abolished the separate women's gallery in the synagogue and the traditional *mechitsa* (partition) between men and women. Although mandating "the seating of men and women on the same floor," the congregation continued to preserve the principle of sexual separation during worship: men occupied the left side of the auditorium, women the right.[7] As late as the early twentieth century, the Hamburg temple, the cradle of German Reform, refused a donation of one million marks from the American banker Henry Budge, who had returned to settle in Hamburg following his father's death, because the sum was conditional on "men and women sitting together" in the new edifice. To Dr. Jacob Sonderling, then rabbi of the temple, that idea was shocking. "In the Hamburg Temple," he reports, "men and women remained separated up to the last moment."[8]

Mixed synagogue seating, or to use the more common nineteenth-century term, "family seating," first developed in Reform Jewish circles in the United States. Rabbi Isaac Mayer Wise, the leading nineteenth-century exponent of American Reform, took personal credit for this particular innovation, claiming to have introduced Jewry's first family pews "in 1850 [sic]...in the temple of Albany."[9] Wise, however, did not *invent* family seating. To understand what he did do, and why, requires first a brief digression into the history of church seating in America.

The earliest New England churches and meetinghouses, following the then-traditional British practice, separated men, women, and children in worship. Men and women sat on opposite sides of a central aisle, and children, also divided according to sex, sat in the back or upstairs. As John Demos points out, "Family relationships were effectively discounted, or at least submerged, in this particular context...the family community and the religious community were fundamentally distinct."[10] Churches sought to underscore the role of the individual as the basic unit in matters of faith and prayer. "God's minister," according to Patricia Tracy, "superseded the role of any other agent; each heart was supposed to be unprotected against the thunder of the Gospel."[11]

Beginning in the mid-eighteenth century, church seating patterns began to change. Families at first won permission to sit together in church on a voluntary basis, and subsequently family seating became the norm.[12] Outside of New England, the history of church seating has not been written, and the pattern may have been more diverse. Missouri Synod Lutherans, for example, maintained separate seating in their churches (which were heavily influenced by German practice) down to at least the end of the nineteenth century. For the most part, however, the family pew won rapid and widespread acceptance in church circles, and Americans, forgetting that there were other possibilities, came to believe that "the family that prays together stays together."[13]

The overwhelming move to adopt family seating stems from great changes in the history of the family that have been amply detailed elsewhere. The growing differentiation between home and work saw families take on a new symbolic role, termed by Demos "the family as refuge," the image being that of family members clustering together for protection against the evils of anomic industrial society. Fear of family breakdown naturally led to a host of new rituals and forms (including the cult of domesticity) designed to "strengthen the family" against the menacing forces threatening to rend it asunder.[14] The family pew was one of these new forms. By raising the family's status over that of the single individual, and by symbolically linking family values to religious values, the family pew demonstrated, as separate seating did not, that the church stood behind the family structure one hundred percent. Family burial plots,[15] which came into vogue at about the same time as family pews, carried the same message of family togetherness on into eternity.

Whether Rabbi Isaac Mayer Wise appreciated the symbolic significance of family pews when he introduced them in 1851 cannot be known. His biographer waxes enthusiastic about how the new system, "enable[d] families to worship together and to have the warmth of togetherness…in the deepest and most sacred of moments,"[16] but Wise himself never said anything of the sort. Instead, as he related the story, family pews became a feature of Congregation Anshe Emeth in Albany almost as an afterthought.

Wise had first come to Albany in 1846 to serve as the rabbi of Congregation Beth El. He was a new immigrant, twenty-seven years old, and thoroughly inexperienced, but he dreamed great dreams and displayed boundless energy. Before long he introduced a series of reforms. Like most early reforms, Wise's aimed mainly at improving decorum and effecting changes in the liturgy. He abolished the sale of synagogue honors, forbade standing during the Torah reading, eliminated various medieval liturgical poems (*piyyutim*), introduced German and English hymns into the service, initiated the confirmation ceremony, and organized a mixed choir.[17] But his effort to effect Berlin-style changes in synagogue seating to make room for the choir ("I suggested to apportion the seats anew, and to set apart half of the floor, as well as of the gallery, for the women") raised a howl of protest and got nowhere, and even within the mixed choir "the girls objected strenuously to sitting among the men."[18] Wise never even raised the issue of family pews.

A series of tangled disputes between Wise and his president, Louis Spanier, led to Wise's dismissal from Beth El Congregation two days before Rosh Hashanah in 1850. Wise considered his firing illegal, and on the advice of counsel took his place as usual on New Year's morning. As he made ready to remove the Torah from the ark, Louis Spanier took the law into his own hands and lashed out at him. The assault knocked off the rabbi's hat, wounded his pride, and precipitated a general melee that the police had to be called out to quell. The next day, Wise held Rosh Hashanah services at his home. The day after that, he was invited to a meeting consisting of "prominent members of the congregation together with a large number of young men,"[19] where a new congregation, Anshe Emeth, came into being with Wise as its rabbi. Anshe Emeth dedicated its new building, formerly a Baptist church, on October 3, 1851. Wise served the congregation there until 1854, when he journeyed west to Cincinnati to assume his life-long position at Bene Yeshurun.[20]

Anshe Emeth is usually credited with being the first synagogue with mixed seating in the world. As Wise relates the circumstances in his *Reminiscences*: "American Judaism is indebted to the Anshe Emeth congregation of Albany for one important reform; viz., family pews. The church-building had family pews, and the congregation resolved unanimously to retain them. This innovation was initiated later in all American reform congregations. This was an important step, which was severely condemned at the time."[21] According to this account, and it is the only substantial one we have, family pews entered Judaism for pragmatic reasons: Members voted to make do with the (costly) building they had bought, and not to expend additional funds to convert its American-style family pews into a more traditional Jewish seating arrangement. Had members considered this a particularly momentous action on their part, they would surely have called attention to it in their consecration proceedings, and Isaac Mayer Wise would have said something on the subject in his dedication sermon. Nothing at all was said, however, and only the sharp eye of Isaac Leeser detected in the description of the synagogue "another reform of the Doctor's, one by no means to be commended." Far from being "severely condemned at the time," the reform seems otherwise to have been uniformly ignored.[22] Pragmatic reforms aimed at improving decorum and bringing the synagogue more closely into harmony with the prevailing American Christian pattern were nothing new, even if this particular reform had not previously been introduced. Nor was there any organized opposition to Wise within his own congregation to generate adverse publicity against him. The "loud remonstrations of all orthodoxy," which Wise purported to remember, actually came later. Anshe Emeth's family pews met with scarcely a murmur.[23]

The introduction of family seating at New York's Temple Emanu-El in 1854 attracted no more notice. When Emanu-El was established in 1845, the very year of the Berlin seating reform, its sanctuary provided for separate seating, women behind the men, in one room. The move to family pews took place, as at Anshe Emeth, when the congregation moved into a new building (the Twelfth Street Synagogue), a former church, and there found enclosed family pews already set up.[24] Although they had no known ideological basis for introducing mixed seating, members presumably found the thought of families worshipping together as a unit in the American fashion far more appealing than the thought of introducing separate seating where none had been before. Convenience triumphed, and justifications followed.

II

Ideological defenses of mixed seating, when they came, concentrated not on family worship, an American innovation, but rather on an older, European, and more widely contended Jewish issue of the day: women's status in the synagogue. Rabbis versed in the polemics of Reform Judaism in Germany felt more at home in this debate, having argued about the status of women at the rabbinical conferences in Frankfurt (1845) and Breslau (1846),[25] and they viewed the principle involved as a much more important one than mixed seating, which they had never before seen, and which seemed to them at the time to be just another case of following in the ways of the Gentiles.[26] As a result, the same basic arguments that justified the abolition of the gallery and "separate but equal" seating in Germany came to be used to justify mixed family seating in the United States. Critical differences between these two new seating patterns proved less important in the long run than the fact that Jews and non-Jews on both sides of the Atlantic came to view the debate over the synagogue seating of women as a debate over the synagogue status of women, and they followed it with interest.

The status of women in the synagogue, and in Judaism in general, attracted considerable attention in early America, much of it negative. As early as 1744, Dr. Alexander Hamilton, a Scottish-born physician, compared the women's gallery in New York's Shearith Israel to a "hen coop." Dr. Philip Milledoler, later president of Rutgers, told a meeting of the American Society for Evangelizing the Jews in 1816 that the "female character" among Jews "holds a station far inferior to that which it was intended to occupy by the God of nature." *The Western Monthly Review*, describing "The Present State of the Jews" in 1829, found that "the Jewess of these days is treated as an inferior being." That was putting it mildly, according to James Gordon Bennett, editor of the *New York Herald*. After visiting Shearith Israel, on Yom

Kippur 1836, he attacked the status of women in Judaism as one of the most lamentable features in the entire religion—and one that Jesus improved:

> The great error of the Jews is the degradation in which their religion places woman. In the services of religion, she is separated and huddled into a gallery like beautiful crockery ware, while the men perform the ceremonies below. It was the author of Christianity that brought her out of this Egyptian bondage, and put her on an equality with the other sex in civil and religious rites. Hence, have sprung all the civilization, refinement, intelligence and genius of Europe. The Hebrew prays "I thank thee, Lord, that I am not a woman"—the Christian—"I praise thee, Lord, that I and my wife are immortal."[27]

There were, of course, other, more positive images of American Jewish women available, including not a few works of apologetica penned by Jews themselves. These explained the traditional rationale behind Jewish laws on women and enumerated long lists of Jewish women "heroes" from the biblical period onward.[28] Literary treatments of Jewish women also offered occasional positive images, usually of noble, alluringly exotic, Semitic maidens, who functioned more as "erotic dream figures," manifestations of romantic ideals, than anything else.[29] Still, to many Americans, Judaism's "mistreatment" of "the weaker sex" was an established fact: evidence of Judaism's "Oriental" and "primitive" character, in stark contrast to "modern" Christianity. By visibly changing the position of women in the synagogue, Jews sought to undermine this fact, to buttress their claims to modernity, and to fend off the embarrassing Christian charges that they had otherwise to face. In abolishing the women's gallery, synagogue leaders thus sought to elevate not only the status of women in Judaism, but also the status of Judaism itself.

The first Jewish leader in America to stress the relationship between changes in synagogue seating and changes in the status of Jewish women seems to have been Rabbi David Einhorn, who immigrated to America in 1855 and rapidly came to dominate the radical wing of the nascent Reform Movement. Einhorn had agitated for "the complete religious equality of woman with man" at the 1846 Breslau Reform Rabbinical Conference, where he declared it his "mission to make legal declaration of the equal religious obligation and justification of women in as far as this is possible."[30] Within the first few years of his tenure at Temple Har Sinai in Baltimore, he endeavored to put this principle into effect, abolishing what he called the "gallery-cage," and bringing women down to share the same floor as men, though apparently not, at first, the same pews.[31]

In discussing the women's issue in *Sinai*, his German-language magazine, Einhorn characteristically stressed the higher "principle" behind his action, in this case abandonment of what he considered to be misguided Oriental rabbinic strictures against women, and a return to what he identified as the more proper biblical lesson of sexual equality. Gallery seating, he sneered, originally stemmed from unseemly acts of levity that marred the celebration of *simchat bet hashoeva* (the water-drawing festival) in temple times. Since staid Occidental modes of worship held forth no similar dangers to modesty, the gallery could be dispensed with. Although clearly less comfortable with the proprieties of completely mixed seating, Einhorn nevertheless allowed that when a husband sat next to his wife and children nothing untoward could be expected. The essential principle, he repeated, was "religious equalization of women." Everything else connected with seating reforms was of secondary importance.[32]

Einhorn's rationale for mixed seating won wide acceptance, perhaps because it offered a specifically Jewish as well as ethically motivated reason to adopt an American practice, and also perhaps because it made a virtue out of what many were coming to see as a practical necessity. Whatever the case, family seating spread. Chicago Sinai, ideologically linked to its Baltimore namesake, never had a gallery and wrote into its basic propositions (1859) that "in the public worship of the congregation, there should be no discrimination made in favor of the male and against female worshippers."[33] A year later, in San Francisco, Rabbi Elkan Cohn, newly appointed to Congregation Emanu-El, introduced mixed seating as one of his first acts, complaining, as he did so, that Judaism "excluded women from so many privileges to which they are justly entitled."[34] The next fifteen years saw mixed seating develop at a rapid pace. In some cases, proponents exclusively stressed women's inequality and the bad image it projected. Rabbi Raphael D'C Lewin, for example, denounced separate seating as "a relic of the Dark Ages."[35] More frequently, pragmatic considerations—purchase of a new synagogue building (perhaps a church containing pews), the need to use the gallery for a choir, the inability of women in the gallery to hear what was going on, or the "undignified" appearance presented by a synagogue where the gallery was far more crowded than the main sanctuary below—worked hand in hand with ideological factors in bringing about reform.[36] In at least one case, Sherith Israel in San Francisco, mixed seating came about because, as the minutes report, "the existing custom of separating the sexes during Divine Services is a cause of annoyance and disturbance in our devotion."[37] Whatever the real reason, however, most synagogues eventually came to justify mixed seating on the basis of women's equality. Isaac Mayer Wise led the way, quite misleadingly retrojecting the women's issue back into his Albany reforms:

> The Jewish woman had been treated almost as a stranger in the synagogue; she had been kept at a distance, and had been excluded from all participation in the life of the congregation, had been relegated to the gallery, even as was the negro in Southern churches. The emancipation of the Jewish woman was begun in Albany, by having the Jewish girls sing in the choir, and this beginning was reinforced by the introduction of family pews.[38]

Although mixed seating looked like an imitation of gentile practices, no proponent of Reform would admit that it was. In seeking to modernize Judaism, reform leaders always insisted that they were strengthening the faith and preventing defections to Christianity; assimilation was as much anathema to them as to their opponents. Knowing how sensitive they were on this issue, critics of mixed seating regularly coupled their references to the innovation with terms like "Gentile fashion," "semblance of a church," and "Christian."[39] They knew that such charges struck home.

Otherwise, traditionalists generally contended themselves to defend their time-honored practices on the basis of Jewish legal precedents and religious prooftexts, chief among them the Talmudic discussion of temple seating practices in Tractate Sukkah 51b. "This is the direct and forcible language of the Talmud," the learned Laemmlein Buttenwieser insisted after quoting his source at length, "and on it we are content to rest our case without further argument."[40]

Proponents of change naturally put forward different interpretations of these texts.[41] Even those most eager to introduce reforms still continued to seek the legitimacy that textural roots provided. The never-ending textual arguments, however, are less important than the fact that the two sides in the seating controversy unwittingly talked past one another. Proponents defended mixed seating as a test of Judaism's ability to meet modernity's challenge to Jewish survival. Opponents defended traditional seating as a test of Judaism's ability to parry modernity's threats to Jewish distinctiveness. Although the two sides seemed only to be debating about laws and practices, the words they used and the passions behind them indicate that the central arguments really reached deeper. Ultimately, they touched on the most basic values—traditional ones and Enlightenment ones—that each side held dear.

III

One of the most historically interesting clashes over mixed seating took place at the venerable B'nai Jeshurun synagogue in New York City in 1875. The dispute eventually reached civil court—one of comparatively few such cases to do so—and involved many of the leading rabbis of the period. It serves as a valuable case study of the whole mixed seating issue as it developed in, disrupted, and ultimately split an individual congregation.

B'nai Jeshurun was the second synagogue founded in New York City (1825) and has proudly boasted of being New York's "oldest Ashkenazic Congregation." From its founding, it followed the path of traditional Judaism, maintaining close ties with the Great Synagogue in London. It grew steadily, various schisms notwithstanding. From 1825 to 1850, its membership increased fivefold to nearly 150, and during the same period its financial condition strengthened appreciably. An even more dynamic period of growth began in 1849 when it elected Rabbi Morris J. Raphall, then rabbi and preacher of England's Birmingham Hebrew Congregation, to serve as its "Lecturer and Preacher." Raphall's salary reputedly was "the most munificent salary received by any preacher in the country"—an investment that handsomely paid off. As America's first "glamour rabbi," he attracted large numbers of new members to the congregation and won B'nai Jeshurun a position of high regard both in the Jewish and the non-Jewish communities. This position was enhanced in 1851 when the congregation dedicated its magnificent new edifice, the Greene Street Synagogue.[42]

As is so often the case, the new situation at B'nai Jeshurun created pressures for ritual reform. Decorum became the watchword as trustees worried more and more about the image projected by the congregation to the world at large. In 1851 and again in 1856 the interests of decorum ("that high standing of respectability which the world has a right to expect and which should correspond with this noble edifice") motivated changes in the distribution of synagogue honors, and in the method of announcing synagogue offerings.[43] Subsequent changes affected the saying of the priestly blessing, henceforward to be repeated "without singing and chanting," and of the Mourner's Kaddish, which mourners were instructed to recite "in unison with the Reader." The institution of a choir, and the introduction of special attire for the cantor and rabbi underlined B'nai Jeshurun's transformation into a showpiece synagogue with a performance-oriented ritual: a move that the congregation's new membership, new building, and new community status had made inevitable.[44]

Once begun, the pressure for reform at B'nai Jeshurun did not so easily abate. The needs and desires of members, coupled with contemporary trends favoring liberalization in synagogues and churches, motivated board members to initiate discussion of seating changes (abolition of the gallery and mixed pews) as early as 1862. At the rabbi's urging, they were not followed up. In 1868, following the death of Rabbi Raphall, the trustees formed a joint committee on ritual, charged with investigating a wide range of possible "improvements" to the synagogue service, alterations in the "internal arrangement of the Synagogue," being only one of them. As a first step, the reader's desk was moved from its traditional place at the center of the synagogue to the front, a move that three years earlier had been voted down. In 1869, the board introduced a confirmation ceremony. Some sixty-three other changes also came up for consideration that year: most dealt with abolition of liturgical poems (*piyyutim*); a few went further, suggesting such things as doing away with the priestly blessing and ending the traditional calling up of seven men to the Torah. After consultation with their new rabbi, Dr. Henry Vidaver, and with Rabbi Jonas Bondi, editor of the *Hebrew Leader*, both of whom evaluated the proposed changes from the perspective of Jewish law, many of these changes, though not the most radical ones, were put into effect.[45]

In November 1871, the congregation took another step along the road to reform. It voted fifty to thirty-one to include women in the choir. Although sanctioned by Rabbi Vidaver, and widely practiced elsewhere, this move by one of America's oldest and most distinguished congregations generated considerable controversy. In spite of Rabbi Vidaver's insistence that Jewish law had not been breached, everyone realized that a mixed choir involved a more substantial departure from Jewish tradition than had previously been allowed. The choir was subsequently abandoned, "as it was found impracticable without an organ," but further steps in the direction of reform seemed inevitable.[46] Nobody should have been surprised when, on November 8, 1874, four months after Rabbi Vidaver had left the congregation for a more lucrative position in San Francisco, B'nai Jeshurun's members met to consider "the propriety of altering the present seats into Pews and also to add an Organ to the Choir.[47]

In reviewing the many changes that took place during this trying period in B'nai Jeshurun's history, Rabbi Israel Goldstein stressed the uncertainty of the congregation, the inner struggle between competing values that pulled members simultaneously in two directions, toward tradition and toward change: "The Congregation's decisions were made and unmade, amidst turbulent sentiment. Many of the members threatened to resign if the changes were not introduced. Others threatened to resign if the changes were introduced. Questions were repeatedly resubmitted and reconsidered, and the sentiment shifted as each faction in turn gained ascendancy."[48]

Even those most favoring change in congregational ritual aimed to stay within the bounds of "our established [Jewish] laws." They wanted the bountiful benefits that they thought reform would bring without sacrificing the comforting legitimacy that they knew tradition provided. Ideally, they somehow sought to be both Orthodox and modern at the same time, enjoying the benefits of both positions, and satisfying everyone.[49]

Although all members of B'nai Jeshurun may have prayed for this Utopia, younger and newer members nevertheless spearheaded the movement for change. One wishes that available evidence on this point were more substantial. Still, of the identifiable members who signed the petition calling for a special congregational meeting to consider instituting family pews and an organ, all five were members of ten years' standing or less (two additional signers cannot be identified). The fact that Joseph Aden, a member of B'nai Jeshurun, laid special stress on his being sixty-two years old when he declared himself in favor of the proposed changes—as if most reformers were far younger—offers additional corroborative evidence.[50]

Reforms in the 1870s all over the American Jewish community stemmed, at least in part, from fears that the young, American-born children of Central European immigrants were being lost to Judaism. Many Jews worried for their faith's future survival. Some foresaw a merger with Unitarianism. Young William Rosenblatt, in an article entitled "The Jews: What They Are Coming To" printed in the widely read *Galaxy*, openly predicted impending doom: "Of that ancient people only the history of their perils and their sufferings will remain."[51] Although various Jews resigned themselves to this "inevitable" fate, others looked to reforms that promised to win the young people back. When, as at B'nai Jeshurun, younger members took upon themselves the initiative to bring about change, their elders usually agreed to support them. They feared, as B'nai Jeshurun's president, Moses Strasburger, candidly admitted, that without changes the congregation would "become disbanded."[52]

Support for reform was by no means unanimous at B'nai Jeshurun: at the tumultuous special meeting called to discuss the question, fifty-five members voted for seating changes and installation of an organ, thirty members remained opposed. The majority viewed the changes they sanctioned as permissible and necessary next steps in the long process of internal transformation that had been going on for a quarter of a century. They believed that by modernizing B'nai Jeshurun—bringing it into harmony "with the requirements of modern taste and culture"—they were saving it for the next generation.[53] The minority, which had grown increasingly restive as the pace of reform quickened, viewed the same changes as confirming evidence of the congregation's final abandonment of Jewish law and tradition. They wondered aloud if the reforms would have been promulgated had an "orthodox lecturer" stood at the congregation's helm.[54]

The B'nai Jeshurun experience illustrates the major issues raised by mixed seating controversies from the late nineteenth century onward. For supporters, the proposed seating change translated into terms like family togetherness, women's equality, conformity to local norms, a modern, progressive image, and saving the youth—values that most Jews viewed positively. For opponents, the same change implied abandonment of tradition, violation of Jewish law, assimilation, Christianization, and promiscuity—consequences that most Jews viewed with horror. Pulled simultaneously in two directions that both seemed right—directions that reflected opposing views on modernity—many of those seeking compromise in the middle took solace in assurances from their leaders that Judaism and mixed seating were fully compatible. Rabbinic arguments and the adoption of mixed seating in synagogue after synagogue made the case for the "Jewishness" of the practice that much more compelling. Feeling reassured that they could reconcile modernity and tradition and still have mixed seating, majorities at congregations like B'nai Jeshurun opted for change. Minorities opposed to the change, meanwhile, found in separate seating a visible and defensible issue around which they could rally. Separate seating imparted just that sense of detached protest against modernity that, supporters felt, Judaism needed to express in order to survive. By exhibiting their reverence for tradition through the basic spatial arrangement of the synagogue, traditionalists made their point of disagreement with innovators plain for all to see. In time, "separate seating" and "mixed seating" became shorthand statements, visible expressions of differences on a host of more fundamental issues that lay beneath the surface.

IV

Mixed seating generally ceased to be a controversial issue in Reform Judaism after the 1870s. By 1890, Isaac Mayer Wise, who was in a position to know, wrote that "today *no* synagogue is built in this country without family pews."[55] Applied to Reform temples, the statement seems to be correct. Orthodox synagogues, of course, continued to separate men and women, and this remained true in the new Orthodox "showpiece" congregations erected, particularly in New York, in the wake of large-scale East European Jewish immigration.[56] In 1895, a proposal for mixed seating did agitate the nation's leading Sephardic Synagogue, Shearith Israel, but the trustees unanimously voted it down. They resolved that in the new synagogue, then under construction, seating would remain, "men in the auditorium and women in the galleries as in the present synagogue." Ninety-six women submitted a resolution supporting the maintenance of this "time-honored custom."[57]

Over the next two decades, debates over mixed seating took place at a good many other modern Orthodox synagogues, especially those that sought to cater to young people. But for the most part—Congregation Mount Sinai of Central Harlem, founded in 1904, being a noteworthy exception—separate seating held. Modernity in these congregations came to mean decorum, use of the English language, and weekly sermons. Proposed seating reforms, by their nature far more divisive, were effectively tabled.[58]

Between the two world wars, the issue of mixed seating arose again, this time in the rapidly growing Conservative Movement. Living in what Marshall Sklare has identified as "areas of third settlement"—younger, more aware of surrounding non-Jewish and Reform Jewish practices, and more worried about the Jewishness of their children—Conservative Jews sought a form of worship that would be "traditional and at the same time modern." Gallery seating for women was not what they had in mind. It violated the American norm of family seating. It ran counter to modern views on the position of women. And it proved dysfunctional to synagogue life, since in America, Jewish women played an increasingly important part in all religious activities, and felt discriminated against by the gallery. Seating reforms thus ranked high on the Conservative Jewish agenda.[59]

In 1921, the question of "whether family pews would be a departure from traditional Judaism" came before the Rabbinical Assembly's [Conservative Jewish] Committee on the Interpretation of Jewish Law. Professor Louis Ginzberg, chairman of the committee, responded that gallery seating was unnecessary, but that "the separation of the sexes is a Jewish custom well established for about 2000 years, and must not be taken lightly."[60] The "separate but equal" seating pattern that Ginzberg and Schechter (like David Einhorn) advocated failed to satisfy proponents of family togetherness in worship, and most Conservative synagogues introduced mixed seating instead, in some cases preserving sexually segregated areas in the synagogue for those who wanted them ("compromise seating")[61]. In 1947, Ginzberg himself told a congregation in Baltimore that if "continued separation of family units during services presents a great danger to its spiritual welfare, the minority ought to yield to the spiritual need of the majority."[62] Privately he admitted that "when you live long enough in America you realize that the status of womanhood had changed so much that separating women from men has become obsolete."[63] By 1955, according to Marshall Sklare, mixed seating featured in "the overwhelming majority of Conservative synagogues," and served "as the most commonly accepted yardstick for differentiating Conservatism from Orthodoxy."[64]

Although recognized Orthodox leaders did indeed tout mixed seating as the "great divide"—the action that put a congregation beyond the pale of Orthodox tradition—many members of Orthodox congregations apparently disagreed. Congregations that both professed to be Orthodox and employed rabbis who graduated from Orthodox rabbinical seminaries still introduced family pews, defending them in one case, on the basis of the "spirit, traditions and procedure of Orthodox Judaism," and in another on the pragmatic grounds that they would "be inviting to the younger members."[65] One source claims that in 1961 there existed "perhaps 250 Orthodox synagogues where family seating is practiced."[66] A different estimate, from 1954, holds that "90% of the graduates of the Chicago Hebrew Theological Institution, which is Orthodox, and 50% of the graduates of the Yeshiva, the Orthodox institution in New York, have positions where family seating or optional family seating prevails." How accurate either estimate was remains unclear, but at least according to one (perhaps biased) observer family seating had "definitely become a form and tradition of Orthodox Israelites adopted and practiced by an overwhelming number of Orthodox Synagogues." Certainly rabbis who served mixed-seating congregations continued to belong to the Orthodox Rabbinical Council of America without fear of expulsion.[67]

Synagogue practices nothwithstanding, Yeshiva University continuously opposed mixed seating. It nominally revoked the ordination of its graduates if they continued to serve mixed-seating congregations after having been warned to leave them. The only temporary justification allowing a graduate to accept a mixed-seating position was if Yeshiva's then president, Bernard Revel, felt that "an able, diplomatic man" could bring the errant congregation "back to the fold."[68] Although in some cases this happened, and in others the rabbi resigned after failing, an apparently substantial but undetermined number of Yeshiva University graduates, torn between piety and prosperity, or influenced by American conditions, made peace with mixed seating. In a few cases, they later defended the practice's orthodoxy in court.

Court proceedings dealing with the mixed-seating problem were, as we know from the B'nai Jeshurun affair, nothing new. A series of cases in the 1950s,[69] however, had the effect of solidifying Orthodoxy's position on the issue, while undermining the comfortable arguments of those who insisted that mixed seating and Jewish tradition could be made compatible. Leading Orthodox spokesmen, in concert with the Union of Orthodox Jewish Congregations of America and the Rabbinical Council of America, so vigorously insisted that mixed seating violated *halachah*, that those who supported the opposite position realized that they were clinging to a view that no institutionalized brand of Orthodoxy would agree to legitimate.

Three cases received particular attention. The first involved Congregation Adath Israel in Cincinnati. Founded by Polish Jews in 1853, and for many years the leading non-Reform synagogue in the city, Adath Israel harbored a range of traditional Jews and had for many years walked a tightrope between the Conservative and Orthodox movements. The synagogue's constitution proclaimed adherence to the "forms and traditions of Orthodox Israelites."[70] At the same time, the synagogue belonged to the Conservative United Synagogues of America. Fishel J. Goldfeder, Adath Israel's rabbi, boasted both an Orthodox and a Conservative training. Members sought to appeal to those with Orthodox leanings and Conservative leanings at one and the same time.

Separate seating of some form or other had been the rule at Adath Israel since its inception. At least since 1896, "separate but equal" seating had been deemed sufficient: "Men sit on one side and the women sit on the other side of the first floor of the Synagogue without any curtain or any partition between them."[71] In 1923, apparently in reaction to liberalization moves in many Conservative synagogues, members voted an amendment to their constitution: "that no family pews be established nor may men remove their hats during services; that no organ be used during services; that no female choir be permitted so long as ten (10) members in good standing object thereto."[72]

Beginning in 1952, however, the congregation, which had been expanding rapidly, began to be agitated by demands for optional family seating, many of them from younger members. The board of trustees, with the blessing of Rabbi Goldfeder, voted 17-9 in favor of optional family seating on December 30, 1953, and a congregational meeting subsequently ratified the action by a vote of 289-100.[73]

Opponents claimed that mixed seating violated the synagogue's constitution. They pointed out that more than the necessary ten members objected to family seating, and besides, they insisted that family seating contravened the "forms and traditions of Orthodox Israelites." They, therefore, moved to block the action, and by mutual agreement finally submitted their dispute to a private court. A three-judge panel ("each side to the controversy shall select one Judge of its own choosing and the third Judge shall be selected by agreement of the counsel for both sides") was given binding authority to decide the case.[74]

The court proceedings brought to the fore the deep divisions within Adath Israel that had long simmered beneath the surface. As the judges noted in their decision, "Some witnesses contended that the.... Synagogue is strictly Orthodox: some said that it is liberal Orthodox, and others believed that it is a Conservative synagogue."[75] Supporters of mixed seating argued, on the one hand, that the congregation was Conservative, since it lacked a formal *mechitsah* (partition), employed a microphone, and confirmed women, and on the other hand, that mixed seating accorded "with the forms and traditions of Orthodox Israelites," as defined by their rabbi. By contrast, opponents of mixed seating argued that the congregation was Orthodox, notwithstanding earlier reforms, and that mixed seating would cause Adath Israel "to lose its status as a proper place of worship."[76] Testimony from leading figures in Orthodox and Conservative Judaism put forth diverging views on mixed seating's *halachic* status, and on the meaning of "Orthodoxy" to different kinds of Jews.

In their decision, Judge Chase M. Davies and Rabbi Joseph P. Sternstein (the third judge, Mr. Sol Goodman, dissented) refused to consider these *halachic* issues at all. Having been instructed to "resolve the controversy involved in the synagogue on a legal basis," they first ruled the 1923 amendment outlawing family pews "not a valid and presently effective amendment to the Constitution and By-Laws of the congregation," since improper procedures had accompanied its adoption. On the more important question of whether family seating violated Orthodox "forms and traditions," the judges, on the basis of American precedents, decided that the issue

> presents a religious question over which a Court of law, and this private Court, which has been instructed to follow legal principles, has no right, power, or jurisdiction. To hold otherwise would be an assumption by this private Court of monitorship of the religious faith of the members of the congregation, since under federal and state Constitutions, there can be no disturbance of or limitation to the power and right of the congregants to exercise that freedom of conscience which is the basis of our liberty.[77]

Given the fact that the board of trustees, the majority of the members and the rabbi all supported "optional family seating," the judges ruled the practice valid. They took pains to point out, however, that as an opinion of a private court, theirs "should not be considered, or cited, as authority in any other case."[78]

In closing, the judges expressed the hope that their decision would "result in a harmonious and unified worship of God by all members of the congregation."[79] That, however, did not come about. Instead, many of the members who had always considered Adath Israel to be Orthodox and opposed mixed seating, withdrew and joined other synagogues. Those who remained at Adath Israel became more closely aligned with the Conservative Movement and referred to themselves increasingly as Conservative Jews. The seating controversy thus unwittingly served as a vehicle for clarifying both religious identity and ideology. By taking a stand on one issue, people expressed their views on a host of other issues as well.

Davis v. Scher[80] the second mixed-seating case, concerned Congregation Beth Tefilas Moses, an avowedly Orthodox Jewish congregation in Mt. Clemens, Michigan, which voted to introduce family seating into its sanctuary in 1955. Baruch Litvin, a businessman who belonged to the congregation and was cordially disliked by many of its members, took up the battle against this decision,[81] basing himself on an established American legal principle: "A majority of a church congregation may not institute a practice within the church fundamentally opposed to the doctrine to which the church property is dedicated, as against a minority of the congregation who adhere to the established doctrine and practice."[82] Litvin's attorneys, supported by the Union of Orthodox Jewish Congregations, introduced a great deal of evidence to support the claim that mixed seating was "clearly violative of the established Orthodox Jewish law and practice" and argued that if mixed seating were introduced, the Orthodox minority would have to worship elsewhere, "deprived of the right of the use of their property...by the majority group contrary to law." The congregation, by contrast, argued that the dispute involved only "doctrinal and ecclesiastical matters," not property rights, and that "it would be inconsistent with complete religious liberty for the court to assume...jurisdiction."[83] Despite court urging, the congregation's lawyers refused to cross-examine witnesses or to introduce any testimony of their own in defense of mixed seating, for fear that this would weaken their argument. They did not believe that the secular courtroom was the proper forum for Jewish doctrinal debates.

Lower courts sided with the congregation and refused to become involved, arguing that Congregation Beth Tefilas Moses' majority voice had the power to rule. The Michigan Supreme Court, however, unanimously reversed this decision and accepted the minority's claims. It stressed that "because of defendants' calculated risk of not offering proofs, no dispute exists as to the teaching of Orthodox Judaism as to mixed seating." By the laws governing implied trusts, therefore, the congregation's majority was denied the power to carry property dedicated for use by Orthodox Jews "to the support of a new and conflicting doctrine." "A change of views on religious subjects," the court ruled, did not require those who still held to older views to surrender property originally conveyed to them.[84]

The third case, *Katz v. Singerman*,[85] had much that was seemingly in common with *Davis v. Scher*. Congregation Chevra Thilim of New Orleans voted in 1957 to introduce family pews, and a minority, led by Harry Katz, went to court to thwart the move. Like Baruch Litvin, Katz argued for minority rights, particularly since the Chevra Thilim charter explicitly included "the worship of God according to the orthodox Polish Jewish ritual" as one of its "objects and purposes," and the congregation had accepted the donation of a building upon the stipulation that it "shall only be used as a place of Jewish worship according to the strict ancient and orthodox forms and ceremonies."[86] The issue to be determined by the court was "whether the practice of mixed or family seating in Chevra

Thilim Synagogue is contrary to and inconsistent with the 'orthodox Polish Jewish Ritual' and 'Jewish worship according to the strict ancient and orthodox forms and ceremonies,' and therefore in violation of the trust and donation…and also the Charter of the Congregation."[87]

Where *Katz v. Singerman* differed was in the strategy employed by defendants. They introduced considerable testimony in support of mixed seating, including evidence supplied by Rabbi Jacob Agus, ordained at Yeshiva University, as well as twenty-seven affidavits testifying that mixed seating "is not contrary to Orthodox Jewish forms and ceremonies."[88] Seventy-five affidavits, and a host of formidable witnesses from across the Orthodox spectrum opposed this testimony, offering abundant evidence in support of separate seating. The court was left to decide who understood Jewish law better.

Lower courts, impressed by the plaintiff's legal display and by the strong pro-Orthodox language employed in the original charter, decided in Katz's favor. The Supreme Court of Louisiana, however, in a decision similar to that rendered in the Adath Israel affair, decided differently. Given the "well-settled rule of law that courts will not interfere with the ecclesiastical questions involving differences of opinion as to religious conduct,"[89] and the famous Supreme Court decision in *Watson v. Jones* (1872), which held that "[i]n such cases where there is a schism which leads to a separation into distinct and conflicting bodies, the rights of such bodies to the use of the property must be determined by the ordinary principles which govern voluntary associations,"[90] the court decided that Chevra Thilim's board of directors alone had the "authority to ascertain and interpret the meaning of 'orthodox Polish Jewish Ritual.'" The fact that Chevra Thilim's rabbi agreed with the board and favored mixed seating held "great weight" with the court, which also cited precedents based on church-state separation and the principle that "churches must in their very nature 'grow with society.'"[91] "This case differs from the case of *Davis v. Scher*," the judges insisted, "for there the evidence was all on one side." Here, with two sides offering conflicting testimony as to what the phrase "orthodox forms and ceremonies" means, the court, following abundant precedent, left the matter for the congregation to decide.[92]

From the point of view of law, *Katz v. Singerman* dealt a severe blow to Orthodoxy, since it made it highly difficult for an Orthodox minority to overturn in court any majority decision, even one found unacceptable in terms of *halacha*. From another point of view, however, the case, like *Davis v. Scher* and the Adath Israel case, actually strengthened Orthodoxy, for it gave publicity to the movement's views and established in the popular mind the fact that "true" Orthodoxy and separate seating went hand in hand. Orthodox Jewish publications denominated those who defended the orthodoxy of mixed seating as "Conservative Jews," and ridiculed "mixed-seating Orthodoxy" as a contradiction in terms.[93] Those who did define modern Orthodox in terms of mixed seating found themselves increasingly isolated. In some cases, congregations that once considered themselves modern Orthodox moved, after adopting mixed seating, firmly into the ranks of the Conservative Movement.[94] In other cases, particularly in congregations served by rabbis from Hebrew Theological College in Chicago, modern Orthodox congregations began to worship under the label of traditional Judaism.[95]

Exceptions notwithstanding, mixed seating, even more than when Marshall Sklare first made the observation, symbolized by the third quarter of the twentieth century that which differentiated Orthodoxy from Jewry's other branches.[96] The symbol that had first signified family togetherness and later came to represent women's equality and religious modernity, had finally evolved into a denominational boundary. Around it American Jews defined where they stood religiously and what values they held most dear.[97]

NOTES

I am grateful to Rochelle Elstein, Barry Feldman, Robert Shapiro, and Barbara E. Ullman for bringing valuable materials to my attention; to Professors Benny Kraut, Jacob R. Marcus, Michael A. Meyer, Jeffrey S. Gurock, Robert Handy, Chava Weissler, Jack Wertheimer, and Lance J. Sussman, for commenting on earlier drafts of this chapter; and to the Memorial Foundation for Jewish Culture for its ongoing support of my work.

1. John M. Neale. *The History of Pews*, 2d ed. (Cambridge, England, 1842), 3.

2. The best available materials on synagogue seating have been prepared by parties in legal disputes; see Baruch Litvin, ed., *The Sanctity of the Synagogue* (New York, 1959); and the special issue of *Conservative Judaism*, 11 (Fall, 1956), devoted to the Adath Israel affair.

3. For two responsa on this issue, see Bernhard Felsenthal, "Muss Man Sich Beim Beten Nach Osten Wenden?" *Sinai*, 6 (May, 1861), 110–11; and Shaul Yedidyah Shochet, *Tiferet Yedidya*, vol. 2 (St. Louis, 1920), 26–32. See also Franz Landsberger, "The Sacred Direction in Synagogue and Church," *Hebrew Union College Annual*, 28 (1957), 181–203.

4. See Jacob Agus. "Mixed Pews in Jewish Tradition," *Conservative Judaism*, 11 (Fall, 1956), 35–36; and Rachel Wischnitzer, *Synagogue Architecture in the United States* (Philadelphia, 1955), 60.

5. For various perspectives, see Leon A. Jick, *The Americanization of the Synagogue* 1820–1870 (Hanover, N.H., 1976); Moshe Davis, *The Emergence of Conservative Judaism* (Philadelphia, 1965); Nathan Glazer, *American Judaism*, 2d ed. (Chicago, 1972); and Allan Tarshish, "The Rise of American Judaism" (Ph.D. diss., Hebrew Union College, 1938).

6. Ismar Elbogen, *Hatefilah Beyisrael* (Tel Aviv, 1972), 350–352; Andrew Seager, "The Architecture of the Dura and Sardis Synagogues," in *The Synagogue*, ed. Joseph Gutmann (New York, 1975), 156–158, 178 nn. 35–36; Salo W. Baron, *The Jewish Community*, vol. 2 (Philadelphia, 1945), 140; Samuel Kraus, *Korot Bate Hatefilah Beyisrael* (New York: Histadrut Ivrit, 1955), 239–240; *Encyclopedia Judaica*, 11, 134–135; Shaye J. D. Cohen. "Women in the Synagogues of Antiquity," *Conservative Judaism*, 34 (November–December, 1980), 23–29; J. Charles Cox, *Bench-Ends in English Churches* (London, n.d.), 17–27.

7. David Philipson, *The Reform Movement in Judaism* (New York, 1931), 245. A similar seating arrangement may have been in effect as early as 1815 in the Reform congregation that met at the home of Jacob Herz-Beer in Berlin. See Nahum N. Glatzer, "On an Unpublished Letter of Isaak Markus Jost," *Leo Baeck Institute Year Book*, 22 (1977), opposite 132. I owe this reference to Professor Michael A. Meyer.

8. Jacob Sonderling, "Five Gates—Casual Notes for an Autobiography," *American Jewish Archives*, 16 (November 1964), 109. On Budge, see Cyrus Adler, *Jacob H. Schiff: His Life and Letters*, vol. 1 (Garden City, N.J., 1929), 7–8. Rebekah Kohut reports in 1929 that "everywhere in Europe, except in the Reform Temples of Paris and London, men and women still worship separately." *As I Know Them* (New York, 1929), 119.

9. *American Israelite*, 37 (27 November 1890), 4.

10. John Demos, "Images of the American Family, Then and Now," in *Changing Images of the Family*, ed. Virginia Tufte and Barbara Myerhoff (New Haven, 1979), 48; Cox, *Bench-Ends*, 17–19; Robert J. Dinkin, Seating the Meeting House in Early Massachusetts," *New England Quarterly*, 43 (1970), 450–464; Peter Benes and Philip D. Zimmerman, *New England Meeting House and Church, 1630–1850* (Boston, 1979), 55–56; Wischnitzer, *Synagogue Architecture*, 12.

11. Patricia J. Tracy, *Jonathan Edwards, Pastor* (New York, 1980), 128. For a similar contemporary argument, see Morris Max, "Mixed Pews," *Conservative Judaism*, 11 (Fall 1956), 70.

12. Dinkin, "Seating the Meeting House," 456; Tracy, *Jonathan Edwards, Pastor*, 244 n. 9.

13. Alan Graebner, *Uncertain Saints* (Westport, Conn., 1975), 17; "Pews," *The American Quarterly Church Review*, 13 (July 1860), 288–289. See Jacob Angus's discussion of the 1885 mixed-seating controversy in Grace Methodist Church of Dayton, Ohio, in Agus, "Mixed Pews in Jewish Tradition," 41.

14. Demos, "Images of the American Family," 43–60, es49; Carl N. Degler, *At Odds: Women and the Family in America from the Revolution to the Present* (Oxford, 1980), 9; and Carl N. Degler, "Women and the Family," in *The Past Before Us*, ed. Michael Kammen (Ithaca, 1980), es317.

15. Hyman B. Grinstein, *The Rise of the Jewish Community of New York* (Philadelphia, 1945),

317–318; see Kenneth L. Ames, "Ideologies in Stone: Meanings in Victorian Gravestones," *Journal of Popular Culture*, 14 (1981), 641–656.

16. James G. Heller, *Isaac M. Wise: His Life, Work and Thought* (New York, 1965), 214.

17. Heller, *Wise*, 124–183; Naphtali J. Rubinger, "Dismissal in Albany," *American Jewish Archives*, 24 (November 1972), 161–162.

18. Isaac M. Wise, *Reminiscences* (1901; 2d ed., New York, 1945), 116–117.

19. Wise, *Reminiscences*, 172.

20. Rubinger, "Dismissal in Albany," 160–183; Heller, *Wise*, 184–234. On the conversion of churches into synagogues, a phenomenon little known in Europe, see Wischnitzer, *Synagogue Architecture*, 61–62. Apparently, Wise did not introduce mixed pews immediately upon his arrival in Cincinnati. They only came to Bene Yeshurun in 1866 when the congregation moved into the Plum Street temple. See James Heller, *As Yesterday When It Is Past* (Cincinnati, 1942), 114.

21. Wise, *Reminiscences*, 212.

22. *Occident*, 9 (December, 1851), 477; *Asmonean*, 10 October 1851, 226; 17 October 1851, 240; see 21 November 1851, 53; 19 December 1851, 83.

23. *American Israelite*, 15 November 1872, 8; 27 November 1890, 4. Naphtali J. Rubinger, "Albany Jewry of the Nineteenth Century; Historic Roots and Communal Evolution" (Ph.D. diss., Yeshiva University, 1970), 120, notes other occasions when Wise retrospectively exaggerated the extent of the opposition against him. Such efforts aimed at creating a personal "hero myth" are common; see Frank J. Sulloway, *Freud, Biologist of the Mind* (New York, 1979), 445–495; Joseph Campbell, *The Hero With A Thousand Faces* (Princeton, 1968).

24. Myer Stern, *The Rise and Progress of Reform Judaism* (New York, 1895), 14; *New Era*, 4 (1874), 126; Grinstein, *Jewish Community of New York*, 267; see also Leopold Mayer's description of Emanu-El in 1850, in Morris U. Schappes, *A Documentary History of the Jews in the United States*, 1654–1875 (New York, 1971), 308.

25. Philipson, *Reform Movement*, 183–184, 219–220; see Kaufmann Kohler, *Jewish Theology* (New York, 1918), 472–473.

26. *See Sinai*, 6 (August 1861), 205–207. For a sociological perspective on the German debate in terms of "identity formation and boundary maintenance," see David Ellenson, "The Role of Reform in selected German-Jewish Orthodox Responsa: A Sociological Analysis," *Hebrew Union College Annual*, 53 (1982), 357–380.

27. Alexander Hamilton, *Itinerarium*, quoted in David and Tamar De Sola Pool, *An Old Faith in the New World* (New York, 1955), 453; *Religious Intelligencer*, 1 (1817), 556; *Western Monthly Review*, 2 (January 1829), 440; *New York Herald*, 22 September 1836. For other negative notices, see Joseph S. C. F. Frey, *The Converted Jew* (Boston, 1815), 15; *The Jew at Home and Abroad* (Philadelphia, 1845), 65; Joseph L. Blau and Salo W. Baron, *The Jews of the United States, 1790–1840: A Documentary History*, vol. 3 (New York, 1963), 677–680; and Lydia M. Child, *The History of the Condition of Women in Various Ages and Nations*, vol. 1 (Boston, 1835), 20. Cf. I. J. Benjamin's Jewish critique (1859) in his *Three Years in America*, vol. 1, transl. Charles Reznikoff (Philadelphia, 1956), 85–89; and see more broadly Joan Jacobs Brumberg, *Mission for Life* (New York, 1984), 79–106.

28. *New York Herald*, 28 September 1836; *Sunday Times and Noah's Weekly Messenger* (New York), 7 July 1850, 26 January 1851; James Parton, *Topics of the Times* (Boston, 1871), 299, 308. The leading Jewish apologia, imported from England, was Grace Aguilar, *The Women of Israel*, 2 vols. (New York, 1851). For a modern analogue, see Lucy Davidowicz, *The Jewish Presence* (New York, 1978), 46–57.

29. Louise Abbie Mayo, "The Ambivalent Image: The Perception of the Jew in Nineteenth Century America" (Ph.D. diss., City University of New York, 1977), 93–104.

30. Philipson, *Reform Movement*, 220.

31. *Sinai*, 3 (1858), 824; Isaac M. Fein, *The Making of an American Jewish Community* (Philadelphia, 1971), 113.

32. *Sinai*, 3 (1858), 818–824; 6 (1861), 205–207.

33. Bernhard Felsenthal, *The Beginnings of the Chicago Sinai Congregation* (Chicago, 1898), 23.

34. *Occident*, 18 (1860), 154; Fred Rosenbaum, *Architects of Reform* (Berkeley, 1980), 26.

35. *New Era*, 1 (February 1871), 193.

36. Jerome W. Grollman, "The Emergence of Reform Judaism in the United States" (Ord. thesis, Hebrew Union College, 1948), 18, 43 passim; *A History of Congregation Beth El, Detroit, Mich., 1850–1900* (Detroit, 1900), 26–28; Jonathan D. Sarna, "Innovation and Consolidation: Phases in the History of Temple Mishkan Israel," *Jews in New Haven*, vol. 3, ed. Barry E. Herman and Werner S. Hirsch (New Haven, 1981), 102; Edward N. Calisch, *The Light Burns On* (Richmond, 1941), 25; Frank J. Adler, *Roots in a Moving Stream* (Kansas City, 1972), 22; Isidor Blum, *The Jews of Baltimore* 1910), 23; *New Era*, 5 (1875), 4; Solomon Breibart, "The Synagogue of Kahal Kadosh Beth Elohim, Charleston." *South*

Carolina Historical Magazine, 80 (July 1979), 228—all describe the adoption of mixed seating in other nineteenth-century American Reform congregations. For the situation at the more traditional congregation Sherith Israel of San Francisco in the 1870s, see Norton B. Stern, "An Orthodox Rabbi and a Reforming Congregation in Nineteenth Century San Francisco," *Western States Jewish Historical Quarterly,* 15 (April 1983), 275–281.

37. Quoted in Grollman, *Emergence of Reform Judaism,* 89.

38. Wise, *Reminiscences,* 212.

39. *Occident,* 13 (1855), 417; 21 (1863), 345; 21 (1864), 500.

40. *Occident,* 21 (1863), 407. On Buttenwieser, see A. Z. Friedman, *Tub Taam,* 2d ed. (New York, 1904), introduction.

41. E.g., *American Israelite,* 13 December 1878, 4.

42. Israel Goldstein, *A Century of Judaism in New York: B'nai Jeshurun, 1825–1925* (New York, 1930), 51–113; see also Grinstein, *Jewish Community of New York*; Moshe Davis, "The Synagogue in American Judaism: A Study of Congregation B'nai Jeshurun, New York City," in *Two Generations in Perspective,* ed. Harry Schneiderman (New York, 1957), 210–235, translated and revised in Moshe Davis, *Beit Yisrael Be-Amerikah* (Jerusalem, 1970), 1–24. On Raphall, see Bertram W. Korn, *Eventful Years and Experiences* (Cincinnati, 1954), 40–41.

43. Goldstein, *B'nai Jeshurun,* 126.

44. Ibid., 126–129; see Jonathan D. Sarna, ed., *People Walk on Their Heads: Moses Weinberger's Jews and Judaism in New York* (New York, 1981), 12–14.

45. Goldstein, *B'nai Jeshurun,* 128, 153–156; *Answers to Questions Propounded by the Ritual Committee on the Subject of the Improvements Intended to Be Introduced in the Synagogue Service of the Cong. "B'nai Jeshurun"* (New York, 1869); Minutes of Congregation B'nai Jeshurun, 1865–1875. Congregation B'nai Jeshurun Papers, microfilm 493c, American Jewish Archives, Cincinnati, Ohio.

46. Goldstein, *B'nai Jeshurun,* 156; Nahum Streisand, *Lilmod Latoim Binah* (New York, 1872); *Jewish Messenger,* 16 July 1875.

47. B'nai Jeshurun Minutes, 8 November 1874.

48. Goldstein, *B'nai Jeshurun,* 157.

49. Ibid., 155; *Answers to Questions,* 1; cf. *New Era,* 1 (1870), 36, for an attack on this phenomenon.

50. *B'nai Jeshurun Minutes,* 8 November 1874, as correlated with the "Register of Congregational Membership," in Goldstein, *B'nai Jeshurun,* 404–436; *Jewish Messenger,* 16 July 1875, 6.

51. William M. Rosenblatt, "The Jews: What They Are Coming To," *Galaxy,* 13 (January 1872), 60; *New Era,* 4 (1874), 14, 513; for a similar later argument (1922), see Aaron Rothkoff, *Bernard Revel* (Philadelphia, 1972), 111.

52. *Jewish Messenger,* 16 July 1875, 6.

53. *Jewish Times,* 21 May 1875, 184.

54. *Jewish Messenger,* 21 May 1875, 21.

55. *American Israelite,* 37 (November 27, 1890), 4, italics added. See Gustav Gottheil, "The Jewish Reformation," *American Journal of Theology,* 6 (April 1902), 279.

56. Jo Renee Fine and Gerald R. Wolfe, *The Synagogues of New York's Lower East Side* (New York, 1978).

57. Pool, *An Old Faith,* 100.

58. Jeffrey S. Gurock, *When Harlem Was Jewish* (New York, 1979), 117; see also Chapter 1 in this volume.

59. Marshall Sklare, *Conservative Judaism* (1955; 2d. ed., New York, 1972), 85–90.

60. *United Synagogue Recorder,* 1 (July 1921), 8.

61. The Cleveland Jewish Center case of 1927, involving Rabbi Solomon Goldman (*Katz v. Goldman,* 33 Ohio A150), drew particular notice. The Ohio Supreme Court ruled in Goldman's favor, refusing to invalidate the changes that he introduced. See Aaron Rakeffet-Rothkoff, *The Silver Era in American Jewish Orthodoxy* (New York, 1981), 112–114, 121 n. 14, 326–347; Jacob J. Weinstein, *Solomon Goldman: A Rabbi's Rabbi* (New York, 1973), 12–17.

62. *Conservative Judaism,* 11 (Fall 1956), 39; Eli Ginzberg, *Keeper of the Law: Louis Ginzberg* (Philadelphia, 1966), 229–230.

63. Sonderling, "Five Gates," 115.

64. Sklare, *Conservative Judaism,* 88; see Rothkoff, *Bernard Revel,* 111; and Norman Lamm, "Separate Pews in the Synagogue [1959]," in *A Treasury of Tradition,* ed. Norman Lamm and Walter S. Wurzberger (New York, 1967), 243–267.

65. *Katz v. Singerman,* 241 Louisiana 154 (1961); Rothkoff, *Bernard Revel,* 164.

66. *Katz v. Singerman,* 241 Louisiana 150.

67. "Opinion in Kahila Kodesh Adath Israel Congregation Matter" (Cincinnati, 1954, mimeographed), 42, Louis Bernstein, *Challenge and Mission: The Emergence of the English Speaking Orthodox Rabbinate* (New York, 1982), 20–21, 36, 46–49, 138–141.

68. Rothkoff, *Bernard Revel,* 164.

69. For the legal background, see Meislin, *Jewish Law in American Tribunals*; and W. E. Shipley, *Change of Denominational Relations or Fundamental*

Doctrines by Majority Faction of Independent or Congregational Church as Ground for Award of Property to Minority, 15 ALR 3d 297 (1967). The Supreme Court's ruling in *Presbyterian Church in the United States v. Mary Elizabeth Blue Hull Memorial Presbyterian Church*, 393 U.S. 440 (1969) resolved several important legal questions bearing on mixed seating disputes; see Paul G. Kauper. "Church Autonomy and the First Amendment: The Presbyterian Church Case," in *Church and State: The Supreme Court and the First Amendment*, ed. Philip B. Kurland (Chicago, 1975), 67–98.

70. "Opinion in Adath Israel Matter," 4. In what follows, I cite this version; a slightly abbreviated and variant version of the decision may be found in *Conservative Judaism*, 11 (Fall 1956), 1–31.

71. "Opinion in Adath Israel Matter," 12. David Philipson found this seating pattern when he preached at Adath Israel's dedication in 1927. He predicted that "ere long the women will sit with their husbands and children." *My Life as an American Jew* (Cincinnati, 1941), 378.

72. Philipson, *My Life as an American Jew*, 8.

73. Ibid., 8–12.

74. Ibid., 1–3. *On the use of arbitration in cases of this sort, see Jerold S. Auerbach, Justice without Law?* (New York, 1983), 69–94.

75. Auerbach, *Justice without Law?* 63.

76. Ibid., 30; *Conservative Judaism*, 11 (Fall 1956), 44.

77. *Opinion in Adath Israel Matter*, 43–66; quotations from 47, 45, 66.

78. Ibid., 59.

79. Ibid., 67.

80. The case is reported in 356 Michigan 291, and is described in great detail, with documents, in Litvin, *Sanctity of the Synagogue*. Much of what follows is based on this volume. See also Bernstein, *Challenge and Mission*, 138–141.

81. Litvin, *Sanctity of the Synagogue*, 11–17.

82. Ibid., 378.

83. Ibid., 382, 412, 408.

84. Ibid., 407–418 reproduces the entire Michigan Supreme Court decision; quotations are from 417, 415.

85. The case is reported in 241 Louisiana 103. For early documents, see Litvin, *Sanctity of the Synagogue*, 61–77; see also Bernstein, *Challenge and Mission*, 138–140.

86. *Katz v. Singerman*, 107, 109.

87. Ibid., 114.

88. Ibid., 136–149. Agus's testimony resembled that which he gave in the Adath Israel matter; see *Conservative Judaism*, 11 (1956), 32–41.

89. *Katz v. Singerman*, 116 quoting *Katz v. Goldman*, above n. 73.

90. *Katz v. Singerman*, 118; cf. *Watson v. Jones* 13 Wall. 679, 20 L ed. 666 (1872).

91. *Katz v. Singerman*, 131. 134.

92. Ibid., 151. Shipley, *Change of Denominational Relations*, 324, 331, overlooks this critical point.

93. E.g., Litvin, *Sanctity of the Synagogue*, 73.

94. See Isaac Klein's letter in *Conservative Judaism*, 11 (Winter 1957), 34.

95. E.g., Joseph Schultz, ed., *Mid-America's Promise: A Profile of Kansas City Jewry* (Kansas City, 1982), 42.

96. Cf. Alan J. Yuter, "Mehizah, Midrash and Modernity: A Study in Religious Rhetoric," *Judaism*, 28 (1979), 147–159; Samuel Heilman, *Synagogue Life* (Chicago, 1976), 28. Charles Liebman, "Orthodoxy in American Jewish Life," *Aspects of the Religious Behavior of American Jews* (reprinted from *American Jewish Year Book*, 66; New York, 1974), 146, notes "some 30 synagogues" which once had mixed seating and, since 1955, have installed *mechitsot*—no doubt to maintain their Orthodox affiliation.

97. In a conversation with me, Prof. Sefton D. Temkin quotes a colleague of his as pointing out that whereas American Orthodoxy defined itself in terms of opposition to mixed seating, British Orthodoxy did so in terms of opposition to the mixed choir, German Orthodoxy in terms of opposition to the organ, and Hungarian Orthodoxy in terms of opposition to the raised, forward pulpit. A comparative study elucidating these differences would be of inestimable value.

CATHOLIC DOMESTICITY

Colleen McDannell

Despite the fact that by 1890 Roman Catholics numbered more than one-quarter of America's church-going population, we still do not know very much about their religious lives. Between 1850 and 1920 successive waves of Irish, German, Italian, Polish, and other immigrants made the Roman Catholic Church by far the largest Christian denomination in the United States. Perceived by turn-of-the-century Protestants as an alien and other-worldly subculture, immigrant Roman Catholicism has also been set apart by scholars as a field of research. Even within the field of American Catholic history most scholarship has privileged the institutional church and its male hierarchy. Though recent work has focused on popular religion and the experience of the laity, the Irish and printed English sources continue to be favored. Despite these drawbacks innovative work is being pursued, especially in the area of gender.

In the following essay, Colleen McDannell explores the changing domestic world of Catholic women. Unlike most scholarship on the religious world of Protestant women, McDannell portrays a Catholic home life that varied by class and ethnicity, and changed over time. Though the arbiters of Catholic culture envisioned a domestic ideal similar to the middle-class Protestant home, working-class Irish and most Italians, Mexicans, and Poles experienced a domestic religious life that differed in subtle and not so subtle ways from the Protestant ideal.

Adapted by permission from Colleen McDannell, "Catholic Domesticity, 1860–1960," in Karen Kennelly, *American Catholic Women: A Historical Explanation* (New York: Macmillan, 1989), 48–80.

15 ❦

CATHOLIC DOMESTICITY, 1860–1960

Colleen McDannell

"MATERNITY, SWEET SOUND!" exclaimed the *Catholic Home Journal* in 1887. "Nature has put the mother upon such a pinnacle, that our infant eyes and arms are, first uplifted to it; we cling to it in manhood, we almost worship it in old age."[1] By the end of the nineteenth century, middle-class American Catholics possessed a domestic ideology as colorful and sentimental as many proper Victorians. Advice books written by Irish priests, popular novels penned by laywomen, and anonymous articles in popular newspapers sang the praise of home and motherhood. Angelic smiles, tender looks, and sacrificial courage demonstrated the irresistible love of mothers. Cloistered in their home, the domestic ideology explained, mothers devoted their energies to their little ones and modeled their homes on the Holy Family. Catholic writers fully agreed with their Protestant counterparts that without good mothers, there could be no family, no religion, and no nation.

Catholic domestic ideology firmly placed the mother at home surrounded by devoted children and husband. Woman's place, it emphasized, was in the home. For many Catholic American women, their place historically *has* been in the home. From the frontier Catholic who let the traveling priest say mass in her house, to the Irish serving girl who cleaned and polished, to the sururban mother baking Easter bread, home life has been the center of many women's lives. That home life, however, has often reflected little of the prevailing domestic ideology. While some Catholic women wrote books on the ideal woman, others struggled to support their families, maintain their own ethnic domestic traditions, and carve out a measure of independence in their households.

To discuss the role of Catholic women within the home is a complicated and far-reaching task. We cannot merely survey the rhetoric used to praise home and mother, nor can we assume that those ideals did not influence the behavior and feelings of real mothers. While the model mother and wife are painted with vivid colors, real Catholic wives and mothers have left to us few statements of their inner feelings. We cannot limit our study to the middle class, since that eliminates a large portion of America's Catholics. Since each ethnic group expresses unique domestic customs, we cannot assume a unified Catholic culture. We cannot even assume that the mother was the chief caretaker of the children, the organizer of home celebrations, and the focus of domestic piety. While a woman's place may indeed have been in the home, her role within that family varied by class, ethnic group, educational level, and age.

To understand the religious role of Catholic women in the home, we have divided the time between 1860 and 1960 into three overlapping periods. From 1860 to 1920 domestic ideology hailed the mother as the center of the home and the perfect family as the foundation of Catholicism. This ideology, created by the arbiters of Catholic culture—middle-class laymen and women, Irish priests and bishops, and the Roman hierarchy—remained for many women too idealistic. Out of necessity it was frequently modified or ignored. Concurrent with the establishment of this "mainstream" Catholic ideology was the influx of new immigrants to America. In the second period, from 1880 to 1940, American Catholicism underwent rapid growth and diversification. Since we cannot describe the domestic religious activities of all the immigrant communities, we will focus on the domestic piety of Italian, Mexican, and Polish women. Although their religiosity differs from Irish and American Catholics, they share two themes: the tendency to imbue everyday home life with a sense of the sacred and the attempt to tame supernatural characters by associating them with the family. Finally, in the period between 1940 and 1960, the principal focus of mainstream Catholic culture with regard to domesticity has been to describe how the values of modern, secular society conflict with family values and how women should respond to such threats. The domestic ideology created in the nineteenth century is still present but less richly articulated. The praising of mothers subsides as Catholic writers begin to encourage men to take over the religious leadership of their families. Women continued to serve a primary role in their family's religious activities, but during the 1940s and 1950s Catholic culture reasserts the patriarchal nature of Catholicism as a balance to suburban domestic life.

A difficult task is thus set before us. We must try to find order and meaning in a domestic ideology that for a modern reader may be hopelessly sentimental. Underneath or around that ideology we must discover what values and behaviors women incorporated into their lives. How did the views of priests, novelists, and critics—both men and women—penetrate into the homes of American women? In this study we can only begin to ferret out the actual behavior of Catholic women within the home. By looking at the development of domestic ideals and the activities of real women at home, a private American Catholicism emerges.

CREATING DOMESTIC IDEOLOGY, 1860–1920

The Catholic ideology that served as a standard measure of womanhood until the Second Vatican Council was a combination of the unique social characteristics of Irish-Americans, the efforts of a Catholic literary elite, traditional European views on women, and a strongly articulated Protestant (*qua* secular) cult of domesticity. Catholic domesticity presented an ideal picture of the behavior and values of women within the home. Spanish-speaking women in the western parts of the United States, newly arrived immigrants from south and central Europe, and rural Catholics contributed little to the creation of domestic ideals. These women carried their domestic values and customs with them from their homelands and maintained them in small, cohesive communities. Either geographically or culturally far from the urban centers of publishing, the seminaries, and the ladies' academies, these women had little contact with emerging Catholic domestic culture. It would be educated Irish and Irish-American Catholics, well acquainted with acceptable European and American standards, who created norms for home life and described women's place within it.

From 1830 to 1920, approximately 4.7 million Irish immigrated to the United States. The vast majority of those men and women felt themselves to be Catholic, although many were unchurched and religiously ill-educated. In spite of the immigrant's dream of a better life in America, life in the New World held little joy for most of the arriving Irish. Those who stayed in the major East Coast cities faced lives riddled with discrimination, Protestant hostility, slum housing, and poverty. Their infant mortality rate was higher than that of any other early immigrant group; Irish crime in New York City at mid-century exceeded by five times that of the American-born and German populations; and their occupational mobility appeared to be as low as that of American blacks. Fleeing poverty and oppression in Ireland, many confronted a similar fate in the United States.

The Irish immigrants who flocked to New York, Boston, Philadelphia, and other industrial cities were unprepared for urban living. Eighty percent of the Irish who emigrated between 1850 and 1920 were unskilled farmers. Few had ever worked in a city or even visited one. Family patterns in Ireland conformed to this social reality: because of the scarcity of land, people married late, if at all. Most of the immigrants arrived in America unmarried and hoped to send money back to their families. Many men and women remained single in America, but those who did marry and bear children did so with enthusiam. By 1940, the Irish were second only to the French Canadians in their rate of reproduction.

The prevalence of permanent celibacy in Ireland encouraged the development of a sex-segregated social structure. Men who waited for marriage in Ireland met together in pubs, at fairs, or in the fields to drink and share stories. Women gathered in their homes, chatting with relatives and friends while working and watching children. Both men and women felt most comfortable with others of the same sex. In most cases, this same-sex bonding continued after marriage. While the marriage rate increased for the Irish in America, same-sex bonding remained strong. Life in urban America did not make it any easier for men and women to socialize freely. Irish men, whose occupational opportunities were initially limited to laboring, found little opportunity to meet or converse with women. Single Irish women, who arrived in America at the same rate as men (coming in even greater numbers during several years), worked primarily as domestic servants or in the needle trades. As servants, their associations with men were severely limited; as seamstresses, their interactions were primarily with other women.

The American Catholic church struggled to minister to the arriving immigrants. With little knowledge of Catholic doctrine and a history of British religious persecution, the Irish were infrequent church-goers and practiced a folk religion their clergy condemned. In New York City during the 1840s the priest-to-people ratio was 1 to 4,500 and in the western territories it grew to 1 to 7,000. After the great potato famine, however, the bishops in Ireland and America conducted a major effort to increase the number of clergy and religious teachers, to teach the people the basics of religion, and to cement their loyalty to the church. In a remarkably short period of time, the Irish in America came to dominate the Catholic church. By the closing decades of the century, the vast majority of priests were Irish and about half of the bishops were of Irish background. Since the appointment of the first U.S. cardinal in 1875, only four out of seventeen cardinals have *not* been Irish. Although the clergy still complained about sporadic mass attendance by men, by the end of the century the Irish had become devoted to the parish and its priests.

The social situation for most of the Irish in America up until the late nineteenth century was not conducive to the establishment of a domestic ideology that promoted the nuclear family, the isolation of women in their homes, and the Christian rearing of children. The importance of the extended family in Ireland, the continuation of same-sex bonding, high rates of permanent celibacy, child labor, and slum living provided an inhospitable environment for the growth of domestic sentiments. There were, however, some Irish Americans who felt that proper home sentiments needed to be articulated and developed among their countrymen. Before the Civil War, Catholic novelists played a crucial role in the development of Catholic domesticity. While the majority of Irish Catholics lived in poverty, these writers detailed what they believed to be a proper home life. They fabricated their images from the ideal of an aristocratic Catholic upper class—Europeans who lived in Old World charm in America—and nostalgic memories of an old-fashioned Irish working class one step out of the bog. While some were priests, the majority were laymen and women who used their writing skills to detail an appropriate Catholic lifestyle and provide strategies for coping with the difficulties of life in the New World.

Mid-nineteenth-century novelists, late-century family newspapers, and translated European advice books echoed a central theme regarding Catholic domesticity. Without a strong family, they exclaimed, religion, the nation, and the economic structure would crumble. The family served as the "nursery of the nation," and the nation was nothing "save a large family." In spite of the economic and social problems that the Irish found in the New World, Catholic culture told them that social, spiritual, and personal ills could be averted if the family coped with hardship and maintained its integrity. The family performed this function not because it was merely a natural or economic unit but because it was an institution founded by God. Writers compared the "true home" to the joys of heaven and the perfect harmony found in Eden. Just as Jesus had lived in a family and followed the dictates of his parents, so the Catholic family was blessed by God.

Some writers went as far as to say that nothing was more sacred than the family—even the church—and that the church was actually created for families. A Miss Barry wrote in 1890 that "all institutions and ordinances which God has created in civil society, and bestowed upon his Church, have for their main purpose to secure the existence, the honor, and the happiness of every home."[3] Laywomen saw their domestic roles as increasingly important as they were told that their homes were sacred schools for the production of good Catholics. In 1877, the editor of *Catholic World* specifically sought to counter the overestimation of home life by reasserting the superiority of celibacy. In an article on French home life, a translation of *La Vie domestique* by Charles de Ribbe, a certain Madame de Lamartine had compared her married life to that of a Sister of Mercy. In a footnote, the editor clearly pointed out that "in regard to the heroic virtue that can be practised in the married state there can be no question. As little can there be any question that in the scale of perfection the religious is the higher state."[4] Catholics encountered a long-standing tradition that accorded the life of the celibate religious the highest merit, while maintaining that the home was "the spot where angels find a resting place/When bearing blessings, they descend to earth."[5]

What was the ideal Catholic home supposed to look like? Since the earthly home was asked to imitate the celestial realms of Eden and paradise, as well as the divine home of Nazareth, it was crucial that it be well ordered. Order in heaven dictated order on earth. To have control over one's environment demonstrated control over personal passions and societal flux. Catholic writers used a theory of correspondence to assert that a well-ordered home created well-ordered citizens, which created a well-ordered nation. The home should always be neat and tidy. Cleanliness and order went hand in hand as the guiding principles by which families controlled their domestic space and thus their personal and political space.

The brunt of demonstrating domestic virtues was borne by women, although good Catholic men were also to manifest orderliness in their lifestyles. Irish women were assumed to possess a high level of purity and simplicity, no matter how refined they became. Their scrupulous neatness and cleanliness would produce a cheerful and restful home for their families. Novelists created pictures of families in their parlors or sitting rooms, enjoying each other's company, but not directly interacting. Father might be reading, mother sewing, and the children playing or studying. The overall effect was one of harmony, peace, and love. Brawls, bickering, noise, and disorder were eliminated from the scenario. No one demanded too much attention from the others nor sat apart in isolation.

This cheerful home provided a source of recreation and relaxation for the working men of the family. In an 1894 sermon, Cardinal James Gibbons colorfully described the model home. "Christian women, when your husbands and sons return to you in the evening after buffeting with the waves of the world," he pleaded, "let them find in your homes a haven of rest. Do not pour into the bleeding wounds of their hearts the gall of bitter words, but rather the oil of gladness and consolation."[6] Note that Gibbons included sons as laborers, referring to male children, but he ignored working daughters. The male world was perceived as being chaotic, threatening, and exhausting—only the ordered space of the home could truly restore the men. Women, understood by the cardinal as naturally more domestic, could somehow cope better with work-related stress. The reality of women's home activities, which frequently included taking in laundry, doing piece-meal finishing work, or coping with boarders, did not fit well into the pattern outlined by the cardinal.

The purpose of keeping a clean, cheerful house was to keep the wandering members of the family—the men and boys—close at home. The logic inherent in the idea was that if the father was happy and relaxed, he would stay in his cheery house and not go out to the cheery pub. Even middle-class women confronted the masculine habit of preferring male companionship to home delights. Many women coped with the reality of caring for large families because their husbands either had deserted, gone west to find employment, or become chronic alcoholics. The creators of domestic ideals pressured women to strive to keep their men at home. Wives and mothers, who saw what happened when men became disenchanted with their families and shirked their responsibilities, must have felt they shouldered a tremendous responsibility. From the pulpit, the popular novel, and the Catholic newspaper, women were told that a poor home life—not poverty, slums, or social disorder—made men forget their families' needs.

Although Catholic domestic ideology assumed that women did not work outside of the home, it did not promote a life of leisure. While the home functioned as a place of rest and repose for men, women were supposed to reflect the work ethic of the family. Catholic writers insisted that increased financial stability did not mean that women became idle objects. Women in the home had to be busy producers. "If half the time and money wasted on music, dancing and embroidery," chided the *Baltimore Mirror* were employed in teaching daughters the useful art of making shirts, and mending stockings and managing household affairs, then…the number of happy homes would be multiplied."[7] Catholic writers did not subscribe to the notion articulated by Thorstein Veblen that idle women symbolized male attainment and status. Catholic women were told to occupy themselves with the practical tasks of housekeeping. Mary Sadlier particularly liked ridiculing in her fiction those seminary-educated daughters who could only play the piano, make wax flowers, and speak a few words of French.

On the other hand, Irish and Irish Americans much admired French culture and the leisured, aristocratic, but Catholic, life it symbolized. Rather than imitating upper-class America, which was decidedly Protestant, Catholics found that French style and customs provided the refinement through which they sought to separate themselves from the "bog Irish." Many advice books were translated from the French. Families sent their daughters to French-language boarding schools where they learned not housekeeping, but the useless embroidery and piano. French religious articles were advertised in Catholic newspapers. Even the French language was considered to be more polite and elegant than English and refined ladies were believed to say their prayers and do their daily devotions in French.

The fascination with French Catholicism also brought a reassertion of the patriarchal household. European advice-book writers were especially rigid in their description of the hierarchical organization of the family. Catholic domestic ideology emphasized traditional lines of authority within the home. Authority in the household permitted the continued assertion of order. The domestic hierarchy reflected the relationship between God and his people and also the church where a pope headed a procession of cardinals, bishops, and clergy. In the introduction to *The Christian Father: What He Should Be and What He Should Do*, Stephen Vincent Ryan, C.M., the bishop of Buffalo stated that "the father actually holds the place of God, and exercises an authority subordinate only to that of God, over his children." In return, he should receive respect and honor "approximating the honor paid to God himself."[8] Children, and wives to some extent, were under the natural and God-given authority of the Father (husband). Breaking away from the family—by men or women— was looked upon as a fundamental domestic sin.

The belief that women were to be under the patriarchal authority of either their father or husband was balanced in Catholic novels by matriarchal trends. In many novels, powerful female characters emerged who were quite independent. These women were always unmarried—either being single or widowed. They ran large households, managed inherited money, traveled, and had adventures. Although the single ones usually ended up married at the end of the story, there was a strong trend to subvert the domestic message by presenting women who were not under the rule of men and yet appeared to be quite independent and happy. Although still within the acceptable realm of the home, as widows or servants, these women were freed from male control. The novelists acknowledged the rule of men over women, but when they wanted to create interesting female characters, they eliminated the authority problem by eliminating the men.

Another way that writers subverted male authority was to emphasize the woman's capacity to "save" her family. This trend had become very popular in Protestant America where women were seen to be more religious and virtuous than men. While Protestants had limited the influence of Mary and the female saints, they had discovered female saving power in mothers, daughters, and wives. Although Catholic literature had a strong streak of the "Eve" character—the seductive, evil woman—popular writing heralded women's redemptive character. Countless stories recalled how sons, remembering their mothers, are saved from evil influence. In 1890, a Philadelphia newspaper carried a story where a mother's "dumb look from her death-bed" motivated the "wretched youth" to become a Jesuit missionary.[9] Likewise, the *Sacred Heart Review* explained in "A Mother's Influence" that the kiss "my mother gave me, has often proved the password to purity and honor in a young man's career and a shield against the many temptations in a young girl's life."[10] The wife or mother not only provided for the physical and psychological well-being of the husband or son, she also shouldered much of the responsibility for his spiritual life.

Catholic culture permitted women such great responsibilities because their everyday lives were perceived as intrinsically religious. Although wives and mothers had chosen the lesser path to heaven, their married life could in many ways duplicate that of a celibate religious. The *Catholic Home Journal* called mothers "home heroes" because they were modestly secluded from "men's praises" and devoted their energies to their children which the "outer world does not know."[11] The mother, like the nun, was retired and secluded, cloistered in her home. Like a saint, her sacrifices went unknown and unacknowledged. The conviction that married women could imitate the life of the nun has a long tradition beginning with Francois de Sales's advice to French women. Following this trend, French priest Paul Lejeune created a "rule" for women that imitated the life of the religious without its precision and severity. Translated in 1913 and published by a major Catholic press, the *Counsels of Perfection for Christian Mothers* encouraged mothers to rise and retire early, to say their morning and evening prayers kneeling, to spend fifteen minutes per day with spiritual reading, to meditate, attend daily mass, and to receive Holy Communion frequently. Although women were encouraged not to let a day pass without reading a page from the Bible, they were warned against reading the mystical writings of John of the Cross and Teresa of Avila because women's imaginations were too sensitive to the "extraordinary phenomena recorded in the works."[12]

Even novelists like Mary Sadlier, who include many independent women in her novels, saw the true Catholic woman as one who retired from the world. Servant girls might be virtuous, but eventually they would marry and step out of the working world. There were no Sadlier women who worked outside of the home for reasons other than poverty. Another writer, Eleanor Donnelly, recalled the life of "Marguerite" who sought fame on the stage as a singer. After a professional tragedy she settled down to housekeeping, telling her new husband "my pride is justly punished."[13] The nun's life of poverty, chastity, and obedience was to be replicable in the Catholic home.

Mary Sadlier acknowledged that this Catholic view of women differed from the Protestant perspective. In 1855, she described a Catholic teaching sister who "had she been a Protestant she would have been a strong-minded woman; beyond all doubt; she might have taken the lead at public meeting, edited a daily newspaper in some of our great cities, delivered public lecturers, and written huge volumes on meta-physics or philosophy." This woman, however, "being a Catholic ...and born in Ireland" chose the better path of feminine modesty and Christian humility. She was "taught to consider human learning as a mere accessory to the grand science of salvation." The true woman chose the higher calling, "the unworldly step of retiring from the world, to live a life of seclusion and of mortification."[14] In the convent or in the home, the woman was to direct her attention not to worldly activities, but to the higher cause of God and family. To say that a woman's place was in the home was similar to saying a woman's place was in the cloister, both assumed an other worldly mentality that isolated women from the public sphere.

Catholic women who for economic or personal reasons sought paid labor were encouraged not to seek careers that took them too far away from the home. In 1886, "Hannah" wrote a letter to "Aunt Bride" that appeared in the *Sacred Heart Review*. Hannah was currently doing domestic work, but she wanted to learn "typewriting" and to become a secretary. "It is not that I am above domestic work," she wrote the newspaper, "but would like to try something different."[15] Aunt Bride spent the bulk of her response telling Hannah how difficult such jobs were—you must learn two languages and have perfect grammar and spelling. Encouraging Hannah to go back to housekeeping, Aunt Bride suggested she learn specialty cooking, become a trained attendant for the sick, or nursery maid. For Aunt Bride—a good representative of Catholic attitudes toward women and the family—if a woman needed to work, let her work in the confines of the home, even if it was a Protestant family who paid her for her labors. Domestic work was approved because it meant that women stayed in the home. Many Irish women, however, well-versed in the difficulties of domestic labor rejected this advice and moved into factory and clerical work, teaching, and other nondomestic positions as quickly as they could get the proper education. While domestic work was presented as an acceptable way for women to earn money if they must, the realities of being a servant—poor pay, no independence, and cranky mistresses—drove Irish working women away from such jobs.

The activities of the Catholic mother were also compared to the role the Virgin Mary played within the Holy Family. The association of women with Mary presented certain problems for domestic writers. The Virgin Mary enjoyed in Catholic tradition a long history that emphasized her powerful and royal characteristics. Mary was the queen of heaven who was often portrayed in medieval and Renaissance art as the "fourth member of the Trinity." Her connection to Christ was more direct than that of her husband Joseph. In order to reduce the feminine power of the Virgin Mary, writers placed her within the domestic structure of life in Nazareth. No longer the queen of the universe, Mary became a Hebrew housewife who looked after the needs of husband and child. "The Blessed Virgin," explained an 1887 article in the *Catholic Home*, "was beyond all measure superior in dignity to St. Joseph, but it is not she who guides and rules in this model family." The author summarized this perspective by finishing with the Pauline quote, "Let women be subject to their husbands as to the Lord."[16] In the *Catholic Girl's Guide* of 1905, Mary made her home inviting and comfortable for St. Joseph when he came home from work. Joseph was pleased to see "his evening meal ready and everything as orderly as possible."[17] Advice book writers stripped Mary of her supernatural powers and presented her in the peaceful house of Nazareth industriously pursuing the vocation of a poor artisan's wife. Mary, seen from this perspective, was the ideal model for women—an ever-virgin mother, obedient, suffering, unselfish, and pious.

If women followed the model of Mary and maintained the spirituality of a nun, they were considered worthy to become priestesses of the domestic shrine. Although they were not real priests, they could officiate at the sanctuary of the home by directing their domestic sacrifices to God. Women were asked to cultivate religious sentiments in their family through their personal religious activities. In 1868, Sister Mary Carroll described a scene from *Pleasant Homes* in which a mother listened to her children recite the catechism and helped them "to ask questions about anything they did not understand, that she might be able to instruct them correctly." She also read from a book for twenty minutes, explaining the evening chapter [from the Bible?], told stories about the saints to "enliven the lesson," and corrected the children's pronunciation of theological terms. The evening ended with prayers.[18] Mothers were to teach their young children how to make the sign of the cross and say the sacred name of Jesus and the holy name of Mary. "What is the Christian mother?" queried a French priest whose advice book circulated in America. She was the one who has chosen "the slavery of home duties" and made "maternity a priesthood" by pouring the "faith of Christ into the very veins of her child as she nurses him at her breast."[19]

The informal religious tasks such as helping children with their catechism or hearing evening prayers were activities that easily fell to the mother to perform. Mothers did this not only because they were close to their children, but because such religious activities were not considered to be the duties of the father. Unlike the Protestant family where the father presided over formal family prayers, family worship was not traditionally promoted among Catholics, who rather were told to say morning and evening prayers as individual, private devotions. Beginning in the late nineteenth century, however, American and international sources began to encourage families to pray together. Papal encyclicals *Supremi apostolatus officio* (1883) and *Fidentem piumque animum* (1896) asked families to pray the rosary together. In 1892, Cardinal Gibbons pleaded for family prayers. In none of these cases was the father asked to direct these activities, although Gibbons specifically called on both the mother and the father to gather their children in the evening for devotions. While some European sources tried to insist that father act as priest to his household, American writers appeared willing to assign this task to both parents or to the mother alone.

When describing the ideal Catholic home, few writers neglected to mention the display of domestic altars. While novelists described how the "better" Catholic families had chapels or oratories, popular newspapers recommended every family to set aside at least a corner for God. Since most Catholic devotions were private and not done by the family as a whole, bedrooms often were described as containing impromptu altars. When the door to the Kielys' "peasant" bedroom stood ajar, one could see "a statue of the Sacred Heart on a little altar with gauze curtains and a red lamp lighting [it]."[20] Lit candles, statues, holy pictures, flowers, as well as the articles advertised by Catholic religious goods stores made the home into a sacred space. After the turn of the century, the cult of the Sacred Heart became popular among Irish Americans, and in 1915 Benedict XV granted special indulgences to those who consecrated their homes to the Sacred Heart. Although house blessings by priests had a long Catholic tradition, house blessings connected with a picture of the Sacred Heart became a symbol of the Irish Catholic home.

The proliferation of religious articles in the home accompanied the rise in Catholic attention toward the family. Homes in rural Ireland during the early and mid-nineteenth century did not display a vast number of religious handicrafts. Poverty limited the expenditures of the family, the lack of mass-produced religious articles restricted the number of goods available, and a lack of interest in religious matters curbed the display of Catholic sentiments. The traditional St. Bridget's cross of blessed palms was often the cottage's only religious adornment. By the end of the century, however, the situation had greatly changed. A coordinated effort by bishops and clergy to reawaken Irish Catholicism had succeeded and sparked a new interest in displaying religious articles in the home. As more Irish recovered from the great famine of the 1850s and entered into the middle class, they found a plethora of mass-produced religious articles to buy, a change that may be seen in the home exhibits at the Glencolumbkille Folk Museum in County Donegal. The prefamine cottage has no religious art except a crucifix; the 1850s cottier's cabin has a crucifix and a statue of Mary (as well as a misplaced 1893 house blessing); and the 1900 home has house blessings, holy pictures, statues, and a crucifix.

A similar development occurred in America. As Irish American Catholics moved into the middle class, they possessed the resources and the proper domestic sentiments to motivate the purchase and display of religious articles. Late-nineteenth-century Catholics readily combined their religion's penchant for sensuality with the Victorian trend for display and surrounded themselves with symbols of their religion and culture. Although few homes could live up to the ideals set before them by the Catholic press and the pulpits, the message was too loud to be ignored. For those Catholics who aspired to religious, economic, and social respectability, striving to present the proper home became an important goal.

It is difficult to evaluate to what extent the message of Catholic domesticity influenced those Irish who were not in the middle class. Photographs of the period show that even in poor families religious prints and statues could be found. In 1903, social workers from Barnard College interviewed working-class Irish families from the West Side of New York City. Although their descriptions reveal a considerable middle-class bias, their observations depict typical conditions that many Irish families experienced throughout the nineteenth century. From one of the interviews, we can get a glimpse of the interaction between Catholicism and home in the life of one Irish woman. It provides us with a brief, if provocative, indication of how domestic Catholicism appeared in the working classes.

Bridget Donelly came by herself to America in 1876. Her father and brother had died in Ireland and her mother had gone mad with grief over their deaths. Upon arrival, she went to work in a silk and wool factory, lived in factory housing, sent money home to her mother and paid for the passage to America of her two elder sisters. After her mother's death and the accumulation of some savings, Bridget felt free to quit her job and marry Martin O'Brien, a friend who had followed her over from Ireland. The next year, at the age of twenty eight Bridget had her first child, who died fourteen months later. Another son was born a year later, who also died in infancy, and a third son was delivered stillborn. Other children came in rapid succession, and by her fifty-third birthday, Bridget O'Brien had six living children all of whom had had bouts of scarlet fever, chronic bronchitis, stomach trouble, and pneumonia.

Bridget O'Brien saw to the religious education of her children. Those children who did not work attended parochial school, but one son refused to learn his catechism well enough to be confirmed. Daughter Ellen, however, learned so well that she received a new white dress and veil for her confirmation. Bridget told her interviewer that she heard her children's prayers every morning and evening, and she and her husband attended their parish church regularly. Her husband, Martin, was strong willed, often drunk, and sporadically employed. Bridget rarely discussed domestic matters with him because he angered easily. Although he stayed home nights, during the day, when he was not working or drunk, he hung out at the local saloon. Bridget insisted that she would stay with Martin even if he drank continuously, but her children ignored him in their nightly prayers. Bridget explained to the interviewer that poor people ought to stay single because their lives are so difficult. If she had known about married life, she would have never married. Nine children were too many to bear; six too many to clothe and feed. But Bridget summarized, "it is God's will if he wants them to come or to go from us."[21]

Irish women in America, like Bridget Donelly O'Brien, had mixed feelings about marriage and family. Many had come from Ireland to escape family problems, the lack of suitable marriage mates, and domestic poverty. In America, they experienced for the first time a semi-independent status by earning their own wages. While some squandered their earnings on clothing, most sent money back to Ireland and gained respectability in their extended family. To marry meant to lose whatever hard-earned freedom they had won, to be subject to frequent childbearing, and to cope with the family instability that chronic poverty produced. Although the prospects of being a spinster domestic servant looked bleak, the alternative of marriage also held little promise of happiness. The realities of everyday life left little room for a sentimental picture of motherhood and family life.

On the other hand, Bridget's efforts to send her children to parochial school, to see that they learn their catechism, and to find the money to purchase a confirmation dress point to a strong commitment to Catholic principles. The Barnard sociologists also reported that in a three-room tenement that held two parents and six children they found a family shrine containing an image of the Virgin, a rosary, a family Bible, a picture of Saint Anthony, several brightly colored vases filled with artificial flowers, two glass crucifixes, a china image of the Virgin, a plaster image of Mary with the infant Jesus, colored pictures of Saint Benedict and other saints, a newspaper print of Leo XIII and of Pius X, photographs of a relative's tombstone in Ireland, and family photographs in a gilt frame decorated by palm leaves. While Bridget and the other Irish of New York's middle West Side might have no use for the sentimental idealization of the home, they did respond to reform efforts in both Ireland and America to involve the poor and working class in Catholic life. The availability of inexpensive mass-produced religious prints and articles made it possible for even the poor to show their piety while infusing color and individuality into their drab surroundings. Although the middle-class social workers might have considered the profusion of religion and color overdone and tacky, this type of religious expression was encouraged by the prevailing Catholic domestic ideology. Women, poor or wealthy, were expected to maintain a visibly Catholic home.

ETHNIC DIVERSITY, 1880–1940

Irish Americans, through their monopoly of the hierarchy and lay leadership, set the standards for Catholic life in the United States. But while they dominated the community, they were not the only Catholic ethnic group in America. At the same time that Irish Americans—with help from European advice books—articulated a domestic ideology, new immigrants were arriving from southern and eastern Europe. Each brought with them customs and traditions that varied both from the Irish and from the accepted traditions of Counter-Reformation Catholicism. The religious activities of women from other ethnic groups provide a rich picture of an active religious life, even if not always approved by Catholic leaders. In their homes, women preserved and modified traditions from the Old World that had been passed down in their families for generations. While many of their husbands and fathers would find little comfort or spiritual uplift in Catholicism, immigrant women maintained their associations with the church—on their own terms. We cannot describe the full religious life of ethnic women, but we can give a flavor of their piety by focusing on a few of the domestic activities of Italian, Mexican, and Polish mothers and wives.

Between 1880 and 1920, approximately four million Italians emigrated to the United States. Increases in population, decreases in available arable land, and changes from the "old way of life" threatened the stability of the southern Italian peasant farmer. Although many Mexicans had resided in what was to be the southwestern United States for generations, the social situations of Mexicans and Mexican lands to the United States after the Mexican-American War (1846–1848) caused many Mexicans to lose control over their land. Like the Italians, many Mexicans became unskilled laborers and, because of their location in the rich agricultural areas of the west, migrant farm workers. Although emigration from Italy radically decreased after the 1920s, Mexican immigration into California, Texas, New Mexico, Colorado, and Arizona continued to grow.

Both southern Italian and Mexican immigrants exhibited a cautious relationship with institutional Catholicism. In both cases, Catholicism in the homeland was associated with the landowning upper classes and the status quo. Immigrants who arrived from Sicily and other regions of southern Italy brought with them anticlericalism, religious indifference, and a folk Catholicism frequently labeled as superstitious. After Mexico claimed its independence from Spain, the recruiting of clergy from Europe stopped and the number of priests decreased. For a few Mexicans, this meant that the father of the family replaced the priest and that home devotions increased, but for most it meant that being Catholic became a biological fact that had little to do with conviction or practice. Like the Italians, the Mexicans felt alienated from a religious tradition perceived to be the support of the rich and powerful. These two immigrant groups differed significantly from the Irish who had found support for their claims against their English rulers and landlords among the Catholic clergy.

Furthermore, the Italian and Mexican immigrants found an American Catholicism thoroughly steeped in Irish ways. The state of one's Catholicism was measured by attendance at mass, respect for the priest, and participation in parish activities. The Italian and Mexican preference for communal religious celebrations (the *festa* or *fiesta*), their elaborate rites of passage (baptisms, weddings, funerals), and their emotional devotion to the saints had little in common with the more restrained Irish. While the Irish were willing to follow their educated clergy and lay leaders, Italian and Mexican immigrants chose to continue the religious traditions brought from their villages. The public space of the streets and the private domain of the home served as the places for religious expression, so that parish life held little importance.

The family was the most important element in Italian and Mexican life—not merely the nuclear family of mother, father, and child, but also the extended family of aunts, uncles, grandparents, and cousins. More important than the Catholic church, American culture, or the individual aspirations of its members, domestic values superseded all others. Men were expected to assume the responsibility for the extended family's economic and general well-being. They were to be aware of the political forces and organizations that could either challenge or support the family's integrity. Jobs, politics, the institutional church—these were the domain of men. Women were responsible for the day-to-day wellbeing of the family. They maintained lines of communications between relatives, saw to the balancing of the family budget, and coped with daily problems. While the men criticized the institutional church, women developed a private relationship with Christ, the Virgin Mary, and the saints. In Mexican and Italian families a division of outlook separated the men's world from the women's world.

Since women were responsible for the everyday well-being of their families, their religious activities within the home centered around family needs and personal concerns. In spite of Mexican or Italian men joking about their wives' attendance at mass, the women found a source of uplift and comfort in their religious activities. In Italian and Mexican families, mothers passed down to their daughters a religious attitude that included church attendance, private prayer, and the knowledge of folklore. Although men probably had more respect for domestic Catholicism than for parish Catholicism, they still tended to leave the creation of a religious home environment to their wives and mothers.

The most visible expression of a woman's piety was the maintenance of domestic shrines. In Mexican families, women often maintained shrines in a corner of their bedrooms. Frequently, the largest statue would be of the Virgin of Guadalupe (the protectress of Mexico) but she would be surrounded by other statues—the miraculous child Santo Niño de Atocha, his mother Santa Maria de Atocha, a Nuestra Señnora de San Juan de Los Lagos, and Saint Anthony of Padua. Candles, fresh or paper flowers, and important documents from the family such as a marriage certificate or letters might be placed with the statues. One or two candles would be lit signifying the continual devotion of the woman to the saints. A rosary, novena cards, special medals, and crucifixes were often placed on the altar and pictures of the saints and family members hung on the wall. Souvenirs from old Mexico added to the eclectic nature of the shrine.

The placement of both religious and family objects together at the shrine emphasized the close association of the family and the supernatural world. The altar was not a separate religious space, but a place where family and religion were brought together. The religious characters were understood as a family and the family was understood as being the source of ultimate meaning. The family itself had a sacred quality. With its sensual, tactile, and colorful aspects, the family shrine underscored the lively character of home religion. Catholicism practiced at home by women was not abstract and intellectual, but immediate, practical, and earthy.

Similar altars were constructed by Italian women. In each room a shrine would contain statues, favorite pictures of the saints, religious candles, and dried palms from several Palm Sundays. The saints most frequently depicted in statues and in engravings were the sacred figures who expressed the relationships of the extended family: The Madonna who held the infant in her arms connected the mother of the family with the divine; the saints Cosmos and Damian were brothers who died together; and the Holy Family of Nazareth reminded the earthly family of the biblical model. For many Italians, the Holy Family itself became the Trinity—mother, father, and child—but always with grandmother St. Ann standing in the background. The Holy Family, like the extended Italian family, had to be multigenerational. Since the saints themselves were understood as being a part of the extended family, if they did not respond to the petitions of their earthly children, they could be chided or ignored like any other family member. Italian women, like Mexican women, saw Catholicism as tightly connected to the well-being of the family. Praying in front of statues or at home was not merely supplementary to church prayers, but in many cases replaced church activities.

Italian and Mexican immigrants who settled in America brought with them fears that could only be controlled by careful behavior and ritual precaution. The world in which they lived was not only filled with saints but also with demons, the evil eye, and ghosts. In Italian homes animal horns were placed in doorways as protection against the evil eye. Amulets were worn, especially by women and children, to ward off evil. Teeth, claws, and replicas of animal horns were sewn on clothing, held in pockets, or included on necklaces or bracelets. Medals were placed in the swaddling clothes of babies, and mothers taught their daughters how to cope with the power of witches. Richard Gambino recalled how his grandmother did not feel that the gold crucifix he wore was sufficient protection; when he was ill, she sewed little sacks filled with an unknown substance to his clothes.

In 1954, a sociologist studying Mexican American families living in public housing in San Antonio, Texas, reported a similar concern of women for protecting their family against the evil eye (*ojo*). To detect whether or not a person was suffering from *ojo* a woman would rub the body of the suspect with an unbroken egg while repeating the Our Father and Hail Mary, finishing at the feet with the Apostle's Creed. The egg would eventually be broken into a glass of water. If, after a number of hours, a round spot resembling an eye appeared on the egg, the conclusion was that the person had been inflicted with the evil eye. Holy water was also valued for its power to help families avoid misfortune and calamity. While present-day readers might scoff at the odd mixture of folklore and standard Catholicism, these rites stress the connection between a woman's concern for her family and her belief in supernatural forces. The orthodox Catholic promotion of the grand scheme of salvation, with its doctrines of sin, atonement, and heavenly reward, held little meaning for immigrants tightly rooted in the here-and-now.

Catholicism for Mexican or Italian women had to "work" for them and their families. Perhaps one of the most important ways that women used religion within their homes was in healing rituals. In 1947, Beatrice Griffith published an account of growing up in a Mexican-American community. Her younger brother Jesusito had been quite ill and nothing the doctors did improved his condition. Each Holy Saturday (*Sâbado de Gloria*) before Easter, her mother organized a healing rite performed by her grandfather. While in Mexico the rite was performed by the grandfather outdoors, in the United States he had to go inside the private space of the home to do the healing. Only old men and young boys—those outside of the mainstream male world—were involved in such rituals in America. The house was prepared by the mother and daughters by sprinkling holy water and arranging white carnations and roses. A son held a baby chick. The grandfather began the rite by praying in Spanish and touching the children present with the white carnations. He touched Jesusito's useless legs and prayed "*Creo Dios Padre.*" Finally he took the baby chick and tried to make it drink water from the mouth of the sick child. "For my mother," Griffith wrote, "it was a good time. Every year it was a good time at *Sâbado de Gloria*, it was a new beginning for everyone, a new chance for good living—a prayer for God's blessings."[22] It was a time when a mother could try to heal her sick child. While the first generation of immigrants insisted on the maintenance of Old World customs, the second and third generation often resented the ways of their parents. The resentment did not stem from the younger generation's involvement with institutional Catholicism, but rather with the desire to become Americanized. Children ridiculed folk Catholicism not because of its unorthodox nature, but because it was old-fashioned and unscientific. In Griffith's account of the *Sâbado de Gloria* ritual, her oldest sister, Carmen, rejected the efforts of her mother to get her involved with the preparations for the healing ceremony. "I'm not going to get cleaned with those flowers and prayers," she yelled from the kitchen, "it's just black magic. I don't want any of that stuff. The kids at school make fun of you if you do that. They think we're dumb anyway."[23] Likewise, Gambino's mother removed the little amulets his grandmother sewed onto his clothes as soon as she discovered them. While the second and third generations of Italian Americans did not become more involved in parish life, they did show some skepticism about the traditions their parents brought from the old country. Private healing rituals in particular appeared to contradict the American preference for a scientific and impersonal medical system. Italian and Mexican women experienced intergenerational conflicts as they tried to negotiate between tight-knit families whose values were based on generations of rural life and the individualistic and work-oriented expectations of urban American society.

A third new immigrant group, the Poles, provide a contrast to the Italians and Mexicans.

Between the 1880s and the 1920s, over 2 million immigrants came to America from the dismembered ancient kingdom of Poland, which had been divided between Germany, Austria, and Russia. Like most immigrants, they came because the economic and social situation in their homeland made it impossible for them to own land. More men came than women, and those who decided to stay permanently sent for wives. Polish women in America did not stay single for long. Polish Catholic men worked primarily as unskilled laborers in the meat packing industry and the steel mills of Chicago, the car manufacturing plants of Detroit, and the coal industry of western Pennsylvania.

Unlike the Mexicans and the Italians, the Poles who came to America accepted the parish as the center of Catholic religious life. In their villages in the Old World, the parish was the focus of both religious and community life. Once in America, the Poles associated themselves so closely with the parish that they defined where they lived not by street designations, but by their parish names. They also respected the clergy: "Who has a priest in the family," according to a Polish saying, "will not be butted by poverty."[24] Polish priests and nuns, familiar with the cultural traditions and expectations as well as the language, ran the parishes and parochial schools. Unlike the Italians, there was no cultural split between the Catholic leaders and their people. Polish values and traditions flourished in mutual benefit societies, women's rosary groups, and church devotions.

As with most immigrants who could not own land in the Old World, home ownership became an important goal; it was an end in itself and not a sign of upward mobility. Polish women, like Irish women, were charged with keeping their homes in absolute order and cleanliness. The Polish home, according to anthropologist Paul Wrobel, "is considered sacred, almost like a shrine, and cleanliness is a sign of respect."[25] Floors were scrubbed, dishes polished until they shone, and yards were kept immaculately trimmed. Once a home was purchased, it was considered to be a treasure not to be misused. To symbolize the importance of the home and to protect it from evil, the priest came with blessed chalk once a year at Epiphany and inscribed "K + M + B" (Kaspar, Melchior, and Balthasar) on all the doors. Before entering or leaving the rooms, guests and family crossed themselves with holy water found in small fonts inside the doors. As late as 1910 in America, Polish women on Whitsuntide decorated their houses and doorways with branches of birch, willow, lilac, and syringa to give their homes a special festive appearance for commemorating Pentecost. This custom was a variation of the Polish rural tradition of women and girls weaving garlands with crosses on them and placing them on the walls of their houses.

Women also maintained family shrines in Polish households. In a Polish home at the turn of the century, there were holy pictures on the walls, often in thick gilded frames, hanging high up near the ceiling. Our Lady of Czestochowa and large oleographs of Jesus and Mary were particularly popular. Candles burned in front of the pictures or statues and pussy willows and a herb bouquet were stuck in the frame. On the feast of the Assumption (known in Poland as *Matka Boska Zielna*, Our Lady of the Herbs), women bought from the markets bouquets made of field flowers and herbs. They took the bouquets to church to be blessed and then placed them with other holy objects in their homes. Prior to the 1930s, pussy willows were used instead of Easter palms on Palm Sunday. Sometimes children were given some of the catkin to swallow to cure or ward off sore throats. When pussy willows were replaced by palms, children received sips of holy water brought from the church on Holy Saturday to help prevent throat ailments.

An important religious role of Polish immigrant women was to manage the elaborate seasonal dinners that gave the family a vivid reminder of the sacred calendar. For Easter, women spent all Holy Week scrubbing the house, decking it with flowers and flowering plants, and making traditional food. Colored eggs, sausages, ham, veal, pig's feet jelly, horseradish, butter shaped like lambs, and babas were prepared by mother and daughters. The mother brought the Easter food in baskets to the church to be blessed or else it was blessed by the priest who came to the home. Blessed Easter eggs were broken and shared at the meal. Easter celebrations were not only conducted in the church, but each family participated in the drama of Holy Week and Easter at home.

Likewise, for the Christmas Eve dinner (*wigilia*) the women prepared cheese and sauerkraut pastries (*pierogi*), fish in various forms, mushroom soup with noodles, herring and boiled potatoes, dumplings with plums or poppy seeds, stewed prunes with lemon peel, and poppy seed cake. Mothers taught their daughters that the meal symbolized the source of the family's food—the grains from the field, the vegetables from the gardens, the mushrooms from the forest, the fruit from the orchards, and the fish from the water. Such meals were not merely elaborate feasts but confirmed that the family recognized its dependence on each other, the natural world, and the divine world of God. This dependence was symbolized in the breaking of the Christmas wafer (*oplatki*). The wafer, made by the nuns or the parish organist, was brought to the homes of the parishioners by alter boys or purchased at the rectory or convent. At the Christmas Eve dinner, the wafer was broken and given to the family and guests. Pieces of the wafer were sent to relatives living out of town as a token of the connectedness of the whole family—including those far away.

Because Polish men were not as estranged from Catholicism as Italian and Mexican men, they participated to a larger extent in domestic religion. Where it was left up to Italian and Mexican women to organize religious rituals, create domestic shrines, and say their private devotions, in the Polish family these activities might be shared by the men. In 1910, the father in a second-generation Polish family took the bread prepared for the evening meal by his wife and ceremoniously made the sign of the cross with a knife over the bread explaining that this bread symbolized the Eucharist. Although women prepared the meal, gathered the family, and passed on detailed knowledge of the customs, men, as the heads of their families, officiated at the family religious rites.

Generational conflicts and the demise of domestic religious traditions also occurred in Polish families. Helen Stankiewicz Zand reports that by 1949 the marking of the doors of Polish homes was rapidly passing away. An aunt of Zand who had come to America at the age of two confessed that she wrote the "K + M + B" on the narrow, top edge of the door facing the ceiling where God would see it, but not scoffers. By 1942, it was no longer the women who carried the heavy baskets of Easter food into the church to be blessed. Zand reports that the children of St. Stanislaus's parish in Buffalo carried small bright colored baskets arranged with token quantities of ham, eggs, sausage, bread, horseradish, salt, and vinegar to church. Children performed a watered-down version of a ritual once carried out by women. The tendency among many ethnic groups, including the Poles, was to simplify ethnic domestic traditions and to have children do what had once been done by adults, especially by women. As home life became more and more geared to children and the succeeding generations became more detached from the traditions of the old country, ethnic domestic traditions became something suitable only for children and old people.

AMERICAN CATHOLIC DOMESTICITY 1920–1960

While ethnic domestic traditions still remained strong in the twentieth century, some Catholics married out of their ethnic group, moved to the suburbs, and left Old World ties in the cities. While grandmothers continued the ways of the old country, granddaughters were attaining more education, going out to work after bearing children, and even divorcing. Catholic leaders, especially the clergy, became hypersensitive to the changes in American life. Their addresses to the family became more impassioned. In 1928, James Gillis, the Paulist editor of *Catholic World*, exclaimed, "there exists today, in all civilized countries, a considerable movement for the abolition of marriage and the disintegration of the family."[26] *The Homiletic and Pastoral Review* of 1935, which provided food for pastors' sermons warned that "Bolshevism appeals directly to young girls. Each dictator sets up his program to win the women, young and old."[27] The situation had not improved by the 1940s. A writer in *America* feared that the "American scene [has begun] to resemble slightly the Soviet one in which public nurseries, birth control clinics and loose marriage arrangements weakened long established ideals of family life and parenthood."[28] Wartime morals, the priest feared, threatened the sanctity of the family.

Even the postwar suburbs of America were not safe. Andrew M. Greeley worried in 1958 that the Americanization of the immigrants might be a mixed blessing and that the suburban Catholic could become *too* American. "Catholics can accept much of the American way of life with little hesitation," he wrote in the family magazine *The Sign*, "but in certain matters—birth control, divorce, and premarital sex experience, for example—we must part company with the average American. We simply cannot accept his ideas." While Catholics in national parishes and old neighborhoods "were somewhat insulated from the infection of pagan influences," Greeley observed, "in the suburbs they are in the main line of the enemy's fire."[29] Suburban Catholics, writers agreed, although free from the economic and social ills of the urban ethnic slum, now faced the spiritual problems of modern life.

In 1948 and 1949, two pastoral letters from the American bishops summarized the pre-Vatican II Catholic attitude toward the family. The family, the bishops explained, was a divine institution that human will cannot alter or nullify. A growing tendency to ignore God and his rights in society provided a "lethal danger" to the family—"more fearsome than the atom bomb." Consequently, every Christian "must make his home holy"; allowing the whole atmosphere to be "impregnated with genuine Christian living." A secularized home was "at the root of so many of our greatest social evils." As the child's first school, the family taught responsibility to God and to others. Family life provided dignity, peace, and security for the mother and exercised an ennobling and steadying influence on the father. For both parents, it awakened and developed a sense of responsibility while fostering their growth in selflessness, sacrifice, and patience. While the government should not interfere with parental authority, it should make provisions for adequate housing and schooling. The family must demonstrate a "staunch loyalty" to God, his commandments, the church, and Catholic doctrine. Daily family prayer, the dedication of the home to the Sacred Heart, group recitation of the rosary, and frequent reception of the sacraments were the means through which pure family life could be established. The bishops concluded by asking Catholics to make their family life "a mirror of the Holy Family of Nazareth" and a "shrine of fidelity, a place where God is the unseen Host."[30]

Catholics responded to the plea to maintain good families by founding organizations dedicated to domestic virtues. During the nineteenth century, countless advice books, novels, newspapers, and sermons explained to women what a Catholic home was and how they could create one. During the twentieth century, Catholic organizations also became involved in promoting Catholic family life. In 1920, the National Council of Catholic Women set up committees on family life and domestic education. A decade later, a group committed to the scholarly and scientific study of family and parent education organized the Catholic Conference on Family Life. Much of this interest in family life by Catholic organizations was stimulated by Pius XI's encyclical letter on Christian marriage, *Casti connubii* (1930). The response to the pope's call for a strengthened Christian family included the rise of popular movements for the promotion of Catholicism in the home. The Christian Family Movement (1940s), Cana Conferences for married couples (1944), Marianist Family Sodality (1950), and the Family Rosary Crusade (1960) were organized efforts to focus attention on the well-being of the family.

The liturgical movement, launched in the 1930s, also helped Catholics create a religious foundation for home life. Through revitalizing the liturgy, the reformers hoped to instill in Catholics a spiritual alternative to the materialism of American society. One of the main American proponents of the movement, Dom Virgil Michel, O.S.B., believed that the family was the "Mystical Body's spiritual miniature." According to his biographer, Michel felt that home devotions were a preparation for, or continuation of, corporate worship in the parish church. "Christian homes," Michel believed, "would be citadels of Christian culture radiating light into their neighborhoods, a kind of sanctuary of God."[31]

The liturgical movement promoted a series of family liturgies that were detached from ethnic ties. By the 1950s, suburban Catholics were reading the numerous books and pamphlets on appropriate family religion published by Liturgical Press out of St. John's Abbey in Collegeville, Minnesota. In exchange for giving up "superstitious" folk customs, the liturgical movement offered families a series of approved Catholic seasonal liturgies. Ethnic traditions were not ignored, but liturgists purified them of any magical or pagan connotations. In the spirit of America as "melting pot," the *Catholic Family Handbook* encouraged families to try the Dutch traditions of St. Nicholas, the Mexican celebration of *Los Posadas*, the German custom of baking lenten pretzels, and the French Canadian Emmaus walk with grandparents on Easter Monday.

What were women asked to do in order to promote their well-being and develop Catholic consciousness in their families? Although it was still assumed that the woman's place was in the home training her children, providing a peaceful environment for her husband, and developing her own spirituality, the rhetoric praising women's piety was gone. By the end of World War I and the demise of Victorian sentimentality, Catholic women were discussed with less ornate prose. As middle-class women in American society stepped down from the pedestal to vote, acquire higher education, and take their place in the work world, Catholic writing responded by toning down its maternal rhetoric. Catholic writers turned away from equating the home with mother and began to point out the importance of the father as the head of the household.

Suburban living in the forties and fifties had placed men in a precarious position with regard to the family. On the one hand, suburban life allowed for a radically improved standard of living over immigrant life in the city. In the suburbs, children could play in their yards instead of in the streets, the air was free from urban pollution, and educational opportunities provided a means of economic improvement. On the other hand, fathers drove long distances to work and frequently juggled two jobs while mothers spent their whole days minding children. While in the city paternal authority could be exerted by an extended network of male relatives even if the father was absent, in the suburbs only women were left to watch over their children. What many Catholics resented was the assumption that women were the head of the home and men the head of the workplace. They insisted that men serve as both the head of the home and the workplace. Andrew Greeley had correctly predicted that Catholics would face important challenges in the suburbs.

To reinstate the paternal authority over the family, Catholic writers tried to minimize the mother's role in domestic religion and emphasize the father's. It was, however, a losing battle. Unlike Protestants who had a long history of family worship with the father substituting for the male minister, Catholics did not have such a tradition. Prayer within the home, until the late nineteenth century had been an individual matter. There was no strong tradition of male leadership in family worship. Because of women's traditional role in informal religious activities—heightened by their isolation in the suburban home—the duty to organize family worship most often fell to them. While fathers might lead the prayers or read from the Bible, it was most likely the mother who would bring the family prayer book, pick out the reading from the Bible, assemble her children, and explain the process to her husband. The enthusiasm with which the advice literature of the 1940s and 1950s insisted that the father organize and lead family prayer only confirms the reality that domestic religion still was the domain of women.

What made it even more difficult to convince men to take over family worship was the stress Catholic writers laid on celebrating seasonal devotions in the family. Catholics traditionally may not have had evening and morning family prayer, but they did have family celebrations oriented to the liturgical year. During the 1950s, Catholic writers made a great attempt at encouraging families to bring Catholicism into their families by conducting seasonal religious rituals. These domestic liturgies had little to do with ethnic traditions and were based on approved church worship styles. Saying the family rosary, reading from the Bible, and having group prayer were considered important for the promotion of home life, but seasonal domestic rituals captured the Catholic preference for the connection of sensuality and the sacred: the everyday with the divine.

The development of a domestic ideology that centered on the love of mothers and the authority of fathers helped create a lay-oriented American Catholicism. By expressing the belief that women, or at least the family, could be a means for the salvation of souls, it weakened the preference for the celibate life promoted by traditional Catholicism. Women were allowed the privilege of "saving souls" because they fully embraced an otherworldly outlook—they were selfless, obedient, charitable, modest, and cloistered in their homes. Women who rejected these otherworldly values and attempted to cultivate a life *in* the world through careers, elaborate social life, or extensive charity obligations relinquished their ability to save their families. Even immigrant women, who may have had no understanding of mainstream Catholic domestic values, perceived that their religious activities in the home could "save" their families. Mothers and grandmothers conducted healing rituals, rites to ward off the evil eye, and petitions to the saints for the good of the family. The home, and the woman as its caretaker, was understood as a sacred space marked by St. Bridget's crosses, Angelus clocks, statues of Our Lady of Guadalupe, or the chalked initials of the three Magi.

Catholic culture, which hailed the importance of the woman in the home, created a fundamental problem for traditional, patriarchal Catholicism. If the home and family reflected the order of heaven and if the home were a miniature church, then women must *not* enjoy such a powerful position within the household. If the mother acted as the main strength of the household, which reflected the cosmic order; then what of the importance of the male deity, the male savior, and the all-male priesthood? Traditional, hierarchical Catholicism demanded that the father serve as the head of his home. Thus, Catholicism fought throughout the nineteenth century to preserve male authority within the home, only to be faced in America with a growing separation of spheres that placed women in control of the home. This same American culture assumed women were more pious, more selfless, more charitable, and thus more religious than men. As Catholic culture encouraged families to worship together at home, and liturgists created formal devotions that duplicated church services, the father was asked to take his position as domestic priest. By the 1940s and 1950s, while women continued to be the domestic priestesses for informal religious instruction, once that instruction became formalized and blessed by the church men were asked to direct family religion. Only the radical rethinking of the mission of Catholicism and the meaning of God beginning after the Second Vatican Council would cause a shift in the understanding of women's religious role within the home.

NOTES

1. "Maternal Affection," *Catholic Home Journal* (May 1, 1887):3.

2. Bernard O'Reilly, *Mirror of True Womanhood* (New York, 1892), p. 12. Maurice Lessage d'Hautecoeur d'Hulst, *The Christian Family: Seven Conferences*, trans. Bertrand L. Conway (New York, 1905).

3. Miss Barry, *Sacred Heart Review* (January 25, 1890):9.

4. "French Home Life," *Catholic World* 25 (1877):767.

5. Mrs. I. J. Hale, *Catholic Home Journal* (January 1, 1886):8.

6. *New York Irish American* (February 20, 1894):2.

7. *Baltimore Catholic Mirror* (January 14, 1881):3.

8. Stephen V. Ryan, intro. to Wilhelm Cramer, *The Christian Father: What He Should Be and What He Should Do*, trans. L. A. Lambert (New York, 1883), p. 4.

9. "A Mother's Look," *Philadelphia Catholic Standard and Times* (December 13, 1890): 7.

10. "A Mother's Influence," *Sacred Heart Review* (July 12, 1890): 13.

11. "Home Heroes," *Catholic Home Journal* (November 1, 1886):8.

12. Paul Lejune, *Counsels of Perfection for Christian Mothers*, trans. Francis Ryan (Saint Louis, 1913), p. 40 on rule, pp. 111–12 on not reading mystic writers.

13. Eleanor Donnelly, "A Lost Prima Donna." In *A Round Table of the Representative American Catholic Novelists* (New York, 1897), p. 46.

14. Mary Sadlier, *The Blakes and the Flanagans, a Tale Illustrative of Irish Life in the United States* (New York, 1855), p. 108.

15. *Sacred Heart Review* (June 6, 1886):12.

16. *Catholic Home* (June 4, 1887):1.

17. Francis X. Lasance, *The Catholic Girl's Guide: Counsels and Devotions for Girls in the Ordinary Walks of Life* (New York, 1906), p. 413.

18. Carroll, *Pleasant Homes*, pp. 18–19.

19. d'Hulst, *Christian Family*, p. 69.

20. "A Peasant Home," *Catholic World* 59:179.

21. Eliza G. Herzfeld, *Family Monographs: The History of Twenty-Four Families Living in the Middle West Side of New York City* (New York, 1905), p. 94.

22. Beatrice Griffith, *American Me* (Westport, Conn., 1944, reprinted, New York, 1973), p. 174.

23. Ibid.

24. William I. Thomas and Florian Znaniecki, *The Polish Peasant in Europe and America* (Boston, 1920), p. 228.

25. Paul Wrobel, *Our Way: Family, Parish, and Neighborhood in a Polish-American Community* (Notre Dame, Ind., 1979), p. 47.

26. James Gillis, *The Catholic Church and the Home* (London, 1928), p. 11.

27. Daniel A. Lord, "The Training of Girls for Catholic Action," *The Homiletic and Pastoral Review* 35 (1934–1935):332.

28. H. C. McGinnis, "War-Time Morals Threaten the Sanctity of the Family," *America* (October 17, 1942):43.

29. Andrew M. Greeley, *The Sign* 37 (February 1958):32.

30. "The Christian in Action" (November 21,

1948) and "The Christian Family" (November 21, 1949). In *Pastoral Letters of the American Hierarchy, 1792–1970* (Huntington, Ind., 1971), pp. 409–10, 416–20.

31. Paul Marx, *Vigil Michel and the Liturgical Movement* (Collegeville, Minn., 1957), p. 270.

MANMADE RELIGION

Mark C. Carnes

At the same time that scholarship on women and religion has grown in complexity, a burgeoning interest in men's lives has lead to an exploration of men's religious experience. Here the most illuminating work has explored the ritual life of fraternal orders. Despite a flurry of recent scholarship, it is still not well known that from the middle to the end of the nineteenth century, the feminization of American Protestantism was paralleled by the growth of fraternal societies. By 1900, one out of every four adult male Americans—a majority of men living in urban settings and working in white-collar occupations—were members of such organizations as the Odd Fellows, Freemasons, Knights of Pythias, Red Men, and hundreds of smaller orders. Among the urban middle class, the women were in the churches and the men were in the lodges. Why were middle-class men attracted to fraternal orders?

A large part of fraternalism's enormous appeal was the romantic attraction of the orders' elaborate rituals. As Mark Carnes argues, young men were drawn to these rituals because they facilitated their "transitions to, and acceptance of, a remote and problematic conception of manhood in Victorian America." The difficulties involved in a boys passage to manhood have been implied though not directly explored by women's historians. The separation of the home from the work place resulted in the creation of a separate "women's sphere" of piety and domesticity; this separation also had the effect of removing the father from the strongest currents of feeling that flowed between generations in the family. As children came to be reared primarily by women, a relational world of mothers and daughters subsumed within a gentler, self-sacrificing and more hopeful Protestant theology was created. Within this world, Carnes holds, young boys faced a particularly disruptive process. Unlike their sisters they could not simply become like their mothers, but instead they had to seek out their own path of masculine identification. Young men were attracted to fraternal orders, Carnes concludes, because these orders facilitated their transition from the emotional orientations instilled by maternal nurture and "feminine" theology to the aggressive and competitive demands of the masculine workplace.

Adapted by permission from Mark C. Carnes, "Words," in his *Secret Ritual and Manhood in Victorian America* (New Haven: Yale University Press, 1989), 37-66.

16 ❦

MANMADE RELIGION
Victorian Fraternal Rituals

Mark C. Carnes

THE YOUNG MAN STUMBLES, but is urged onward by the tribal elders. He is blindfolded, and his arms are bound behind his back. His arms and legs glisten from the light of the campfire. Lightning flashes and thunder rumbles in the distance. The tribesmen push him onto a stone slab. The chief elder comes forward, raises his arms for silence, and offers a prayer, evidently from memory. All men, he says, must obey God, to whom the young man is to be sacrificed. The tribesmen, who have been silent, now beat on drums, harder and faster. The elder draws a knife, raises it above his head, and suddenly subjects the man to an ordeal. Then the men rush forward to welcome the initiate, the newest member of their tribe.

Such rituals are common among primitive peoples. But this one was, perhaps, different. For the camp was located in the lodgeroom of the Improved Order of Red Men. The thunder was provided by a gong, and the lightning by gas lights. The tribesmen were shopkeepers, factory managers, or workmen; the initiate was probably a clerk or apprentice in their employ. And the ritual had been written by a formal committee, including clergy, that had met in Baltimore in 1834.

The Improved Order of Red Men was one of thousands of ritualistic societies that proliferated during the last half of nineteenth-century America. In 1897 the *North American Review* described the decades since the Civil War as the "Golden Age of Fraternity," and reported that of a population of nineteen million adult male Americans, five and a half million belonged to fraternal orders—the Red Men (165,000), Odd Fellows (810,000), Freemasons (750,000), Knights of Pythias (475,000), and hundreds of smaller orders.[1] Millions more belonged to the Grand Army of the Republic, the Knights of Labor, and insurance societies. The distinguishing feature and central activity of all these organizations was the performance of elaborate sequences of initiation rituals. All fraternal orders required initiates to profess a belief in God; and all of the rituals were pervaded with explicit religious symbols and references.

Fraternal ritual, though remarkably widespread, was chiefly a phenomena of the middle classes. The rise of the rituals coincided with the orders' adoption of middle-class values. Formerly drinking societies, the Freemasons and Odd Fellows during the 1830s and 1840s banned alcohol, attempted to ascertain the moral character of new members, created juridical proceedings to expel dissolute or wayward members, and replaced the rented tavern rooms by building elaborate "temples." Scholars have confirmed that membership in most orders was drawn largely from the urban middle classes.[2]

But why were such men impelled to perform elaborate initiations? Contemporaries, such as the writer for the *North American Review*, observed that

> There is a strange and powerful attraction for some men in the mysticism of the ritual. There is a peculiar fascination in the unreality of the initiation, an allurement about fine "team" work, a charm of deep potency in the unrestricted, out-of-the-world atmosphere which surrounds the scenes where men are knit together by the closest ties, [and] bound by the most solemn obligations to maintain secrecy....

The lodges did not promote friendship, nor even serve the needs of business, he added. So much time was spent on initiation that members never got a chance to know each other or to cultivate contacts. Often they became so intent on satisfying a "craving" for ritual that they neglected their professions or businesses.[3] Why some men were predisposed to be "charmed" by and "powerfully attracted" to such rituals he did not say.

CHANGES IN RITUAL

Several fraternal orders had initiation ceremonies prior to the 1830s and 1840s, the most important being Freemasonry and Odd Fellowship. But at that time their rituals, especially as practiced in the United States, were quite brief; most of the lodges rented rooms in taverns and the orders functioned largely as drinking societies. Sometimes the early rituals included religious references: some Masonic rituals explicitly endorsed a Deistic God of the Great Watchmaker variety; the early degrees of Odd Fellowship were imbued with a generally benign view of mankind and of a loving God. The order was initially a social club, a place to join, in the words of a favorite song, "with friends so blithe and jolly,/ Who all delight for to dispel/ The gloom of melancholy." Such men, presumably, found the pleasures of this world more compelling than the terrors of the next. But during the 1830s and 1840s a new group of middle-class men swarmed into the orders such as the Freemasons, the Odd Fellows, and the Red Men. They complained that the simple existing rites were "formal" and "unmeaning." They eliminated the drinking songs and the simple oaths and replaced them with religious initiatory dramas, such as the one at the beginning of this essay. The Odd Fellows created a Committee on Ritual that in 1845 came up with a new Initiatory Degree. The initiate became Adam, and the ritual elaborated on the consequences of his fall.[4] Like Adam, the candidate was "naked" (his shirt had been removed) and he was repeatedly told that "thou art dust" and placed on the floor—"Low! level with the earth! This is the state of man" (and, in Genesis, the fate of snakes).[5] The "emblematic" chains around the initiate's body represented his "guilty soul." The blindfolded initiate was then asked: "If you had light, should you know the person that recommended you?" After he had responded "Yes," his blindfolds were removed and a skeleton was thrust into his face. "Contemplate that dismal, ghastly emblem of what thou art sure to be, and what thou mayst soon become."[6]

The initiate, "bound by ignorance and fear," required the sudden revelation of light, and of God. No longer a mute spectator, he had become the central figure in an ancient drama, "coeval with the first inhabitants of the earth."[7] His development in Odd Fellowship, and in life, would not be easy: obstacles were inevitable; pain and death man's destiny. The skeleton served as a reminder that no comfort could be expected even after death. And the easygoing God that had smiled upon the drinking frolics had been replaced by a "Supreme, Intelligent Being," whose "holy name" was to be mentioned only with "that reverential awe which is due from the creature to the Creator."[8]

During the next ten or fifteen years an almost identical transformation pervaded the upper levels of Scotch Rite Freemasonry. This is most evident in the "modern ritual" of the 28th degree of the Scottish Rite ("Knights of the Sun"). The chief official of the lodge, the Worshipful Master, represented Father Adam; the initiate was his child, whose eyes were bandaged and whose arms were bound with chains. A mask was fastened to his face, and a crown placed upon his head. He wore a ragged and bloody robe. In his left hand he held a purse, in his right, a sword.

When asked what he most desired, the conductor (speaking for the initiate) answered: "To divest myself of original sin." The "child" of Adam was conducted around the temple while another official described God as "the living and awful being, from whom nothing in the universe is hidden." Man had "wandered far into darkness;" around him hovered "sin and shame."

By mid-century the rituals of American Freemasonry and Odd Fellowship had been completely transformed: man's goodness had been replaced with an assumption of his innate sinfulness; his innocent enjoyment of life's pleasures with a "dreadful track" of trials and tortures; a solicitous God with an "awful being" who was prepared to "thrust a red hot iron through the initiate's tongue, pluck out his eyes, cut off his hands, and leave him to be devoured by voracious animals" should he reveal the secrets of the order.[9]

The ritualists during the 1840s and 1850s established the theological foundation for the rituals that proliferated during the last third of the nineteenth century. And despite the public endorsement by all fraternal orders of good works and tolerant morality, the *rituals* of all major and most minor orders offered a form of religious expression far removed from the liberal beliefs which had come to prevail in the churches of the middle classes.

The secret deity of the orders was distant and impersonal, a God to whom access, save at death, was impossible. It more closely resembled the God of the Puritans than the benevolent and human Christ of liberal Protestantism. Fraternal rituals sought to redress "the Divine displeasure,"[10] or to propitiate an "offended Great Spirit."[11] The fire triangle, base upon the ground, which appeared in many Masonic rituals delineated an "angry God."[12] A funeral hymn of the Odd Fellows implored of the "Great God" to

> ...afflict not in Thy wrath,
> The short allotted span,
> That bounds the few and weary days
> Of pilgrimage to man.[13]

The lurid descriptions of corpses and the insistence upon confronting one's mortality were also suggestive of Puritan mores and theology.

One Masonic editor, who happened upon John Bunyan's *Pilgrim's Progress*, was struck by the ritualistic possibilities of Christian's humiliation, his struggle to cross the black river Death, and then his ascent to the Celestial City. "How analogous is all this to the Masonic system!" he wrote. He thought it odd that the degree makers of the past hundred years, in response to the "wholesale demand" for rituals, had neglected Bunyan's classic.[14]

But American fraternal leaders had little use for an explicitly Christian ritualism. Prior to 1845, initiates for the Odd Fellow's Priestly Order, or Scarlet Degree, were told that the scarlet ribbon with which they were invested symbolized "the Royal Dignity of Jesus Christ, and the bloody suffering of him and his church." But the revisions of 1845 eliminated the Scarlet Degree; and Christ ceased to have a place in the rituals of the order. By the 1850s Christ's name had also been excised from most Masonic rituals. After the Civil War only a handful of rituals offered prayers specifically addressed to Christ.[15]

Scholars within the fraternal groups justified the omission of Christ by emphasizing the universal character of their orders; all men, whether Christian, Mohammedan, or Jew, were theoretically welcome to share in the fellowship of the lodge. But the theorists also alluded to a theological difficulty with a Christian interpretation of Masonry. Fraternal initiations, one Masonic official observed, came to a climax when the initiate was confronted with a flash of light, a skeleton, the mysteries of the ark, or some other revelation marking "the disruption of the candidate from the ties of the world, and his introduction into the life of Masonry. It is the symbol of the agonies of the first death and of the throes of the new birth."

> There is to be, not simply a change for the future, but also an extinction of the past; for initiation is, as it were, a death to the world and a resurrection to a new life.[16]

The allusion to Christ was surely intentional, and its implication significant: Christ's own "initiation," by ensuring man's salvation, rendered all other initiatory experiences superfluous. If Masonry were merely an allegorical rendering of Christ's message, then members might just as well attend church. By insisting upon a disruption of the initiate's "ties to the world" and an "extinction" of his past, Mackey had implied the insufficiency of Christian worship.

The orders' exclusion of Christ gained significance because it occurred just as Protestant worship "increasingly centered" on Him.[17] The Calvinists' anguished doubts about the workings of an unknowable God ceased to concern liberal theologians, who advised churchgoers to think less about sin and depravity, and "more of Christ, his character, his love, his suffering."[18]

The theological tension between liberal Protestantism and fraternal rituals is all the more remarkable since the latter were often written by liberal ministers. The five-member committee which in 1845 revised the rituals of the Odd Fellows included Edwin Hubbell Chapin, a prominent Universalist minister, and John McCabe, a banker who in three years would be ordained as an Episcopalian minister.[19] Chapin's background was particularly incongruous. Though raised in a stalwart Puritan family, he rebelled against his family's orthodoxy. "I reject the doctrine of the trinity, of a vicarious sacrifice to appease the wrath of God, of total depravity, original sin," he said in 1840. His was a "religion of love, and not of fear."[20] Yet four years later, as chairman of the Odd Fellows Committee on Ritual Revision, he helped create a ceremony that asserted man's innate depravity and culminated in the frightening encounter with a skeleton.

Many ministers also served as High Priests, Prophets, and Chaplains. In New York State in 1891 a large proportion of the ordained clergy belonged to the Freemasons, including approximately 26% of the Universalist, 22% of the Episcopalian, and 18% of the Methodist clergy. The percentage was much lower among Congregational (6%), Presbyterian (7%)

Lutheran (13%), and Baptist (15%) clergymen.[21] And fraternal members were themselves drawn largely from the urban middle classes where religious liberalism found its greatest support.[22]

How, then, did fraternal members and liberal ministers reconcile in their own minds their participation in one form of religions expression on Sundays, and its antithesis later in the week?

Anthropologists have shown that the meaning of symbols is largely dependent upon the cultural context in which they are employed.[23] Nearly all fraternal symbols were clearly associated in the minds of most members with the church. Lodge members usually knelt before an altar. Without exception, American fraternal orders required that members affirm their belief in God, and take their oaths upon the Bible. Many fraternal rituals were based on familiar Biblical stories. As in church, the ceremonies of the lodge commenced and ended with songs; frequently fraternal hymns were based on popular Protestant hymns. Sunday morning's "All hail the power of Jesus' name/ In whom all blessings fall" on lodge nights became "When met in friendship's sacred name/We round an altar stand."[24] Yet these common symbols—Bible, altar, cross, chalice, candles, hymns—helped conceal the deeper tension between the ideology of church and lodge.

Lodge members and clergymen, reassured of the propriety of their rituals by the familiar symbols of the church, created and repeatedly practiced rituals which altered the context— and the meaning—of those symbols. Probably most Christians who joined orders believed that the rituals posed no challenge to their religious convictions. Symbols linked lodge and church, and the professed purpose of the rituals—to make men mindful of ethical principles—accorded with the teachings of Christianity. But with each successive degree the context of the symbols changed. By the time a Mason had performed the revised version of the 30th degree of the Scottish Rite (Knights Kadosh), in which he drank wine and broke bread, the Christian significance of that act had diminished considerably. In a setting of coffins and skulls, bloody oaths and frightening scenery, the symbols of the chalice, wine, Bible, and candles, connoted antithetical ideas about the past, death, and divinity. By disguising the contradictory ideas of liberal Protestantism and initiatory ritual, fraternal symbols evoked the unity of church and lodge even as they refuted liberal theology.[25]

An example can be found in interpretations of the cross which, bearing the letters INRI, appeared over the Worshipful Master's chair in Masonic lodges. New Masons probably assumed that the letters stood for the Latin inscription on the cross of Jesus: (*Jesus Nazarenus Rex Iudoeorum*). According to Masonic scholars, however, INRI stood for the Hebrew words *iammim* (water), *nour* (fire), *rouach* (air), and *iebeschah* (dry earth), as well as for the Latin *Igne Natura Renovatur Integra* (entire nature is renovated by fire).[26] Similarly, the cross figured prominently in many fraternal rituals, but initiates gradually learned that it did not refer to Christ. The cross, the foremost Masonic scholar Albert Pike wrote, was a sacred symbol among the druids, Indians, Egyptians and Arabians "thousands of years before the coming of Christ."[27] The superficial Christian meaning of these symbols merely concealed a deeper association with ancient—and pagan—religions.

Fraternal ritualists and scholars acknowledged the multivocalic nature of their symbols. Pike wrote that the symbols of Masonry "have more than one meaning" and "conceal rather than disclose the Truth.... In all time truth has been hidden under symbols and often under a succession of allegories: where veil after veil had to be penetrated, before the true Light was reached, and the essential truth stood revealed."[28]

But what secret did the orders take such pains both to conceal, and then, following an elaborate succession of initiatory journeys, to reveal? What essential truth did the awful God of the orders impart to initiates?

FRATERNAL RITUAL AND GENDER

All of the orders excluded women from the initiations. Because the religion of the lodge was exclusively for men, the ceremonies can be regarded as loosely analogous to the male initiation ceremonies of primitive societies. Thus the subject of fraternal ritual begs to be examined in light of anthropological research on primitive male initiation ceremonies.

The most important work in this field was a cross-cultural study by cultural anthropologist John Whiting and his associates during the 1950s. They determined that male initiation ceremonies were most commonly found in societies where women exerted an almost exclusive control over male infants and boys, and men controlled the economic and political resources (as evidenced by patrilocal residence).[29] Whiting subsequently hypothesized that in societies where the father is absent or plays a minor role in child rearing, the male infant perceives the mother as all-powerful and comes to envy her role. Yet when that boy begins to notice the world outside the home, perhaps around the age of five, he becomes aware that men control resources and clearly occupy an enviable position. A secondary identification with the masculine role thus becomes superimposed on the female identification. Male initiation ceremonies "serve psychologically to brainwash the primary feminine identity and to establish firmly the secondary male identity."[30] In societies where this "cross-sex identity conflict" becomes sufficiently widespread, initiation rituals will emerge in response to this psychological need. The rituals, by resolving these emotional conflicts, promote the well-being of young men and, presumably, of society itself.

At first glance, Whiting's discussion of mother-son sleeping arrangements and patrilocal residence seems far removed from Victorian America. But critics have contended that Whiting's coding categories were merely manifestations of larger societal characteristics. Exclusive mother-son sleeping patterns could be viewed as an analogue for father absence in early child rearing and patrilocal residence for disproportionate male authority in the adult world.[31]

This reformulation makes it possible to move the analysis of male initiation ceremonies beyond primitive societies. In particular, the division of gender roles in Victorian America in many ways approximated the structural preconditions for Whiting's paradigm. Women's historians have shown a deep psychological division between Victorian men and women. Relegated to the "domestic sphere" of child-rearing, many women sought emotional fulfillment and personal justification by devoting themselves to their children. To the task of child rearing, mothers imparted an intensity born of religious conviction, a belief that by instilling in their children the sweet virtues of Jesus, they would ultimately reshape a masculine order that had grown neglectful of his mission.[32]

On the other hand, men, having relinquished supervision of the home, increasingly defined themselves in terms of work and political affiliations. Economic growth and structural change contributed to the separation of men from the home during much of the day. As the distance between home and workplace increased, and the workday itself was lengthened, fathers found little time to be with their children. "Paternal neglect," one observer complained in 1842, had become epidemic.[33] And when fathers returned home they were often unable to provide meaningful guidance to sons who were striking out in the emerging professions and corporations.

Not all middle-class boys had ineffective or mostly absent fathers, or received so powerful a dose of evangelical maternal guidance. Nor did all middle-class men join a lodge or become enthralled by its rituals. But many did experience some aspect of this developmental paradigm; Victorian America corresponded at least in some general way to the structural preconditions of Whiting's cross-sample.

Given its sweeping implications, Whiting's explanation and particularly his psychological assumptions warrant closer consideration. His model is drawn from identification theories which assert that if the fathers are ineffective or absent in child rearing, boys will envy the power of their mothers, imitate their behavioral traits, and identify with the feminine role.[34]

The concept of identification involves distinctions and refinements that are far removed from historical evidence; it seems doubtful that historians can ever determine whether boys or men, at the core of their being, perceived themselves as "masculine." Moreover, psychologists have recently questioned the concept of gender identification. Joseph Pleck has argued forcefully that gender roles are socially constructed; there is no core masculinity to which a "normal" male aspires.[35] In view of these other criticisms, I propose to replace Whiting's "cross-sex identity conflict" model with the less problematic gender-role perspective.[36]

Restated in gender-role terms, the dilemma for boys in Victorian America was not simply that their fathers were absent, thereby depriving them of psychological guides to their core masculinity, but that adult gender roles were invariant and narrowly defined, and that boys were mostly taught the sensibilities and moral values associated with the adult female role. As teenagers, or perhaps somewhat earlier, they perceived the disjunction in adult gender roles and fantasized about how they would fit into the world of men. In the absence of fathers and of adult male role models in general, they contrived a "boy culture" which in its stylized aggression and competition provided an unconscious caricature of men's roles in business and politics.[37] As young men, they were drawn to male secret orders, where they repeatedly practiced rituals that effaced their religious values and emotional ties associated with women.

Fraternal rituals affirmed that while woman gave birth to a man's body, initiation gave birth to his soul, surrounding him with brothers who would lavish the "utmost affection and kindness" upon him. Sometimes, as in the Adoption Degree of the Red Men, the initiate's entry into a new family was explicit. But all fraternal orders appropriated the language of family relations: members were brothers; officers, fathers; and initiates, sons.[38]

The fraternal member's developmental path to masculine identification was identical in dramatic structure to his search for religious truths, which consisted of a similar four-part sequence (see Table): After 1) the initiate was shown to be innately sinful, 2) he commenced a difficult pilgrimage for religious truth, which 3) culminated through a wrenching conversion experience in his death; and thus 4) led him to an understanding of a distant God.

The initiate's partial nakedness simultaneously depicted his sinfulness and his immaturity; conversely, his acquisition of sacred aprons and patriarchal robes confirmed both his newfound religious comprehension and his acceptance by the men of the order. Similarly, skulls and skeletons helped contradict liberal beliefs on the changelessness of death even as they expressed a death to feminine identifications. And the Light in which all fraternal rituals culminated symbolized the acquisition of religious truths and the moment

Table: Diagram of Religious and Emotional Journeys

	1.) DEFICIENCY OF INITIATE	2.) JOURNEY/ ORDEAL	3.) SHOCK/ DEATH	4.) REBIRTH
Religious journey:				
	innately sinful	need for conversion	wrenching conversion	religion of patriarchs
Emotional journey:				
	innately unmasculine/ effeminate	recapitulation of alternative childhood	effacement of feminine childhood	reconcile with patriarchs

of masculine rebirth. The highly condensed symbolic meanings of fraternal ritual suggests that the entire ritualistic sequence carried two different but closely related sets of meanings.

Victor Turner observed that ritual symbols could express many ideas at once; this is clearly evident in fraternal rituals. But more important than the fraternal ritual's use of symbols with multiple meanings was its ability to carry two different but coherent symbolic messages simultaneously. It perhaps could not be otherwise, for evangelical women had devised a childrearing style which joined liberal religious truths to maternal nurture. The men who were reared in such an environment could not confidently enter the world of manhood until they had broken with both.

Historians of American Protestantism have described the years following the Civil War as the "summit of complacency," or, more positively, as a "golden age" of liberal theology.[39] But just a few blocks from the comfortable and tranquil Protestant churches, in nearly every town and city, fraternal lodges offered a dramatic religious experience that functioned to transform the beliefs and emotional underpinnings of American men.

If such men built new temples, it was because existing ones had proven deficient; if they created strange new gods, it was because the ones with which they were familiar had failed them; and if they chose to evoke spiritual wastelands, it was because such representations in some way resembled the world in which they lived.

NOTES

1. W.S. Harwood, "Secret Societies in America, *North American Review* 164 (May 1987):620,623; Albert C. Stevens, *Cyclopedia of Fraternities* (New York: E.B. Treat, 1907 [1897].

2. By the late nineteenth century, membership in ritualistic organizations was so widespread as to make generalization impossible. It is possible to discern a membership shift in the Red Men and the Odd Fellows, during the formative 1830s and 1840s, from laborers and artisans to clerks, shopkeepers, and lawyers; membership in the Freemasons differed from region to region and from lodge to lodge. On the essentially middle-class character of fraternal orders, see Lynn Dumenil, *Freemasonry and American Culture, 1880–1939* (Princeton: Princeton University Press, 1984), 229; Mary Ann Clawson,

"Brotherhood, Class, and Patriarchy in Europe and America" (Ph.D. diss. State University of New York at Stony Brook, 1980), 393–99; John Gilkeson, "A City of Joiners: Voluntary Associations and the Formation of the Middle-Class in Providence, 1830–1920" (Ph.D. diss. Brown University, 1981), 121; Don Harrison Doyle, *The Social Order of a Frontier Community: Jacksonville, Illinois, 1825–1870* (Urbana: University of Illinois Press, 1985), 182–83, 187, 269; and Brian Greenberg, *Worker and Community: Response to Industrialization in a Nineteenth-Century American City, Albany, New York, 1850–1884* (Albany: State University of New York Press, 1985), 89–101. On the infusion of the middle classes into the Odd Fellows, see James L. Ridgely, *History of American Odd Fellowship* (Baltimore:

Grand Lodge, I.O.O.F., 1878), 7, 32, 142–143.

3. Harwood, "Secret Societies in America," 620–22; one year later another observer proposed an inquiry into the cause of this strange "attraction," adding that it raised the question of "whether the mystical side to our natures has not expanded relatively more rapidly than that which looks mainly to material comfort"; in Stevens *Cyclopedia of Fraternities* (from the preface to the first [1897] edition, xvi).

4. The Initiatory Degree did not refer to Adam by name, but the references were unmistakable. On the inadequacies of the White Degree, see J. Fletcher Williams, "The Encampment Branch of the Order," in Henry L. Stillson, ed. *The Official History and Literature of Odd Fellowship* (Boston: Fraternity Publishing Co., 1897), 427.

5. According to Genesis, God punished Adam for his sin by forcing him to work "till thou return unto the ground; for out of it wast thou taken: for dust thou art, and unto dust shalt thou return;" unceasing toil was a prelude to mortality.

6. These and other passages from the 1845 ritual were from *Dr. Willis' Expose of Odd Fellowship*, 18–25. Willis' expose is substantially the same as that found in John Kirk, *Kirk's Exposition of Odd-Fellowship* (NY: by author, 1857).

7. *Willis's Expose of Odd Fellowship*, 23.

8. *Willis's Expose of Odd Fellowship*, 9–10, 24.

9. [Ezra A. Cook, comp.] *Scotch Rite Masonry Illustrated* (Chicago: Ezra A. Cook, 1892), 217.

10. Joseph D. Weeks, *History of the Knights of Pythias* (Pittsburgh, Pa: Joseph D. Weeks and Co., 1874) 17–19.

11. [Ezra A. Cook], *Red Men Illustrated: The Complete Illustrated Ritual of the Improved Order of Red Men*, (Chicago: Ezra A. Cook, 1896), 84.

12. The fire triangle was opposed to the water triangle, point downward, which denoted a "kind, good, gracious, and merciful God," Macoy, *Encyclopedia of Freemasonry*, 618–619. Significantly, the water triangle rarely appeared in Masonic rituals.

13. Sovereign Grand Lodge, Independent Order of Odd Fellows, *Funeral Ceremony to be Observed at the Burial of Members*, 23.

14. "The Pilgrim's Progress as a Masonic Allegory," *Voice of Masonry* (May, 1867).

15. Among the major orders, only the Knights Templars and the Good Templars referred to Christ in the initiatory rituals.

16. Mackey, *The Masonic Ritualist*, 23–24.

17. Donald M. Scott, *From Office to Profession* (Philadelphia: Univ. of Pennsylvania Pr., 1978), 138–139.

18. Catharine Beecher, ed., *The Biographical Remains of Rev. George Beecher* (New York: Leavitt, Trow & Co., 1844), 150–151; cited in Scott, *From Office to Profession*, 139.

19. Then a banker, John McCabe became a prominent Episcopalian minister three years later. See A. B. Grosh, *The Odd–Fellow's Improved Manual* (Philadelphia: J. Bliss, 1871), 40–41; *Dictionary of American Biography*, s.v. "McCabe, John;" Sumner Ellis, *Life of Edwin H. Chapin, D.D.* (Boston: Universalist Publishing House, 1882), 282–284.

20. Ellis, *Life of Chapin*, 87–89.

21. These estimated figures are based on the following table:

Table : **Ministerial Affiliation with Freemasonry, 1890**

Denomination	(a)# FM Ministers	(b)# total min (estimated)	% Masons
Baptists	112	755	15
Congregation.	21	358	6
Episcopalian	146	665	22
Lutheran	11	183	13
Methodist	288	1635	18
Presbyterian	59	838	7
Unitarian	1	26	4
Universalist	31	118	26

On the denominational division of clergyman-masons in New York State in 1891, see Stevens, *Cyclopaedia of Fraternities*, 12n. The 1890 Federal Census of Religious Bodies does not include a denominational breakdown of ministers by state. For a detailed explanation of how this data was compiled see Mark C. Carnes, *Secret Ritual and Manhood in Victorian America* (New Haven: Yale University Press, 1989), 189.

22. See also Dorothy Ann Lipson, *Freemasonry in Federalist Connecticut* (Princeton, N.J.: Princeton University Press, 1977), 127–129; Sydney E. Ahlstrom, *A Religious History of the American People* (New Haven: Yale University Press, 1972), 775.

23. Victor Turner, *Process, Performance and Pilgrimage* (New Delhi: Concept, 1979), 14–15. An alternative view is found in C. J. Jung, who held that the meaning of some symbols lies deep in the roots of the human psyche; *Psyche and Symbol: A Selection from the Writings of C.G. Jung*, Violet S. de Laszlo, ed. (NY: Doubleday, 1958).

24. See John W. Dadmun, *The Masonic Choir: A Collection of Hymns and Tunes for the Use of the Fraternity* (Boston: G. D. Russell & Company, 1864), 4.

25. Critics of secret societies noted the inherent contradictions of fraternal rituals. "Truth and error,"

one wrote, "have been artfully commingled," see Jonathan Sarver, "Sermon on Odd-Fellowship and Other Secret Societies," (Chicago: Ezra A. Cook, 1876) 4.

26. Albert Pike, *Morals and Dogma of the Ancient and Accepted Scottish Rite of Freemasonry* (Charleston, S.C.: Southern Jurisdiction of the A.A.S.R., 1878), 291; Albert MacKey, *Encyclopedia of Freemasonry*, (Philadelphia: L.H. Everts, 1886) 139.

27. Pike, *Morals and Dogma of Freemasonry*, 504–505. So pervasive was the fraternal use of the cross symbol that one Pythian scholar was surprised that his order did not develop its symbolism more elegantly: "Pythianism has its cross although one seldom hears of it. For some cause this primitive symbolical religious ornament has been overlooked," Creller, *The Golden Shield of Pythian Knighthood* (S.F.: The Rosemont Pr., 1928), 92.

28. Pike, *Morals and Dogma of the Ancient and Accepted Scottish Rite of Freemasonry* , 104–105, 148, 246, 819.

29. J.M.W. Whiting, Richard Kluckhorn, and Albert Anthony, "The function of Male Initiation Ceremonies at Puberty," in Eleanor E. Maccoby, T.M. Newcomb, and E.L. Hartley, eds. *Readings in Social Psychology* (New York: Henry Holt and Co., 1958). For a criticism of the study on technical grounds see Edward Norbeck, D.E. Walker, and M. Cohen, "The Interpretation of Data: Puberty Rites," *American Anthropologist* 64:3 (1962).

30. Robert V. Burton and J.M.W. Whiting, "The Absent Father and Cross-Sex Identity," *Merrill-Palmer Quarterly* 7 (1961): 87–90.

31. See Frank W. Young, "The function of Male Initiation Ceremonies: A Cross-Cultural Test of an Alternative Hypothesis," *American Journal of Sociology* 68 (January 1962): 381–86.

32. The literature is substantial and increasing rapidly. The early or most influential works include: Anne L. Kuhn, *The Mother's Role in Childhood Education* (New Haven: Yale University Press, 1947); Barbara Welter, The Cult of True Womanhood: 1820–1860," *American Quarterly* 18 (summer 1966); Ruth Bloch, "American Feminine Ideals in Transition: The Rise of the Moral Mother," *Feminist Studies* 4 (June 1978); Nancy Cott, *The Bonds of Womanhood* (New Haven: Yale University Press, 1977); and Mary P. Ryan, *Cradle of The Middle Class: The Family in Oneida County, New York, 1790–1865* (Cambridge: Cambridge University Press, 1981).

33. Rev. John S.C. Abbott, Paternal Neglect," *Parents' Magazine* (March 1842), cited in Kuhn, *The Mother's Role in Childhood Education*, 4; also Bernard W. Wishy, *The Child and the Republic: The Dawn of Modern American Child Nurture* (Philadelphia: University of Pennsylvania Press, 1968), 26–29.

34. See G.R. Bach, "Father-Fantasies and Father Typing in Father-Separated Children," *Child Development* 17 (1946): 63–80; David B. Lynn, A Note on Sex Differences in the Development of Masculine and Feminine Identification," *Psychological Review* 66 (1959):126–35; R.R. Sears, M.H. Pintler, and P.S. Sears, "Effect of Father Separation on Pre-School Children's Doll Aggression," *Child Development* 17 (1946):219–43; Talcott Parsons believed that when fathers were mostly absent during child rearing, excessive maternal affection would discourage sons from entering into the instrumental world inhabited by men. Talcott Parsons and R.F. Bales, *Family, Socialization and Interaction Process* (Glencoe, Ill., 1955).

35. For a forceful exposition of this argument, see Joseph H. Pleck, *The Myth of Masculinity* (Cambridge: Massachusetts Institute of Technology Press, 1984).

36. Some learning theorists insist that children identify with nurturing and affectionate parents rather than with those who are perceived as powerful; see E.M. Hetherington and G. Frankie, "Effects of Parental Dominance, Warmth, and Conflict on Imitation in Children," *Journal of Personality and Social Psychology* 6 (1967): 119–125; P.H. Mussen and L. Dister, "Masculinity, Identification, and Father-Son Relationships," *Journal of Abnormal and Social Psychology* 59 (1959): 350–56. A Bandurra and R.H. Walters, *Adolescent Aggression: A Study of the Influence of Child-Training Practices and Family Interrelationships* (New York: Ronald Press, Co., 1959).

37. See E. Anthony Rotundo, "Boy Culture: Middle-Class Boyhood in Nineteenth-Century America" in Mark C. Carnes and Clyde Griffen eds. *Meanings for Manhood: Constructions of Masculinity in Victorian America* (Chicago: University of Chicago Press, 1990), 15–36.

38. *Odd Fellowship Illustrated* (1875), 44; also *Willis's Expose of Odd Fellowship*, 35.

39. The phrase "summit of complacency" is used in the title of chapter 2, Henry F. May, *Protestant Church and Industrial America* (New York: Harper & Row, 1949), and "the golden age of liberal theology" in the title of chapter 46, Sydney E. Ahlstrom, *A Religious History of the American People* (New Haven: Yale University Press, 1972).

THE LAKOTA GHOST DANCE

Raymond J. DeMallie

For Native American peoples the nineteenth century was a period of continual change marked by the takeover of their country by white people, the disappearance of the buffalo, and finally, adjustment to reservation life. Until recently the ghost dance that emerged among many tribes in the late nineteenth century (and was most dramatically enacted during the Lakota Sioux massacre at Wounded Knee in 1890), has been interpreted as a reaction by Native Americans to hunger and the loss of their land. In contrast, Raymond DeMallie argues that this interpretation does not give justice to the religious nature of the movement nor see it as part of the whole of Lakota culture. Instead, DeMallie sees the Sioux Ghost Dance as a new religious movement that drew upon and reformulated the pre-existing rituals and myths of the Lakota religious tradition.

Reprinted by permission from Raymond J. DeMallie, "The Lakota Ghost Dance: An Ethnohistorical Account," *Pacific Historical Review* 51(1982): 385–405.

17 ❦

THE LAKOTA GHOST DANCE
An Ethnohistorical Account

Raymond J. DeMallie

THE LAKOTA GHOST DANCE (*wanagi wacipi*)[1] has been the subject of extensive study, first by newspapermen, who made it a true media event, and later by anthropologists and historians. The chronology of the contextual events in Lakota history—the 1888 and 1889 land cession commissions and their subsequent delegations to Washington, the beef ration cuts at the agencies, the spread of the ghost dance ritual among the Lakotas in 1890, the death of Sitting Bull, the calling in of U.S. troops, the flight of Lakota camps to the badlands, the blundering massacre at Wounded Knee, and the eventual restoration of peace under U.S. army control of the Sioux agencies—is voluminously detailed in the printed literature.[2]

The historiography of the Lakota ghost dance period begins with two contemporary works drawn primarily from newspaper sources, James P. Boyd's *Recent Indian Wars* (1891) and W. Fletcher Johnson's *Life of Sitting Bull and History of the Indian War of 1890–91* (1891). Despite the sensationalist tone, both volumes compiled a substantial body of important historical material. James Mooney, in his anthropological classic, *The Ghost-Dance Religion and the Sioux Outbreak of 1890* (1896), included a balanced historical discussion based on unpublished government records, newspaper accounts, and interviews with Indians. Mooney stressed the revivalistic aspects of the ghost dance and the hope it offered for regeneration of Indian culture. Subsequently there have been numerous historical studies of the Lakota ghost dance, most of which are partisan, focusing either on the Indian or military point of view. George E. Hyde's *A Sioux Chronicle* (1956) attempted to reconcile both perspectives and present the ghost dance in its political and economic context. The definitive modern historical study is Robert M. Utley's *The Last Days of the Sioux Nation* (1963), the best presentation of the military perspective.[3]

The so-called "Sioux Outbreak" with the associated troop maneuvers and the resultant Wounded Knee massacre were, from the moment they began, linked with the ghost dance. This new religion had come into Sioux country from the West, originating with Jack Wilson (Wovoka), a Paiute prophet living in Nevada. Lakota acceptance of the ritual has been interpreted as a response to the stress caused by military defeat, the disappearance of the buffalo, and confinement on a reservation. The ghost dance religion itself has been seen as an epiphenomenon of social and political unrest. As the redoubtable Dr. Valentine T.

McGillycuddy, the former dictatorial agent of Pine Ridge, diagnosed the situation in January 1891: "As for the ghost dance, too much attention has been paid to it. It was only the symptom or surface indication of deep-rooted, long-existing difficulty…."[4]

Such an analysis has become standard in the writings of both historians and anthropologists. Mooney wrote that among the Sioux, "already restless under both old and new grievances, and more lately brought to the edge of starvation by a reduction of rations, the doctrine speedily assumed a hostile meaning."[5] Similarly, Robert H. Lowie asserted in *Indians of the Plains* (1954), a standard text: "Goaded into fury by their grievances, the disciples of Wovoka in the Plains substituted for his policy of amity a holy war in which the Whites were to be exterminated."[6] However, this consensual interpretation of the ghost dance has not gone unchallenged. For example, in an anthropological overview, Omer C. Stewart explicitly rejected the characterization of the ghost dance as a violent, warlike movement.[7] Nonetheless, this is a minority viewpoint in the literature.

Re-evaluation of the ghost dance starts with an examination of the consensual interpretation exemplified in Robert M. Utley's work. He wrote:

> Wovoka preached a peaceful doctrine, blending elements of Christianity with the old native religion…. The Ghost Dance gripped most of the western tribes without losing this peaceful focus. Among the Teton Sioux, however, it took on militant overtones…. In their bitterness and despair, the Sioux let the Ghost Dance apostles, Short Bull and Kicking Bear, persuade them that the millennium prophesied by Wovoka might be facilitated by destroying the white people. Wearing "ghost shirts" that the priests assured them would turn the white man's bullets, the Sioux threw themselves wholeheartedly into a badly perverted version of the Ghost Dance.[8]

Before this analysis can be evaluated, a number of fundamental assumptions underlying it must be made more explicit. First, the statement that Wovoka's doctrine blended Christianity with "the native religion" implies that there was some fundamental similarity between the native religions of the Paiutes and the Lakotas. This assumption underestimates the significance of the vast cultural differences between these two tribes.

Second, the analysis asserts that the Lakotas perverted a doctrine of peace into one of war. This assertion incorrectly implies that the Lakota ghost dance religion was characterized by a unified body of doctrinal teaching. Lakota accounts of visits to the prophet clearly show that his teachings were not formulated into a creed; each man went away from meeting Wovoka with a personal interpretation of the ghost dance religion. For the Lakotas, this behavior was very much in accord with traditional religious practices, which defined loci of power (*wakan*) in the universe and devised rituals to tap this power, but which left each individual free to contribute to the understanding of the totality of the power (*Wakan Tanka*) through his own individual experiences.[9] Within the context of a nondoctrinal religion, there can be no heretics, only believers and nonbelievers.

Third, the analysis asserts that the leaders of the ghost dance misled their followers for political reasons, even to the point of making false claims that their sacred shirts would ward off bullets. This assertion assumes *a priori* that to its leaders the ghost dance was a political movement merely masquerading as religion.

Fourth, the claims that the ghost dance "gripped" the tribes and that "the Sioux threw themselves wholeheartedly into" the ritual suggests irrational fanaticism. But the historical record makes it clear that the period of Lakota participation in the ghost dance was basically confined to the fall and early winter of 1890 and that the majority of the Lakota people in the ghost dance camps had only gone to them because they feared that an attack from the U.S. army was imminent. This factor explains why these camps fled to the safety of the bad-lands.

The standard historical interpretation of the Lakota ghost dance takes too narrow a perspective. It treats the ghost dance as an isolated phenomenon, as though it were divorced from the rest of Lakota culture. It also refuses to accept the basic religious nature of the movement. The so-called ghost dance outbreak has broader implications and interconnections than historical studies have indicated. To dismiss the ghost dance as only a reaction to land loss and hunger does not do it justice; to dismiss it as merely a desperate attempt to revitalize a dead or dying culture is equally unsatisfactory. Even though it was borrowed from outside sources, the ghost dance needs to be seen as part of the integral, ongoing whole of Lakota culture and its supression as part of the historical process of religious persecution led by Indian agents and missionaries against the Lakotas living on the Great Sioux Reservation.

The primary reasons why previous historical analyses of the Lakota ghost dance have been inadequate lie in our reluctance to consider seriously the symbolic content of Indian cultures—in this instance, to allow the Lakotas their own legitimate perspective. Instead, empathetic writers have characterized the Lakotas as though they were either uncomprehending children or were motivated by precisely the same political and economic drives as white men. Both attitudes are as demeaning as they are misleading, and they fail to treat Indian culture with the same serious consideration afforded other cultures.

Writing history that deals with the meanings and conflicts of peoples with different cultural systems is a complex task. In recent years historians of the American Indian have turned to ethnohistory to provide methods for understanding the complexities of interactions between participants coming from totally different cultures. In a discussion of the new perspectives available from political, ecological, economic, and psychological anthropology, Calvin Martin has demonstrated the utility and contributions of each to the writing of ethnohistory.[10] Within the discipline of anthropology, however, there is a more general theoretical perspective that may profitably be applied to ethnohistorical study—namely, symbolic anthropology. This method attempts to isolate differing significant symbols—units of meaning—that define perspectives on reality within different cultural systems.[11] In the context of ethnohistory, it attempts to compare epistemological and philosophical bases for action from the perspective of the different cultures involved. Its focus is on ideas systematically reconstructed for each cultural system. It does not reduce history to ideological conflicts, but uses ideology to understand the motivation that underlies behavior.[12]

It must not be assumed that the intention of a symbolic approach to ethnohistory is to penetrate the minds of individuals in the past. Psychological approaches to history are necessarily highly speculative, and any claim to intersubjectivity is no more possible with individuals in the past than with those of the present. Rather, the symbolic approach attempts to delineate collective understandings from each of the cultural perspectives involved, and thus to describe the cognitive worlds of the participants in the events under study. Using this as background, the ethnohistorian has a basis for ascribing motives and meanings to past actions. Robert Berkhofer expressed it well when he wrote: "Historical study, then, in my view, is the combination of the actors' and observers' levels of analysis into a unified representation of past reality."[13]

In attempting to reconcile and combine both Lakota and white perspectives on the ghost dance, it is essential to compare causal notions of change as understood by the two cultures. During the late nineteenth century the basic issues on the Great Sioux Reservation were what kinds of change would occur in Indian culture and social life and who would direct this change. Whites assumed that Indian culture was stagnant and that the Indians could be transformed for the better only by the imposition of Western civilization. Indians, on the other hand, sought to control the process of change themselves.

For the Lakota people, the nineteenth century had been a period of continual changes: further explorations on the Plains, the complete integration of the horse into their culture, the flourishing of the sun dance as the focal point of ritual activity, the slow take over of their country by the whites, the disappearance of the buffalo, and finally the adjustment to reservation life. A discussion of the Lakota view of the relationship between mankind and the natural world, particularly the buffalo, can help us begin to understand these changes from the Lakotas' perspective.

During the 1860s, when commissioners traveled up the Missouri River to sign treaties with the Indians, they found the attitude of the Lakotas toward the buffalo to be particularly unrealistic. To the commissioners it was evident that the buffalo were being exterminated and would soon be gone from the region. To the Indians this decline did not appear to be an irreversible process. For example, the chiefs told the commissioners that they hoped the whites would take away the roads and steamboats and "return us all the buffalo as it used to be."[14] Baffled at this illogic, the commissioners reported that the Indians "are only too much inclined to regard us possessed of supernatural powers."[15] This complete failure to communicate stemmed from the commissioners' assumption that the facts of the natural world must have appeared the same to the Indians as they did to the whites. Yet the Indians themselves recorded testimony which showed dramatically that the Lakotas thought of the land, the animals, and the people as a single system, no part of which could change without affecting the others. Thus when the commissioners asked if the Indians would consent to live on the Missouri River, they were told: "When the buffalo come close to the river, we come close to it. When the buffaloes go off, we go off after them."[16] The Indians, the animals, and the land were one; while the people lived, talk of buffalo extinction was without meaning. Much later, Black Elk expressed the same attitude when he commented to poet John G. Neihardt: "Perhaps when the wild animals are gone, the Indians will be gone too."[17]

To understand this interrelatedness of man, land, and animals—particularly the buffalo—it is necessary to understand the Lakota view of their origins. During the early twentieth century, the old holy men at Pine Ridge instructed Dr. James R. Walker, the agency physician, in the fundamentals of their religion. A cornerstone of their belief was that both mankind and the buffalo had originated within the earth before they emerged on the surface.[18] When the buffalo became scarce, it was believed that they went back inside the earth because they had been offended, either by Indians or whites. At any given time, this explanation accounted for the scarcity of buffalo. Later, Black Elk told Neihardt about a holy man named Drinks Water who had foretold during the mid-nineteenth century that "the four-leggeds were going back into the earth."[19] But this explanation also allowed for the return of the buffalo. The ghost dance Messiah's promise of a new earth, well stocked with buffalo, was completely consistent with the old Lakota system of cause and effect by which they comprehended the ecology. If the buffalo had been driven back into the earth by the white man, they could be released again by the Messiah.

The Lakotas' causal model of change was vastly different from the white man's. The Lakota world was a constant, with relationships among its parts varying according to external pressures. As the nineteenth century wore on, these pressures came more and more from the whites. But these pressures were not conceived of by the Lakotas as cumulative or developmental. All that *was* existed in its potentiality before the whites intruded; if they would leave, the world could be again as it had been. From the 1850s through the 1870s the Lakotas tried to get rid of the whites by war; in 1890 they tried ritual dancing and prayer. The white view, of course, was diametrically opposed. This was the age of the developmental social philosophers preaching the doctrine of individual competition for the evolution of humanity. The history of mankind was religiously believed to be progressive; changes were accepted as good and cumulative, leading from earlier stages of savagery and barbarism (in which the Indians still lived) to civilization, which was believed to be becoming progressively better, not only technologically, but morally as well.

It is within this general context of cross-cultural misunderstanding that a symbolic approach can contribute to an analysis of the Lakota ghost dance and subsequent military action. The dance itself, the actual ritual, became the focus of misunderstanding between Indians and whites. Most importantly, dance was a highly charged symbol. For the Lakotas the dance was a symbol of religion, a ritual means to spiritual and physical betterment. Even Lakota nonbelievers accepted the religious motivation of the ghost dance. For the whites, on the other hand, Indians dancing symbolized impending war. Similarly, Indian and white conceptions of ghosts were different. For the Lakotas, the ghost dance promised a reunion with the souls of their dead relations. For the whites it suggested that the Indians were expecting to die, caught up in a frenzy of reckless fatalism.

This clash over the meaning of the ghost dance is fully documented in the literature. For example, in 1890, according to James Boyd's *Recent Indian Wars:*

> The Indians mingled tales of their hard treatment with their religious songs, and their religious dances assumed more and more the form of war dances.... The spirit of fatalism spread and they courted death at the hands of white men, believing that it would be a speedy transport to a happier sphere.[20]

However, Boyd's sources—both Indian and white—do not provide factual support for his interpretation. Nonetheless, this seems to have been the general opinion held by whites living on the frontiers of the Great Sioux Reservation. Boyd wrote:

> Older residents, and those acquainted with Indian warfare, knew well that an outbreak was always preceded by a series of dances. While these men were quite familiar with Indian nature, they failed to discern between a religious ceremony and a war dance.[21]

Boyd reviewed the progress the Sioux had made in Christianity, home building, farming, and ranching, and he raised the question of why they would wish to precipitate war. One possible answer came from Red Cloud, who said in an interview:

> We felt that we were mocked in our misery.... There was no hope on earth, and God seemed to have forgotten us. Someone had again been talking of the Son of God, and said He had come.

The people did not know; they did not care. They snatched at the hope. They screamed like crazy men to Him for mercy. They caught at the promises they heard He had made.[22]

Towards the end of the book, Boyd revealed his personal interpretation of the cause of the trouble: "The Indians are practically a doomed race, and none realize it better than themselves."[23]

Doubtlessly, some individual Lakotas shared this sense of despair. There were no buffalo; the government systematically broke its promises to support the Sioux until they could provide for themselves; and the Indians were starving. The ghost dance, arising at this opportune time, held out hope for the Lakotas. But if the Lakotas truly had believed themselves to be a doomed people, they would have paid no attention to the ghost dance. The religion was powerful because it nurtured cultural roots that were very much alive— temporarily dormant, perhaps, but not dying.

Is it reasonable to dismiss the Lakota ghost dance as insignificant, the mere "symptom" of other troubles, to use McGillycuddy's medical metaphor? This depiction does not explain the popularity of the ghost dance as a religious movement among other tribes. Perhaps it could be used to explain the warlike twist that the ghost dance took among the Lakotas. But when the record is evaluated objectively, it seems clear that the Lakota ghost dance did not have warlike intentions. Hostility was provoked only when Indian agents demanded that the dance be stopped, and violence came only after extreme provocation—the assassination of Sitting Bull by the Standing Rock Indian Police and the calling in of the army. For all intents and purposes, Sitting Bulls's death was unrelated to the ghost dance. Agent McLaughlin had been clamoring for the old chief's arrest and removal from the reservation for some time, ever since Sitting Bull had refused to take up farming and be a model "progressive" Indian, to use McLaughlin's own term.[24]

Lakota ghost dancers were enjoined to put away whatever they could of the white man's manufacture, especially metal objects. George Sword, captain of the Pine Ridge Indian Police, noted that some of the ghost dancers did have guns.[25] When the agent demanded that the dance at No Water's camp cease, he was threatened with guns and retreated to the agency.[26] Apparently, the purpose of the weapons was to ward off outside interference with the ritual. However, Boyd quoted a ghost dancer named Weasel: "We did not carry our guns nor any weapon, but trusted to the Great Spirit to destroy the soldiers." This statement was made after troops had arrived at Pine Ridge. Weasel related: "The priests called upon the young men at the juncture not to become angry but to continue the dance, but have horses ready so that all could flee were the military to charge the village."[27] However, even this precaution was not considered necessary by fervent believers. Short Bull, one of the ghost dance leaders, assured his people that they would be safe from the white soldiers:

> If the soldiers surround you four deep, three of you, on whom I have put holy shirts, will sing a song, which I have taught you, around them, when some of them will drop dead. Then the rest will start to run, but their horses will sink into the earth. The riders will jump from their horses, but they will sink into the earth also. Then you can do as you desire with them. Now you must know this, that all the soldiers and that race will be dead.[28]

Historical sources provide more information about the ghost dance from Short Bull than from any other of the leaders. Talking to Walker, he outlined his understanding of the prophet's teachings: "It was told that a woman gave birth to a child and this was known in heaven."[29] Short Bull went to meet him. "This man professed to be a great man, next to God." The prophet told Short Bull and the other Lakotas "that he wished to be their intermediary. He said 'Do nothing wrong.'" On another occasion Short Bull said:

> Who would have thought that dancing could have made such trouble? We had no wish to make trouble, nor did we cause it of ourselves.... We had no thought of fighting.... We went unarmed to the dance. How could we have held weapons? For thus we danced, in a circle, hand in hand, each man's fingers linked in those of his neighbor.... The message that I brought was peace.[30]

The messianic and strongly Christian nature of the ghost dance is very clear in Short Bull's teachings:

> The Father had commanded all the world to dance, and we gave the dance to the people as we had been bidden. When they danced they fell dead and went to the spirit-camp and saw those who had died, those whom they had loved....
>
> In this world the Great Father has given to the white man everything and to the Indian nothing. But it will not always be thus. In another world the Indian shall be as the white man and the white man as the Indian. To the Indian will be given wisdom and power, and the white man shall be helpless and unknowing with only the bow and arrow. For ere long this world will be consumed in flame and pass away. Then, in the life after this, to the Indian shall all be given.[31]

Through the teachings of the ghost dance, and statements about it by Lakotas recorded from 1889 until about 1910, it is possible to proliferate evidence to demonstrate the peaceful intentions of the leaders of the ghost dance. The historical record does not support the accusation that the Sioux "perverted" the ghost dance doctrine of peace to one of war.

Simple refutation of the consensual historical interpretation does little to advance an understanding of the ghost dance. Since it had a short life among the Lakotas, at least as far as active performance of the ritual, perhaps it might be dismissed as an isolated reaction to social stress, a revitalization movement that failed. After all, Mooney estimated that only half of the Sioux were affected by the ghost dance and his sources suggest that of these, only a small number were real believers in the religion.[32] But this conclusion ignores the extreme importance that the Lakotas of 1890 placed on the dance, as well as the extent to which its suppression had served in later years as a symbol of white oppression. When Mooney visited Pine Ridge in 1891 as part of his comparative study of the ghost dance, he found the Lakotas uncooperative. He wrote: "To my questions the answer almost invariably was, 'The dance was our religion, but the government sent soldiers to kill us on account of it. We will not talk more about it.'"[33]

The study of Lakota history from 1880 to 1890 suggests that it is a mistake to treat the ghost dance as an isolated phenomenon. Its prohibition was only another step in the systematic suppression of native religious practices that formed an integral part of the U.S. government's program of Indian civilization. Missionary observers felt that the ghost dance was only one more eruption of the "heathenism" that necessarily underlay the Indian pysche, a heathenism to be conquered and dispatched when Indians, as individuals, raised themselves from barbarism to civilization. The evolutionary social theory of the times held sway in the rhetoric of Indian policy.[34] *The Word Carrier*, a Protestant missionary newspaper published at the Santee Agency in Nebraska, argued in 1890 (before Wounded Knee) that it was the government's responsibility to end the ghost dancing because of its political potential. The argument was an insidious one, expressed as follows:

> Their war dances have been suppressed simply as a political measure. The sun dance was forbidden in the name of humanity, as cruel and degrading. The Omaha dances should be summarily suppressed in the name of morality. But all of these alike, as well as all other of their heathen dances, should be prevented as far and as fast as possible until utterly eradicated, because they are potentially dangerous. We ought not to touch them as religious ceremonials, but, as breeders of riot and rebellion, we must.[35]

The callousness of missionary zeal for the suppression of heathenism is nowhere more dramatically revealed than in *The Word Carrier's* editorial on the Wounded Knee massacre printed in the January 1891 issue:

> The slaughter of a whole tribe of Indians at Wounded Knee was an affair which looks worse the more it is investigated. But aside from the question of culpability there is a providential aspect which demands notice. Taking it in its bearings on the whole condition of things among the rebellious Titon [*sic*] Sioux it was a blessing. It was needful that these people should feel in some sharp terrible way the just consequences of their actions, and be held in wholesome fear from further folly.[36]

Commentary is perhaps unnecessary, but we can suggest that the fanaticism of Christian missionaries was no less than that of the ghost dancers themselves. Stanley Vestal, in his biography of Sitting Bull, takes the Christian aspects of the ghost dance at face value and seizes the opportunity to comment on the missionaries:

> The Ghost dance was entirely Christian—except for the difference in rituals. However, it taught nonresistance and brotherly love in ways that had far more significance for Indians than any the missionaries could offer. No wonder the missionaries became alarmed; they were no longer sure of their converts.[37]

However, the dominant interpretation of the ghost dance, contemporarily and historically, places little significance on Christian parallels.

Some contemporary observers felt that the ghost dance showed striking resemblances to the sun dance, a suggestion that seems at first unfounded, but which gains credibility by reading descriptions of the ritual. Mary Collins, a missionary, witnessed the ghost dance in Sitting Bull's camp and recorded the following description:

> I watched all the performance, and I came to the conclusion that the "ghost dance" is nothing more than the sun dance revived. They all looked at the sun as they danced. They stopped going round now and then, and all faced the sun, with uplifted faces and outstretched arms, standing in straight lines and moaning a most horrible sound. Then they raised themselves on the toes, and then lowered themselves, raising and lowering their bodies in this way, and groaning dismally, then joined hands with heads strained backwards, watching the sun and praying to it

until, with dizziness and weariness, one after another fell down, some of them wallowing and rolling on the ground and frothing at the mouth, others throwing their arms and running around and whooping like mad men, and all the time, as much as possible, still gazing sunward. They have not yet cut themselves, as in the old sun dance, but yesterday I heard this talk: some said, "If one cuts himself, he is more 'wakan,' and can see and talk with the Messiah."[38]

These similarities to the sun dance—gazing sunward and the dance step of the sun dance—are suggestive. Also, Mooney notes that of all the tribes who adopted the ghost dance, the Sioux were one of the few to dance around a sacred tree (or pole), the structural form of the old sun dance.[39] This element may be superficial, serving only to indicate that when people borrow new ideas, they adapt them to older cultural forms as closely as possible. However, it reinforces the Lakotas' sense of religious loss and their deep felt need to establish continuity with their past. It seems that the new religion, believed to come from a reincarnated Christ wearied of the faithlessness of the whites and ready to aid his Indian children, was incorporated in a ritual form that merged the circle dance of the Paiutes (in which men and women danced together in a circle, holding hands—an innovation for the Lakotas) with the sacred dance circle and center pole of the traditional Lakota sun dance.

A speech by Short Bull to his people on October 31, 1890, points out the importance of the tree or center pole as defining the sacred space for the ghost dance ritual: "Now, there will be a tree sprout up, and there all the members of our religion and the tribe must gather together. That will be the place where we will see our dead relations." Short Bull's ghost dance preachings incorporated traditional Lakota symbolism of the four directions to suggest the unifying effects of the ghost dance on all Indian tribes. "Our father in heaven has placed a mark at each point of the four winds," indicating a great circle around the central tree. To the west was a pipe, representing the Lakotas; to the north, an arrow, representing the Cheyennes; to the east, hail, representing the Arapahoes; and to the south, a pipe and feather, representing the Crows. "My father has shown me these things, therefore we must continue this dance." He promised that the ghost dance shirts would protect them from the soldiers. "Now, we must gather at Pass Creek where the tree is sprouting. There we will go among our dead relations."[40] Many years later one Lakota who had participated in the ghost dance as a boy commented: "That part about the dead returning was what appealed to me."[41]

In practice, the millenialism of the ghost dance was merged with the symbols of the old religion. The tree, which had symbolized the body of an enemy in the old sun dance, became in the ghost dance symbolic of the Indian people themselves; this tree was dormant, but it was about to sprout and bloom. The tree symbol is best known from Black Elk, who found the outward symbols of the ghost dance so strikingly similar to his own vision during childhood that he was immediately caught up in the new religion. He felt it as a personal call, a reminder that he had not yet begun the work assigned him by his vision. "I was to be intercessor for my people and yet I was not doing my duty. Perhaps it was the Messiah that had appointed me and he might have sent this to remind me to get to work again to bring my people back into the hoop and the old religion."[42]

It seems clear in Black Elk's case that the ghost dance, while seen as a new ritual, inaugurated by a new prophet—perhaps Christ himself—was in no way felt to be a sharp break with the old religion. It was rather a means to bring the old religion to fulfillment. There is no denial that this new hope for religious fulfillment was born of frustration and unhappiness bordering on despair. The ghost dance was to bring about the transformation to a new life on a rejuvenated earth filled with all the Lakota people who had ever lived before—living again in the old ways, hunting buffalo unfettered by the demands of whites, and freed from the cares of the old earth. Years later, one ghost dancer recalled the wonderful promise of the ghost dance visions:

> Waking to the drab and wretched present after such a glowing vision, it was little wonder that they wailed as if their poor hearts would break in two with disillusionment. The people went on and on and could not stop, day or night, hoping perhaps to get a vision of their dead, or at least to hear of the visions of others. They preferred that to rest or food or sleep. And I suppose the authorities did think they were crazy—but they weren't. They were only terribly unhappy.[43]

In order to put the ghost dance in its proper perspective in Lakota religious history, it is imperative to review the process of religious persecution that marked the Lakota experience during the 1880s. At Pine Ridge, from the beginning of the decade, Agent McGillycuddy preached against the evils of the sun dance. Finally, in his annual report for 1884, he wrote that "for the first time in the history of the Ogalalla Sioux and Northern Cheyennes" the sun dance was not held.[44] Though McGillycuddy did not fully understand the reasons why, the prohibition of the sun dance was indeed a drastic blow. As a public festival it brought together Lakotas from all the agencies into old-time encampments, with opportunities for courting and fun. In addition to the actual ritual of the ceremony, the sun dance provided the time and place for many additional rituals, including the acting out of visions, dances by groups of people with shared vision experiences, demonstrations of the powers of medicine men (healers), the piercing of babies' ears (essential for identity as a Lakota), and lavish giveaways. Camped around the sacred circle with the sacred tree at its center, the occasion of the sun dance was a real affirmation of Lakota identity and power, in both physical and spiritual senses. In the words of Little Wound, American Horse, and Lone Star, as they explained their traditional religion to Dr. James R. Walker in 1896: "The Sun Dance is the greatest ceremony that the Oglalas do. It is a sacred ceremony in which all the people have a part…. The ceremony of the Sun Dance may embrace all the ceremonies of any kind that are relative to the Gods."[45]

In 1888, as the Oglala winter counts—native pictographic calendars—record, a further government prohibition was enforced on the Lakotas: "Bundles were forbidden."[46] It had been the custom when a beloved person died to cut a lock of his or her hair and save it in a ritual bundle for a year, thus causing the spirit (*wanagi*) to remain with the people. At the end of the period, the spirit was released, and a great giveaway was held; throughout the year goods were amassed to give away in honor of the departed one. In some cases, as upon the death of a first-born son, the parents gave away everything they owned, although, according to tribal customs of sharing, they would in return be given the necessities of life and thus reestablished in a new home to help put the past out of their minds. Agent H. D. Gallagher at Pine Ridge decided in 1888 that although this custom had been allowed unchecked by his predecessors, he would put an immediate stop to it. Yet, he wrote in his annual report, "I found myself opposed by every Indian upon the reservation."[47] To the Lakotas it was a final horror: not even in death was there escape from the white man's restrictions. The giveaway after death was prohibited and became an offense punishable by arrest. Ten years later, in

1898, Short Bull, in his capacity as religious leader, sent a plea to the agent begging for understanding:

> The white people made war on the Lakotas to keep them from practicing their religion. Now the white people wish to make us cause the spirits of our dead to be ashamed. They wish us to be a stingy people and send our spirits to the spirit world as if they had been conquered and robbed by the enemy. They wish us to send our spirits on the spirit trail with nothing so that when they come to the spirit world, they will be like beggars.... Tell this to the agent and maybe he will not cause us to make our spirits ashamed.[48]

Such requests fell on deaf ears. From the agents' point of view, every vestige of heathen religion had to be eliminated before civilization could take firm root. The powers of the agents were dictatorial in the matter.

Following the prohibition of public rituals surrounding the sun dance, as well as the rituals of death and mourning, came the prohibition in 1890 against the new ritual of the ghost dance. Then came the murder of Sitting Bull and the massacre at Wounded Knee. It was a period of grave crisis for the Lakota people, physically and emotionally. Their religion had been effective before the whites came, but now the *Wakan Tanka* seemed no longer to hear their prayers. Under the restraints of reservation life, traditional customs relating to war and hunting were abandoned. For spiritual renewal there were only two places to turn: secret rituals of the purification lodge, vision quest, *yuwipi*, and attenuated versions of the sun dance, or alternatively to the various Christian churches which were clamoring for converts.

But the years immediately following the ghost dance were bad ones for missionaries to make new converts. According to Agent Charles G. Penney, in his annual report for 1891, there were yet "a considerable number of very conservative Indians, medicine men and others, who still insist upon a revival of the Messiah craze and the ghost dancing."[49] The following year the missionary John P. Williamson, a perceptive observer, reported from Pine Ridge that "the effect of the ghost dances in the former years was very deleterious to Christianity, and is still felt among the Ogalallas. The excitement of a false religion has left a dead, indifferent feeling about religion."[50]

The Lakota religious leaders at Pine Ridge who shared their thoughts with Dr. Walker at the beginning of the twentieth century were disappointed, but not defeated. Little Wound, after revealing the sacred secrets of the *Hunka* ceremony, said to Walker:

> My friend, I have told you the secrets of the *Hunkayapi*. I fear that I have done wrong. But the spirits of old times do not come to me anymore. Another spirit has come, the Great Spirit of the white man. I do not know him. I do not know how to call him to help me. I have done him no harm, and he should do me no harm. The old life is gone, and I cannot be young again.[51]

Afraid of Bear commented: "The spirits do not come and help us now. The white men have driven them away."[52] Ringing Shield stated: "Now the spirits will not come. This is because the white men have offended the spirits."[53]

One of the most eloquent testimonies comes from a speech by Red Cloud, recorded by Walker, in which he outlined his understanding of the Lakota *Wakan Tanka*. Then he added:

When the Lakotas believed these things they lived happy and they died satisfied. What more than this can that which the white man offers us give?... *Taku Skanskan* [Lakotas' most powerful god] is familiar with my spirit (*nagi*) and when I die I will go with him. Then I will be with my forefathers. If this is not in the heaven of the white man, I shall be satisfied. *Wi* [Sun] is my father. The *Wakan Tanka* of the white man has overcome him. But I shall remain true to him.[54]

Outwardly, the white man's victory over Lakota religion was nearly complete. Inwardly, even among those who—like Red Cloud—accepted Christianity for what it was worth, the recognition of the existence of *wakan* in the life forms of the universe provided foci of belief and hope.

Any meaningful understanding of the Lakota ghost dance period must begin with an analysis of the foundations for cultural conflict. Lakotas and white men operated under radically different epistemologies; what seemed illogical to one was sensible to the other and vice versa. Objects in the natural world symbolized totally different realms of meaning in the two cultures. This difference has important implications for the writing of history. For example, Utley suggests that "when the hostile Sioux came to the reservation, they doubtless understood that the life of the future would differ from that of the past."[55] But we can raise a reasonable doubt that this statement truly characterized the Lakota point of view. When Utley writes: "That the vanishing herds symbolized their own vanishing ways of life cannot have escaped the Sioux,"[56] we must deny the assertion. This is the unbeliever's attitude, totally dependent on acceptance of western philosophy. Similarly, it is necessary to take issue with Utley's claim that "after Wounded Knee...the reality of the conquest descended upon the entire Nation with such overwhelming force that it shattered all illusions."[57] This is political rhetoric to justify the defeat of the Indians, not reasoned historical assessment.

The vast differences between the rhetoric of whites and Indians gives special significance to the ghost dance as the last step in a decade-long series of events aimed at crushing every outward expression of Lakota spirituality. From the believer's standpoint, the social and political problems—the so-called outbreak and the Wounded Knee massacre—were but epiphenomena of religious crisis. The ghost dance was inextricably bound to the whole of Lakota culture and to ongoing historical processes in Lakota society. Although it was introduced from the outside, it was rapidly assimilated to the Lakota system of values and ideas, especially because it promised resolution to the grave problems that beset the people. To recognize it as a religious movement in its own right does not deny its interconnection with all other aspects of Lakota life or negate its intended practical consequence to free the Lakotas from white domination. However, such recognition does retain the Lakotas' own focus on the ghost dance as a fundamentally religious movement which was to bring about radical transformation completely through religious means. Virtually all historical data point to the non-violent intentions of the ghost dance religion and the commitment of the believers to achieving their ends non-violently. It was the explicit command of the Messiah. In a cultural sense, this understanding of the ghost dance was shared by all Lakotas, believers and nonbelievers alike.

The importance of the ghost dance is not to be measured in the simple number of participants or in the unhappiness or despair that it reflected, but rather as part of the religious history of the Lakota people. For a time it held out such hope to the Lakotas that its ultimate failure, symbolized by the tragic deaths of the believers at Wounded Knee, generated a renewed religious crisis that forced a final reali: n that the old ways, with the hunting of the buffalo, were actually gone forever. Out of this religious collapse, new beliefs, new philosophies, eventually developed that would entail a major intellectual reworking of the epistemological foundations of Lakota culture.

Among the writers on the Lakota ghost dance, only John G. Neihardt accepted it as a legitimate religious movement and saw it as an attempt by the holy men of the Lakotas to use sacred means to better the condition of their people.[58] A symbolic approach forces examination of the religious aspects of the ghost dance, not only because it *was* primarily religious from the Lakotas' perspective, but also because at least some contemporary white observers—the missionaries—understood that the ritual's true power lay in its religious nature. To the white men the ghost dance was seen as the last gasp of heathenism; to the Indians it offered renewed access to spiritual power.

The ghost dance ritual itself was a powerful symbol, but one on whose meanings the whites and Lakotas were incapable of communicating. They shared no common understandings. That the ghost dance could be a valid religion was incomprehensible to the whites, just as the whites' evolutionary perspective on Lakota destiny—that the barbaric must develop into the civilized—was incomprehensible to the Lakotas. Religion, dancing, ghosts, the processes of social change, and animal ecology were all important symbols to both whites and Indians but the meanings of these symbols in the two cultures were diametrically opposed. By focusing on these symbols it is possible for the ethnohistorian to reconstruct the meanings of events from the perspective of the participants and to arrive at an analysis that has both relevance and insight, and which contributes to an understanding of the historical realities of the Lakota ghost dance.

NOTES

1. Literally, "spirit dance." The term *wanagi* refers to the immortal spirit of a human and may be translated as "spirit," "ghost," or "soul." See James R. Walker, *Lakota Belief and Ritual*, ed. by Raymond J. DeMallie and Elaine A. Jahner (Lincoln, 1980), 70–71.

2. For a historiographical survey of the literature on the Lakota ghost dance, see Michael A. Sievers, "The Historiography of 'The Bloody Field... That Kept the Secret of the Everlasting Word': Wounded Knee," *South Dakota History*, V1 (1975), 33–54.

3. James P. Boyd, *Recent Indian Wars, Under the Lead of Sitting Bull, and Other Chiefs; with A full Account of the Messiah Craze, and Ghost Dances* (Philadelphia, 1891); W. Fletcher Johnson, *Life of Sitting Bull and History of the Indian War of 1890–'91* (Philadelphia, 1891); James Mooney, *The Ghost-Dance Religion and the Sioux Outbreak of 1890*, Bureau of American Ethnology Annual Report 14, pt. 2 (Washington, D.C., 1896); George E. Hyde, *A Sioux Chronicle* (Norman, 1956); Robert M. Utley, *The Last Days of the Sioux Nation* (New Haven, 1963).

4. Mooney, *Ghost-Dance Religion*, 833.

5. *Ibid.*, 787.

6. Robert H. Lowie, *Indians of the Plains* (New York, 1954), 181.

7. Omer C. Stewart, "The Ghost Dance," in W. Raymond Wood and Margot Liberty, eds., *Anthropology on the Great Plains* (Lincoln, 1980), 184.

8. Robert M. Utley, *Frontier Regulars: The United States Army and the Indian, 1866–1890* (New York, 1973), 402–403,

9. See Walker, *Lakota Belief and Ritual*, 68–73; Raymond J. DeMallie and Robert H. Lavenda, "Wakan: Plains Siouan Concepts of Power," in Richard Adams and Raymond D. Fogelson, eds., *The Anthropology of Power: Ethnographic Studies from Asia, Oceania and the New World* (New York, 1977), 154–165.

10. Calvin Martin, "Ethnohistory: A Better Way to Write Indian History," *Western Historical Quarterly*, IX (1978), 41–56.

11. For an introduction to the field, see Janet L. Dolgin, David S. Kemnitzer, and David M. Schneider, eds., *Symbolic Anthropology: A Reader in the Study of Symbols and Meanings* (New York, 1977) and Clifford Geertz, *The Interpretation of Cultures* (New York, 1973).

12. See, for example, DeMallie, "Touching the

Pen: Plains Indian Treaty Councils in Ethnohistorical Perspective," in Frederick C. Luebke, ed., *Ethnicity on the Great Plains* (Lincoln, 1980), 38–53.

13. Robert E. Berkhofer, Jr., *A Behavioral Approach to Historical Analysis* (New York, 1969), 73.

14. *Proceedings of a Board of Commissioners to Negotiate a Treaty or Treaties with the Hostile Indians of the Upper Missouri* (Washington, D.C., 1865), 104.

15. Indian Peace Commission, in *Annual Report of the Commissioner of Indian Affairs* (1866), 169.

16. *Proceedings of A Board of Commissioners*, 34.

17. Transcript of interviews of Black Elk by John G. Neihardt, 1931, pp. 3–4, Western History Manuscripts Collection, University of Missouri, Columbia.

18. Walker, *Lakota Belief and Ritual*, 124, 144.

19. Black Elk interview transcripts, 161.

20. Boyd, *Recent Indian Wars*, 198.

21. *Ibid.*, 180.

22. *Ibid.*, 181.

23. *Ibid.*, 289.

24. A good analysis is provided by Stephen D. Youngkin, "Sitting Bull and McLaughlin: Chieftainship Under Siege," (M.A. thesis, University of Wyoming), 1978.

25. Mooney, *Ghost-Dance Religion*, 798.

26. *Ibid.*, 847.

27. Boyd, *Recent Indian Wars*, 194–195.

28. Mooney, *Ghost-Dance Religion*, 789.

29. Walker, *Lakota Belief and Ritual*, 142.

30. Natalie Curtis, *The Indians' Book* (New York, 1935), 45.

31. *Ibid.*, 46–47.

32. Mooney, *Ghost-Dance Religion*, 917, 927.

33. *Ibid.*, 1060.

34. See Francis Paul Prucha, *American Indian Policy in Crisis: Christian Reformers and the Indian, 1865–1900* (Norman, 1976), 155–158.

35. *The Word Carrier*, XIX, no. 12 (Dec. 1890), 34.

36. *Ibid.*, XX, no. 1 (Jan. 1891), 1.

37. Stanley Vestal, *Sitting Bull: Champion of the Sioux* (new ed., Norman, 1957), 272.

38. *The Word Carrier*, XIX, no. 11 (Nov. 1890), 30.

39. Mooney, *Ghost-Dance Religion*, 823.

40. *Ibid.*, 788–789.

41. Ella C. Deloria, *Speaking of Indians* (New York, 1944), 83.

42. Black Elk interview transcripts, 182.

43. Deloria, *Speaking of Indians*, 83.

44. Valentine T. McGillycuddy, in *Annual Report of the Commissioner of Indian Affairs* (1884), 37.

45. Walker, *Lakota Belief and Ritual*, 179–180.

46. James R. Walker, *Lakota Society*, ed. by Raymond J. DeMallie (Lincoln, 1982), 151.

47. H. D. Gallagher, in *Annual Report of the Commissioner of Indian Affairs* (1888), 49.

48. Walker, *Lakota Belief and Ritual*, 141.

49. Charles G. Penney, in *Annual Report of the Commissioner of Indian Affairs* (1891), 410.

50. John P. Williamson, in *ibid.* (1892), 459.

51. Walker, *Lakota Belief and Ritual*, 198.

52. *Ibid.*, 202.

53. *Ibid.*, 206.

54. *Ibid.*, 140.

55. Utley *Last Days of the Sioux Nation*, 22.

56. *Ibid.*

57. *Ibid.*, 5.

58. John G. Neihardt, *The Song of the Messiah* (New York, 1935).

THE FEMINIST THEOLOGY OF THE BLACK BAPTIST CHURCH

Evelyn Brooks Higginbotham

In her study of the Women's Convention in the National Baptist Church, Evelyn Brooks Higginbotham goes well beyond previous understandings of both the African American church and women's religious experience by focusing on the roles of black women within what was the largest organization of African Americans at the turn of the century. While many historians have explored the African American church, most focus on the leadership of black men and overlook the contribution of the black women who made up most of the church's membership. In contrast, Higginbotham argues that the black Baptist church was not the creation of male ministers but rather "the product and process of male and female interaction." Similarly, while a growing number of scholars have explored the various ways in which men and women shaped and were shaped by the nineteenth-century religious world of the European-American middle class, their studies do not help us understand how women and men beyond the borders of the white, middle-class appropriated the ideology of separate spheres. Here Higginbotham shows how a rising gender consciousness lead black women to be "at once separate and allied with black men in the struggle for racial advancement while separate and allied with white women in the struggle for gender equality." Living within multiple racial and gender realities, Higginbotham's depiction of black Baptist women confounds simplistic renderings of separate men's and women's spheres.

Adapted by permission from Evelyn Brooks Higginbotham, "Feminist Theology, 1880–1900," in her *Righteous Discontent: The Women's Movement in the Black Baptist Church, 1880-1920* (Cambridge, MA: Harvard University Press, 1993), 120–149.

What if I am a woman; is not the God of ancient times the God of these modern days: Did he not raise up Deborah, to be a mother and a judge in Israel [Judges 4:4]? Did not queen Esther save the lives of the Jews? And Mary Magdalene first declare the resurrection of Christ from the dead?

—Maria Stewart, "Farewell Address," 21 September 1833

18

THE FEMINIST THEOLOGY OF THE BLACK BAPTIST CHURCH, 1880–1900

Evelyn Brooks Higginbotham

BOSTON BLACK MINISTER Peter Randolph cited gender proscriptions among the "strange customs" that he confronted when he returned to his Virginia birthplace soon after the Civil War to assume the pastorate of Richmond's Ebenezer Baptist Church. Randolph noted the segregated seating for men and women and the men's refusal to permit women at the business meetings of the church. Charles Octavius Boothe, a black Baptist minister in Alabama, recalled that in the early years of freedom women were not accustomed to the right to pray publicly.[1] Even as late as the 1880s in Tennessee and in Arkansas, black women met with virulent hostility in their efforts to establish separate societies.

During the last two decades of the nineteenth century black Baptist women increasingly challenged such examples of gender inequality. Working within the orthodoxy of the church, they turned to the Bible to argue for their rights—thus holding men accountable to the same text that authenticated their arguments for racial equality. In drawing upon the Bible—the most respected source within their community—they found scriptural precedents for expanding women's rights. Black women expressed their discontent with popular conceptions regarding "woman's place" in the church and society at large. They challenged the "silent helpmate" image of women's church work and set out to convince the men that women were equally obliged to advance not only their race and denomination, but themselves. Thus the black Baptist women developed a theology inclusive of equal gender participation. They articulated this viewpoint before groups of men and women in churches, convention anniversaries, and denominational schools, and in newspapers and other forms of literature.

The religious posture of black Baptist women was contextualized within a racial tradition that conflated private/eschatological witness and public/political stand. Saving souls and proselytizing the unconverted were integral to black women's missions, but their work was not limited to the private sphere of spiritual experience. The public discourse of church leaders and members, both male and female, had historically linked social regeneration, in the specific form of racial advancement, to spiritual regeneration. According to the ethicist Peter Paris, the principle of human freedom and equality under God constituted the "social teaching" of the black churches. This social teaching survived as a "nonracist appropriation of the Christian faith" and as a critique of American racism. The social teaching of human equality distinguished black churches from their white counterparts and represented a liberating principle "justifying and motivating all endeavors by blacks for survival and transformation."[2]

While the "nonracist" principle called attention to a common tradition shared by black churches, it masked the sexism that black churches shared with the dominant white society. Black women reinterpreted the church's social teaching so that human equality embraced gender as well. In the process, they came to assert their own voice through separate women's societies and through their recognition of an evangelical sisterhood that crossed racial lines. Within a female-centered context, they accentuated the image of woman as saving force, rather than woman as victim. They rejected a model of womanhood that was fragile and passive, just as they deplored a type preoccupied with fashion, gossip, or self-indulgence. They argued that women held the key to social transformation, and thus America offered them a vast mission field in which to solicit as never before the active participation of self-disciplined, self-sacrificing workers.[3] Through the convention movement, black Baptist women established a deliberative arena for addressing their own concerns. Indeed, one could say that the black Baptist church represented a sphere for public deliberation and debate precisely because of women.

ORTHODOXY'S GENDERED VISION

The feminist theology in the black Baptist church during the late nineteenth century conforms to Rosemary Ruether's and Eleanor McLaughlin's concept of a "stance of 'radical obedience.'" Referring to female leadership in Christianity, Ruether and McLaughlin distinguished women's positions of "loyal dissent" that arose within the mainline churches from women's positions of heresy that completely rejected the doctrines of the traditional denominations. They argued for the wider influence of women inside rather than outside the denominations, since women in the "stance of 'radical obedience'" seized orthodox theology in defense of sexual equality.[4]

If black Baptist women did not break from orthodoxy, they clearly restated it in progressive, indeed liberating language for women. In many respects their gendered vision of orthodoxy was analogous to the progressive racial theology already espoused by black ministers. In the Jim Crow America of the late nineteenth century, the Reverend Rufus Perry's *The Cushites, or the Descendants of Ham as Found in the Sacred Scriptures* (1893) dared to interpret the Bible as a source of ancient black history—as the root upon which race pride should grow.[5] Nor was a progressive, liberating theology new to blacks. For generations under slavery, African Americans rejected scriptural texts in defense of human bondage. Despite the reluctance of the slavemaster to quote the biblical passage "neither bond nor free in Christ Jesus," the slaves expressed its meaning in their spirituals and prayers. However, in the black Baptist church of the late nineteenth century, the women in the leadership called attention to the verse in its more complete form: "Neither bond nor free, neither male nor female in Christ Jesus."

By expounding biblical precedents, black women presented the intellectual and theological justification for their rights. But they expressed, too, a gendered interpretation of the Bible. The multivalent religious symbols within the Bible had obviously caused slavemasters and slaves, whites and blacks to invoke "orthodoxy" with meanings quite different from one another. It is perhaps less obvious that the Bible served dually to constrain and liberate women's position vis-a-vis men's in society. Caroline Bynum acknowledges gender differences in the way people appropriate and interpret religion in its symbolic and practical forms, inasmuch as people are gendered beings, not humans in the abstract. Bynum calls attention to the radical potential in this acknowledgment: "For if symbols can invert as well as reinforce social values…if traditional rituals can evolve to meet the needs of new participants…then old symbols can acquire new meanings, and these new meanings might suggest a new society."[6]

Even more important than the multivalent character of biblical symbolism are the very acts of reappropriation and reinterpretation of the Bible by black women themselves. As interpreters of the Bible, black women mediated its effect in relation to their own interests.

WOMEN'S THEOLOGIZING

Women members of the male-dominated American National Baptist Convention, forerunner of the National Baptist Convention, U.S.A., were the first to question the illusory unity of the convention as the voice of all its people. Within this national body, Virginia Broughton of Tennessee and Mary Cook and Lucy Wilmot Smith of Kentucky were the most vocal in defense of women's rights. Broughton, Cook, and Smith were active in organizing separate Baptist women's conventions in the face of varying levels of male support and hostility. They spoke for an expanding public of women who stood in opposition to exclusive male power and dominance.

All three women were born in the South during the last years of slavery, but Broughton's background was the most privileged. She described her father as an "industrious man" who hired out his time from his master and subsequently bought his wife's and his own freedom. Raised as a free black, Broughton enrolled in a private school taught by a Professor Daniel Watkins during her adolescent years. She graduated from Fisk University in 1875—claiming to be the first woman of any race to gain a collegiate degree from a southern school. She was married to John Broughton, a lawyer active in Republican Party politics in Memphis, although she continued to work as a teacher and full-time missionary throughout her married life. In 1885, Broughton's feminist attitude surfaced when she challenged the appointment of a less experienced, black male teacher over herself. Supported by her husband, she eventually won her case as head teacher in the Kortrecht school—the only black public school in Memphis to have one year of high school instruction.[7]

After working for twelve years as a teacher in the public school system and as a part-time missionary for at least five of those years, Broughton left the school system to become a full-time missionary. She was immensely popular among southern black and northern white Baptist women. Her stature as a national figure among black Baptists continued to rise in the upcoming century.[8] Broughton's gendered appropriation of biblical symbols shaped her understanding of the women of her own day; she traced the Baptist women's movement and its providential evolution to Eve in the Garden of Eden. In *Women's Work, as Gleaned from the Women of the Bible* (1904), Broughton summed up the ideas that had marked her public lectures, correspondence, and house-to-house visitations since the 1880s, and she sought to inspire the church women of her day "to assume their several callings."[9]

Mary Cook was born a slave in Kentucky in 1862. Raised in a very humble environment, she was able to acquire a college education partly through the philanthropy of white Baptist women in New England and partly through the support of the Reverend William J. Simmons, black Baptist minister and president of the State University at Louisville. Cook graduated from the Normal Department of the State University at Louisville in 1883 and subsequently taught Latin and literature at her alma mater.[10] Like Broughton, Cook worked closely with the black Baptist women of her state and enjoyed communication with northern white Baptist women. In 1898 she married the Reverend Charles H. Parrish, a leader among black Baptists in Kentucky. She was active in the national convention of black Baptist women, which was founded in 1900, and also in secular black women's clubs, especially the National Association of Colored Women.

Cook, the most scholarly of the three women, expressed her views in the black press, in an edited anthology, and in speeches before various groups, including the American National Baptist Convention. She served on the executive board of the ANBC and was honored by being selected to speak on women's behalf in the classic statement of black Baptist doctrine, *The Negro Baptist Pulpit* (1890). In often militant language, Cook strove to enlarge women's power in the church. She termed the Bible an "iconoclastic weapon" that would destroy negative images of her sex and overcome the popular misconceptions of woman's place in the church and society. Like Broughton, Cook derived her position from the "array of heroic and saintly women whose virtues have made the world more tolerable."[11]

Although it is not clear whether Lucy Wilmot Smith was born a slave, she is reported to have grown up in a very poor household. Born in 1861, Smith was raised by her mother, who as sole provider struggled to give her daughter an education. Smith graduated from the Normal Department of the State University at Louisville, taught at her alma mater, and also worked as a journalist. She never married. At the time of her premature death in 1890, she was principal of the Model School at the State University at Louisville. A leader in the Baptist Woman's Educational Convention of Kentucky, she sat on its Board of Managers and served as the secretary of its children's division. Like Cook, she was one of very few women to hold an office in the male-dominated American National Baptist Convention. She served as Historian of the ANBC, wrote extensively in the black press, and delivered strong feminist statements at the annual meetings of the ANBC.[12] She ardently supported woman's suffrage. Her death in 1890 prevented her from joining Broughton and Cook in the later movement to organize a national women's convention. Cook eulogized her: "She was connected with all the leading interests of her race and denomination. Her pen and voice always designated her position so clearly that no one need mistake her motive."[13]

None of the women was a theologian in any strict or formal sense, and yet their theocentric view of the world in which they lived justifies calling them theologians in the broad spirit that Gordon Kaufman describes:

> Obviously, Christians are involved in theologizing at every turn. Every attempt to discover and reflect upon the real meaning of the Gospel, of a passage in the Bible, of Jesus Christ, is theologizing; every effort to discover the bearing of the Christian faith or the Christian ethic on the problems of personal and social life is theological. For Christian theology is the critical analysis and creative development of the language utilized in apprehending, understanding, and interpreting God's acts, facilitating their communication in word and deed.[14]

As Kaufman implies, the act of theologizing was not limited to the formally trained male clergy. Nor did it extend only to college-educated women such as Broughton, Cook, and Smith. Scriptural interpretation figured significantly in the meetings of ordinary black women's local and state organizations. Virginia Broughton noted a tremendous groundswell of black women engaged in biblical explication in their homes, churches, and associational meetings.[15] In 1884 Lizzie Crittenden, chairman of the board of managers of the women's convention in Kentucky, identified the women's gendered interpretation of orthodoxy as revelation of their continued organizational growth: "It has really been marvelous how much has been found in the sacred word to encourage us that before had been left unsaid and seemed unheeded."[16] The reports of northern white missionaries in southern black communities confirmed these observations. Mary O'Keefe, a white missionary in Tennessee, wrote to her Chicago headquarters that black women in Bible Bands recited and interpreted passages of Scripture at their meetings. O'Keefe was fascinated by their black expressive culture. One elderly black woman, interpreting a scriptural text, became louder and louder in her delivery. "The last word came out with a whoop," O'Keefe recounted, "which was echoed and re-echoed by the others until it was quite evident that her view was accepted."[17] Mary Burdette, a leader of white Baptist women in the Midwest, also found black Baptist women engaged in biblical study during her tour of Tennessee. The women discussed ancient role models in justification of current demands for participatory parity within the denomination. Burdette described their round-table discussion: "Six sisters added to the interest by brief essays and addresses relating to women's place and work in the church as illustrated by the women of the Bible. Mrs. Broughton spoke of Eve, the mother of us all and the wife given to Adam for a help-meet, and following her we heard of Deborah, and that from her history we could learn that while men might be called to deliver Israel, they could not do it without the presence and assistance of Christian women."[18]

The enthusiasm with which black women of all educational backgrounds and ages claimed their right to theological interpretation was characterized by Virginia Broughton as part of the "general awakening and rallying together of Christian women" of all races. There were other black women who joined Broughton, Cook, and Smith in voicing gender concerns. Black women interpreters of the Bible perceived themselves as part of the vanguard of the movement to present the theological discussion of woman's place.[19] They used the Bible to sanction both domestic and public roles for women. While each of the feminist theologians had her own unique style and emphasis, a textual analysis of their writings reveals their common concern for women's empowerment in the home, the church, social reform, and the labor force. The Baptist women invoked biblical passages that portrayed positive images of women and reinforced their claim to the public realm. This realm, according to the literary critic Sue E. Houchins, provided black religious women like Broughton and others an arena in which they could transcend culturally proscribed gender roles and "could 'function as person[s] of authority,' could resist the pressures of family and society…and could achieve legal and structural support from the church for their work as spiritual advisors, teachers, and occasional preachers."[20]

THE GOSPEL ACCORDING TO WOMAN

The feminist theologians of the black Baptist church did not characterize woman as having a fragile, impressionable nature, but rather as having a capacity to influence man. They described woman's power of persuasion over the opposite sex as historically positive, for the most part, although they also mentioned a few instances of woman's negative influence, notably, the biblical stories of Delilah and Jezebel. But even this discussion emphasized man's vulnerability to woman's strength, albeit sometimes pernicious, and never recognized an innate feminine weakness to fall to temptation. Mary Cook asserted that woman "may send forth healthy, purifying streams which will enlighten the heart and nourish the seeds of virtue; or cast a dim shadow, which will enshroud those upon whom it falls in moral darkness."[21]

According to the feminist theologians, while the Bible depicted women in a dual image, it also portrayed good and evil men, and thus only affirmed woman's likeness to man and her oneness with him in the joint quest for salvation. Virginia Broughton insisted that the Genesis story explicitly denied any right of man to oppress woman. Her interpretation of woman's creation stressed God's not having formed Eve out of the "crude clay" from which he had molded Adam. She reminded her readers that God purposely sprang Eve from a bone, located in Adam's side and under his heart, for woman to be man's companion and helpmate, and she noted that God took the bone neither from Adam's head for woman to reign over him, nor from his foot for man to stand over her. Broughton observed that if woman had been Satan's tool in man's downfall, she was also God's instrument for human regeneration, since God entrusted the germ for human redemption to Eve alone. By commanding that "the seed of woman shall bruise the serpent's head," God had linked redemption inseparably with motherhood and woman's role in the physical deliverance of the Redeemer.[22]

Feminist theologians praised and took pride in the mothers of Isaac, Moses, Samson, and other greater or lesser heroes of the Old Testament. They described the women of the Old Testament as providing far more than the bodily receptacles through which great men were born into the world. They were responsible for rearing and molding the sons who would deliver Israel from its oppressors. The mother's determining hand could extend as far back as the child's prenatal stage—or so concluded Virginia Broughton in a reference to Samson's mother: "An angel appeared to Manoah's wife, told her she should have a son and instructed her how to deport herself after the conception, that Samson might be such a one as God would have him be, to deliver Israel from the oppression of the Philistines."[23]

Since motherhood was regarded as the greatest sanctity, Mary the mother of Jesus personified the highest expression of womanhood. Of all biblical mothers, she assumed the position of the "last and sublimest illustration in this relation."[24] Hers was motherhood in its purest, most emphatically female form, for it was virginal and thus without the intercession of a man. To the feminist theologians of the black Baptist church, Jesus, conceived from the union of woman and the Angel of God, became the fruition of God's commandment in Genesis. Mary Cook used her knowledge of ancient history and the Latin classics to add further insight concerning the virgin mother theme: she revealed its roots in antiquity by calling attention to the concept of virgin mother as a literary motif. Citing parallels with the story of the twins, Remus and Romulus, the mythical founders of Rome, Mary Cook posited, "Silvia became their mother by the God Mars, even as Christ was the son of the Holy Ghost."[25]

Although motherhood remained the salient image in their writings and speeches, Broughton, Cook, and Smith did not find their own personal lives consumed with maternal responsibilities. Lucy Wilmot Smith never had a husband or child, nor did Mary Cook during the period when she wrote her feminist theological texts. Broughton, on the other hand, was married with five children, and even lectured on the subject of "the ideal mother." Yet she spent little time in the actual role of mothering. She admitted taking her son periodically with her on missionary trips, but more often the care of the younger children fell to older siblings, other family members, and a number of "good women secured from time to time." In fact Broughton noted that all her children were taught domestic duties at an early age. The eldest daughter, Elizabeth, fixed suppers for the family and "was always solicitous about her mother's comfort."[26] Although she wrote lovingly of her children in her autobiography, Broughton undoubtedly valued her missionary work above every other responsibility. This is clearly revealed in the case of her daughter's illness. Broughton canceled a missionary engagement to join her sick daughter Selena, who died a few days after her mother's return home. She never again canceled a missionary engagement, for her daughter's death had taught her that "she could stay home and sit by the bedside of her children and have all the assistance that medical skill could render, and yet God could take her children to himself if he so willed it."[27] What may seem callous by today's standards was not viewed as such by Broughton's household. Broughton describes her last hours with her daughter as loving spiritual moments that influenced all of the family members to "think seriously of heavenly things." Her single-minded devotion to missions did not result in censure or condemnation by her community. Broughton commanded the respect of the women in her community and black Baptist women across the nation.

For feminist theologians such as Cook and Broughton, the image of woman as loyal, comforting spouse transcended the husband-wife relationship to embrace that of Jesus and woman. They were quick to point out that no woman betrayed Jesus and noted that a woman had bathed his feet with her tears and wiped them with her hair, while Mary and Martha had soothed him in their home after his long, tiring journey. Biblical women had expressed their faith through acts of succor and kindness much more than had men. Yet Cook and Broughton coupled woman's domestic image as comforter with the public responsibility of prophesying and spreading the gospel. Cook remarked that in Samaria, Jesus engaged in conversation with the woman at the well, "which was unlawful for a man of respect to do," and by so doing set a new standard for encouraging woman's intellect and permitting "her to do good for mankind and the advancement of His cause."[28]

Their emphasis on woman's relationship with Jesus ironically, albeit subtly, shifted women's duties outside the home, since woman's primary obligation was interpreted to be to God rather than husband. This was evident in Virginia Broughton's own marriage. Broughton resisted pressures of family and society by proclaiming her allegiance to God above family. She boldly alluded to her work as independent of her husband's wishes. Not yet converted when she began mission work, Broughton's husband demanded that she cease this endeavor, since it took her away from home and family for several days at a time. When he asked, "When is this business going to stop?" Broughton replied with what she termed a divinely inspired answer. "I don't know," she hurled at him, "I belong to God first, and you next; so you two must settle it." According to Broughton, her husband eventually came around to her way of thinking, "after a desperate struggle with the world, the flesh, and the devil." Broughton was able to convince her husband that she was called by God for missionary work and that "to hinder her would mean death to him."[29]

During the late nineteenth century feminist theology turned to the example of women leaders in the Old and New Testaments as sanction for more aggressive church work. Both Cook and Broughton reinterpreted biblical passages that had traditionally restricted woman's role—particularly Paul's dictum in the book of Corinthians that women remain silent in church. For Cook, an analysis of the historical context of Paul's statement revealed that his words were addressed specifically "to a few Grecian and Asiatic women who were wholly given up to idolatry and to the fashion of the day." Her exegesis denied the passage universal applicability. Its adoption in the late nineteenth century served as merely a rationalization to overlook and minimize the important contribution and growing force of woman's work in the church. Both Cook and Broughton argued that Paul praised the work of various women and, at times, depended upon them. The feminist theologians particularly enjoyed citing Paul's respect for Phoebe, the deaconess of the church at Cenchrea. Having entrusted Phoebe with an important letter to Rome, Paul demanded that everyone along her route lend assistance if needed. The Baptist women added the names of others who aided Paul, for example, Priscilla, Mary, Lydia, and "quite a number of women who had been co-workers with the apostle."[30]

The black feminist theologians also found biblical precedent for leadership outside the church in charitable philanthropic work. Olive Bird Clanton, wife of the Reverend Solomon T. Clanton of New Orleans, addressed the American National Baptist Convention in 1887 and maintained that Christian doctrine "has placed the wife by the side of her husband, the daughter by the side of her father, the sister by the side of her brother at the table of the Lord, in the congregation of the sanctuary, male and female met together at the cross and will meet in the realms of glory." Unlike Broughton and Cook, Olive Clanton's northern upbringing made her sensitive to the plight of foreign immigrants and to the squalid conditions in urban tenements. She had little faith in ameliorative legislation if unaccompanied by the activity of women in social reform, especially female education, the care of children, and the cause of social purity. Clanton advocated an aggressive, outgoing Christianity to reach the oppressed and needy class of women and children who did not go to church and thus remained outside the purview of the minister. These types could be helped by women, whose kindness and compassion uniquely qualified them for uplift work. In Clanton's opinion, "the wearied wife, and anxious mother, the lonely woman, often feeling that she is forgotten by the world and neglected by the church will open her heart and life to the gentle Christian woman that has taken the trouble to visit her." She encouraged women to organize social purity socities, sewing schools, and other types of unions in order to uplift the down-trodden.[31] The tireless work of Dorcas, who sewed garments for the needy, became a standard biblical reference for women's charitable work.

Proponents of a feminist theology endeavored to broaden employment opportunities for women. Lucy Wilmot Smith, Historian of the American National Baptist Convention, put the issue squarely before her predominantly male audience in 1886 when she decried the difference in training between boys and girls. She noted that the nineteenth-century woman was dependent as never before upon her own resources for economic survival. Smith believed that girls, like boys, must be taught to value the dignity of labor. She rejected views that considered work for women disdainful, or temporarily necessary at best—views that conceded to women only the ultimate goal of dependency on men. "It is," she wrote, "one of the evils of the day that from babyhood girls are taught to look forward to the time when they will be supported by a father, a brother, or somebody else's brother." She encouraged black women to enter fields other than domestic service and suggested that enterprising women try their hand at poultry raising, small fruit gardening, dairying, bee culture, lecturing, newspaper work, photography, and nursing.[32]

Mary Cook suggested that women seek out employment as editors of newspapers or as news correspondents in order to promote women's causes and to reach other mothers, daughters, and sisters. She advocated teaching youths through the development of juvenile literature and urged women in the denomination's schools to move beyond subordinate jobs by training and applying for positions as teachers and administrators. Cook praised women with careers as writers, linguists, and physicians, and she told the gathering of the American National Baptist Convention in 1887 that women must "come from all the professions, from the humble Christian to the expounder of His word; from the obedient citizen to the ruler of the land."[33]

Again, the Baptist women found biblical precedents to bolster their convictions and to inspire the women of their own day. Cook and Broughton pointed to the biblical woman Huldah, wife of Shallum. Huldah studied the law and interpreted the Word of God to priests and others who sought her knowledge. In the Book of Judges another married woman, Deborah, became a judge, prophet, and warrior whom God appointed to lead Israel against its enemies. Depicting Deborah as a woman with a spirit independent of her husband, Cook asserted: "Her work was distinct from her husband who, it seems, took no part whatever in the work of God while Deborah was inspired by the Eternal expressly to do His will and to testify to her countrymen that He recognizes in His followers neither male nor female, heeding neither the 'weakness' of one, nor the strength of the other, but strictly calling those who are perfect at heart and willing to do his bidding."[34]

Biblical examples had revealed that God used women in every capacity and thus proved that there could be no issue of propriety, despite the reluctance of men. Mary Cook urged the spread of women's influence in every cause, place, and institution that respected Christian values, and she admonished her audience that no profession should be recognized by either men or women if it lacked such values. She concluded her argument with an assertion of women's "legal right" to all honest labor, as she challenged her sisters in the following verse:

> Go, and toil in any vineyard
> Do not fear to do and dare;
> If you want a field of labor
> You can find it anywhere.[35]

AN AGE OF LIBERAL THEOLOGY

The feminist theology of the black Baptist church reflected several intellectual trends of the late nineteenth century. Like other Americans, the Baptist thinkers accepted a priori the notion of certain intrinsic differences between the male and female identity. The dominant thought of the age embraced an essentialist understanding of gender; it ascribed to womanhood a feminine essence that was virtuous, patient, gentle, and compassionate, while it described manhood as rational, aggressive, forceful, and just. Unlike man, woman was considered naturally religious, bound by greater emotionalism, and with a greater capacity to sympathize and forgive. Since the manifestation of the feminine essence became most readily apparent in the act of raising children in the home, feminine virtues were easily equated with maternal qualities.[36] It appeared axiomatic that God and nature had ordained woman's station in life by providing her with a job and workplace incontestably her own.

At the same time, the Baptist feminist theologians were influenced by the secular woman's movement, which rejected the bifurcation of the private sphere of home and family from the public sphere of business and politics. The goals of organizations such as the National American Woman Suffrage Association and other secular clubs gained momentum during the latter decades of the century among white and black women. These organizations sought to steer women's entrance into the public domain by such routes as voting rights and equal educational and employment opportunities. Yet even though their agenda questioned gender-prescribed roles, most adherents of nineteenth-century feminism remained bridled in a gender-specific, "domesticating" politics.[37] They continued to adhere to essentialist conceptions of gender—defining woman's "nature" as separate and distinct from man's. They translated the preeminence of the maternal responsibility for molding the future character of youth into woman's superior ability to shape the destiny of society. Frances Willard, the suffragist and temperance leader, asserted her belief in "social housekeeping" when she maintained that woman carried her "mother-heart" into the public realm and lost none of her femininity in the process. On the contrary, woman's "gentle touch" refined and softened political institutions, professions, indeed every arena it entered.[38]

Even more directly, the writings and speeches of black Baptists formed part of a feminist-theological literary tradition that spanned the entire nineteenth century. Feminist theological literature especially proliferated in the century's latter decades—the years that the historian Sydney Ahlstrom termed the "golden age of liberal theology." Liberal theology emerged in response to Darwinist biological theories of evolution, Social Darwinism, and a host of geological discoveries and historical studies that challenged what had previously appeared to be the timeless infallibility of the Bible. A radical tendency to deny any sacred authority to the Scriptures found advocates among "infidels" such as Robert Ingersoll and the suffragist Elizabeth Cady Stanton. At the other end of the spectrum stood the fundamentalists, many of whom were southern Protestants, holding tenaciously to the literal truth of each biblical statement despite disclosures of particular inaccuracies and contradictions.[39]

Between these extremes were liberals who came from the pulpits and seminaries of northern Protestant denominations—in fact, some of the same groups responsible for establishing institutions of higher learning for black people in the South. The great majority of these liberals attempted to reconcile their traditional religious beliefs with the new social and scientific theories. By articulating a resilient and vibrant orthodoxy, evangelical liberalism, led by such ministers as Henry Ward Beecher, Newman Smyth, William Newton Clarke, and Washington Gladden, effected the survival of traditional Protestantism in an age of questioning and positivistic devotion to accuracy. Discussing the largely "conservative intent" of this liberalizing influence, Winthrop Hudson argued that the primary interest of the evangelical liberals was not to destroy Christian doctrines, but to restate them "in terms that would be intelligible and convincing and thus to establish them on a more secure foundation."[40]

This exact intent may be attributed to the writings of feminist theologians. Frances Willard, also a contributor to feminist theology, reconciled gender equality with the vital spirit of the Bible. She noted that the insistence on "real facts" had changed not only views toward science and medicine but also those toward theology, causing theology to become more flexible and to see the Bible as an expansive work that "grows in breadth and accuracy with the general growth of humanity." Willard advocated the "scientific interpretation of the Holy Scriptures" and urged women to lend a gendered perspective to the modern exegesis of the Bible.[41]

Feminist theologians who emerged in the mainline denominations argued for women's rights from the standpoint of liberal orthodoxy. They stood in dramatic opposition to

Elizabeth Cady Stanton's elaborate condemnation of the Bible in *The Woman's Bible* (1895). Stanton rejected orthodoxy, liberal or conservative. A compilation of interpretive essays from many contributors, *The Woman's Bible* critically questioned the Bible as the divinely inspired authority on women's position in society. Although some of the essays called attention to heroines and positive female images, *The Woman's Bible* pointed overwhelmingly to biblical images that were negative. The Bible, according to Stanton, had served historically as a patriarchal instrument for women's oppression. She condemned it for inspiring women only with the goals of obedience to husbands, subordination to men in general, and self-sacrifice at the expense of their own self-development. *The Woman's Bible* challenged women to reject Christian teachings as set forth in the Bible and to assert full equality with men.[42]

Feminist theology within the mainstream Protestant churches differed significantly from that of Stanton. Its goal was to make religion less sexist, not to make women any less religious. While feminist theology did not make converts of all who professed Protestant liberalism, it represented a significant movement within liberal evangelicalism's effort to relate theology to social issues. During the age of liberal theology, religious education and critical theological scholarship grew with unprecedented dynamism. Referring to the term "Christology" as a coinage of his day, Augustus Strong noted in 1884 that the study of Christ had become a science in its own right.[43] As biblical scholars investigated and debated the human and divine nature of Jesus, some of them also drew attention to his masculine and feminine qualities. In doing so they drew upon Protestant discourses that had their origin early in the nineteenth century and indeed can be traced to the eighteenth century's rooting of morality in the sentiments. The historians Ann Douglas and Barbara Welter, for example, have disclosed a wealth of early nineteenth-century religious and literary materials that identified the church and Christ himself with feminine attributes—representing Christ, that is, as soft, gentle, emotional, and passive.[44] The feminization of Christianity, needless to say, did not go unchallenged either before or after the Civil War. In fact, the debate concerning the association of the church and Savior with feminine virtues lost none of its vibrancy after 1875, as feminist theologians and women generally used a feminine image of Christ to justify their struggle for social justice in general and for women's rights in particular.

Opponents of the feminine version of religion often conceded the feminine attributes in Christ but reaffirmed the predominance of the masculine. Gail Bederman argues that movements such as the Men and Religion Forward Movement and other advocates of a "mascular Christianity" adopted cultural constructions of gender in order to reconcile religion to the modern "corporate, consumer-oriented order" of the twentieth century.[45] The masculinist perspective countered efforts to subsume Christ's manliness in the glorification of the feminine by contending that his feminine virtues, namely, tenderness, sympathy, and forgiveness, were subordinate to his masculine attributes of assertive leadership, strong intellect, and business acumen. Defenders of the masculine orientation evoked the image of the "church militant" in the religious conquest of the world, and they offered a "tough Christianity" with stern, uncompromising features as a counterpoint to the softness and emotionalism of a feminized church.[46]

DOUBLE GENDER CONSCIOUSNESS

Black Baptist men and women did not debate Christ's feminine versus masculine nature, but the duality captured the complexity of images surrounding their own racial and gender identities. A dialogic imagery of Christ as simultaneously feminine and masculine, passive and aggressive, meek and conquering informed African Americans' self-perceptions and self-motivations. This was true for them as individuals and as a group. Black Baptist women continually shifted back and forth from feminine to masculine metaphors as they positioned themselves simultaneously within racial and gendered social space. Whether united with black men, or working separately in their own conventions or cooperatively with white Baptist women, black Baptist women expressed a dual gender consciousness—defining themselves as both homemakers and soldiers. Their multiple consciousness represented a shifting dialogic exchange in which both race and gender were ultimately destabilized and blurred in meaning.

On the one hand, black Baptist women spoke in unambiguous gendered symbols. Virginia Broughton called attention to the feminine symbolism in the Bible (for example, the designation of the church as the "bride" of Christ), and she regarded such metaphors as conveying biblical esteem for women.[47] The black feminist theologians also contextualized women's gains in society within an evolutionary framework that repeatedly referred to the degraded status of women in ancient civilizations and in contemporary non-Christian cultures, and they argued that the standard of womanhood evolved to a higher plane with the spread of Christianity. This view undergirded their emphasis on motherhood and domesticity. Since mothers were considered to be the transmitters of culture, woman's virtue and intelligence within the home measured the progress of African Americans and all of civilization.[48]

Black Baptist women shared common bonds with white Baptist women who worked in similar societies. They were familiar with the history of white Baptist women's societies and praised their work for the freedpeople at the end of the Civil War. The white Baptist missionary Joanna P. Moore played an influential role in the lives of a number of southern black women. Moore cited biblical precedents for women as teachers and church leaders, although her conviction that women should engage in teaching, house-to-house visitation, and temperance work never minimized for her the singular importance of woman's domestic role. Her views coincided with the views of the black feminist theologians whose image of women's religious duties posited them within the traditional home setting, at the same time as they beckoned women into the world to spread the faith.[49]

The feminist theologians of the black Baptist church considered the combined efforts of black and white women critical to the progress of black people and to harmonious race relations. By Christianizing the home and educating the masses, women provided the key to solving the race problem in America. Black women likened their role to that of the biblical queen Esther, who had acted as an intermediary between the king and her people. They envisioned themselves as intermediaries between white America and their own people. Expressing the biblical analogy, Mrs. H. Davis compared Ida B. Wells to queen Esther and praised her crusade against lynching on the front page of the *National Baptist World:* "We have found in our race a queen Esther, a woman of high talent, that has sounded the bugle for a defenceless race."[50]

Women such as Virginia Broughton, Mary Cook, and Lucy Wilmot Smith epitomized the high quality of woman's rational powers. Widely read, this educated female elite implicitly and explicitly challenged the conviction that assigned intellect to men and emotionalism to women. Mary Cook explained the cultivation of the female intellect as Christ's special mission to women and blamed sexism, not Christianity, for hindering women's intellectual development. "Emancipate woman," she demanded, "from the chains that now restrain her and who can estimate the part she will play in the work of the denomination."[51]

Yet the feminist sentiments articulated by these black Baptist theologians were neither uniform nor rigid. At times Virginia Broughton appeared to soften her demands for women's presence within the highest denominational councils and to adopt a more conciliatory attitude toward men. She urged, if sometimes with tongue in cheek, complementary work with a deeper sensitivity to what she called man's "long cherished position of being ruler of all he surveys." She referred to the "womanly exercise" of talent, and at a time when woman's role was emergent but not clearly defined, she tended to assure men that women would not seek unauthorized office.[52]

Lucy Wilmot Smith spoke less circumspectly. In strong feminist language, she insisted upon new expectations of women. Smith revealed her outspoken belief in the need for women to adopt attitudes identified as male in outlook: "Even in our own America, in this last quarter of the Nineteenth Century ablaze with the electric light of intelligence, if she [woman] leaves the paths made straight and level by centuries of steady tramp of her sex, she is denominated strong-minded or masculine by those who forget that 'new occasions make new duties.'"[53]

However, Lucy Smith could subordinate easily, almost imperceptibly, her feminist consciousness to that of race. On one such occasion she stated that educated black women held certain advantages over white women. She believed that the identical labor reality for male and female slaves created a solidarity not found in the white race, and she praised the black man of her day for continuing to keep his woman by his side as he moved into new types of work. Smith noted that the white woman "has had to contest with her brother every inch of the ground for recognition."[54] Mary Cook spoke of the freedom women exercised within the Baptist denomination and told the men of the American National Baptist Convention: "I am not unmindful of the kindness you noble brethren have exhibited in not barring us from your platforms and deliberations. All honor I say to such men."[55] Thus racial consciousness equally informed their identity and their understanding of gender.

Racial consciousness placed black women squarely beside black men in a movement for racial self-determination, specifically in the quest for national black Baptist hegemony. From the perspective of racial self-help, this movement so blurred values and behavior exclusively associated with either the masculine or the feminine identity that it implicitly undermined the validity of gender dichotomies. Despite nineteenth-century essentialist assumptions about woman's moral superiority, the black Baptist women's preoccupation with "respectability," as the cornerstone for racial uplift, never tolerated a double standard of behavior on the part of men and women.[56] In the same vein, concepts such as self-sacrifice and patience lost their traditionally feminine connotations and became sources of strength endorsed by men, not only women. Black ministers championed self-denial as a prerequisite for race development, while they hailed patience as the self-control necessary to build a strong black denominational force.

For nineteenth-century African Americans, distinctions between the feminine and masculine identity were complicated by a racial system that superimposed "male" characteristics upon all whites (male and female) and "feminine characteristics" upon all blacks (male and female). Theories of racial essence, what George Fredrickson termed "romantic racialism," paralleled and overlapped essentialist gender assumptions. During the nineteenth century and into the twentieth, both blacks and whites subscribed to theories of innate characteristics and behaviorism that captured the soul of each race. Within the human family, so romantic racialists theorized, black people embodied an essence that was musical, emotional, meek, and religious. In contrast, the white race was perceived to be intellectual, pragmatic, competitive, and with a disposition to dominate. The counterposing of the two races paralleled the feminine-masculine dichotomy. During the Civil War, the white abolitionist Theodore Tilton described blacks as the "feminine race of the world." In the early twentieth century, Robert Park, the white sociologist, similarly described the Negro as an "artist, loving life for its own sake…. He is, so to speak, the lady of the races."[57]

Although blacks usually rejected the explicit analogy between their "soul qualities" and the feminine essence, they invariably re-presented and re-constructed a group identity with qualities reminiscent of those ascribed to women. Harvard-trained W. E. B. Du Bois championed theories of racial distinctiveness. In his article "The Conservation of Races," published in 1897, Du Bois disclosed his recognition and admiration for what he believed to be the "spiritual, psychical" uniqueness of his people—their "special gift" to humanity.[58] In *The Gift of Black Folk* (1924) he opined that the meekness and "sweet spirit" of black people "has breathed the soul of humility and forgiveness into the formalism and cant of American religion."[59] For blacks, the idealization of race served to negate notions of white superiority and, in turn, the legitimacy of white male power and racist institutions. Like the feminine ideal, the racial ideal valorized a more equitable, inclusive society.[60]

Perceiving themselves to be joined in a struggle for the economic, educational, and moral advancement of their people, black Baptist men as well as women employed masculine symbols when characterizing black women's efforts to combat the legacy of slavery and the continued rise of racism at the turn of the twentieth century. By so doing, black women and men once again confounded interpretations of race and gender essentialism that had their origins in white discourses. The black women in the Baptist church fused the rhetoric of war with that of domesticity. They represented themselves as the "home force" while at the same time exhorting one another to assume the role of valiant "soldier"—to go out into the "highways and hedges" and forge the "link between the church militant and the church triumphant."[61] Virginia Broughton looked to both the Bible and history for validation: "But what about man going alone to war? We answer by asking who was it that drove the nail into Sisera's temple? And what of the heroism of Joan of Arc? War is one of man's inventions; it is not good in itself, neither is it good for man to go to war alone, most especially in the Lord's work."[62]

This aggressive attitude, commonly identified with male subjectivity, underlay the black women's determination to insert their voices boldly into the deliberative arena of the convention movement. The Old Testament figures Deborah and Huldah became the recurrent reference points illustrating woman's capacity to combine humility and grace with aggressive zeal and strong intellect. The examples of Deborah and Huldah were also cited by the black Baptist women to prove that marriage need not negate public leadership for women.

The feminist theology of the black Baptist church never altered the hierarchical structure of the church by revolutionizing power relations between the sexes, nor did it inhibit ministers from assuming men's intellectual and physical superiority over women.[63] To the ire of black women, the black newspaper *Virginia Baptist* in 1894 presented a two-part series that adopted biblical arguments for restricting women's church work to singing and praying. The newspaper claimed divine authority in denying women the right to teach, preach, and vote.[64] Although the black feminist theologians opposed this line of thought, they did not challenge the basis for male monopoly of the clergy, nor did they demand equal representation in conventions in which both men and women participated. But feminist theology stirred women to find their own voice and create their own sphere of influence.

Feminist theology had significant implications for black Baptist women's future work. It buttressed their demand for more vocal participation and infused their growing ranks with optimism about the dawning twentieth century. It also encouraged women to establish and control their own separate conventions at the state and national levels. Black Baptist women did not, in the end, demand a radical break with all the sexist limitations of their church, but they were surely ingenious in fashioning the Bible as an "iconoclastic weapon" for their particular cause. The feminist theologians had operated "from a stance of 'radical obedience.'" And indeed it was this vantage of orthodoxy that compelled the brethren to listen.

NOTES

1. Peter Randolph, *From Slave Cabin to the Pulpit: The Autobiography of Rev. Peter Randolph* (Boston: James H. Earle, Publisher, 1893), p. 89. Charles O. Boothe, *The Cyclopedia of the Colored Baptists of Alabama* (Birmingham: Alabama Publishing Company, 1895), 252; also see Jacqueline Jones, *Labor of Love, Labor of Sorrow: Black Women, Work, and the Family from Slavery to the Present* (New York: Random House, 1985), 67.

2. Peter J. Paris, *The Social Teaching of the Black Churches* (Philadelphia: Fortress Press: 1985), 11–13.

3. Mary V. Cook, "Work for Baptist Women," in Edward M. Brawlet, ed., *The Negro Baptist Pulpit* (Philadelphia: The American Baptist Publication Society, 1890), 271–285; American National Baptist Convention (hereafter ANBC), *Journal and Lectures of the Second Anniversary of the 1887 American National Baptist Convention, Held with the Third Baptist Church, Mobile, Ala., August 25–28, 1887* (n.p., n.d.), 57.

4. Rosemary Ruether and Eleanor McLaughlin, eds., *Women of Spirit: Female Leadership in the Jewish and Christian Traditions* (New York: Simon and Schuster, 1979), 19; also see this argument applied to white women during the Second Great Awakening in Carroll Smith-Rosenberg, "The Cross and the Pedestal: Women, Anti-Ritualism, and the Emergence of the American Bourgeoisie," in Smith-Rosenberg, *Disorderly Conduct: Visions of Gender in Victorian America* (New York: Oxford University Press, 1986), 129–164.

5. Rufus Perry traced the ancestry of black Americans to the biblical Cushites, who were the descendants of Cush, Ham's eldest son. According to Perry, the Cushites were the ancient Ethiopians and indigenous Egyptians whose history exemplified prowess in medicine, war, art, and religious thought. Identifying the Cushite leaders of the Bible, Perry considered the greatness of the African past to be the foundation stone of the African American's future. See Rufus L. Perry, *The Cushites, or the Descendants of Ham as Found in the Sacred Scriptures and in the Writings of Ancient Historians and Poets from Noah to the Christian Era* (Springfield, Mass.: Willey, 1893), 17–18, 158–161.

6. Caroline Walker Bynum, Steven Harrell, and Paula Richman, eds., *Gender and Religion: On the Complexity of Symbols* (Boston: Beacon Press, 1986), 15–16.

7. See Kathleen Berkeley's discussion of the Broughton case. Berkeley argues that the case was more than simply one of gender discrimination, but a power struggle between the white superintendent of schools and a black member of the school board. Kathleen C. Berkeley, "The Politics of Black Education in Memphis, Tennessee, 1868–1891," in Rick Ginsberg and David N. Plank, eds., *Southern Cities, Southern Schools: Public Education in the Urban South* (Westport, Conn.: Greenwood Press, 1990), 215–217.

8. Broughton was elected to office in the Woman's Convention, Auxiliary of the National Baptist Convention, U.S.A., when it was organized in 1990. She held the office of recording secretary in this organization, which represented more than one million black women across the United States. See National Baptist Convention, *Journal of the Twentieth Annual Session of the National Baptist Convention, Held in Richmond, Virginia, September 12–17, 1900* (Nashville: National Baptist Publishing Board, 1900), 195–196. See also Thomas O. Fuller, *History of the Negro Baptists of Tennessee* (Memphis: Haskins

Print-Roger Williams College, 1936), 238.

9. Virginia Broughton, *Women's Work, as Gleaned from the Women of the Bible, and Bible Women of Modern Times* (Nashville: National Baptist Publishing Board, 1904), 3, 23, 36.

10. I. Garland Penn, *The Afro-American Press and Its Editors* (Springfield, Mass.: Willey, 1891), 367–374; G. R. Richings, *Evidences of Progress among Colored People*, 12th ed. (Philadelphia: Geo. S. Ferguson, 1905), 224–227; Charles H. Parrish, ed., *Golden Jubilee of the General Association of Colored Baptists in Kentucky* (Louisville: Mayes Printing Company, 1915), 284–285; State University Catalogue, 1883–1884, Simmons University Records, Archives Department, University of Louisville.

11. Brawley, ed., *The Negro Baptist Pulpit*, 271–286; ANBC, *Journal and Lectures, 1887*, 49.

12. Penn, *The Afro-American Press*, 376–381.

13. See Mary Cook's eulogy of Lucy Wilmot Smith in *Home Mission Echo* (January 1890): 4–5; Penn, *Afro-American Press*, 378–381; Woman's American Baptist Home Mission Society (hereafter WABHMS), *Twelfth Annual Report of the Woman's American Baptist Home Mission Society with the Report of the Annual Meeting, Held in the First Baptist Church, Hartford, Connecticut, May 7–8, 1890* (Boston: C. H. Simonds, 1890), 26.

14. Gordon D. Kaufman, *Systematic Theology: An Historicist Perspective* (New York: Charles Scribner's Sons, 1968), 57.

15. Virginia W. Broughton, *Twenty Years' Experience of a Missionary* (Chicago: The Pony Press Publishers, 1907), 32.

16. *Minutes of the Baptist Women's Educational Convention of Kentucky. First, Second, Third, Fourth, Fifth Sessions, 1883–1887* (Louisville: National Publishing Company, Print, 1887), 13.

17. Miss M. O'Keefe to Mary Burdette, 4 April 1891, Mary Burdette File, Correspondence 1891–1898, WABHMS Archives, American Baptist Archives Center, Valley Forge, Pa.

18. See report of Mary Burdette, "Our Southern Field," *Tidings* (January 1894): 9.

19. Mary Cook stated: "As the Bible is an iconoclastic weapon—it is bound to break down images of error that have been raised. As no one studies it so closely as the Baptists, their women shall take the lead." ANBC, *Journal and Lectures, 1887*, 49.

20. See introduction by Sue E. Houchins, *Spiritual Narratives* (New York: Oxford University Press, 1988), xxxii. *Spiritual Narratives* includes Virginia Broughton's autobiography, *Twenty Years' Experience of a Missionary*, along with those of Maria Stewart, Jarena Lee, Julia A. J. Foote, and Ann Plato.

21. ANBC, *Journal and Lectures, 1887*, 53–54; also see the evaluation of woman's influence by black Baptist minister William Bishop Johnson, editor of *The National Baptist Magazine*, when he stated: "Man may lead unnumbered hosts to victory, he may rend kingdoms, convulse nations, and drench battlefields in blood, but woman with heavenly smiles and pleasant words can outnumber, outweight, and outstrip the noblest efforts of a generation." William Bishop Johnson, *The Scourging of a Race, and Other Sermons and Addresses* (Washington, D.C.: Beresford Printer, 1904), 78.

22. Broughton, *Women's Work*, 5–7.

23. Ibid., 11–16.

24. Ibid., 25.

25. Mary Cook described Mary, the mother of Jesus, as "non-excelled maternal devotion." See ANBC, *Journal and Lectures, 1887*, 47–48.

26. Broughton, *Twenty Years' Experience*, 48–51.

27. Ibid., 42–45, 48.

28. Broughton, *Women's Work*, 31–32; Brawley, ed., *Negro Baptist Pulpit*, 273.

29. Broughton, *Twenty Years' Experience*, 46–47. Sue Houchins argues that Broughton and women like her drew confidence to transcend prescriptive gender roles from belief in the "privileged nature of their relationship with God." See introduction by Houchins, *Spiritual Narratives*, xxxiii.

30. The argument that attempted to restrict Paul's words exclusively to "immoral" women of Corinth was used by both black and white advocates of greater church roles for women. See, for example, Frances Willard, *Women in the Pulpit* (Boston: D. Lothrop, 1888), 159, 164; ANBC, *Journal and Lectures, 1887*, 48–50.

31. Olive Bird Clanton was raised in Decatur, Illinois, where she obtained a high school education. Her husband was elected secretary of the American National Baptist Convention in 1886. In a biographical sketch of Solomon Clanton, William J. Simmons, then president of the American National Baptist Convention, described Olive Clanton as "one of the most discreet, amiable, and accomplished women in the country." See William J. Simmons, *Men of Mark: Eminent, Progressive and Rising* (Cleveland: Geo. M. Rewell, 1887), 419–421; ANBC, *Journal and Lectures, 1887*, 56–57.

32. ANBC, *Minutes and Addresses of the American National Baptist Convention, Held at St. Louis, Mo., August 25–29, 1886 in the First Baptist Church* (Jackson, Miss.: J. J. Spelman, Publisher, 1886), 68–74.

33. ANBC, *Journal and Lectures, 1887*, 50–53, 55–56.

34. Ibid., 47; Broughton, *Women's Work,* 27–28.

35. ANBC, *Journal and Lectures, 1887,* 55–56.

36. For discussions on the cult of motherhood and domesticity, as well as treatment of woman's unique qualities relative to man's, see the following: Ann Douglas, *The Feminization of American Culture* (New York: Alfred A. Knopf, 1977), 87–89; Barbara Welter, "The Cult of True Womanhood, 1820–1860," *American Quarterly,* 18 (Spring 1966): 151–174; Katherine Kish Sklar, *Catherine Beecher: A Study in American Domesticity* (New York: W. W. Norton, 1976), 134–137; Anne Firor Scott, *The Southern Lady: From Pedestal to Politics, 1830* (Chicago: University of Chicago Press, 1970), 37; also see this discussion as part of the evolving themes in women's history in Linda K. Kerber, "Separate Spheres, Female Worlds, Woman's Place: The Rhetoric of Women's History," *Journal of American History,* 75 (June 1988): 9–39.

37. See Paula Baker, "The Domestication of Politics: Women and Political Society, 1780–1920," *American Historical Review,* 89 (June 1984): 620–647; Michael McGerr, "Political Style and Women's Power, 1830–1930," *Journal of American History,* 77 (December 1990): 864–885.

38. Willard, *Women in the Pulpit,* 54, 64; Douglas, *Feminization of American Culture,* 51–52.

39. Sydney E. Ahlstrom, *A Religious History of the American People* (New Haven: Yale University Press, 1972), 763–787; Arthur Meier Schlesinger, "A Critical Period in American Protestantism, 1875–1900," *Massachusetts Historical Society Proceedings,* 64 (1930–1932): 523–548; Richard Hofstadter, *Social Darwinism in American Thought, 1860–1915* (Philadelphia: University of Pennsylvania Press, 1944), 1–16, 88; Barbara Welter, "Something Remains to Dare," introduction to Elizabeth Cady Stanton et al., *The Woman's Bible* (1895; rpt. New York: Arno Press, 1974), v–xi.

40. The label "progressive orthodoxy," coined by the faculty of Andover Seminary in 1884, characterized the majority of evangelical liberals who sought to retain Christian doctrine as much as possible while allowing for adjustment when necessary. See Winthrop S. Hudson, *Religion in America: An Historical Account of the Development of American Religious Life,* 2nd ed. (New York: Charles Scribner's Sons, 1973), 269–274.; Martin E. Marty, *Modern American Religion,* vol. 1 (Chicago: University of Chicago Press, 1986), 17–43.

41. Mary Cook also encouraged the belief in a living, rather than static doctrine and argued that women's freedom would grow with the "vitalizing principles" of the Baptist denomination. Frances

Willard's position was more extreme than Cook's, however. In order to discourage literalism, Willard presented a two-page chart that graphically revealed changing, ambivalent, and contradictory biblical references to women. Willard also rejected literalism's opposite tendency, or what she termed "playing fast and loose." ANBC, *Journal and Lectures, 1887,* 49; Willard, *Woman in the Pulpit,* 17–38, 50.

42. See Matilda Jocelyn Gage, *Woman, Church, and State,* 2nd ed. (New York: The Truth Seeker Company, 1893); and Welter, "Something Remains to Dare," *Woman's Bible,* xxv–xxxiv; Aileen S. Kraditor, ed., *Up From the Pedestal: Selected Writings in the History of American Feminism* (Chicago: Quadrangle Books, 1968), 108–121.

43. Augustus H. Strong, *Philosophy and Religion* (New York: A. C. Armstrong and Son, 1888), 201.

44. Douglas, *Feminization of American Culture,* 9–13; Barbara Welter, "The Feminization of American Religion: 1800–1860," in Mary Hartman and Lois Banner, eds., *Clio's Consciousness Raised: New Perspectives in the History of Women* (New York: Harper and Row, 1974), 137–157.

45. Bederman notes that church membership remained more than 60 percent female for nearly two centuries and that the perceived crisis of a "feminized church" reflected in actuality the "gendered coding of contemporary languages of religion and of power." In short, feminized Protestantism was deemed acceptable to men during the era of laissez faire capitalism. It went hand in hand with the old middle-class virtues of hard work, thrift, and self-sacrifice. While these values served "an individualistic, producer-oriented middle class," they were rendered anachronistic to the emergent corporate capitalism of the Gilded Age. See Gail Bederman, "The Women Had Charge of the Church Work Long Enough': The Men and Religion Forward Movement of 1911–1912 and the Masculinization of Middle Class Protestantism," *American Quarterly* 41 (September 1989): 432–461; also T. Jackson Lears, *No Place of Grace: Anti-Modernism and the Transformation of American Culture 1880–1920* (New York: Pantheon Books, 1981), 104.

46. Twenty years before Matheson, a white Baptist minister, the Reverend Augustus Strong, stated that Christ had brought new respect to passive virtues at a time when the world had hitherto exalted only manly virtues. Strong's writings nonetheless insist on Christ's dominant masculinity. Strong incurred the ire of suffragists, since he opposed woman's suffrage and believed in woman's subordination to man in office based on biblical authority. See Strong, *Philosophy and Religion,* 400–416,

549–550. Another white Baptist minister, Jesse Hungate, denied woman's right to ordination, maintaining that the ministry was the divine calling of men. Hungate stressed the necessity of woman's subordination to her husband. Included in his book are the responses of seventy-two Baptist ministers who overwhelmingly agreed with Hungate's opposition to women in the clergy. See Jesse Hungate, *The Ordination of Women to the Pastorate in Baptist Churches* (Hamilton, N.Y.: James B. Grant, University Bookstore, 1899), 4–5, 11, 13–14, 29–36, 46, 69–84, 101–102.

47. Such metaphors could present interesting consequences. For Virginia Broughton, they seemed to offer unambiguous masculine and feminine images: "By no title could our risen Lord endear himself more to women than that of bridegroom and thus it is he likens his return in the parable of the 'Ten Virgins.'" For the sexist, masculine bias of white Baptist Jesse Hungate, the common designation of the church as the "bride" of Christ led him to assert his demand for a manly Christianity, stating: "She is the church militant; who is also the conquering one." See Broughton, *Women's Work*, 43–44; Hungate, *Ordination of Women*, 35.

48. The argument that woman's status evolved with Christianity was advanced by critics for and against woman's rights. It put religious emphasis on the general impetus of Social Darwinism. The anti-women's rights group argued that Christianity's civilizing influence heightened differences between men and women. The higher the culture, the more women were removed from the hardening contact with labor alongside men. Women were able to confine their duties to home and family and thus became more refined and delicate. The black Baptist writers did not stress this particular theme as much as they argued the direct relation between Christianity and the sanctity of marriage and home life. They focused on women's victimization in non-Christian cultures in antiquity and the present. In non-Christian cultures, women were described as merchandise subject to barter, polygamy, and marriage without love or "delicacy." See ANBC, *Minutes and Addresses, 1886*, 69; ANBC, *Journal and Lectures 1887*, 45–46; ANBC, *Journal, Sermons, and Lectures, 1888*, 89–90; also see Hofstadter, *Social Darwinism*, 24–29; Strong, *Philosophy and Religion*, 405–406; Hungate, *Ordination of Women*, 41–42; Case, *The Masculine in Religion*, 5–7.

49. The title of Joanna Moore's autobiography showed that she viewed her own work as surrogate to Christ's. See Joanna P. Moore, *In Christ's Stead* (Chicago: Women's Baptist Home Mission Society,

1895), 131–133, 139–140, 146.

50. Another comparison of Ida B. Wells with Esther in the Bible appeared in H. J. Moore, "Let America Beware," *National Baptist World*, 12 October 1894; [Mrs.] H. Davis, "A Moses Wanted," *National Baptist World*, 5 October 1894.

51. ANBC, *Journal and Lectures 1887*, 48–49.

52. Broughton, *Women's Work*, 37–40, 43.

53. ANBC, *Minutes and Addresses, 1886*, 69, ANBC, *Journal and Lectures, 1887*, 48.

54. Penn, *Afro-American Press*, 380–381.

55. ANBC, *Journal and Lectures, 1887*, 49.

56. Broughton, *Women's Work*, 32.

57. George Fredrickson discusses "romantic racialism" within the context of the "benign" view of black distinctiveness. This view was upheld by romanticism, abolitionism, and evangelical religion and should be distinguished from anti-black sentiments which vilified blacks as beasts and unworthy of human dignity. See *The Black Image in the White Mind: The Debate on the Afro-American Character and Destiny, 1817–1914* (New York: Harper and Row, 1972), 101–115, 125–126; Everett C. Hughes et al., eds., *The Collected Papers of Robert Ezra Park* (Glencoe, Ill.: Free Press, 1950), 280, quoted in Stanford M. Lyman, *The Black American in Sociological Thought* (New York: Capricorn Books, 1973), 42.

58. DuBois stated: "But while race differences have followed mainly physical race lines, yet no mere physical distinctions would really define or explain the deeper differences—the cohesiveness and continuity of these groups. The deeper differences are spiritual, psychical, differences—undoubtedly based on the physical but infinitely transcending them." W. E. B. DuBois, "The Conservation of Races," in Philip S. Foner, ed., *W. E. B. DuBois Speaks: Speeches and Addresses, 1890–1919* (New York: 1970), 77–79, 84.

59. W. E. Burghardt DuBois, *The Gift of Black Folk: The Negroes in the Making of America* (New York: Washington Square Press, 1970), 178.

60. Blacks, more often than whites, counterposed a black ideal against white in distinguishing the two races. Outstanding black leaders such as W. E. B. Du Bois, Edward Wilmot Blyden, Benjamin Brawley, son of Baptist leader Edward M. Brawley, and Nannie H. Burroughs, the corresponding secretary of the Woman's Convention of the black Baptist church, expounded theories of "romantic racialism." See James McPherson, *Abolitionist Legacy: From Reconstruction to the NAACP* (Princeton, N.J.: Princeton University Press, 1975), 67–68, 344; Nannie H. Burroughs, "With All Thy Getting," *Southern Workman*, 56 (July 1927): 301.

61. ANBC, *Journal and Lectures, 1887*, 46–47, 49–50, 54–55, 57; Brawley, *The Negro Baptist Pulpit*, 285. Black Baptist minister William Bishop Johnson also used the warfare motif when addressing women, and he challenged them to fulfill their obligations to God "by going forth into the highways and hedges and compelling men to bow allegiance to Calvary's cross." Johnson, *Scourging of a Race*, 78–79.

62. Broughton, "Woman's Work," *National Baptist Magazine* (January 1894): 33.

63. Anthony Binga does not describe women outside the role of homemaker; William Bishop Johnson contended that men did not give women their proper estimation in society, and yet he also assigned to man the qualities of "understanding" and "mind," and to woman, "will" and "soul." See Binga, *Sermons*, 293; Johnson, *Scourging of a Race*, 76.

64. See the response of black club women to the *Virginia Baptist* articles in "Editorial—Woman's Place," *The Woman's Era*, 1 (September 1894).

PART FOUR

CONTEMPORARY LIFE
1945–PRESENT

OLD FISSURES AND NEW FRACTURES

Robert Wuthnow

Before the Second World War, much of American religious life was divided into the three dominant groups of Protestants, Catholics, and Jews. After the war, this division was replaced by a cross-cutting ideological fracture separating religious conservatives from religious liberals. Unlike older interpretations that saw the principal tensions in American life as those dividing Protestants from Catholics and Christians from Jews, Robert Wuthnow employs a sociological and empirical analysis to document this new mapping of American religious life as polarized along liberal and conservative lines. Conservatives are more likely to go to church or synagogue, believe in the literal truth of the Bible, are opposed to abortion, and in favor of prayer in public schools. Liberals, in contrast, are less likely to regularly attend church or synagogue yet say that religion is important in their lives; they see the Bible as inspired by God, and take the liberal positions in moral and political debates. Wuthnow traces the origins of this split to both long-term patterns and recent developments in American religious life. Though neither side is monolithic, he concludes that both conservatives and liberals tend to see the worst in the other and there are few indications that reconciliation is on the horizon.

Reprinted by permission from Robert Wuthnow, "Old Fissures, New Fractures," in his *The Struggle for America's Soul: Evangelicals, Liberals, and Secularism* (Grand Rapids: Eerdmans, 1989,) 19–38.

19 ❧

OLD FISSURES AND NEW FRACTURES IN AMERICAN RELIGIOUS LIFE

Robert Wuthnow

IN THE OPENING LINES of his hauntingly memorable description of the Battle of Waterloo, Victor Hugo makes a startling observation: "If it had not rained on the night of June 17, 1815, the future of Europe would have been different. A few drops more or less tipped the balance against Napoleon. For Waterloo to be the end of Austerlitz, Providence needed only a little rain, and an unseasonable cloud crossing the sky was enough for the collapse of a world."[1] What is startling is not the idea that the future of Europe, or even the outcome of the battle, hinged on something as seemingly trivial as an unexpected rainstorm.

Such explanations fill the annals of military history. Had not the British expeditionary force been able to evacuate from Dunkirk under cover of heavy fog during the week of May 26, 1940, the German army might well have gone on to win the war. Those who tread the battlefields near Gettysburg, Pennsylvania, view the heights along Culp's Hill and Cemetery Ridge, and wonder what the outcome would have been had Lee's troops occupied those favored positions instead of Meade's. The great turning points of history sometimes appear to hinge less on what people do than the conditions under which they have to do it. The flukes of nature—or the hand of God—interven willfully at fortuitous moments.

Yet we in contemporary society, schooled as we have been in the complexities of history, know how tenuous these arguments often prove to be. Battles may be won or lost on the basis of a sudden turn of weather, but wars are not and neither is the course of history.

What if, by some chance, Lee's troops had occupied the heights at Gettysburg? Would Meade's then have run the bloody gauntlet that became immortalized as "Pickett's charge"? Or would the Federal army have faded away to fight on more opportune terms? We learn from modern analysts of the battle that Lee was forced to fight, despite the unfavorable terrain, because he desperately needed to win. Supplies were running low and Confederate agents needed to be able to demonstrate to their European creditors that they could win. The reason supplies were running low lay deep in the South's agrarian economy (cf. the North's industrial economy) and even deeper in the triangular trade that had developed between the South, Great Britain, and West Africa. Lee was forced to fight; Meade could have slipped away.

As we proceed with Victor Hugo's account, what actually startles us is that he succeeds so well in defending his thesis. A soggy battlefield was indeed a decisive factor. But as so often is the case in Hugo's narratives, it was the larger terrain—and the uncertainties inherent in this terrain—that constituted the framework in which the decisions of the two commanders had to be made. An unexpected rainstorm made it impossible for Napoleon to deploy the full force of his artillery. He could not have anticipated this factor, an element of the battle that in essence remained obscure.

The *quid obscurum* in Hugo's account, though, is at once more simple and straight-forward than this and more elusive. Running through the battlefield, interposed directly between the two armies, was a ditch. It extended across the entire line that Napoleon's cavalry would have to charge. It was a deep chasm, made by human hands, the result of a road that had been cut like a knife through the natural terrain. It was hidden from view. The cavalry charged, and then faced the terror. Hugo recounts:

> There was the ravine, unexpected, gaping right at the horses' feet, twelve feet deep between its banks. The second rank pushed in the first, the third pushed in the second; the horses reared, lurched backward, fell onto their rumps, and struggled writhing with their feet in the air, piling up and throwing their riders; no means to retreat; the whole column was nothing but a projectile. The momentum to crush the English crushed the French. The inexorable ravine could not yield until it was filled; riders and horses rolled in together helter-skelter, grinding against each other, making common flesh in this dreadful gulf, and when this grave was full of living men, the rest marched over them and went on. Almost a third of Dubois's brigade sank into the abyss.[2]

The *quid obscurum* was quite literally a hidden fracture with enormous consequences.

The second, and deeper, meaning of Hugo's reference to the *quid obscurum* is that of the broader uncertainties evoked by the clash of two armies. Only in the heat of battle do the unforeseen contingencies become evident; only then do the plans of the commanding generals prove to have missed important features of the broader terrain. In the struggling line of soldiers engaged in hand-to-hand combat one begins to realize that the expenditures are greater than expected. The consequences of seemingly unimportant conditions turn out to be incalculable. It is left to the historian to calculate, with the advantage of hindsight, the role of these previously obscured realities.

THE GREAT FRACTURE IN AMERICAN RELIGION

My purpose in drawing attention to Hugo's discussion is also twofold. At the more literal level, like the ravine cutting across the plateau of Mont-Saint-Jean, a great fracture runs through the cultural terrain on which the battles of religion and politics are now being fought. It is a fracture that deserves our attention. For it is of recent creation, a human construction, unlike the timeless swells of culture through which it has been cut. It has become a mire of bitter contention, consuming the energies of religious communities and grinding their ideals into the grime of unforeseen animosities. At a broader level, this fracture also symbolizes the unplanned developments in the larger terrain that did not become evident until the battles themselves began to erupt. With the advantage of hindsight, we can now discover the importance of these developments. We can see how the present controversies in American religion were affected by broader changes in the society—the consequences of which remained obscure at the time but have now become painfully transparent.

The ravine running through the culturescape of American religion is as real as the one made by the road between the two villages on the Belgian border, though it differs from that Belgian ravine in one important respect. It is not simply a fissure in the physical environment, a ditch that creates the downfall of one of the protagonists. It is to a much greater extent the product of the battle itself. The chasm dividing American religion into separate communities has emerged largely from the struggle between these two communities. It may have occurred, as I shall suggest shortly, along a fault line already present in the cultural terrain. But it has been dug deeper and wider by the skirmishes that have been launched across it.

Depending on whose lens we use to view it, we can describe this fissure in any number of ways. Television evangelist Jimmy Swaggart has described it as a gulf between those who believe in the Judeo-Christian principles on which our country was founded and those who believe in the "vain philosophies of men." On one side are the "old-fashioned" believers in "the word of Almighty God" who are often maligned as "poor simpletons"; on the other side are the "so-called intelligentsia," those who believe they are great because they "are more intelligent than anyone else," "socialists," believers in "syphilitic Lenin," and the burdened masses who have nothing better to get excited about than football and baseball games.[3] In contrast, a writer for the *New York Times* depicted it as a battle between "churches and church-allied groups" who favor freedom, democracy, and the rights of minorities, on the one hand, and a right-wing fringe interested in setting up a theocracy governed by a "dictatorship of religious values," on the other hand.[4]

Apart from the colors in which the two sides are portrayed, though, one finds general agreement on the following points: (a) the reality of the division between two opposing camps; (b) the predominance of "fundamentalists," "evangelicals," and "religious conservatives" in one and the predominance of "religious liberals," "humanists," and "secularists" in the other; and (c) the presence of deep hostility and misgiving between the two.

An official of the National Council of Churches summarized the two positions, and the views of each toward the other, this way: "Liberals abhor the smugness, the self-righteousness, the absolute certainty, the judgmentalism, the lovelessness of a narrow, dogmatic faith. [Conservatives] scorn the fuzziness, the marshmallow convictions, the inclusiveness that makes membership meaningless—the 'anything goes' attitude that views even Scripture as relative. Both often caricature the worst in one another and fail to perceive the best."[5]

To suggest that American religion is divided neatly into two communities with sharply differentiated views is, of course, to ride roughshod over the countless landmarks, signposts, hills, and gullies that actually constitute the religious landscape. Not only do fundamentalists distinguish themselves from evangelicals, but each brand of religious conservatism is divided into dozens of denominational product lines. Similar distinctions can be made on the religious left. In the popular mind, though, there does seem to be some reality to the cruder, binary way of thinking.

A national survey, conducted several years ago (even before some of the more acrimonious debates over the role of religion in politics had arisen), found both a high level of awareness of the basic division between religious liberals and conservatives and a great deal of genuine hostility between the two. When asked to classify themselves, 43 percent of those surveyed identified themselves as religious liberals and 41 percent said they were religious conservatives. The public is thus divided almost equally between the two categories, and only one person in six was unable or unwilling to use these labels.[6]

The ways in which self-styled liberals and conservatives answered other questions also seem to lend some validity to the two categories. As one would expect, conservatives were much more likely than liberals to identify themselves as evangelicals, to believe in a literal interpretation of the Bible, to say they had had a "born-again" conversion experience, to indicate that they had tried to convert others to their faith, and to hold conservative views on issues such as abortion and prayer in public schools. Liberals were less likely than conservatives to attend church or synagogue regularly, but a majority affirmed the importance of religion in their lives, tended to regard the Bible as divinely inspired (but not to be taken literally), and held liberal views on a variety of political and moral issues.

Some denominations tended to consist of more conservatives than liberals, or vice versa. But generally, the major denominational families and faith traditions—Methodists, Lutherans, Presbyterians, Baptists, Catholics, Jews—were all divided about equally between religious conservatives and religious liberals. In other words, the cleavage between conservatives and liberals tends not, for the most part, to fall along denominational lines. It is a cleavage that divides people within the same denominations—as recent struggles within the Southern Baptist Convention, the Episcopal Church, the Presbyterian Church, U.S.A., and the Roman Catholic Church all attest.

The study also demonstrated the extent to which the relations between religious liberals and religious conservatives have become rife with conflict. A majority of the public surveyed said the conflict between religious liberals and conservatives is an area of "serious tension." A substantial majority of both groups said they had had unpleasant, or at best "mixed," relations with the other group. These relations were said to have taken place in fairly intimate settings: in one's church, among friends and relatives, even within the same Bible study or fellowship groups. Moreover, each side held a number of negative images of the other. Liberals saw conservatives as rigid, intolerant, and fanatical. Conservatives described liberals as shallow, morally loose, unloving, and unsaved.

The study also demonstrated that, unlike other kinds of prejudice and hostility, the ill feelings separating religious liberals and religious conservatives *did not mitigate* as the two groups came into greater contact with one another. The more each side came into contact with the other, and the more knowledge it gained about the other, the less it liked the other.

Viewed normatively, such levels of animosity and tension between religious liberals and conservatives are disturbing. We might expect nothing better from communists and capitalists or Democrats and Republicans. But deep within the Hebrew and Christian traditions lies an ethic of love and forgiveness. In congregation after congregation prayers are routinely offered for unity among the faithful. Creeds are recited stating belief in the one, holy, catholic church. And homilies are delivered on Jesus' injunction to love one's neighbor as oneself.

If these findings are disturbing, they are not, however, surprising. They accord with the way in which American religion is portrayed in the media and in pulpits, and with the way in which American religion seems to function. The major newspapers and television networks routinely publicize the bizarre activities of fundamentalists and evangelicals: the conservative governor who prays with his pastor and hears God tell him to run for the presidency, the television preacher who prays (successfully, it turns out) that an impending hurricane will be averted from the Virginia coast, the fundamentalists in Indiana who deny their children proper schooling and medical care, the evangelical counselor in California who is sued by the family of a patient who committed suicide, the deranged member of a fundamentalist church in Maine who shoots down his fellow parishioners with a shotgun.

Conservative television preachers and conservative religious publications make equally vitriolic comments about their liberal foes: how an Episcopal bishop is condoning sexual permissiveness within his diocese, how Methodist liberals are encouraging homosexuality among the denomination's pastors, how zealous clergy in the nuclear disarmament movement are selling the country out to the Russians, how religious conservatives are being discriminated against in colleges and universities. It is little wonder that the labels begin to stick. Sooner or later it does in fact begin to appear as if the world of faith is divided between two belligerent superpowers.

But this picture of the religious world is not simply a creation of the sensationalist media. At the grass roots, one can readily find denunciations of liberalism from conservative pulpits and diatribes against fundamentalism from liberal pulpits. One can readily observe the split between liberals and conservatives in church meetings and discussion groups. Liberals freely express doubts about the historical authenticity of the Bible. Conservatives appeal for greater faith in the supernatural, the miraculous, and argue for more emphasis on sin and personal salvation. Beneath the innocent statements of each are deeper feelings about right and wrong, truth and error.

Beyond these simple exchanges, the two also isolate themselves in different communities of support and action: liberals in the nurturing environment of the local peace concerns fellowship, the forum on AIDS, the movement to lobby for equitable and affordable housing; conservatives in the womb of Bible study groups and prayer fellowships.

One can also readily observe the polarizing tendencies of national issues on the religious environment. Pick up the latest issue of *Christian Century* or *Christianity Today*; observe the number of articles that deal with politics and note the paucity of material on theology or even personal spirituality. Or open the mail and count the letters from Moral Majority, Christian Voice, People for the American Way, the American Civil Liberties Union. The issues are now national rather than local or regional. They concern an appointment to the Supreme Court, a constitutional amendment on abortion, a preacher running for president. They are supported by one faction of the religious community and opposed by another. They induce polarization.

But to say that the chasm between religious liberals and conservatives exists for many reasons is still only to describe it—to parade the colors of the troops engaged in the great battle of which this conflict consists. It is a chasm deepened and widened by political debate. It is a chasm around which religious communities' participation in public affairs divides. It has become a predictable feature of the contemporary debate over church-state relations. To understand it, though, we must look at broader developments in the social terrain. We must try to discover why this particular fracture line existed in the cultural geography in the first place.

A CLOSER LOOK AT THE CULTURAL GEOGRAPHY

In one sense, of course, the fracture line can be found in the soil of American religion as far back as the years immediately after the Civil War. Even in the eighteenth century and during the first half of the nineteenth century one can identify the beginnings of a division between religious conservatives and religious liberals insofar as one considers the effects of the Enlightenment on elite culture. Skepticism, atheism, anticlericalism, and of course deism constitute identifiable alternatives to the popular piety of Methodists and Baptists and to the conservative orthodoxy of Roman Catholics, Jews, Presbyterians, and others during this period. But to an important degree the potential division between conservatism and liberalism before the Civil War is overshadowed by the deeper tensions to which the society is subject. Nationalism and regionalism, differences between the culture of the Eastern seaboard and the expanding Western territories, and increasingly the tensions between North and South provide the major divisions affecting the organization of American religion.

Not until the termination of these hostilities and the resumption of material progress after the Civil War does it become possible for the gap between religious conservatives and liberals to gain importance. Gradually in these years the discoveries of science, the new ideas of Charles Darwin, and by the end of the century the beginnings of a national system of higher education provide the groundwork for a liberal challenge to religious conservatism. Of course, the culmination of these changes comes at the turn of the century in the modernist movement and its increasingly vocal opponent, the fundamentalists.

In the long view, the present division between religious liberals and religious conservatives can be pictured simply as a continuation or outgrowth of this earlier conflict. The inevitable forces of modernization produced a secular tendency in American religion, a tendency that condoned greater individual freedom in matters of the spirit and voiced skepticism toward a faith based in divine revelation, and this tendency evoked a reactionary movement in which religious conservatism was preserved.

That, as I say, is the impression gained from taking a long view of American history. If one takes a more limited perspective, though, a rather different impression emerges. One is able to focus more directly on the immediate contours of the religious environment and to see how these contours are in the short term shaped by specific events. I suppose that this is the advantage of taking the perspective of the sociologist—which seldom extends much before World War II.

At the close of that war, the condition of American religion was quite different than it is now. It contained seeds that were to germinate and grow, like weeds in the concrete, widening the cracks that have now become so visible. But the basic divisions ran along other lines. Tensions between Protestants and Catholics had reached new heights as immigration and natural increase contributed to the growth of the Catholic population. Tensions between Christians and Jews also ran deep, even though they were often less visible than the conflicts dividing Protestants and Catholics. There was, as Will Herberg described it a few years later, a "tripartite division" in American religion: to be American was to be Protestant, Catholic, or Jewish.[7]

In addition, denominational boundaries also played an important role in giving structure to the Protestant branch of this tripartite arrangement. Ecumenical services were beginning to erode some of these boundaries (often for the explicit purpose of displaying Protestant unity against the threat of papal expansion). But ethnic, national, and geographic divisions—as well as theological and liturgical divisions—continued to reinforce denominational separatism.

In all of this, there was little evidence of any basic split between liberals and conservatives.

To be sure, fundamentalism was alive and well. But its very success proved in a deeper sense to be its limitation. By the mid-1930s, fundamentalist spokesmen had largely conceded their defeat in the major Protestant denominations and had withdrawn to form their own organizations. As the Great Depression, and then the rationing imposed by the war, made travel more difficult, these organizations also grew farther apart from one another. By the end of the war, they consisted mainly of small, isolated splinter groups on the fringes of the mainline denominations.

Most of the population that continued to believe in such doctrinal tenets as biblical inerrancy, the divinity of Jesus, and the necessity of personal salvation remained within these larger denominations. Even the official policies of these denominations reflected what would now be considered a strong conservative emphasis. Evangelism, door-to-door canvassing of communities, revival meetings, biblical preaching, missions—all received prominent support.

Also of significance was the fact that many of the more out-spoken conservative religious leaders were unobtrusively beginning to build their own organizations. At this point, however, these leaders were able to build quietly and were content largely to maintain ties with the major denominations, rather than break away like their fundamentalist counterparts.

There were certainly differences of opinion among believers about such matters as the literal inspiration of the Bible or the role of churches in political affairs. But these were as yet not the subject of mass movements or of widely recognized cultural divisions. Only the terms "fundamentalist" and "liberal" suggest continuity between this period and our own; a more careful examination of issues, personalities, and organizations indicates discontinuity.

FISSURE LINES IN THE RELIGIOUS LANDSCAPE

In the years immediately following World War II we do find evidence of the conditions that were to predispose American religion to undergo a major transformation in the decades that followed. Three such predisposing conditions stand out.

First, American religion was on the whole extraordinarily strong. The largest churches now counted members in the thousands. Overall, the number of local churches and synagogues ranged in the hundreds of thousands. Some denominations sported budgets in the tens of millions. Collectively, religious organizations took in approximately $800 million annually—as historian Harold Laski observed, this figure exceeded the budget of the entire British government.[8]

In comparison with Europe, the American churches were especially strong. They had not been subjected to the same limitations on government spending that the churches in England, France, and Germany had faced, nor had they encountered the mass withdrawal of the working classes that these churches had experienced; and of course they had not been subject to the extensive destruction resulting from the war. They had been weakened by the Depression and by shortages of building materials during the war. But curiously, perhaps, this very weakness turned out to be a strength as well. It prompted major building programs after the war, allowed the churches to relocate in growing neighborhoods, and generally encouraged what was to become known as the religious revival of the 1950s.

The critical feature of the churches' massive institutional strength for the coming decades was religion's ability to adjust to a changing environment. Rather than simply wither away—or maintain itself in quiet contemplative seclusion—it adapted to the major social developments of the postwar period. In this sense, we owe much of the present controversy in American religion to the simple fact that it had remained a strong institutional force right up to the second half of the twentieth century.

The second predisposing condition was the strong "this-worldly" orientation of American religion. Not only was it able to adapt to changing circumstances; it also engaged itself actively in the social environment by its own initiative. When the war ended, religious leaders looked to the future with great expectancy. They recognized the opportunities that lay ahead. They were also mindful of the recurrent dangers they faced.

Indeed, a prominent theme in their motivational appeals focused on the combination of promise and peril. For instance, a resolution passed by the Federal Council of Churches in 1945 declared: "We are living in a uniquely dangerous and promising time."[9] It was a dangerous time because of the recurrent likelihood of war, the widely anticipated return to a depressed economy after the war-induced boom had ended, and of course the invention of nuclear weapons. It was a promising time because of new opportunities for missionary work and evangelism.

The stakes were high, so persistent activism was the desired response. In the words of a Methodist minister, who reminded his audience of the perilous opportunities facing them: "That requires…a great godly company of men and women with no axe to grind, desiring only to save, serve, help and heal."[10] The result was that religious organizations deliberately exposed their flanks to the influences of their environment. Programs were initiated, education was encouraged, preaching confronted issues of the day—all of which, like the rain on Napoleon's troops, would reveal the churches' dependence on the conditions of their terrain.

The third predisposing factor was reflected in the relation understood to prevail between religion and the public sphere. This factor is especially important to understand, because it provides a vivid contrast with the ways in which we now conceive of religion's influence in the political arena. In the 1940s and 1950s there appears to have been a fairly widespread view among religious leaders, theologians, and even social scientists that values and behavior were closely related. Find out what a person's basic values were, and you could pretty well predict that person's behavior. If persons valued democracy, they could be counted on to uphold it in their behavior. If a person worked hard and struggled to get ahead, you could be pretty sure that person valued success and achievement.

More broadly, writers also extended this connection to society. A nation's culture consisted essentially of values, and these values were arranged in a hierarchy of priority. The society was held together by this hierarchy of values. It generated consensus and caused people to behave in similar ways.

For religious leaders, this way of conceiving things was very convenient. It meant that the way to shape people's lives was by shaping their values, and this was what the churches did best: they preached and they taught. They influenced the individual's system of values. They shaped the individual's conscience.

The churches' conduit to the public arena was thus through the individual's conscience. Shape a churchperson's values, and you could rest assured that your influence would be carried into the public sphere. That person would vote according to his or her conscience, would manifest high values in his or her work, would behave charitably, ethically, honestly. All the churches needed to do was preach and teach.

This view also gained support from the public arena itself. Public officials spoke frequently and fervently about their commitment to high moral principles. They lauded the work of religious leaders in reinforcing these principles. Truman, Eisenhower, Dulles, and others spoke of their own religious faith and commended this faith as a source of societal cohesion and strength. It was easy for religious leaders to believe that their efforts were really having an impact.

Already, though, there were signs that this worldview was coming apart. The problem was not that political leaders were suspected of hypocrisy, although this may have been the case. Nor was the problem, as some have suggested, that this was basically a Protestant view, and thus was being undermined by the growing pluralism of the society. Catholic and Jewish leaders in the 1950s articulated it too. The idea was not that religious faith channeled behavior in specifically Protestant or Catholic or Jewish directions. The idea—at least the one expressed in public contexts—was that a deep religious faith gave the individual moral strength, conviction, the will to do what was right.

But the premises on which this worldview itself was based were beginning to be questioned. Doubts were beginning to be expressed about the basic connection between values and behavior. What if one's basic values did not translate into actual behavior? What if one's behavior did not stem from one's convictions but was influenced by other factors?

At this time, these questions were only raised occasionally. But the very fact that they could be raised suggested the presence of a cultural fissure, a fault line along which a more serious fracture could open up. Values constituted one category, behavior another. The two categories were connected—had to be connected closely for arguments about the impact of conscience on public affairs to be credible. But this connection itself was becoming tenuous.

YEARS OF STRUGGLE

How then did these predisposing conditions in the 1950s become transformed to produce the chasm between religious liberals and conservatives that we experience at the present? How did Herberg's tripartite system, in which the basic religious and *religio-political* divisions occurred between Protestants and Catholics and between Christians and Jews, come to be replaced by what some have called a "two-party system"?

The answer is complex, of course, because it involves not only the relations among all the major religious groupings but also the relations between religion and the forces shaping the broader society. It is, however, enormously important, for it brings together all the decisive factors that have shaped American religion in the period since World War II. We can touch on only the basic contours here.

In picturing the transformation as a tripartite division being replaced by a two-party system, we should not think that the latter simply superimposed itself on the former or that the one led directly into the other. It is helpful to divide the process in two and seek answers for each of its phases separately. The first phase (not chronologically but analytically) amounted to an erosion of the basic divisions constituting the tripartite system. The second phase amounted to developments reinforcing a new, different cleavage between liberals and conservatives. These processes combined to create what many have sensed is a new dynamic in the relations between church and state, or between religion and politics more generally. But they are also analytically separable.

It also helps to identify an interim phase between the two. Three categories of religious organization did not simply meld into two. Thinking of it in those terms causes us to miss the violence associated with any social change as basic as this one. Natural communities were torn asunder, their parts flung into the air and scattered in strange configurations, before the subterranean forces at work in the society finally rearranged them in the patterns we see today. We have to recognize the upheaval and displacement associated with this process if we are to tap the wellsprings from which much of the present political fury arises.

The erosion of the divisions separating Protestants and Catholics, Jews and Christians, and members of different denominations came about gradually. It was legitimated from within by norms of love and humility that promoted interfaith cooperation. It was reinforced from without by changes in the larger society. Rising educational levels, memories of the Holocaust, and the civil rights movement all contributed to an increasing emphasis on tolerance. Regional migration brought Catholics and Protestants, and Christians and Jews, into closer physical proximity with one another. Denominational ghettos, forged by immigration and ethnic ties, were gradually replaced by religiously and ethnically plural communities. Rates of interreligious marriage went up. It became increasingly common for members of all religious groups to have grown up in other groups, to have friends from other groups, and to have attended other groups.

The denominational hierarchies, seminaries, pension plans, and so forth still played a significant role in the organization of American religion. But the ground was in a sense cleared of old demarcations, thereby making new alliances and cleavages easier to emerge.

For those who had spent their entire lives within particular denominational ghettos, these changes in themselves represented major disruptions, of course, especially when it was their pastor who began welcoming outsiders, their denomination that lost its identity by merging with another, or their child who married outside the faith.

Most of the upheaval, though, came during the 1960s and was closely associated with the upheaval that pervaded the society in general. Young people were particularly subject to this upheaval. Many were the first ever in their families to attend college. For many, attending college meant leaving the ethno-religious ghetto for the first time. The campuses themselves were growing so rapidly that alienation and social isolation were common experiences. Of course, the civil rights movement and antiwar protests added to the turmoil.

Among the many ways in which this upheaval affected religion, two are especially important. First, the tensions of the 1960s significantly widened the gap between values and behavior that was mentioned earlier. The two major social movements of this period were the civil rights movement and the antiwar movement, and significantly, both dramatized the disjuncture between values and behavior. The civil rights movement brought into sharp relief what Gunnar Myrdal had called the "American dilemma"—the dilemma of subscribing to egalitarian values in principle but engaging in racial discrimination in practice.[11] Here was a clear example of values and behavior being out of joint.

The antiwar movement pointed up a similar disjuncture. On the one hand, Americans supposedly believed deeply in such values as democracy and the right of people to determine their own destiny. On the other hand, the country was engaged in a war in Southeast Asia that to many seemed to deny these principles. Military force was being used, at best, in an effort to determine another people's destiny for them, or at worst, to prop up an ineffective nondemocratic regime. Both movements drove home, often implicitly, the more general point that people of high values and good consciences could not always be counted on to manifest those virtues in their day-to-day behavior.

The wedge that these movements drove into the earlier connection between values and behavior was to prove increasingly important in separating religious liberals from religious conservatives. Although this picture was to be modified somewhat by the 1980s, in the late

1960s it essentially consisted of conservatives grasping the values side of the equation and liberals seizing the behavioral side. That is, conservatives continued to emphasize preaching and teaching, the shaping of high personal moral standards, and above all the personally redemptive experience of salvation. Whether behavior would result that could alleviate racial discrimination or the war in Southeast Asia was not the issue; the issue was what one believed in one's heart and the motives from which one acted. In contrast, liberals increasingly attached importance to behavior. Believe what one will, it does not matter, they said, unless one puts one's faith on the line, takes action, helps bring about change. Changing social institutions was especially important, because they were the reason values and behavior did not correspond. People with good intentions were caught up in evil systems that needed to be overthrown.

For the time being at least, liberals argued for religious organizations' taking direct action in politics, while conservatives remained aloof from politics entirely, preferring instead to concentrate on matters of personal belief. Indeed, the two often gave lip service to the higher principles held by the other but expressed disagreement over the tactics being used. Thus, conservatives often expressed sympathy with the ideal of racial equality, but argued against the direct-action techniques in which liberal clergy were becoming involved. Liberals often continued to express sympathy with the ideal of personal salvation, but argued that personal salvation alone was not enough of a witness if church people did not become actively involved in working for social justice as well.

The second consequence of the turmoil of the 1960s that stands out is the increasing role of higher education in differentiating styles of religious commitment. In the 1950s, perhaps surprisingly so in retrospect, those who had been to college and those who had not were remarkably similar on most items of religious belief and practice. By the early 1970s, a considerable education gap had emerged between the two.

The college educated were much less likely, even than the college educated of the previous decade, to attend religious services regularly. Their belief in a literal interpretation of the Bible had eroded dramatically. They were more tolerant of other religions, and they were more interested in experimenting with the so-called new religions, such as Zen, Transcendental Mediation, Hare Krishna, and the human potential movement. Those who had not been to college remained more committed to traditional views of the Bible, were more strongly interested in religion in general, continued to attend religious services regularly, and expressed doubt about other faiths, including the new religions.

In short, educational differences were becoming more significant for religion, just as they were being emphasized more generally in the society. Higher education was becoming a more significant basis for creating social and cultural distinctions. In regard to religion, education was beginning to reinforce the cleavage between religious liberals and religious conservatives.

For a time, perhaps even as recently as 1976, it appeared that the gap between religious liberals and conservatives might be bridged by a significant segment of the evangelical community. Many of its leaders had participated in the educational expansion of the previous decade. They were exposed to the current thinking in higher education, had been influenced by their own participation in the civil rights movement and the antiwar movement, and had come to hold liberal views on many political issues, and yet retained a strong commitment to the biblical tradition, including an emphasis on personal faith.

Their voice, however, was soon drowned out by the more strident voices of the religious right. Television hookups and direct-mail solicitations replaced the evangelical periodical, seminary, and scholarly conference as more effective means of forging a large following and extracting revenue from that following. Issues such as abortion and feminism provided platforms on which the religious right could organize.

Educational differences continued to separate the more conservative from the more liberal. But other issues began to reinforce these differences. Issues arose that also reflected the experience of women in gaining higher education and becoming employed in professional careers, or the exposure one gained in college to the social sciences and humanities as opposed to more narrowly technical educations in engineering or business.

The religious right also borrowed the more activist style of political confrontation that the left had used during the 1960s. It began to renew the connection between values and behavior. Its commitment to personal morality remained strong, but it now urged believers to take political action, to organize themselves, to infuse their morality into the basic institutions of government. Each side developed special purpose groups to gain its objectives, either within more narrow denominational contexts or in the national arena.

Thus, deeper features of the social and cultural terrain underlie the present fracture between religious liberals and religious conservatives. Had it simply been, say, the Supreme Court's 1973 decision on abortion that elicited different responses from liberals and conservatives, we might well have seen a temporary flurry of activity followed by a gradual progression of interest to other matters. Instead, the religious environment is characterized by two clearly identified communities. Each has developed through the events spanning at least a quarter of a century. The two are located differently with respect to the basic social division that has been produced by the growth of higher education. Other bases of differentiation, such as regionalism, ethnicity, and denominationalism, that might have mitigated this basic division have subsided in importance. Each side has mobilized its recources around special purpose groups.

It is, therefore, highly likely that specific issues concerning the relations between church and state, cases in the federal courts involving religion, and religious issues in electoral campaigns will continue to evoke strong—and opposing—responses from these two communities.

FACTORS MITIGATING THE STRUGGLE

At the same time, we should not avoid mentioning several forces that may work to contain or reduce this polarization of religion in the public arena. One is the fact that neither community is actually organized as a single party. Each side is still divided into dozens of denominations, is represented by dozens of different national leaders, has mobilized its political efforts through dozens of special purpose groups, and at the grass roots consists of thousands of separate congregations. For either side to operate effectively as a political bloc, it must forge coalitions among these various organizations. And, despite the fact that both sides have been able to transcend old divisions, matters of theology, of liturgical tradition, and even of region still present formidable barriers to be overcome.

Another mitigating factor is that both sides continue to register, at least at the grass roots, a healthy suspicion of government. It sometimes appears that each side is anxious to use government to achieve its goals. But grass-roots mobilization of church people, whether liberals or conservatives, has been more effective in opposing government than in cooperating with government.

During the civil rights movement, churchgoers who became most active in politics at the grass roots were those who opposed the actions being taken by the government. During the Vietnam War, churchgoers most active in politics were again those who opposed the government's actions. In recent years, the most politically active churchgoers have been those who opposed the government's role on abortion and welfare spending. In each of these periods, moreover, churchgoers who felt government was becoming too powerful were more likely to become politically active than churchgoers who did not feel this way. I suspect that the reason for this political activism lies in the fact that there is a long history of concern, expressed specifically in the First Amendment to the Constitution, over the threat that government poses to religious freedom. In any case, this suspicion of government seems likely to dampen enthusiasm for any strong theocratic orientation of the kind that has sometimes been projected.

Finally, we must remember that the involvement of either religious faction in political life cannot succeed without active support from leaders in the political arena itself. During the 1980s, under the Reagan administration, at least an impression of such support was often taken for granted. At the same time, officials of both political parties have often expressed consternation over the activities of religious groups. Lack of political experience, extremist rhetoric, disinterest in routine party activities, and single-issue orientations have been cited as reasons for this consternation.

Moreover, religious liberals and religious conservatives have often been courted by factions within the political community for entirely secular purposes: because they supported stronger defense initiatives, or because they favored a freeze on nuclear weapons, or because they wanted a tougher policy against communism in Latin America. Either military or economic changes in the larger international arena can radically alter the nature of these issues, and therefore the likelihood of religious factions being courted.

I return, then, to the point at which I began. The relations between faith and politics are contingent on the broader terrain on which they occur. Like the Battle of Waterloo, the battle between religious conservatives and religious liberals is subject to its environment. A deep cultural ravine appears to separate the two communities. Whether this ravine can be bridged depends on raising it from obscurity, bringing it into consciousness, and recognizing the surrounding contours on which these efforts must rest.

NOTES

1. Victor Hugo, *Les Miserables* (New York: New American Library, 1987), 309.

2. Ibid., 328–29.

3. From a broadcast in February 1987 titled "What is the Foundation for Our Philosophy of Christianity?" I wish to thank Victoria Chapman for the transcription of this sermon.

4. E. J. Dionne, Jr., "Religion and Politics," *New York Times*, 15 September 1987.

5. Peggy L. Shriver, "The Paradox of Inclusiveness-that-Divides," *Christian Century* (January 21, 1984): 194.

6. At the extremes, the public was also about equally divided: 19 percent said they were very liberal; 18 percent, very conservative. These figures are from a survey conducted in June 1984 by the Gallup Organization under a grant from the Robert Schuller Ministries. Some of the study's findings were reported in the May and June, 1986, issues of *Emerging Trends*, a publication edited by George Gallup, Jr. The results of additional analyses of these data appear in Robert Wuthnow, *The Restructuring of American Religion: Society and Faith since World War II* (Princeton: Princeton University Press, 1988).

7. Will Herberg, *Protestant-Catholic-Jew* (Garden City, NY: Doubleday-Anchor, 1955).

8. Harold Laski, *The American Democracy* (New York: Viking, 1948), 283.

9. "The Churches and World Order," reprinted in *Christian Century* (February 7, 1945): 174–77.

10. C. Stanley Lowell, "The Conversion of America," *Christian Century* (September 29, 1949): 1134.

11. Gunnar Myrdal, *An American Dilemma* (New York: Harper & Brothers, 1944).

SEEKING JEWISH SPIRITUAL ROOTS

Deborah Dash Moore

Following the Second World War, large numbers of Jews from New York and Chicago joined the migrations of people from the Northeast and Midwest to the sunbelt cities of Miami and Los Angeles. Cut loose from the older European religious cultures of their families, these "permanent tourists," as Deborah Dash Moore calls them, created a new and distinctly American Jewish identity in the loosely structured Jewish communities of Miami and Los Angeles. In this fresh look at transformations within modern American Judaism, Moore directs our attention to the young, ambitious rabbis who, like their fellow migrants, were eager to break out of the patterns of belief and behavior that had been established in the Northeast. In a world with few enduring traditions or social hierarchies, these pioneering rabbis created new religious traditions and reclaimed old ones. They understood implicitly that in order to attract a town of rootless migrants to their synagogues they needed to offer Jews a social and religious identity. In this new environment, the common denominational distinctions between Orthodoxy and Conservatism, and Conservatism and Reform became less visible and, instead, "an easy eclecticism took hold." By imagining religion as a form of "spiritual recreation" that complemented the leisure lifestyle, sunbelt Judaism distinguished itself from the older, European Judaism of the Northeast and Midwest.

Reprinted by permission from Deborah Dash Moore, "Seeking Spiritual Roots," in her *To the Golden Cities: Pursuing the American Jewish Dream in Miami and L.A.* (New York: The Free Press, 1994), 93–122.

Here there are no vested interests, here there are no sacred cows, here there is no cold hand of the past. There is an opportunity to develop new forms of Jewish communal living geared in a realistic fashion to the actual needs of the Jewish community.

—Charles Brown, Head of the Los Angeles
Jewish Community Council, 1952
(quoted in Max Vorspan and Lloyd P. Gartner,
A History of the Jews of Los Angeles)

20

SEEKING JEWISH SPIRITUAL ROOTS IN MIAMI AND LOS ANGELES

Deborah Dash Moore

AS JEWS PULLED UP THEIR ROOTS and turned their backs on the old home and neighborhood to migrate across the continent, many left their parents' religious traditions behind, those familial religious and ethnic practices that seemed an integral part of the northern urban life and territory. Some, growing up in secular Jewish households, had only known religious tradition from their neighbors and the synagogue down the street. Others remembered sabbaths and seders from childhood in another time and place. Upon arrival in the open golden spaces of Miami and L.A., these childhood religious traditions seemed less appropriate, more of an anachronism. As one self-styled upper-middle-class San Fernando Valley Jewish mother explained, "Our children know and appreciate their heritage, but the realities of university academic competition, part-time jobs and family and household obligations cannot be ignored. Nor can my husband and I set aside the rigorous full-time effort we must put forward to provide the home, education and general lifestyle we've chosen for ourselves" in order to "return to the kind of practicing Judaism we knew as youngsters. Anyway," she cheerfully confessed, "let's be really honest and admit that those practices were forcibly imposed upon us by our parents, and this was the case for most of our peers."[1]

Jews in Miami and L.A. embraced a kind of rootlessness that proved even more pervasive than the upbeat confession of one San Fernando mother would suggest. Their apparently casual abandonment of religious tradition left them more open to an innovative personalism and eclecticism than would be countenanced by their more rooted relatives in the Northeast and Midwest, many of whom also discarded parental religious traditions. The permanent tourist mentality bred insecurity as well as the sense that every day was a holiday; it undermined the significance of religious traditions by changing their social and cultural context. In the diffuse and loosely structured Jewish communities of Miami and L.A., communities that lacked any real authority, those seeking religious roots necessarily engaged in an individual, personal quest, not a collective endeavor.

Without familiar institutional guides or fixed patterns of living derived from close-knit Jewish families and neighborhoods, newcomers turned to new and ambitious leaders eager to teach and inspire them. A handful of religious entrepreneurs felt the magnetic pull of Los

Angeles to be irresistible. Like their fellow Jewish migrants, they liked the atmosphere—often discovered during a stint as chaplain in the armed services—and sought to escape stifling family ties. Many of these young rabbis were more liberal than their peers and possessed a flair for showmanship, a skill vital to those who wish to attract widely dispersed people with no institutional loyalties to join a congregation. They saw in the City of Angels a market economy in religious culture that encouraged inventiveness and salesmanship and placed few restraints upon them. Self-reliant, flexible, and self-confident, they knew how to mobilize people to build a congregation around themselves. Seeking new lives for themselves and dissatisfied with established rabbinical patterns of behavior and belief, they were eager to break out of the rabbinic mold that had been established in the Northeast. Many also were willing to take risks, to experiment with new forms of Judaism, to start with the individual and his or her desires, to craft religious practices in response to the needs of their rootless fellow newcomers.[2]

In the freewheeling atmosphere of Los Angeles, Jews invented new religious traditions and rediscovered old ones. Denominational distinctions common between Orthodoxy and Conservatism, and Conservatism and Reform lacked clarity in L.A. In the Northeast and Midwest, Orthodoxy's emphasis upon the immutability of sacred law, the divine character of the oral and written Torah, and the necessity of upholding ritual observance—especially separate seating of men and women in the synagogue—set it apart from Conservatism, which stressed the changing character of Jewish law, evidenced a willingness to modify ritual observance through mixed seating, and staunchly supported Zionism. Reform championed modernity, rejected most rituals and laws as outdated, argued for a form of Judaism without an ethnic dimension, and took a non-Zionist posture.[3] But in L.A., where Jews were unconstrained by the past, an easy eclecticism took hold, based in more congenial peer group structures than in traditional hierarchies. Rabbis mixed old and new, invented and restored, to see what would work, what would attract other Jews, what would bring people into the fold.

As a new generation of pioneer rabbis settled in this outpost of American Jewry, they transformed the prevalent rabbinic image by their flexibility and adaptiveness to the new climate. The older view considered L.A. a desolate place where only desperate circumstances would force a rabbi to settle. Jews used to joke that the only rabbis who were attracted to such a city as Los Angeles—known for its clean air, offbeat society, meager numbers of Jews, and lackluster Jewish religious life—were those with either one lung or two wives. Nevertheless, the arrival of thousands of newcomers every month created enormous opportunities for empire building and changed L.A.'s reputation into an attractive one. Most rabbis who came, however, departed from patterns of rabbinic leadership established in the Northeast. Los Angeles was still a town for the rebellious and outrageous.

Los Angeles's preeminent rabbi, whose unbroken tenure at the city's most prestigious Reform temple gave him enormous prominence within the community, viewed many of the changes brought by newcomers with alarm. He disdained the innovations and eclecticism, the mixture of ethnicity and religion that characterized the newcomers' search for religious roots. A blunt, outspoken man, who personified a type of rabbi rarely found in the northeastern and midwestern centers of Jewish life, Edgar Magnin of the Wilshire Boulevard Temple looked back at the changes since the end of World War II. "This is a different ballgame today," he told reporters; "you've got another Brooklyn here. When I came here, it was Los Angeles." Magnin had more than the Dodgers' franchise in mind. Were the Jewish mores of Brooklyn infesting the palm trees of Los Angeles? The newcomers' persistent and public search for a Jewish identity in the era of ethnic revival irked Magnin. "I see these guys with their yarmulkes eating bacon on their salads at the [Hillcrest Country] club. They want to become more Jewish, whatever that means. It's not religious, it's an ethnic thing. What virtue is there in ethnic emphasis?" he asked. "You know," he concluded, "it's insecurity, the whole thing is insecurity. Roots, roots, roots—baloney!"[4]

Magnin's outrageous and improbable juxtaposition of yarmulkes and bacon spoke to potential contradictions in the newcomers' experimental and eclectic approach. Associating yarmulkes with visibly orthodox, ethnic, east European, and, for Magnin, Brooklyn Jews, he scoffed at the inappropriateness of eating any food in a *tref* (unkosher) country club.[5] But in Los Angeles who possessed the authority to say that such contradictions mattered?

Rabbis with a vision welcomed the challenge of an unformed Jewish community and its religious contradictions. They saw an opportunity to unify Jews and develop a community around a synagogue. Their vision usually included distinctive traditions, which they designed and nurtured. Once they glimpsed the possibilities of shaping their own congregation, they found it hard to leave; they were "built into the bricks," as one rabbi put it. Under these circumstances, the identity of rabbi and congregation gradually merged. "[I have] become too involved with too many people in the life of Temple Isaiah," Rabbi Albert Lewis wrote, trying to explain to Maurice Eisendrath, the head of the Reform Union of American Hebrew Congregations (UAHC) in New York City, why he was turning down a much more prestigious position with a Detroit congregation. "Essentially it is a close-knit group and many of us have been working together for more than five years. We are just now at the fruition of a part of our program as our Temple nears completion. We have laid plans for the future and these people are looking to me to carry them out." The intimacy and commitment, the opportunity to lead people who really cared and who depended upon a spiritual leader, and the potential to shape a meaningful Jewish religious community from scratch tempted young, imaginative, and aggressive men more than did traditional paths of professional mobility in the established communities left behind.[6]

Miami too had the attraction of being practically virgin territory for eager young rabbis. Its promise enticed in particular three who left their strong imprints on the community's religious life. Irving Lehrman, Joseph Narot, and Leon Kronish successfully built distinctive synagogues and crafted a Jewish tradition that spoke to their congregants' rootlessness. Despite their allegiance to different religious ideologies—Narot to Reform, Kronish to a version of Reform that he called Liberal Judaism, and Lehrman to Conservatism—the synagogues they created exhibited surprising similarities. Kronish and Lehrman arrived during the war, a few years after the founding of the congregations they came to lead. They began, as it were, from scratch. Narot came after the war to the oldest, and for many years the only, Reform congregation in Miami. All initiated and oversaw the physical, spiritual, and educational institutions in which to shelter and sustain their congregations.

These three rabbis presided over substantial construction programs, determining thereby the physical appearance of the synagogues and their attached schools and community buildings. All three assiduously pursued members. Kronish organized his temple into "congregational commandos" to enlist unaffiliated Jews. Lehrman regularly carried membership blanks in his pocket, prepared, for example, to sign up new members at a *simha* (a festivity). As membership grew, so did the programs offered by the congregations. That the rabbis were remarkably effective preachers was attested to by the crowds that regularly came to hear them. Each used his pulpit as a base to participate in the wider world of city and national affairs. All three expected to become leaders of American Jewry as had their mentor, Stephen Wise, yet their individual stories reveal widely different values, styles, and outlooks.[7]

Lehrman arrived in Miami in 1943, thirty-two years old and fresh out of rabbinical school. The son of Abraham Lehrman, an Orthodox rabbi, Irving graduated from the high school program of the Orthodox Rabbi Isaac Elchanan Theological Seminary (RIETS) and studied at City College.[8] He married Bella Goldfarb, daughter of a prominent Brooklyn rabbi. Despite the presence of ten generations of rabbis in his family, Lehrman initially decided to go to law school. However, drawn by his father's friendship with the Talmudic scholar Chaim Tchernowitz, Lehrman entered the Jewish Institute of Religion (JIR), the rabbinical school established by the liberal Zionist rabbi Stephen Wise. Wise had designed the Jewish Institute of Religion to train rabbis for all Jews, across the denominational spectrum, but few fully observant Jews studied there. The institute emphasized Zionism and Jewish peoplehood, especially the common ethnic bonds uniting Jews despite their religious and ideological differences, and encouraged in its students an openness to religious innovation and a disregard for denominational labels. Students tended to model themselves on Wise, and like him, they imagined the rabbinate as committed to Zionism, the Jewish people, and social justice. The school's flexibility provided ideal training for pioneering among Jews without religious roots.[9]

Wise's close connections to the Miami Beach Jewish Center brought young Lehrman to the attention of leading men in the congregation who wanted a Conservative rather than an Orthodox synagogue (at least they wanted men and women to sit together). Invited to apply for the position—but only on the condition that he pay his own way down to Miami Beach for the interview—Lehrman agreed to take the gamble. He arrived in August with his wife and two children and never left.[10]

Lehrman rapidly began to shape the congregation. Most of the men came from immigrant Orthodox backgrounds familiar to him. Financial success in business encouraged them to embrace a more modern traditionalism. As observant Jews and accomplished businessmen, they wanted their synagogue to blend Jewish traditionalism and American success. Lehrman decided to steer toward Conservatism, a middle path between his father's Orthodoxy and his liberal rabbinical training, a choice that would be especially acceptable to his congregants. He started the late Friday evening service that had become a hallmark of Conservatism. Earlier the congregation had only held a traditional Friday eve service before the festive Sabbath meal. Now they enjoyed Lehrman's persuasive sermons and a musical service that occurred after dinner, extending the joyful Sabbath spirit. On Shabbat Shuva, the sabbath of return that falls between the High Holidays of Rosh Hashanah and Yom Kippur, he introduced the Conservative prayer book in place of the Orthodox *siddur*. Its more contemporary English translation of the standard prayer service signaled the congregation's new modern posture.[11]

Lehrman's engaging good looks and effective oratory drew one hundred additional members to the center within a few months of his arrival. One early congregant, who grew up in Brooklyn, remembered how she fell in love with him as a young woman. "Pearls came out of his mouth!"[12] Lehrman initiated popular breakfast services for teenagers on Sunday morning in an attempt to foster a peer group community within the synagogue's orbit and to inspire adolescents to become committed Jews. An enthusiastic congregation raised his four thousand dollar salary after two months in appreciation of his unanticipated success.

By the end of the year, Lehrman elicited a commitment from his congregants to build a synagogue north of 14th Street, in the affluent part of Miami Beach where the synagogue's dome would stand out as a religious symbol among the glitter of the hotels.[13] The men of the synagogue, threatened with Lehrman's departure if he did not get his way, pledged $200,000 toward the million dollars needed.

When the war ended and the center unveiled its plans to build a new synagogue, Lehrman came under attack for misguided priorities. How could a synagogue launch a major fund-raising drive at a time when Jewish survivors in the DP camps desperately needed help? Although shaken by the attacks, Lehrman defended the drive. Those who give to build a synagogue would be the same to give to rescue survivors, he argued. One gift did not preclude the other. The sermon was effective, but the controversy reflected the sometimes conflicting pulls of past and future, Europe and Miami Beach, on these pioneering communities. Trying to build anew, they were often seen as self-absorbed and indifferent to the past. The epic struggle for nationhood, by contrast, galvanized Jews in Miami Beach; Zionist rhetoric inspired thousands as well as politicizing and secularizing their faith. Beside such an heroic battle to rescue survivors of the Holocaust languishing in DP camps and bring them to the newborn State of Israel, a drive to build a bigger synagogue paled in comparison. The Miami Beach Jewish Center moved into its impressive new synagogue on Washington Avenue and 17th Street in 1948. Further construction and fund-raising occupied the leadership throughout the 1950s due to the ever-expanding Jewish population and the synagogue's increased membership.

Lehrman's influence could be measured by the constant construction of elegant facilities for worship as well as for festive events and even meetings, or by the crowds that snaked around the block waiting with their tickets to get in to hear him preach on Friday evenings, or by the steadily increasing numbers who joined the synagogue, or by the life tenure awarded him by a deeply grateful congregation—all signs of Lehrman's success in building a Jewish religious community within the brief span of the postwar period.[14] Seeking to establish Judaism in America's popular playground, Lehrman made synagogue life an acceptable leisure activity for Jews in Miami Beach, both residents and regular visitors. After an elegant meal at one of the many restaurants on the Beach, well-dressed congregants strolled over to the synagogue to hear Lehrman preach on topics of the day. Others joined many of the clubs sponsored by the Miami Beach Jewish Center, including a popular little theater group that "included people from all walks of life, rich and poor."[15] Its entertainments extended the synagogue's reach, bringing both secular and religious leisure activity under congregational auspices.

One of Lehrman's most significant innovations concerned the position and education of women within his synagogue. Here Lehrman worked with Bella, his wife, who helped to pioneer a distinctive role for the rabbi's wife beyond her traditional supportive position. Prewar Conservative congregations had taken tentative steps toward expanding the religious participation of women and enhancing the education of girls. Lehrman went further and encouraged his congregants to treat the supplementary Jewish education of their daughters with the same seriousness as that of their sons. If he was going to build anew, he would incorporate the postwar appreciation of women as active workers in all causes and missions. Man's work, even in such a domain as the synagogue, which traditionally excluded women from active participation, was no longer for men alone. Lehrman reminded members that "the Jewish girl of today is the Jewish mother of tomorrow and it is most important that she receive an intensive education." At the beginning of the school year, which corresponded to the start of the Jewish year, Lehrman regularly urged: "Give your children a Jewish education! Do not disinherit them from the wealth of knowledge and tradition that is rightfully theirs!" Education, he noted, offered children "stability by giving them roots!"[16]

Educating girls and boys together implicitly diminished traditional distinctions between the roles of men and women in Judaism. Women played a secondary role in Jewish public religious observance; the home was their religious realm. But intensive education without participation in synagogue ritual suggested empty promises. Though boys continued to outnumber girls in the afternoon Hebrew school, Lehrman moved toward equality of women within the synagogue.[17] In 1952 he instituted a custom of asking the entire congregation to rise on *Simhat Torah* during the Torah reading, in contrast to the usual practice of calling individuals to receive that honor of an *aliyah* (literally, "going up"; that is to read from the Torah). The entire congregation then repeated the blessings said by one given an *aliyah*, and as Lehrman explained, each member should consider himself or herself personally called to the Torah in the Jewish tradition. To his surprise he received a letter of thanks from Bess Gersten for the "thrill" of having been called to the Torah for the first time in her life. Gersten also enclosed a check for fifty dollars, the usual practice upon receiving such an honor.[18]

Later that year the congregation celebrated its first bat mitzvah, a new religious ceremony for girls modeled on the bar mitzvah ritual for boys who reach the age of thirteen. A bat mitzvah recognized the accomplishments of girls in mastering a more intensive educational program by honoring them within the synagogue and inviting them to accept their religious responsibilities as Jewish adults. Among the first to become bat mitzvah was Marjorie Friedland, daughter of the synagogue's president, a major supporter of Lehrman and the center. Despite the encouragement, only a devoted few gave their daughters a bat mitzvah though all parents wanted their sons to become bar mitzvah.[19] The introduction of so radical an innovation occurred as the men leading the congregation debated whether to continue the venerable practice of *shnoddering*, or bidding competitively for the honor of an *aliyah*.[20] Thus, old and new, tradition and innovation, coexisted at the center.

Lehrman wanted his congregants to pray, to *daven*, to become intoxicated with Judaism. He wanted them to embrace a personal spirituality. He started a junior congregation run by children at the school, in which "the girls, too, have an opportunity to participate." He admitted that he was "envious" of the thirty thousand young Christians who turned out for a Miami revival meeting of Billy Graham's Youth for Christ movement "to participate in a most moving demonstration of prayer." Lehrman compared Graham's movement to "our synagogue youth organizations...our young people who are given all sorts of lectures and forums and discussion groups—everything except good old-fashioned prayer." Despite the attraction of Protestant evangelicalism, Lehrman stopped short of transforming his congregation into a center of fundamentalist fervor. Crowds of four thousand on the High Holidays was his limit. Yet his recognition of a deep need for Jews to find meaning in a Judaism that spoke to them as individuals, comparable to the personal spirituality of Protestant evangelicalism, suggests how attuned he was to what might motivate his fellow permanent tourists in Miami Beach.[21]

If he eschewed a crusading pietism, he and Bella did try to teach congregants the art of Jewish living. They sought, that is, to instruct women in the kind of experiential spirituality associated in the past with the woman's role in Judaism. Through women they hoped to spiritualize the entire family. By the 1950s it was apparent that mothers, previously responsible for home ritual, no longer knew what to do. Somehow—perhaps through neglect or disinterest, perhaps as a result of migration—women had lost the skills to celebrate home rituals. The pious home had all but vanished in this city by the sea. Prodded by the rabbi and his wife, the religious school PTA and synagogue sisterhood sponsored workshops explaining how to observe holidays at home. The workshops demonstrated how to set the table, what food to cook, what blessings to say. Women learned by actually doing. The workshops began with the Hanukkah holiday with its focus on children, but soon expanded to include Pesach (Passover), with its elaborate home seder ritual, and Rosh Hashanah.[22]

Bella Lehrman introduced into the center a novel and entrepreneurial institution: the sisterhood gift shop. The gift shop addressed simultaneously several congregational needs: It provided a steady source of income for the synagogue; it made available ritual objects not easily purchased in Miami; and it helped to link the congregation's younger and older married women. It encouraged as well the development of the women's business skills because running the gift shop required knowledge of purchasing, bookkeeping, and merchandising. Since very few married women worked in an era that promoted women's domestic nature and role and many had maids to help take care of housework, the gift shop provided a rare workplace outside the home for their entrepreneurial energies and skills. Many Jewish women actively sought such volunteer work.[23]

The women running the gift shop sold merchandise that they thought would appeal to other women, their target audience, as the chief purchaser for the household, but they also tried to expand their customers' repertoire of ritual objects. Jews do not actually need all of the ceremonial objects that they possess, although many reflect a desire to beautify ritual activity. Most of the required items—like *tallit*, the prayer shawl, and *tefillin*, the small leather boxes holding scriptural inscriptions that are strapped with thongs to the forehead and arm—belong in the almost exclusive domain of men. The gift shop encouraged Jewish women to change their attitude toward ritual objects, to see them as decorative, functional, and experiential. Women were invited to explore a world of possibilities opened up by postwar affluence, to beautify their homes with Jewish symbols. A pair of silver candlesticks, for example, might decorate a mantlepiece during the week, hold a pair of candles, and even stimulate a woman to kindle and bless the sabbath lights. The shop enhanced the art of living Jewishly even as it contributed to the buying and selling of Jewish culture.[24]

The shop highlighted the commonality of Jews, a people with its own crafts and decorative arts. It became a means to showcase Israeli ceremonial and art objects, linking Israel to American Jews by encouraging women to consume these products of the new Jewish state. Like a miniature museum, the shop displayed artifacts of Jewish culture. Visitors to the shop implicitly learned that Judaism concerned itself with aesthetic issues. The shop's location within the synagogue symbolically placed a religious seal of approval upon its contents. For some a gift shop visit became part of a ritual associated with the synagogue or with shepherding children to religious school. A purchase satisfied both the customer and individual who received the present, creating a Jewish network linking them with the synagogue. The profit from sales contributed to a worthwhile congregational endeavor, such as the synagogue library.

The shop began, as did the workshops, with Hanukkah and bar mitzvah, offering gifts of toys, books, and records for children, jewelry from Israel, and items to decorate the house.[25]

It soon expanded to include bride's Bibles and kiddush cups for weddings, tie clips and ID bracelets for bar mitzvahs, Israeli menorahs and art objects, and cookbooks for the housewife. By the late 1950s the gift shop contained such elegant items for the home as sterling silver trays, candy dishes, and Israeli coffee spoons that had merely tangetial Jewish symbolic significance. In addition, it included specialized ritual objects used only by more observant Jews, like silver spice boxes for the *havdala* ceremony marking the end of the sabbath and matzo covers for Pesach. With an eye on the ornamental, women also bought mezuzot, small cases holding scriptural inscriptions that are placed on door lintels to fulfill a religious commandment, and spice boxes to decorate their home. But the shop never became exclusive in its merchandise and continued to carry such American inventions as Jewish New Year's greeting cards and personalized Bar Mitzvah napkins. The wide range of items available for purchase, in terms of cost, quality, and religious culture, suggested the diversity of commercial Jewish symbols and the eclecticism of popular piety. Although not an exclusive feature of the Miami Beach Jewish Center, the sisterhood gift shop found a broad audience in this innovative and adaptable community because it offered types of portable, symbolic insignia of roots that newcomers welcomed.[26]

A year after Lehrman found his place in the sun, Leon Kronish and his wife, Lillian, arrived in the "spiritual wilderness" of Miami Beach. A New York native like Lehrman, Kronish also graduated from JIR. Unlike Lehrman, neither he nor his wife came from a rabbinical family, although like Bella, Lillian was a college graduate. Without the pull of parental orthodoxy, Kronish moved easily toward liberalism, not conservatism. When he came to the Beth Sholom Center, it had perhaps forty members in good standing. The fledgling synagogue had been established only three years earlier, and despite its name, which meant "house of peace," it was weakened by internal conflict. The handful of founding members, like those of the Miami Beach Jewish Center, thought, but could not agree, to have an Orthodox-Conservative congregation. They hired Kronish in the summer of 1944, and by the fall he was telling the first general congregational meeting of the new year that they were "a Modern Conservative Jewish organization."[27]

Like Lehrman, Kronish immediately made an impact upon the congregation. A tall, handsome man and a persuasive speaker with a good sense of humor—he often began his sermons with a joke—Kronish rapidly attracted followers. He regularly greeted each congregant after services and quickly learned the names of all. Within a few months one hundred new members joined—the new rabbi actively solicited them—and by the spring Kronish was encouraging the board to give the center a more specifically religious name.[28] With the change from Beth Sholom Center to Temple Beth Sholom came a commitment to become a "liberal congregation" that would guarantee freedom of the pulpit.[29] The congregation minutes suggest that Kronish desired to follow his mentor Stephen Wise's path to Reform Judaism, accompanied by a strong commitment to Zionism, Jewish peoplehood, and social justice. During the summer Kronish returned to New York City, charged by the temple's religious committee with purchasing prayer books published by the Reform UAHC. Despite the decision to become a liberal congregation, members continued to quarrel over whether that actually meant what the label *Reform* implied. Many associated *Reform* not with liberalism, social justice, and openness but with elitism, non-Zionism, and a religious service devoid of Hebrew that resembled high-church Protestantism with its organ music, strict rules of decorum, and formal quality of worship.[30]

The issue of denominational labels irritated Temple Beth Sholom throughout the 1940s.

Although Kronish urged the board to affiliate with the UAHC, several men resisted the stigma associated with *Reform*.[31] They preferred *liberal* because it lacked the ideological freight associated with *Reform*, especially Reform's long opposition to Zionism and the establishment of a Jewish state, a position that had changed only under the pressures of World War II. Kronish, however, carried his congregation into the Reform Union.[32] When issues arose that might have aligned Temple Beth Sholom with more Conservative practices—such as how many days of a Jewish holiday to observe—Kronish persuaded the board to follow Reform custom, though he rarely justified his argument by referring to Reform authority.[33] By the 1950s, once the hurdle of affiliation was overcome, Kronish pointedly referred to Temple Beth Sholom as a liberal congregation, not a Reform one, since he, too, disliked Reform's lukewarm support of Israel.

Kronish gradually began to give both form and substance to *liberal* through the Friday night and Sabbath services and an extensive educational program. The late Friday eve services were largely in English, accompanied by an organ and dominated by the sermon. After the crowds departed, Kronish and his family, often with a few of his devoted followers, would go to Juniors Restaurant, located on Collins Avenue not far from the Temple, to discuss the sermon, an indication of the vigorous debate and enthusiasm generated by the young rabbi. Saturday mornings Kronish reserved for a more traditional service that included the weekly reading of several chapters of the Torah as well as a sermon, or *d'var Torah*, designed to explain some aspect of sacred scriptures; he also used more Hebrew prayers in that service. The congregation left the decision regarding the wearing of prayer shawls up to individuals but insisted that anyone ascending the pulpit for the honor of an *aliyah* don one.[34]

Kronish started to experiment with the religious content of such holiday services as Shavuot, which celebrates the time when the Israelites received the Torah from God at Mount Sinai, and Purim, which commemorates the Jews' rescue from an antisemitic pogrom. For Shavuot, he wrote a cantata on the theme of Israel Reborn; for Purim he crafted a new megillah, that is, he retold the story found in the biblical Book of Esther in a modern idiom. Kronish also experimented with the popular holiday of Hanukkah, writing a poetic dramalogue. Touched by the positive response to his innovations, he thanked his congregants for their "understanding spirit which makes possible these creative experiments in religious worship." Many of the men leading Temple Beth Sholom were second-generation Jews, familiar with religious changes introduced by Conservatism during the interwar years. Thus they accepted the young rabbi's innovations and supported his efforts to develop "a dynamic ritual that is traditional in spirit, rich in Jewish warmth, and liberal in form." Kronish wanted to create a new *minhag*, or rites, for American Jews, that would be the substance of a religious ritual "that would win the hearts of the masses." Miami Beach, with its cross section of Jews drawn from all corners of the United States, provided an ideal setting for such an ambitious national endeavor. Kronish rapidly filled the temple to capacity, supervised a successful building expansion program, and received recognition from the Miami Jewish community.[35]

Given his articulate and self-conscious religious liberalism, Kronish moved openly and rapidly to enhance the status of women within the congregation. He instituted some innovations even a few years before Lehrman did. Although an early proposal that women be guaranteed places on the board of directors did not change the congregation's governance, Kronish announced in 1948 a special bat mitzvah class. "Mothers are the cornerstone of the Jewish family," he explained. "Women, too, are becoming more prominent in Jewish community life. To provide intelligent leadership and to equip our girls for these responsibilities, we are instituting this year a special BAS MITZVAH program" with a newly designed ceremony. The following year, when members complained about the presence of women on the pulpit during the High Holidays, he recommended that they enroll in his adult education classes to learn the reasons behind Beth Sholom's practices.[36]

Lillian Kronish, like Bella Lehrman, introduced a sisterhood gift shop and holiday workshops. The gift shop started in 1947 with presents appropriate for bar mitzvahs, weddings, holidays, and, of course, Hanukkah. "Gracious Living Means Giving," the sisterhood advertised. "Make it a habit to choose your gifts at the Sisterhood Gift Shop." The shop was open daily from nine to five and on Sunday mornings when children came to school. Holiday workshops began the same year. The rabbi helped guide families in planning their own home seder for the second night of Pesach, following the congregational seder on the first night. He urged members to "make Passover an unforgettable experience, a joyous experience, a family get-together. Children will subconsiously know that God and Israel, freedom and family joy are all one." Herein lay the true art of Jewish living, an experience that was joyous, spiritual, homey, and aesthetically appealing.[37]

Kronish practiced what he preached. "Undoubtedly, the most lasting legacy that I have from my father, the educator, is that Jewish education begins in the home," recalled his daughter. In describing her childhood home, Maxine Kronish Snyder portrayed the art of Jewish living that the rabbi and his wife tried to inspire in their congregants. "The walls, with the Jewish art and books, convey Jewish learning and Jewish feeling; the music on the stereo is Jewish, and it has helped link us to our roots in Europe and Israel," she wrote; "the conversations at the Shabbat and holiday meals are experientially Jewish, and they helped us keep Judaism, Israel, and especially Jerusalem, uppermost in our minds; the kitchen"— not a kosher one but Jewish nonetheless, "where my mother has always been in charge—is intensely Jewish, not just in its delicious foods and smells, but also in its human atmosphere, brimming with caring, concern and sensitivity." This vision of the Jewish home as the source of Jewish spirituality animated efforts to educate Jewish women. Maxine considered herself "fortunate" to have been able "to learn and experience" as she grew up "the power and value of a Jewish education that is centered in an intensely Jewish home."[38]

Given the similarities of the synagogues that Lehrman and Kronish built—of Temple Emanu-El (the more religious name adopted by the Miami Beach Jewish Center in 1954) and Temple Beth Sholom—wherein lay the differences? Jews living on Miami Beach during the 1950s used to point to the fact that worshipers needed a ticket to attend Friday night services at Temple Emanu-El whereas they could just walk in to the services at Temple Beth Sholom. Indeed, Beth Sholom made a commitment to such democratic practices part of its creed. An early membership brochure affirmed: "We demand that [the synagogue] be Democratic. That means an equitable dues system."[39] It also meant no financial barriers to membership, no assigned pews, and no tuition fees. Temple Beth Sholom's modern low-profile brick buildings, recessed from the street, physically expressed similar liberal democratic sentiments and presented a contrast with the tall, elegantly appointed buildings of Temple Emanu-El, especially its multistoried, domed synagogue that sat diagonally at the corner intersection.

The Jewish religious ideals of the congregations also differed, reflecting their rabbis' perspective. In 1948 Temple Beth Sholom published in its bulletin a definition of a good

Jew. Such a person was impatient with the sociopolitical ills plaguing society and eagerly sought remedies for them. The definition assumed both marriage and family because it listed educating one's children Jewishly as part of being a good Jew. The good Jew was seen to respond to the needs of his people, read Jewish books, and not be demoralized by antisemitism. Such a Jew is intelligently Jewish, affiliates with a synagogue, and has self-knowledge. Compare this to the Miami Beach Jewish Center's checklist for Jewish adults published in 1951. Its minimum rating scale of Jewish practice included a "fair knowledge" of synagogue ritual, familiarity with the background of Jewish observances, knowledge of general Jewish history, a "working knowledge" of Hebrew, and familiarity with Jewish music. A Jewish adult with this background ideally attends every sabbath service he can, enrolls his children in a Jewish school, reads at least five books of Jewish content each year, and fluently expresses ideas about Judaism. Finally, a Jew should both know and recite the kiddush and blessing for his children each sabbath eve. The concern with specific Jewish knowledge and ritual behavior versus liberal values and general Jewish commitment in part distinguished Conservatism from liberalism in postwar Miami.[40]

Despite these differences, not to mention those of style and temperament, Lehrman and Kronish had more in common with each other, especially their strong Zionist commitment to Israel, than they did with the third influential Miami rabbi, Joseph Narot. Ironically, Kronish and Narot joined the Reform rabbinical association, and both led congregations affiliated with the UAHC. Yet the two stood poles apart on many of the most important issues facing American Jews.

Narot came to Miami in 1950 at the age of thirty-seven with ten years of experience as a rabbi of a Reform congregation in Atlantic City. Born in a small town near Vilna, Lithuania, Narot grew up in poverty in Warren, Ohio. He received a traditional Jewish education from his Orthodox parents. In 1969 Narot looked back upon his life in an extraordinary sermon, a personal confession rarely made by rabbis before their congregants. The sermon revealed some of the motives driving these pioneering rabbis. Surveying the rows upon rows of over four thousand congregants gathered in the Miami Beach Convention Center on the eve of Rosh Hashanah, Narot began to preach.[41] "Where shall I begin?" he asked, addressing the thousands sitting before him. What have I learned from my life? "My parents never left the old world—spiritually speaking. They always referred to Europe as 'home'—'in der haym.' For that reason I thought that the gap between them and me was due to culture and language," he admitted. "Years later, when I confronted my own children, I learned how mistaken I had been." Narot rebelled against his father and his father's Orthodoxy. When he was eighteen, he discovered Reform Judaism and "took to it with the zeal of the convert." This zeal never abated. "Reform's fervor for social justice, its loyalty to all knowledge and experience, its readiness to innovate and modify, its faith in reason, filled my imagination."

But Narot confessed to more than a fervent devotion to Reform. He acknowledged as well that the Reform rabbinate promised a poor boy a way out of Warren and a chance to earn a decent livelihood. Narot characterized himself as "a self-made man," a vision that drew upon American frontier imagery but discarded any notion of tradition handed down through the generations, a notion that was critical to Jewish continuity and that Jews usually assumed animated their rabbis. Yet in Miami, a city without traditions and roots, Narot's vision of self-creation hardly outraged his congregants. Perhaps more shocking, he admitted learning "that a man can never get enough money. There is no end to the wanting of things." He confessed, too, "in my secret depths I have yearned to be the world-renowned rabbi and have even envied the acclaim which other colleagues seem to get." Such ambitions, appropriate to secular newcomers, rarely came from a rabbi. Narot's decision to confess his eagerness for fame and fortune, measured by conventional standards, set him apart from his northeastern and midwestern peers, who often championed learning, piety, communal service, and spiritual sacrifice as their motivation for serving in the rabbinate.

As the oldest and most prestigious Reform congregation in Miami, Temple Israel did not suffer from the chaotic conditions of newness faced by Lehrman and Kronish. When Narot arrived to take the pulpit there, he could build upon a solid base, and build he did. Like Lehrman and Kronish, Narot was a handsome man. (Good looks appeared to be a requisite for the Miami rabbinate; it certainly helped attract congregants). Narot expanded the Temple's membership, constructed new school buildings, and attracted increased attendance at Friday evening services—the main sabbath services for Reform congregations. He also strengthened Temple Israel's position as the representative Jewish institution to Miami's Christian religious world. Though in perhaps less dramatic fashion than the congregations on the Beach, Temple Israel grew rapidly under Narot despite heavy membership turnover typical of established synagogues. Measured by the same criteria of numbers, buildings, attendance, congregational support, and communal recognition used to gauge Lehrman's and Kronish's achievement, Narot's success was considerable.[42]

But Narot did not change the position of women or the education of girls. Temple Israel fixed minimal educational requirements of several hours once a week for both boys and girls that Narot considered appropriate. He steadfastly opposed using Jews' desire to see their sons become bar mitzvah as a means of encouraging them to give their children more Jewish education, and he attacked this process sharply, ridiculing such synagogue schools as bar mitzvah "factories." Similarly, the radically reduced home rituals of Reform, consisting of a festive meal on the High Holidays and, occasionally, Hanukkah celebrations, sufficed. There were no workshops in the art of Jewish living. Narot urged, instead, making attendance at Friday night services a "fashionable" weekly activity.[43]

Narot managed to leave his stamp upon the synagogue, a more formidable task than that faced by his Miami Beach peers since Temple Israel had a number of local traditions from its previous quarter century.[44] He adamantly adhered to the radical teachings of classic Reform Judaism, especially its rejection of religious ritual and Jewish law, its emphasis upon ethics and the primacy of belief in monotheism, its non-Zionism and lukewarm acceptance of Israel, and its opposition to Jewish ethnicity associated with the idea of Jewish peoplehood. He resisted congregants' efforts to give centrality to bar mitzvah, relegating Hebrew instruction to voluntary weekday classes. He also insisted that such religious symbols as prayer shawls and head covering for men be eliminated as they were in classic Reform temples. Finally, Narot championed the right of Reform Jews not to observe more than one day of each Jewish holiday, since classic Reform had eliminated the traditional second day. In sermons and in printed "letters to my congregation," Narot explained the modern vision of Reform Judaism, its rational religious message, its aesthetic and ethical ideals. Some members thought he apologized for Reform Judaism too much and that he was forever rejecting his own non-Reform origins. But perhaps this psychological spur gave his personal charisma its attractive edge.[45]

This hint of insecurity suggested the drive of the self-selected pioneer to carve out his own domain. Narot's passion for radical Reform was integral to his leadership. He could not take his faith for granted but abrasively and defensively wore it on his sleeve. When he went to the racetrack on Saturday—an unusual Shabbat activity for a Reform rabbi—he defended his sport as legitimate: "Relaxation and recreation must…be part of our Sabbath regimen, along with study, prayer, and synagogue attendance."[46] Indeed, his demand that congregants choose Reform as he had chosen it identified him as akin to Lehrman or Kronish in his desire to found a distinctive congregation in his own image.

In the mid-1960s Narot invited a well-known sociologist to survey Temple Israel's Sunday School, Miami's largest.[47] The survey delineated the Jewish values held by the students. Most essential, they said, was a belief in God, in order to be "a good Jew." This emphasis upon belief in God contrasted with the values encouraged by Kronish, who stressed the pursuit of social justice as critical, or by Lehrman, who focused on observing Jewish religious ritual. Neither Kronish's nor Lehrman's congregation bothered to include belief in God as part of their definition of a good Jew. Narot's students, however, learned effectively his interpretation of Judaism, for following their faith statement was an affirmation of identity, that is, accepting oneself as a Jew and not trying to hide one's Jewishness. The students ranked worshiping God, knowing the fundamentals of Judaism, attending services on the High Holidays, and leading an ethical life after these two fundamentals of being a good Jew. Over half thought it essential to gain the respect of their Christian neighbors, thus exhibiting Jews' traditional concern with their Christian neighbors' attitudes toward them. Other issues so central to the congregations of Kronish and Lehrman, including support for Israel, synagogue membership, contributions to Jewish philanthropies, efforts in behalf of equality for all minority groups, and marriage "within the Jewish faith" received recognition as desirable but not essential.

Like the programmatic statements of the two Miami Beach congregations, this list faithfully reflects Narot's concerns and the values of radical Reform. Its focus on belief in God and one's social identity as a Jew, coupled with concern for basic Jewish beliefs and how Jews appeared before their Christian neighbors, indicates Temple Israel's distinctiveness in Miami.

Narot's dedication to Reform, Kronish's commitment to liberal Judaism, and Lehrman's attachment to Conservatism set these three rabbis apart, but their extraordinary ambition, drive, and success in the business of the rabbinate united them. They understood implicity that in a town of rootless Jews, a rabbi had to be a showman to draw crowds into his synagogue. He had to offer Jews a social as well as a religious identity, political values as well as moral ones. They shared a similar vision of the place of the synagogue in Jewish life: It was a broad, all-encompassing, representative Jewish institution. And despite their different interpretations of Judaism, they imagined religion as spiritual recreation, an opportunity to enjoy learning and working together, men and women, boys and girls, the ideal complement to Miami's leisure lifestyle. These values distinguished them from many of their fellow rabbis but linked them with the characteristic rabbinic figures of Los Angeles.

Edgar Magnin, Los Angeles's leading rabbi for over half a century, was perhaps prototypical of the pioneer American rabbi. Born and raised in San Francisco, Magnin attended the University of Cincinnati and Hebrew Union College (HUC). Like Narot, he saw the rabbinate as a vehicle for social mobility; he wanted to be a Reform rabbi because "the class of people were more refined." Unlike Narot, Magnin inclined toward tradition and away from classic Reform. When Magnin came to Los Angeles in 1920 as rabbi of the city's leading Reform congregation, he opposed changing the Jewish sabbath to Sunday, an action that had been championed by several leading classical Reform rabbis. He consistently leaned toward Conservatism in the context of Reform and thus reintroduced abandoned traditions. Magnin restored the bar mitzvah ritual that classic Reform had rejected in favor of a new ceremony of confirmation and reinstituted blowing the shofar rather than a trumpet on the High Holidays.[48]

Magnin built an impressive sphere of influence for himself. He oversaw the construction of an imposing new synagogue building with "proportions like a theater" on a prestigious site on Wilshire Boulevard, and he urged his congregation to change its name to the Wilshire Boulevard Temple. "I wanted people to know the location," he remarked. He socialized with his wealthy congregants, joining the Hillcrest Country Club at a time when no other rabbis were members in pursuit of the power and influence he needed to build his synagogue and its importance. A large, gregarious man who spoke colloquially, Magnin symbolized the rabbinate in Los Angeles for many years; most non-Jews knew of no other. Neal Gabler dubbed him "rabbi to the stars."[49]

Magnin spoke bluntly about his own singular accomplishment: over fifty years in one pulpit at a prestigious synagogue. His self-assessment and perspective offer insight into the values of pioneer rabbis and their contrast to prevalent American rabbinic norms. Magnin castigated the misplaced rabbinic agenda of the eastern establishment. At annual national meetings, he felt, rabbis discussed silly things like theology or Jewish survival rather than talking about the purpose of the rabbinate or how to succeed in religion, which was, to Magnin's way of thinking, a business like lawyering. When Jews go to a synagogue service, he explained, "they must come out touched. If they don't come out laughing or crying, then there's something wrong." He elaborated: "You should go *away* with some *feeling* of lift and some feeling of 'I'm glad I'm a Jew. There is something to life, some meaning.'" The rabbi produced this effect through his preaching. Magnin, who taught homiletics, saw the rabbinate as "a leadership job." It was his duty to inspire his congregants and give them pride in their Judaism, not to make pronouncements. He disdained those eastern "rabbis who compare themselves to prophets" as "idiots and phonies" and much preferred his own pioneering type of rabbi, who enjoyed the good life. Prophets, after all, "never received a salary, they never had a pension, they never lived in nice homes, they never ate at Perinos or the Bistro out in Beverly Hills."[50] Nor, one might add, did they ever go to racetracks.

Magnin's pragmatic and personal approach to the rabbinate did not preclude a commitment to more intensive and advanced Jewish education or to a more experiential form of Judaism than had traditionally been available in Reform. In 1954 he criticized Reform's tendency to become static and its failure to make demands upon its adherents. Under his guidance Wilshire Boulevard Temple continued to grow and to make new demands upon its members, especially its youth.[51] In the two most significant developments—the College of Jewish Studies and Camp Hess Kramer—Magnin recognized and encouraged the vision of another Reform rabbi eager to draw uprooted Jews into a community around the congregation, Alfred Wolf.

Wolf had come to Los Angeles in 1946 to organize the West Coast Region of the UAHC and collaborated with Magnin and other Reform rabbis in establishing the College of Jewish Studies, which was aimed at Reform Sunday School teachers and interested adults. In 1949 Magnin encouraged Wolf to initiate a camping program under Wilshire Boulevard Temple auspices. Wolf first discovered camping as a teenager in Nazi Germany. "Called upon to organize Jewish youth groups in Heidelberg," he reflected, "I realized how much of Jewish values I could get across to young people as we were hiking or camping together under the open sky." Exposure to American Protestant church groups' use of camp meetings confirmed Wolf's convictions that Jews could learn from them. That fall Wolf presented his idea for "camping in the spirit of Reform Judaism" to the temple's men's club. The men agreed to sponsor the program.[52]

While well established prior to World War II as a Jewish summer activity, camping under specifically religious auspices—especially sponsored by a synagogue—was a new, postwar innovation. Wolf recalled that "there was no tradition then of any temple activity after Confirmation."[53] Even a temple leader like J. Robert Arkush, head of the men's club and a supporter of the camp project, had difficulty convincing his daughter to go. Once the teenagers got to the primitive campsite in the Pacific Palisades, however, they discovered the friendship and closeness camp could engender. Their enthusiasm for camping convinced several temple members to provide their children with a decent campsite.

The decision to purchase property for a camp revealed a serious rift between those who saw religious school as ideal for Jewish youth and camp as a commercial gimmick and those who considered Sunday School ineffective and camp as an inspiring Jewish communal alternative. Wolf tried to mediate by suggesting that camp and school could complement each other. School provided "periodic religious reminders in an otherwise secular week" while camp represented the integration of Jewish "religious principles and practices with daily living."[54] It also allowed teenagers to remain connected with the temple after confirmation and it strengthened loyalty to Reform institutions. Despite lack of enthusiasm among some members, an absence of qualified camp directors, and the problem of time for supervision by the rabbis, the men's club directors in 1951 voted to purchase a campsite. The following year Camp Hess Kramer opened on 110 acres in Ventura County.

Magnin never spent a night at camp—he was a "Waldorf Astoria camper"—but he supported the venture. He thought that the camp provided an ideal setting to cultivate religious feelings. Several hundred campers and their counselors experienced Judaism within a surrogate home. "You can give the kids all the tools in the Religious School that you want," an early camping convert argued. "But until they actually have an opportunity to live what they've learned, they just don't get the relationship, they don't get the values. At Camp the kids *live* the Sabbath and they find out it works."[55] Some were inspired to participate more actively in temple educational activities and to exercise youth leadership after their camp experience. Occasionally individuals recruited for positions in camp moved over to full-time employment at the temple as youth directors, teachers, and even cantors. Camp also offered a venue for year-round conferences. Its separate incorporation as a temple subsidiary allowed it to initiate community projects that asserted Reform Judaism's importance in Los Angeles. In 1953 the camp started its annual interracial and inter-religious weekend conference on human relations for university students and faculty. Camp Hess Kramer brought influence, personnel, leadership, and, of course, members to Wilshire Boulevard Temple.[56] Its creation expanded the synagogue's orbit as it taught youth how to be Jewish. Like gift shops and holiday workshops, summer camping under synagogue auspices sought to fill space left by absent religious traditions in Miami and L.A.

Facing the disruptive effects of migration, admitting the absence of a "natural" public Jewish environment in Los Angeles, and unable to depend upon transmission of a pattern of Jewish living by newcomers to their children, ambitious and pragmatic rabbis, eager to experiment, initiated novel programs to fit needs of potential members. On the way they built their own distinctive congregations, establishing their sphere of influence. They borrowed the idea of summer camps from youth leaders in Y's, community centers, and settlement houses, from innovative Jewish educators, from Zionists, Socialists, and Communists in order to nurture and incorporate their own youthful elite.[57] Camping under synagogue sponsorship would show Jews how to live as religious Jews by giving them at least a minimum ritual competence and allowing them to enjoy a Jewish spirituality. It would imbue youngsters with loyalty toward their brand of Judaism, a loyalty that might even extend beyond devotion to "their" rabbi. Though a rabbi like Magnin preferred Judaism without any Jewish ethnicity, camping inevitably introduced elements of shared sociability associated with a sense of family, belonging, and peoplehood.

Wolf's success in carving out his own domain under the institutional umbrella of Temple Wilshire was unusual—a tribute both to his and Magnin's abilities. Magnin's willingness to share his power was exceptional. More often, an ambitious rabbi coming to Los Angeles built his own synagogue and imprinted his personality on the institution. As did their peers in Miami, most Los Angeles rabbis yoked their congregations to a national denominational movement. A few tried to promote what they considered to be a unique Los Angeles vision.[58] "Since its inception the Valley Jewish Community Center has refused to adopt any label other than that of 'Jewish,'" proclaimed its rabbi, Sidney Goldstein. A graduate of the Jewish Institute of Religion, Goldstein championed an inclusive vision for the center. "Its services are traditional yet liberal and its program is many faceted. It seeks to serve all the Jews in the Valley." But most rabbis did not follow his lead. Goldstein himself left the center less than six months later after fighting with members who disputed the substance of his sermons and disagreed with his interpretation of the rabbi's prophetic role.[59]

Deciding to throw "its lot in with the Conservative Movement" and to reject a nondenominational vision, the center board recognized that "naturally, there are many in our midst who do not know what Conservatism represents.... This confusion exists in many parts of the country but reaches its acme here on the West Coast." The board solved its dilemma by employing a new rabbi, Aaron Wise. In those years "they accepted whatever I recommended and whatever I did because I was their spiritual leader," Wise recalled.[60] Not only did Wise oversee all of the details of building a congregation, but he also linked his efforts and the resources of the Valley Jewish Community Center (VJCC) to the growth of Conservative institutions in Los Angeles, specifically the fledgling University of Judaism. Less than three months after he arrived, Wise praised plans announced by the Conservative Jewish Theological Seminary (JTS) to establish a branch in Los Angeles. "We who have faith that the Jewry of Southern California has a great future are reassured by the Seminary's program," he told his congregants. "Not only will we become a great physical center for Jewish life but also a spiritual and cultural center." Even before his formal installation, the board voted unanimously to support the seminary. As Kronish had affiliated with the Reform UAHC in Miami, so Wise supported the University of Judaism in Los Angeles. He grabbed hold of the national movement to clarify the center's identity as a Conservative synagogue.[61]

Wise discovered California in 1945 when he spent a summer in Santa Barbara as a civilian chaplain. He came to the Valley Jewish Community Center with his wife, Miriam, and children in the summer of 1947 at the age of thirty-four because he wanted to work with his own peers, congregants who "were my age, and not the age of my parents and grandparents."[62] The center had almost ten years of history when Wise arrived. As the first congregation in the San Fernando Valley, it was ideally situated to benefit from the large numbers of Jews finding new homes there. The center also attracted Jews who worked in the motion picture industry. Their impact registered most visibly in the center's music program. However, despite a membership of approximately three hundred, the center was located on a dead-end street in a modest building. Like the Miami Beach Jewish Center, the Valley Jewish Community Center possessed unrealized potential.

Wise quickly began to shape the center into a Conservative synagogue, koshering the kitchen and insisting that men cover their heads during worship. He started regular Sabbath morning services and required all bar mitzvah and confirmation candidates to attend. After the short (one hour), largely English service, Wise told stories drawn from Jewish folklore. Soon membership began to grow. Like his Miami peers, Wise rapidly achieved success. By 1958 the center had the reputation of being *the* synagogue in the Valley; so many had joined that, with a surplus of funds, it temporarily closed membership. Wise used the center's bulletin to reach out to and educate members, supplementing its schedule of events and personal notices with didactic messages. "A cardinal tenet of our faith is Zionism, and its hope for the rebirth of the Jewish people on its own soil, for the renascence of Hebrew culture and art," he wrote on one occasion. Conservatism, he explained, respects Reform for its innovation and is drawn to the tradition of Orthodoxy, but it loves America. "In this, of all nations on earth, we are native-born: for American democracy is in a profound sense the child of the Judaic tradition."[63]

Yet Wise recognized that the Judaic tradition had "faded from the lives of most" of his congregants. "You would expect that an individual Jew, a father, a grandfather, would belong to a synagogue and have so much to communicate to his children, his own family in the home. But most of that is lost now," he reflected. Wise suggested compensating for the absence of a male Judaic heritage by expanding women's religious education. These innovations resembled those introduced by Lehrman and Kronish in Miami. Like them, Wise relied on his wife to develop new roles for women. Before the first Hanukkah, Aaron and Miriam Wise started a "novel book and gift shop service" under sisterhood supervision. Among the initial items offered for sale were mezuzahs and Magen Davids—six-pointed Jewish stars—as well as Hanukkah gifts and books for children and adults. A year later the merchandise included a larger array of ceremonial objects, such as yarmulkes, *tallithim* (prayer shawls), candlesticks, menorahs, and *yarzeit* (annual memorial) bulbs to honor the dead, along with games, Bible coloring books and statuttes. A poster promoting the shop proclaimed "Make your Jewish home beautiful."[64]

The sisterhood continued to expand the possibilities of making a Jewish home beautiful. Upon completion of construction of a new synagogue building with its stained glass windows by Mischa Kallis, an artist working for Universal Pictures, the sisterhood transferred the design of the stained glass windows to plates. These they offered for sale, inviting members to decorate their homes with the beauty—and, implicitly, the spirituality—of the synagogue by purchasing the dishes. In 1948 the sisterhood introduced a competitive note by sponsoring a contest for the most beautiful Hanukkah home decorations. Over sixty families participated. By 1949 it was clear that these measures were insufficient. Recognizing "a definite need in our Jewish homes to know how to celebrate Hanukkah," the sisterhood initiated a workshop. Over ninety women came to learn how to cook *latkes*, sing songs and blessings, and decorate their homes while they heard the story of the Maccabees and discovered the holiday's contemporary meaning. One workshop's success led to another one for Rosh Hashanah so that members wouldn't feel lost on the

"Days of Awe." This workshop, a joint venture of PTA and the sisterhood, included model table settings, explanations of prayers, the design and creation of New Year's greeting cards, and even a skit on High Holiday etiquette. These activities bespoke a determined effort by Aaron and Miriam Wise to create among their congregants a distinctive Jewish lifestyle in a place where such natural rhythms of Jewish living were not part of the landscape.[65]

Wise encountered more difficulty convincing members to give their daughters an intensive religious education. The year he arrived, only one girl out of forty-five students attened Hebrew school. The following year saw little improvement: four out of sixty-two students were female. In 1950 Wise introduced a bat mitzvah program for the four girls. That June, on a Friday night, Connie Chais became the center's first bat mitzvah. The daughter of Zionist activists George and Ruth Chais, Connie read some prayers and spoke on the founder of Hadassah, Henrietta Szold. Although the bulletin noted that "the equality of women in Jewish religious life has been emphasized," the Friday night bat mitzvah ritual hardly approached equality with a sabbath morning bar mitzvah. Wise soon closed the gap by calling women to the Torah during sabbath morning services—as is done for a bar mitzvah—giving them the honor of an *aliyah* in recognition of their learning how to read from the Torah scrolls.[66]

Miriam Wise took bolder and more innovative steps to encourage women's equality within the synagogue. Like her Miami peers, she had received an advanced Jewish and secular education. Like them, she consciously positioned herself as an authoritative model for women congregants, opening possibilities for voluntary synagogue leadership while raising her children. She regularly reviewed books of Jewish interest, and she fostered an appreciation of Jewish learning. Most significant, however, she recruited five women to study Hebrew and Torah together. The four years of study culminated in an adult bat mitzvah in which the group of women were called up to the *bimah*, the raised platform where the Torah scroll was read, in order to read from the Torah. They were not the first women to receive such an honor of an *aliyah*, however. That occurred in the mid-1950's during High Holiday services in the El Portal Theater, rented for the occasion. "I was standing in the lobby," remembered Irma Lee Ettinger, the center's administrator, "when all of a sudden the doors opened and several hundred people streamed out. I stopped one of them," she recounted, "and asked him what was happening. He said, 'There's a woman on the bimah and she has an aliyah.' I said, 'Who is the woman?' and he said, 'Miriam Wise.' The crowd gathered in front of the theater, discussed the major change in religious policy and after they calmed down, they returned to the services," she recalled. "That was the rabbi's rather unique way of advising VJCC that women were going to be given equal rights," she observed.[67] In Los Angeles, a rabbi like Wise could pursue equal rights for women without waiting for congregants to confer.

In Miami as in Los Angeles, rabbis and their wives did their best to whet an appetite for things Jewish, to awaken a desire to experience Judaism, to develop an experiential spirituality, to encourage Jews to choose the art of Jewish living. The cities' Jewish frontier setting drew rabbis seeking fame and influence, men willing to take risks and to innovate in order to pull newcomers to the cities into their synagogues. Seeking to further Judaism, rabbis hitched their personal ambition to the migrants' inchoate desires and needs. They intuitively grasped the mentality of permanent tourists and offered a form of Judaism that fit a leisure lifestyle. Entertaining, uplifting, enriching, such a Judaism appealed to uprooted men and women. Rabbis like Lehrman, Kronish, and Narot in Miami, Wise and Wolf in Los

Angeles, along with Albert Lewis and Jacob Pressman and later Isaiah Zeldin and Harold Schulweis, joined earlier figures like Magnin and Max Nussbaum in pioneering new types of congregations. In a world with few constraints, traditions, or established patterns of deference, the eclectic possibilities depended largely upon the imaginations of ambitious pioneer rabbis. Eager to build synagogues of their own, they experimented to create new liturgies, to give Judaism an aesthetic dimension, to fashion novel educational programs. They brought the American Jewish culture of the East, of their upbringing and education, to the South and West where they adapted it to new circumstances.

These men and their wives seized the opportunity to experiment with new ways to be Jewish and to pioneer self-consciously in a world where "the very meaning of Jewishness is changing."[68] The entrepreneurial spirit moved rabbis as much as other Jews. They saw the promise of a frontier society—its openness, venturesomeness, and willingness to tolerate innovation. Rabbis grasped this promise, each in his own way, and offered a personalized path to Jewish fulfillment to the engaged minority seeking religious roots.

NOTES

1. Letter to the editor of the *Los Angeles Times* in 1970, quoted in Stephen J. Sass, "Southern California," *Present Tense*, 9 (Spring 1982): 33.

2. I am grateful for insights regarding characteristics of L.A. rabbis to Wolfe Kelman, who oversaw the placement of Conservative rabbis in the postwar era. Wolfe Kelman, interview with author, 5 March 1988. Bruce Phillips, lecture at conference on Jews in Los Angeles, UCLA, 6 May 1990.

3. Marc Lee Raphael, *Profiles in American Judaism: The Reform Conservative, Orthodox, and Reconstructionist Traditions in Historical Perspective* (San Francisco: Harper & Row, 1984).

4. Quoted in "The Jews of Los Angeles: Pursuing the American Dream," *Los Angeles Times*, 29 January 1978.

5. "Yarmulke comes from Poland to Brooklyn to Los Angeles. It's Brooklynese and Polish. Since the founding of the State of Israel it's become kind of a badge to some Jews." Edgar F. Magnin, "Leader and Personality," an oral history conducted 1972–1974 by Malca Chall, 10, Regional Oral History Office, The Bancroft Library, University of California, Berkeley, 1975. Courtesy of The Bancroft Library.

6. Irving Lehrman quoted in Paul S. George, "An Enduring Covenant" in *Event of the Decade* (1988), 19; Albert Lewis to Maurice Eisendrath, 30 December 1952, General Correspondence, 1/7, Box 212, Albert M. Lewis MSS, AJA.

7. *Temple Beth Sholom Bulletin*, 10 December 1948; Report of Leon Ell, Membership Committee, 24 April 1945; Minutes of Meeting of Board of Directors of Temple Emanu-El, 21 August 1958. Lehrman and Kronish studied at Wise's Jewish Institute of Religion; Narot learned from Wise dur-

ing the years Narot served as rabbi in Atlantic City. See Joseph R. Narot, "First Teachers in Last Resorts," *CCAR Journal*, Winter 1978: 46–47.

8. He also frequently attended the Brooklyn Jewish Center, one of the foremost and innovative Conservative synagogue centers in the borough, to hear the preaching of its rabbi, Dr. Israel Levinthal. Irving Lehrman, "The Sermon," in *In the Name of God* (New York, 1979), 216.

9. *Center Review*, 23 September 1943: 4; Helen Goldman, telephone conversation, 10 January 1993; Michael A. Meyer, "A Centennial History," *Hebrew Union College-Jewish Institute of Religion at One-Hundred Years*, ed. Samuel E. Karff (Hebrew Union College Press, 1976), 150, 159.

10. George, "An Enduring Covenant," 9–78. Unless otherwise noted, material is drawn from this commissioned history.

11. This was the first sabbath observed in the new synagogue building. *Center Review*, 21 October 1948: 3.

12. Elaine Glickman, interview with author, 19 March 1991.

13. Lehrman found the architect Charles Greco, who had designed a large synagogue in Cleveland. George, "An Enduring Covenant," 19; Polly Redford, *Billion Dollar Sandbar* (New York: E. P. Dutton, 1970), 274.

14. The board of directors unanimously voted to give Lehrman life tenure in January 1951, less than ten years after his arrival. *Center Review*, 19 January 1951: 5.

15. Glickman, interview; quote from George, "An Enduring Covenant," 48.

16. See, for example, *Center Review*, 15 October

1947 and 5 October 1951. By 1952 the *Review* reported many more girls enrolling in the more intensive Hebrew department of the school, rather than just in the once-a-week Sunday school; 19 September 1952. See also *Jewish Center Review*, 8 May 1953 and 17 September 1954.

17. In 1961–62, after more than a decade of exhortation, there were still over twice as many boys (194) as girls (74) enrolled in the afternoon Hebrew school. Girls, on the other hand, dominated the Sunday school, 155 to 91. Louis Schwartzman, *Seventeenth Annual Report*, Bureau of Jewish Education, Miami, Florida (July 1961–1962), n.p., Rosen files.

18. *Jewish Center Review*, 17 October 1952.

19. *Jewish Center Review*, 4 December 1953; Glickman, interview.

20. Lehrman had convinced the congregation to eliminate *shnoddering*, which was considered undignified, but those who were given an *aliyah* were expected to announce their contribution from the *bima*. The men leading the congregation did not want to forgo this traditional source of synagogue income. See "President's Report" in the *Review*, 7 April 1948, and Minutes of the Executive Committee Meeting, 14 November 1954.

21. *Jewish Center Review*, 11 January 1952; Irving Lehrman, "The 'Power of Prayer,'" in *In The Name of God*, 197. Graham did invite Lehrman to speak at the 1961 Crusade held in the Miami Beach Convention Center. George, "An Enduring Covenant," 61.

22. See *Temple Emanu-El Review*, 17 September 1954, 10 December 1954, 17 December 1954, 24 March 1955, 31 March 1955, 5 September 1956.

23. Glickman, interview.

24. I appreciate Richard Cohen's insights on the multiple meanings of ritual objects. For an early perceptive discussion see Abraham G. Duker, "Emerging Culture Patterns in American Jewish Life," *Publications of the American Jewish Historical Society* 39:4 (June 1950), 351–88.

25. *Jewish Center Review*, 7 December 1951, 3 December 1954.

26. *Temple Emanu-El Review*, 19 October 1956, 4 January 1957, 8 March 1957, 22 March 1957, 9 September 1957.

27. Letter from Morris Berick to officers and members of Temple Beth Sholom, 27 March 1946, Minutes of Temple Beth Sholom; History in Minutes of the Beth Sholom Center, 6 April 1942; Temple Beth Sholom, *Twentieth Anniversary, 1942–1962*, Jubilee Book and Calendar (1962–63), n.p.; Minutes of the First General Meeting of the 1944–45 Season, 8 November 1944, in Minutes of Temple Beth Sholom.

28. See instructions in temple etiquette, *Beth Sholom Bulletin*, 11 February 1949; also Maxine Kronish Snyder, "My Father and My Family: Growing Up Jewish," in *Towards the Twenty-First Century: Judaism and the Jewish People in Israel and America*, ed. Ronald Kronish (Hoboken: KTAV, 1988), 332; report of Leon Ell, Membership Committee, Minutes of Meeting of Board of Directors of Beth Sholem Center, 24 April 1945.

29. Constitution, n.d., in back of Minutes of Temple Beth Sholom. The Miami Beach Jewish Center also changed its name to Temple Emanu-El, but not until 1954.

30. He didn't actually purchase them, and when he returned, he thought "out loud" about using another prayer book. However, the religious committee did order the prayer books, although the temple declined for several years to join the UAHC because of the vehement opposition of one member who thought that such membership would label it Reform. See letter from Morris Berick, 27 March 1946. On the UAHC issue see Minutes of Meeting of Board of Directors of Temple Beth Sholom, 27 December 1945, 22 January 1948, 29 January 1948, 9 March 1950.

31. See Minutes of Special Meeting of Board of Directors of Temple Beth Sholom, 29 January 1949; also, Minutes of Regular Meeting of Board of Directors of Temple Beth Sholom, 24 May 1945, 6 August 1945, 27 December 1945, 21 March 1946, 22 January 1948, 9 March 1950.

32. *Temple Beth Sholom Bulletin*, 10 December 1948. Kronish actually anticipated an American Union of Liberal Synagogues that would absorb Conservative, Reform, and unaffiliated into a renascent *klal yisroel*.

33. In this case Kronish argued that the congregation should follow the pattern of the State of Israel. There are interesting theological implications of such an argument, but Kronish did not discuss them. Minutes of Regular Meeting of Board of Directors of Temple Beth Sholom, 17 March 1949. See also an earlier argument in *Temple Beth Sholom Bulletin*, 15 September 1947. "Since Palestine is now THE CENTER of our spiritual and cultural life, and can safely be said to determine the norm of Jewish existence, as a gesture of Jewish solidarity, we deem it important to follow the Palestinian custom."

34. Ronald Kronish, interview with author, 2 March 1992; Minutes of Meeting of Board of Directors of Temple Beth Sholom, 1 October 1945.

35. *Temple Beth Sholom Bulletin*, 14 March 1947, 23 May 1947, 14 January 1949, 17 September 1948, 1 September 1947.

36. Minutes of General Membership Meeting, 27 March 1946, Minutes of Temple Beth Sholom; *Temple Beth Sholom Bulletin*, 17 September 1948; Minutes of the Regular Meeting of the Board of Directors of Temple Beth Sholom, 20 October 1949.

37. *Temple Beth Sholom Bulletin*, 5 December 1947, 14 January 1949, 4 April 1947.

38. Maxine Kronish Snyder, "My Father and My Family," 329.

39. Included in *Temple Beth Sholom Bulletin*, 17 October 1947.

40. *Temple Beth Sholom Bulletin*, 17 September 1948; *Jewish Center Review*, 16 November 1951.

41. Biographical details and quotes from Joseph R. Narot, "The Meaning of My Life," in *High Holy Day Sermons Preached at Temple Israel of Greater Miami, 1969/5730*, Joseph R. Narot and Steven B. Jacobs (n.d.), 1–5.

42. Narot's concern to expand the membership appears regularly in Minutes of the Meeting of the Board of Trustees of Temple Israel of Miami, 6 November 1951, 4 December 1951, 6 May 1952, 11 November 1952, 10 August 1953, 12 October 1954. See also Joseph R. Narot, "The Earnestness of Being Important," in *Letters to My Congregation* (1959–60), 3.

43. The sisterhood did open a gift shop. Minutes of the Meeting of the Board of Trustees of Temple Israel of Miami, 4 December 1951.

44. For example, in the matter of synagogue ritual, Temple Israel only had mourners stand to say kaddish, the traditional practice. Narot convinced the board to have the entire congregation stand for the kaddish, an innovation of classical Reform. Minutes of the Meeting of the Board of Trustees of Temple Israel, 9 September 1952, for reaffirmation of earlier policy; Minutes of the Regular Meeting of the Board of Trustees of Temple Israel of Greater Miami, 9 February 1959, for the change.

45. Joseph R. Narot, "What I Believe About Bar Mitzvo," in *An Introduction to a Faith* (Miami, n.d.), n.p., and "Bar Mitzvo Again—Once Over Heavily," in *Letters to My Congregation* V (Miami, 1962), 2; Minutes of the Regular Meeting of the Board of Trustees of Temple Israel of Miami, 12 September 1955, 14 February 1955; Joseph R. Narot, *Letters to My Congregation* (Miami, n.d. [1960?]), *An Introduction to a Faith* (Miami, n.d. [1961?]), *A Primer for Temple Life* (Miami, n.d.), "Do I Protest Too Much?" in *Letters to My Congregation* (Miami, n.d.), 15.

46. See Joseph R. Narot, "Horse Races, Barber Shops, and Reform Judaism," in which he defends his decision to go to the races and get his hair cut on the sabbath. *Letters to My Congregation* V, 34.

47. Morris Janowitz, *Judaism of the Next Generation* (Miami: Rostrum Books, 1969), 37, Table 3.2.

48. Magnin, Oral History, 27.

49. Magnin, Oral History, 85, 89; Neal Gabler, *An Empire of Their Own* (New York: Crown, 1988), chapter 8.

50. Magnin, Oral History, 126–27, 186 (emphasis in the original), 56, 53.

51. Magnin, Oral History, 259. Wilshire Boulevard Temple introduced a High School department and a Hebrew department, the former requiring additional study after confirmation and the latter requiring more intensive study for two and a half more hours per week. In 1960 the Academy School for gifted children was started, an even more intensive program in religious education. The academy enrolled thirty children in its first year and required attendance three days each week. See Wilshire Boulevard Temple, President's Annual Report (1961), 3, Wilshire Boulevard Temple, Box 841, George Piness MSS, AJA.

52. The account is drawn from Alfred Wolf and Dan Wolf, "Wilshire Boulevard Temple Camps, 1949–1974," in *Wilshire Boulevard Temple Camps*, ed. Alfred Wolf (Los Angeles: Wilshire Boulevard Temple, 1975), 5–17, quote on 5, Los Angeles, Wilshire Boulevard Temple Camps, Nearprint Box—Geography, AJA. *Bulletin of the Valley Jewish Community Center*, 6 December 1946.

53. Wolf and Wolf, "Wilshire Boulevard Temple Camps," 6.

54. Wolf and Wolf, "Wilshire Boulevard Temple Camps," 8.

55. Tom Redler quoted in Wolf and Wolf, "Wilshire Boulevard Temple Camps," 17.

56. One needed to be a temple member to send one's child to camp. Occasionally this requirement generated resentment. Ellie Hudson, interview with author, 10 July 1989.

57. See Jenna Weissman Joselit, ed., *A Worthy Use of Summer: American Jewish Summer Camping, 1900–1950* (Philadelphia: National Museum of American Jewish History, 1993).

58. Jacob Sonderling followed a similar path. He founded the Society for Jewish Culture that offered dramatic lectures in worship and "conservative reform." Vorspan and Gartner, *Jews of Los Angeles*, 235.

59. *Bulletin of the Valley Jewish Community Center*, 3 January 1947, 21 March 1947, 28 March 1947, 18 April 1947.

60. The account, unless otherwise noted, is

drawn from Cynthia and Robert Rawitch, *The First Fifty Years, Adat Ari El* (North Hollywood, 1988), quote on 55.

61. *Bulletin of the Valley Jewish Community Center*, 3 October 1947, 10 October 1947, 5 December 1947.

62. Quoted in Rawitch and Rawitch, *Adat Ari El*, 9.

63. Biography of Irma Lee Ettinger by Elaine Brown, *Adat Ari-El Yearbook* (1981), n.p.; *Bulletin of the Valley Jewish Community Center*, 24 October 1947. For other explanations of Conservatism, see 31 October 1947, 7 November 1947, 21 November 1947.

64. Wise quoted in Rawitch and Rawitch, *Adat Ari El*, 56; *Bulletin of the Valley Jewish Community Center*, 24 October 1947, 1 December 1948.

65. *Bulletin of the Valley Jewish Community Center*, 1 November 1951, 1 January 1949, 15 September 1951.

66. *Bulletin of the Valley Jewish Community Center*, 1 January 1949, 1 June 1950.

67. Quoted in Rawitch and Rawitch, *Adat Ari El*, 70–71.

68. Fred Massarik, "The Jewish Population of Los Angeles: A Panorama of Change," *Reconstructionist* 18:15 (28 Nov. 1952): 14.

MARTIN AND MALCOLM

James H. Cone

Since their deaths in the 1960s, Martin Luther King, Jr., and Malcolm X have symbolized for many people two distinct and conflicting black perspectives on America. King, the nonviolent advocate of equal rights, has been honored as an American hero with his own national holiday. Malcolm, the symbol of defiant self-defense, has become the patron saint of angry young people. Rather than emphasize the conflict between these two men, James Cone argues instead that Martin and Malcolm represent two broad streams of thought within a common African American struggle against racism and for the freedom of black people. Aspects of both perspectives have appeared in the writings of black intellectuals throughout African American history. When it has appeared that blacks would soon be included in American society on an equal basis with whites, Martin's integrationist views have been foreshadowed. In contrast, harbingers of Malcolm's nationalist thinking can be heard whenever despair over the possibility of genuine equality has been warranted. "To understand Martin Luther King's and Malcolm X's perspectives on America and their relation to each other," Cone believes, "it is important to see them in the light of these two different but interdependent streams of black thought."

Reprinted by permission from James H. Cone, "America: A Dream or a Nightmare?" in his *Martin & Malcolm & America: A Dream or a Nightmare* (New York: Orbis, 1991), 1–18.

I have a dream that one day this nation will rise up and live out the true meaning of its creed, "We hold these truths to be self-evident, that all men are created equal." I have a dream that one day…sons of former slaves and the sons of former slave owners will be able to sit down together at the table of brotherhood…. This is our hope…. With this faith we will be able to work together, to pray together, to struggle together, to go to jail together, to stand up for freedom together, knowing that we will be free one day…. This will be the day when all God's children will be able to sing with new meaning, "My country 'tis of thee, sweet land of liberty, of thee I sing."

—Martin Luther King, Jr.
March on Washington
Washington, D.C.
28 August 1963

No, I'm not an American. I'm one of the 22 million black people who are the victims of Americanism. One of the…victims of democracy, nothing but disguised hypocrisy. So, I'm not standing here speaking to you as an American, or a patriot, or a flag-saluter, or a flag-waver—no, not I! I'm speaking as a victim of this American system. And I see America through the eyes of the victim. I don't see any American dream; I see an American nightmare!

—Malcolm X
Cory Methodist Church
Cleveland, Ohio
3 April 1964

21

MARTIN AND MALCOLM

Integrationism and Nationalism
in African American Religious History

James H. Cone

THE MEETING OF MALCOLM AND MARTIN

"Well Malcolm, good to see you," Martin said. "Good to see *you*," Malcolm replied.

After nearly eight years of verbal sparring through the media, two great African American leaders, Martin Luther King, Jr., and Malcolm X, finally met for the first and only time in Washington, D.C., 26 March 1964. Both were attending the U.S. Senate's debate of the Civil Rights Bill. Initiated by Malcolm following Martin's press conference, the meeting was coincidental and brief. There was no time for substantive discussions between the two. They were photographed greeting each other warmly, smiling and shaking hands. The slim, six-foot three-inch Malcolm towered over the stocky, five-foot eight-inch Martin. They walked together a few paces through the corridor, whispering to each other, as their followers and the media looked on with great interest. As they departed, Malcolm teasingly said, "Now you're going to get investigated."

Although the media portrayed them as adversaries, Martin and Malcolm were actually fond of each other. There was no animosity between them. They saw each other as a fellow justice-fighter, struggling against the same evil—racism—and for the same goal—freedom for African Americans.

"I'm throwing myself into the heart of the civil rights struggle and will be in it from now on," Malcolm told James Booker of the *Amsterdam News* the day before he departed for the nation's capital. Recently expelled from the Black Muslim movement, he was trying to develop a new image of himself so he could join the mainstream of the civil rights movement. In Washington, Malcolm observed the debate from the Senate gallery and held impromptu press conferences during much of the day. He was pleased that the Senate voted against sending the bill to the Judiciary Committee and then voted to start debate on the bill in the full Senate. He told the media that the Senate should pass the House-passed bill "exactly as it is, with no changes." But he predicted glumly, "If passed, it will never be enforced." "You can't legislate good will—that comes through education."[1]

In another section of the Senate gallery, Martin King was observing the same debate. Like Malcolm, he also held several press conferences and cheered the Senate's decision to take up the bill. But he expressed concern about the southern filibuster which threatened to weaken it. Martin told the media that a month of "legitimate debate" was acceptable. But he vowed that "if the Senate is still talking about the bill after the first week of May," he would initiate a creative direct-action program in Washington and throughout the country "to dramatize the abuse of the legislative process." He did not rule out civil disobedience. "At first we would seek to persuade with our words and then with our deeds." Martin also promised that he would fight for more civil rights legislation the following year. "We cannot stop till Negroes have absolute and complete freedom."[2]

The meeting of Martin and Malcolm has profound, symbolic meaning for the black freedom movement. It was more than a meeting of two prominent leaders in the African American community. It was a meeting of two great resistance traditions in African American history—integrationism and nationalism. Together Martin, a Christian integrationist, and Malcolm, a Muslim nationalist, would have been a powerful force against racial injustice. When they were separated, their enemies were successful in pitting them against each other and thereby diluting the effectiveness of the black freedom movement. Both Martin and Malcolm were acutely aware of the dangers of disunity among African Americans. They frequently spoke out against it and urged African Americans to forget their differences and to unite in a common struggle for justice and freedom. Why then did Martin and Malcolm not set an example by joining their forces together into a black united front against racism? The answer to this question is found partly in the interrelationship of integrationism and nationalism in African American history. These two resistance traditions also provide the historical context for a deeper understanding of Martin's dream and Malcolm's nightmare.

INTEGRATIONISM AND NATIONALISM
IN AFRICAN-AMERICAN INTELLECTUAL HISTORY

No one stated the dilemma that slavery and segregation created for Africans in the United States as sharply and poignantly as W.E.B. Du Bois. In his classic statement of the problem, he spoke of it as a "peculiar sensation," a "double-consciousness," "two souls, two thoughts, two unreconciled strivings; two warring ideals in one dark body, whose dogged strength alone keeps it from being torn asunder." The "twoness" that Du Bois was describing stemmed from being an African *in* America "Here, then, is the dilemma," he wrote in "The Conservation of Races." "What, after all, am I? Am I an American or am I a Negro? Can I be both?"[3]

Integrationist thinkers may be defined as those who answer "Yes" to the question, "Can I be both?" They believe it is possible to achieve justice in the United States and to create wholesome relations with the white community. This optimism has been based upon the "American creed," the tradition of freedom and democracy as articulated in the Declaration of Independence and the Constitution, and is supported, they believe, by the Jewish and Christian Scriptures. The integrationist line of thought goes something like this: If whites really believe their political and religious documents, then they know that black people should not be enslaved and segregated but rather integrated into the mainstream of the society. After all, blacks are Americans, having arrived even before the Pilgrims. They have worked the land, obeyed the laws, paid their taxes, and defended America in every war. They built the nation as much as white people did. Therefore, the integrationists argue, it is the task of African American leaders to prick the conscience of whites, showing the contradictions between their professed values and their actual treatment of blacks. Then whites will be embarrassed by their hypocrisy and will grant blacks the same freedom that they themselves enjoy.

On the other hand, nationalist thinkers have rejected the American side of their identity and affirmed the African side, saying "No, we can't be both." They have contended that 244 years of slavery, followed by legal segregation, social degradation, political disfranchisement, and economic exploitation means that blacks will never be recognized as human beings in white society. America isn't for blacks; blacks can't be for America. The nationalists argue that blacks don't belong with whites, that whites are killing blacks, generation after generation. Blacks should, therefore, separate from America, either by returning to Africa or by going to some other place where they can create sociopolitical structures that are derived from their own history and culture.

Integrationism and nationalism represent the two broad streams of black thought in response to the problem of slavery and segregation in America. Of course, no black thinker has been a pure integrationist or a pure nationalist, but rather all black intellectuals have represented aspects of each, with emphasis moving in one direction or the other, usually at different periods of their lives. What emphasis any black thinker made was usually determined by his or her perspective on America, that is, whether he or she believed that blacks would soon be included in the mainstream of American life on a par with whites. When blacks have been optimistic about America—believing that they could achieve full equality through moral suasion and legal argument—they have been integrationists and have minimized their nationalist tendencies. On the other hand, despair about America—believing that genuine equality is impossible because whites have no moral conscience or any intention to apply the laws fairly—has always been the seedbed of nationalism. To understand Martin King's and Malcolm X's perspectives on America and their relation to each other, it is important to see them in the light of these two different but interdependent streams of black thought.

INTEGRATIONISM BEFORE MARTIN KING

Integrationists have had many able advocates since the founding of the republic. Among them were the great abolitionist Frederick Douglass, many prominent black preachers, and representatives of the National Association for the Advancement of Colored People (NAACP), the National Urban League, and the Congress of Racial Equality (CORE).

Frederick Douglass was the outstanding advocate of integrationism during the nineteenth century. Born a slave, Douglass escaped from slavery and became an international figure with his powerful speeches and writings in defense of the full citizenship rights of blacks. For him the existence of slavery was a staggering contradiction of the principles of the Constitution and the concept of humanity.

Unlike the white abolitionist William Lloyd Garrison, who denied his allegiance to a Constitution ratified by slaveholders, Douglass embraced it as an "anti-slavery document" and then proceeded to quote it as supporting evidence for the abolition of slavery. The Constitution reads, "'We the people'; not we the white people," Douglass proclaimed; "and if Negroes are people, they are included in the benefits for which the Constitution of America was ordained and established."[4]

No one was as persuasive as Frederick Douglass in pointing out to whites the hypocrisy of extolling the "principles of political freedom and of natural justice" articulated in the Declaration of Independence while holding blacks as slaves. His well-known Independence

Day speech in Rochester, New York, on the topic "What to the Slave Is the Fourth of July?" was calculated to cut deeply into the conscience of whites who thought of themselves as civilized. "To [the slave], your celebration is a sham," he proclaimed to a stunned white audience. "Your denunciation of tyrants, brass-fronted impudence; your shouts of liberty and equality, hollow mockery.... There is not a nation on the earth guilty of practices more shocking and bloody than are the people of the United States."[5]

Douglass's scathing words did not mean that he had given up on America and would accordingly seek separation from the land of his birth. He was offered an opportunity to stay in England where he was given many honors, but he rejected the idea. Douglas believed that blacks could find justice in the United States and safely intertwine their future with that of the white majority. He was severely critical of blacks and whites who proposed the colonization of blacks in Africa or some other place. "It's all nonsense to talk about the removal of eight million of the American people from their homes in America and Africa," he said. "The destiny of the colored Americans...is the destiny of America. We shall never leave you.... We are here.... To imagine that we should ever be eradicated is absurd and ridiculous. We can be modified, changed, assimilated, but never extinguished.... This is our country; and the question for the philosophers and statesmen of the land ought to be, What principle should dictate the policy of the nation toward us?"[6]

Although Douglass experienced many disappointments in his fight for justice, he never lost his love for America or his belief that blacks would soon achieve full freedom in the land of their birth. "I expect to see the colored people of this country enjoying the same freedom [as whites]," he said in 1865, "voting at the same ballot-box..., going to the same schools, attending the same churches, traveling the same street cars, in the same railroad cars,... proud of the same country, fighting the same foe, and enjoying the same peace, and all its advantages."[7]

Optimism about blacks achieving full citizenship rights in America has always been the hallmark of integrationism. This optimism has been based not only on the political ideals of America but also upon its claim to be founded on Christian principles. Blacks have believed that the Christian faith requires that whites treat them as equals before God. No group articulated this point with more religious conviction and fervor than black preachers.

According to black preachers, Christianity is a gospel of justice and love. Believers, therefore, must treat all people justly and lovingly —that is, as brothers and sisters. Why? Because God, the creator of all, is no respecter of persons. Out of one blood God has created all people. On the cross Jesus Christ died for all —whites and blacks alike. Our oneness in creation and redemption means that no Christian can condone slavery or segregation in the churches or the society. The integration of whites and blacks into one community, therefore, is the only option open for Christians.

As early as 1787, Richard Allen (an ex-slave and a Methodist minister) led a group of blacks out of St. George Methodist Church in Philadelphia, and in 1816 he founded the African Methodist Episcopal (AME) Church. He did this because he and his followers refused to accept segregation in the "Lord's house." A few years later, James Varick and other blacks in New York took similar action and organized the African Methodist Episcopal Zion (AMEZ) Church. Black Baptists also formed separate congregations.

Independent black churches were not separatist in the strict sense. They were not separating themselves from whites because they held a different doctrinal view of Christianity. Without exception, blacks used the same articles of faith and polity for their churches as the white denominations from which they separated. Separation, for blacks, meant that they were rejecting the *ethical* behavior of whites—they were rejecting racism that was based on the assumption that God created blacks inferior to whites. Blacks also wanted to prove that they had the capability to organize and to operate a denomination just like whites. In short, black Christians were bearing witness to their humanity, which they believed God created equal to that of whites. The motto of the AME Church reflected that conviction: "God our Father, Christ our Redeemer, Man our Brother." "When these sentiments are universal in theory and practice," the AME bishops said in 1896, "then the mission of the distinctive colored organization will cease."[8]

Not all black Christians chose the strategy of separation. Instead, some decided to stay in white denominations and use them as platforms from which to prick the conscience of whites regarding the demands of the gospel and to encourage blacks to strike a blow for freedom. "Liberty is a spirit sent out from God," proclaimed Henry Highland Garnet, a Presbyterian minister, "and like its great Author, is no respecter of persons."[9]

Following the Civil War, the great majority of black Christians joined black-led churches among the Methodists and Baptists. The independence of these churches enabled their pastors to become prominent leaders in the black struggle for integration in the society. Prominent Baptists included Adam Clayton Powell, Sr., and Jr., of the Abyssinian Baptist Church (New York), Martin Luther King, Sr., of Ebenezer Baptist Church (Atlanta), William Holmes Borders of the Wheat Street Baptist Church (Atlanta), and Vernon Johns of the Dexter Avenue Baptist Church (Montgomery). Reverdy C. Ransom, an AME minister, was a "pioneer black social gospeler." Other significant voices included Benjamin E. Mays, president of Morehouse College, and Howard Thurman, dean of Rankin Chapel and professor of theology at Howard University. All spoke out against segregation and racism in the white churches and the society, insisting that the integration of blacks and whites into one community was the demand of the Christian faith. In his book *Marching Blacks*, Adam Powell, Jr., accused white churches of turning Christianity into "churchianity," thereby distorting its essential message of "equality" and "brotherhood." "No one can say that Christianity has failed," he said. "It has never been tried."[10]

How can whites claim to be Christians and still hold blacks as slaves or segregate them in their churches and the society? That has been the great paradox for black Christians. Since whites attended their churches regularly, with an air of reverence for God, and studied the Bible conscientiously, blacks expected them to see the truth of the gospel and thereby accept them into their churches and the society as brothers and sisters. Many black Christians believed that it was only a matter of a little time before Jesus would reveal the gospel truth to whites and slavery and segregation would come tumbling down like the walls of Jericho. That was the basis of the optimism among black Christians.

Too much confidence in what God is going to do often creates an otherworldly perspective which encourages passivity in the face of injustice and suffering. That happened to the great majority of blacks from the time of the Civil War to the coming of Martin Luther King, Jr. The organized fight for justice was transferred from the churches to secular groups, commonly known as civil rights organizations, especially the NAACP, the National Urban League, and CORE. Each came into existence for the sole purpose of achieving full citizenship rights for African Americans in every aspect of American society. They often have used different tactics and have worked in different areas, but the goal has been the same—the integration of blacks into the mainstream of American society so that color will no longer be a determining factor for success or failure in any human endeavor.

Founded by prominent whites and blacks in 1909, the NAACP was the first and has been the most influential civil rights organization. Branded as radical before the 1960s, it has been a strong advocate of integration, using the courts as the primary arena in which to protest segregation. The NAACP is best known for its successful argument before the United States Supreme Court against the doctrine of "separate but equal" schools for blacks and whites, claiming that such schools are inherently unequal and therefore unconstitutional. The 17 May 1954 school desegregation decision has often been called the beginning of the black freedom movement of the 1950s and 1960s.

One year after the founding of the NAACP, the National Urban League was organized. Less aggressive than the NAACP, the Urban League was founded "for the specific purpose of easing the transition of the Southern rural Negro into an urban way of life. It stated clearly that its role was to help these people, who were essentially rural agrarian serf-peasants, adjust to Northern city life." Using the techniques of persuasion and conciliation, the Urban League appealed to the "enlightened self-interest" of white business leaders "to ease the movement of Negroes into middle class status."[11]

A generation later, in 1942, the Congress of Racial Equality was founded in Chicago. The smallest and most radical of the three groups, CORE is best known for introducing the method of nonviolent direct action, staging sit-ins in restaurants and freedom rides on buses. This new dimension of the black struggle for equality had a profound effect on the civil rights movement in the 1950s and 1960s and particularly on Martin King.

Unlike the black churches, which had few white members and no white leaders, the civil rights organizations included whites in every level of their operations. For example, a white person has often served as the president of the NAACP, and each of the three organizations has had a significant number of whites serve on its board of directors. They claimed that the implementation of integration must apply to every aspect of the society, including their own organizations. The inclusion of whites also limited their independence and made them vulnerable to the nationalist critique that no black revolution can be successful as long as its leadership is dependent upon white support.

BLACK NATIONALISM BEFORE MALCOLM X

The roots of black nationalism go back to the seventeenth-century slave conspiracies, when Africans, longing for their homeland, banded together in a common struggle against slavery, because they knew that they were not created for servitude. In the absence of historical data, it is not possible to describe the precise ideology behind the early slave revolts. What we know for sure is that the Africans deeply abhorred slavery and were willing to take great risks to gain their freedom.

This nationalist spirit was given high visibility in the slave revolts led by Gabriel Prosser, Denmark Vesey, and Nat Turner during the first third of the nineteenth century. But it was also found in the rise of mutual-aid societies, in the birth and growth of black-led churches and conventions, and in black-led emigration schemes. Unity as a people, pride in African heritage, the creation of autonomous institutions, and the search for a territory to build a nation were the central ingredients which shaped the early development of the nationalist consciousness.

There have been many articulate voices and important movements of black nationalism throughout African American history. Among them were David Walker and Martin Delany during the antebellum period and Henry McNeal Turner, Marcus Garvey, Noble Drew Ali, and Elijah Muhammad during the late nineteenth and early twentieth centuries.

The central claim of all black nationalists, past and present, is that black people are primarily Africans and not Americans. Unlike integrationists, nationalists do not define their significance and purpose as a people by appealing to the Declaration of Independence, the Constitution, Lincoln's Emancipation Proclamation, or even the white man's religion of Christianity. On the contrary, nationlists define their identity by their resistance to America and their determination to create a society based on their own African history and culture. The posture of rejecting America and accepting Africa is sometimes symbolized with such words as "African," "black," and "blackness." For example, Martin Delany, often called the father of black nationalism, boasted that there lived "none blacker" than himself. While Douglass, in typical integrationist style, said, "I thank God for making me a man simply," he reported that "Delany always thanks Him for making him a black man."[12]

The issue for nationalists was not only human slavery or oppression. It was also the oppression of *black* people by *white* people. Nothing aroused the fury of nationalists more than the racial factor in human exploitation. Their identity as black touched the very core of their being and affected their thoughts and feelings regarding everything, especially their relations with white people. Nationalists, unlike integrationists, could not separate their resentment of servitude from the racial identity of the people responsible for it. "White Americans [are] our *natural enemies*," wrote David Walker in his *Appeal* in 1829. "By treating us so cruel," we "see them acting more like devils than accountable men." According to Walker, "whites have always been an unjust, jealous, unmerciful, avaricious and blood-thirsty set of beings, always seeking after power and authority."[13]

Black nationalism was defined by a loss of hope in America. Its advocates did not believe that white people could ever imagine humanity in a way that would place black people on a par with them. "I am not in favor of caste, nor a separation of the brotherhood of mankind, and would as willingly live among white men as black, if I had an *equal possession and enjoyment* of privileges," Delany wrote in 1852 to the white abolitionist William Lloyd Garrison; he went on: "but [I] shall never be reconciled to live among them, subservient to their will—existing by mere *sufferance*, as we, the colored people, do, in this country.... I have no hopes in this country—no confidence in the American people."[14]

This difference in emotional orientation between nationalists and integrationists led to disagreement in their definition of freedom and their strategies for achieving it. For nationalists, freedom was not black people pleading for integration into white society; rather it was separation from white people so that blacks could govern themselves. For many nationalists, separation meant emigration from the United States to some place in Africa or Latin America. "Every people should be the originators of their own designs, the projector of their own schemes, and creators of the events that lead to their destiny—the consummation of their own desires," Delany wrote in his best-known work, *The Condition, Elevation, Emigration, and Destiny of the Colored People of the United States* (1852). "No people can be free who themselves do not constitute an essential part of the *ruling element* of the country in which they live," said Delany. "The liberty of no man is secure, who controls not his political destiny.... To suppose otherwise, is that delusion which at once induces its victim, through a period of long suffering, patiently to submit to every species of wrong; trusting against probability, and hoping against all reasonable grounds of expectation, for the granting of privileges and enjoyment of rights, that will never be attained."[15]

The ebb and flow of black nationalism, during the nineteenth century and thereafter, was influenced by the decline and rise of black expectations of equality in the United States. When blacks felt that the achievement of equality was impossible, the nationalist sentiment among them always increased. Such was the case during the 1840s and 1850s, largely due to the Fugitive Slave Act (1850) and the Dred Scott Decision (1857).

During the Civil War and the Reconstruction that followed it, black hopes soared and even Delany stopped talking about the emigration of blacks and began to participate in the political process in South Carolina, running for the office of lieutenant-governor.

Black expectations of achieving full citizenship rights, however, were short-lived. The infamous Hayes Compromise of 1877 led to the withdrawal of federal troops from the South, thereby allowing former white slaveholders to deal with their former slaves in any manner they chose. The destructive consequences for blacks were severe politically, economically, and psychologically. Accommodationism emerged as the dominant black philosophy, and Booker T. Washington became its most prominent advocate. Washington replaced Frederick Douglas as the chief spokesperson for blacks, and ministers were his most ardent supporters.

During the period of the "nadir" and the "long dark night" of black people's struggle for justice in America, Henry McNeal Turner, a bishop in the AME Church, and Marcus Garvey of the Universal Negro Improvement Association (UNIA) articulated nationalist perspectives that were more directly linked with the subsequent philosophy of Malcolm X. Like Malcolm's, their perspectives on America were derived from the bottom of the black experience. They spoke a language that was full of racial pride and denunciation of white America. It was intended to elevate the cultural and psychological well-being of down-trodden blacks burdened with low self-esteem in a society dominated by the violence of white hate groups and the sophisticated racism of the Social Darwinists.

A native of South Carolina, Turner grew up on the cotton fields with slaves and learned to read by his own efforts. He was a proud and fearless man, and his nationalism was deepened as he observed the continued exploitation of blacks by whites, North and South, during and following Reconstruction. When the Supreme Court ruled in 1883 that the Civil Rights Act of 1875 was unconstitutional, Turner felt that that "barbarous decision" dissolved the allegiance of black people to the United States. "If the decision is correct," he wrote, "the United States Constitution is a dirty rag, a cheat, a libel, and ought to be spit upon by every negro in the land."[16]

The betrayal of Reconstruction, the "enactment of cruel and revolting laws," lynching and other atrocities, reenslavement through peonage, and political disfranchisement encouraged Turner to conclude that blacks would never achieve equality in the United States. He became an ardent advocate of emigration to Africa. "There is no more doubt in my mind," Turner said, "that we have ultimately to return to Africa than there is of the existence of God."[17]

Although Turner was elected a bishop in the AME Church, he was not the typical holder of that office. The more whites demeaned blackness as a mark of inferiority, the more Turner glorified it. At a time when black and white Christians identified God with European images and the AME Church leaders were debating whether to replace the word "African" in their name with "American," Turner shocked everyone with his declaration that "God is a Negro."[18]

Although Turner addressed his message to the sociopolitical problems of the black masses in the rural South, he did not create an organization to implement his African dream. That distinction fell to Marcus Garvey.

On 23 March 1916, one year after Turner's death, Marcus Garvey came to the United States from his native Jamaica. While Turner's base was the rural South, Garvey worked in the urban North, mainly in Harlem. While the geography was different, the people were essentially the same, being mostly immigrants from the South in search of the American dream of economic security, social advancement, and political justice. Instead they entered a nightmare of racism and poverty which they thought they had left behind in the South.

Garvey understood the pain of color discrimination because he experienced it personally and observed it in the lives of other blacks in Jamaica and also during his travels in Central America, Europe, and the United States. It seemed that everywhere he traveled blacks were being dominated by others. "Where is the black man's Government?" he asked. "Where is his King and his kingdom? Where is his President, his country, and his ambassador, his army, his navy, his men of big affairs?" Unable to find them, Garvey, with the self-assurance of a proud black man, then declared: "I will help to make them."[19]

Garvey knew that without racial pride no people could make leaders and build a nation that would command the respect of the world. This was particularly true of blacks who had been enslaved and segregated for three hundred years. In a world where blackness was a badge of degradation and shame, Garvey transformed it into a symbol of honor and distinction. "To be a Negro is no disgrace, but an honor, and we of the Universal Negro Improvement Association do not want to become white."[20] He made blacks feel that they were somebody and that they could do great things as a people. "Up, you mighty race," Garvey proclaimed, "you can accomplish what you will," and black people believed him.

As whites ruled Europe and America, Garvey was certain blacks should and would rule Africa. To implement his African dream, he organized the UNIA, first in Kingston, Jamaica, and later in New York. "Africa for the Africans" was the heart of his message. In 1920 Garvey called the first International Convention of Negro Peoples of the World, and 25,000 delegates from twenty-five countries met in New York City. A redeemed Africa, governed by a united black race proud of its history, was the theme which dominated Garvey's speeches. "Wake up Ethiopia! Wake up Africa!" he proclaimed. "Let us work towards the one glorious end of a free, redeemed and mighty nation. Let Africa be a bright star among the constellation of nations." "A race without authority and power is a race without respect."[21]

No one exceeded Garvey in his criticisms of the philosophy of integration, as represented by the members of the NAACP and other middle-class black leaders and intellectuals. He believed that any black organization that depended upon white philanthropy was detrimental to the cause of Africa's redemption and the uplifting of the black race. "No man will do as much for you as you will do for yourself."[22] By depending on whites, blacks were saying that they could not do it alone, thereby creating a sense of inferiority in themselves.

According to Garvey, integration is a self-defeating philosophy that is promoted by pseudo-black intellectuals and leaders. He accused integrationists of wanting to be white and completely ignoring the socio-economic well-being of poor blacks at the bottom. W.E.B. Du Bois, then the editor of the NAACP's *Crisis* magazine, was one of Garvey's favorite targets of criticism. Garvey urged his followers that "we must never, even under the severest pressure, hate or dislike ourselves."[23] His criticism of the NAACP and Du Bois was very similar to Malcolm X's attack upon the same organization and its executive director, Roy Wilkins, during the 1960s. Black nationalists are defined by race confidence and solidarity, and they are often intemperate in their criticisms of black integrationists, for they believe integrationists compromise the self-respect and dignity of the race by wanting to mingle and marry white people—the enemy.

In 1920, Garvey's UNIA claimed a membership of four million and a year later six million, with nine hundred branches. While most scholars insist that the numbers were inflated, no one denies that Garvey organized the largest and most successful mass movement of blacks in the history of the United States. Garvey did what all black nationalists after him have merely dreamed of doing, and that is why they continue to study his life and message for direction and inspiration.

Concerned about Garvey's popularity, the government, with the help of black integrationist leaders, convicted him of mail fraud. Upon his imprisonment and deportation, black nationalism entered a period of decline. But the problems of oppression and identity which gave rise to it did not disappear.

In addition to Marcus Garvey's UNIA, two movements were important in defining the nationalism that influenced Malcolm X: the Moorish Science Temple founded by Noble Drew Ali in Newark, New Jersey, and the Nation of Islam—the "Black Muslims"—founded in Detroit in 1930 by the mysterious Wallace D. Fard and later headed by his disciple, Elijah Poole, a former Baptist minister from Sandersville, Georgia. Elijah Poole as Elijah Muhammad achieved his authority in the Black Muslim religion because he convinced Black Muslim believers, including Malcolm, that Allah came to North America "in the person of Wallace D. Fard," taught him for three and a half years, and then chose him as his Messenger.

Both movements rejected Christianity and white people and affirmed the religion of Islam and an African-Asian identity. Both movements were primarily religious, having less political emphasis than Garvey's UNIA. Although the Moorish Science Temple is still in existence, it was important mainly as a forerunner of the Nation of Islam. The Nation of Islam received many members from the Moorish Science Temple following the assassination of Noble Drew Ali.

The Nation of Islam was the most important influence on the life and thought of Malcolm X. Its importance for Malcolm was similar to the role of the black church in the life of Martin King. While Garvey influenced Malcolm's political consciousness, Elijah Muhammad defined his religious commitment. Elijah Muhammad was the sole and absolute authority in defining the doctrine and practice of the Nation of Islam. While affirming solidarity with worldwide Islam, he proclaimed distinctive doctrines. The most important and controversial one was his contention that whites were by nature evil. They were snakes who were incapable of doing right, devils who would soon be destroyed by God's righteous judgment. White people, therefore, were identified as the sole cause of black oppression.

In Black Muslim theology the almighty black God is the source of all good and power. To explain the origin of the evil of black oppression, Muhammad rejected the Christian recourse to divine mystery or God's permissive will, instead setting forth his own distinctive explanation, which focused on the myth of Yacob. Out of the weak individuals of the black race, Yacob, a renegade black scientist, created the white race, thereby causing all of the evil which has flowed from their hands: "The human beast—the serpent, the dragon, the devil, and Satan—all mean one and the same: the people or race known as the white or Caucasian race, sometimes called the European race. Since by nature they were created liars and murderers, they are the enemies of truth and righteousness, and the enemies of those who seek the truth."[24] This myth was important for Malcolm's view that the whites are evil by nature. The myth and its doctrinal development came exclusively from Elijah Muhammad.

The logical extension of this doctrine is that since black people are by nature good and divine, they must be separated from whites so they can avoid the latter's hour of total destruction. The solution to the problem of black oppression in America, therefore, is territorial separation, either by whites financing black people's return to Africa or by providing separate states in America.

Although the Nation of Islam and other nationalist movements (especially Garvey's) were the dominant influence in shaping Malcolm's life and thought, he was also indebted to the integrationist protest tradition. The same kind of cross current of nationalist and integrationist influences bore upon the career of Martin King, though he was indebted far less to the nationalist tradition. No sharp distinction can be drawn between the traditions, because representatives of both were fighting the same problems—the power of "white over black" and its psychological impact upon the self-esteem of its victims. Nationalists and integrationists were aware of the truth of each other's viewpoint, even though they did not always acknowledge it. Integrationists realized the danger of complete assimilation into American society. Like nationalists, they did not want to destroy the cultural and spirtual identity of blacks. That was perhaps the major reason why black churches and fraternal and sororal organizations remained separate from whites. Despite their repeated claim about 11:00 A.M. on Sunday morning being the most segregated hour of the week, black ministers in black denominations made no real efforts to integrate their churches. They knew that if they did, their power as blacks would have been greatly curtailed and their own cultural and spiritual identity destroyed. The advocates of integration, therefore, focused their energies primarily on the political and economic life of America. They believed that justice was possible if whites treated blacks as equals under the law.

Likewise, black nationalists realized the danger of complete isolation from the political and economic life of America. That was perhaps the major reason for the frequent shifts in their philosophy. Black nationalism was not primarily a Western, "rational" philosophy, but rather a black philosophy in search of its African roots. It was a cry for self-esteem, for the right to be recognized and accepted as human beings. Its advocates knew that blacks could not survive politically or economically in complete separation from others, especially whites in the United States. Neither could any other people (including whites) survive in isolation from the rest of the world. Everyone was interdependent. The black masses, therefore, did not follow nationalists because of their call for separation from America. Rather it was because of the nationalists' ability to speak to their "gut level" experience, that is, to express what it *felt* like to be black in white America.

Integrationists and nationalists complemented each other. Both philosophies were needed if America was going to come to terms with the truth of the black experience. Either philosophy alone was a half-truth and thus a distortion of the black reality in America. Integrationists were *practical*. They advocated what they thought could be achieved at a given time. They knew that justice demanded more. But why demand it if you can't get it? Why demand it if the demand itself blocks the achievement of other desirable and achievable goals? In their struggle for justice, they were careful not to arouse the genocidal instincts inherent in racism. Thus they chose goals and methods which many whites accepted as reasonable and just. The strengths and weaknesses of the integrationist view are reflected in the life and ministry of Martin King.

Nationalists were *desperate*. They spoke for that segment of the African American community which was hurting the most. Thus, they often did not consider carefully the consequences of their words and actions. The suffering of the black poor was so great that practical or rational philosophies did not arouse their allegiance. They needed a philosophy that could speak to their existence as black people, living in a white society that did not recognize their humanity. They needed a philosophy that empowered them to "respect black" by being prepared to die for it. Overwhelmed by misery, the black poor cried out for relief, for a word or an act that would lift them to another realm of existence where they would be treated as human beings. In place of an American dream, nationalists gave the black poor an African dream. The strengths and the weaknesses of this perspective were reflected in the life and ministry of Malcolm X.

Martin King and Malcolm X were shaped by what Vincent Harding has called the "Great Tradition of Black Protest,"[25] a tradition that comprised many variations of nationalism and integrationism. Their perspectives on America were influenced by both, even though they placed primary emphasis on only one of them. Both integrationism and nationalism readied Martin and Malcolm for leadership in the black freedom movement of the 1950s and 1960s—with Martin proclaiming an American dream from the steps of the Lincoln Memorial and Malcolm reminding him of an American nightmare in the streets of Harlem.

NOTES

1. NYAN, 28 March 1964, 50; WP, 27 March 1964, 4, 6; NYT, 27 March 1964, 10; "Integration: Long Day," *Newsweek*, 6 April 1964, 22; Peter Goldman, *The Death and Life of Malcolm X*, 2d ed. (Urbana: University of Illinois Press, 1979), 95; "The Time Has Come, 1964–66," pt. 2 of *Eyes on the Prize*, Channel 13, New York, 15 January 1990.

2. WP, 27 March 1964, 6; NYT, 27 March 1964, 10.

3. W. E. B. DuBois, *The Souls of Black Folk* (1903; reprint, New York: Fawcett Premier Book, 1968), 16, 17; idem, "The Conservation of Races" (1897), in Julius Lester, ed., *The Seventh Son: The Thought and Writings of W. E. B. DuBois* (New York: Vintage Book, 1971), vol. 1, 182.

4. Philip S. Foner, ed., *Frederick Douglass: Selections from His Writings* (New York: International Publishers, 1964), 57.

5. Ibid., 52–53.

6. Cited in Lerone Bennett, Jr., *Pioneers in Protest* (Chicago: Johnson Publishing Co., 1968), 208–9.

7. Foner, ed., *Frederick Douglass*, 44.

8. Cited in Peter J. Paris, *The Social Teaching of the Black Churches* (Philadelphia: Fortress Press, 1985), 25, n. 26.

9. Henry Highland Garnet, *An Address to the Slaves of the United States of America* (1843), reprinted with David Walker's *Appeal* (1829), in *Walker's Appeal & Garnet's Address to the Slaves of the United*

States of America (New York: Arno Press/New York Times, 1969), 93.

10. Adam Clayton Powell, Jr., *Marching Blacks*, rev. ed. (New York: Dial Press, 1973), 194.

11. Kenneth B. Clark, "The Civil Rights Movement: Momentum and Organization," *Daedalus*, 95 (Winter 1966), 245.

12. Cited in Theodore Draper, *The Rediscovery of Black Nationalism* (New York: Viking Press, 1970), 22; for an interpretation of the origin of black nationalism, see August Meier, "The Emergence of Negro Nationalism," Parts I and II, *Midwest Journal*, 45 (Winter 1951 and Summer 1953), 96–104 and 95–111.

13. *Walker's Appeal and Garnet's Address*, 71, 73, 27–28; see also Sterling Stuckey, *The Ideological Origins of Black Nationalism* (Boston: Beacon Press, 1972), 97, 99, 55–56.

14. Carter G. Woodson, ed., *The Mind of the Negro as Reflected in Letters Written during the Crisis, 1800–1860* (1926; reprint, New York: Russell & Russell, 1969), 293.

15. Martin Robison Delany, *The Condition, Elevation, Emigration, and Destiny of the Colored People of the United States* (1855; reprint, New York: Arno Press/New York Times, 1969), 209; see also John H. Bracey, Jr., August Meier, and Elliott Rudwick, eds., *Black Nationalism in America* (Indianapolis: Bobbs-Merrill Co., 1970), 89.

16. Henry McNeal Turner, "The Barbarous

Decision of the Supreme Court" (1883), in Edwin S. Redkey, ed., *Respect Black: The Writings and Speeches of Henry McNeal Turner* (New York: Arno Press/New York Times, 1971), 63.

17. Ibid., 165; Edwin S. Redkey, *Black Exodus: Black Nationalist and Back-to-Africa Movements, 1890–1910* (New Haven: Yale University Press, 1969), 29.

18. Henry McNeal Turner, "God Is a Negro" (1898), in Redkey, ed., *Respect Black*, 176–77.

19. Amy Jacques Garvey, ed., *Philosophy and Opinions of Marcus Garvey* (New York: Arno Press/New York Times, 1969), vol. 2, 126.

20. Ibid., 325–26.

21. Ibid., vol. 1, 5, 2.

22. Cited in E. David Cronon, *Black Moses: The Story of Marcus Garvey and the Negro Improvement Association* (Madison: University of Wisconsin Press, 1955), 173.

23. Garvey, ed., *Philosophy and Opinions*, vol. 2, 326.

24. Cited in Louis E. Lomax, *When the Word Is Given...* (New York: Signet Book, 1964), 56. The classic study on the Nation of Islam is C. Eric Lincoln, *The Black Muslims in America* (Boston: Beacon Press, 1961, Rev. ed., 1973). See also E. U. Essien-Udom, *Black Nationalism: The Search for an Identity in America* (Chicago: University of Chicago Press, 1962); James Baldwin, *The Fire Next Time* (New York: Dell, 1962). An early significant study is Erdmann Doane Beynon, "The Voodoo Cult Among Negro Migrants in Detroit," *American Journal of Sociology* (May 1938), 894–907. See also Monroe Berger, "The Black Muslims," *Horizon* (Winter, 1964), 48–65. The best source for the teaching of Elijah Muhammad is his *The Supreme Wisdom: The Solution to the So-Called Negroes' Problem* (Chicago: University of Islam, 1957); also his *Message to the Blackman* (Chicago: Muhammad's Temple No. 2).

25. Vincent Harding, *There Is a River: The Black Struggle for Freedom in America* (New York: Harcourt Brace Jovanovich, 1981), 83.

WHEN BLACK ELK SPEAKS, EVERYBODY LISTENS

William K. Powers

Since its publication in 1932, John G. Niehardt's *Black Elk Speaks* has become the most widely read book on American Indian religion. This life story of the Oglala Sioux holy man Black Elk is a compelling narrative, but it does not provide an accurate description of Black Elk or his religion. As William Powers argues, Neihardt recounts only the "traditional" side of Black Elk's story, and he does this by molding Black Elk's Native American story to the Judaeo-Christian model of worldliness, suffering, and salvation. Moreover, Niehardt suppresses the fact that after 1904 Nicholas Black Elk served in the Catholic church as a catechist for two decades. Like many Christian Native Americans, Black Elk lived creatively within two religious worlds. In its highly interpretive and selective telling of Black Elk's story, Niehardt's book obscures rather than explains the Lakota religion. Hence, "when Black Elk speaks, everybody listens, and everybody hears precisely what he or she feels inclined to hear with little regard for the meanings of the Lakota words."

Reprinted by permission from William K. Powers, "When Black Elk Speaks, Everybody Listens," in Chris Vecsey, ed., *Religion in Native North America* (Moscow, ID: University of Idaho Press, 1990), 136–151.

22 ❦

WHEN BLACK ELK SPEAKS, EVERYBODY LISTENS

William K. Powers

THIS PAPER[1] briefly discusses the Christian life of the Lakota, Black Elk, who was made famous by the poet, John G. Neihardt, and others, after the publication of *Black Elk Speaks*, which in the opinion of some is the most influential book ever published on American Indian religion. I realize that a critical evaluation of an Indian and a book that have reached the zenith of popularity in the United States and Canada, and a good part of Europe, risks touching the nerves of those who today hail Black Elk as a true prophet of a universal way of thinking about the world—far beyond the boundaries of the Pine Ridge reservation where he lived most of his life. But, though nerves may be touched, even exposed, my critique is not so much of a man who lived through the classic period of Lakota history and culture, but of the disciples who were to follow him, praise him, adulate him, idolize him, deify him, and frequently misunderstand him and the culture in which he lived at the time of his interviews with Neihardt.

My overall contention is that the book *Black Elk Speaks*, and the plethora of other books, articles, reviews, essays, songs, plays, and poetry, in fact, obscure Lakota religion rather than explain it. Further, I will argue that much of what passes as Lakota religion today is the product of the white man's imagination, and that soon the Lakota religion, if it follows the path of *Black Elk Speaks* shall simply be absorbed by other religions or philosophies, and it will be no fault of Black Elk the man, but rather Black Elk the myth, Neihardt, and his disciples. If the term "disciples" seems to convey at once a Christian image, it is precisely because I believe that *Black Elk Speaks* and the Black Elk myth, as opposed to the Black Elk truth, are so successful because Neihardt and others have consciously molded a character that conforms to the Judaeo-Christian model of worldliness, suffering, and salvation. There are those who would argue that the writing of Black Elk's "teachings," as they have come to be called, was not a conscious attempt to satisfy a largely white and Christian audience, but simply a coincidental merger of world views that exist in some mystical way to explain the irrationality of the white man's world.

I would argue that the best judge of such irrationality might be the *Indian himself* rather than white disciples of Black Elk. However, most elderly Indians on the Pine Ridge reservation who knew Black Elk, and this would include other medicine men and singers, some of them still living and practicing native Lakota religion, would wonder why all the fuss about Black Elk. They would insist that Nick (or Nic), as Black Elk was commonly called even during the time of the famous Neihardt interviews, was a charismatic and versatile man. He was a medicine man, although most would not have remembered him as a ritual curer or dreamer, as has been stated by his disciples. Rather they would know him first as an Episcopal layman and perhaps catechist. They would remember him as someone who took up the Ghost dance religion but explained it to his followers in decidedly Christian terms of damnation. They would indeed remember him as a Roman Catholic catechist, who along with his second wife, spent most of their lives from 1905 until his death in 1950 as leaders in the Catholic church, participating fully in the various Catholic programs that brought thousands of Indians together every several years. More importantly, he was known as someone who could teach in Lakota what he believed to be the tenets of the Catholic church. And he would be remembered for his important role of godfather to the newly baptized, as well as ersatz priest when inclement weather or other responsibilities of the church made it impossible for the Jesuits at Holy Rosary Mission to travel to the outlying districts to perform their priestly duties, particularly in the reservation town of Manderson.

Although time and space prevent me from presenting in detail a biographical sketch of Black Elk that would do him justice, I will attempt here to touch upon the most salient features of his participation in Lakota and Christian religion. DeMallie's recent book[2] provides the best, although brief, history of Black Elk, drawing heavily upon missionary literature. Also of some note, although likewise rather brief, is Steinmetz's treatment of Lakota religion as a kind of pre-Christian belief system in which the sacred pipe is regarded as a harbinger of Christ.[3]

There is, of course, the potential danger of converting Black Elk too severely—balancing his overdramatized traditional role as medicine man with an equally overweighted dedication to Christianity. However, I shall try here to look at his other life, drawing occasionally on interesting shreds and patches of information from my own field work, which include assessments of Black Elk by Lakota people who knew him. Unfortunately, this is a population that is usually not included among the experts and interpreters that have introduced Black Elk to the white man's world, and of course to the younger generation of Lakota and other Indians.

Black Elk Speaks, contrary to most claims, is not Black Elk's story, or even an outline of the most salient features of his life.[4] The importance of Black Elk Speaks lies in its description of a *holy vision* of Black Elk's which he revealed to Neihardt. This vision came to him in an attenuated form when Black Elk was nine years old. He then went by the boyhood name of *Kahnigapi* (Chosen), a point which Neihardt is not aware of but which is important to the Lakota. Interestingly, despite the claims of Black Elk disciples that the book has invoked a spiritual renascence among its followers, only a few chapters of Black Elk Speaks are focused on Lakota religion. The majority discuss in a rather abbreviated way the growing up of an average Lakota.

If we pare his life story down to its significant elements, we find that Black Elk was born on the following dates: 1856, according to the archives of Holy Rosary Mission where finally he was given religious instructions; 1858, according to the information found on his tombstone; 1862, according to the information give by Black Elk to Brown; and 1863, according to the information given to Neihardt. DeMallie convincingly demonstrates that Neihardt was right, and that 1863 is the correct date. These inconsistencies in his birth date represent only minor controversies that generally surround his life.

I shall not dwell on his early years, which we must surmise were like that of any other Lakota boy growing up on the Great Plains in the last half of the nineteenth century. What we know of specific importance is that when he was nine he received part of a vision, and in 1881 when he was eighteen years of age, he received a great, full-blown vision, which was interpreted by another medicine man, who told Black Elk that he must publicly perform his vision, a common practice in Lakota religion. That year Black Elk performed the Horse dance. The description of the great vision and the Horse dance figure prominently in Neihardt's book and are frequently interpreted in other works.[5]

Sometime during the next five years, Black Elk converted to Episcopalianism. We have little information about this period of time, but we assume that he participated in all the Lakota rituals. However, two facts help us to reconstruct this period in his life. First is the fact that the Episcopalians were the first and only active Christian missionaries on the Great Sioux Reservation between 1879 and 1888 when the first Catholic mission, Holy Rosary Mission, was built four miles north of Pine Ridge Agency.

Secondly, the Buffalo Bill Wild West Show, which Black Elk was to join around 1886, also required that all Indians must be Christian. In 1886 Black Elk sailed with Buffalo Bill for Europe and stayed for three years. In letters he sent home during this time, he is already quoting, albeit crudely, passages from the Bible.

The disciples of Black Elk usually interpret this period as one in which Black Elk sought to learn more about the white man, more about his origins, more about his power. But in fact, there is no reason to believe that Black Elk behaved any differently from the other Indians who accompanied the Wild West shows to Europe. The reservation system had created a vacuous period. There were no buffalo to hunt and no enemies to kill. The Lakota and others were at last at peace with each other, and they were frankly bored. Old song texts which I have collected from this period of time indicate clearly that the Indians leaving for Europe saw it as a challenge, a potential adventure that had all the daring and adventure of the hunt and the warpath. Some of the men even sang death songs at the train station, believing that indeed they might never return from this far off place located rather abstractly across an ocean they had never seen yet had named in Lakota, the Great Water.

The three years in Europe must have been exciting. Black Elk travelled in England, Italy, Germany, and France, and unluckily was stranded. We know nothing about this period except that later he rejoined Buffalo Bill and finally returned home to Pine Ridge. There he arrived just in time to hear about the new messiah in the guise of the prophet Wovoka in Nevada. Black Elk joined in the Ghost dance, but according to informants on the Pine Ridge reservation his manner of preaching the Ghost dance doctrine was decidedly Christian.

For example, in order to make his Christian followers understand the nature of the cataclysmic event that was to manifest itself in the form of a great upheaval of the earth, with the white man churned under, while the Indian remained safely on the surface to rejoin the old people who had died and the buffalo that had nearly disappeared, Black Elk would fill a paunch with water and bury it in the ground. As he preached he would suddenly stamp on the ground around the paunch of water, forcing its contents to spill over. He would then instruct his followers that the portending cataclysm might very well take the form of the Great Flood of Biblical times, and that all disbelievers would perish in the tide. He also carried gunpowder with him and after building a fire would quickly throw it into the blaze, comparing the explosion and scattering of hot ashes to the punishment of fire in hell. All these methods greatly impressed the Lakota people and even today they remember the proselytizing techniques of these stories.

But after the Ghost dance failed, ending with the massacre of the Lakota by the United States cavalry at Wounded Knee Creek, Black Elk, at least temporarily, again began to exhibit an interest in the old times, conducting Yuwipi meetings, curing rituals held in a darkened room for the purpose of calling spirits who in Lakota belief would instruct the medicine man as to the precise method for curing his ailing patients. At this point Black Elk, like so many other medicine men, was participating simultaneously in both religious systems, drawing upon the protocol and ritual of traditional Lakota religion, as well as on Christianity to help meet daily problems as they arose.[6] The necessity of Neihardt and others to make him uniquely Lakota has obscured the fact that most Lakotas have been and continue to be quite capable of moving between two or more religious systems on a situational basis, drawing from each or all those prayers, songs, rituals, histories, myths, and beliefs that satisfied the needs of the particular time and its attendant crises. The western position that people are supposed to belong to one religion, or at least to one religion at a time in serial allegiance to a singular belief system, has contributed significantly to the myth of Black Elk.

At any rate, Black Elk did not spend all his time cogitating over the mysteries of the universe and particularly that part of the world called the white man. Three years after returning from Europe, in 1893, at the age of 28 or 29, although the exact day is not known, Black Elk married a woman named Kate Warbonnet.[7] A son named Never Showed Off was born in 1893, and another son, Good Voiced Star, was born in 1895. His more famous son, Benjamin, who served as the interpreter for both Neihardt and Brown, was born in 1899. His wife, Kate, was apparently one of the first converts to Catholicism, that is to say, was formally recognized and baptized by the newly arrived German Jesuits. Thus in 1895, the first two sons were baptized in the Catholic church, receiving the names William and John respectively. William died in 1897, and Benjamin was baptized on March 11, 1901: Kate later died in 1903, leaving John and Benjamin.

After Kate's death, Black Elk must have felt very much alone in the world with only his sons. He continued to practice various traditional Lakota rituals, a fact pointed out by John Lone Goose, a neighbor who was also a Catholic and a lay catechist. Apparently, Lone Goose had talked with Black Elk about Catholicism and criticized him for participating in what the Jesuits were almost casually to regard as acts of the devil. It was in 1904, after curing a young Indian through traditional methods, that he chanced upon a Jesuit, named Father Lindebner, whom the Indians called Short Father. Lindebner convinced Black Elk to become a Catholic, and after two weeks of instruction at Holy Rosary Mission he was baptized by Father Lindebner on December 6, 1904, the feast of St. Nicholas. Black Elk was given the saint's name and from then on was known to the residents of the Pine Ridge reservation as Nicholas Black Elk, or less formally, Nick. His godfather was the son of a French trader named Peter Pourier, a Catholic catechist.

On July 2, 1905, Nick Black Elk was confirmed in the Catholic Church at St. Francis Mission on the Rosebud reservation, receiving the confirmation name of William. A year later he married Anna Brings, also known as Anna Brings Back Horses, or Brings Back White Horses. She had been married previously under the name of Anna Water Man, or Waterman, and brought to the marriage one daugher, Emma. Apparently, she was baptized a Catholic, but not confirmed, and in the year of their marriage, 1906, she was confirmed at an Indian Congress on July 7, receiving the name Rosa, afterward frequently going by the name, Rosa Anna.

Together, Nick and Rosa Anna had four children, Lucy, Henry, Mary, and Nic Tom, all of whom were baptized on the day of their births. Much later, Benjamin, or Ben as he was commonly know, was confirmed Benjamin Aloysius on June 15, 1911.

The preceding detailed examination of Black Elk's family lineage conveys the idea that Catholicism played an important part in his life, as did his early participation in other religious pursuits such as Episcopalianism, the Ghost dance, Yuwipi, the Vision Quest, and the public enactment of his most powerful visions. Black Elk was consistent in all his beliefs, but toward the end of his career, Catholicism prevailed. And involvement in his newfound religion was systematic, that is, he participated fully in it according to the rules. All his children were baptized and confirmed. Even his interpretations of old Lakota religion were couched in decidedly Christian terms, such as his fire and brimstone interpretations of the Ghost dance.

Between 1907 and 1930, Black Elk was almost totally consumed by his duties in the Catholic church. He was a member of the St. Joseph's Society, a confraternity of Lakota catechists who served as custodians of the local chapels, and who even held prayer services on Sundays and other important holidays when the priests could not make the journey. His wife became a member of the St. Mary's Society, the women's counterpart. These societies had originated with the Benedictine fathers, who found them a convenient way of organizing cadres of the faithful to serve the needs of the Mother Church. During this time, Black Elk was so popular among the Jesuits that he and one or two colleagues were constantly in demand to travel to other reservations to help missionize the other Indians. Black Elk traveled among the Arapahoes and Shoshonis of Wyoming, the Winnebagos of Nebraska, and even the Dakotas of eastern South Dakota. It is reputed that he was Father Eugene Buechel's favorite.

Black Elk's role as a godfather for baptism was particularly important, his record outstanding. For example, in less than one month after Black Elk had been confirmed, he served as godfather for one Jacob Stead (Steed) at Manderson, the community with which he is most readily identified. Over the next year, he served as godfather for seventeen other persons. Between 1906 and 1910, according to the baptismal records of Holy Rosary Mission, he served as godfather for a total of fifty-nine people. Among these were Mark Big Road, a leading medicine man on the Pine Ridge reservation; a German woman known as Agnes Mary Tasica Win; still another by proxy; for Silas Fills the Pipe, who later would become a fellow catechist and colleague in travels to other reservations; his own mother, Mary Leggings Down, known as Mary Nahco Win or Tipi Gloucia; and for his own son, Henry. In 1911, at St. Peter's Church in Manderson, he served as godfather for twenty people at one mass baptism.

Between 1913 and 1920 he served as godfather for fifteen people, one of whom was his own son's wife. On May 31, 1917, he was godfather for ten persons. During the years 1920 to 1928, he stood up for twelve people, including Jonas Ground Spider, also known as Jonas Walks Under Ground, a leading peyotist in his later years, and Crispina Pourier, the daughter of his own godfather.

On September 1, 1930, he was godfather for the last time for Mary Iron Crow who was sixty-five years old. This date is important because it was the month *after* Black Elk was first visited by John G. Neihardt. In all, Black Elk, for over twenty-five years, not eight, as has been claimed,[8] stood up for a total of 134 people for which we have documentation.

Black Elk Speaks was published in 1932. There is no trace of Black Elk's Christian life in it. But Neihardt was clearly aware of the old man's participation in the Catholic church. Although DeMallie states (1984, 27) that Neihardt probably did not know about Black Elk's participation in the Catholic church, later in the book he states:

> Black Elk told Neihardt little about his later life, his experiences in the Catholic Church, his travels to other Indian reservations as missionary, and his work as a catechist at Pine Ridge. Neihardt was curious about why Black Elk had *put aside his old religion.* According to Hilda (Petri), Black Elk merely replied, "My children had to live in this world," and Neihardt did not probe any further. (DeMallie, 1984, 47, italics added)

Although *Black Elk Speaks* met with critical acclaim, the Jesuits at Pine Ridge must have been shocked. There is no evidence that they even knew the Neihardt interviews were being conducted. To them, Black Elk was one of their prize catechists, even though they occasionally chided him for spending too much money on the conversion of new souls.[9] He was part of their showcase, and there was no reason for them to believe that he was anything but sincere. Although a claim has been made that there was a misunderstanding between Black Elk and Neihardt, the latter wanting simply to write a biography of the old man, and the former believing that Neihardt wanted to be instructed in the old religion, this claim is not supported empirically. Neihardt wanted to write a good book, one that would increase his own status as a poet and writer. It was not the money, he once told Black Elk, because he could make much more money writing other kinds of things. But later, when looking for a publisher for the work, he approached the publisher William Morrow, suggesting the chapter on the Horse dance might make a good movie and thus help promote book sales. Morrow published the book but died before any agreement with a motion picture producer could be arranged. The book, despite its critical acclaim, was not an immediate financial success.[10]

Countering the admonition Black Elk received from astonished clergy at Holy Rosary Mission, the old man issued a letter in 1934, two years after publication of *Black Elk Speaks*. The letter, witnessed by Reverend Joseph Zimmerman, S. J., at Holy Rosary was written by his daughter, Lucy (Looking Horse).[11] Its contents are instructive because it totally disclaimed Neihardt and the book that had made Black Elk famous, It stated:

> I shake hands with my white friends. Listen! I will speak words of truth. I told about the people's ways of long ago and some of this a white man put in a book but he did not tell about current ways. Therefore I will speak again, a final speech.
>
> Now I am an old man. I called my priest to pray for me and so he gave me Extreme Unction and Holy Eucharist. Therefore I will tell you the truth. Listen, my friends!
>
> For the last thirty years I have lived very differently from what the white man told about me. I am a believer. The Catholic priest Short Father baptized me thirty years ago. From then on they have called me Nick Black Elk. Very many of the Indians know me. Now I have converted and live in the true faith of God the Father, the Son, and the Holy Spirit. Accordingly, I say in my own Sioux Indian language, "Our Father, who art in heaven hallowed be thy name," as Christ taught us and instructed us to say. I say the Apostles' Creed and I believe it all.
>
> For very many years I went with several priests to fight for Christ among my people. For about twenty years I helped the priests and I was a catechist in several communities. So I think

I know more about the Catholic religion than many white men.

For eight years I participated in the retreat for Catechists and from this I learned a great deal about the faith. I am able to explain my faith. From my faith I know Who I believe in so my work is not in vain.

All of my family is baptized. All my children and grandchildren belong to the Catholic Church and I am glad of that and I wish very much that they will always follow the holy road.

I know what St. Peter has to say to those men who forsake the holy communities. My white friends should read carefully 2 Peter 2:20–22. I send my people on the straight road that Christ's church has taught us about. While I live I will never fall from faith in Christ.

Thirty years ago I knew little about the one we call God. At that time I was a very good dancer. In England I danced before Our Grandmother, Queen Victoria. At that time I gave medicines to the sick. Perhaps I was proud, I considered myself brave and I considered myself to be a good Indian, but now I think I am better.

St. Paul also became better after his conversion. I know that the Catholic religion is good, better than the Sun dance or the Ghost dance. Long ago the Indians performed such dances only for glory. They cut themselves and caused the blood to flow. But for the sake of sin Christ was nailed on the cross to take our sins away. The Indian religion of long ago did not benefit mankind. The medicine men sought only glory and presents from their curing. Christ commanded us to be humble and He taught us to stop sin. The Indian medicine men did not stop sin. Now I despise sin. And I want to go straight in the righteous way that the Catholics teach us so my soul will reach heaven. This is the way I wish to be. With a good heart I shake hands with all of you.

[signed]Nick Black Elk
Lucy Looks Twice
Joseph A. Zimmerman,
S.J. (Wanblee Wankatuya [High Eagle])

Despite all this empirical evidence for Black Elk's self-proclaimed allegiance to the Catholic Church, admittedly a Catholicism that could coexist with traditional Lakota religion, Neihardt returned a second time to record the "teachings" of Black Elk, this time hoping to write a more popular book on the Sioux. Disappointed that *Black Elk Speaks* was not a commercial success, he wanted to gather information for another book, *When the Tree Flowered*,[12] which he desperately wanted to become popular. Yet again we find no references to Black Elk the catechist even though by his own admission Neihardt knew that Black Elk was still a strong Catholic.

If this were not enough, just three years later, Joseph Epes Brown came to the Pine Ridge scene, actively looking for Black Elk, and ultimately wrote another popular book, *The Sacred Pipe*.[13] We know less about the methodology concerning the writing of this latter book, another which attempts to immortalize the "teachings" of Black Elk. Brown's foreword, presumably "told" by Black Elk, states quite unequivocally:

We have been told by the white man, or at least by those who are Christian, that God sent to men His son, who would restore order and peace upon the earth; and we have been told that Jesus the Christ was crucified, but that he shall come again at the Last Judgement, the end of this world or cycle. This I understand and know that it is true…. (Brown 1953, xix)

This statement was collected by Brown in 1947. On August 19, 1950, Black Elk died and was buried in St. Agnes cemetery in Manderson, South Dakota, with a full Christian burial. He never lived to see the publication of Brown's book in 1953, and one wonders why and under what circumstances the Black Elk myth was repeated so few years after the old man had refuted Neihardt's book.

Did Black Elk enjoy dictating his teachings to men who mysteriously had been "sent" to him? Or were his teachings carefully edited to conform to the white man's expectations of his life? In believing that Black Elk was indeed an honorable man, one possessing the charisma that attracted these authors, I opt for the latter.

Since *Black Elk Speaks* was written, countless numbers of articles and references to it have proliferated in American literature. Interestingly, anthropologists, although keen on using the book in their classes on American Indians have rarely entered into the controversy. One of the most critical disciplines has ironically almost totally ignored the possibility that much of what Black Elk had to say was manufactured by a white man. Those least interested in Black Elk, either as a person or as a phenomenon, have been the Oglalas at Pine Ridge themselves. Although Black Elk's "teachings" still remain an important part of American literature and poetry, they have not impressed the average Lakota, who today wonders why so many people would be interested in the life of, what to them, was just another Oglala.

According to traditional Lakota doctrine, medicine men do not rise above each other. They practice their religion, they follow the way of the pipe, and sooner or later they become old and impotent and are replaced by other younger medicine men who take up the rituals of their predecessors. There is no room in Lakota religion or Lakota philosophy for medicine men who place themselves above other medicine men and the common people. It is a contradiction in terms. Lakota medicine men should above all be humble, and to have a book written about them extolling their virtues above others is unthinkable in Lakota terms. The idea of focusing on one medicine man as some kind of paragon of Lakota virtue is strictly a white man's idea. And this idea has been replicated over and over now with the publication of other books that are epigonic of *Black Elk Speaks* and whose authors also were mystically sent to write the teachings of their respective gurus.[14]

Despite the adulation of Black Elk by his white disciples, he is still remembered by Lakotas primarily as a Catholic catechist, but not greater than Silas Fills the Pipe, Ivan Star Comes Out, Peter Pourier, Joseph Horn Cloud, and others who were his contemporaries, but who have had no biographers to tell their deeds. They were all humble men, caught up in the period of time in which Christianity arrived upon the scene to compete with Lakota religion. In some cases, Lakota people were converted to orthodox Christianity, but perhaps in most cases, they compromised; they joined Christian denominations, but without totally forsaking their native religion.

Since the turn of the century, much of what passes today for Indian culture and religion has been fabricated by the white man, or Indians who have been trained in the white man's schools. If we were to focus only on the literature of the Lakota and Dakota, written by Indians or whites, pseudo-autobiographies[15] or biographies, we find an amazing, continuous list of titles, reissues, and translations appearing nearly every year. Chronologically, some of those include Charles Eastman's works, *Indian Boyhood* (1902), *The Soul of the Indian* (1911), and *From the Deep Woods to Civilization* (1916). These are characteristic of the Indian who has become educated and writes about his youth for a white audience. Next are Luther Standing Bear's "autobiographies," all obviously written by a New

York editor, including *My People the Sioux* (1928) and *Land of the Spotted Eagle* (1933), among others. Between the publication of these is *Black Elk Speaks*, published in 1932, and Mari Sandoz's book, *Crazy Horse*, in 1942, which is also a romanticization of Lakota culture, written for whites, and refuted by some Indians who did not believe that Crazy Horse was a chief to be revered. *The Sacred Pipe* followed in 1953.

There was a German edition of Neihardt's *Black Elk Speaks* in 1955 prior to reissue in America in 1961, and in Germany in 1962. Neihardt's work appeared in Italian in 1968, and was again published in London in 1972 and reissued in 1974. *The Sacred Pipe* appeared in German in 1956, in Italian in 1970, and has been reissued in English in 1971, 1972, 1973, 1976, 1977, 1979, 1980, 1981, and 1982, at last count.

Then new medicine men happened upon the scene, all having in common the same as-told-to "autobiographies," and all written by white men sent for the purpose of recording Lakota religion. An example of this phenomenon is of course *Lame Deer: Seeker of Visions* with Richard Erodes, published in 1972 and translated into German in West Germany in 1979 and in East Germany in 1982. *Lame Deer* is currently being translated into Hungarian.

Even without including the French translations, this incomplete publication record gives some indication of the popularity of the books under question, suggesting just how many *more* translations have stood between what Black Elk and others said and what the ultimate reader hears. Today, when Black Elk speaks everybody listens, and everybody hears precisely what he or she feels inclined to hear with little regard for the meanings of the Lakota words.

Essentially, in *Black Elk Speaks* and other books written by white men for a white audience, the ideas, plots, persons, and situations of these books have been constructed to conform to the expectations of a white audience that generally knows little about what it means to be brought up as a Lakota over the past one hundred years. Of particular significance, I think, is that the only language to which *Black Elk Speaks* and other books have not been translated is Lakota, the native language of the people who presumably are the originators and benefactors of these religious ideas. *Black Elk Speaks*, although translated into many languages of the world with the belief that we can hear what Black Elk said through what has often been called the *authentic* voice of Neihardt, cannot be translated back into the original. *The Sacred Pipe* fares better, perhaps because there is no pretense in creating a voice, only a culture-history, whose contents include the seven sacred rites of the Oglala in which all Lakota medicine men believe.

But it is not only that the work cannot be translated back into the language of the people themselves. There is no interest in Black Elk on the reservation as a philosopher or spokesman for the traditional way of life, at least not by his living contemporaries. Hierarchical ranking of medicine men is, again, antithetical to Lakota thought. Furthermore, there are practical problems with Black Elk's interpretations of his life and vision. Some of his ideas, taken to be applicable to all Lakota by his various interpreters, are, in fact, idiosyncratic and mean very little to the uninitiated Lakota. The attempt to regard basic Judaeo-Christian tenets of Neihardt's culture as somehow characteristically Lakota makes the work unacceptable to the Indians on the reservation. They frankly do not need spiritual leaders like Black Elk. They have their own leaders, and their medicine men frequently disagree with Black Elk's philosophy.

There are, however, some Lakota today who do look to spiritual guidance from books. The new generation of Indians has moved to the cities away from their direct source of inspiration on the reservations. In many ways their needs are greater, for they must live in constant contact with the people who have attempted to destroy their culture and their religion. For these young Indians, *Black Elk Speaks* and other fabrications of the white man become not only increasingly acceptable but even desirable in the form of literature, given the Judaeo-Christian substructures introduced by contemporary white writers. To survive in the world today, a white man need only be a white man, but for an Indian to survive he must be both Indian and white. In many ways *Black Elk Speaks* is a form a literary imperialism as are so many other books on Indians. But it also represents literary compromise in that Indians are allowed to be Indians because the white man has dictated through clever prose and poetry the very parameters of being Indian. And through this process, the young Indian accepts a religion, one he calls Lakota religion, manifested in an acceptable form of literature and written by a white man who knows little or nothing of the real religion practiced by older and younger Lakotas today on the reservation. And this younger generation of Lakota does not even know the difference.

With each new translation and yet another subtitle, another translator's preface, another advertising copywriter's impression of the book that will make it sell, it is undeniable that the myth of Black Elk has captured the minds and emotions of white Americans and Europeans. Contemporary medicine men at Pine Ridge, however, would be surprised to know about this. This type of romantic culture has always appealed to the Euroamerican world. Not surprisingly, for example, the complete works of Karl May are recently undergoing a rejuvenation in Europe, as are the works of James Fennimore Cooper in the United States. But even from this Euroamerican background is it not immoral to witness the creation of an Indian religion by a romantic white man? The religious zeal of even more romanticists is overshadowed by their total ignorance of a Lakota religion learned first hand from those ritual specialists who are not the subjects of books, and who are therefore more nearly akin to the ideal type of Lakota medicine man accepted by Lakota culture.

When Nick Black Elk first spoke to Neihardt, only the old man's son and some of the other old timers who were present really heard what Black Elk had to say. But today when Black Elk speaks everybody listens-they listen in English, German, French, Italian, Russian, Hungarian, Spanish, and in Portuguese, and each one hears and interprets Black Elk's meaning within the context of his or her own language and culture. And even the Indian who listens and others who are caught up in the old man's "teachings" are unaware that the true spiritual nature of the Lakota, or at least part of it, has been manufactured in the literary workshops of the white man. And that is precisely the way the white man wants it to be.

NOTES

1. This is an excerpt of a larger paper by the same title that was originally presented to a number of universities in Germany during May and June, 1985. I am particularly thankful to Drs. Christian and Johanna Feest for their hospitality and use of their library where I wrote the initial draft. I am also grateful for the hospitality provided by our German hosts, particularly Professor and Mrs. Helmbracht Breinig. Only publications relevant to this article will be cited. References to *Black Elk Speaks* and their works about Black Elk could themselves fill a not-so-modest volume.

2. DeMallie (1984).

3. See particularly Steinmetz (1980).

4. *Black Elk Speaks* and *The Sacred Pipe* lack any major criticisms. The major perpetuators of the Black Elk myth are found in Deloria (1984), which contains a comprehensive bibliography. For a critical evaluation of as-told-to autobiographies, the best work is by Krupat (1985). An interesting debate over the authenticity of Black Elk also appears in Swann (1983). For a critical evaluation of Neihardt's work in general see the infrequently-cited book by Whitney (1976).

5. There are a few other interpretations of the Horse dance which is still remembered by living

Lakotas. It was a dramatic event in which persons who dreamed of the Thunderbeings wore masks and rode horses that danced to the songs. For references to the Horse dance see Feraca (1963) and Powers (1982).

6. For an analysis of dual participation in Lakota religion and Christianity, see Powers (1987).

7. The biographical material as well as his role in the Catholic church has been gleaned from archives at Holy Rosary Mission, Pine Ridge, South Dakota, *Liber Baptismorum*, 16 volumes, and *Registrum Confirmatorum*. Information related to marriages is contained on a special file index.

8. The claim was made in a review of DeMallie's book *The Sixth Grandfather* by Lueninghoener (1984).

9. Detailed records of expenditures and loans incurred by Lakota catechists were kept by the Jesuits and Holy Rosary Mission.

10. There are various references to Morrow and Neihardt in DeMallie (1984).

11. In the Jesuit Archives at Marquette University and published in DeMallie (1984).

12. Neihardt (1951).

13. For a discussion about the tension between Neihardt and Brown see McCluskey (1972).

14. In addition to Brown (1953), see also Lame Deer and Erdoes (1972) and Mails (1979).

15. See Krupat (1985).

BIBLIOGRAPHY

Brown, J. E. 1953. *The Sacred Pipe.* Norman: University of Oklahoma Press.

Deloria, Jr., Vine, ed. 1984. *A Sender of Words.* Salt Lake City: Howe Brothers.

DeMallie, Raymond J., ed. 1984. *The Sixth Grandfather.* Lincoln: University of Nebraska Press.

Feraca, Stephen E. 1963. *Wakinyan: Contemporary Teton Dakota Religion.* Browning, Montana: Museum of the Plains Indian.

Krupat, Arnold. 1985. *For Those Who Come After.* Berkeley: University of California Press.

Lame Deer, John (Fire), and Richard Erdoes. 1972. *Lame Deer: Seeker of Visions.* New York: Simon and Schuster.

Lueninghoener, Florence Boring. 1984. Review of *The Sixth Grandfather,* ed. Raymond J. DeMallie. *Nebraska History* 65(4):545–56.

McCluskey, Sally. 1972. "Black Elk Speaks and So Does John G. Neihardt." *Western American Literature* 6:231–42.

Mails, Thomas E. 1985. *Fools Crow.* Garden City: Doubleday and Company.

Neihardt, John G. 1932. *Black Elk speaks.* New York: William Morrow and Company.

———. 1951. *When the Tree Flowered.* New York: MacMillan.

Powers, William K. 1982. *Yuwipi: Vision and Experience in Oglala Ritual.* Lincoln: University of Nebraska Press.

1987. *Beyond the vision: Essays on American Indian culture.* Norman: University of Oklahoma Press.

Steinmetz, S. J., Paul. 1980. *Pipe, Bible and Peyote among the Oglala Lakota: A Study in Religious Identity.* Motala, Sweden: Borgstroms Tryckeri.

Swann, Brian, ed. 1983. *Smoothing the Ground.* Berkeley: University of California Press.

Whitney, Blair. 1976. *John G. Neihardt.* Boston: Twayne Publishers.

SEARCHING FOR EDEN WITH A SATELLITE DISH

Grant Wacker

Pentecostal Christianity began at the beginning of this century and now has more more than 30 million American adherents and a worldwide following of 430 million. These numbers rank Pentecostals behind only Roman Catholics as the largest gathering of Christians in the world. Though considerable attention has been given to the public ministries of Jim Bakker, Jimmy Swaggert, and Pat Robertson, and to the extraordinary practice of speaking in tongues, relatively little is known about ordinary Pentecostal church members. In the following essay, Grant Wacker traces the mushrooming growth of Pentecostalism to two impulses that have continually struggled for the movement's soul: primitivism and pragmatism. As Wacker states, the primitive impulse is "a powerfully destructive urge to smash all human-made traditions in order to return to a first century world where...dreams and visions exercised normative authority, and the Bible stood free of higher criticism." The pragmatic impulse, in contrast, is a desire to do whatever is needed to meet the movement's goals. By the end of the twentieth century, Wacker argues, these two impulses have resulted in a movement whose primitivism has meant that Pentecostal theology and worship patterns have remained "largely untouched by the assumptions of the secular culture" and yet whose pragmatism has led a rush "to embrace the therapeutic rewards and technological amenities of modernity with scarcely a second thought."

Adapted by permission from Grant Wacker, "Searching for Eden with a Satellite Dish: Primitivism, Pragmatism, and the Pentecostal Character," in *The Primitive Church in the Modern World*, Richard Hughes, ed. (Urbana: University of Illinois, 1995).

23

SEARCHING FOR EDEN WITH A SATELLITE DISH

Primitivism, Pragmatism, and the Pentecostal Character

Grant Wacker

THE DATE, Monday, April 9, 1906. The place, a four-room house on Bonnie Brae Street in downtown industrial Los Angeles. After the supper dishes had been cleared away, black saints gathered to seek the Baptism of the Holy Ghost. They assumed that when the power fell they would be enabled to speak an array of unlearned foreign languages, just as the apostles had done in the *Book of Acts*. In the preceding weeks the little band had met many times without success. But on that memorable spring evening the Spirit finally moved. First one, then another, and then another began to stammer in unfamiliar tongues. Before the night was over nearly all found themselves singing and shouting in the mysterious cadences of Africa, Asia, and the South Sea Islands. The worshipers concluded, naturally enough, that after a spiritual drought of nearly two thousand years the wonder-working power of the Holy Ghost once again had fallen upon Christ's humblest followers.

Word raced through the black community. Visitors gathered night after night, spilling out onto the porch and front lawn. Tradition has it that the weight of the enthusiasts soon crushed the porch. Realizing that they needed larger quarters, the band scraped together funds to lease an abandoned meeting house several blocks away on a short dirt road called Azusa Street. The following Tuesday evening, eight days after the initial manifestation of tongues, the Lord chose to advertise the mission through a most unsuspecting instrument, a secular newspaper reporter who may have been strolling home from work at the nearby *Los Angeles Times* building. "The night is made hideous...by the howlings of the worshipers," he wrote. "The devotees of the weird doctrine practice the most fanatical rites, preach the wildest theories and work themselves into a state of mad excitement." Not surprisingly, the devotees of the weird doctrine saw things differently. Within a week the San Andreas fault shifted, San Francisco lay in shambles, and anyone with a pure heart and an open mind could see that the long-awaited worldwide revival had finally begun.[1]

The tinder that caught fire in that ramshackle mission on Azusa Street is commonly said to have been the beginning of the worldwide pentecostal movement. Whether the revival really started among blacks at Azusa, or among whites in faith healing services in Topeka, Kansas years earlier, or even in a series of white-hot meetings among North Carolina hill folk in the 1890s, as various historians have contended, there can be little dispute that the pentecostal insurgence mushroomed into one of the most powerful religious upheavals of the twentieth century. A 1979 Gallup poll revealed that in the United States alone, nineteen percent—or twenty-nine million—adult Americans called themselves "Pentecostal or charismatic Christians."[2] Twelve years later the Assemblies of God, the largest and strongest of the pentecostal denominations, posted two million American adherents and another twenty-two million in affiliated bodies in other parts of the world.[3] In 1993, according to David Barrett, a leading scholar of world Christianity, the movement registered 430 million converts worldwide. Except for Roman Catholics, it ranked as the largest aggregation of Christians on the planet. Barrett projected that the revival would claim 560 million adherents by the year 2000 and well over a billion by the year 2025.[4] Almost certainly those figures swelled in the telling, perhaps wildly so, yet other studies consistently confirmed that within a century of its beginnings pentecostals had managed to claim a massive slice of the religious pie, both at home and abroad.[5]

Exactly who were the Christians who called themselves pentecostals? In the early 1990s scores of denominations—or fellowships, as they preferred to be called—claimed the label. The best known was the Assemblies of God, which was national in scope but strongest in the Sunbelt states. Other well-known bodies included the mostly black Church of God in Christ, clustered in the states of the Old South; the Church of God, concentrated in the Southern Highlands; the Pentecostal Holiness Church, centered the Southeast; and the International Church of the Foursquare Gospel, most visible on the West Coast. The United Pentecostal Church and the largely black Pentecostal Assemblies of the World, commonly known as "Oneness" groups because of their insistence that Jesus alone was God, identified themselves as pentecostal but maintained (or were allowed to maintain) few relations with other pentecostal bodies. Both were concentrated in the urban Midwest. Literally scores of smaller sects, many of which were non-English speaking, dotted the religious landscape.[6]

What did pentecostals believe and practice? In the early days they often dubbed their missions Full Gospel Tabernacles, which meant that they preached the "full" or "foursquare" gospel of 1) salvation through faith in Jesus Christ, 2) baptism of the Holy Spirit with the evidence of speaking in unknown tongues, 3) divine healing, and 4) the promise of the Lord's soon return. Late twentieth century adherents still shared those notions but in other ways they had grown extremely diverse. Run-down urban missions competed with opulent suburban churches; rough-tongued country preachers vied with unctuous television celebrities. More importantly, after World War II an emphasis upon the supernatural gifts of the Spirit as described in *I Corinthians* 12 and 14—preeminently the casting out of demons, divine healing, speaking in tongues, and the interpretation of tongues—penetrated some of the long established Protestant denominations and the Roman Catholic Church. The newer enthusiasts commonly called themselves charismatic Christians, partly to distinguish themselves from their unscrubbed pentecostal cousins.[7] Virtually every week in the 1980s and early 1990s the secular press carried an article about pentecostals or charismatics. Often those items focused upon the avarice of a Jim Bakker, the antics of a Jimmy Swaggert, or the Presidential ambitions of a Pat Robertson. Yet behind those very public and often sorry tales lay the private stories of millions of ordinary believers whose commitment to the work of the church typically dwarfed the involvement of non-pentecostal mainline Christians.

Scholars have offered various explanations for pentecostalism's apparent success. Some historians have pointed to the numerous continuities between the Wesleyan holiness and the pentecostal traditions back at the turn of the century, noting that the latter got a head start, so to speak, by appropriating the vast network of periodicals, churches, campmeetings, Bible schools, and faith homes that holiness folk had carefully cemented in place decades earlier. Other historians have suggested that pentecostalism provided spiritual compensations for the material good things that believers felt they had been denied this side of heaven's gate. Sociologists in turn have focused upon pentecostals' aptitude for providing a place in the sun for ordinary folk displaced by social disorganization or cast adrift by cultural dislocations. Friendly theologians have pointed to the revival's ability to meet enduring needs of the human spirit, while unfriendly ones have suggested that it exploited the gullibility of the masses, offering bogus cures for incurable diseases.[8]

All of these explanations bear a measure of truth, yet none seems entirely adequate.[9] In this essay I wish to offer an additional possibility. I do not propose that it supplants any of the others, but I do think that it illumines a neglected dimension of the question.

Simply stated, pentecostalism flourished because two impulses perennially warred for mastery of its soul. I shall call the first the *primitivist* and the second the *pragmatic*. The labels themselves are not crucial, but they seem as useful as any in suggesting a range of meanings that we shall explore more fully in a few moments. Here it suffices to say that the primitivist impulse represented a powerfully destructive urge to smash all human-made traditions in order to return to a first century world where the Holy Spirit alone reigned. In that realm supernatural signs and wonders formed the stuff of daily life, dreams and visions exercised normative authority, and the Bible stood free of higher criticism. The pragmatic impulse, in contrast, reflected an eagerness to do whatever was necessary in order to accomplish the movement's purposes. Though pragmatism did not logically require acceptance of the technological achievements and governing social arrangements of the postindustrial West—structural differentiation, procedural rationality, centralized management, and the like—as a practical matter that is the way things usually worked out. Moreover, once pentecostals learned that pragmatic attitudes not only worked, but also paid large dividends in subjective well-being, they found themselves drawn inch by inch into the assumptions of the therapeutic society where the quest for personal fulfillment reigned supreme.[10]

There are numerous ways to make this argument. In this essay I shall try to achieve this by asking a simple question: What kind of persons joined the revival in the first place? The answer—to jump way ahead in the story—is that the pioneer generation evinced, to a striking degree, *both* primitive and pragmatic character traits . More significantly, they displayed those traits at the same time, without compromise, in a knot of behavior patterns so tangled and matted as to be nearly inseparable. Not everyone fit the prototype of course. As with any large social aggregation—fifty thousand by 1910, maybe twice that number by 1920[11]—a great rainbow of human types joined the revival. Some exhibited consistently primitivist urges, while others found more pragmatic values congenial. Thus the doubleness of the pentecostal character did not necessarily manifest itself with equal force within the same persons all of the time. But within the aggregate it did.

Before turning to those early materials one caveat is needed. Exactly how the founding figures came to acquire these traits falls outside the scope of this essay. Some clearly brought them to the movement.[12] But others just as clearly absorbed them after they joined.[13] Probably most fell somewhere in-between, discovering something like an elective affinity between long-standing predispositions on one hand and newly acquired ideals on the other. At this distance it is hard to sort out the exact mix, and probably matters little if we could.

The main point is that apparently conflicting impulses energized the initial generation as a whole, and that pattern persisted into the 1990s. The clue lies in the faces of the day laborers and washerwomen who crowded the Azusa mission. In their determination to see the lame healed and the dead raised, whatever the cost—and that is the key phrase: *whatever the cost*—they proved themselves as worldly-wise as their well-heeled great grandchildren who frequented the glass-and-steel Christian Life Centers scattered along the Interstate by-passes.

THE PRIMITIVIST IMPULSE

Pentecostals themselves acknowledged only the primitivist side of their lives, so we shall begin with that part of their story. Primitivism has borne a score of meanings in the historical and theoretical literature of religious studies.[14] I shall define it quite simply as a yearning somehow to return to a time before time, to a space outside of space, to a mythical realm that Alexander Campbell memorably called the "ancient order of things." It is important to note that among early pentecostals primitivism was not simply restorationism, or at least what is commonly called restorationism. The latter suggested a rather self-conscious effort to sit down, figure out what the New Testament blueprint called for, then quite rationally reproduce it in the modern world. Campbellites, Mormons, Landmark Baptists, and other so-called restorationist sects of the nineteenth century readily come to mind.[15] Pentecostal primitivism certainly included all of that, but it was more. It was the dark subsoil in which restorationist and, for that matter, millenarian visions germinated. It was the urge to destroy all recently-made traditions in order to return to the ancient tradition of the New Testament where the Holy Ghost, and only the Holy Ghost, ruled the hearts and minds of the faithful. That long-lost world was, in a sense, an Edenic realm pulsating with supernatural signs and wonders, yet it was also an apocalyptic realm regimented by the timeless truths and universal values of Scripture. First generation stalwarts sought to re-enter that world as literally as possible by breathing its holy air, smelling its sacred fragrances, luxuriating in its spiritual delights. In the process, they fashioned their own social networks, cultural symbols, and religious rituals. To a remarkable extent they succeeded in creating a primitive garden in a modern wilderness.

On first reading, early pentecostals' rhetoric suggests that they were, above all, heavenly-minded pilgrims pursuing other-worldly satisfactions because they harbored little interest in this-worldly delights. Their storefront missions and backlot tents served as sequestered havens where they found inestimable rewards, at least by any ordinary calculus of things. What emerges from the literature is an image of questers determined to exchange the fleeting pleasures of life in the present world for the enduring fulfillments of life in the world to come. Of course they never explained themselves exactly that way. Indeed, they rarely explained themselves at all. But they did leave a long trail of hints, mostly in letters, diaries, and testimonials, suggesting the kind of satisfactions they sought in the sweat-soaked bedlam of the meeting. Those hints enable us to infer the sort of people they were, the hurts they endured, the aspirations they nurtured.

Examples surface everywhere we look in the primary literature. One Chicago partisan put it as plainly as language permitted: "Those who speak in tongues seem to live in another world."[16] Living in another world took a number of forms, however. For some, it engendered something like a sixth sense, a fundamentally new way of seeing even the natural landscape around them. "It seemed as if human joys vanished," a Florida advocate wrote. "It seemed as if the whole world and the people looked a different color."[17] A Wesleyan

Methodist pastor in Toronto spoke of a surge of feelings she had never known: "overwhelming power," "absence of fleshly effort," a sensation of walking "softly with God."[18] Some devotees appear to have entered into a sacred zone where time itself was calibrated according to divine rather than human standards. Looking back to the first blush of the revival from the vantage point of the mid 1920s, evangelist Frank Bartleman judged that he would "*rather live six months at that time than fifty years of ordinary time.*"[19] Members commonly spoke of spending hour after hour, sometimes entire days, in prayer and singing without thought of food.[20] Many had no awareness that night had fallen or that daylight had dawned.[21] Converts found themselves in a breathtaking era of history where the old structures had been swept away and new ones erected. In their nightly prayer meetings, a Webb City, Missouri, devotee wrote, "it seemed impossible to distinguish between the earthly and the heavenly anthems…. The celestial glory…filled the room with a halo of glory. [Some] could scarcely endure the 'weight of glory' that rested upon them."[22] Another recalled that when he underwent the baptism experience, "the fire fell and burned up all that would burn and what would not burn was caught up into heaven…It [was] a salvation indescribable…. My spirit long[ed] to be free from a sin-cursed world and be at home with Jesus."[23] One venerable pentecostal historian may have said more than he intended but surely touched an essential chord, when he wrote that many onlookers believed they were "either insane over religion, or drunk on some glorious dream."[24]

If the other world of supernatural delights and timeless truths functioned as the all-consuming locus of interest, it is hardly surprising that pentecostals betrayed little interest in earthly affairs such as Presidential elections or local politics. Their response to the war then raging in Europe is instructive. A few forthrightly supported American entry into the conflict and a handful opposed it, but the great majority held no opinion at all. What they worried about in letters to the editors was not bloodshed but the likelihood that the conflict would open up new opportunities for sin. "War is a feeder of hell," stormed the *Church of God Evangel*. "This last awful struggle has been the cause of millions of mother's boys dropping into the region of the damned where they are entering their eternal tortures."[25] Peace proved no more interesting than war. The November 1918 issue of Aimee Semple McPherson's *Bridal Call* characteristically said nothing about the Armistice that had just been signed. Six months elapsed before McPherson finally got around to reminding her readers that there was a Red Cross hospital atop Calvary's hill too.

Spirit-filled believers lost interest in the kind of day-to-day activities that most evangelical Protestants regarded as simple and legitimate pleasures of life. I am not thinking here of a pipe by the fireplace on a winter's night, or a frosty beer out on the front porch on a summer afternoon. Worldly enjoyments of that sort remained inconceivable. Rather, the point is that even officially sanctioned satisfactions such as family, children, and marital sex often lost all appeal.

Diaries and autobiographies reveal a good deal. Aimee Semple McPherson may not have cared much about the war, but she did care about Holy Ghost revivals. She boasted that she kept on traveling and preaching, month after month, even though her young daughter back at home seemed to be dying of influenza. The reason? Abraham had never hesitated to sacrifice Isaac.[26] The journal of pioneer educator D. C. O. Opperman, which carefully chronicled his ceaseless travels back and forth across the South between 1905 and 1912, displayed a man so preoccupied with the work at hand that he gave only perfunctory notice to his marriage and the birth of his first two children. He even failed to note the name of his third child.[27] The diary of Pentecostal Holiness Church leader, George Floyd Taylor, revealed a similar pattern: a litany of reports on sermons preached, biblical passages meditated upon, Sunday School classes taught, cronies talked with, prayer meetings attended. The entry for August 27, 1908, taken virtually at random, proclaimed, "My soul is a sea of glass.... Glory! Glory!... My soul secretly cries out for God to hide me away in His presence."[28] Except for a daily report on the weather, Taylor's journal avoided any hint of mundane detail. One would never suspect that this husband and father had ever suffered a trace of disappointment, a pang of hunger, or a tug of lust.

Even in death the pattern persisted. Just before his own death, Richard G. Spurling, Jr., a founder of the Church of God, asked that he not be buried facing east, as the custom was among his people, but buried facing his homeplace. With that gesture Spurling meant to signal that he had spent too much time caring for his family and not enough time doing the only thing that really mattered, preaching the gospel.[29]

Enthusiasts subordinated romance to a calculus of heavenly rewards. Neither the wedding nor the wedding night could be taken as events memorable or pleasurable in their own right. The notice of an Inglewood, California, ceremony reported that it was preceded by a time of "rejoicing and praise before God." Many were saved.[30] A newspaper published by a pentecostal band in San Francisco happily observed that when two of its members married, the ritual concluded with an impassioned "exhortation for sinners to seek the Lord."[31] Things were no different in Britain. In the Welsh hamlet of Llandilo, one paper reported, celebrants carved up the wedding home into a prayer room and a food room. To everyone's joy one "brother received the baptism of the Holy Ghost" in the prayer room—while the rest presumably attended to their appetites in the food room.[32] Back in Oklahoma, a new husband-wife evangelist team trumpeted that their wedding had been a "glorious occasion" because it reminded all present of "Jesus our Heavenly Bridegroom coming in the air."[33] Evangelist Howard Goss primly recorded that his bride Ethel spent their wedding night preaching a fiery sermon at a revival in Eureka Springs, Arkansas, with telling effect upon local sinners.[34] A young brother from Canada begged the readers of the *Christian Evangel* to pray that "God will give me the girl of my choice—a baptized saint—for a wife." Why? For love? For family? Perish the thought! If they married, he solemnly explained, they could start a rest home for missionaries.[35]

If pentecostals discountenanced the routine pleasures of life, they were equally prepared to forgo the bonds that tethered them to earth. This helps explains why believers could dismiss digging a storm cellar, an act that surely seemed prudent enough, as a "habit of the flesh."[36] It also helps explain why a sister who claimed to be heaven-bound yet worried about the eternal fate of her children could become a target of ridicule. If a mother were *truly* heaven-bound, the argument ran, she would not be compromised by any earthly interest, even a concern for the souls of her offspring.[37]

Night after night enthusiasts lustily sang, "Take the world, but give me Jesus." But there really was not much to take. They were already living on that distant shore.

THE PRAGMATIC IMPULSE

If an initial reading of the letters, diaries, and testimonial columns of early pentecostalism leaves an image of pilgrims singlemindedly trekking toward heaven's gate, a second reading creates a strikingly different image. The latter suggests that first generation converts are better interpreted as eminently practical-minded folk who used the limited resources at their disposal to gain their purposes, sacred or otherwise. According to this second perspective, when all was said and done, pentecostals proved themselves a persistently ambitious lot, considerably less interested in what was said than in what was done. A scenario of mundane sagacity and this-worldly hardheadedness dominates the picture.

Admittedly, it requires a bit of reading between the lines to see how prevalent the pragmatic character trait really was. Pentecostals almost never described themselves with the repertoire of words we associate with this-worldliness: shrewdness, adroitness, savvy, and the like. Indeed, they typically went to great lengths to suggest the opposite. They wanted to believe and, more importantly, they wanted the world to believe, that the Holy Spirit alone governed all aspects of their lives. They also hoped to convince themselves and their neighbors that they never gave a second thought to their own interests. But if we turn the data under the light just a little, they tell a very different story. It was no accident that Aimee McPherson, a pentecostal barnstormer, put up the first religious radio station in the United States, nor that two generations later Pat Robertson, a pentecostal TV preacher, launched the first privately owned communications satellite in the world. That sure sense of knowing the ropes, knowing how to get things done, knowing how to negotiate with local power brokers, existed from the beginning, always poised just beneath the surface.

As a deeply rooted character trait, mundane sagacity manifested itself in countless ways. For brevity I shall discuss only two. The first was a maverick streak so pronounced that it bordered upon outright rebelliousness. Historian Timothy L. Smith once wrote that nineteenth century holiness come-outers typically found themselves "unable to accept much real discipline save their own."[38] That characterization fit early pentecostals even better than their holiness parents. Thumbing through the biographical data, one is struck by pentecostals' self-taught inventiveness, their stubborn unwillingness to be instructed, much less bound, by the conventions of the past. While they were never as theologically unbuttoned as other homegrown sects like Mormons and Jehovah's Witnesses, they routinely winked at or even discarded inherited orthodoxies whenever it suited their purposes. Indeed, the tradition's cardinal doctrinal distinctive—namely, that speaking in tongues invariably accompanied the baptism of the Holy Spirit—stood unprecedented in the entire history of Judaism and Christianity. From time to time individual partisans espoused highly imaginative positions, to put it as charitably as possible, on matters as diverse as the origin of the human species, the destiny of Israel, the gold standard, and much else. Standing alone like that may have taken a toll at some deep psychological level. But on the surface pentecostals seem not to have suffered a twinge of self-consciousness, let alone embarrassment, as they marched in solitary zeal across the theological landscape.

The point I wish to emphasize here is not so much the singularity of pentecostals' theological ideas, as such, but the frame of mind they brought to the task of formulating those ideas. The fundamental animus can be described as exuberant creativity, a kind of swashbuckling inventiveness that prompted them to draw their own conclusions from their own sources in their own way, the devil and the established churches be damned. To take one of countless examples, probably only a small minority ever shared founder Charles Fox Parham's view that the unregenerate dead suffered annihilation rather than eternal torment. But the way that he came to that conclusion was altogether typical. Parham had been reared and schooled as an orthodox Methodist. Upon marriage, his wife's grandfather, a Quaker with annihilationist leanings, challenged him to read the Bible without commentaries in hand or creeds in mind. Parham did, and soon reached an annihilationist position himself, which he stubbornly upheld the rest of his life despite relentless vilification from other evangelicals.[39]

The maverick disposition manifested itself in other ways. A disproportionate number of the early leaders had been voluntary immigrants to the United States to begin with, typically coming from Australia, Britain, or Western Europe. Most came over not to escape penury or military service in the Old World but either to do better financially or to find ampler scope for their ministries in the rolling religious spaces of the New World.[40] Many proved inveterate travelers, crisscrossing the United States and frequently the Atlantic and Pacific oceans year in, year out. For example A. A. Boddy, sometimes hailed as the father of British pentecostalism, sailed the ocean at least fourteen times, not counting side trips to Africa, Siberia, and the European Continent.[41] Some of course were forced to travel constantly, whether they liked it or not, because they were overseers or itinerant preachers by trade.[42] But autobiographies make clear that the opposite dynamic often dominated: many became overseers or itinerants in the first place because they could not abide the confinement of a settled pastorate for more than a few weeks at a stretch.[43] Some clearly became foreign missionaries for pretty much the same reason. China missionaries Alfred and Lillian Garr wrote that they gladly suffered the loss of their "old Holiness friends" in order to be the first to herald the pentecostal message in Asia. One can almost feel their expansionist exuberance: "It was like beginning life over, a new ministry...not limited to a small fraction of the Holiness people, nor to one country...but the 'World our parish.'"[44] Sometimes globe-trotting obviously got out of hand. Complaints about the needlessly peripatetic ways of overseas missionaries regularly spiked the editorial columns of early newspapers.[45]

The maverick demon in the pentecostal soul recoiled at the specter of regularization. For the better part of a decade zealots fought off efforts to standardize the funding of missionaries, or to impose even minimal rules of financial accountability upon evangelists or local churches.[46] Until after World War I the majority of periodicals were launched, edited, and run as one-man or, equally often, as one-woman operations.[47] A remarkable number of those editors continued to publish and jealously guard their subscription lists long after joining a pentecostal denomination with its own official publication.[48] Pentecostals were never as prone to put up schools as they were to float periodicals. Yet at least a score of elementary and secondary academies and Bible institutes, originally founded and run as largely one-person operations, persisted long after the founder had joined a body with its own centrally-sponsored institutions. These independent schools sorely irked denominational bureaucrats determined to rein in such endeavors.[49] Yet in their heart of hearts they too knew that the movement had been born of a defiant temper. In later years patriarch Howard Goss, a denominational bureaucrat himself, acknowledged that the very "foundation for the vast Pentecostal Movement" had been laid by loners and free-lancers, by missionaries without board support and pastors without degrees or salaries or "restful holidays."[50]

Besides a maverick disposition, the evidence discloses another pragmatic character trait. Any number of adjectives will do: intrepid, audacious, assertive, pushy. I shall lump them all under the rubric of willfulness. What these terms all suggest, rightly enough, is a singleminded determination to gain the goal at hand, regardless of the obstacles or even of the human cost. One nameless writer hit the nail squarely on the head when he or she judged that the baptism experience steeled believers with "holy boldness."[51] And they were plenty proud of it too. For Church of God General Overseer A. J. Tomlinson, the lassitude that came with "long study and…deep tiresome thinking" had grievously undermined established Christianity. In his mind it was high time for Christians to get moving, "fired up with holy zeal and undaunted courage."[52] The faint-hearted might lament the rush of technology or the secular world's obsession with progress, but not Tomlinson. Why should we, he demanded, allow others, "by going hungry and arising early, to win the prize for energy, wit, longsuffering, perseverance, grit and determination?"[53]

For most enthusiasts holy boldness was as much a practical as a spiritual mandate. Thus M. L. Ryan, pastor of a flock in Spokane, Washington, and editor of one of the earliest periodicals, *Apostolic Light,* led a band of eighteen missionaries to Japan in the summer of 1907 without the endorsement of any board or denomination, and apparently without any certain destination in mind or clear notion of how they would support themselves when they got there. No matter. When the band reached Tokyo, Ryan discovered that he would have to pay high customs fees. Undeterred, he offered his typewriter and tent as collateral, somehow secured a two-masted lifeboat and immediately proceeded to sail around Tokyo harbor preaching the pentecostal message (presumably with an interpreter in tow). Within days Ryan had managed to turn out two issues of an English-and-Japanese edition of *Apostolic Light.*[54]

Pentecostals' notorious anti-intellectualism was more stereotypical than typical. Yet insofar as they were anti-intellectual, much of that trait can be attributed to impatience, to a brash determination to get on with the job at hand rather than waste time on pointless theorizing. One leader probably revealed more than he intended when he declared that "God made grappling hooks of His Pentecostal preachers rather than bookworms."[55] Not all preachers and certainly not all laypersons were grappling hooks. As in any large social movement, pentecostalism also attracted the timid and the bookish.[56] But no one thought to preserve their memory in the evidence because it did not fit the ideal. What we read about, rather, are leaders variously described as "vivid, magnetic…incisive."[57] Many are "erect, clear-eyed, tense and enthusiastic."[58] Others are "[filled with] intense dogmatic zeal [and] a firm determination to rule or ruin."[59]

Willfulness fired stamina. Though the evidence is too spotty to warrant confident generalizations about the rank-and-file, pentecostal leaders appear remarkably vigorous. To be sure, most had experienced serious illness before converting to the movement and many suffered recurring bouts afterward. Yet there is good reason to believe that significantly fewer of them endured debilitating illness than the national norm. Moreover, virtually all enjoyed stunning divine healings in their own bodies.[60] Those landmark events not only brought physical restoration but also stirred converts to proclaim the pentecostal message with renewed vigor. Thus willfulness—defined in this case as a determination to believe that one had been healed, regardless of symptoms, or the certainty that one had been divinely commissioned to do the Lord's work, come what may—ignited and sustained extraordinary levels of physical exertion.

Again, examples readily come to hand. One thinks of missionary heroes like Victor Plymire, who toiled forty-one years on the Tibetan-Chinese border, despite hardship, disease, and persecution from local magistrates, with only a handful of converts to show for his life's work.[61] Yet the exertions of less heralded leaders illustrate the point better precisely *because* they were less heralded. One evangelist remembered that if workers could not afford trains or carriages, "they rode bicycles, or in lumber wagons; some went horseback, some walked. Often they waded creeks. Often men removed their clothes, tied their bundles above their heads and swam rivers" to get to the next night's meeting.[62] In 1908 Winnipeg pastor and businessman A. H. Argue casually remarked that he had led nine services per week every week for the past nine months.[63] Mary "Mother" Barnes achieved local notoriety for shepherding a revival in Thayer, Missouri, from nine a.m. until midnight, seven days a week, for eight months straight.[64] In 1912 E. N. Bell proudly grumbled that as sole editor of *Word and Witness*, he had mailed out nineteen thousand copies of the paper each month, personally answered six to seven hundred letters each month, and held down a full time pastorate in Malvern, Arkansas, where he preached five times per week and maintained a regular hospital visitation ministry.[65] The diary of A. J. Tomlinson stands as a chronicle of tireless travel on foot, mule, train, auto, ship—whatever was available—and the preaching on the average of one sermon a day for nearly forty years. The entries for a July 1925 weekend were typical. At age sixty-five, between Thursday and Sunday, he delivered ten sermons amidst swarming mosquitoes and drenching humidity. "The only rest I got," he added in a telling postscript, "was while the saints were shouting, dancing and talking in tongues."[66]

Allowing for some forgivable exaggeration in such accounts, it is clear that extraordinary faith—read willfulness—prompted extraordinary activity. To be sure, common sense tells us that men and women who could ford rivers and shout the devil into submission were blessed with a tough constitution to begin with. But it was an iron-willed frame of mind that put that constitution rightly to work. One author allowed that feeling blue from time to time was to be expected, yet immediately added that melancholy was a sin to be borne and fought off like any other temptation. "[The Christian] is never to be sorrowful for a moment, but to be ALWAYS REJOICING."[67] The steel rod that stiffened the pentecostal spinal column revealed itself in India missionary Elizabeth Sisson. In the dentist's chair, Sisson boasted, she had never used Novocain because she was determined to retain complete control of her mind and body at all times.[68] That last statement is particularly significant given that Sisson also wrote with luxuriant detail about the frequency and intensity of her ecstatic experiences, events that outsiders would readily categorize as disassociative if not pathological.[69]

Willfulness manifested itself in other ways. Sometimes pentecostal writers sounded like hawkers for a Dale Carnegie course. "It is always better to encourage people to do what they can for themselves," one averred. "People are pauperized by teaching them.... to ask the Lord to do for us many things which we ought to do for ourselves."[70] Often willfulness expressed itself in a simple syllogism that outsiders found scandalous if not blasphemous. The syllogism ran like this. God has uttered certain promises in Scripture. If believers act in the prescribed manner, God has bound himself to respond in the prescribed manner. "Getting things from God is like playing checkers," wrote F. F. Bosworth, the most respected healing evangelist of the 1920s. "He always moves when it is His turn.... Our move is to expect what he promises."[71]

Pentecostals applied that reasoning most frequently to the matter of physical health. Since God had promised to heal the body if one prayed with genuine faith, the only possible result was immediate and complete restoration of the body. Carrie Judd Montgomery, one of the most prolific and articulate figures in the early history of the movement, made the case with memorable clarity: "If, after prayer for physical healing, we reckon the work as already accomplished in our bodies, we shall not fear to act out that faith, and to make physical exertions which will justify our professed belief in the healing."

Then came the knock-out punch: "I have never failed to receive according to my faith."[72] The import was as clear and hard as glass: the genuineness of one's faith was directly and exactly commensurate with one's ability to get up and subdue the afflicting disease. If the symptoms persisted that meant either that one's faith was weak or that they were nothing but "counterfeit symptoms" to begin with. As one physician convert put it, "[You must not] wait to see the evidence of your healing. There will be no evidence until it is done, and it will not be done until you believe without visible or tangible evidence of any sort."[73] One nameless grandmother, who had worn eyeglasses for twenty years, tossed them out when she decided to pray for restoration of her eyesight. From that point on, she forced herself to read ten chapters of her Bible each day without glasses because God had promised that he would answer the prayer of faith. Therefore He *did*. "Why, salt water is good for the eyes," she wrote, tears tumbling onto the page.[74]

Express your needs in prayer. Assume that you possess your healing the instant you pray for it. Get up and act on that assumption. If counterfeit symptoms persist, disregard them. After all, the Lord promised: "'I'll do anything you want me to do.'"[75]

The formula worked every time—if one possessed the grit and the moxie to make it work.

CONCLUSION

The better part of a century has passed since that nameless grandmother flung her glasses aside. The world has changed dramatically since then, and in many ways pentecostals have changed with it. But only superficially.

At the end of the twentieth century the essential structural tension between the primitive and the pragmatic persisted as acutely as ever. On one hand, the theology and worship patterns or what religion scholars might call the myths and rituals that energized the movement's inner life survived largely untouched by the assumptions of the secular culture. Biblical inerrancy and literalism hovered as close to the ground as they did at the turn of the century. Darwin, Marx, and Freud, not to mention more recent icons of the secular academy such as Mary Daly, Richard Rorty, and Stephen Jay Gould, remained wholly outside the horizon of pentecostal consciousness. More significantly, the longing for vital manifestations of the supernatural gifts of the Holy Spirit flourished with unabated fervor. Pentecostal periodicals brimmed with stories of stunning healings and divine interventions in daily life. Miracles may not have danced before believers' eyes quite as often as they once did, but one thing was sure: No child of the revival would have counted it a good thing if it were true.[76]

At the same time, however, latter day enthusiasts rushed to embrace the therapeutic rewards and technological amenities of modernity with scarcely a second thought. Although a few still gathered in storefront missions and avoided the trappings of the good life, the majority worshipped in carpeted, air-conditioned buildings indistinguishable from the local United Methodist Church. Adherents propagated their message with state-of-the-art publishing and communications technology. They hob-nobbed with the rich and the powerful. Indeed, many of them *were* the rich and the powerful. On the whole, then, they dressed, worked, and played like anyone else who hailed from the same region and occupied the same position in the social system. Sometimes it appeared that the only difference between pentecostal Christians and mainline Christians was that the former got there first and did it bigger, better, and less tastefully.[77]

Taken together, then, pentecostals of the 1990s presented an arresting spectacle. They appeared to believe and worship by one set of rules but to work and play by quite another. Stalwarts spent their evenings at full gospel rallies rapturously speaking in tongues, and spent their days in university computer labs unraveling mysteries of another sort. Spirit-filled medical missionaries cast out demons in the morning and adjusted CAT scanners in the afternoon. Partisans asked the Holy Spirit to help them find their car keys as nonchalantly as they invited a neighbor to drop by for coffee. Though scenarios of this sort could have been witnessed in virtually any large urban pentecostal church—and for that matter a great many small rural ones too—we are not limited to impressions. The hard data sniffed out by social scientists told very much the same story. Case studies of pentecostal converts strongly suggested that the primitive and the pragmatic actually co-varied: the more fervent the former, the more determined the latter.[78]

Any number of outsiders looked at this spectacle and came away scratching their heads, wondering how it all fit together. In their minds it was nothing short of remarkable that pentecostals' taste for other-worldly ecstasies and for ahistorical dogmatisms had survived as long as it had. Surely it could not last indefinitely, they supposed. Surely pentecostals were destined either to go the way of the United Methodists—that is, move uptown culturally as well as socially—or, like Old Order Mennonites, to recede to a picturesque but obscure corner of contemporary life.[79] What most of those observers presupposed, of course, was that cultural modernism and social modernization came together as a package deal, something like a solid-state appliance with no customer-removable parts.

But that is precisely where the problem arises. Recent history proves that no one owns the franchise on modernity. Everywhere we look we see ardent Christians selectively shopping in the warehouse of the times, choosing what they like, ignoring what they do not like, and rarely giving the matter a second thought. The plain fact is that religious folk put their lives together in a dizzying variety of ways.

Examples abound. In the mid nineteenth century Oneida Perfectionists, fired by a potent mix of apocalyptic Scripture readings and ecstatic religious experience, implemented systematic work habits and careful accounting procedures that led to the redoubtable Oneida Silverware Company. In the late nineteenth century evangelical missionaries fanned out around the world heralding a darkly primitivist vision of the imminent fiery climax of history. Yet the very urgency of their message also impelled them to adopt the most efficient means of transportation and publication known, along with a streamlining of mission boards at home that should have made Wall Street envious. Anyone familiar with the corpus of missionary biographies and autobiographies of the last two centuries knows how often the primitive and the pragmatic, or at least facsimiles thereof, presented themselves in the same souls. "A strange compound of fiercely practical common sense and profound mysticism," was the way that Pearl Buck described her China missionary mother.[80] After World War II ultra-traditionalist insurrectionaries around the world distinguished themselves by their deployment of the best and latest in mass communications technology—not to mention weaponry. And lest anyone doubt that all sorts of primitivisms could promenade arm-in-arm with the most advanced forms of social modernization, we need only observe the daily lives of millions of mainline Christians in the 1990s. Episcopalians confronted the mystery of the Eucharist on Sunday mornings and ran corporate board meetings on Monday afternoons. Roman Catholics earnestly confessed the Apostles' Creed one day and negotiated high priced real estate deals the next.

All of this is to say that at one time or another virtually every tradition within the Christian family (and for that matter a good many *outside* the Christian family) confronted a roughly similar set of polarities: piety versus intellect, supernature versus nature, prophetic critique versus priestly legitimation, ancient wisdom versus modern insight, right belief versus right results. In this respect, Spirit-filled believers proved themselves no different from countless faithful before them.

But the story does not end there. In other ways first-, second-, and third-generation pentecostals consistently showed themselves very different indeed. If they drew threads of inspiration from the heritage of Christian belief and behavior, they also wove those threads into a distinctive tapestry that was very much of their own making. And one feature of that distinctiveness was the sheer bravura with which they maintained *both* the primitive and the pragmatic sides of their identity at once. Though it would be difficult to prove, looking back over the twentieth century, it is at least arguable that the contrast between transcendent visions and mundane sagacity manifested itself more dramatically among pentecostals than among any other large group of Christians of modern times (except perhaps the Mormons). That was particularly true in the Third World where, especially after World War II, the transcendent and the mundane flourished side by side with riotous abandon.[81]

To be sure, the exact nature of the interaction between the primitive and the pragmatic in the pentecostal subculture is not entirely clear. We grope for metaphors. Is that relationship best construed as a struggle between antagonists? Or as an alliance between partners? Or is it more accurate to picture it as both at once—something like the inexplicable chemistry of a combative yet invigorating marriage?

Subtler images that intimate more complex modes of interaction also come to mind. The trickster figure of American folklore offers one possibility. In those stories a mythic character such as Brer Rabbit presents itself in one form in one context, but in a dramatically different form in another context. This analogy suggests that perhaps we should think of the primitive and the pragmatic not as two distinct impulses at all, but rather as a single reflex that changed faces according to situation. The signal benefit of the trickster construct is that it reminds us that a given act, such as obliviousness to conventional family ties, may have served primitive ends in one setting and pragmatic ones in another.[82]

Another possibility presents itself. Literary critics have taught us that all texts can be read at two levels (or at *least* at two levels.) Wherever there is a surface text there is also always a submerged text; what is said gains force and meaning when we peel back the explicit words, so to speak, and expose the implicit ones beneath. Religious cultures too can be read as "texts." In that case, pentecostals' primitivist behavior can be construed as the surface text, while their pragmatic inclinations can be construed as the submerged text. The task then is not to prove that one was more real or even more important than the other, but to recognize that the revivals' spiritual power and cultural meaning emerged from the perennial interplay of the two.[83]

A metaphor drawn from the realm of the theater offers one more option and, given the intractable doubleness of the evidence, a particularly compelling one. By this reckoning the primitive invariably stood front and center stage, carrying the burden of the plot, reveling in the applause of the faithful and, of course, bravely bearing the jeers of the faithless. The pragmatic, on the other hand, normally served as the stage manager, standing behind the curtains, orchestrating all of the moves—but with the cash till never far from mind. This scenario suggests that when pentecostals were wearing their primitivist garb, they may have been, first and foremost, following a script: a pre-approved story carefully designed to edify the committed and win the uncommitted. It also suggests that if believers played to the galleries more often than they admitted, journalists and historians bought the ruse more often than they knew.[84]

All of these metaphors may well help us conceptualize the inner workings of pentecostal culture, but they also pose risks, for they may beguile us into thinking that the primitive and the pragmatic were somehow substantive things in themselves. Obviously they were not; they are only labels that we apply to conspicuous and persistent patterns of behavior. Thus pinning down the exact configuration of the interaction—be it antagonistic, complementary, competitive, invertible, dialectical, theatrical, or whatever—seems less important than recognizing its pervasive and vital presence in the movement's life. The real task before us then is to divine the functions that the interaction performed in the lives of ordinary believers.

At least two functions come to mind. The first might be called institutional success, the second ethical immaturity.

Institutional success arose from a delicate balancing of primitive and pragmatic energies. On one side, the primitive fueled the revival by offering certitude about the truthfulness of inherited theological claims and the reality of the supernatural. It gave ordinary Christians life-giving energies. It guaranteed that the pentecostal message would not fall into the deadening routines of pragmatic implementation or, worse, of self-serving manipulation. Moreover, other-worldly yearnings distanced the tradition from the conventions of the surrounding culture, making it possible for believers to chart their own spiritual course in a world that was not so much hostile as simply uncomprehending. The pragmatic, in contrast, stabilized the movement by keeping adherents from squandering their energies in ecstatic excesses. It imposed standards of efficiency, economy, and institutional order. It kept the revival from rendering itself, in Emerson's fine words, "frivolous and ungirt." Most importantly, perhaps, the pragmatic enabled believers to reproduce their culture among succeeding generations by fostering stable educational structures. If primitivist aspirations inspired a vision of life as it might be, pragmatic values afforded the means for preserving it.

Less happily, the interplay of impulses also engendered ethical immaturity. The primitive freed enthusiasts from worrying very much about the propriety of their social attitudes. To be sure, they avoided personal vices such as drinking and smoking and, except for the question of conscription during World War I, they took pride in their obedience to the laws of the land. But until very recently at least, pentecostals displayed little or no concern with larger questions of responsible social and political behavior. It almost never occurred to them that a Christian ought to take a thoughtful stand, or *any* stand, regarding suffrage, prohibition, civil rights, environmental pollution, or famine in other countries. Only the Holy Spirit reigned in their lives, they wanted to believe, and because the Holy Spirit had nothing to say about those pesky questions, there was no reason to trouble themselves with them either. In the meantime, the pragmatic impulse spurred pentecostals to build the biggest and buy the best of everything, mainly for the Lord of course, but sometimes a little for themselves too. Where other more historically seasoned Christians had learned that it was not so easy to live godly lives in a godless world, pentecostals experienced few qualms about their ability to shuttle from celestial heights to terrestrial plains and back again. The impregnable conviction that they—and often enough, that they alone—had seen the Promised Land enabled them to relish the satisfactions of spiritual separation from modern life and, at the same time, to savor most of its benefits without a trace of guilt. The formula proved golden, in more ways than one.[85]

As the movement matures, of course, some of this may change. We need not accept the conclusions of extreme cultural evolutionists who expect the primitive side of the pentecostal character to wither up and die in the bright sun of modern civilization in order to suppose that time and experience will temper the wildest of visionaries. And in the process, pentecostals are sure to tumble into the dark turbulences of history, where life is not simple nor solutions clear-cut. Awareness that the movement did not fall from the skies like a sacred meteorite but emerged at a particular time and place, and thus bore the earmarks of its time and place, may make it more difficult to sustain the power of first century signs and wonders. But if immersion in the messy details of history threatens a slow-down of institutional growth, it also promises a deepening of ethical self-awareness.[86]

At the same time, modern secular culture, smugly secure in its relativist premises and its quest for personal gratification, may find that unruly movements like pentecostalism really do have something to say that is worth hearing. "The Lord hath more light yet to break forth out of his Holy Word," Pilgrim John Robinson observed four centuries ago.[87] Pentecostals were not the first and almost certainly will not be the last of American-born sectarians to capture the religious world's attention. But they may demonstrate, in ways that other Christians have not often matched, that the ancient book and the ecstatic visions it harbored still bears the power to change lives and to transform cultures.

NOTES

A number of colleagues critiqued earlier versions of this essay. Among those I especially wish to thank William R. Hutchison and George M. Marsden.

1. *Los Angeles Times*, April 18, 1906, 1.

2. The Gallup poll is described in Kenneth S. Kantzer, "The Charismatics among Us," *Christianity Today*, February 22, 1980, 24–29.

3. *The Assemblies of God: Current Facts 1991*, a pamphlet published by that body's Office of Information in Springfield, Missouri, in 1992, claims a U. S. constituency of 2,234,708, a US membership of 1,324,800, and a world constituency of 22,723,215.

4. David B. Barrett, "Annual Statistical Table on Global Mission: 1993," *International Bulletin of Missionary Research*, 17 (January 1993) : 23. It should be remembered that many charismatics are Roman Catholics.

5. In 1991 membership for the major pente-costal bodies in the United States totaled 7,698,547. *Yearbook of American and Canadian Churches, 1991* (Nashville: Abingdon, 1991), 258–264. A research assistant and I compiled these figures by adding up the totals for all of the groups that are traditionally categorized as pentecostal. Random telephone sampling of the adult United States population in 1990 yielded adherence figures of 4,032,000. *Research Report, the National Survey of Religious Identification, 1989–90, The Graduate School and University Center of the City University of New York*. (I have not included 442,000 self-professed adherents of the "Church of God," since there are several decidedly nonpente-costal Wesleyan holiness bodies that go by the same name.)

6. For a concise, perceptive overview of the history of American pentecostalism, see R. G. Robins, "Pentecostal Movement," in *Dictionary of Christianity in America*, edited by Daniel G. Reid and others (Downers Grove, IL: Inter Varsity Press, 1990).

7. The insurgence of the world charismatic movement is ably described in Vinson Synan, *The Twentieth-Century Pentecostal Explosion* (Altamonte Springs, FL: Creation House, 1987).

8. I have briefly addressed the range of explanations that have been offered by scholars in "Bibliography and Historiography of Pentecostalism (US)," in *Dictionary of Pentecostal and Charismatic Movements*, edited by Stanley M. Burgess and Gary B. McGee (Grand Rapids: Zondervan, 1988), 65–76.

9. Reductionist approaches predominate, at least in the nontheological scholarly literature. For critiques of such see Virginia H. Hine, "The Deprivation and Disorganization Theories of Religious Movements," in *Religious Movements in*

Contemporary America, edited by Irving I. Zaretsky and Mark Leone (Princeton, NJ: Princeton University Press, 1974), 646–664; Margaret M. Poloma, "An Empirical Study of Perceptions of Healing Among Assemblies of God Members," *Pneuma: The Journal of the Society for Pentecostal Studies*, 7 (Spring 1985): 61–77; and Grant Wacker, "Taking Another Look at the Vision of the Disinherited," *Religious Studies Review*, 8 (1982):15–22. See also the fine survey of the assumptions and conclusions of the dominant social scientific literature in H. Newton Malony and A. Adams Lovekin, *Glossolalia: Behavioral Science Perspectives on Speaking in Tongues* (New York: Oxford University Press, 1985), chapter 7. More generally see R. Stephen Warner, "Theoretical Barriers to the Understanding of Evangelical Christianity," *Sociological Analysis*, 15 (Spring 1979): 1–9.

10. My understanding of the differences between cultural modernism on one hand and technological and social modernization on the other has been informed by Mary Douglas, "The Effects of Modernization on Religious Change," *Daedalus*, 3 (Winter, 1982):1–19; Bruce B. Lawrence, *Defenders of God: The Fundamentalist Revolt Against the Modern Age* (San Francisco: Harper & Row, 1989), especially chapter 1; and John F. Wilson, "Modernity and Religion: A Problem of Perspective," in *Modernity and Religion*, edited by William Nicholls (Waterloo, Ontario : Wilfrid Laurier University Press, 1987), 9–18. Obviously there is no necessary link between pragmatism and modernity. Many ancients displayed highly pragmatic behavior and many moderns do not. But the present point is that pentecostals' pragmatic behavior *normally* led to an appropriation of the technological achievements and social arrangements of the post-industrial West.

11. Reliable figures on the size of the movement in the early years of the century are hard to come by, to say the least. In 1908, in the first attempt to construct a historical overview, India missionary Max Wood Moorhead estimated 50,000 adherents in the United States alone. Two years later Arthur S. Booth-Clibborn, a thoughtful and widely-traveled early leader, put the figure at 60,000 to 80,000 fully committed members, plus another 20,000 to 40,000 active supporters worldwide. Moorhead, "A Short History of the Pentecostal Movement," *Cloud of Witnesses*, 1908, 16; Booth-Clibborn, *Confidence*, August, 1910, 182. In 1936 the United States Bureau of the Census, listed 356, 329 members for 26 known pentecostal sects. Given pentecostals' propensity to worship in homes, skid-row missions, and rural meeting houses, many of which surely escaped the eye of the enumerators, it is safe to assume that the actual number was greater. I have taken these census figures from Robert Mapes Anderson's *Vision of the Disinherited: The Making of American Pentecostalism* (New York: Oxford University Press, 1979), 117.

12. The entwining of primitivist and of pragmatic strains revealed itself in the behavior of holiness pastor A. G. Garr years before his conversion to pentecostalism. See for example the wide-eyed supernaturalism *and* the streetwise bravura of Garr's actions at a 1903 street meeting in Dillon, MT, in *Burning Bush*, September 10, 1903, 7.

13. Some of the faithful acquired the signature blending of primitive and pragmatic traits only after they converted. Consider for example one missionary correspondent in China who wrote to Nazarene leader A. M. Hills about the personality transformation that overtook holiness defectors to pentecostalism: "Quiet, retiring, teachable natures, who were charitable to a fault, were transformed into dogmatic, unteachable, schismatic and anathema-breathing souls." A. M. Hills, *The Tongues Movement* (Manchester [UK]: Star Hall, no date [presumably 1914]), 26.

14. "Primitivism," by George Boas, in *Dictionary of the History of Ideas*, edited by Philip Wiener (New York: Scribners, 1973).

15. The story of these and other explicitly restorationist bodies is ably told by Richard T. Hughes and C. Leonard Allen in *Illusions of Innocence: Protestant Primitivism in America, 1630–1875* (Chicago: University of Chicago Press, 1988).

16. *The Apostolic Faith* [Los Angeles] , June–September l907, 3.

17. *The Apostolic Faith* [Los Angeles], January 1907, p.1, quoted in Edith L. Blumhofer, *The Assemblies of God: A Chapter in the Story of American Pentecostalism* (Springfield, MO: Gospel Publishing House, 1989), I:143.

18. Addie A. Knowlton, *The New Acts*, June 1907, 8.

19. Frank Bartleman, *Azusa Street* (Plainfield, NJ: Logos International, 1980), 21, Bartleman's emphasis. The main body of this work is an unaltered reprint of Bartleman's 1925 classic, *How "Pentecost" Came to Los Angeles—How It Was in the Beginning*.

20. Ardell K. Mead, *The Apostolic Faith* [Los Angeles] , November l906, 3; A. A. Boddy, quoting the letter of "a working-man," *The Christian* [UK], August 1, 1907, page number unreadable; Mrs. Hebden, *The Promise* [Toronto], May 1907, 2.

21. *Word and Work*, May 1910, p.14; *The Apostolic Faith* [Los Angeles], December 1906, 3;

typescript of interview with Azusa pioneer A. G. Osterberg, "Second Tape," Assemblies of God Archives, Springfield, MO.

22. A. R. Haughawout, *The Apostolic Faith* [Baxter Springs, KS], June l914, 3.

23. J. M. Vawter, *The New Acts*, August 16, 1906, 6.

24. Howard A. Goss, *The Winds of God: The Story of the Early Pentecostal Days (1901–1914) in the Life of Howard A. Goss, As Told by Ethel E. Goss* (New York: Comet Press Books, 1958), 78.

25. *The Church of God Evangel*, February 24, 1917, 1.

26. Aimee Semple McPherson, *This Is That: Personal Experiences, Sermons and Writings* (New York: Garland Publishing, 1985, unaltered reprint of 1919 original), 205–7.

27. Daniel C. O. Opperman, "Diary," 1905–1912, Assemblies of God Archives, Springfield, MO.

28. George Floyd Taylor, "Diary," North Carolina State History Archives, Raleigh, NC. This diary was kept for the years 1896, 1901, and 1908. Of course pentecostals' autobiographies and diaries, like all such texts, may have been penned more for the edification of potential readers than as a record of actual experiences. If so, that would make my argument stronger, for it shows that they regarded singlemindedness other-worldliness as the ideal.

29. James and June Glover Marshall, "R. G. Spurling Jr.: The Origins of the Church of God," *Reflections...Church of God Heritage*, Winter, 1990, 3.

30. *Glad Tidings* [San Francisco], July 1928, 10.

31. *Glad Tidings* [San Francisco], May 1926, 8.

32. *Showers of Blessings*, #8 [about 1910], 9.

33. Agnes N. O. LaBerge, *What God Hath Wrought: Life and Work of Mrs. Agnes N. O. LaBerge* (New York: Garland Publishing, 1985, unaltered reprint of 1920 original), 54.

34. Goss, *Winds*, 136.

35. *Christian Evangel*, October 17, 1914, 2.

36. *The Pentecostal Evangel*, April 4, 1914, 6.

37. *The Pentecostal Evangel*, November 1, 1919, 5.

38. Timothy L. Smith, *Called Unto Holiness: The Story of the Nazarenes: The Formative Years* (Kansas City, MO: Nazarene Publishing House, 1962), 37.

39. Charles Fox Parham, *The Life of Charles F. Parham Founder of The Apostolic Faith Movement*, compiled by Mrs. Charles Fox Parham (Baxter Springs, KS: The Apostolic Faith, 1930), 14.

40. For example, John Alexander Dowie, Fred Vogler, and Frank Ewart emigrated from Australia; Stanley Frodsham, A. W. Frodsham, Noel Perkin, and George T. Studd from Britain; Andrew Urshan from Persia.

41. A.A. Boddy, *Confidence*, September 1914, 176. For Boddy's incessant globe-trotting, which was, if not typical, at least not rare among early leaders, see the typescript biography by his daughter, Mother Joanna Mary Boddy, "Alexander Alfred Boddy, 1854–1930," Assemblies of God Archives, Springfield, MO.

42. See for example the fat file of newspaper clippings tracking the continental crisscrossings of evangelists John S. and Hattie McConnell, Assemblies of God Archives, Springfield, MO.

43. Bartleman, *Azusa*, 146–7.

44. Alfred and Lillian Garr, quoted in B. F. Lawrence, *The Apostolic Faith Restored* (St. Louis: Gospel Publishing House, 1916), 98.

45. Gary B. McGee, *"This Gospel...Shall Be Preached": A History and Theology of Assemblies of God Foreign Missions to 1959* (Springfield, MO: Gospel Publishing House, 1986), 77.

46. For missionaries, see Joseph H. and Blanch L. King, *Yet Speaketh: Memoirs of the Late Bishop Joseph H. King* (Franklin Springs, GA: Pentecostal Publishing House, 1949), p.191. For local churches see *Glad Tidings* (Kenedy [correctly spelled], TX]) September 1924, 1–2. See also the verbal altercation between patriarchs J. R. Flower and George Brinkman over financial accountability, recounted from one perspective in *The Pentecostal Evangel*, November 15, 1918, 7, and from the opposite in *The Pentecostal Herald*, October 1919, 3.

47. See Wayne E. Warner, "Publications," in *Dictionary of Pentecostal and Charismatic Movements*. Examples of publications launched by women include *The Apostolic Faith* [Portland, OR], edited by Florence Crawford and Clara Lum; *The Bridal Call* edited by Aimee Semple McPherson with assistance from her mother, Minnie Kennedy; *Bridegroom's Messenger*, edited by Elizabeth A. Sexton; *Elbethel*, edited by Cora McIlray; *The Latter Rain Evangel*, edited by Lydia Piper and Anna C. Reiff; *Triumphs of Faith*, edited by Carrie Judd Montgomery; and *Trust* edited by Elizabeth V. Baker and Susan Duncan.

48. For example, D. W. Kerr edited and published *The Pentecostal Missionary Report* out of his church in Cleveland, OH; Robert Craig edited and published *Glad Tidings* out of his church in San Francisco; Samuel G. Otis edited and published *Word and Work* at the campmeeting grounds in Framingham, MA.

49. Michael G. Owen, "Preparing Students for the First Harvest," *Assemblies of God Heritage*,

Winter, 1989–90, 3–5, 16–18; Lewis Wilson, "Bible Institutes, Colleges, Universities," in *Dictionary of Pentecostal and Charismatic Movements.*

50. Goss, *Winds,* 154.

51. *The Apostolic Faith* [Los Angeles], October 1906, 2.

52. A. J. Tomlinson, *The Last Great Conflict* (New York: Garland Publishing, 1985, unaltered reprint of 1913 original), 68–69.

53. Tomlinson, *Last,* 38.

54. *The Apostolic Faith* [Houston], October, 1908, 2; *Midnight Cry,* November, 1907, 2; *Pentecost,* April–May, 1909, 4, *Seattle Post Intelligencer* August 29, 1907, 6, and September 3, 1907, 4. There is no reason to believe that Ryan knew a word of Japanese, which makes his venture to Japan all the more audacious. I owe the *The Pentecost* reference to Wayne Warner, and the *Post Intelligencer* references to Professor Cecil M. Robeck of Fuller Seminary.

55. Goss, *Winds,* 65.

56. Stanley F. Frodsham, long-time editor of the Assemblies of God's *The Pentecostal Evangel,* won lasting notoriety for remaining lost in the heavenlies. "Brother Frodsham had many gifts," a colleague recalled years later, "but discernment was never one of them." Interview with Wayne Warner, August 29, 1992.

57. Goss, *Winds,* 17, regarding Parham.

58. Lewiston, Maine, newspaper reporter describing Frank S. Sandford, quoted in Shirley Nelson, *Fair, Clear, and Terrible: The Story of Shiloh, Maine* ([Lathan, NY]: British American Publishing, 1989), 78.

59. Charles William Shumway, "A Study of 'The Gift of Tongues,'" A. B. thesis, University of Southern California, 1914, 179, regarding William H. Durham.

60. Anderson, *Vision,* 103–104. It is difficult to determine the life expectancy of first generation leaders, partly because the records are spotty, and partly because there is no consensus as to who should be included. With those qualifications in mind, I selected one hundred persons from the *Dictionary of Pentecostal and Charismatic Movements* whose birth and death dates are known and who, in my judgment, served as pathfinders during the formative years from 1905 to 1920. The median birth and death dates for those leaders was 1869 and 1943, yielding a life-span of seventy-four years. In contrast, the typical American born in 1866 (the year closest to 1869 for which census figures are available) lived only fifty-four years. Though this is hardly a scientific sampling, these figures do suggest that far from being sickly, as charged, pentecostal trail blazers exhibited unusual vigor. See "Years of Life Expected

at Birth," compiled by National Center for Health Statistics, in *The World Almanac and Book of Facts 1992* (New York: World Almanac, 1992), 956.

61. Victor G. Plymire, typed autobiography, no title, Assemblies of God Archives, Springfield, MO.

62. Goss, *Winds,* 73.

63. *The Apostolic Messenger,* February–March 1908, 2? (page number not clear).

64. *The Pentecost,* August 1909, page number not available.

65. *Word and Witness,* December 20, 1912, 2. Bell did not acknowledge that volunteers helped him mail out the periodical—which may say a good deal about the image he desired to project. Interview with Wayne Warner, August 31, 1992.

66. *Diary of A.J. Tomlinson,* edited by Homer A. Tomlinson (Jamaica, NY: Erhardt Press, 1955), III:104–5. See also 140.

67. Henry Proctor, *Trust,* May–June 1930, 14.

68. Elizabeth Sisson, *The Latter Rain Evangel,* May 1909, 6–10. Members of the quasi-pentecostal Shiloh community near Durham, Maine, routinely refused Novocain for the same reason. Nelson, *Fair,* 332 of publisher's galley edition, omitted from published edition.

69. See for example Elizabeth Sisson, *The Latter Rain Evangel,* May 1909, 10. A graduate student who read this paper responded that Sisson's willfulness in the dentist's chair seemed more a reflection of primitivist other-worldliness than of pragmatic this-worldliness. Perhaps so. At the margins the two traits blended and often it is hard to know where to draw the line.

70. Anonymous, *Living Water,* reprinted without further citation in *Triumphs of Faith,* June, 1908, 123.

71. F. F. Bosworth, *Christ the Healer: Sermons on Divine Healing* (published by author, 1924), 98–99.

72. Carrie Judd Montgomery, *Faith's Reckonings* [tract], no date [about 1920], 9.

73. Dr. J. A. Krumrine, *Trust,* September 1915, 12–13.

74. Anecdote related by the daughter, Mildred Edwards, *Trust,* February 1915, 13.

75. Maude Craig, *Tongues of Fire,* August 15, 1900, 146, "me" emphasized in the original. This periodical, which bore the subtitle *From "The Church of the Living God The Pillar and Ground of the Truth,"* was published by the quasi-pentecostal Shiloh community.

76. Margaret Poloma, *The Assemblies of God at the Crossroads: Charisma and Institutional Dilemmas* (Knoxville: University of Tennessee Press, 1989), chapter 9, especially 161, and Arthur E. Paris, *Black*

Pentecostalism: Southern Religion in an Urban World (Amherst: University of Massachusetts Press, 1982), throughout.

77. Edith L. Blumhofer, *Restoring the Faith: The Assemblies of God, Pentecostalism, and American Culture* (Urbana, IL: University of Illinois Press, 1993), 254–260; Mickey Crews, *The Church of God: A Social History* (Knoxville: University of Tennessee Press, 1990), throughout, but especially chapter 7, "From Back Alleys to Uptown." For a one-sided though partly defensible expose of pentecostals' relentless pursuit of the good life, see Robert Johnson, "Heavenly Gifts," *Wall Street Journal*, December 11, 1990, 1. See also Poloma, *Assemblies of God*, 153.

78. See for example Poloma, *Assemblies of God*, 48–49; William J. Samarin, *Tongues of Men and Angels: The Religious Language of Pentecostalism* (New York: Macmillan, 1972), 213; Luther Gerlach and Virginia H. Hine, *People, Power, Change: Movements of Social Transformation* (Indianapolis: Bobbs-Merrill, 1970), 4–5; H. Newton Malony, "Debunking Some of the Myths about Glossolalia," in *Charismatic Experiences in History*, edited by Cecil M. Robeck, Jr. (Peabody, MA: Hendrickson, 1985), 105–106. This article was originally published in the *Journal for the Scientific Study of Religion*, 34 (1982) : 144–148. According to this data, better educated and more prosperous adherents are *more*, not less, likely to speak in tongues and to espouse first century (or at least what outside journalists and academics like to think are first century) assumptions in religious matters than their less accomplished counterparts. Admittedly, these studies tested for the correlation between speaking in tongues and position in the social system, which is not exactly the same as pragmatism as I have defined it (that is, a willingness to appropriate the technological achievements and social arrangements of the modern West whenever it suits their purposes). But it is plausible to assume that above average education and wealth normally betoken a measure of pragmatic aptitude for getting along in the modern social system.

79. See for example Vance Packard, "The Long Road from Pentecostal to Episcopal," in *The Status Seekers* (New York: David McKay, 1959), 200–201, described in Martin E. Marty, *A Nation of Behavers* (Chicago: University of Chicago Press, 106. The same outlook undergirds Robert Anderson's otherwise superior study of pentecostal origins, *Vision of the Disinherited*. Anderson claims that pentecostals sought redress for the various deprivations they suffered in "other-worldly, symbolic, and psychotherapeutic" measures. By implication, once those depri-

vations disappear, the otherworldly measures will disappear too. See especially 229. See also James Davison Hunter, *American Evangelicalism: Conservative Religion and the Quandary of Modernity* (New Brunswick, NJ: Rutgers University Press, 1983), especially 5–6, 131, and, for a sophisticated reworking of the argument, see *Evangelicalism: The Coming Generation* (Chicago: University of Chicago Press, 1987), especially 238–241. William G. McLoughlin used a different path to arrive at the same destination. He claimed that pentecostals, however numerically impressive, would remain mere "effluvia" incapable of "seriously threatening the old order" as long as they distanced themselves from modern mainstream culture. McLoughlin, "Is There a Third Force in Christendom?," in *Religion in America*, edited by McLoughlin and Robert N. Bellah (Boston: Beacon Press, 1968, first edition 1966), 45–72, especially 47, and McLoughlin, *Revivals, Awakenings, and Reform: An Essay on Religion and Social Change in America, 1607–1977* (Chicago: University of Chicago Press, 1978), chapter 6, especially 212–216.

80. Pearl S. Buck, *The Exile* (New York: John Day, 1936), 58.

81. David Martin, *Tongues of Fire: The Explosion of Protestantism in Latin America* (Cambridge, MA: Basil Blackwell, 1990), 122, 140, 164; David Stoll, *Is Latin America Turning Protestant? The Politics of Evangelical Growth* (Berkeley, CA: University of California Press, 1990), 13, 36, 94; Everett A. Wilson, "Sanguine Saints: Pentecostalism in El Salvador," *Church History* 52 (1983) : 186–198; Everett A. Wilson, "The Central American Evangelicals: From Protest to Pragmatism," *International Review of Mission*, January 1988, 93–106. More generally see Martin E. Marty's astute assessment of the functions of the interaction of primitivism and pragmatism in "Sophisticated Primitives Then, Primitive Sophisticates Now," *The Christian Century*, June 7–14, 1989, 586–591.

82. See for example Catherine Albanese, *America: Religions and Religion* (Belmont, CA: Wadsworth, 1992, second edition), 28–32.

83. See for example Virginia Lieson Brereton, *From Sin to Salvation: American Women's Conversion Narratives, 1800–1980* (Bloomington: Indiana University Press, 1991), chapters 3 and 7.

84. I owe this insight to David D. Hall, *Worlds of Wonder, Days of Judgment: Popular Religious Belief in Early New England* (New York: Alfred A. Knopf, 1989), 239–245. The signal exception to my generalization about historians of pentecostalism is Robert Mapes Anderson who, in *Vision of the Disinherited*,

moved to the other extreme, discountenancing the approved script almost entirely.

85. Dan Morgan, *Rising in the West* (New York: Alfred K. Knopf, 1992), offers an intriguing case study of an extended family of share croppers who migrated from Oklahoma to California in the 1930s and quite literally made a fortune in construction, junk dealing, real estate, sports franchises, and retirement homes in the burgeoning economy of the Southwest. Morgan shows that the family's fervent pentecostal faith provided spiritual and communal legitimation for their perfectly legal yet financially aggressive (if not avaricious) behavior every step of the way.

To be fair, pentecostals often responded to the material needs of their own members at least by providing food, clothing, rent money, and the like, when those privations arose. But typically they acted on a purely case by case basis, uninformed by any systematic social ethic or recognition of the structural dislocations that might have caused such problems in the first place. More significantly, their leaders consistently refused to permit self-criticism of ease of lifestyle or the use of money by themselves or by the rank-and-file. In the 1970s and 1980s a few "mainline" pentecostal writers critiqued the "Faith Confession" movement, a subtradition that explicitly sanctified the pursuit of boundless personal wealth. But that critique proves my larger point precisely because it focused upon—and only upon—egregious and flaunted excess, not routine preoccupation with the good life. A signal exception to all of this is the work of pentecostal ethicist Murray Dempster of Southern California College. See for example his "Pentecostal Social Concern and the Biblical Mandate of Social Justice," *Pneuma: The Journal of the Society for Pentecostal Studies*, 9 (Fall 1987): 129–154, and "Christian Social Concern in Pentecostal Perspective: Reformulating Pentecostal Eschatology," *Journal of Pentecostal Theology*, 2 (1993) : 51–64.

86. A profounder ethical sense may be coming into being. Pentecostals' preoccupation with laws pertaining to abortion and homosexuality in the 1980s and 1990s betokened a narrow yet very important entry into the broader sphere of public policy.

87. Robinson is quoted in Winthrop S. Hudson and John Corrigan, *Religion in America* (New York: Macmillan, 1992, fifth edition), 32–33.

THE CHALLENGE OF EVANGELICAL/PENTECOSTAL CHRISTIANITY
TO HISPANIC CATHOLICISM

Allen Figueroa Deck, S. J.

Since 1970 the number of Hispanic immigrants from Mexico, Cuba, and other Latin American countries to the United States has more than doubled to 22.4 million or 9 percent of the U.S. population. Next to the 30 million African Americans, Hispanics now constitute the second largest minority group in the nation. Within the Catholic Church, many believe that by the year 2000 Hispanic Catholics may very well outnumber all other Catholics in the United States combined. Despite this phenomenal growth, very little is known about the Hispanic Catholic acculturation to the North American Catholic Church. What has been observed, however, is the growing defection of Hispanics from the Catholic Church and into the burgeoning evangelical and pentecostal Protestant denominations.

Allen Deck explores the reasons why Hispanic Americans are attracted to evangelical and pentecostal Christianity and the challenges this new movement presents to the North American Catholic Church. In Deck's estimation, Hispanics' perceive a middle-class elitism and professionalism in the American Church that neglects popular forms of Hispanic Catholic religiosity. Hispanic Catholicism, like evangelical and pentecostal forms of worship, is more concerned with the emotions and the immediate experience of God. Hispanic Catholics, moreover, see in the intimate evangelical and pentecostal Protestant faith communities the opportunity to both retain their cultural homogeneity and adapt to the modern demand for a more personal, individualized relationship to God. As Deck sees it, the challenge to the North American Catholic Church is to first listen to and respect the needs of the Hispanic community and then adapt to those needs by emphasizing both the older communal and the modern individualized dimensions of the Catholic faith.

Adapted by permission from Allen Figueroa Deck, S.J., "The Challenge of Evangelical/Pentecostal Christianity to Hispanic Catholicism," in Jay P. Dolan and Deck, eds., *Hispanic Catholic Culture in the United States: Issues and Concerns* (Notre Dame: University of Notre Dame Press, 1994), 409–439.

The churches ought to discover what is now being said "in God's laboratory in Brazil." The unexpected growth of the churches is possible only if the old missionary approaches are abandoned, only if the "cultural coldness, the systematized, privileged and secularized Christendom of North America is renounced."

William R. Read[1]

24 ❦

THE CHALLENGE OF EVANGELICAL/PENTECOSTAL CHRISTIANITY TO HISPANIC CATHOLICISM

Allan Figueroa Deck, S.J.

ONE OF THE MORE STRIKING DEVELOPMENTS in the history of Christianity worldwide is the dramatic emergence of a flourishing pentecostal/charismatic movement particularly in the latter half of the twentieth century. Church demographer David Barrett estimates the total population of pentecostal/charismatic Christians in excess of 150 million, with more than a third of this population in Latin America. Pentecostalism is by far the fastest-growing movement in worldwide Christianity. Barrett projects that if current growth rates are sustained, pentecostal Christianity will account for 21 percent of all Christians in the world by the end of the century.[2] Latin American Catholics are flocking to pentecostalism in very significant numbers in both Latin America and in the United States. Two of pentecostalism's largest congregations are found in Latin America.[3] Father Flavio Amatulli, a leading Catholic expert on Protestantism in Mexico, estimates the number of Protestants there in the order of 6 million, of whom 70 percent are pentecostals.[4]

In the United States, a recent study made for the U.S. Catholic bishops in 1990 indicates that the vast majority of Protestant congregations that have attracted immigrant U.S. Hispanics are pentecostal or evangelical (mainly Baptist).[5] What are the background, the context, and possible reasons for this astonishing development?

While Protestant missionary endeavors can be traced back to the early nineteenth century in several areas inhabited by Hispanics, the astonishing growth of Hispanic Protestantism, particularly in the second half of the twentieth century, is not primarily the result of the earlier efforts. Rather, Protestant proselytism of Hispanics began a sustained period of growth only at the end of the last century, when pentecostalism was born and when evangelical Protestantism under pressure from modernist trends ceased being the principal, mainline form of American Protestantism. For the time being hegemony passed to the urban, liberal, intellectual elites in the various denominations. The 1925 Scopes trial was a watershed in this development, according to historian George Marsden.[6] The public's negative reaction to the trial was a defeat for the evangelicals who attempted to hold back the onslaught of modernism by reverting to a particularly rigid form of biblical fundamentalism.

Perhaps the subsequent success of evangelical outreach to Hispanics can be traced to evangelicalism's decline among mainstream, affluent, educated, urban Protestants. New immigrant groups, poorer and often rooted in rural experiences, would likely become a new audience for the evangelicals, the source of new vitality. Both they and the pentecostals recruited from the ranks of the poor with much more ease than the mainline churches.

The vast majority of today's Hispanic Protestants trace their origins to this period in the history of American Protestantism. Whereas the first Protestant outreach was principally in the hands of the mainline churches of the nineteenth century, the second outreach has occurred in this century and its main protagonists have been the evangelicals and pentecostals. Hispanics have generally chosen to enter into the evangelical/pentecostal current. They are thus contributing to a significant revitalization of evangelical Protestantism, the predominate, classic form of U.S. Protestantism. Modernism or, to use Paul Ricoeur's expression, "the acids of modernity," contributed much to evangelicalism's precipitous decline in the early decades of this century. Now Hispanics, more than any other U.S. minority, are contributing to its revival and making evangelicalism, particularly in its pentecostal manifestation, the fastest growing and arguably the most dynamic division of Christianity in the United States and in the world today.

The success of evangelicals and pentecostals in Hispanic ministry can begin to be grasped through a study of the gradual flowering of this trend in several Latin American nations.[7] One of the more basic observations to make about this vast movement of evangelical and pentecostal Christians is the symbiosis between their North American and Latin American missionaries. U.S.-born Latinos and native Latin Americans have crossed the Rio Grande in both directions. The approaches eventually hammered out, so successful in many parts of Latin America, are the same ones used here in the United States.[8] Church historian Justo L. González, while speaking about the more mainline United Methodist Church, documents this in his study of Hispanic Methodists: "One characteristic of Hispanic United Methodism...is that its strength is in direct proportion to its connection with centers of Hispanic culture outside the United States."[9]

Despite some gains on the part of Justo L. González's United Methodists, however, it is not they who are attracting impressive numbers of Hispanics. This is part of a larger picture: the historic decline of mainline Protestantism in general and the vigorous upsurge of more marginalized denominations and independent congregations of either an evangelical or pentecostal stripe.[10] Today when one speaks of Hispanic Protestantism one is not usually talking about the "historical" churches at all, but rather, about some strain of evangelicalism and especially pentecostalism. These are churches which exhibit some of the classic features of the *sect*. They are headed by gifted, winning, charismatic leaders and are often independent of hierarchies or higher church governments. They enjoy, moreover, the benefit of not being perceived as institutions and escape or are somewhat untainted by the postmodern disenchantment with institutional religion.[11] Donald W. Dayton has gone farther and called this charismatic Christianity a kind of "third force": "I am often inclined to suggest that churches like my own, in the holiness movement, or those of Pentecostalism, are so different from magisterial Protestantism that they constitute some new strand in the church—a sort of 'third force' that is neither Catholic nor Protestant."[12]

Justo L. González, in his history of Hispanic Methodism, sheds light on some of the reasons for the reluctance of mainline churches to allow Hispanics their own space and their own way of doing things. It was assumed that Hispanics would simply adapt to the preexisting patterns of ministry, church government, organization, and funding. This assumption neglected the concrete social class and cultural location of Hispanics and led to failure after failure.[13] Those assumptions in the United States are driven by the middle-class horizon of most church leaders and the increasingly strong pragmatic, managerial, and technological orientation of planners who get the attention of bishops and church administrators. In this regard it can be noted that evangelical/pentecostal efforts have been characterized by a *respect* for some important idiosyncracies of the local community and its natural, indigenous leaders. Today we might call that respect a feature of a dialogical, inculturating mode, that is, the ability to rethink ministry as insiders from within the culture to be evangelized instead of imposing preconceived ideas and inappropriate approaches on benighted outsiders.

Thomas H. Groome, a leading pastoral theologian, gives a possible explanation for this failure to engage in meaningful dialogue on the part of mainline (both Protestant and Roman Catholic) churches. He refers to an attitude underlying much of mainstream, contemporary religious education and church leadership. Following Max Horkheimer, Groome calls it *instrumental reasoning* or *technical rationality*.

> Technical rationality is moved by an instrumental interest in "what works" to produce "results." It does not engage knowers as "thinking-persons-in-relationship" with reality but functions as an adversial stance toward nature, society and other people; it obliterates the dialectical relationship that should exist between knower and known if knowledge is to be life-giving and historically responsible.... [I]t employs the mind in a one-dimensional, utilitarian logic that excludes memory and imagination and concentrates only on what it claims are objective and empirical "facts" in order to promote commodity production and bureaucratic management.... [I]t results in a refusal to think of outcomes beyond what "works for control" and demands a suspension of imagination.[14]

Most Catholic commentaries on evangelical/pentecostal proselytism have not pursued these more serious and perhaps subtle explanations of the nature of this development. They have not sought to frame the issue in its deeper social, cultural, and historical underpinnings. Catholic reflections on this trend have tended, rather, to be argumentative, to be a form of latter-day apologetics.[15] For decades Roman Catholic writers have been bemoaning the proselytism of what they disdainfully call *the sects*. They note the inroads made with Hispanics.[16] This is an issue repeatedly mentioned by Catholic clerical authorities from the local parish priest to the pope himself, but serious self-evaluation and soul searching has usually not characterized their reflections.

The available data on the appeal of evangelical Protestantism to U.S. Hispanics indicate that appreciable numbers of them are indeed either joining these churches or at least flirting with them. Andrew Greeley maintains that more than a million have left the Roman Catholic Church in the fifteen-year period between 1973 and 1988 and that the larger percentage of these are joining either evangelical or pentecostal churches.[17] Gerardo Marín and Raymond J. Gamba found that only 72.9 percent of Hispanics in the San Francisco area identified themselves as Roman Catholics.[18] This is down from projections of twenty years ago in which 92 percent considered themselves Catholic. The 1985 survey of Roberto Gonzalez and Michael La Velle showed that more than half of all U.S. Hispanics have been contacted by one of these evangelical or pentecostal groups.[19] The data included in Martin's and Stoll's works reveal that the largest and fastest growing type of Protestantism in Latin America is precisely evangelical/pentecostal.[20] The study recently completed for the United

States bishops' Ad Hoc Committee on Proselytism confirms the seriousness of the challenge these groups are posing for immigrant Catholics in general in the United States and especially for Hispanics.[21]

Before proceeding any further, however, it may be helpful to focus briefly on the nature of evangelical and pentecostal Christianity. In a general overview of Hispanic Catholic "defections" to these churches it is impossible always to make the relevant distinctions between these two related but quite distinct trends in contemporary Christianity. What, then, does one mean by evangelical and pentecostal? For the purposes of this discussion I refer the reader to the writings of George M. Marsden. This prolific student of evangelical religion in the United States has demonstrated that evangelical Christianity is an extremely influential form of American Protestantism, perhaps *the* most influential form. Marsden outlines its salient features:

> The essential evangelical beliefs include (1) the Reformation doctrine of the final authority of the Bible, (2) the real historical character of God's saving work recorded in the Scripture, (3) salvation to eternal life based on the redemptive work of Christ, (4) the importance of evangelism and missions, and (5) the importance of a spiritually transformed life.[22]

In an earlier work Marsden provides a richly textured account of evangelicalism at one of the decisive moments in its gestation in the United States, the period between 1870 and 1925.[23] For the purposes of our study he makes four points that are quite relevant. The first is that evangelical Protestantism is intimately linked to certain features of the Anglo-American cultural ethos with its orientation toward individual responsibility, work, civic pride, egalitarianism. It grew out of Calvinism and Puritanism. Second, it has a great appeal for ordinary people, since from an early stage evangelicalism adopted a popular philosophy of life called *Scottish Common Sense Realism.* Third (as mentioned above), evangelicalism gave rise to fundamentalism in the heat of Protestantism's struggle with modernism and liberalism. Fourth, pentecostalism, while being distinct in terms of its practical, less fundamentalist, use of the Bible, is an outgrowth of the holiness movement in evangelical Protestantism, specifically Methodism.[24] In very simple terms, pentecostalism gives much greater importance to the doctrine of the Holy Spirit and to the outward manifestation of the Spirit in power. It is also worth noting that African Americans have played a substantial role in both evangelical and pentecostal Christianity. They have had a strong presence in both but especially in pentecostalism where the spontaneous expression of feeling has been a hallmark. Baptists, who are evangelicals, generally eschew the emotion. But this distinction becomes blurred in the case of the black Baptists.

INTERPRETING THE PHENOMENON

Perhaps the single most important issue affecting the critical analysis of the challenge of evangelical Protestantism for Hispanic Catholics or for mainline Christians of any cultural background is the failure to take the phenomenon seriously. Everyday experience seems to demonstrate that those who find this issue of interest or are even alarmed by it do little more than bemoan it, wring their hands, or dismiss it with a simplistic explanation. When discussing the movement of significant numbers of Latin Americans to these religions it has been quite common to ascribe it to a plot by the C.I.A. Or it is understood as another example of how ignorant, superstitious people can be manipulated into preposterous religious beliefs by crafty agents of well-financed fringe denominations. Stoll and others have documented real C.I.A. and evangelical church efforts of this kind.[25] Thoughtful analyses of the phenomena, nevertheless, reveal that the massive movement of Hispanic Catholics away from their ancient Church both in Latin America and the United States is a much more complex and subtle reality than many would like to believe. How do we explain the resistance even on the part of often well-informed Catholics and others to a more nuanced understanding of these facts?

Ronald A. Knox alludes to the problem of interpretive posture or stance in his now classic study of what he called *enthusiasm or ultrasupernaturalism* in the history of Christianity. As a fiercely committed English Roman Catholic he tells us in the foreword that he planned to line up all the "rogues," that is, demonstrate the nature of the error involved in the various enthusiastic expressions of Christianity that did not remain in union with Rome. He wanted to create a "rogues' gallery" he tells us. But as he got deeper into the topic he came to respect the underlying experiences and concerns of those who over the centuries had promoted this enthusiastic Christianity: "somehow in the writing, my whole treatment of the subject became different; the more you got to know the men, the more human did they become, for better or worse; you were more concerned to find out why they thought as they did than to prove it was wrong."[26]

A similar experience is reported in a more recent study of evangelical religion in the U.S. by historian Randall Balmer. He was raised in a narrow, evangelical Christian home that, as is common, tended toward being fundamentalist as well. He rejected all of that and became an Episcopalian. Later in life he returned to his roots with his book *Mine Eyes Have Seen the Glory: A Journey into the Evangelical Subculture in America.* In the epilogue he tells us:

> Evangelicalism will also persist, I think, because of its timeless appeal. It promises intimacy with God, a support community, an unambiguous morality, and answers to the riddles of eternity.... Evangelicalism simply will not go away. In the 1920's H. L. Mencken, no friend of evangelicals, remarked that if you tossed an egg out of a Pullman window almost anywhere in the country, you would hit a fundamentalist. Pullman cars are obsolete in America today. Fundamentalists are still around.[27]

Both Knox and Balmer are dealing with a critical issue, namely, the hermeneutic or the interpretive perspective taken toward this reality. My contention is that most mainline Christian writers, be they Roman Catholic or Protestant, have approached the topic with suspicion and even prejudice. It is my contention that the relevance and import of the phenomenon called evangelical religion among Hispanics or any other people cannot be assessed as long as the attitude is basically condescending, patronizing, or outright hostile (as has been especially the case among Catholic Hispanics).

The question then emerges, Why so much negativity toward evangelical and especially pentecostal Christianity? Surely there are good, even excellent, reasons for this resistance. Among mainline Catholics and Protestants in the U.S. it has to do with the perception— often true, no doubt, but also exaggerated or even unfounded—that evangelicals oversimplify the Christian tradition, tend toward excessive emotionalism and a fractious sectarianism, are sometimes linked with nationalistic and even racist elements of society. Clifton L. Holland in the study of Hispanic Protestantism in Los Angeles, confirming an earlier conclusion of researchers Leo Grebler, Joan Moore, and Ralph Guzman[28] discovered that it tended to flourish among rather introverted, conservative Hispanics who were clinging together in a kind of fortress mentality:

> Much of recent Hispanic church growth has taken place among conservative Hispanic churches which represent various degrees of introversion, rather than among the so-called "liberal" Hispanic churches related to the mainline Protestant denominations.[29]

Another source of negativity toward evangelical Protestantism and especially toward its pentecostal expression, however, is its historic identification with the popular classes, the poor and less educated members of society. The style of prayer and socialization typical of rural or blue-collar communities where evangelicalism thrives the most are usually problematic for the more educated classes. Learned discussions of the phenomenon of evangelical religion are often led by the academicians at university, seminary, and theologate. They often view these matters from the perspective of the class that dominates in their institutions and churches. Usually this is the middle and upper middle classes with which they themselves are identified in terms of vital interests and tastes.

For Hispanics the principle source of resistance to evangelical Protestantism has to do with its intimate connection with the North American ethos, especially its perceived individualism and consumerism. Hispanics in this regard view evangelical Protestantism as the quintessential expression of U.S. religion and culture, an interpretation masterfully developed by George Marsden in *Fundamentalism and American Culture*. Given the need to resist the onslaught of Americanization and certain forms of modernization, the thoughtful Hispanic will view evangelical efforts to convert Hispanics as a particularly vicious attack on his or her cultural identity. Even though the Hispanic American may not be active in practicing the Catholic faith, he or she perceives that the culture is permeated by a kind of Catholic ethos that revolves around a rich collection of rites and symbols. Many of those rites and symbols are imbued with a certain Catholic spirit. The evangelical penchant for reducing the mediation between God and humanity to the Scriptures is antithetical to the Hispanic Catholic tendency to multiply mediations. Not only the Church but the saints, angels, and especially the Virgin Mary are viewed as mediators in addition to Jesus Christ himself. The more democratic, egalitarian ethos of evangelicalism is somehow foreign to the hierarchical configuration of both the Hispanic family and society. Hispanics have often experienced serious family divisions when a member becomes a Protestant. In Hispanic culture this is not just a religious matter. It is a profound cultural, social, and familial rupture.

These are only some of the reasons for the suspicion and lack of openness toward the evangelical phenomena. They are certainly appreciable. In the effort to fairly assess the reality one must ask, however, Upon what grounds may one approach the issue with openness and generosity in the effort to shed greater light on the reality and better grasp its significance? The resistance to evangelical/pentecostal Christianity is quite intense. For Hispanics, however, and despite the many serious reasons they have to resist this trend, there appears to be a way to overcome the barriers. The key to overcoming these seeming contradictions is what I call the *unanalyzed affinity*.

THE UNANALYZED AFFINITY:
POPULAR RELIGIOSITY AND EVANGELICALISM

Scholarly efforts to compare and contrast evangelical Protestantism with Hispanic Catholicism will be well advised to take Hispanic popular Catholicism, not the standard, textbook version, as the norm. As I have argued in my book *The Second Wave*, this is the lived religion of most Hispanics.[30] It is important to acknowledge the distinctive character of the existential Catholicism of most Hispanics. Their Catholicism is hardly the reflection of a rigorous religious formation based upon accepted catechetical texts. Rather, theirs is a popular faith mediated especially by grandmother, mother, and women in general. Its standards and practices are not articulated in books or in any other form of print medium. This deeply rooted form of Catholicism is communicated orally, from person to person, within the context of family, rancho, town, or barrio. It almost totally lacks rational articulation but is not for that less convincing and motivating. For this simple faith is quite captivating and graphic, dramatic and emotive. It eschews the cognitive in its effort to appeal to the senses and the feelings. It does this through symbol and rite. Its main qualities are a concern for an immediate experience of God, a strong orientation toward the transcendent, an implicit belief in miracles, a practical orientation toward healing, and a tendency to personalize or individualize one's relationship with the divine. These qualities, Peter W. Williams tells us, are also present in normative Catholicism, but they are much more present in Hispanic popular religiosity. They are notably absent in mainline Protestantism, however, which, unlike Catholicism, tended to succumb to modernity's programmatic leveling of belief through relentless inquiries into the historicity of every Christian doctrine and practice.[31]

The point I want to make here is that the movement from popular Catholicism to some form of evangelical or pentecostal Protestantism is not as strange and drastic as it may seem. In a certain sense the movement of Hispanics to evangelical religion is a way to maintain a continuity with their popular Catholic faith which in the period both before and after the Second Vatican Council has been disparaged, opposed, dismissed, or ignored by many official teachers of the Church.[32] This is the point that Harvey Cox makes in *Religion in the Secular City:* "The history of the antagonism [between modern rationality and popular religion] makes it hard for the modern theological enterprise to recognize and draw on people's religion as a key source in the building of a postmodern theology."[33]

What Cox affirms about theologians may also be applicable to pastoral agents, mainline priests, and religious educators who tend to see popular religiosity as a problem to be uprooted, not a strength upon which to build. The period after the Second Vatican Council has been an "age of the theologian," a time of serious efforts to adapt their concepts to the everyday life of the Church. The effort, however, has not always been informed by knowledge of other cultures and social classes, or by respect for the somewhat anomalous religion of ordinary people.

The tension between normative and popular faith has been one of the main features of Hispanic Catholicism since the first evangelization of the sixteenth century. The powerful presence of pre-Columbian religious forms and sensibilities in the Catholicism of the first indigenous converts and the absence of native, indigenous priests throughout the colonial period created a permanent suspicion among the clergy and other learned Catholics about the syncretic religion of the natives and of their progeny, the *mestizos*.[34] This tension was magnified by migration to the United States where Catholicism had achieved an extraordinary level of coherence among the faithful masses through the Catholic school system and well-organized religious education programs for Catholic children in the public schools. This remarkable cohesiveness between the normative faith of the official Church and that of the ordinary faithful was achieved through many means, but the famous Baltimore catechism is the example that readily comes to mind.

In the period after the Second Vatican Council, U.S. Catholics have generally pursued a course of renewal which once again gave emphasis to the cognitive, rational articulation of the new norms of the Council. Hispanic Catholicism can seem anomalous and even heterodox to the confirmed Anglo-American Catholic whether one looks at it from the pre- or post-Vatican II perspective.

Another factor that helps explain the distance between mainstream U.S. Catholicism and popular Hispanic Catholicism is social class location. In a certain sense it was easier for U.S. Catholics of a century ago to receive Hispanics. Both groups tended to be outsiders to the American way of life. Traditional U.S. Catholic ethnic groups—Irish, German, Italian, or Slavic—were uniformly working class. The style of their faith, manners, and experiences were not as separate as the distinct languages they spoke. Today's Catholic immigrants, Hispanics, for instance, find their U.S. Catholic counterparts much more affluent, more educated, and, as a result, more distant from them socially and culturally than was the case a century or even half a century ago.[35]

Needless to say, U.S. Hispanics, especially the recent immigrants among them, find mainline Protestants equally or even more distant than their U.S. Catholic contemporaries. There are some Protestants, however, who have overcome this distance—the evangelicals and especially the pentecostals. For that is the branch of Protestantism that historically, especially in the last hundred years, has appealed to the working class, the poor, and the marginated in U.S. society. Consequently one will find evangelical and pentecostal churches in the barrios or on Main Street inner-city store-fronts. In these urban neighborhoods small, inviting congregations of a hundred or so Hispanics have emerged; almost invariably they are led by a Hispanic who reaches out to them in Spanish without hesitation. These are all circumstances that render the evangelization quite effective.

FROM CULTURAL TO PERSONAL CONVERSION

The winning ways of these small Protestant congregations, their communitarian flavor, and their accessibility are features which help the Hispanic overcome some strong resistances. Mexican Catholics, for example, natives of the Catholic heartland of Mexico—the states of Jalisco, Michoacán, Guanajuato, and Zacatecas—often have a horror of Protestants. They are afraid that conversion to Protestantism on the part of a family member will tear apart the entire family. Do not the Protestants denigrate and disdain Mary, the Mother of Jesus? Do they not attack veneration of the saints, one of the hallmarks of Mexican Catholicism? These Catholic Mexicans may also still prize the memory of the Cristero Rebellion, a war their grandparents fought precisely in defense of the Church and against an anti-Catholic government in the 1920s. Are they now to walk away from this heritage and change religion the way one would change clothes?

Yet evangelical/pentecostal Protestants are breaking down these historic resistances. Perhaps the contemporary ability of Hispanic Catholics to convert to some form of Protestantism can be explained to some extent by Hispanic Catholicism's penchant for syncretism. It should be recalled that many, if not most, Third World cultures manifest a remarkable ability to combine diverse religious beliefs and traditions. Western Christianity, with its strong philosophical orientation, is sensitive to what it views as inconsistencies in religious theory and practice. Not so for the native peoples of the Americas and for the Africans who populated the Caribbean islands and the coasts of Central and South America. Their religious beliefs are expressed through symbol and therefore enjoy a kind of open-endedness that at different times has scandalized the European Christian. In the encounters of today's Catholic Hispanic with diverse and even antithetical strands of Christianity perhaps a similar syncretic tendency is still at work.[36]

In addition, evangelical and pentecostal churches stress something that Hispanic Catholics intuit to be of great importance today, specifically within the context of their confrontation with the culture of modernity. Their ancient Catholicism came about as the result of the conversion of a people, of an entire culture. The method used by the mendicant orders was one of the last great flowerings of Constantinianism. What mattered was not the individual, personal transformation of the Indian, but rather the transformation of the collective symbols and rituals of their culture. This distinction is difficult for modern people to grasp given the highly personal and individual horizon of modern cultures. The concept of personal conversion would have been foreign to Aztecs, Mayans, or any other indigenous and African peoples. It was also rather foreign to the sixteenth-century friars whose mindset was still imbued with the ideology of Christendom and the principle *cujus regio, ejus religio*. Hispanics today, however, are at various stages of modernization. They sense that their communal orientation to religion is inadequate. They seek a more self-conscious, individualized faith. The subjection to forces outside themselves, the heteronomy of their traditional Catholic worldview, becomes increasingly dysfunctional. They sense the need to move beyond their collective, ancestral conversion of centuries ago. For it is not adequate to the challenges of the modern world with its stress on human autonomy, mobility, personal freedom, and human rights.

Consequently today's Hispanic in the United States, in contrast to what was possible or even thinkable at other times, seeks to appropriate *personally* his or her faith. But the large, impersonal, Catholic parish is simply not the most likely place for this to occur. The smaller assembly favored by the evangelicals and pentecostals is ideally suited for the modern context. Yet they do not destroy the communitarianism of the earlier conversion. Being relatively small, these evangelical/pentecostal congregations come closer to the rural, small community context that is most familiar to the people.

Hispanic Catholicism flourished in the premodern context characterized by a belief in hierarchy, respect for elders, and an orientation toward the collectivity and the common good. Hispanic Catholicism enters into crisis when confronted with the drastically different order of modernity, its emphasis on individual rights and equality. In the shift from premodern to modern society the vital psychological space goes from family and significant others to oneself, from the well-being of the collectivity to one's own personal fulfillment. Hispanic Catholicism is simply identified with the premodern, the more ancient way of life, while Protestantism is actually the form of Christianity that arose with modernity itself. For Protestantism emphasized the possibility of entering into a personal, direct relationship with God by diminishing many of the mediations (sacraments, images, saints, visible Church) that seemed to stand in the place of such a direct friendship. Consequently, Hispanics attracted to evangelical religion are looking for something they realize has been lacking if not denied them in the past: personal conversion. Yet they do not desire to abandon completely their communitarian ethos. Nor do they have to in order to become Protestants. To the contrary, the small faith-sharing orientation of many evangelical churches affirms the communal thrust of Hispanic popular Catholicism while at the same time orienting the people toward more self-determination.

In a similar way, the popularity of cursillos and the charismatic renewal among Hispanic Catholics in the past thirty years is due in large measure to the way that these movements satisfy the need for a more personally appropriated faith.[37] Something of the same dynamic may be the case in the Hispanic people's attraction for evangelical and pentecostal religion. In addition to strong conversion experiences, these churches also provide a vigorous community setting. These two features (personal conversion and community) appear to be the ones most sought by Hispanics in their search for a deeper spirituality, as reported by the 1986 Vatican study.[38] By providing those experiences the evangelical/pentecostals become an effective bridge for Latin American Christianity shaken to its core by the challenges of modernity.

Theologian Avery Dulles detects an evangelizing turn in the thought and ecclesial vision of recent popes. Pope Paul VI's *On Evangelization in the Modern World* is considered one of the most important church documents of the post-Vatican II era.[39] Pope John Paul II has taken up the theme of evangelization with characteristic vigor. In some measure the pope's emphasis on evangelization is due to the extraordinary success and dynamism of evangelical and pentecostal Christianity. He is very aware of this trend and mentions "the challenge of the sects" frequently. Dulles describes this shift to an evangelizing, missionary mentality as "one of the most surprising and important developments in the Catholic Church since Vatican II." The phrase *new evangelization*, which is the name given this emerging ecclesial orientation, has received a great deal of attention in Europe and Latin America. It is only now being taken seriously in the United States.[40]

The emphasis given evangelization in today's Roman Catholic Church is due to many factors. It is not unreasonable to suggest that one of them is the Catholic Church's recognition of the dramatic success of evangelical/pentecostal efforts to promote personal conversion and appropriation of the faith. The so-called cultural Catholicism of traditional Catholic peoples must somehow be transformed into a more responsible, mature faith suitable to a modern, secularized world given to various forms of practical atheism. In this respect evangelical/pentecostal evangelization efforts reflect a successful response to the challenges modernity poses for Christianity. In turn, evangelicalism and pentecostalism pose several challenges to mainline Christianity and to Catholicism in particular. These challenges include but go beyond the context of Catholicism's confrontation and tensions with modernity.

THE MAJOR CHALLENGES

Perhaps the underlying appeal of evangelical religion resides in the fact that it is a way of standing up to a kind of elitism that arises in the mainline churches, both Roman Catholic and Protestant. Much of the literature cited above suggests that the main characteristic of evangelical and pentecostal Christianity is not its conservatism but rather its populism. It has a certain down home flavor, a simpler appeal, and greater accessibility to those with limited educational backgrounds. In the Latin American world the resistance to elite religion took the form of *religiosidad popular*. In the United States among Protestants it takes the form of evangelicalism and pentecostalism. The mainline religious thinkers of the

United States, unaware, perhaps, of their social class location and its powerful affect on their attitudes, have tended to conceive of evangelicalism in terms of conservative-liberal antagonisms. What really is at stake, however, is the search of ordinary people for a faith that is characterized by an explicit affirmation of God's transcendence, strong convictions about God's will in certain matters of morality founded on biblical teaching, a confidence in God's power to work miracles and especially to heal, and the possibility of establishing a personal relationship with God appropriate for the highly individualized modern world. For Hispanics these needs were in some sense met by their popular Catholicism. Evangelical religion, as mentioned above, may seem more suitable for the modern world given that religion's strong emphasis on personal relationship with Christ.

Bishop Roberto O. González pursues this thought and summarizes the challenge of the so-called sects in these words:

> ...part of the success of the sects is their evangelical rootedness in the Gospel—that they seem to present Christ in all his power as the foundation of a new life, of conversion, of forgiveness of sins. Their preaching seems to be based solely upon the person and power of Christ.[41]

Further on in the same article Bishop Gonzalez provides a trenchant description of evangelical religion. The points he highlights are expressive of the nature of the challenge posed by the evangelical trend:

> What are they [the sects] saying? That the heart of Christianity is a personal relationship with Jesus Christ, as Saviour and Lord, in whom I find forgiveness of sins and newness of life. That Christ is everything! Then everything else that the Church stands for, in terms of faith and morals, comes out of the relation with that center of universal history, which is the person of Jesus Christ. He has the power to grant me radically new existence, to free me from all imperfections, to purify me from my sins and to free me from all limitations that the world and the law and custom seem to impose on me.[42]

Bishop González's observation about freedom from the law and custom is relevant to another challenge posed by evangelical religion, namely, its relevance to the encounter of Hispanics with the culture of modernity. More and more attention is being focused upon this encounter which is perhaps the single most dramatic process currently underway in Latin America and among Latin Americans in the United States. The analyses of David Martin and other students of modernity in Latin America reveal that evangelical/pentecostal Christianity provides a new orientation for ordinary people seeking to deal with the stresses involved in the rapid changes brought about by urbanization, secularization, and immigration. The movement away from traditional Catholicism accordingly has something to do with finding a new religious organizing principal. Conversion to evangelical religion allows Hispanics (gives them permission, as it were) to free themselves from the hierarchical, strongly communal, rural, traditional social and family structure, a system that seems more and more dysfunctional in the new circumstances of immigrant life in the United States or, for that matter, in the huge Latin American metropolis. This shift has elements of continuity as well as change. On the one hand, the affectivity of traditional religion is sustained as is the strong orientation toward transcendence. Yet a new personal freedom is experienced, one founded on the strong catharsis, the conversion experience of the born-again Christian.[43]

The mainstreaming of United States Catholicism, its strong middle-class orientation today, the increasing professionalization of its ministers both clerical and lay are the source of considerable discomfort for Hispanics. The horizon of Church leaders unwittingly absolutizes the middle-class norm. This leads to parish situations, approaches to prayer, worship, and preaching, styles of architecture, church administration, and fund raising that clash with Hispanic sensibilities. In the face of this discomfort evangelical/pentecostal churches provide a most attractive alternative.

The arrival of so many diverse ethnic groups to the United States in the last twenty-five years and the consequent emergence of multicultural ministries is a challenge related to the previous one. Outreach specifically targeted on Hispanics is sometimes combined with outreach to other groups. Pastors justify not doing more for Hispanics on the grounds that they have a responsibility to all. Thus services for Hispanics are watered down. Directions and orientations for the church, parish councils, diocesan pastoral councils, diaconate programs may move away from particular groups like Hispanics and develop somewhat amorphous, nondescript programs that offer "something for everybody."[44]

Contrasting with the multicultural ideology that appears to be endemic to a growing number of U.S. Catholic Church leaders is the remarkably successful approach of the evangelicals and pentecostals formulated by the church growth movement of Donald McGavran: "If people preferred to become Christians as part of social groups, without having to cross racial, linguistic, or class barriers, then the most successful, fastest growing churches would be socially homogeneous."[45]

In the United States, particularly in the period after the civil rights movement of the 1960s and 1970s, such as approach, predicated on what seems to be a "separate but equal" principle, is problematic. The challenge consists, then, in programmatically gearing the outreach and the church context to integration of the various ethnic and social class communities while respecting their often urgent need for their own turf. Historically, the Catholic Church pursued a policy not unlike the one championed by McGavran: the national parish. When Hispanic ministry became a larger piece of the Church's overall ministry in the period after the Second World War, however, this policy was already being abandoned. Jay Dolan demonstrates the importance of both the national parish and enthusiastic religion, revivalism, for ethnic Catholics of other times in his groundbreaking work entitled *Catholic Revivalism:*

> Historians have always considered revivalism as a major force in American religious history. Yet, they have consistently limited their vision to the Protestant phase of this phenomenon, believing that Roman Catholics were not so evangelically oriented. This study corrects that limited view and suggests that the religion of revivalism not only found a home among Catholics, but indeed was a major force in forming their piety and building up the church.[46]

Hispanic Catholics are challenged by an evangelical Protestantism that continues to practice the "wisdom" of nineteenth-century American Catholicism by affirming the national parish approach, that is, having congregations established just for the Spanish-speaking and promoting among them an enthusiastic, highly affective religiosity.

The Hispanic Catholic response to these challenges is taking various forms. One of them is expressed through the concept mentioned above and presently gaining currency among Hispanic ministry leaders: the "new evangelization." Pope John Paul II gave the impetus for this concept in his 1983 allocution opening the novena, the years of preparation for the fifth centenary of the coming of the gospel to the Americas in 1992. Bishop Roberto González has formulated what this concept might mean for Hispanic Catholics struggling to lead better lives and attracted to some of the features of evangelical/pentecostal Christianity. He stresses the need to acknowledge the positive values in much of what the evangelicals are saying and doing. At the same time he suggests that a fuller, more challenging and rooted Christian life can still be discovered in Catholicism. The challenges he sees facing United States Hispanics are secularism, consumerism, and sectarianism. He believes that the Catholic tradition has something to offer in response to these challenges. While respecting and even learning from the insights and faith tradition of evangelicals, González believes that ultimately the greatest challenge to Hispanic Catholics does not come from the sects but, rather, from what he calls "radical secularism and the concomitant consumerism that tend to exclude all forms of transcendence and religiosity from the dominant culture and from the public and civic life.[47]

The Latin American bishops seem to suggest something similar in their treatment of the appeal of evangelical religion in their preparatory document for Santo Domingo. In general they have taken the "high road" and responded to the phenomenon not by condemning the evangelical/pentecostal churches but by showing how the phenomenon relates to deeper trends in the culture, especially to the challenges of modernity. Among the factors contributing to the rise of evangelical Protestantism in Latin America is the ongoing search for meaning, especially for ultimate meaning and transcendence, among the youthful masses of Latin Americans.[48] In the context of dramatic changes taking place in their societies, politics, and culture, people continue to seek God and not just earthly solutions. Perhaps this insight relates as well to Hispanics in the United States who face similar upheavals. The explicit faith orientation of evangelical religion responds directly to the need for religious orientation of a people who historically have been extremely faith oriented.

The stress on God's transcendence is enhanced by three typical features of evangelical Christianity that clearly appeal to Hispanics: 1) the emphasis on feelings expressed in music; 2) the stress on the accessibility of the Bible to the ordinary believer (not just to the exegete and the *savant*),[49] and 3) the small faith community orientation which creates an atmosphere where peer witnessing and reinforcement can occur. These elements are often absent in the religious milieu of the more affluent and educated.

Mainline religion—Protestantism going back to nineteenth-century liberalism, and Roman Catholicism more recently in Europe and the United States—has tended toward elitism, has often distanced itself from the concerns of ordinary people becoming the refined religion of those in the know. It has made its peace with the anonymity and mobility of the city and modern life. The future vitality of the churches, then, depends upon their ability to immerse themselves again in the human experience of a faithful for whom middle-class ways and full-fledged modernity are still an illusive possibility, not the unquestioned norm. Evangelical religion and pentecostalism are leading the way in this as the dramatic data on the growth of worldwide pentecostalism indicate.

It must be noted, however, that the basic ecclesial communities constitute another, perhaps not totally unrelated, response to the challenges outlined here. Their path has been traced in several studies, most recently by Marcello Azevedo.[50] Their importance for ministry among Hispanic Catholics in the United States has been repeatedly underscored by both the bishops and the Hispanic Catholic leadership itself. Certainly some of the same qualities found in evangelical Christianity can be found in these small Christian faith communities: a sense of community, less anonymity, and a more affective style. The basic ecclesial communities also promote a clear, direct sense of social commitment, something that evangelical religion does not, at least initially, seem to stress.[51] David Stoll, as mentioned earlier, has noted that the base communities have not been as successful among the poor as the evangelical/pentecostal congregations because the base communities have sometimes lost sight of the euphemistic, symbolic, and ritual way popular religion deals with oppression. These base communities, however, have not lost sight of the communal thrust of Hispanic cultures. Roberto S. Goizueta calls this the intrinsic communal character of praxis and links it to the principle of solidarity in Catholic social teaching. He believes that "in the praxis of U.S. Hispanics community has ontological priority, for it gives birth to subjectivity." Goizueta quotes Virgilio Elizondo: "For our native forefathers,... it was the community that called forth the individuality of the person."[52]

Putting together David Stoll's critique of liberation theology and the base communities with the observations of Roberto Goizueta and Virgilio Elizondo, one might conclude that a future path for Christianity in Latin America and among United States Hispanics can be found in a dialectical relationship, a dialogue, a give-and-take between the insights of liberation theology and the experiences of the base ecclesial communities on the one hand and, interesting enough, the evangelical/pentecostal communities on the other. This path will perhaps be the fruit of a mature analysis and evaluation of the complex religious, social, economic, political, and cultural ferment experienced by Hispanics in North and South America. The path may become a new, vital form of ecumenism.

Finally, the quotation from William R. Read at the beginning of this chapter captures the essence of the long-range issue raised for Hispanic Catholics in the United States by evangelical and pentecostal Christianity. The evangelization of U.S. Hispanic Catholics demands that one "abandon the cultural coldness, the systematized, privileged and secularized Christendom" of the mainline religions of North America. That means promoting a countercultural gospel message. Interestingly enough, then, Hispanic Catholicism with both its popular religiosity and zeal for social justice on the one hand and evangelical Protestantism on the other may have more in common than is usually thought. Donald Dayton was attempting to articulate the basis for this surprising confluence in these words:

> As these movements (Pentecostalism and liberation theology) come more and more into dialogue, they may discover that they have more in common than they think. A central feature of Pentecostalism is its doctrine of "divine healing" which to my mind asserts very fundamentally the salvific intention of God to save and transform the body and this world—an assumption that the movement shares in some sense with the theology of liberation and social transformation.[53]

Dayton goes on to note that liberation theologians like Gustavo Gutiérrez are becoming more aware of the need to develop a deeper spirituality; while pentecostals and evangelicals are speaking more and more of the need for a social ethic. A recent work by pentecostal Hispanic theologian Eldin Villafañe, *The Liberating Spirit: Toward an Hispanic American Pentecostal Social Ethic*, is an example of this trend that may come as a surprise to mainline Christians unfamiliar with the work of pentecostal thinkers.[54]

The subtle and often perplexing reality of evangelical religion's appeal to Hispanic Catholics is, consequently, an issue that involves some of the weightier questions regarding how Hispanics will change and live their Christian faith in the context of U. S. culture as it too changes and moves toward the next millennium. In the interplay between seemingly disparate religious traditions—the evangelical/pentecostal and the Catholic—a vision of Christianity, its possible future tone and texture, emerges to our surprise and wonderment. That battle is being fought in the minds and hearts of today's Hispanic Americans. As they go, so goes the Christianity and religion of the Americas, both North and South.

NOTES

1. William R. Read, *Brazil 1980: The Protestant Handbook*, (Monravia, Calif.: Mission Advanced Research and Communications Center, 1973), xxix.

2. See Vinson Synan, "Varieties and Contributions," *Pneuma* 9, no. 1 (Spring 1987), 31–49.

3. See David Barrett, *World Christian Encyclopedia* (New York: Oxford University Press, 1982), 815–848.

4. Flavio Amatulli, *El sectarismo nos cuestiona* (Mexico, D.F.: Apostoles de la Palabra, 1988), 12.

5. Eleace King, I.H.M. *Proselytism and Evangelization: An Exploratory Study* (Georgetown: CARA/Georgetown University, 1991), 40.

6. George M. Marsden, *Fundamentalism and American Culture* (New York: Oxford University Press, 1980), 184.

7. David Stoll outlines the history and salient features of contemporary evangelical and pentecostal missionary outreach to Latin American in chapter 4 of *Is Latin America Going Protestant?*, (Berkeley: University of California, 1990), 68–98.

8. The fall 1986 issue of *Pneuma* has two articles on Latin American pentecostalism especially in light of its ecumenical relations. The first is by Everett A. Wilson, "Latin American Pentecostals: Their Potential for Ecumenical Dialogue"; the second, by Carmelo E. Alvarez, "Latin American Pentecostals: Ecumenical and Evangelical." These articles tend to support the notion that pentecostalism on both sides of the Rio Grande is a complex movement with similar challenges and difficulties (see 85–95). Pablo A. Derios summarizes the current status of evangelicalism in Latin America in "Protestant Fundamentalist in Latin America."

9. Justo L. González, *Each in Our Own Tongue* (Nashville, Tenn.: Abingdon, 1991), 30.

10. See James Davidson Hunter, *The Coming Generation* (Chicago: University of Chicago Press, 1987).

11. Another trend worth noting here is that growing numbers of mainline Protestant Hispanic congregations are becoming "evangelical" or "charismatic," that is, they subscribe to the styles and theological emphases of evangelicalism and/or pentecostalism but remain within the mainline Church. A similar observation may be made regarding Roman Catholic charismatics.

12. Donald W. Dayton, "Is Latin American Turning Pentecostal? The Ecumenical Significance of a Religious Revolution," unpublished paper given at National Academy of Ecumenism (NAAE) annual meeting, St. Louis, Mo., September 28, 1991, 17–18.

13. González, *Each in Our Own Tongue*, 35–37.

14. Thomas H. Groome, *Sharing Faith* (San Francisco: Harper, 1991), 81–82.

15. The work of Father Flavio Amatulli, an Italian missionary in Mexico, is an excellent example of an approach taken by the Church in Latin America. See Flavio Amatulli, *Catolicismo y Protestantismo* (Acayucan, Veracruz: Apóstoles de la Palabra, 1985).

16. See Carlos Martínez García, "Secta: Un concepto inadecuado para explicar el protestantismo mexicano," *Boletín Teológico*, 23, no. 41 (March 1991), 55–72. He objects to the uncritical use of the term *sects* to refer to evangelical and pentecostal religious groups in Mexico and, by inference, in Latin America. He suggests that the term reflects a prejudice not only on the part of Roman Catholic church leadership but also on the part of social scientists, journalists, and other writers who insist on viewing the growth of this form of Protestantism over so many decades of the twentieth century with disdain and fear.

17. Andrew Greeley, "Defection among Hispanics," *America*, July 30, 1988, 61–62.

18. Gerardo Marín and Raymond J. Gamba, *Expectations and Experiences of Hispanic Catholics and Converts to Protestant Churches* (San Francisco: University of San Francisco, Social Psychology Laboratory, Technical Report no. 2, February 1990), 4.

19. Roberto O. González and Michael LaVelle, *The Hispanic Catholic in the United States: A Socio-Cultural and Religious Profile* (New York: Northeast Hispanic Pastoral Center, 1985), 134.

20. Stoll, *Is Latin America Turning Protestant?*

21. Eleace King, *Proselytism and Evangelization.*

22. George M. Marsden, *Understanding Fundamentalism and Evangelicalism* (Grand Rapids, Mich.: Eerdsmans, 1991), 4–5.

23. See Marsden, *Fundamentalism and American Culture.*

24. Ibid., 3–8.

25. Stoll, *Is Latin America Turning Protestant?* 250–251.

26. Ronald A. Knox, *Enthusiasm* (Westminster, Md.: Christian Classics, 1951), vi.

27. Randall Balmer, *Mine Eyes Have Seen the Glory: A Journey into the Evangelical Subculture in America* (New York: Oxford University Press, 1989), 233–234.

28. Leo Grebler, Joan Moore, and Ralph Guzman, *The Mexican American People: The Nation's Second Largest Minority* (New York: Free Press, 1970), 494–507.

29. Holland, *Religious Dimension in Hispanic Los Angeles*, 444. Also see Grebler, Moore, and Guzman, *Mexican American People*, 498–499.

30. Allan Figueroa Deck, *The Second Wave* (Mahweh, N.J.: Paulist Press, 1989), 56–57.

31. Peter W. Williams, *Popular Religion in America* (Chicago: University of Illinois Press, 1989), 9–14.

32. The negativity toward popular religion in the period after Vatican II has not been as strong among the bishops who have generally insisted on the need to respect it. See John Eagleson and Philip Scharper, eds., in *Puebla and Beyond* (Maryknoll, N.Y.: Orbis, 1979), 184–188. Papal pronouncements on popular religion since Pope Paul VI's period have been generally positive. See Pope Paul VI, *On Evangelization in the Modern World* (Washington, D.C.: USCC Publications, 1976), no. 48.

33. Harvey Cox, *Religion in the Secular City* (New York: Simon and Schuster, 1984), 241.

34. This is exactly the point made by Robert Ricard in *La conquista espiritual de México* (México, D.F.: Fondo de Cultura Económica, 1986), 23, where he stresses one of the major findings of his lifelong study of the evangelization of Mexico: "...he tratado de mostrar que la debilidad principal de la obra evangelizadora de los religiosos españoles estribaba en el fracaso del Seminario de Tlaltelolco y en la enorme laguna que representaba la ausencia de un clero indígena completo.... La iglesia de México resultó una fundación incompleta. O mejor dicho, no se fundó una Iglesia mexicana, y apenas se sentaron las bases de una iglesia criolla; lo que se fundó, ante todo y sobre todo, fue una Iglesia española...donde los fieles indígenas hacían un poco el papel de cristianos de segunda catetgoría."

35. Sociologists Roger Finke and Rodney Stark have studied the affect of middle-class mores and mindsets on evangelism, the outreach of mainline churches to immigrants, in "The Upstart Sects Win America—1776–1850," in *The Churching of America, 1776–1990*, 54–108. They discuss Catholic outreach to immigrants and compare it to that of the evangelical/pentecostal denominations in "The Coming of the Catholics, 1850–1926," in the same book, 109–144. Sociologist Joseph P. Fitzpatrick explains the relevance of social class distance for contemporary Catholic approaches to Hispanic ministry in "The Hispanic Poor in the American Catholic Middle-Class Church," *Thought* 63, no. 249 (Spring 1988), 189–200.

36. Andrew Greeley, following the lead of David Tracy, sheds light on the way Catholics develop their faith. Catholics have an *analogical* imagination, while Protestants seem to have a *dialectical* one. One of the characteristics of Catholics, then, is the ability to hold contradictions in tension. This is what makes the Church "catholic." Perhaps this tendency is at work with Hispanics who even when they become Protestants do not cease being Catholic in a certain sense, that is, a Catholic ethos continues to inspire them. See Andrew Greeley, *The Catholic Myth* (New York: Charles Scribner's Sons, 1990), 34–47. Hence Hispanics in evangelical and pentecostal churches may be "Trojan horses" on behalf of Catholicism. Eleace King found, for example, several pentecostal and other Protestant Hispanic churches with images of the Virgin Mary (Our Lady of Guadalupe) and other Catholic symbols (*Proselytism and Evangelization*, 53).

37. Deck, *Second Wave*, 67–69.

38. *Vatican Report on Sects, Cults, and New Religious Movements*, 4–5.

39. See Kenneth Boyack, C.S.P., *Catholic Evangelization Today*, (Mahwah, N.J.: Paulist Press, 1987), 5–7.

40. Avery Dulles, "Pope John Paul II and the New Evangelization," *America*, February 1, 1992, 70.

41. Roberto O. González, "The New Evangelization and Hispanics in the United States," *America*, October 19, 1991, 268.

42. Ibid., 269.

43. In addition to David Martin's treatment of the move to evangelical Christianity as a moment in

the modernization of Latin America (*Tongues of Fire*, 284–285), Marcello Azevedo also treats of the effectiveness of the sects in dealing with the reality of Latin America's intense urbanization in *Basic Ecclesial Communities in Brazil* (Washington, D.C.: Georgetown University Press, 1987), 125–126. My thesis is that an analogous situation obtains in the United States.

44. Allan Figueroa Deck, "The Crisis of Hispanic Ministry: Multiculturalism as an Ideology," *America*, July 21, 1990, 33–36.

45. David Stoll, *Is Latin America Turning Protestant?* 75.

46. Jay P. Dolan reviews the salient features of the Church's historic, nineteenth-century outreach to Catholic ethnics including the national parish experience in *Catholic Revivalism* (Notre Dame, Ind.: University of Notre Dame Press, 1978), xix.

47. R. González, "New Evangelization and Hispanics," 268.

48. *Documento de consulta*, 139.

49. In this connection C. Gilbert Romero develops the relationship between popular Hispanic religiosity and the Bible. He shows how biblical symbolism and imagery are constitutive elements of Hispanic religiosity. See his *Hispanic Devotional Piety: Tracing the Biblical Roots* (Maryknoll, N.Y.: Orbis, 1991), 19–20ff.; and by the same author, "Tradition and Symbol as Biblical Keys for a U.S. Hispanic Theology," in Alan Figueroa Deck, ed.,

Frontiers of Hispanic Theology in the United States, (Maryknoll, N.Y.: Orbis, 1992), 41–61.

50. M. Azevedo, *Basic Ecclesial Communities in Brazil*.

51. The bishops speak encouragingly of the small faith communities in the pastoral letter on Hispanic ministry, *The Hispanic Presence: Challenge and Commitment* (Washington, D.C.: USCC Publications, 1983), 27. The more than 1200 Hispanic Catholic leaders assembled in Washington, D.C., for the Third National Pastoral Encuentro in 1985 produced a document, the *National Pastoral Plan for Hispanic Ministry* (Washington, D.C.: USCC Publications, 1987). In this document the basic ecclesial community is singled out as an especially apt tool for effective evangelization (see, 10).

52. Roberto S. Goizueta, "Rediscovering Praxis," in *We are a People*, ed. Roberto S. Goizueta, (Minneapolis: Fortress Press, 1992), 64–65. For Hispanic culture's affinity with the Catholic concept of solidarity, see Roberto S. Goizueta, "The Church and Hispanics in the United States: From Empowerment to Solidarity," in *That They Might Live*, ed. Michael Downey (New York: Crossroad, 1991), 168–169.

53. Dayton, "Is Latin America Turning Protestant?" 22–23.

54. Eldin Villafañe, *The Liberating Spirit* (Lanham, Md.: University Press of America, 1992).

THE POWER TO HEAL IN HAITIAN VODOU

Karen McCarthy Brown

The recent migration of Haitians to the United States has brought the Vodou religion to these shores. Vodou combines the African religious beliefs and practices of the slaves, who were brought to Haiti in the eighteenth century to work the sugar plantations, with the French Catholicism of their masters. According to the anthropologist Karen McCarthy Brown, the urban Vodou temples of New York, Miami, and other cities attempt to recreate the extended families of the Haitian countryside by envisioning each individual as embedded in an extensive web of relationships with families, ancestors, and the spirits. In this context, the urban Vodou healer addresses a range of medical, psychological, social, and spiritual difficulties that trouble those who frequent their home-based temples. By vividly reminding their followers of the true nature of the world, the healer helps them to find their way.

In the following essay, Karen Brown enters into this urban world of Haitian Vodou to contrast the narrow understanding of what healing means in Western medicine. Western interpretations of healing power as property have been particularly damaging to women. In Western medicine, the total physical, psychological, social, and historical nature of disease is divided up and parceled out to experts; few persons pay attention to their interrelations or to the larger spiritual framework. In contrast, Brown presents us with the Brooklyn Vodou healer Mama Lola who ministers to the many needs of a substantial immigrant community through various means, including dreams and possession-trances. Because Vodou is based on acceptance of the fact of death, Brown explains, all attempts at healing take place within the boundaries of fate. "Facing and accepting (though not surrendering in front of) the givens of the human condition and the limitations of one's own power," Brown concludes, "is the source of the Vodou power to heal."

Reprinted by permission from Karen McCarthy Brown, "The Power to Heal: Reflections on Women, Religion, and Medicine," in Clarissa W. Atkinson, Constance Hall Buchanan, and Margaret R. Miles, eds., *Shaping New Vision: Gender and Values in American Culture*, Studies in Religion, No. 5 (Ann Arbor, MI: Produced and Distributed by UMI Press, 1987), 124–141.

25 ❦

THE POWER TO HEAL IN
HAITIAN VODOU

Reflections on Women, Religion, and Medicine

Karen McCarthy Brown

WOMEN'S DIFFICULTIES in relation to western medicine, including psychoanalysis, are well documented in feminist literature. The relationships between particular sexist ideologies and medical perceptions, diagnoses, and treatments have been uncovered.[1] Women's difficulties in breaking into the medical profession are equally well known.[2] When women have sought access to the power to heal by becoming doctors, they have met resistance in one form or another in every place and every period of the history of Western scientific medicine.

The root metaphors of Western civilization are more visible in medicine than in many areas of life. On the most basic level, cultures are shaped by their root metaphors. These are the unarticulated yet deeply formative images that direct the flow of thought and action in any given culture. As in any operational thought system, there is a time lag between the root metaphors and current theory of Western medicine. There is a naive empiricism still deep in the medical ethos even though it has been set aside to some extent in medical textbooks. Feminist research, or research in general for that matter, has yet to reveal all the ramifications of Western medicine's intense physicalization of disease or of its view of healing as something done by an heroic actor who "possesses" power to an essentially passive, physical body that has no personal identity, social context, or history.

In Western medicine, healing power, like diseases and patients, is controlled by defining it as a piece of property. The power to heal is understood to reside in things—medical implements, drugs, and machines—whose use is restricted to those who possess other things—diplomas, licenses, and white coats—that indicate their ownership of a particular body of knowledge. It is the view of healing power as material property which can be owned and used by an elite few that I wish to explore in this essay. Seeing healing power as property, subject to all the dynamics of a capitalist system, is one of the most significant root metaphors of Western medicine and one of the most damaging to women.

It is extremely difficult to become conscious of the root metaphors of one's own people and place. Once grasped, they are even harder to hold on to and pursue through the complex layers of daily life and collective history. It is precisely because they operate below consciousness that these metaphors are so efficient in the processes of culture formation and maintenance. If our root metaphors were available to us easily, if every day we could accept, reject or amend them, there would be no shared culture. Yet to see them as essential to communal life and to see their elusive character as integral to their functioning is not to conclude that they should not be tampered with. Change of the magnitude feminists call for requires that we pursue them. Yet this is not easy. One way to crack open the Western medical system to its root metaphors is to place it in relation to a healing system from another culture which is strikingly different. This is what I propose to do here.

The heart of this essay is a case study of healing in Haitian Vodou, the African-Catholic religion that grew up on the slave plantations of the eighteenth-century French sugar colony then called Saint Domingue. This case, drawn from a New York-based Haitian healer, will be preceded by a discussion of women healers in Haiti in which I will attempt to uncover the reasons for women's relatively easy access to this power domain and also show something of the women's style, as distinct from the men's, of using power within it. The actual case study will be followed by some analytical comments about healing in the Vodou system which will be used to locate and describe a healing power that cannot be privately owned and tightly controlled. The conclusion will address western scientific medicine and particularly the feminist critique of it. This section will include suggestions that feminists ought to focus on understanding the oppressive nature of power in Western medicine and on clarifying our own tendency to think of power as property.

WOMEN HEALERS IN HAITI

While in some parts of rural Haiti women can gain recognition and prestige as *manbo* (priestesses) and they can be herbalists and *fèm saj* (midwives) throughout the island, nowhere in the countryside do they effectively challenge the hegemony of the male in the healing sphere. This is not so in the cities where there are probably as many women as men doing healing work. The urban Vodou context is the heritage of Alourdes, the woman healer who will be described in the case study which is the focus of this paper. This relatively recent phenomenon of large numbers of women heading Vodou temples is due in part to chance.

Haiti is a poor country with an extremely depressed economy where the agricultural productivity which once made it the "Pearl of the Antilles" is now long gone. The reasons are long-term political corruption, overpopulation, and soil erosion. The large, patriarchal extended family dominated in Haiti's past, and this is still thought of as the ideal family. Even moderately successful men in the countryside can enter into multiple *plasaj* (common-law) unions with women. Each of these women is then set up in a house of her own in which she raises the children born of their union. Having her own household gives the rural woman limited autonomy, and her freedom and responsibility are increased by the fact that it is women who run the markets.[3] In the markets, women sell such things as baskets, candies, and bread along with the family farm produce. A market woman learns selling skills and money management through this work. The small profits she makes from the things she has produced with her own hands are hers to keep as insurance against natural and social catastrophe. These monies are often the only thing that prevent her children from starving.

As more and more young people have been forced off the family land, away from the rural extended families and toward the greater autonomy of city life, women have generally fared better than men. Their adaptable, small-scale market skills are one reason. The preference of piece-work factories for women, who are thought to be steadier workers and less likely to cause problems, is another. Women have become breadwinners and their relationships with men, many of whom have significantly less earning power, have become more unstable as a result. Women in the cities have thus found themselves the heads of their own houses, as they were to some extent in the country, but with no supporting (and confining) extended family to back up that household unit.

Urban Vodou is, at its core, an attempt to recreate the security gained from the extended families of the countryside. In the cities, it is the Vodou temple and the fictive kinship network it provides that compensate for the loss of the large rural family. The head of the temple is called "mother" or "father" and the initiates are addressed as "children of the house." The Vodou initiate owes service and loyalty to his or her Vodou parent after the pattern of filial piety owed all parents by their children in Haiti. In turn, Vodou parents like actual ones, owe their children protection, care, and help in times of trouble. In certain circumstances this help is of a very tangible sort: food, a place to sleep, assistance in finding work.

In rural Haiti the patriarch has unquestioned control, a control that extends to his role as priest when the family serves the Vodou spirits. But in urban Haiti, women's increased autonomy and access to money have made it possible for them to become heads of Vodou "families." Furthermore, I believe that certain aspects of healing and priestcraft have changed as a result of women's greater participation. I do not wish to overstate this conclusion, yet neither do I want to dismiss it simply because it is based on impressions. Starting when I first went to Haiti in 1973 and long before I considered undergoing initiation myself, many male and female friends offered this advice: "If you *kouche* [undergo initiation], do it in a woman's temple. The men will want to use you."

The urban Vodou temples run by men tend to mimic the patriarchal structure of the rural extended families. The authority of the priest is absolute. Also, the urban priest is notorious for fathering many children and recruiting desirable young women to be among his *hunsi* (brides of the gods), the ritual chorus and general workforce of a Vodou temple.[4] He thus creates for himself a highly visible father role which he then extends to all those who serve the spirits under his tutelage. While the priestess who heads a temple is not necessarily more democratic in all of her relationships with those who serve in her house, she does tend to be so in the ways that a mother's role with her children is normally less inflexibly hierarchical than that of a father. For example, some temples headed by women function as day-care centers for the working mothers associated with them. The woman-headed temple tends to reiterate the tone and atmosphere inside the individual home, a place where women have usually been in charge. This is an atmosphere that allows the priestess more flexibility and play in human relationships than the priest who acts out of the more public, and therefore more static and controlled, role of the patriarch.

Thus it has been social change that has created a chink in the patriarchal armor. Women have slipped through and, in urban temples, created "families" of their own modeled partially on the patriarchal family but with important modifications. Women's healing style is subtly but significantly different due to the age-old roles they have played in child rearing and barter marketing. Haitian market women, like many North American Black women who support their families, probably have a greater sense of being effective in the world than do the white, middle-class, North American women whose voices dominate in feminist scholarship. This self-assurance is the firm base on which their flexibility operates. Furthermore, the greater flexibility and play of women's roles as compared to those of men have meshed with central attitudes in the larger culture, specifically attitudes toward healing. This meshing has taken place in such a way that key aspects of the character of the people as a whole have been enhanced under the leadership of women. The following study of a woman healer at work will support these observations.

THE SOLDIER WHO WAS HUNGRY FOR FAMILY

Late in March of 1984, I went to visit Alourdes[5] at her home in the Fort Greene section of Brooklyn. Alourdes is a Vodou priestess and healer. In this African-American spiritual system, the terms priest or priestess and healer are synonymous. Mama Lola, as Alourdes is sometimes called, ministers to the many needs of a substantial immigrant community of taxi drivers, dishwashers, gas station attendants, nurses' aides, telephone operators and the chronically unemployed. She reads cards, practices herbal medicine, manufactures charms and talismans, uses her considerable intuitive powers ("the gift of eyes"), and the well-honed empathy of a strong woman of fifty who is now a homeowner and head of a sizeable household, yet spent the first half of her life in Haiti where at times she was driven to prostitute herself to feed her children. In addition to her personal skills and strengths, Mama Lola also provides her healing clients with access to the wisdom and power of the Vodou spirits, a configuration of African spirit entities loosely identified with Catholic saints, each of whom presides over a particular life domain such as child-bearing and rearing, family roots, anger and assertion, humor, and death. (Humor and death necessarily go together in the Haitian view of things.) Alourdes gains access to the spirits through dreams and through possession-trance, which is central in Vodou. In treatment sessions, she will frequently "call" the spirits for diagnosis, insight or specific instructions as to what is to be done to bring about healing.

I have known Alourdes for nearly ten years. She presided over my initiation into Vodou and now calls me her "daughter." We have been working together on a book about her life for the past eight years. I have an easy familiarity in her home. So when we sat at her kitchen table in March of 1984, it was not unusual for her to tell me what was currently going on in her healing practice. Alourdes can be discreet if that is what is called for; however, if there is nothing about a client's problem that needs protecting, she sometimes teaches by sharing the details of cases. "I got somebody," she said. "I'm doing some work for him. He is in the army. Oh boy, Karen! That man so big! When he go downstairs, he got to go like this." With her usual refusal to reduce a story to words, Alourdes' stout and squat body sprang up from her chair and hobbled across the kitchen imitating a tall man in fear of hitting his head on the ceiling. Mama Lola continued:

> He from Virginia, but his mother in New York. She live in Brooklyn. But when he come he don't stay with her. He stay in hotel. I say to him, "Why you don't stay with your mother? Let her take care of you." He say, "Not me. I not dependent on nobody. What I need that for? The army is my family. I love the army and I going to stay in it until I die…er…until I retire." That what he say. I look at him and I think, "That funny!", because I never meet nobody…that's the *first* person I meet who say, "I love the army." So you know what I think? I think he just hungry for family.

As is the custom, the lieutenant had presented himself to Alourdes with an introduction from a mutual friend and a non-specific problem. He had "no luck." Although she sometimes knows what is wrong with clients as soon as she meets them, Mama Lola told me she always performs the expected diagnostic card reading so they will not be intimidated by her. She did such a reading for the lieutenant.

As she told me the story I could imagine the two of them in her cramped altar room tucked away in one corner of the basement, the one tiny window blocked by a heavy curtain, bunches of odorous herbs and a collection of baskets hanging from the ceiling, smoke-darkened color lithographs of the Catholic saints attached to the walls above altar tables dense with tiny flickering flames, smooth dark stones sitting in oil baths, bottles of rum, vodka and perfume, herbal brews and sweet syrups. She would have sat in the big armchair with the stuffing coming out of one arm, her broad mocha face lighted from underneath by a candle stub that burned on one corner of the small table in front of her. I smiled to think of the big army officer hunched on the tiny bench opposite her where clients always sit.

After a preliminary sign of the cross, Alourdes would have shuffled the cards and offered them to him to cut. When they were spread in front of her in four rows of eight, she would already have been in a withdrawn, concentrated state of mind. After some minutes of silence, Alourdes would have begun to tap the cards ("heat them up") in an order determined by her inner vision and ask him questions, such as "You have some trouble in your house? You fight?"

At this stage of the divination process, the healer faces a large number of choices as to the direction of questions. Just as a healer such as Mama Lola is a combination medical doctor, psychotherapist, social worker, and priest, so the "problems" or "bad luck" she is faced with may manifest across a spectrum ranging from the physical to the social to the spiritual. No matter how the bad luck is eventually defined, it will always be diagnosed as ultimately due to a disruption in relationships, whether these are relationships with the living, the dead, or the spirits. The presenting symptom, though carefully articulated and then attended to by the healer, is to some extent arbitrary. In other words, trouble with one's father could equally well result in stomach pains or difficulty on the job. Haitians thus see the person as defined by a relational matrix and disturbance at any point in that matrix can create problems anywhere else.

During diagnostic card readings, the client is free to answer yes or no to the healer's probing questions without prejudice. Thus the client is active in the diagnosis yet does not dictate the description of the problem. When the questions and answers have gone on for some time, a joint definition of the problem will usually emerge. Most clients would acknowledge a significant difference between the problem they thought they came with and the one that was defined through divination. The outsized lieutenant from Virginia was no exception, although it took him a while to realize this.

After many questions and many negative responses from the lieutenant, it finally came out during his first session with Alourdes that he wanted a promotion to a higher rank in the army and thought one of his superiors was standing in his way. Alourdes was not sure.

> I read card for him, but I don't see nothing. You know some people, they really got bad luck and you just see it. But with him, I don't see nothing like that…little thing maybe, but no real big thing in his path…nobody at work want to stop him. So I say to him, "How long you feel you got back luck?" He think…he think…he think and he say, "Since I was a little boy." I say, "You can't have bad luck since you little boy!" Then I say, "What happened when you was a little boy?" Oh sweetheart, he tell me a story that was so sad…so awful.

The lieutenant had grown up in poverty in the Bahamas. A key event happened when he was no more than six or seven. One day his mother had nothing to give her children to eat. Neither did she have money to buy food. "He was so hungry…so hungry," Alourdes said. The enterprising and desperate young boy went, without his mother's permission or knowledge, to the factory where his father worked to ask for money for food. The man, shamed in front of his co-workers, turned on the boy with a terrible, hurtful truth that had been hidden until that moment. "Why you calling me Daddy?", he snapped. "I'm not your father." The young boy hid his hurt in anger and retaliated in a way that reveals much about the ideology of male power in Caribbean societies. He yelled at the man he had always thought to be his father: "You going to be sorry. Someday I going to be rich and I going to support you. I not going to be a hungry man like you!" Then, Alourdes said, he went home and cried. But he never said anything to his mother about the incident.

A few years later the boy found out by chance who his real father was. There was a woman who lived not far from his house whom the child had always addressed as Auntie without knowing if she really was an aunt or only a friend given the honorary title as is common in the islands. One day as he walked by her house, a young blonde woman sitting on the porch called him over, took his chin in her hand, lifted his face for careful inspection and said to Auntie: "That brother of yours can't deny this one. Oh no!" Alourdes reported that Auntie then told the boy, "That your daddy's new wife. He marry her in Germany. She come to visit me." That afternoon, for the first time, the boy heard the name of his biological father.

As a young adult already showing signs of promise in an army career, he went to Germany with the intention of looking up his father. But he procrastinated and left the country without making contact. According to Alourdes, her client explained his actions by saying: "What I need to find that man for? He not my father…not really."

Alourdes began her treatment, in pace with her client, by addressing the problem the lieutenant had acknowledged: his failure to get promoted. I was temporarily living in Massachusetts, working on Alourdes' biography, so I did not stay in close touch with the details of his case. It is likely that Alourdes gave him a "good luck bath"—herbal infusions and perfume mixed with fresh basil leaves (a general prophylactic) and water—which was spread upward, in small handfuls, over his body. After such a "bath" he would be instructed not to bathe with soap and water for three days.[6] She probably made one or more good luck charms for him as well. Surely she made an herb-doctored cologne that he could wear every day to enhance his luck. If she chose to take his story about the ill will of the senior officer seriously, she may also have manufactured a charm to "tie" or "bind" the supposed enemy. Making these charms is an interesting process for it requires exhausting amounts of concentration on the part of the client. The lieutenant may well have been given a container of straight pins and told to count out two piles of 101 pins each and then count the piles again, and then again. Once absolutely certain that he had the exact number he would have been instructed to push each one (it takes effort) into a thick wax candle, while repeating aloud his desire that the man get out of his way and doing so in the name of the appropriate saint at each thrust of metal into wax. Among other things, this would have helped the lieutenant get clear as to whether it was his superior officer who was the source of his problems.

Some months after our first conversation about the soldier, Alourdes reported that deeper problems had been uncovered in the course of a subsequent card reading and they were now starting to work on those. It seems the woman known as Auntie had quarrelled with the boy's mother[7] not long after the chance meeting in which he learned the name of his father. The now grown man had a dim memory of the boy witnessing an act of magic, the placement of a charm. The boy remembered seeing Auntie write his name several times on a piece of paper and bury it along with a tiny oil lamp beneath one of the trees in her courtyard. Alourdes had to work on a larger canvas now. There were relational problems within the extended family and, since the charm was buried under a tree which everyone knew was the dwelling place of a spirit, the spirits themselves were now involved. This would take time.

Again, I was not in New York and did not observe any of the particulars of the army officer's treatment. But it is unthinkable that it would have gone on without Alourdes calling Papa Gède, Master of the Cemetery, one of the two main Vodou spirits with whom she works. Once this spirit had struggled with and displaced Alourdes' *gro bonanj*, big guardian angel, an aspect of the human soul that is roughly equal to consciousness and/or personality, he would have begun to speak and act through Alourdes' body, slugging down herb- and pepper-laced rum (Alourdes herself drinks little and then only sweet wine or liqueur) and searching about for his bowler hat and his dark glasses with one lens missing.[8] Some say Gède's glasses have only one lens because the penis has only one eye. Others take a metaphysical approach and suggest that Papa Gède sees between the worlds of the living and the dead and that this sense of disjuncture accounts for his randy behavior and merciless joking. Gède delights in going after straight-laced people like the lieutenant who exercise strong control over themselves and their lives. It is likely that Gède teased him relentlessly, though not without point or lesson.

Ezili Dantò[9], the fearsome dark-skinned spirit associated with the Catholic Madonna known as Mater Salvatoris, may also have made a visit to Alourdes' tiny altar chamber while the lieutenant squatted on the low red wooden stool. If she did, she did not mince words with a man who neglected his mother and rejected invitations to sleep in her house and eat her food. Ezili Dantò can deliver frightening diatribes.

Whatever its specifics, the treatment went on for some months, with hiatuses when the lieutenant was not able to be away from the base in Virginia. In the course of things, Alourdes got to know her client well and when he came for treatments, she offered him coffee and they sat at the upstairs kitchen table before descending to the basement where the proud soldier had to hunch and squat in order to squeeze himself into the presence of the healing spirits. I asked about him in one of the regular phone calls that went from Cambridge to Brooklyn during the summer of 1984. Alourdes reported a recent conversation she had had with him:

> I talk to him real good. Oh sweetheart, I talk to him. I tell him to forgive his mother. She lie to him and tell him that other man his father. But she say that cause she ashame. So he got to forgive his mother and forgive that man who tell him, "I am not your father." Forgive him, cause he hurt and angry. I tell him, "Even he angry at you and your mother, that not your fault. You was just a child. No child responsible for that. Maybe at first your mother lie to him too. Maybe she say 'I'm pregnant for you,' when it really not his baby. But…maybe she hungry. Maybe she got to do that so he could feed her all that time she pregnant. Maybe he not know you was not his baby til after you born and then he hurt and angry. Don't judge her. Women got to do all kind of thing." I know…cause when I got Robert [the third of Alourdes' four children and the last one born in Haiti] I tell somebody "I pregnant for you," but it not true. What I going to do?

I got to eat or that baby going to die! I tell him, "You got to love your mother…do everything to see she happy before she dead…she an old lady now…send her money…go see her." But you know who I hate, Karen? Who the bum? That man who go to England! He the bum! Cause maybe he find out she pregnant and maybe he think that going to be expensive. So he just run away. And you know what? He a racist. He got to go marry a white woman. Black woman not good enough. Ehh!

The course of treatment had been decided on. Healing, forgiveness, and reconnection were the desired ends (as well as disconnection and moral censure for the biological father and his family) and, undoubtedly, Alourdes worked on these goals through her usual combination of prayers and charms and visits from the spirits who would variously tease, empathize, and deliver stern lectures.

To ask whether this clarification of the nature of the problem, when it finally did come, or the cure itself, when that finally was effected, should be credited to Alourdes or to the spirits is to ask a confusing question from the Vodou point of view. Those who serve the spirits do not make such neat distinctions between the person and the *lwa* (spirit) who resides "in" or "around the head" all the time and who "rides" the back of the neck during possession.[10]

Nearly a year later the name of Alourdes' sad and ungainly soldier friend came up in a conversation. "What ever happened to him?", I asked. "Did he get his promotion?" Alourdes responded in a vague and distracted fashion. She thought he did get it. She was not sure. Maybe he did not. "But," and here she brightened up and turned her full attention to me, "when he in New York now, he stay with his mother. His mother the only family he got. That man who raise him dead long time. He don't come to see me no more but he okay now. Don't you worry, sweetheart."

HEATING UP: HEALING IN HAITIAN VODOU

The word "power" (*pouvwa* in Haitian Creole) is rarely used to refer to the ability to heal. In fact it would hint of associations with malevolent magic if someone were to say of Alourdes, "li genyen pouvwa," she has power. Yet many do say of her, "li genyen konesans," she has knowledge. In Vodou circles *konesans* refers to sacred knowledge, the knowledge of how to heal. It is a word with a wide referential field including complex information about herbs, arcane teachings (including what we might call theology), and, most importantly, open channels of communication with the ancestors and the spirits which provide information as to what is going on at the deepest levels of a person or even what will happen in the future.

"Heating up" is another term used in relation to healing. It is always used in an active mode, as in the following example: "The spirits will not come to help us until the ceremony is *byen echofe*," well heated up. It is only when the singers, dancers, and drummers at a Vodou ceremony have moved beyond the fatigue and preoccupations of their difficult lives and are performing enthusiastically, drawing on a spiritual energy reserve tank,[11] that the spirits will be enticed to "ride" one of the faithful. Yet it is not only large groups that are able to heat things up sufficiently to bring about transformation. Alourdes' own energy can be similarly raised and heated by gazing into a candle flame when she wishes to call one of the spirits for help in performing a treatment. And if charms are expected to work over time, they also must be periodically "heated up" by being focused on and prayed over. Often a candle is lighted by the charm or "point" as part of this process.

With the concepts of "knowledge" and "heating up" we move close to the root metaphors that shape the Haitian understanding of healing power. *Konesans* is a wide-ranging and mostly non-specific thing. Even those few priests and priestesses who have "the gift of eyes," highly developed intuitive powers, know that this knowledge, like the energy that enables a manual laborer to dance all night, comes from sources beyond themselves and is not something to be counted on in every situation. Thus a Vodou healer can never really be said to "own" such knowledge. Furthermore heat, even though its presence in the body is a basic life sign and its transformative presence in the hearth makes cooking, eating, and therefore survival possible, is also an evanescent thing. It must be sought again and again, rekindled and recycled. Waxing and waning is part of the nature of heat and so, if healing is accomplished through heating, then it is never appropriate to think of the healer as "having" healing power in the way one can "have" a piece of property. The most that can be said of a Vodou priestess such as Alourdes is that she has mastered some techniques for enticing the heat to rise. In working with the soldier, Alourdes' initial problem was to heat him up enough for the real sources of pain and blockage to rise to the surface.

In Vodou, heat is life energy and it is intimately connected to death, humor, and sexuality. I do not have the leisure here to support these connections by teasing them out of the intricate details of ritual, although this can be done and presents the most convincing case since there is no scriptural canon or written doctrine in Vodou. I can make a few general comments, however, which will show the connections on a broad scale. The easiest place to begin is with Gède. This spirit is guardian of the cemetery; he is a trickster, and the dance performed for him is a mime of sexual intercourse. During the long and taxing rituals for the Vodou spirits, Gède appears in the interstices, between dramatic and somber possessions that touch deep emotional chords in those gathered to "serve the spirits." His role is not unlike that of a cheerleader who entertains the crowd and gets it revved up for the second half of the game. He also appears at the end of ceremonies, in the early morning hours, when the social and personal wounds cauterized during the long night of spirit contact must be covered with the soothing salve of humor so the participants can return protected to jobs and family. Gède was the humorous but effective medicine most likely applied early in the soldier's cure. Its purpose was to soothe him, but also to energize him, to shake him up.

The word *balanse*, to balance, has special meanings in Vodou circles. It refers to an active balancing as when something or someone is swung equally far between two poles. When sacred objects are taken off the Vodou altars and introduced into the ritual action, they must first be "heated up." To do this the ritual assistant is directed to *balanse*, dance, with the object in a side to side swinging motion. The word is also used in wider contexts. A Vodou priest once told me about the death of a mutual friend and, in commenting on the grieving family, he said "Gède, Master of the Cemetery, came to the house and balanced it," i.e. sent the household reeling.

Energy is what is sought in Vodou healing ceremonies, but like electricity this energy can be constructive or destructive. It all depends on how it is used.[12] The analogy of electricity is useful and yet, from another perspective, it hides something of the wisdom of the system. Those who serve the spirits do not understand the life energy they work with as morally indifferent so much as they see it as actually created from clash and contradiction. And death is the biggest contradiction of all.

Death and sexuality work together to raise life energy. Without death, there would be no point to sex and birthing. Death and humor go together because humor is the only appropriate and strong response to what is both dreadful and inevitable. Gède's is not an easy dismissive humor based on a false sense of superiority, but one that arises when a person hits rock bottom and rebounds because, put simply, there is nothing else to do. As a result of their cruel history of slavery, oppression, and poverty (Haiti is the poorest country in the western hemisphere), Haitians individually and collectively have repeatedly hit rock bottom. The humor and energetic creativity that characterize their culture, and particularly the Vodou dimensions of it, come from acceptance of the conditions of life. "Moun fèt pou mouri," people are born to die, Haitians are fond of saying with a shrug of the shoulders.

Vodou is based on an open-eyed acceptance of the fact of death and, in a related way, all attempts at healing in Vodou begin with the recognition that there are limits to what human knowledge, effort, and will can accomplish. For example, the first determination that a healer makes is whether a problem is "from god" or "from the spirits." God, Bondye, is the distant and omnipotent creator. The spirits are god's "angels" or emissaries in the world. Healers cannot change the mood or will of god. If a problem is discovered to be from god, the healer simply leaves it alone. But healers can feed the spirits, coax and cajole them into being more gentle and forgiving with one of their "children." In the second stage of the soldier's treatment, this is what Alourdes had to do with the spirit whose ill will had been set in motion by the charm "Auntie" buried under the tree in her courtyard.

The Vodou understanding of the multiple dimensions of the human soul parallels the limits the healer faces in problems from god. In addition to several other facets of soul (including the *gro bonanj* that is displaced during possession) there is also *zetwal*, star, a person's fate. At birth, the larger outline of a human life is already determined from beginning to end. All maneuvering, whether it is that of a Vodou healer such as Alourdes or of an ordinary individual, is done within the confines of what is fated to be. Each client is thus a given, someone unique who simply is what he or she is. Clients of Vodou healing do not lose personal history or social identity, and this may partially explain why, at all stages of the cure, the patient is an active participant. The lieutenant from Virginia helped define his problem through his responses to questions during the card reading; he participated in the manufacture of the baths and charms designed to prompt healing; and he engaged in conversation with Alourdes as well as with the Vodou spirits who were called in the course of his healing.

Modern Vodou healers acknowledge other limits to their powers. While most are skilled and effective herbalists, when certain symptoms are present, Alourdes and the hundreds of others like her who serve urban communities where there are scientific medical resources available will recommend that a patient see a medical doctor for x-rays or antibiotics.

Because Mama Lola operates out of a healing system based on an acceptance of limits, she is able to handle the power to heal in a flexible way that is neither grasping nor controlling. In curing the soldier, Alourdes employed a range of powers. She used "the gift of eyes," what I have been calling intuition, for her diagnosis of his problem. She used personal experience and empathy to understand the situation. She drew on community norms for judgment against the irresponsible biological father. She used herbs and charms. She also called on the spirits. Spirit possession when combined with her other skills provided range and flexibility in the postures she could take in relation to her client. At one time she could be a friend whose own experience of having a child in the womb and no man willing to take responsibility for it became the resource for wise counsel and deep compassion for the soldier. At another time she could be an awesome spirit, such as Ezili Dantò, censuring behavior and dictating the terms on which help would be given. This fluidity of roles means that any power a Vodou healer such as Alourdes exercises over a client is applied in a specific place and time, for a specific purpose. Her power as a healer does not adhere to her as a permanent attribute nor does it generalize itself to all her social relations.

Furthermore, because healing power in Vodou cannot be controlled and owned, neither can the object of that power be confined and controlled. Physical problems are taken seriously (and they are treated), but problems are not reduced to their physical manifestations. In Vodou there is a flow between the material and the non-material, the inside and the outside, the intrapsychic and the person, society, and history. Charms of the sort described in the story of the soldier's cure are examples of the internal externalized, of the temporary concretizing of a problem in order that it can be addressed directly. The "good luck bath" is an example of the reverse where an olfactory statement about how things *should* be is manufactured, administered, and breathed in by a patient for a period of three days.

In sum, healing power, the process of applying that power, and the problems to which it is applied are all characterized by fluidity and flexibility. And, as I have argued above, the power can be held so lightly because those who orchestrate this power are neither denying their own or another's ultimate vulnerability, nor are they pretending there are no limits to their skills. Facing and accepting (though not surrendering in front of) the givens of the human condition and the limitations on one's own power is the source of the Vodou power to heal, just as death is the source of Gède's humor and drive to propagate life. Acceptance of the rules of the game, the clash of opposites that is life, enhances life energy, heats things up, and heals.

CONCLUSIONS

The point of these thoughts is, of course, not to convince anyone to throw over Western scientific medicine and attempt to introduce traditional Vodou healing into the mainstream of North American culture. The purpose of the exercise lies in using the stark contrast with Haitian Vodou to unearth the property metaphor deep in western medicine (and western civilization in general) and to examine the tendencies to parcel out, fence in, control, and defend which are fostered in the medical arena by this root metaphor. In Western medicine, unlike Vodou healing, the patient's body is fenced off from his or her identity, history, and social context. We have separate healers to deal with each piece of territory. The physical-psychological-social-historical-spiritual disease cycle is similarly broken apart and parceled out among the experts with few persons paying attention to the interrelations. Within medicine, those specialties which of necessity deal with the interrelations have the least prestige. Think of environmental studies, nutrition, public health, and preventive medicine in general. Furthermore, as a result of being divided, conquered, and colonized, the patient is rendered passive in the curing process.

None of these points is new, nor is it news that women have been especially strongly controlled within such a control-oriented system. If Friedrich Engels was right in connecting the rise of women's oppression with the development of the notion of property,[13] then we can appreciate why women have had so much trouble with western scientific medicine. This comparative exercise may make a modest addition to the feminist critique of medicine in demonstrating that otherwise diffuse insights into the nature of western medicine are knit together by the hidden cultural metaphor that defines patients and diseases as pieces of property subject to ownership, use, and alteration.

The more substantial contribution may come in realizing that, unlike the fluid and flexible "heat" in Haitian Vodou, the power to heal in western medicine is also treated like a piece of prime real estate. Doctors own their power as if it were a thing and control access to it through the medical fraternities. One result of this unarticulated assumption about the nature of healing power is that it leaves doctors with a prestigious but rigid and greatly diminished human role. Doctors are required to deny significant portions of their humanity in order to function according to accepted standards. Doctors cannot bring their broader life experiences, their humor, or their own embodiedness into the healing process except as "bedside manner," and that is stage management having nothing directly to do with curing. Furthermore, the role of the western medical doctor, once defined and controlled, becomes the possession of the person with the diploma, a permanent attribute of that person. This in turn causes the power of the doctor while actually doctoring—a situation in which he or she has awesome power over the vulnerable patient—to generalize itself to other areas of life where it manifests as class status and economic bounty. Along this line, it is interesting that Alourdes strictly follows the unwritten rule of Vodou healing that the healer should never take undue profit from curative work.

Western medical consciousness is carefully controlled like the role of the doctor. Medicine is a science and science enshrines reasons, a focused and consistent use of the mind that eschews wider and deeper though less controllable ways of knowing. The supposed universal claim of the well-reasoned argument, its ability to detach itself from the specificity of the person who thought it and function in an equally powerful way no matter where it is applied, is another attempt to reify a power and establish control over it. Western civilization as a whole therefore fears so-called altered states of consciousness (altered from what norm?) of the sort that are central to Vodou possession-trance. For example, while there are substantive reasons for our wariness of "recreational drugs" and alcohol, it is also clear that we fear them because they make people inconsistent and unreasonable. We even apologize when we have a cold for "not being ourselves today." It may well be that one of the reasons Vodou has attracted so many negative stereotypes in this culture is that, in heating things up, it brings out the many and not always consistent persona that inhabit each of us. Yet when trance and other altered states of consciousness are discussed in the academic and scientific communities, the question that seems to need answering is why some have chosen to spend time and effort exploring them. Rarely does anyone turn the question around and ask why we, in the western world, have narrowed our consciousness to such a pure and unflickering beam of light. Erika Bourguignon's work seems to indicate that most groups at most times and in most places have utilized altered states in ways central to their societies.[14] It would seem that our passion for consistent and controlled knowing is more anomalous in the larger human picture than is Alourdes' ability to move in and out of trance states in which spirit entities speak and act through her.

In Vodou healing, the power is not so controlled. Healing power is an evanescent thing raised for the moment through the humor and strength that lie on the other side of an honest facing of death and one's own more short-range limitations. This sense of limits is exactly what we do not have in western medicine where the doctor is a superhero and every disease is an enemy just about to be conquered, if it has not already submitted to the power of medicine to enforce change. In discussions about abortion and euthanasia as well as in such celebrated cases as that of Baby Jane Doe (an infant born with serious physical deformities), western culture reveals itself struggling but largely unable to integrate death into life or to acknowledge limits to the power of medicine.

Western civilization has generated a great deal of power and property. This has given us the opportunity to create the illusion that we can avoid the harsh limits that have become the source of strength and healing in places like Haiti. Such a statement is not intended to glorify Haitians, who are as human as any other group, but rather to point to the need for a kind of wisdom in our medical establishments that, among third-world liberation communities, has been called the "epistemological privilege of the oppressed."

One of the reasons it is so difficult for Western medical doctors to face and accept such major limits as death is that we have cut the healing arts off from spirituality, which would provide the only framework large enough and safe enough to make the confrontation possible. When religion and healing are separated, both appear to lose. The humorless, de-sexed, and death-denying monotheism that we currently pursue in western culture may well have parallels with the lonely beacon of reason that we follow in scientific thought. But I will leave that connection for others to explore.

Feminists who have found this comparison of healing in Vodou and in western medicine helpful may wish to ponder the formative powers of the property metaphor at greater length. When we fight the medical establishment for "control of our bodies" or for "control of reproduction," when we identify "our bodies" with "our selves," even when we address a misogynist society by declaring our intention to "take back the night," we sound more as if we are battling over property than changing the terms of the debate. Changing root metaphors is not easy, but we might begin the task by taking a clue from Alourdes and attempting an act of radical empathy with those who wield the power that damages us. It seems to me that it is time for feminists to examine the ways in which we demonize men and male behavior. For a while we have needed to do that to gather strength and reach clarity, but the easy caricaturing of men which passes for humor in some (certainly not all) feminist circles is a thin and brittle humor far removed from the richness of Gède's laugh. If we could look at one male-controlled institution, the medical establishment for example, and see through the heroic antics and controlling ethos to the genuine human hunger for life and life energy from which they spring, then we might be able to do what Alourdes did. She treated the lieutenant from Virginia by exposing his hunger for prestige, power, and independence as what it truly was, a hunger for human connection.

NOTES

1. Among the best examples of this work are G. J. Barker-Benfield, *The Horrors of the Half-Known Life: Male Attitudes Toward Women and Sexuality in Nineteenth-Century America* (New York: Harper and Row, 1976) and Barbara Ehrenreich and Deirdre English, *For Her Own Good: 150 years of the Experts' Advice to Women* (New York: Doubleday, 1978).

2. See for example, Barbara Ehrenreich and Deirdre English, *Witches, Midwives and Nurses: A History of Women Healers* (New York: The Feminist Press, 1973).

3. For further insight into market women see Sidney W. Mintz, "The Employment of Capital by Market Women in Haiti," in *Capital, Saving and Credit in Peasant Societies*, edited by Raymond Firth and B. S. Yamey (Chicago: Aldine Publishing

Company, 1964).

4. This point needs to be qualified by recognition of the large numbers of homosexual priests who have genuine power and prestige within Vodou. This is somewhat surprising given the homophobia observable in the larger Haitian culture. However this is only a partial qualification since many of these same priests would be more precisely called bisexual. They father children and have traditional families over which they exercise more or less traditional forms of power.

5. Alourdes is not yet certain if she wishes her full name to be known. I hope no one will see my use of only her first name in this article as a sign of disrespect.

6. A "bath" is applied in an upward direction,

starting at the feet and ending with the head, when it is designed to enhanced good luck and in a downward direction when it is supposed to remove bad luck. Leaving the bath on the skin for three days is in my view (I have taken many "baths" myself) a powerful form of aroma therapy. All are pungent. One lives with the smells, waking and sleeping, for a long enough period of time for them to address the deep self, more technically, the limbic mind where the sense of smell is located.

7. Punitive magic, something not nearly as central to Vodou as its image in North America would lead us to believe, is most often carried out between families or groups. But its target, intentional or de facto, is often the youngest and most vulnerable member of that family. This explains Auntie's charm being directed against the boy even though the quarrel had been between herself and the boy's mother.

8. Possession in Haitian Vodou is not a matter of putting on an act or assuming a ritual posture. It is a deep trance state which most often leaves the one possessed unable to remember anything that happened while being ridden by the spirit. It is a fascinating state from a psychological perspective because the spirit will often contradict and even, at times, severely chastise the very person being ridden.

9. Ezili Dantò is the woman who bears children. Her iconography and possession-performance work through all the permutations of mother-child relations from the most fiercely defensive to the most fiercely rejecting. Dantò is a member of the Petro pantheon of spirits, one of two major groups recognized in urban Vodou. Petro spirits are not evil but they are recognized as having "hot" temperaments and uncompromising standards.

10. The question as to whether persons and spirits are truly separate and distinct is answered in paradoxical ways in Vodou. Beliefs surrounding possession trance and the struggle of the *gro bonanj* with the possessing spirit point to a separation. Yet initiation rituals simultaneously "feed the spirits in the head" of the person and establish a repository for them outside the person. Also, when the ceremony is performed for an ancestor that calls his or her spir-

it "up from the water" and establishes it on the family altar, that entity is called both by the name of the ancestor and by the name of the chief Vodou spirit with whom he or she worked. Thus reference may be made to "Marie's Dantò" or to "Pierre's Gède."

11. Although the terminology is mine, the notion of a spiritual energy reserve tank is one that is actually quite developed in Vodou. In Vodou belief, one of the dimensions of the human soul is called the *ti bonanj*, little guardian angel. For a long time I had trouble understanding what this was. Then Alourdes gave me the following example of how it works: "When you walking a long way or you carrying something very heavy…and you know you not going to make it…then the *ti bonanj* take over so you can do what you got to do."

12. The notion that power has no moral direction of its own and thus can be used either constructively or destructively may account in part for the bad reputation that Vodou has in North America. There are instances of punitive magic being carried out by Vodou priests and priestesses but there is also a strong belief in the overall interconnectedness of things and events which makes them rare. The use of the will to damage another necessarily produces an equally damaging counter-effect on the one manufacturing the charm unless that person is either righteous beyond a doubt or very well protected.

13. F. Engels, *The Origin of the Family, Private Property and the State* (New York: Pathfinder Press, 1972).

14. I believe this to be a fair conclusion to draw from Erika Bourguignon's research even if it must by necessity be an impressionistic one. The reader should know that Bourguignon herself is far too cautious a statistician and researcher to claim to have actually proven anything as sweeping as this statement. See Erika Bourguignon, *Possession* (San Francisco: Chandler and Sharp, 1976) and "World Distribution and Patterns of Possession States," in *Trance and Possession States*, edited by Raymond Prince (Montreal: R. M. Bucke Memorial Society, 1968).

FRONTIERS OF ENCOUNTER

Diana L. Eck

The dramatic growth of the world's religions in America during the past quarter century is an astonishingly little noticed phenomena. Since the 1965 immigration act lifted national quotas and restrictions on Asian immigration, the ethnic make-up of the United States has come to include many more immigrants from Asia, the Pacific, and the Middle East. Today Muslim mosques and Hindu and Buddhist temples can be found in nearly every American city, though most are hard to see because they are in homes, former churches, or movie theaters. Some estimate that there will be more Muslims than Jews in the United States within a generation. In some parts of the United States, like New York, followers of Asian religions already outnumber Episcopalians and Presbyterians. Taken together, this growth of the world's religions in America has created new "frontiers of encounter."

Diana Eck reflects on this religious encounter between East and West in America in the one hundred years since the 1893 World Parliament of Religion in Chicago. She tells this story in the context of her own Swedish Christian upbringing in Bozeman, Montana, and her training in comparative religion. The need for comparative study is particularly acute because these newcomers bring with them religious ideas that are "foreign" to most Americans. And yet, as Eck points out, there has always been religious diversity in the world. What is new today is "our sharply heightened awareness of religious diversity in every part of our world and the fact that today everyone—not just the explorers, the missionaries, the diplomats, and the theologians—encounters and needs to understand people and faiths other than their own."

Reprinted by permission from Diana L. Eck, "Frontiers of Encounter: The Meeting of East and West in America since the 1893 World's Parliament of Religions," in her *Encountering God: A Spiritual Journey from Bozeman to Benares* (Boston: Beacon Press, 1993), 22–44.

26

FRONTIERS OF ENCOUNTER

The Meeting of East and West in America since
the 1893 World's Parliament of Religions

Diana L. Eck

ALL OF MY ANCESTORS were immigrants from Småland and Varmland in Sweden.
On my father's side, they came to Minnesota and then Montana. On my mother's side, they
came to Illinois, moved on to Iowa, and finally ended up in the Pacific Northwest. They were
among the 1.3 million Swedish immigrants who came to America between 1840 and 1930.
They were all Swedish Lutherans. I was sharply confronted with their heritage and my own
not long ago when I spent the morning at the annual Paryushana rites at the Jain Center of
Greater Boston, which is in the town of Norwood on a quiet residential street called Cedar
Street, in a church that had formerly been a Swedish Lutheran Church.

The Jains, a community of Gujarati immigrants from India with religious roots going
back at least to the sixth century B.C.E., have owned the building for ten years now. The
cut-crystal chandeliers reminded me of those in the church in Sünne, where Grandma Eck
grew up. Nothing else in the sanctuary, however, would have been familiar to her. The pews
had been removed and the entire room carpeted. On the raised altar area were tables bearing
fine marble images of the Jain saints called *tirthankaras,* "those who have made the crossing"
from this life of birth and death to the utter freedom of the far shore. At the altar, Jain laity,
their mouths and noses covered with a white band of cloth so as not to inadvertently injure
microscopic life-forms, were making traditional offerings of flowers, incense, and water to
the *tirthankaras.* The sanctuary was crowded with people and filled with song and incense.

Paryushana is the holy day marking the end of the annual period of austerity and fasting,
so everyone was in an ebullient mood. A feast was to follow in the back yard, where a huge
yellow and white striped tent, America's version of the Gujarati *shamayana*, had been
erected. The Jain community of the Boston area, an unusually high percentage of them in
the computer industry, turned out by the hundreds for the occasion. As Gujarati families
poured out of the church and toward the feast, the women wearing bright saris and shawls,
I strolled up Cedar Street to take perspective on the colorful scene. A few doors up I met one
of the neighbors, a Catholic woman who had never been into the temple, but who waved
her hand with satisfaction toward the old Swedish church and its new congregation and
said, "This is what makes America!"

In 1893 the World's Parliament of Religions convened in Chicago in connection with the World's Fair which celebrated the four hundredth anniversary of Columbus' arrival in the Americas. For most Americans this two-week assembly was their first encounter on this continent with people of the great religious traditions of Asia. One hundred years ago most of the 150,000 American visitors who attended one or more sessions of the Parliament had never before heard the voice of a Buddhist, a Hindu, or a Muslim; one could probably count the number of Hindus in North America on the fingers of one hand. In the 1890s T.C. Iliff and Brother Van still wrapped their leather reins around the hitching posts in downtown Bozeman. Contemplating the centennial of this Parliament, this one-hundred-year span seems a very long time indeed. The world has turned over and over again with social, political, and cultural revolution. The "New World," built on the backs of ancient native cultures, has grown quickly, energetically, and, for some, ruthlessly.

What was a fair and a somewhat artificial parliament in 1893 is today the reality of Chicago. The metropolitan yellow pages list dozens of entries under the headings "Churches: Buddhist" or "Churches: Islamic." There are said to be seventy mosques in Chicago today and almost half a million Muslims. The suburbs of the city boast two sizable and elaborate Hindu temples, to say nothing of the dozen smaller places of Hindu worship. There are at least twenty Buddhist temples and meditation halls—from those of the Japanese Zen tradition to those of the Cambodian, Vietnamese, and Laotian Buddhist refugee communities. There is a Zoroastrian fire temple. There are Baha'is and Jains, Sikhs and Afro-Caribbean Voodoo practitioners. The Chicago planning committee convened nearly fifty cosponsoring religious groups to organize the centennial of the Parliament in 1993. This local committee, called the Council for a Parliament of the World's Religions, was more representative of the world's religions than the Parliament itself had been.

Much has happened to the United States in the one hundred years since the Parliament. One hundred years ago, my own great-grandparents were just getting settled in what to them was a new world. They were among the millions of immigrants who came from Sweden, Ireland, Poland, and Italy—Protestant, Catholic, and Jewish. America became a nation of immigrants, though not without prejudices and bigotry and exclusion. Beginning in the 1880s, the U.S. Congress passed a series of Asian exclusion acts that attempted to limit and even eliminate immigration from Asia. Such an immigration policy remained substantially in effect through the 1950s. John F. Kennedy was writing on the history of immigration and the need for the liberalization and reform of American immigration law at the time of his assassination: "To know America...it is necessary to know why over 42 million people gave up their settled lives to start anew in a strange land. We must know how they met the new land and how it met them, and, most important, we must know what these things mean for our present and for our future."[1] When the immigration act proposed by President Kennedy was finally passed and signed into law in 1965, a new era of immigration began, bringing people from all over Asia to the United States. The Jain temple on Cedar Street in Norwood, with its Swedish cut-glass chandeliers, stands as a symbol of the changes over these one hundred years. The Roman Catholic neighbor down the street expressed what Kennedy would surely have wanted to say as well—"This is what makes America."

THE WORLD'S PARLIAMENT OF RELIGIONS

The World's Parliament of Religions convened for more than two weeks in September of 1893. It was not really a world event except in intention and vision. It was planned by

American Christians, mostly Protestants, and it could as easily be seen as one of the opening events of the modern Christian ecumenical movement as the first act in the modern interreligious movement. There were relatively few Asians present, and the sole Muslim speaker was a New Englander who had converted to Islam. Even so, the vision of the Parliament was lofty and it set forth questions of interreligious relations that are as vivid today as they were in 1893. In convening the Parliament, chairman John Henry Barrows proclaimed, "Our meeting this morning has become a new, great fact in the historic evolution of the race which will not be obliterated."[2]

There were some for whom this "new, great fact" was questionable and even objectionable. The Archbishop of Canterbury had declined to come because "the Christian religion is the one religion." He went on to say, "I do not understand how that religion can be regarded as a member of a Parliament of Religions without assuming the equality of the other intended members and the parity of their positions and claims."[3] Apparently the Sultan of Turkey also objected to the Parliament, and as a result, representatives of the Arab Muslim world did not attend. The General Assembly of the Presbyterian Church, meeting in Portland, Oregon, in 1892, expressed its disapproval. The monks of the Engaku-ji Buddhist monastery in Kamakura, Japan, were likewise sceptical and sought to dissuade their abbott, Soyen Shaku, from going; they thought it would be "improper for a Zen priest to set foot in such an uncivilized country."[4] Despite their apprehensions, Soyen Shaku insisted on going and the young monk who drafted his letter of acceptance in English was D. T. Suzuki, who later became the preeminent cultural translator of the Zen Buddhist tradition from Japan to North America.

When the Parliament opened, a replica of the Liberty Bell tolled ten times, once for each of the great religions represented. Charles Carroll Bonney, the president of the Parliament and one of its first visionaries, began his address, "Worshippers of God and Lovers of Man, let us rejoice that we have lived to see this glorious day!" He saw the Parliament as evidence that "the finite can never fully comprehend the infinite," and declared, "Each must see God with the eyes of his own soul. Each must behold him through the colored glasses of his own nature. Each one must receive him according to his own capacity of reception. The fraternal union of the religions of the world will come when each seeks truly to know how God has revealed himself in the other."[5] John Henry Barrows then welcomed the delegates and confessed, "When, a few days ago, I met for the first time the delegates who have come to us from Japan, and shortly after the delegates who have come to us from India, I felt that the arms of human brotherhood had reached almost around the globe. But there is something stronger than human love and fellowship, and what gives us the most hope and happiness today is our confidence that 'the whole round world is every way bound by gold chains about the feet of God.'" He described the days which lay ahead as "the first school of comparative religions, wherein devout men of all faiths may speak for themselves without hindrance, without criticism, and without compromise, and tell what they believe and why they believe it."[6] And so they did.

One of the most vibrant and dramatic of the Parliament participants was Swami Vivekananda, who was among those who spoke for the Hindu tradition. His challenge was that of a widely pluralistic worldview. In addressing his "sisters and brothers of America," he declared that he was proud "to belong to a religion that has taught the world both tolerance and universal acceptance." The Archbishop of Canterbury would indeed have been uncomfortable hearing Vivekananda proclaim so forcefully, "It is the same light coming through different colors.... But in the heart of everything the same truth reigns; the Lord has declared to the Hindu in his incarnation as Krishna, 'I am in every religion as the thread through a string of pearls. And wherever thou seest extraordinary holiness and extraordinary power raising and purifying humanity, know ye that I am there.'"[7]

Among the Buddhists at the Parliament was the Sri Lankan Buddhist reformer Dharmapala, who asked the audience in a large lecture hall, "How many of you have read the life of the Buddha?" When only five raised hands, he scolded, "Five only! Four hundred and seventy-five millions of people accept our religion of love and hope. You call yourselves a nation—a great nation—and yet you do not know the history of this great teacher. How dare you judge us!"[8] One of the Buddhists from Japan was equally challenging, pointing explicitly to the anti-Japanese feeling in America and deploring the signs that read "No Japanese is allowed to enter here." "If such be the Christian ethics—well, we are perfectly satisfied to be heathen," he said. The Japanese are not so concerned, he said, whether someone is called a Buddhist, a Shintoist, or a Christian, "the consistency of doctrine and conduct is the point on which we put the greatest importance."[9]

There was little Muslim participation at the Parliament. Islam was represented by the American convert Mohammed Webb, who spoke directly to the prejudices and images of Islam in the West. "There is not a Muslim on earth who does not believe that ultimately Islam will be the universal faith." But he went on, "I have not returned to the United States to make you all Mussulmans [Muslims] in spite of yourselves.... I do not propose to take a sword in one hand and the Koran in the other and go through the world killing every man who does not say 'There is no God but one and Mohammed is the prophet of God.' But I have faith in the American intellect...and in the American love of fair play, and will defy any intelligent man to understand Islam and not love it."[10]

Among the scholars who sent messages to the Parliament was J. Estlin Carpenter from Oxford University, who made it clear that the comparative study of religion had opened up the concept of revelation to what he called the "Bible of humanity." "Philology has put the key of language into our hands," said Carpenter. "Shrine after shrine in the world's great temple has been entered; the songs of praise, the commands of law, the litanies of penitence, have been fetched from the tombs of the Nile, or the mounds of Mesopotamia, or the sanctuaries of the Ganges. The Bible of humanity has been recorded. What will it teach us? I desire to suggest to this Congress that it brings home the need of a conception of revelation unconfined to any particular religion, but capable of application in diverse modes to all."[11]

Despite such visions of a much wider conception of revelation, the Parliament was dominated, on the whole, by Christian participants with a universalist fulfillment theology—the view that Christianity represents the flower and fulfillment of the religious hopes and aspirations present in other faiths. One eloquent expression of such a view was that of the Reverend Joseph Cook of Boston: "Old man and blind, Michael Angelo in the Vatican used to go to the Torso, so-called—a fragment of the art of antiquity—and he would feel along the marvelous lines chiseled in by-gone ages, and tell his pupils that thus and thus the outline should be completed. I turn to every faith on earth except Christianity, and I find every such faith a Torso. But if its lines were completed it would be a full statue corresponding in expression with Christianity."[12] Even Mr. P.C. Mozoomdar of the reformist Brahmo Samaj movement in India said in the course of the Parliament, "I regard Christ as an essential factor in the future of India.... The Parliament of Religions opens up the gate of a golden era, an era which shall purge off all the un-Christian elements of the different faiths, both Christian and non-Christian, and unite them all in Christ."[13] Professor Goodspeed, a historian of religion at the University of Chicago, foresaw at the Parliament a universal ethical religion for the future. "That religion," he said, "is not so much Christianity as Christ. Such was the deepest voice of the Parliament."[14]

As for the relation of Christianity to other faiths, the Parliament was very cautious. In his summary report, chairman Barrows was careful to state that "there was no suggestion on the part of Christian speakers that Christianity was to be thought of as on the same level with other religions."[15] For the most part, Christians claimed universality for Christianity, while listening with earnestness to the witness of Muslims, Buddhists, and Hindus. It was with satisfaction that Barrows recalled how all the representatives of the great historic religions prayed together daily the Lord's Prayer. "The Christian spirit pervaded the conference from the first day to the last. Christ's prayer was used daily. His name was always spoken with reverence. His doctrine was preached by a hundred Christians and by lips other than Christian. The Parliament ended at Calvary."[16]

Apparently not everyone felt that the Parliament pointed unequivocally to the manifest destiny of Christianity. Barrows allowed in his report that "it was felt by many that to claim everything for Christianity and deny any good in other religions is not Christian, and is an impeachment of that Divine goodness which is not confined to geographical limits and which sends its favors upon the just and upon the unjust. Christians came to rejoice with an increased hopefulness as they perceived that religion, however imperfect, is, after all, the best there is in man, and that God is not confined in his mercy and benefactions to any favored race or people."[17] He added these lines of verse:

So many roads lead up to God
T'were strange if any soul should miss them all.

Despite the dominance of Christian discourse, the spirit of the Parliament was really something quite new. In his summary statement, Barrows wrote, "It was a novel sight that orthodox Christians should greet with cordial words the representatives of alien faiths which they were endeavoring to bring into the light of the Christian Gospel; but it was felt to be wise and advantageous that the religions of the world, which are competing at so many points in all the continents, should be brought together, not for contention but for loving conference, in one room."[18] The atmosphere was described as one of "mutual tolerance, extraordinary courtesy, and unabated good will."[19] In closing, Vivekananda thanked the "noble souls whose large hearts and love of truth first dreamed this wonderful dream, and then realized it," and proclaimed, "The Parliament of Religions has proved to the world that holiness, purity, and charity are not the exclusive possessions of any church in the world."[20] At the final session, Rabbi Emil Hirsch of Chicago announced, "The day of national religions is past. The God of the universe speaks to all mankind."[21]

In the overall composition of the Parliament there were many omissions. Of the major speakers only two were African Americans. Commenting on the World's Fair as a whole, the president of Haiti, Frederick Douglas, called the "White City" created for the event a "whitened sepulchre" for blacks.[22] Fannie Barrier Williams, one of the two African Americans to address the Parliament, declared, "It is a monstrous thing that nearly one-half of the so-called evangelical churches of this country repudiate and haughtily deny fellowship to every Christian lady and gentleman happening to be of African descent.... The hope of the negro and other dark races in America depends upon how far the white Christians can assimilate their own religion."[23]

About ten percent of the participants in the Parliament were women. Theirs were some of the clearest and most powerful voices. Julia Ward Howe spoke with a certain scepticism about the noble ideals of all the religious traditions and asked provocatively "why the practice of all nations, our own as well as any other, is so much at variance with these noble precepts?" She continued, "I think nothing is religion which puts one individual absolutely above another, and surely nothing is religion which puts one sex above another."[24] Elizabeth Cady Stanton, who was then working on *The Woman's Bible* (published in 1895), addressed the Parliament, insisting that attention to the poor is the only way to salvation. She quoted the scriptural passages "God is no respecter of persons" and "He has made of one blood all the nations of the earth." And she challenged the assembly by declaring, "When the pulpits in our land shall preach from these texts and enforce these lessons, the religious conscience of the people will take new forms of expression, and those who in very truth accept the teachings of Jesus will make it their first duty to look after the lowest stratum of humanity."[25] The Reverend Antoinette Brown Blackwell, one of the few ordained women to speak, seemed to confirm Stanton's vision: "Women are needed in the pulpit as imperatively and for the same reason that they are needed in the world—because they are women. Women have become—or when the ingrained habit of unconscious imitation has been superseded, they will become—indispensable to the religious evolution of the human race."[26]

Finally, despite the overflowing sentiments of universal fellowship expressed at the Parliament, there were no Native Americans there. Indeed, one of the shocking facts of the Chicago World's Fair was the display of American Indians on the midway as curiosities. For many from the "Old World," they were as exotic as Vivekananda. No native elder or chief, however, spoke at the Parliament, and as far as I know no Parliament participant spoke to regret the absence of this religious perspective. Native American religiousness was clearly not seen as a religious perspective at all. Just three years earlier Chief Sitting Bull had been arrested and killed, the Ghost Dance had been suppressed, and 350 Sioux had been massacred at Wounded Knee Creek. On September 16, 1893, while the Parliament met, six and a half million acres of Cherokee, Pawnee, and Tonkawa reservation lands were opened for homesteader settlement and 50,000 settlers rushed to claim homestead lands on that day alone. Nothing of the trampling of native peoples was mentioned in the Parliament. No Black Elk, no Red Cloud, no White Calf was invited to speak of the vision of the native peoples of America. Not until eighty-five years later, with the American Indian Religious Freedom Act of 1978, was the integrity of Native American religiousness legally recognized. And even since then, native peoples have struggled constantly to prevent the degradation of sacred sites, to stop the display of sacred artifacts and bodily remains in museums, and to use ceremonial peyote in their rites.

A few months before the Parliament, in July of 1893, Frederick Jackson Turner delivered a much-discussed address to the American Historical Association in Chicago in which he asserted that the "frontier" was now closed: The 1890 census report had said, "The unsettled area has been so broken into by isolated bodies of settlement that there can hardly be said to be a frontier line." The movement toward the frontier line, beyond which lay what the American mythic imagination deemed "unsettled" territory, had been definitive for American consciousness. "Up to our own day American history has been in large degree the history of the colonization of the Great West. The existence of an area of free land, its continuous recession, and the advancement of American settlement westward, explain American development," said Turner. "And now...the frontier has gone, and with its going has closed the first period of American history."[27]

There in Chicago, in the summer of 1893, the western frontier was pronounced closed, and a new frontier of America's encounter with the East was about to open.

SWEDES ON THE FRONTIER

In the summer of 1893, my great-grandmother Hilda Olson Fritz was picking blackberries for a living on the fire-scarred hillsides of the Olympic Mountains of Washington State, with a pistol on one hip and a baby on the other. The most precious cash commodity of these pioneers was blackberry jam, which they used in trade at the general store down on the bay. Hilda wrote of her long days, "I assure you, it was not easy to pick blackberries and carry a small child. When I set the baby down, I feared a cougar would bounce out, so my big revolver was always in the belt around my waist."[28]

Of all of the great-grandparents who were of Swedish immigrant stock, Hilda was the only one I knew when I was a child. I was four years old when I held her big pioneer hand and posed for a photograph with her on the front porch of the log cabin in the foothills of the Olympics. As Hilda told it, her father, Olaf Olson, left Sweden with "a great desire to come and aid Lincoln in the war for freedom from slavery." By the time he arrived, however, the war was over and Olaf had to settle for employment as a gardener in Des Moines. When he had earned some money he sent for his wife and children. Their decisions about where to settle—first in Rock Island, Illinois, and then in Stanton, Iowa—were motivated in part by the presence of a good Swedish Lutheran church. They were like so many European immigrants who settled in those decades in the Midwest; their farm life in Iowa, first in Staton and then in Pochontas County, was both rewarding and very difficult. There were blizzards, tornados, and crop failures. One year, Hilda wrote, "the grasshoppers left nothing. The turkeys ate so many grasshoppers they died, the hogs ate the dead turkeys and got the cholera."

After twenty years of struggle, the whole family moved further west, looking for the "free land" that pressed its imprint upon the imagination of these immigrant pioneers. Hilda and her husband-to-be, Olaf Edward Fritz—"Ed" for short—rode west with a cattle train. They made their way to the Pacific Northwest, where they settled in Port Townsend in 1889. The family leased a three-story building and started a hotel, where, as Hilda later put it, "no liquor was served and no Chinaman employed."

Further up the Olympic peninsula and inland, there was still homestead territory in the valley of the Dungeness River. Marian Taylor, the local historian of the Dungeness area, writes, "In 1891 four new families, three of them related, came as a group after having been told of the valley by an old prospector."[29] The three related families were Fritzes and Olsons, and the fourth would eventually be related too—the Hokansons, whose daughter Ida married Hilda and Ed's son Ike. When they all arrived in the summer of 1891, it was wild country. There were no roads from Port Townsend into the forests of the Olympic Mountains, so they took their supplies by boat up to Sequim Bay and hauled them on horse-back up into the hills. It was a steep climb up from the bay. For five generations now our family has called the Fritz place by the name it must have had that first summer—Up in the Hills. Theirs was the life of real pioneers. Recalling their first cabin, Hilda wrote:

The cabin was 12 by 14 feet. On the north side was the door, a large cedar slab hewed smooth. Also the fireplace and a wide cedar board to hold tin plates, tin cups, and other things. Under the window was a broad cedar log, very nice and smooth. That was our table. For seats we used small trees sawed off at the right heights. For beds we used fir branches that were woven together in a way that made them springy. I sewed gunny sacks together for two beds and found that the dry ferns made a good thin pad for the top of the fir-boughs. The branches from the fir trees, chopped fine, made a good covering for the floor and the smell of balsam was soothing.

Hilda made jam and bought their first pony with the proceeds. She planted a garden in what she called "the wilderness." She learned how to shoot and treed a wildcat. Her husband, Ed, got grouse and deer; she said if she had only one bear she could make it last through the whole winter. Toward evening on August 19, 1893, she built a fire for making jam, put the water on to boil, and headed out to the garden with her shotgun to get radishes and cabbage for supper and to see if she could shoot the rabbit that had been ravaging the garden. The sparks from the fire caught the cedar shakes on the roof and the chain burned to the ground. "All that we had toiled so hard for through many years went up in smoke in less than an hour. But our courage, hope, and faith lived on and is still living."

Hilda was clearly a woman of faith. When I thumb through her old Swedish prayer book and her Evangelical hymnal, I wish I had really known her. I think about the similarities and the differences between her religious faith as a Swedish Lutheran and mine. In her journal she wrote a prayer that is, for me, a window into the religious sensibility of a woman who lived her adult life in relative isolation. "Grant us the peace of solitude. Give us the strength of the forest. Give us trust and faith that will stand by us in all tribulation. Help us to know that you, the Giver of joy and sorrow, are very near us and willing to help. For you know, O Lord, that we love not our fellow beings less, but nature more."

On September 11, 1893, Hilda would have been trying to keep house in a makeshift camp next to a burned-out cabin in the back hills of the Olympic Mountains as the World's Parliament of Religions opened in Chicago. By the winter, they had built the house of solid squared logs of Douglas fir where my grandfather Ike was born. Hilda may well have read something about the Parliament in the occasional copies of the *Seattle Times* that made their way "up in the hills," but I imagine she was preoccupied with building a new life in what was left of the frontier. The newspapers described the color and the spectacle of the Parliament— the eloquent turbaned Vivekanada, the scarlet robes of Cardinal Gibbon, the fiery Dharmapala from Ceylon swathed in white garments, the rainbow of pure silk worn by the delegates from China and Japan.

There were new worlds launched that September in Chicago and in the hills of the Olympics. Different as they were, they are both worlds that have come to be not only mine but ours as Americans. My great-grandparents and grandparents were at the last edge of the closing frontier in the West. The frontier of encounter with the East, the Orient, was just beginning.

At the time of the Parliament, the Swedes on the other side of the family, my father's side, were also beginning to come from the "old country" one at a time, Ecks and Nordquists. The Nordquists were a big clan, ten brothers and sisters in all. As soon as those who were here earned enough, they sent for the next in line. My grandmother Anna Nordquist was the last to come. She and her sister Signe and their mother, Louisa, sailed from Sweden to New York on the Lusitania in 1914. They traveled from coast to coast on the train. Both the newness and the caution they felt as Swedish women traveling alone across the whole stretch of this new world was conveyed by Grandma Anna's tale of buying a bagful of what they thought were apples in New York before getting on the train. When Anna tried one and found it soft, she spit it out and insisted they throw the whole bag away; only later did she discover that the rotten apples were peaches. Anna worked for a time as a maid in Portland, Oregon, before moving to Anaconda, Montana, where there was a large Swedish settlement. There she met my grandfather Theodore Eck, a carpenter and general contractor, at a big Swedish community picnic.

The world of my grandparents was the bipolar world of the "old country" and the new. Anaconda and Butte, Montana, dominated by the Anaconda Copper Company, were characterized by ethnic rivalries and mutual suspicion among the Swedes, Italians, Poles, and Irish. Asia did not figure in that world, despite the presence of a small Chinese population in Butte. Hindus, for the most part, lived in India, Muslims in the wide stretch from Indonesia to Morocco, and Buddhists in South and East Asia. My grandmother Anna Nordquist Eck had never met a Hindu or a Buddhist, or, very likely, anyone from Asia. In thinking through the meanings of life and death, she did not come in contact with the ideas of the Bhagavad Gita, or the Upanishads, or the Four Noble Truths. Though Hindu ideas had come gently into American literature through the writings of Emerson and Thoreau, Grandma Eck did not read the literature of American transcendentalism. In those days Americans encountered Asia, if at all, in the images gleaned from the relationships of mission. So vibrant was the idea of mission to Grandma Eck that when I returned from my first year in India she always introduced me proudly to her friends as "my granddaughter who is a missionary in India."

ASIAN EXCLUSION

The late nineteenth- and early twentieth-century image of America as a nation of immigrants simply did not include, in the American mythic imagination, immigrants from Asia. The torch-bearing arm of the statute of Liberty was raised in New York harbor toward the Atlantic, not the Pacific. When Israel Zangwill, the nineteenth-century playwright, spoke of America as "God's melting pot"—melting, refining, and reshaping immigrant races and peoples into a new race—it was assumed that the peoples of the melting pot were European. A similar welcome was not extended westward toward Asia.

In 1882, the first Chinese exclusion act was passed. It specifically prohibited the entry of skilled and unskilled laborers from China into the U.S. and those who were already here were barred from eligibility for naturalization as citizens and their wives were made ineligible for entry. The debate in Congress over the bill was thick with anti-Chinese rhetoric. A member of the House of Representatives declared, "They do not wear our kind of clothes...and when they die, their bones are taken back to their native country."[30] The period of exclusion was reduced from twenty years to ten in the final bill. Only thirty-seven members of the House of Representatives opposed it, among them Congressman Joyce, who stated the case eloquently: "I would not vote for it if the time were reduced to one year or even one hour, because I believe that the total prohibition of these people from our shores for any length of time...is a cowardly repudiation...of a just and long established principle in our government."[31]

Chinese workers had come to Hawaii and then to the U.S. beginning in the 1840s as agricultural laborers and as miners. Chinese labor had built the railways across the West and up and down the Pacific coast. In Montana, Chinese had come to the gold and copper mines in Helena and Butte, where sizable "Chinatowns" developed. An 1869 Helena newspaper article gives a glimpse of emerging Chinese culture: "Today is the (Chinese) annual Josh Day [sic], on which occasion their custom is to visit the burial places—as our China men and women have done, closing their ceremonies about 2 p.m.—burn incense and innumerable small wax candles about the head stones or boards of the graves, depositing a liberal lunch of choice eatables and drinkables, designed for the spirits of the departed; recite propitiatory prayers to their savior (Josh), and otherwise show themselves sacredly minded of the welfare of their dead."[32]

In 1870, when the first census of the Montana territory took place, the Chinese were 10 percent of the population. They contributed to the economy with Chinese businesses; there were two dozen Chinese-owned laundries in Helena alone. But Montana also experienced this rising xenophobia that led to the Chinese Exclusion Act. The Butte newspaper published articles filled with invective: "The Chinaman's life is not our life, his religion is not our religion. His habits, superstitions, and modes of life are disgusting. He is a parasite, floating across the Pacific and thence penetrating into the interior towns and cities, there to settle down for a brief space and absorb the substance of those with whom he comes into competition. His one object is to make all the money he can and return again to his native land, dead or alive…. Let him go hence. He belongs not in Butte."[33]

In 1892, the Geary Act extended the exclusion for another ten years. At the time of the World's Parliament of Religions, the Honorable Pung Kwwang Yu, a Chinese representative in Washington, D.C., spoke at the closing session of the pain of such prejudice: "I have a favor to ask of all the religious people of America, and that is that they will treat, hereafter, all my countrymen just as they have treated me."[34] In that same year, 1893, the Butte newspaper editorialized, "The Chinaman is no more a citizen than a coyote is a citizen, and never can be."[35] Montana historian Robert Swartout, Jr., looking back on this period, writes that anti-Chinese prejudice was "so pervasive that recognition of the Chinese role in the development of modern Montana would come only after most of the Chinese pioneers and their descendents had left the state."[36]

The exclusion that began with anti-Chinese legislation gradually dilated to include Filipinos, Japanese, Koreans, and other "Asiatics" as well, even "Hindoos" (meaning anyone from India). In the fall of 1907 my grandfather Ike would have been scarcely twelve in that cabin in the hills of the Olympics. That September, across Puget Sound in Bellingham, a mob of five hundred lumbermen attacked the simple homes of immigrant Hindu mill workers. Joan Jensen, who has documented the experience of Asian Indian immigrants in North America, tells the tale: "Battering down the doors, the mob threw belongings into the street, pocketed money and jewelry, and dragged Indians from their beds. The Indians fled, some injuring themselves by jumping from buildings in an attempt to escape. Those who did not move fast enough were beaten."[37] Hundreds of Indians were driven from town. The editor of the *Bellingham Herald* insisted, "The Hindu is not a good citizen. It would require centuries to assimilate him, and this country need not take the trouble. Our racial burdens are already heavy enough to bear….Our cloak of brotherly love is not large enough to include him as a member of the body politic."[38] This perception of the Hindu must have held sway in Port Angeles, the lumber town on the Olympic peninsula. In 1913, the real estate brokers of Port Angeles and Clallam County pledged not to sell property to "Hindoos or to Negroes."[39]

The exclusion of Asians that had been launched with the anti-Chinese campaign of the 1880s was extended repeatedly by legislation pressed by an organization called the Asiatic Exclusion League. In 1924, the National Origins Act established permanent restrictions on immigration from outside the Western hemisphere, and prohibited the entry of aliens not eligible for U.S. citizenship, which included Asians. Severe restrictions on Asian immigration and naturalization lasted through World War II. During the war, anti-Japanese fear and suspicion spread to include hundreds of thousands of Japanese Americans who were citizens of the United States. The internment camps in which American citizens were placed during World War II recapitulated the sentiments that had generated the whole history of Asian exclusion.

Exclusion also meant, in some cases, denial of citizenship to those who were already here. In 1923, the Supreme Court of the United States ruled that "Hindus" could not be American citizens. The decisive case involved a certain Mr. Thind, a Sikh gentleman who had settled in California, married an American woman, and become a naturalized citizen. "Hindu" was understood as a racial, not a religious, group. Mr. Thind was now to be stripped of his citizenship because of his race. Hindus, the court reasoned, were not "free white men" and therefore did not qualify for American citizenship. Scholars apparently reminded the court that Indians and Europeans both came from the Indo-European language and racial family, but the judges ruled that such was not the perception of the "common man." "It may be true that the blond Scandinavian and the brown Hindu have a common ancestor in the dim reaches of antiquity, but the average man knows perfectly well that there are unmistakeable and profound differences today."[40]

A NEW "NEW WORLD"

In 1965, a new immigration act initiated by John F. Kennedy was signed into law by Lyndon Johnson. Robert Kennedy, in supporting the act before the U.S. Congress, said, "Everywhere else in our national life, we have eliminated discrimination based on national origins. Yet, this system is still the foundation of our immigration law."[41] The new policy eliminated national origins quotas and opened the door again for immigration from Asia.

Gradually, in the course of the next two decades, the ethnic makeup of the United States came to include many more immigrants from Asia, the Pacific, and the Middle East. These new Americans have changed the religious landscape of the United States. Today there are Hindu and Buddhist temples and Muslim mosques in virtually every American city, most of them largely invisible because they are in homes and office buildings, or in former churches, Masonic lodges, and movie theaters. In the 1980s, however, evidence of the new religious reality began to become visible as majestic and imposing temples were consecrated, such as the Hindu Sri Meenakshi Temple in Houston and the Buddhist Hsi Lai Temple in Hacienda Heights, and as mosques were built, such as the one that rises from the cornfields outside Toledo or the one that occupies a whole city block at Third Avenue and Ninety-sixth Street in Manhattan. Immigrant America of the late nineteenth century often thought of itself as a new world when in fact it was the old world of Europe transplanted into a new environment. But the world of multireligious America in the late twentieth century is truly a new frontier.

One hundred years ago, Swami Vivekananda was a novelty and was treated like an exotic prophet in the parlors of Brattle Street in Cambridge and in the wealthy suburbs of Boston. Now there is a large South Asian minority population in Boston's wealthy suburbs. Hindus have consecrated a fine temple in Ashland, designed by a traditional Hindu temple architect from South India, built by a Wellesley engineering firm, and finished with religious images and ornamentation by a team of artisans trained in the workshops of Mahabalipuram. An adjacent residential compound houses three full-time priests. The Ganesha temple in Flushing, New York, and the Sri Venkateshwara Temple in Pittsburgh were the first full-scale Hindu temples in the United States, both built in the late 1970s. Now there are large Hindu temples with their elaborate towers in virtually every major metropolitan area—in Aurora outside Chicago, in the hills of Malibu near Los Angeles, in Lanham, Maryland, outside Washington, D.C. There are temples in Flint, Michigan; Allentown, Pennsylvania; Whittier, California; Beavercreek, Ohio; Smyrna, Georgia; Kenner, Louisiana. There are summer camps for Hindu young people. Were he to tour the United States today, Swami Vivekananda would be greeted at Bengali summer picnics and Hindu heritage family camps.

A century ago, Dharmapala denounced America's ignorance of the life and teachings of the Buddha. Today many Americans would do no better if quizzed on the life of the Buddha, and yet today virtually the whole of the Buddhist world has roots in North America, from the Theravada traditions of South Asia to the Vajrayana traditions of Tibet and the Mahayana traditions of China, Japan, and Korea.

On a Sunday in Los Angeles not long ago, I set out with my mother and a detailed city map to explore the Buddhist world in what must be the most complex Buddhist city on earth. At the Wat Thai temple in North Hollywood, hundreds of Thai-American children were learning the Thai language and drawing crayon pictures of the life of the Buddha in the educational wing, while their parents listened to a sermon in the temple or chatted under the trees next to open-air Thai kitchens and snack stalls. At the Kwan Um Sa Korean temple on Olympic Boulevard we saw the large and stately temple room, formerly a Masonic lodge, lined with posh red chairs facing an altar with a huge standing Buddha. At the Sri Lankan temple, a house on Crenshaw Avenue, we spoke with one of the resident saffron-robed monks about his Buddhist chaplaincy at UCLA.

We arrived at the Vietnamese temple on Berendo Street, the oldest of the thirty or forty Vietnamese Buddhist temples in the L.A. area, as a group of volunteers was mailing thousands of invitations for the upcoming celebration of the Buddha's birthday. At the International Buddhist Meditation Center we met an American-born nun who had been initiated into a Vietnamese Buddhist lineage and is an energetic organizer of the city's Buddhist Sangha Council, an ecumenical organization unlike any other in the world, bringing monks and nuns from across the Buddhist spectrum together in a local forum. A few blocks away we visited the Zen Center of Los Angeles, where the houses of half a city block are occupied by the Zen students of Maezumi Roshi. At the Hsi Lai Temple in Hacienda Heights, we met Taiwanese nuns who led the Chinese Buddhist community in the construction of the largest Buddhist temple complex in the Western Hemisphere—a massive and elegant palace-style hilltop temple and convent complex. When my mother went home to Montana with the photographs of her trip to Los Angeles her friends gasped, "This is L.A.?"

The first mosque in the United States was built by Lebanese immigrants in Cedar Rapids, Iowa, in 1934. In the 1950s the same Iowan community of Muslims started the first Muslim publishing house. By 1971, they had dedicated another new mosque in Cedar Rapids. The history of Iowa Muslims is but a part of the history of American Islam, for we now know that long before the rise of the Black Muslim movement in Detroit in the 1930s there were African-American Muslims who had come as slaves from Africa. There are now more than six hundred mosques in the United States—in Houston, Chicago, Toledo, Tempe, Savannah.

In Washington, D.C., the Islamic Center is a beautiful building, its minaret rising above the tree-lined streets of the embassy district. The mosque in Quincy, south of Boston, sits in the shadow of the great cranes of the Quincy shipyards, which employed many of the early Muslim immigrants to the Boston area from Jordan, Syria, and Lebanon. It is but a short walk from the birthplace of the sixth president of the United States, John Quincy Adams, and is one of some twenty mosques in the Islamic Council of New England. The nationally organized Islamic Society of North America has its headquarters in Plainfield, Indiana, and has large conventions every Labor Day weekend. There is an Association of Muslim Scientists and Engineers, an Islamic Medical Association, a Muslim Students Association. There are more Muslims in the United States today than Episcopalians. According to some estimates, there will soon be more Muslims than Jews. On June 25, 1991, the U.S. House of Representatives, which opens each day with an act of prayer, for the first time heard a prayer offered by a Muslim religious leader, Siraj Wahaj, an African-American imam from the Masjid al-Taqwa in Brooklyn.

There are also many smaller Asian communities, such as the Jains, the Zoroastrians, and the Sikhs, in the United States. The Sikh community dates back to the early decades of the twentieth century, when the first Sikh immigrant workers arrived in California and the Pacific Northwest. They were disparagingly called "rag-heads" and the newspapers spoke threateningly of a "tide of turbans." Many were among the "Hindus" thrown from their boarding houses in the Bellingham riots. The Pacific Khalsa Diwan Society was founded in Stockton, California, in 1912 and the *gurudwara* (Sikh house of worship in Stockton is one of the oldest in the United States. There are more than fifteen *gurudwaras* in California and nearly as many on the East Coast, the largest being the Richmond Hill *gurudwara* in Queens, which gathers as many as five thousand Sikh Americans for large festival days. There are some sixty Jain temples and centers in the United States, like the one on Cedar Street in Norwood, Massachusetts. Both the Jain Association of North American and the Zoroastrian Association of North America have biannual congresses.

Of course there are many parts of the United States where this new world of religious diversity has yet to be visible. But even in those places—perhaps the hills of the Olympic peninsula or the streets of Anaconda, Montana—the cultural awareness of such diversity is generated through the modern media. When my Grandma Anna came from Sweden in 1914, she and her mother, Louisa, brought the family Bible. For them, and for almost everyone in their generations, the Bible was the most important book they owned. For some it was the *only* book they owned. In any case, it was the main book on the subject of religion. Today the bookstores, even in Anaconda and Port Townsend, are stocked with paperback books on the world's religions. There are scriptures such as the Bhagavad Gita and the Holy Qur'an. There are collections of religious poetry telling of the heart's love of Lord Krishna. There are books on Zen Buddhist meditation, Islamic calligraphy, Sufi poetry, and Jewish holidays. There are books describing the legends, rites, and myths of the Plains Indians, the Yoruba, and the Maori. Newspapers, even the Butte *Montana Standard* and the Port Angeles *Peninsula Daily News*, contain stories of the Dalai Lama's Nobel Peace Prize, the Islamic resurgence in the Middle East, the rising Sikh self-consciousness in India, and the opening of a Buddhist peace pagoda in Massachusetts. Everywhere consciousness of the world's religious diversity is greater than ever before.

In North America this plurality is a relatively new phenomenon of the past quarter-century. Even so, it is astonishing that we have paid so little notice. During the 1970s and early 1980s there was a great deal of attention and concern about what were called "cults," some of them being new guru-centered religious movements from India. When young people, Protestant, Catholic, and Jewish, followed enthusiastically after Hindu gurus or new-style Tibetan Buddhist teachers, it was newsworthy and, to some, alarming. An anti-cult movement complete with "deprogrammers" was mobilized. And yet all the while we failed to notice that Hindu Americans were becoming our surgeons, engineers, and newsdealers, Buddhist Americans our bankers and astronauts, Muslim Americans our teachers, lawyers, and cabdrivers. By now we are all virtually next-door neighbors.

The "Old World" is also becoming a new world. Western European countries such as Britain, France, Germany, and Sweden are all struggling with the meaning of their new religious plurality. Britain, long dominantly and officially Christian, is a barometer of the changes that are taking place. When Fielding wrote *Tom Jones* two centuries ago, his Parson Thwackum could say, "When I mention religion, I mean the Christian religion; and not only the Christian religion, but the Protestant religion, and not only the Protestant religion, but the Church of England." Today, however, when religion is mentioned in Parliament or in relation to school assemblies, it can no longer be presumed to be the Protestant religion of the Church of England. In Britain, there are over a million Muslims, 400,000 Hindus, and 400,000 Sikhs. Leicester is said to be the second-largest Hindu city in the world outside India (second only to Durban in South Africa). There are substantial numbers of Muslims in Bradford and Birmingham, of Sikhs in Southall and Handsworth. In the city of Coventry, 10 percent of the population is from the Indian subcontinent. Pluralism is an issue at virtually every level of British life—from the election of city officials and the construction of school curricula to the theological discussions of the Church of England. So persistent have the questions of interfaith relations become that the Church of England issued a 1992 publication entitled *Multi-Faith Worship*, raising questions, exploring dilemmas, and offering advice. How should Hindu and Sikh prayers be included in the annual Boy Scout services? What kind of installation service is appropriate for a newly elected Sikh mayor? How might a memorial service for disaster victims be shaped to include Christian, Muslim, Hindu, and Sikh prayers?[42]

Religious plurality is an older but not necessarily an easier issue in Asia. India's long and legendary pluralism, rooted in a broadly Hindu ethos, was torn by rising communal self-consciousness during the struggle for independence. Religious communalism literally divided the land into India and Pakistan. But the political use of religious identity—Muslim, Sikh, and Hindu—has not waned in supposedly secular India since then; indeed, it seems to be on the rise. Elsewhere in Asia, Indonesia has built its government on what it calls the Panchashila—the "five principles" of a general monothesim and humanitarianism—which it claims unite Islam, the dominant religion, with Hinduism, Buddhism, Christianity, and Indonesian traditional religion. Nearby Malaysia is officially Muslim, but struggling with Hindu and Chinese minorities. The Philippines are predominantly Catholic and struggling with the aspirations of a Muslim minority demanding its political rights. Sri Lanka has seen over a decade of violence between the predominantly Buddhist Sinhalese majority and the Tamil minority population, which is largely Hindu. With the disintegration of the Soviet bloc, the "politics of identity" seems to be the dominant source of energy and of conflict in the struggle of cultures and ethnic groups for independence and for power.

FRONTIERS OF ENCOUNTER

The world has always been one of religious diversity and interaction. From ancient times to the present, people have encountered and have had to interpret for themselves the religions of their neighbors. Herodotus, encountering the mysteries of Egypt, identified Egyptian gods as ancestors of the more familiar gods of Greece, assimilating the foreign into the familiar. When early Buddhist monks travelled along the Silk Road from India to China in the third century, they had to speak of the Middle Way of Buddhism in language that would be understood by Taoist and Confucian sages. Buddhism changed and so did China. When the first Muslim generals and their armies came to India in the eleventh century, the scholar Alberuni was with them, taking upon himself the task of trying to understand the religiousness of the Hindus, whom he found "totally differ from us in religion, as we believe in nothing in which they believe and *vice versa*."[43] His *Kitab al-Hind* (Book of India), might be seen as one of the earliest works of comparative religion. It is a book which closes with a prayer to God "to pardon us for every statement of ours which is not true."[44]

The Hebrew prophets interpreted the Canaanite gods as important idols, nothing but dust, blocks of wood. The early Christians interpreted their Hebrew background in light of what they saw as a new reality, the Messiah, the crucified and risen Christ. Christianity is an interpretation of Jewish traditions and Jewish hopes, but the church also moved in the Greco-Roman world among people who had never held those traditions and hopes, who did not know the language of the Hebrew prophets, and Christians had to offer an interpretation to them as well. In Athens, Paul stood in the agora and spoke of the god to whom the Athenians had erected a shrine marked "To the Unknown God," and he quoted the Greek poets who spoke of the one "in whom we live and move and have our being" (Acts 17:28). In the second century, the Christian theologian Justice Martyr insisted that the God of the Bible was surely the God of Plato as well, and that the activity of God, the Logos, fully present in Christ, is universal and is seen wherever intelligence and goodness are seen. Interpreting the "other" in light of our own experience and tradition has always been a religious necessity and a religious challenge.

What is new today is not the diversity of our religious traditions nor the task of interpretation. What is new is our sharply heightened awareness of religious diversity in every part of our world and the fact that today everyone—not just the explorers, the missionaries, the diplomats, and the theologians—encounters and needs to understand people and faiths other than their own. In the hundred years since the days of Great-grandma Hilda and the World's Parliament of Religions, all of us have come to a very new place in our religious history. For much of the world's population, our religious ghettos are gone or almost gone, and the question of how we respond to religious difference is unavoidable. Hasidic Jews live in neighborhoods adjacent to those of Korean Buddhists and African-American Muslims. Some may retreat into voluntary isolation again, claiming the loyalties of religion, ethnicity, race, or language ever more insistently, but the exigencies of an interdependent world will not permit such a response for long. The question of difference is not only a cultural, social, and political question. It is also a theological question, as people in each religious tradition think about what it means to embrace a particular faith in full recognition of the power and dignity of other faiths in the lives of their neighbors.

Diversity, of course, is not pluralism. Diversity is simply a fact, but what will we make of that fact, individually and as a culture? Will it arouse new forms of ethnic and religious chauvinism and isolation? Or might it lead to a genuine pluralism, a positive and interactive interpretation of plurality? These are critical questions for the future, as people decide whether they value a sense of identity that isolates and sets them apart from one another or whether they value a broader identity that brings them into real relationship with one another.

Swami Vivekananda ended one of his electrifying speeches at the parliament of 1893 with a flourish of romantic, visionary hope, a tribute to America: "It was reserved for America to call, to proclaim to all quarters of the globe that the Lord is in every religion....Hail Columbia, mother-land of liberty! It has been given to thee, who never dipped her hand in her neighbor's blood, who never found out that shortest way of becoming rich by robbing one's neighbors, it has been given to thee to march on at the vanguard of civilization with the flag of harmony."[45] America has grown up to disappoint this vision in the past century, dipping her hand repeatedly in the blood of her neighbors, discovering in her own way the shortcuts to getting rich. In 1893, the United States used military force in Hawaii, in 1894, in Nicaragua; in 1898, Cuba and then the Philippines. All this before the new century had begun. In fact, American history told from the standpoint of its native peoples would have amply demonstrated the soiling of Vivekananda's vision from the very day that European settlers came to these shores. Even so, there is one part of the vision—the flag of harmony part—that may still be claimed as a distinctively American vision, though not a reality, one hundred years after the Parliament. As rocky and sometimes ugly as the history of immigration has been, with its racism, prejudice, and exclusion, America has kept on growing and changing into an ever-becoming nation of immigrants. This process of growth has created in the United States what is by now the most ethnically diverse nation on earth—and simultaneously one of the most religiously minded. With conscious and energetic attention to the question of difference and diversity, it is just possible that the United States may become a culture not simply of diversity, but of genuine pluralism. This would surely be America's most significant contribution to world civilization.

In 1893 the census declared that the frontier line was no longer traceable on the map of America. But there were other frontiers that were just beginning to be visible. These were the frontiers of encounter, where it was no longer a question of pushing out the known borders of settlement into what was "unsettled land," but of reaching the known borders of one community and encountering others. These were the frontiers that were just beginning to be visible in 1893—in America's encounter with the native peoples of the continent; in European America's encounter with Asian immigrants; and in Christian and Jewish America's encounter with people of other great faiths and civilizations. Today these frontiers of encounter and many others like them are everywhere. They are local and global, east and west, north and south. It is at these frontiers that our common future will be defined.

NOTES

1. John F. Kennedy, *A Nation of Immigrants* (New York: Harper Torchbooks, 1964), 3.

2. John Henry Barrows, ed., *The World's Parliament of Religions* (Chicago: Parliament Publishing Company, 1893), vol. I, 73. For an understanding of the currents and undercurrents of the Parliament, I am indebted to my colleague Richard Seager, who has edited a volume of Parliament speeches, *The Dawn of Religious Pluralism* (Chicago: Open Court, 1992), and written an interpretive work on the Parliament, "The World's Parliament of Religions, Chicago, Illinois, 1893: America's Coming of Age" (Ph.D. diss., Harvard University, 1986).

3. Barrows, *The World's Parliament of Religions*, 20–21.

4. Rick Fields, *How the Swans Came to the Lake* (Boston: Shambala, 1986), 113.

5. Barrows, *The World's Parliament of Religions*,

vol. 1, 67–72.

6. Ibid., 72–79.

7. Ibid., vol. 2, 977.

8. Ibid., 1571.

9. Ibid., vol. I, 444–50.

10. Ibid., vol. 2, 989–90.

11. Ibid., 843.

12. Ibid., vol. 1, 540.

13. Ibid., vol. 2, 1580.

14. Ibid., 1575.

15. Ibid., 1573.

16. Ibid., 1578.

17. Ibid., 1565.

18. Ibid., 1559.

19. Ibid., 1560.

20. Ibid., 973.

21. Ibid., 1304.

22. Cited by Seager, "The World's Parliament of Religions," p.47.

23. Barrows, *The World's Parliament of Religions*, vol. 2, 635–36.

24. Ibid., 1250.

25. Ibid., 1235–36.

26. Ibid., 1150.

27. Frederick Jackson Turner, "The Significance of the Frontier in American History," in *The Frontier in American History* (Huntington, N.Y.: Robert E. Krieger, 1976), 1–38.

28. Hilda Lavisa Olson Fritz's "A Family History" was written in the 1940s and was later typed by my aunt, Irene Fritz Conca. The manuscript is currently being edited by my mother, Dorothy Fritz Eck. All the material about Hilda Olson Fritz is from this manuscript.

29. Marian Taylor in Virginia Keeting, ed., *Dungeness: The Lure of a River* (Port Angeles, WA: Olympic Printers, 1976), 48.

30. Jack Chen, *The Chinese of America* (San Francisco: Harper and Row, 1980), 147.

31. Ibid., 148.

32. Robert R. Swartout, Jr., "From Kwangtung to the Big Sky: The Chinese Experience in Frontier Montana," in Robert R. Swartout, Jr., and Harry W. Fritz, eds., *Montana Heritage: An Anthology of Historical Essays* (Helena: Montana Historical Society, 1992), 75.

33. Ibid., 78.

34. Fields, *How the Swans Came to the Lake*, 123–24.

35. Swartout, "From Kwangtung," 77.

36. Ibid., 79.

37. Joan M. Jensen, *Passage from India: Asian Indians in North America* (New Haven Yale University Press, 1988), 46.

38. Ibid., 48.

39. Joan M. Jensen, "Apartheid: Pacific Coast Style," *Pacific Historical Review* 38 (August 1969), 339–40.

40. *The Supreme Court Reporter*, October 1923, "United States v. Bhagat Singh Thind (argued Jan. 11, 12, 1923; decided Feb. 19, 1923), 338–42.

41. Ronald Takaki, *Strangers from a Different Shore: A History of Asian American* (New York: Viking Penguin, 1989), 418.

42. *"Multi-faith Worship"?: Questions and Suggestions from the Inter-faith Consultative Group* (London: Church House Publishing, 1992).

43. Edward Sachau, ed., *Alberuni's India* (Delhi: S. Chand & Co., 1964), 19.

44. Ibid., 246.

45. Barrows, *The World's Parliament of Religions*, vol. 2, 978.

Karen McCarthy Brown is Professor of the Sociology and Anthropology of Religion in the Graduate and Theological Schools of Drew University. She is the author of *Mama Lola: A Vodou Priestess in Brooklyn* (California, 1991), and is working on a book on race in America. The context for the discussion of race will be her relationship with Mama Lola extended through historical explorations of both their families back to the eighteenth century.

Mark C. Carnes is Professor and Chair of the History Department at Barnard College, Columbia University. He is the author of *Secret Ritual and Manhood in Victorian America* (Yale, 1989), and the editor (with Clyde Griffen) of *Meanings for Manhood: Constructions of Masculinity in Victorian America* (Chicago, 1990) and *Past Imperfect: History According to the Movies* (Holt, 1995). His current project is titled "Gendered Lines, Gendered Signs: The Victorian Creation of the Code."

James H. Cone is Briggs Distinguished Professor at Union Theological Seminary. His books include *Black Theology and Black Power* (Seabury, 1969), *A Black Theology of Liberation* (Orbis, 2d ed. 1986) and *Martin & Malcolm & America* (Orbis, 1991).

Allen Figueroa Deck, S.J., is Adjunct Professor in the Department of Theological Studies at Loyola Marymount University. He is the author of *The Second Wave: Hispanic Ministry and the Evangelization of Cultures* (Paulist, 1989), editor of *Frontiers of Hispanic Theology in the United States* (Orbis, 1992), and coeditor (with Jay P. Dolan) of *Hispanic Catholicism in the U.S.: Issues and Concerns* (Notre Dame, 1994). He is working on linking Hispanic popular religion (Roman Catholic and Protestant) with traditional Catholic spirituality.

Raymond J. DeMallie is Professor of Anthropology and Director of the American Studies Research Institute at Indiana University. He is the editor (with Elaine A. Jahner) of James R. Walker, *Lakota Belief and Ritual* (Nebraska, 1980), the editor of *The Sixth Grandfather: Black Elk's Teachings Given to John Neihardt* (Nebraska, 1984), and the editor (with Douglas R. Parks) of *Sioux Indian Religion: Tradition and Innovation* (Oklahoma, 1987). He is working on a translation and edition of the writings of the early twentieth-century Oglala religious and political leader George Sword.

Diana L. Eck is Professor of Comparative Religion and Indian Studies at Harvard University where she is also Chair of the Committee on the Study of Religion in the Faculty of Arts and Sciences and a member of the Faculty of Divinity. She is the author of *Darsan: Seeing the Divine Image in India* (Anima, 1981), *Banares, City of Light* (Knopf, 1982), and *Encountering God: A Spiritual Journey Bozeman to Banaras* (Beacon, 1993). She is directing a research team at Harvard to explore the new religious diversity of the United States and its meaning for the American pluralist experiment.

Tamar Frankiel is Adjunct Lecturer at the School of Theology at Claremont. Among her publications are *Gospel Hymns and Social Religion: The Rhetoric of Nineteenth-Century Revivalism* (Temple, 1978), *California's Spiritual Frontiers: Religious Alternatives in Anglo-Protestantism, 1850–1910* (California, 1988), and *The Voice of Sarah: Spirituality and*

Traditional Judaism (HarperSanFrancisco, 1990). She is doing research on the concept of holiness in Judaism.

William B. Gravely is Professor of Religious Studies at the University of Denver. He is the author of *Gilbert Haven, Methodist Abolitionist* (Abingdon, 1973) and of many journal articles concerning African American religion, abolitionism, and Methodist studies. He is completing an interpretive study of the 1947 lynching of Willie Earle, the last lynching in South Carolina.

Ramón A. Gutiérrez is Professor of Ethnic Studies and History at the University of California, San Diego. He is the author of *When Jesus Came, the Corn Mothers Went Away: Marriage Sexuality, and Power in New Mexico, 1500-1846* (Stanford, 1991) and coeditor of *Feasts and Celebrations in North American Ethnic Communities* (New Mexico, 1995). He is working on a social and cultural history of New Mexico's Indian slaves.

David G. Hackett is Associate Professor of Religion at the University of Florida. The author of *The Rude Hand of Innovation: Religion and Social Order in Albany, New York 1652–1836* (Oxford, 1991), he is writing a book on fraternalism and religion in the late nineteenth century.

David D. Hall is Professor of American Religious History at Harvard Divinity School. He is the editor of *The Antinomian Controversy: A Documentary History, 1636–1638* (Wesleyan, 1968) and the author of *Worlds of Wonder, Days of Judgment: Popular Religious Belief in Early New England* (Knopf, 1989). He is working on a "new history of Puritanism," an effort to link social and intellectual history while drawing on perspectives from women's history and cultural studies.

Evelyn Brooks Higginbotham is Professor of Afro-American Studies at Harvard University and Professor of African American Religious History at Harvard Divinity School. Professor Higginbotham is the author of *Righteous Discontent: The Women's Movement in the Black Baptist Church, 1880-1920* (Harvard, 1993). She is completing a book of essays on race, history, and feminist theory and a coauthored textbook on African American History.

Charles Joyner is Burroughs Distinguished Professor of History and Culture at Coastal Carolina University. He is the author of *Down By the Riverside: A South Carolina Slave Community* (Illinois, 1984) and *Remember Me, Slave Life in Coastal Carolina* (Georgia Humanities Council, 1989). He is writing about "the South as a folk culture."

Joel W. Martin is Associate Professor in the Department of Religious Studies and the Program of American Studies at Franklin and Marshall College. He is the author of *Sacred Revolt: The Muskogees' Struggle for a New World* (Beacon, 1991) and coeditor (with Conrad Ostwalt, Jr.) of *Screening the Sacred: Religion, Mythology, and Ideology in Popular American Film* (Westview, 1995). He is researching a project to be called "The Breathmaker, the Bible, and Bre'er Rabbit: Cultural Contact and Religious Exchange Among Southeastern Indians, Settlers, and Slaves."

Colleen McDannell is Sterling M. McMurrin Chair in Religious Studies and Associate Professor of History at the University of Utah. She is the author of *The Christian Home in Victorian America, 1840–1900* (Indiana, 1986), (with Bernhard Lang) *Heaven: A History* (Yale, 1988), and *Material Christianity: Religion and Popular Culture in America* (Yale, 1995). She is doing research on the history of camp.

Deborah Dash Moore is Professor of Religion and Director of the Program in American Culture at Vassar College. She is the author of *At Home in America: Second Generation New York Jews* (Columbia, 1981) and *To the Golden Cities: Pursuing the American Jewish Dream in Miami and L.A.* (Free Press, 1994). With Paula Hyman, she is coediting "Jewish Women in America: An Historical Encyclopedia."

William K. Powers is Distinguished Professor of Anthrolopology at Rutgers University. His books include *Oglala Religion* (Nebraska, 1977), *Yuwipi, Vision and Experience in Oglala Ritual* (Nebraska, 1982) and *Sacred Language: the Nature of Supernatural Discourse in Lakota* (Oklahoma, 1986). He is working on "When the People Gather," a study of continuity and change in the forerunner to the contemporary pow-wow.

Albert J. Raboteau is Henry W. Putnam Professor of Religion at Princeton University. He is the author of *Slave Religion: The "Invisible Institution" in the Antebellum South* (Oxford, 1978) and *Fire in the Bones* (Beacon, 1995). With David Wills, he is coediting "Afro-American Religion: A Documentary History Project."

Daniel K. Richter is Associate Professor of History and a Member of the American Studies Department at Dickinson College. He is coeditor (with James H. Merrill) of *Beyond the Covenant Chain: The Iroquois and Their Neighbors in Indian North America, 1600-1800* (Syracuse, 1987) and he is the author of *The Ordeal of the Longhouse: The Peoples of the Iroquois League in the Era of European Colonization* (University of North Carolina Press for the Institute of Early American History and Culture, 1992). He is writing "Facing East: Perspectives on the European Colonization of North America."

Mary P. Ryan is Professor of History at the University of California, Berkeley. She is the author of *Cradle of the Middle Class: The Family in Oneida County, New York, 1790–1865* (Cambridge, 1981) and *Women in Public: Between Banners and Ballots, 1825–1880* (Johns Hopkins, 1990). She is completing a book on democracy and difference in three American cities over the nineteenth century.

Jonathan D. Sarna is Joseph H. and Belle R. Braun Professor of American Jewish History at Brandeis University. His publications include *Jacksonian Jew: The Worlds of Mordecai Noah* (Holmes and Meier, 1981) and *JPS: The Americanization of Jewish Culture* (Jewish Publication Society, 1989). He is working on a new history of American Judaism.

Leigh Eric Schmidt is Associate Professor of Religion at Princeton University. He is the author of *Holy Fairs: Scottish Communions and American Revivals in the Early Modern Period* (Princeton, 1989) and *The Buying and Selling of American Holidays* (Princeton, 1995). He is researching issues of hypocrisy, deception, imposture, simulation, and scandal in American religion.

Jan Shipps is Professor Emeritus of Religious Studies and History at Indiana University-Purdue University, Indianapolis. She is the author of *Mormonism: The Story of a New Religious Tradition* (Illinois, 1985) and the coeditor (with John W. Welch) of *The Journals of William E. McClellin, 1831–1836* (Illinois University Press and Brigham Young University Studies, 1994). She is writing "Being Mormon: The Latter-Day Saints since World War II."

Grant Wacker is Associate Professor of American Religious History at Duke Divinity School. He is the author of *Augustus H. Strong and the Dilemma of Historical Consciousness* (Mercer, 1985). He is completing a book to be called, "Heaven Below: The Inner Worlds of Early Pentecostalism."

Charles Reagan Wilson is Professor of History and Southern Studies at the University of Mississippi. He is the author of *Baptized in Blood: The Religion of the Lost Cause, 1865–1920* (Georgia, 1980) and *Judgment and Grace in Dixie: Southern Faiths from Faulkner to Elvis* (Georgia, 1995). He is writing "The Southern Way of Life," a history of regional culture and consciousness.

Robert Wuthnow is Gerhard R. Andlinger Professor of Social Sciences and Director of the Center for the Study of American Religion at Princeton University. His many publications include *The Restructuring of American Religion: Society and Faith Since World War II* (Princeton University Press, 1988), *Christianity in the 21st Century: Reflections on the Challenges Ahead* (Oxford University Press, 1993), and *God and Mammon in America* (Free Press, 1994). He continues to do research on the changing character of American religion since World War II.